HEINZ HÖHNE

THE ORDER OF THE DEATH'S HEAD

The Story of Hitler's SS

Translated from the German by
RICHARD BARRY

UNABRIDGED

PAN BOOKS LTD : LONDON

Published in German under the title
Der Orden unter dem Totenkopf.
First published in Great Britain 1969
by Martin Secker & Warburg Ltd.
This edition published 1972 by Pan Books Ltd,
33 Tothill Street, London, SW1.

ISBN 0 330 02963 0

Made and printed in Great Britain by
Cox & Wyman Ltd, London, Reading and Fakenham

CONTENTS

ILLUSTRATIONS IN PHOTOGRAVURE

(*between pages* 314 *and* 315)

AUTHOR'S ACKNOWLEDGEMENTS

I would like to take this opportunity of thanking all those persons and institutions without whose active assistance this book could not have been written. My thanks go: first to Herr Rudolf Augstein, the editor of *Der Spiegel*, whose patient criticism both facilitated and improved my work; secondly, to Herr Hans Detlev Becker, the publication director of *Der Spiegel*, who initiated the SS Series, took immense interest and was always ready with advice. I equally feel under an obligation to all those men and women – former members, opponents and victims of the SS – who were prepared, time and again, to provide information; they are too numerous to be mentioned individually. They have contributed much to this book but they carry not the smallest responsibility for any errors or misinterpretations of which I may have been guilty.

TRANSLATOR'S NOTE

In most cases German technical terms, titles and ranks have been retained in this book. On the first occasion when such words appear, a literal translation is given in brackets. A glossary of German words regularly used in the book is on page xv. A table of SS ranks with their approximate equivalents in the British and American Armies is at Appendix 2.

CALENDAR OF EVENTS

1889 *April 20th* Birth of Adolf Hitler

1900 *October 7th* Birth of Heinrich Himmler

1923 *November 9th* Hitler 'putsch' in Munich

1925 *February* Reconstitution of National-Socialist Party
Summer Formation of first SS units

1929 *January 6th* Himmler becomes 'Reichsführer-SS'

1930 *Late autumn* The SS in practice becomes independent of the SA

1931 *Autumn* SS Security Service set up under Reinhard Heydrich
December 31st SS 'Race and Resettlement' Office set up under Walter Darré

1933 *January 30th* Hitler becomes Reich Chancellor
February 27th The Reichstag fire
February 28th The 'Ordinance for the Protection of People and State' lays the foundation for National-Socialist dictatorship
March 9th Himmler becomes Police President of Munich
March 17th Formation of the 'Leibstandarte Adolf Hitler' under Sepp Dietrich
March 20th Dachau Concentration Camp set up
April 1st Himmler becomes Commander of the Bavarian Political Police
April 26th Formation of the Gestapo, Berlin

1934 *April 20th* Himmler becomes Inspector of the Prussian Gestapo
April 22nd Heydrich becomes Head of the Gestapo
June 9th The SD constituted sole political intelligence and counter-espionage service of the Nazi Party

June 30th The 'Röhm putsch'. Formation of armed SS units begins. All concentration camps placed under the SS

July 20th The SS formally constituted as a force independent of the SA

August 2nd Death of Hindenburg. Hitler becomes Führer and Chancellor of the Reich and Supreme Commander of the Wehrmacht

1935 *March 16th* Introduction of universal military service

1936 *Early March* Formation of VOMI (Volksdeutsche Mittelstelle)

March 7th Reoccupation of the Rhineland

March 29th SS Guard formations renamed 'SS Totenkopfverbände' and expanded to 3,500 men

June 17th Himmler nominated Reichsführer-SS and Chief of the German Police

1938 *February 2nd* The Blomberg-Fritsch crisis

March 13th The Austrian Anschluss

September 28th/
October 1st The Munich Agreement. Germany occupies the Sudetenland

November 9th Anti-Jewish pogrom ('Kristallnacht')

1939 *March 15th* Occupation of the 'remainder of Czechoslovakia'; formation of the 'Protectorate of Bohemia and Moravia'

May 22nd The 'Pact of Steel' between Germany and Italy

August 23rd Non-Aggression Pact between Germany and the Soviet Union

September 1st Outbreak of war. SS 'Verfügungstruppe' raised from 8,000 to 9,000, SS 'Totenkopfverbände' to 6,500. Security Police and SD 'Einsatzgruppen' commence activity in Poland

September 22nd Formation of the RSHA under Heydrich

October Formation of the SS Division 'Das Reich' and of one SS 'Totenkopf' division

October 7th Himmler becomes 'Reich Commissar for the strengthening of Germanism' (RKF)

1940 *January* Introduction of the title 'Waffen-SS'
April 9th Invasion of Denmark and Norway
May 10th Attack on Holland, Belgium and France
June 1st Strength of Waffen-SS 100,000 (raised to 150,000 by end of year)
September 27th Three-Power Pact between Germany, Italy and Japan

1941 *June 22nd* German attack on Russia. Four 'Einsatzgruppen' of the Security Police and SD move into the Soviet Union
Summer Beginning of the 'Final Solution of the Jewish question'
December 7th-11th Japanese attack on Pearl Harbor. Hitler declares war on USA
December 19th Hitler takes over as Commander-in-Chief of the Army
End year Overall strength of SS troops 230,000

1942 *February 1st* Formation of SS Economic and Administrative 'Hauptamt' (WVHA)
March 16th All concentration camps placed under the WVHA
June 6th Assassination of Heydrich
November 8th Anglo-American landing in North Africa

1943 *January 31st/February 1st* Surrender of Stalingrad
May 13th End of the war in North Africa
August 25th Himmler becomes Minister of the Interior
September 8th Surrender of Italy
September 12th Rescue of Mussolini by Skorzeny

1944 *June 6th* D-Day
June 30th Overall strength of the Waffen-SS 594,000, 'Allgemeine SS' 200,000, concentration-camp guards 24,000
July 20th Bomb attack on Hitler
July 21st Himmler becomes C-in-C Replacement Army
August 25th Allies enter Paris
October Peak of Waffen-SS manpower 910,000. Total of 38 SS divisions
December 16th Ardennes offensive

1945	*February 2nd*	Yalta Conference
	April 30th	Suicide of Hitler
	May 23rd	Suicide of Himmler

GLOSSARY

Abschnitt	A regional sub-division of the SS territorial organization, subordinate to an Oberabschnitt. Also a regional HQ of the SD.
Abteilung	A branch, section or sub-division of a main department or office (Amt, Amtsgruppe or Hauptamt). Alternatively a military unit or detachment up to battalion strength.
Abwehr	The Intelligence and Clandestine Warfare Service of the German High Command – Amt Ausland/Abwehr.
Abwehrpolizei	Counter-espionage police. A function of the Frontier Police – controlled by the Gestapo.
Ahnenerbe	'Ancestral heritage.' An organization, created by Himmler, the primary object of which was to search for early German relics and research into early German history.
Allgemeine SS	The general body of the SS consisting of part-time, full-time and inactive or honorary members, as distinct from the Waffen-SS.
Allgemeine Wehrmachtsamt	The General Armed Forces Office (in OKW) concerned principally with personnel, training and equipment.
Amt (pl. Amter)	An office, branch or directorate of a Ministry; in certain cases an independent ministry, eg, Auswärtiges Amt [Foreign Ministry].
Amtsgruppe	A branch of a Hauptamt.
Anwärter	A cadet or candidate.
AO	Auslandsorganisation (qv).
AOK	Armee-Oberkommando (qv).
Armee-Oberkommando	An Army Headquarters.
Ausland/Abwehr	See Abwehr.
Auslandsorganisation	The Nazi Party agency concerned with the

	care and supervision of Germans abroad. Ranked as a Gau (qv).
Ausland-SD	The branch of the SD dealing with foreign intelligence.
Aussendienststelle	An out-station of a Ministry or agency.
Aussenstelle	Alternative form of Aussendienststelle (qv).
Auswärtiges Amt	The Foreign Ministry.
AWA	Allgemeine Wehrmachtsamt (qv).
Barbarossa	Code word for the German attack on Russia, June 22nd, 1941.
Bauinspektion	Building Inspectorate – part of Amtsgruppe C of the WVHA.
BdO	Befehlshaber der Ordnungspolizei (qv).
BdS	Befehlshaber der Sicherheitspolizei (qv).
Beamter	Official or functionary.
Befehl	An order or command.
Befehlshaber	A senior military commander.
Befehlshaber der Ordnungspolizei	Commander of the uniformed police at regional and Wehrkreis level and in occupied territories – subordinate to the HSSPF – previously entitled Inspekteur der Ordnungspolizei.
Befehlshaber der Sicherheitspolizei und des Sicherheitsdienstes	Commander of the Security Police and Security Service in occupied territories – subordinate to the HSSPF for particular tasks but under direct RSHA control. Latterly the title of the IdS in certain areas of the Reich.
Bereitschaft	An emergency or alarm detachment of the Party or police (see also under Politische).
Bereitschaftspolizei	Mobile barrack police units of the Landespolizei administered by the Länder until the centralization of the police in 1935–6.
Bezirk	A district or administrative unit.
Brigadeführer	See Appendix 2.
Burgomeister	Mayor of a town or city.
Bürgerwehr	Citizens defence force (of the early post-1918 period).

Chef des Generalstabes des Heeres	Chief of Staff of the Army.
Chef der Sicherheitspolizei und des SD	Chief of the Security Police and Security Service – Heydrich until 1942, then Kaltenbrunner.
Chef der Zivilverwaltung	Head of the Civilian Administration in an occupied territory.
CSSD	Chef der Sicherheitspolizei und des SD (qv).
DAG	Deutsche Ansiedlungsgesellschaft (qv).
DAW	Deutsche Ausrüstungswerke (qv).
DEST	Deutsche Erd- und Steinwerke (qv).
Deutsche Ansiedlungsgesellschaft	The German Settlement Company, affiliated to the RKF in 1940.
Deutsche Ausrüstungswerke	The German Armaments Works. An SS enterprise established in 1939.
Deutsche Erd- und Steinwerke GmbH	German Excavation and Quarrying Company Ltd. An SS enterprise formed in 1938. Used concentration-camp labour.
Deutsche Umsiedlungs-Treuhand GmbH	German Resettlement Trust Ltd – affiliated to the RKF.
Deutsche Wirtschaftsbetriebe	German Economic Enterprises. A holding company formed to cover all SS economic enterprises.
Dienststelle	A headquarters, administrative office or station.
DUT	Deutsche Umsiedlungs-Treuhand GmbH (qv).
DWB	Deutsche Wirtschaftsbetriebe (qv).
Ehrenführer	Honorary SS officers, usually of senior rank. A distinction granted by Himmler to leading Party and State personalities, eg, Bormann, Ribbentrop.
Einsatzgruppe	An operational group or task force of the Sipo and SD for special missions (usually liquidations) in occupied territory. Consisted of up to six Einsatzkommandos.
Einsatzkommando	A detachment of the Sipo. Part of an Einsatzgruppe.

Einsatzstab	An operational staff of the Sipo and SD employed in occupied territory; also used for an RSHA operational staff dealing with the appropriation of real estate in the Eastern territories.
Einwandererzentralstelle	Central Immigration Office controlled by the RSHA; also part of the RKF.
Einwohnerwehr	Citizens Defence Force (or the early post-1918 period).
Ersatzheer	The Replacement Army.
EWZ	Einwandererzentralstelle (qv).
Fachreferat	A specialist sub-section or 'desk' in an office or headquarters.
Feldjägerkorps	A shock formation of the SA, disbanded in 1935 and incorporated in the police.
Feuerschutzpolizei	Fire Fighting Police – a branch of the Orpo.
Feuerwehr	Fire Brigade; these were controlled by the Orpo.
FHA	Führungshauptamt (qv).
FHQ	Führerhauptquartier (qv).
Fördernde Mitglied (of the SS)	Patron or sponsoring member of the SS; administered by the WVHA; paid a monthly contribution.
Führer	Leader, commander or chief. 'Der Führer' [The Leader] was used only in relation to Hitler.
Führerhauptquartier	Hitler's Field Headquarters.
Führungshauptamt	Operational headquarters of the whole SS, responsible for training, organization and employment with the exception of tactical employment of the Waffen-SS divisions in the field. Its head was Obergruppenführer Hans Jüttner.
Gau	The main territorial division of the Nazi Party. Germany was divided into 42 Gaue.
Gauleiter	The highest ranking Party official in a Gau, responsible for all political and economic activity, mobilization of labour and civil

	defence.
Geheime Feldpolizei	Secret Field Police. The executive arm of the Abwehr. Largely taken over by the Sipo and SD in 1942.
Geheime Staatspolizei	Secret State Police. Became Amt IV of the RSHA. Its head was Obergruppenführer Heinrich Müller.
Geheimes Staatspolizeiamt	The national headquarters of the Secret State Police. Absorbed into the RSHA in 1939.
Gemeinde	A municipality or community.
Gemeindepolizei	Municipal police.
Gendarmerie	The rural police, including motorized traffic-control units.
Generalgouvernement	The Government General – German-occupied Poland and its administration.
Generalkommando	An Army Corps Headquarters.
Generaloberst	Colonel-General. An army rank senior to General but below Field-Marshal – no precise equivalent in the British or U.S. armies.
Generalquartiermeister (of the Army)	Quartermaster-General of the Army or Deputy Chief of Staff.
Gericht	A court of law or tribunal.
Germanische Leitstelle	The 'Germanic' Liaison Office in the SS Hauptamt responsible for the supervision of the 'Germanic' SS.
Germanische SS	The 'Germanic' formations in the Waffen-SS; also the indigenous 'Germanic' organizations in the occupied territories.
Gesamt SS	Lit. overall SS, a term used to cover all SS branches.
Gestapa	Geheimes Staatspolizieamt (qv).
Gestapo	Geheime Staatspolizei (qv).
Grenzpolizei	Frontier or Border Control Police – controlled by the Gestapo.
Grenzpolizeikommissariat	A territorial division of the Grenzpolizei.
Gruppe	An elastic term used for a territorial HQ of

	the SA, an *ad hoc* military formation, or a section in a ministry.
Gruppenführer	See Appendix 3.
Hauptabteilung	A main division of a department or office.
Hauptamt SS	The Central Office of the SS responsible for recruitment, training, education, welfare, etc., of the entire SS. Its head was Obergruppenführer Gottlob Berger.
Hauptamt SS-Gericht	The SS Legal Department administering the special disciplinary and penal code governing all SS and police personnel. Its head was Obergruppenführer Franz Breithaupt.
Hauptamt Haushalt und Bauten	SS Department of Budget and Buildings. Controlled construction work and the allocation of concentration camp labour, later part of the WVHA. Its head was Obergruppenführer Oswald Pohl, later head of the WVHA.
Hauptamt Sicherheitspolizei	The Headquarters of the Security Police (Gestapo and Kripo), integrated into the RSHA in 1939.
Hauptamt Verwaltung und Wirtschaft	See WVHA.
Hauptaussenstelle	A main outstation of the SD.
Hauptscharführer	See Appendix 2.
Hauptsturmführer	See Appendix 2.
Haupttreuhandstelle Ost	Main Trust Office for the East. A public corporation created by Göring for the seizure and administration of Polish and Jewish property.
HIAG	Hilfsgemeinschaft auf Gegenseitigkeit – Mutual Help Association. The present welfare organization for former Waffen-SS personnel. Located in Lüdenscheid, Westphalia.
Höhere SS- und Polizeiführer	Senior SS and Police commander. Himmler's personal representative in each Wehrkreis and liaison officer with the military

	and senior regional authorities. Also established in occupied territories. Nominally the commander of all SS and police units in his area.
HSSPF	Höhere SS- und Polizeiführer (qv).
HTO	Haupttreuhandstelle Ost (qv).
IA Abteilung	The section of the former Berlin Police Presidency responsible for the collection of political police intelligence. Taken over by the Gestapa in 1933-4.
Ic	The Intelligence officer in a military HQ or formation. Used to designate an intelligence service, eg, that set up by Heydrich as the forerunner of the SD.
IdO	Inspekteur der Ordnungspolizei (qv).
IdS	Inspekteur der Sicherheitspolizei (qv).
Inspekteur der Ordnungspolizei	The original title of the BdO.
Inspekteur der Sicherheitspolizei und des Sicherheitsdienstes	Inspector of the Security Police and Security Service at regional and Wehrkreis level. Under direct RSHA control but subordinate to the HSSPF for particular tasks. See also BdS.
Jagdverbände	SS sabotage and subversive units. Their chief was Otto Skorzeny.
Junkerschule	An SS officer-cadet training school.
Kasernierte Polizei	Militarized barrack police organized in motorized units. Extensively employed in the eastern occupied territories.
KdO	Kommandeur der Ordnungspolizei (qv).
KdS	Kommandeur der Sicherheitspolizei (qv).
Kommandeur	Officer commanding a unit.
Kommandeur der Ordnungspolizei	Commander of the uniformed police in a General Kommissariat – subordinate to the BdO.
Kommandeur der Sicherheitspolizei und des Sicherdienstes	Commander of the Security Police and Security Service in a sub-district (General Kommissariat) of a Reichskommissariat in

	occupied territory. Also the commander of an Einsatzkommando.
Kommandoamt	The department within the Führungshauptamt responsible for the general operational control of the Waffen-SS.
Kommissariat	A regional HQ of the Frontier Police (see also Reichskommissariat).
Kreis	A district or county. The principal sub-division of a Gau.
Kreishauptmann	The principal district official in the Government-General.
Kreisleiter	The lowest salaried official of the Nazi Party. Responsible for a Kreis.
Kriminalkommissar	The lowest rank in the upper officer class of the Criminal Police.
Kriminaloberkommissar	The next senior rank in the Criminal Police above Kriminalkommissar.
Kriminalpolizei	The Criminal Police which, together with the Gestapo, formed the Security Police (Sipo). In 1939 became Amt V of the RSHA. Its head was Gruppenführer Arthur Nebe.
Kriminalrat	Kriminalrat. A senior rank in the Kriminalpolizei, below Kriminaldirektor.
Kripo	Kriminalpolizei (qv).
Land (pl. Länder)	One of the fifteen territorial divisions of Republican Germany, each with its own Government. From 1933 the Central Government controlled the Länder through Reichsstatthalter.
Landeskriminalpolizeiamt	Criminal Police HQ in a Land prior to the centralization of the police in 1936.
Landeskriminalpolizeistelle	A local office of the Criminal Police in a Land.
Landkreis	Rural sub-division of a Regierungsbezirk in Prussia.
Landrat	The chief authority in the administration of a Landkreis. Frequently the same man as the Party Kreisleiter.

Landtag	Chamber of Deputies or diet in a Land – abolished by the Nazis.
Lebensborn	Lit. 'Spring of Life' – the SS maternity organization.
Legationsrat	Embassy or Legation Counsellor. A Foreign Service rank.
Leibstandarte SS Adolf Hitler	The Adolf Hitler Bodyguard Regiment. The oldest of the SS militarized formations, formed in 1933. Reached divisional status in 1941. Commanded from 1933 to 1943 by Oberstgruppenführer Sepp Dietrich.
Leitabschnitt	A regional HQ of the SD, coinciding approximately with a Wehrkreis.
Leitstelle	A regional HQ of the Gestapo or Kripo established at the HQ of a Wehrkreis or capital of a Land.
LKPA	Landeskriminalpolizeiamt (qv).
Ministerialdirektor	A senior official in the civil service. Head of a department in a ministry.
Ministerialrat	Senior counsellor in the civil service. Usually head of a section in a ministry.
Ministerpräsident	Minister-President. The Prime Minister of a Land government.
Nationalsozialistische Deutsche Arbeiter Partei	National-Socialist German Workers' Party – the official title of the Nazi Party.
Nationalsozialistische Kraftfahr-Korps	National-Socialist Motor Corps. One of the para-military formations of the Nazi Party.
Nationalsozialistische Volkswohlfahrt	National-Socialist People's Welfare Organization, responsible largely for the care of mothers and juveniles.
NSDAP	Nationalsozialistiche Deutsche Arbeiter Partei (qv).
NSKK	Nationalsozialistische Kraftfahr-Korps (qv).
NSV	Nationalsozialistische Volkswohlfahrt (qv).
ObdH	Oberbefehlshaber des Heeres (qv).
Oberabschnitt	The main territorial division of the SS,

	approximately equivalent to a Wehrkreis.
Oberbefehlshaber des Heeres	The Commander-in-Chief of the Army (von Brauchitsch 1938–41 *vice* von Fritsch, then Hitler).
Oberführer	See Appendix 2.
Obergruppe	A main territorial division of the SA.
Obergruppenführer	See Appendix 2.
Oberkommando des Heeres	The High Command of the Army.
Oberkommando der Wehrmacht	The High Command of the Armed Forces (Hitler was supreme commander with Keitel as Chief of OKW).
Oberkriegsverwaltungsrat	A senior administrative counsellor in occupied territory.
Oberpräsident	The senior administrative official in a Prussian province.
Oberregierungsrat	Government counsellor – a senior civil service rank.
Oberscharführer	See Appendix 2.
Oberste SA Führer	Supreme Commander of the SA (Hitler from 1930).
Oberstes Parteigericht	The Supreme Court of the Nazi Party under Reichsleiter Walter Buch.
Oberstgruppenführer	See Appendix 2.
Obersturmbannführer	See Appendix 2.
Obersturmführer	See Appendix 2.
Oberverwaltungsrat	A senior administrative counsellor.
OKH	Oberkommando des Heeres (qv).
OKW	Oberkommando der Wehrmacht (qv).
Ordnungspolizei	Lit. 'Order police'. The regular uniformed police comprising the Schutzpolizei, Gendarmerie and Feuerschutzpolizei together with certain technical and auxiliary services.
Organisation Todt	A semi-military government agency established in 1933 and used mainly for the construction of strategic highways and military installations.

Orpo	Ordnungspolizei (qv).
Ortsgruppenleiter	A Nazi Party official in charge of one or more parts of a town, subordinate to a Kreisleiter.
Ortspolizei	Local police.
OSAF	Oberste SA Führer (qv).
Ostindustrie GmbH	Eastern Industries Ltd – an SS concern formed with the primary purpose of exploiting Jewish labour in Poland.
Ostministerium	Ministry for the East – see Reichministerium für die besetzten Ostgebiete.
OT	Organization Todt (qv).
Personalhauptamt	The main SS personnel department responsible for the records of all SS officers. Its head was Gruppenführer Maximilian von Herff.
Politische Bereitschaft	Political alarm squad. The precursor of the SS-Verfügungstruppe.
Polizeipräsident	Police President. The head of the regular police in a large city.
Rasse- und Siedlungshauptamt	SS department for Race and Re-settlement. The office responsible for the racial purity of the SS and the settlement of SS colonists in the conquered eastern territories.
Referat	A sub-section or 'desk' within a Gruppe.
Referent	The official in charge of a referat.
Regierungsbezirk	Sud-division of a Prussian province. Also a Bavarian administrative district.
Regierungspräsident	The senior government official in a Regierungsbezirk.
Regierungsrat	Government counsellor. The lowest rank in the higher civil service.
Reichsführer-SS und Chef der Deutschen Polizei	'Reich SS Leader and Chief of the German Police'; Himmler's full title from June 1936.
Reichsfürung-SS	The High Command of the SS, comprising Himmler's Personal Staff and the Hauptämter (including the RSHA).

Reichsgau	One of eleven regions formed from territories annexed after 1939. Administered by a Reichstatthalter.
Reichskommissar für die Festigung Deutschen Volkstums	Reich Commissar for the Strengthening of Germanism. An office created in 1939 under Himmler for the repatriation of 'racial Germans' and settlement of German colonies in eastern occupied territories.
Reichskommissariat für das Ostland	The German Civil Administration in occupied Soviet territories (except the Ukraine) and ex-Russian-occupied Poland. Divided into 'General Kommissariats'.
Reichskriminalpolizeiamt	The headquarters of the Criminal Police. Became Amt V of the RSHA.
Reichsleiter	The highest-ranking Nazi Party official.
Reichsministerium für die besetzten Ostgebiete	Reich Ministry for the Occupied Eastern (Soviet) Territories. Created in 1941 under Rosenberg.
Reichssicherheitshauptamt	Reich Central Security Department. Formed in 1939. Combined the Security Police (Gestapo and Kripo) and the SS Security Service (SD). It was both an SS Hauptamt and a branch of the Ministry of the Interior.
Reichsstatthalter	The Governor of a Land or Reichsgau. Frequently identical with the Party Gauleiter.
Reichswehr	The 100,000 army to which Germany was restricted under the Treaty of Versailles.
RFSS	Reichsführer-SS.
RKF	Reichskommissar für die Festigung Deutschen Volkstums.
RMO	Reichsministerium für die besetzten Ostgebiet.
Rottenführer	See Appendix 2.
RSHA	Reichssicherheitshauptamt (qv).
RuSHA	Rasse- und Siedlungshauptamt (qv).
SA	Sturmabteilung (qv).
Scharführer	See Appendix 2.
Schupo	Schutzpolizei (qv).

Schutzpolizei	Lit. 'Protection Police'. The regular uniformed municipal and country constabulary, forming the bulk of the Ordnungspolizei.
Schutzstaffel	Lit. 'Protection' or 'Guard Detachment'– the SS.
SD	Sicherheitsdienst RFSS (qv).
Selbstschutz	A self-defence militia recruited from the German minority in Poland.
Sicherheitsdienst RFSS	The SS Security Service formed in 1932 under Heydrich. Intended to be the sole Party Intelligence organization. The HQs of the Sipo and SD formed the core of the RSHA in 1939.
Sicherheitshauptamt	The SS Security Department under Heydrich. Also known as the SD Hauptamt.
Sicherheitspolizei	The Security Police consisting of the Gestapo and the Kripo – under Heydrich.
Sipo	Sicherheitspolizei.
Sonderkommando	A special detachment of the SS employed for police and political tasks in occupied territory.
SS	Schutzstaffel.
SSPF	SS- und Polizeiführer (qv).
SS- und Polizeiführer	District SS and Police Commanders in Eastern occupied territories – subordinate to the HSSPF.
Staatsanwalt	Public Prosecutor.
Staatsschutzkorps	State Protection Corps – an unofficial term used to describe the combined functions of the Gestapo, Kripo and SD.
Staatspolizei	Initially the Prussian Political Police. Later the Nazi Political Police ie the Gestapo.
Staatspolizeileitstelle	The regional HQ of the Gestapo in a Wehrkreis, Prussian province, Land or Reichsgau, controlling a number of Aussendienststellen.
Staatspolizeistelle	The regional HQ of the Gestapo in a

	Regierungsbezirk, smaller Land or Reichsgau. Coordinated by but not subordinate to a Leitstelle.
Staatssekretär	State Secretary. The permanent head of a ministry – Permanent Under-Secretary.
Stabshauptamt	The Staff Office of the RKF.
Stabswache	'Headquarters Guard'. The original Party guard detachment formed from the SA in 1923. Forerunner of the Leibstandarte.
Stahlhelm	The Nationalist ex-servicemen's organization founded by Franz Seldte in 1918. Compulsorily absorbed into the SA in 1933.
Standarte	An SS (and SA) formation approximately equivalent to a regiment.
Standartenführer	See Appendix 2.
Standgericht	Court-martial.
Standrecht	Martial law.
Stapo	Staatspolizei (qv).
Stapostelle	Staatspolizeistelle (qv).
Stelle	Place, position, appointment, establishment.
Stellvertreter	Deputy or representative.
StHA	Stabshauptamt (qv).
Stosstrupp	Assault or shock troop, battle group.
Streifendienst	Patrol Service manned by the Hitler Youth, trained and officered by the SS.
Sturm	An SS (or SA) unit equivalent to a company.
Sturmabteilung	Lit. 'Storm Detachment'. The SA (the 'Brown-shirts'). The original Nazi paramilitary organization founded in 1921.
Sturmbann	An SS (or SA) unit approximately equivalent to a battalion.
Sturmmann	See Appendix 2.
Technische Nothilfe	Technical Emergency Corps. An auxiliary police force of the Orpo consisting of engineers, technicians and specialists for construction work, public utilities, communications, salvage, etc.

Teno	Technische Nothilfe.
TN	Technische Nothilfe.
Totenkopfverbände	'Death's-Head Formations'. The concentration-camp guard units. In 1939 formed the nucleus of the SS Totenkopf Division, one of the first field formations of the Waffen-SS.
Truppführer	See Appendix 2.
TV	Totenkopfverbände.
Umwandererzentralstelle	Central Re-settlement Office concerned with the re-settlement of Polish deportees from the Wartheland. Part of the RKF organization controlled by the RSHA.
Unterscharführer	See Appendix 2.
Untersturmführer	See Appendix 2.
UWZ	Umwandererzentralstelle (qv).
VDA	Volksbund für das Deutschtum im Ausland (qv).
Verfügungstruppe	The militarized formations of the SS renamed Waffen-SS in the winter of 1939/40.
Verwaltung	Administration.
Volksbund für das Deutschtum im Ausland	League for Germans Abroad. A pre-Nazi organization dealing with the Volksdeutsche. Taken over by the Party in 1930. Its head was Obergruppenführer Lorenz who was also head of VOMI (qv).
Volksdeutsche	'Racial Germans'. German minorities in foreign countries.
Volksdeutsche Mittelstelle	Racial German Assistance Office. One of the organizations through which contact was maintained with Germans abroad. Largely run by the SS. Head – Obergruppenführer Lorenz.
Volkssturm	Home Guard.
VOMI	Volksdeutsche Mittelstelle (qv).
VT	Verfügungstruppe (qv).
Waffen-SS	Fully militarized SS formations, initially composed of the Verfügungstruppe and the

	Totenkopfverbände, later including non-German units. Provided nearly 40 divisions during the second World War.
Wehrbezirkskommando	Military District – subordinate to a Wehrkreis – concerned primarily with recruiting.
Wehrkreis	Military region, indicated by roman numeral. The main military territorial organization in Germany. In peacetime each Wehrkreis contained an active infantry corps.
Wehrmacht	The armed forces (Army, Navy, Air Force).
Wehrmachtführungsstab	The armed forces operations staff. Part of OKW under Colonel-General Alfred Jodl.
Wirtschafts- und Verwaltungshauptamt	SS Economic and Administrative Department formed from the SS Hauptamt in 1940. Controlled the SS economic enterprises and administered the concentration camps. Its head was Obergruppenführer Oswald Pohl.
WVHA	Wirtschafts- und Verwaltungshauptamt.
Zentralabteilung	Coordinating section of an office or agency.

THE STRUCTURE OF THE SS IN 1944

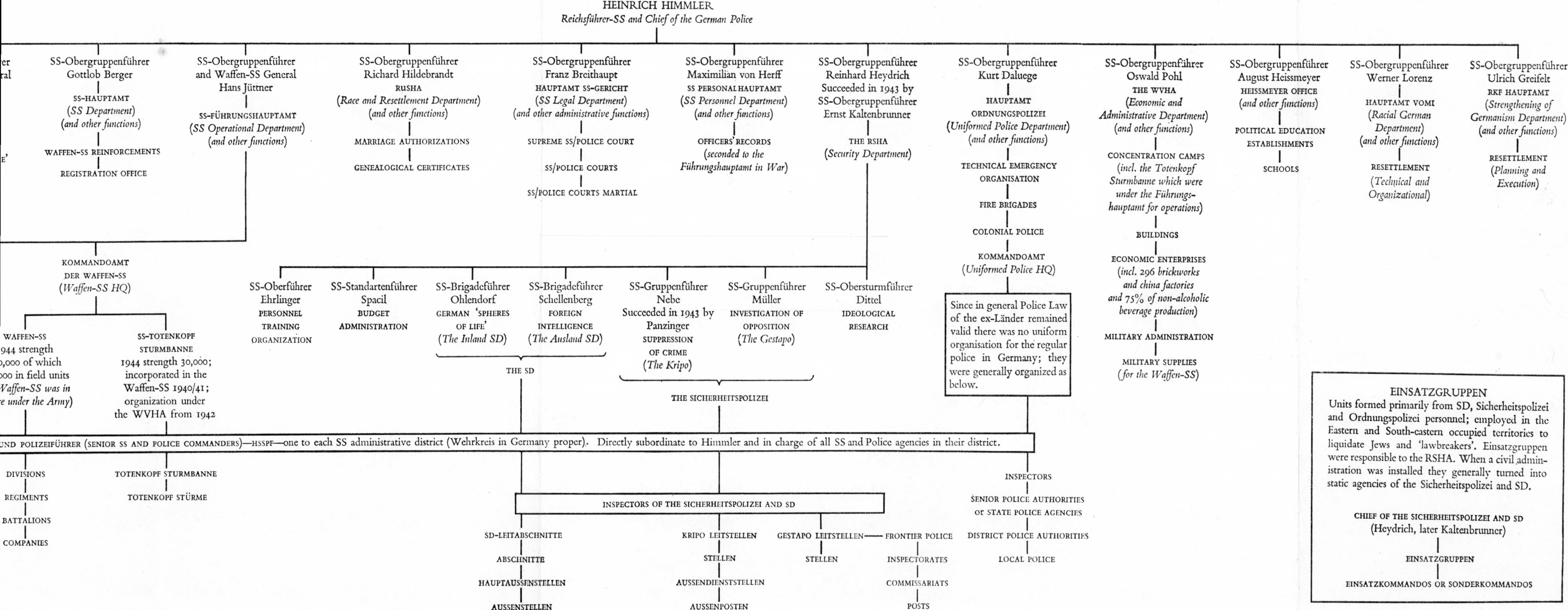

1

INTRODUCTION

THEIR uniform was black and they were the terror of a nation. Their badge was the Death's Head and they swore eternal allegiance to the Führer. Their flash was the runic double-S and they murdered men in millions. Hardly an aspect of the nation's life seemed safe from their interference; they were in charge of the police and the Secret Service; they provided the sentries on the Reich Chancellery and the guards in the concentration camps; they manned the divisions which carried the Death's Head symbol to Europe; they occupied key positions in agriculture, the health service, racial policy and scientific affairs; they crushed their way into traditional diplomatic festitives; they had their watchdogs among the ministerial bureaucrats.

They called themselves the 'Schutzstaffel' [Guard Echelon SS] of the National-Socialist Party and in the words of SS-Hauptsturmführer [Captain] Dieter Wisliceny they considered themselves a 'new form of religious sect with its own rites and customs'.

No layman was allowed a glimpse of the inner working of this secret society; the Führer's SS was intended to be mysterious, sinister and incomprehensible to the ordinary citizen, like the Order of Jesuits which the SS officially abominated but actually imitated down to the smallest detail. The lords of this black-uniformed secret Order deliberately cultivated the fear evoked by their mere existence. SS-Obergruppenführer [General] Reinhard Heydrich head of the Sicherheitspolizei [Security Police] boasted: 'The Gestapo, the Kriminalpolizei [Criminal Police] and the security services are enveloped in the mysterious aura of the political detective story.'[1] Heinrich Himmler, the Reichsführer-SS [Reich SS Leader] and Grand Master of the Order said with some satisfaction: 'I know that there are many in Germany who feel uncomfortable when they see this black tunic; we understand that and do not expect to be beloved by over-many people.'[2] The German people sensed that the SS had enveloped the Reich in a fine-spun web, whose individual threads they could not see. The Germans merely heard the tramp of the black columns resounding on the cobbles of their towns and villages; they simply heard hundreds of thousands of masculine voices roar:

SS marschiert, die Strasse frei!	Clear the streets, the SS marches
Die Sturmkolonnen stehen!	The storm-columns stand at the ready.
Sie werden aus der Tyrannei	They will take the road
Den Weg zur Freiheit gehen.	From tyranny to freedom.
Drum auf bereit zum letzten Stoss!	So we are ready to give our all
Wie's unsere Väter waren!	As did our fathers before us.
Der Tod sei unser Kampfgenoss!	Let death be our battle companion.
Wir sind die schwarzen Scharen.	We are the Black Band.[3]

Thousands upon thousands of unseen eyes seemed to watch every step taken by every German. The tentacles of the police octopus wrapped themselves round the community; any trace of anti-Nazi sentiment was duly noted by 45,000 officials and employees of the Gestapo distributed over 20 Leitstellen [regional offices] and 39 Stellen [sub-regional offices] fed by so-called 'antennae' in a further 300 Leitstellen and 850 Frontier Police 'Commissariats'.[4] The security of the State was guarded by 65,000 men in the Sicherheitspolizei and 2,800,000 men in the Ordnungspolizei [regular police] headed by 30 HSSPF [Höhere SS- und Polizeiführer – senior SS and Police commanders].[5] 40,000 guards terrorized hundreds of thousands of actual or supposed enemies of the régime in 20 concentration camps and 160 affiliated labour camps.[6] Alongside the Wehrmacht, and eyeing their military rivals,[7] stood 950,000 soldiers of the Waffen-SS [Armed SS] including 310,000 'racial Germans' and 200,000 foreigners. A shadowy army of 100,000 SD [Sicherheitsdienst – the SS security service] informers kept a continuous check on the population's thinking.[8] Whatever the sources – universities, businesses, farms or local authorities – every detail of any significance was sucked in and pumped to the Berlin central office.

But the outer world was never allowed to know anything of what went on inside the SS; nothing was allowed to emerge which might indicate the thinking within Heinrich Himmler's empire. Himmler took care to ensure that no member of his Order came in too close contact with laymen; SS leaders were not allowed to go to law with ordinary people lest the courts gain an insight into SS internal affairs;[9] the Reich Ministry of Economics was refused information on SS industrial concerns.[10] An order from Himmler to the concentration-camp guards, the Totenkopfverbände [Death's-Head formations – TV] laid down that: 1. No unit was to be located in its home area; a Pomeranian

Sturm [SS unit equivalent to a company] would therefore never serve in Pomerania, for instance. 2. Units were to be moved every three months. 3. Individual men were never to be employed on street duties.[11] Even the most exalted dignitaries of the Third Reich did not know what went on in the SS; in 1945 Göring said: 'I had no insight into the SS. No outsider knew anything of Himmler's organization.'[12]

Not until the collapse of the Third Reich was the curtain concealing the SS empire removed. Then the men who had commanded the SS over the years appeared in the dock at Nuremberg accused of instigating war and other almost inconceivable crimes.

The Allied military courts set out in detail all that the SS safety curtain had so carefully concealed. From the statements of the witnesses and the documents brought in evidence by the prosecution emerged an apocalyptic picture of racial mania, the grisly story of the SS as the guillotine used by a gang of psychopaths obsessed with racial purity. The bill of horror showed: 4–5 million Jews murdered, 2,500,000 Poles liquidated, 520,000 gipsies eliminated, 473,000 Russian prisoners of war executed, 100,000 incurables gassed under the euthanasia programme.[13] On September 30th, 1946, the Allied judges pronounced sentence on Himmler's SS, declaring it to be a criminal organization on the grounds that: 'The SS was used for purposes which were criminal, involving the persecution and the extermination of the Jews, brutalities and killings in concentration camps, excesses in the administration of occupied territories, the administration of the slave labour programme and the maltreatment and murder of prisoners of war.'[14] As a result, the judgement continued, suspicion of crime attached to all persons 'who had been officially accepted as members of the SS . . . who became or remained members of the organization with knowledge that it was being used for the commission of acts declared criminal by Article 6 of the [London War Crimes] Charter.'[15]

By this judgement of the Nuremberg court the badge of the SS became the sign of a criminal political organization, a mark of Cain henceforth branded upon anyone who had ever worn the black uniform. Once the breeding-ground of a self-styled élite, the SS became the 'army of outlaws', in the self-pitying words of SS General Felix Steiner.[16] Nevertheless the Allied judgement suffered from a serious defect; it did not explain why more than a million men had turned, collectively and almost overnight, into mass murderers; it did not explain the source of the power which enabled the SS to turn the racial fantasies of the National-Socialist régime into dreadful fact.

Ex-members of the SS either could not or would not explain the mystery. They evaded the issue, either pretending that they knew nothing about it, or off-loading the responsibility upon others who were dead. In 1948 came a somewhat timid effort at self-criticism from ex-SS-Untersturmführer [Lieutenant] Erich Kernmayr, alias Kern, with his book *Der Grosse Rausch* (The Great Frenzy);[17] but then West Germany, with its atmosphere of rehabilitation, provided a kind of protective twilight from which emerged a body of exculpatory literature written by ex-SS commanders who clearly believed that memories are short. At Nuremberg, for instance, Oberstgruppenführer [General] Hausser, the senior Waffen-SS General, referred to Himmler as 'completely unmilitary' and could hardly ever remember having seen him with troops;[18] SS-Sturmbanführer [Major] Brill described the Allgemeine SS [general SS] as 'a voluntary organization entirely distinct from the Waffen-SS';[19] SS men invariably stated that they had 'never been taught racial hatred'.[20]

But then came the ex-inmates of the concentration camps, the survivors of the SS terror, and the explanation of the mystery which they gave to the German nation was this:

The SS was a monolithic organization directed by the demoniac will of one man; it was composed of fanatical ideologists and unscrupulous power-hungry functionaries; the SS had gradually laid hands upon every position of power in the Third Reich, until finally it had constructed a 'super-organized master and slave system, every part at all times controllable.'[21] These are the words of Eugen Kogon, an ex-inmate of Buchenwald and now Professor of Politics at the Darmstadt Political High School, in his well-known book *Die SS Staat*; Kogon has an analytical mind and in his book he pictures the SS leaders as a homogeneous clique 'pursuing a plan consistently step by step at any cost. Each partial step was sought with a degree of ruthlessness completely transcending ordinary concepts.'[22] Kogon concluded that only by such methods could the 'well-built structure of the SS State' have arisen 'which permeated first the Nazi Party, next Germany and finally the whole of Europe.'[23] In other words the concentration camps were a 'scale model'[24] of the SS State and the SS the real rulers in Adolf Hitler's Germany.

Kogon thus produced a striking theory, apparently the first to give a comprehensible explanation of the SS phenomenon. In 1948 Otto Ohlendorf himself wrote in his death-cell: 'We must take a man like Kogon seriously.'[25] Kogon, to give him his due, did make certain small reservations and introduce some minor nuances, but others soon followed to paint an even blacker picture of SS omnipotence.

Gerald Reitlinger in *The Final Solution* described Himmler's empire as 'a State within a State ... the only thing with which it could be compared was the Russian NKVD';[26] Comer Clarke, Eichmann's biographer, saw the SS carrying 'the shadow of the Nazi terror into nearly every home on the continent';[27] in the eyes of the French writer Joseph Kessel, the whole of Europe lay under the SS jackboot – 'from the Arctic Ocean to the Mediterranean, from the Atlantic to the Volga and the Caucasus, all were at his [Himmler's] mercy.'[28]

The greater the power ascribed to the SS, the clearer and more horrifying became the picture of the SS man painted both by German and foreign writers. Rudolf Pechel, editor of the *Deutsche Rundschau* and a former inmate of Sachsenhausen, thought that 'with their dull cold-fish stare, betraying the absence of any spiritual life within, the eyes were the SS men's common denominator' and he believed that he could spot an SD informer 'simply from the look in his eye'.[29] Kogon described SS men as 'maladjusted and frustrated, men whom circumstances had deprived of success, whose innate endowment was slight, who often enough were total social failures.'[30] The lower-level Gestapo officials he called 'a catch-all of down-and-outs';[31] SD informers were 'the worst scum collected from the aristocracy and the bourgeoisie, the working and white-collar classes.'[32]

Having exhausted the stock of derogatory adjectives, the supporters of the SS-State theory then turned to the formulae of modern psychoanalysis. Elie Cohen, an ex-inmate of Auschwitz, considered that 'SS men (apart from certain exceptions) consisted of normal individuals who, because of their criminal super-ego, had become normal criminals.'[33] Another psychologist, Leo Alexander, regarded the SS as a completely ordinary collection of gangsters, who collectively behaved exactly as criminal cliques usually do: 'If a member did anything which put his loyalty to the organization in a questionable light, he was either liquidated – killed – or he had to undertake a criminal act which definitely and irrevocably tied him to the organization. According to the age-old custom of criminal gangs, this act had to include murder.'[34]

Meanwhile, however, other voices were raised to dispute the theories of the Kogon school. In a sociological study published in 1954, Karl O. Paetel questioned whether collectively the SS could be written down so far. He considered that the SS did not consist of a 'single type of man; there were criminals and idealists, blockheads and intellectuals.'[35] In 1956 Dr Ermenhild Neusüss-Hunkel published a book on the SS in which she stated that the difference in function between the numerous branches of Himmler's organization meant that 'an unequivocal estimate of the character of the SS membership as a whole was not possible.'[36] She calculated that no more than 15 per cent of SS members had actively contributed to the National-Socialist system of tyranny: in

1944 there were 800,000 enrolled members of the SS,[37] of whom 39,415 were serving in the SS central offices, 26,000 in the so-called 'police reinforcements', 19,294 in Sicherheitspolizei and SD units in occupied territory, less than 6,000 with the Sicherheits- and Ordnungspolizei in Germany and 2,000 as concentration-camp guards.[38]

At about this time the SS files were released by the Allies and study of these led to further alterations in the post-war picture of the SS. The first result was to throw doubt on Kogon's book; the files showed numerous inaccuracies in his dates, statistics and descriptions of personalities, when not based on his personal experiences in Buchenwald; moreover it had already become noticeable that each fresh edition of Kogon's book contained numerous amendments.

Remarkably enough the Germans practically ignored the new picture of the SS presented by the realist historians – and for good reason – the historians were threatening to destroy the alibi of a nation, the theory of SS omnipotence.

The Germans had been both horrified and relieved by the revelations of SS crimes – horrified because the reputation of their country would be besmirched for years to come in the eyes of the world, relieved because, at least for the older generation, the news of the terrifying power of the SS offered a tiny loophole for escape from a past with which they had not been able to come to terms. If, they said to themselves, the SS had really been so all-powerful, if it had really held the country in an unassailable iron grip, then for the ordinary citizen of the Third Reich criticism of the régime's policy or active opposition to the misdeeds of the Nazi State was simply tantamount to suicide.

Exposure of the SS crimes was no unwelcome development for many Germans; these horrors formed the great alibi, a nation's excuse to itself and to the world. Compared to the activities of Himmler's corps of thugs, the failings of so many other Germans under the Third Reich paled into insignificance. As early as 1946 Laternser, the Defence Counsel for OKW [Oberkommando der Wehrmacht – Armed Forces Defence Staff] said in Nuremberg that the SS commanders would have to die anyway and therefore everything should be laid at their door – the Wehrmacht [regular armed forces] escutcheon must remain clean.[39] When it later became known from American sources that Himmler himself had temporarily flirted with the July 20th, 1944 conspiracy to kill Hitler, Hans Rothfels adjured his German fellow-historians not to attach too much weight to this theory, saying that: 'there is in fact no chapter entitled "Himmler" in the history of the German underground movement.'[40]

For the general run of German historians the subject of the SS was taboo. The intellectual descendants of Ranke and Treitschke carefully concealed their thoughts regarding the most horrifying organization ever invented by Germans – they wrote no book on the SS, no major work on Himmler's Eastern policy, no study of the National-Socialist police machine. The German historians left the field wide open to their foreign colleagues, who began, with varying degrees of sympathy, realism and intensity of research, to study the most recent period of German history with the SS as the centrepiece. One or two standard works were produced, such as Raul Hilberg's *The Destruction of the European Jews*[41] and Alexander Dallin's *German Rule in Russia*[42] (both authors were American); many other books were translated and published by reputable German firms but the majority of their authors lacked adequate source material and so they contributed little to the formation of a more factual picture of the SS.

The Frenchman Jacques Delarue; for instance, produced a *History of the Gestapo* without even having examined the most important source for his subject, the files of Himmler's private office.[43] In his history of the Gestapo the British journalist Edward Crankshaw seems unable to distinguish between the duties of the Gestapo and those of the Einsatzgruppen [Action Groups – SS liquidation squads];[44] another Frenchman, Benoist-Méchin, produced a ten-volume *History of the German Army*, in which he passes over the whole Röhm affair with a couple of Hitler speeches and some out-of-date newspaper quotations.[45] The result was, of course, fatal. The book simply confirmed what the Nazis had always been saying. When history is written with such levity, the experts are bound to discover mistakes.

The first serious work was that of Hannah Arendt, the German sociologist who emigrated to America. Her book *Eichmann in Jerusalem* published in 1963, was the first to produce a credible picture of an SS commander as a human being.[46] In the same year Enno Georg, in his book on the SS economic concerns, showed how diverse were the components which went to make up the SS.[47] Shortly thereafter, led by Hans Buchheim with his *SS und Polizei im NS-Staat* (SS and Police in the National-Socialist State) the historians of the Institut für Zeitgeschichte (Institute for Contemporary History), Munich, attacked the problem and produced *Anatomy of the SS State*[48] as a 'counterweight to the widespread habit of painting a highly emotionalized picture of the past in order to highlight certain major truths but at the price of historical exactitude regarding facts and circumstances' – as their foreword puts it.[49] From America came the first real history of the Waffen-SS written by George H. Stein.[50] Stein summarizes the matter: 'The doctrine of criminal conspiracy and collective guilt formulated during the Nuremberg era no longer satisfies serious investigators. Without minimizing the extent of the staggering crimes committed by Himmler's minions, recent research has shown that the SS was in fact more varied and complex than the monolithic criminal organization indicted before the International Military Tribunal.'[51]

Nevertheless the investigators are still only in the early stages. Many are still unable to put their false picture of the SS State entirely out of their mind; many still believe with Karl Paetel that at any rate in the final phases of the Third Reich 'only two men mattered – Adolf Hitler and Heinrich Himmler.'[52] For a long time now many historians have supported the mistaken notion that the SS was the sole undisputed source of authority under the National-Socialist dictatorship; they can hardly be expected to abandon their favourite theory too quickly.

The Third Reich has been pictured as a totalitarian State, 'super-organized' (Kogon's phrase),[53] all-embracing, encompassing every individual citizen and subjecting him to a single coordinated central directing force. The National-Socialists seemed to have made the age-old dream of the Germans come true: a strong State in which only one man's will prevailed – that of the Führer, in which only one political ideology was authoritative – that of the National-Socialist Party, in which only one force ruled over law and order – that of the SS/Police.

But the dream of the strong State remained a figment of the imagination. The Third Reich was not a totalitarian State; it was a caricature of one – a caricature reflecting all the dreams, hopes and ideas of the early Nazi leaders as they constructed their authoritarian State. Hans Buchheim concluded that the totalitarian Führer State was 'not a machine perfected down to the smallest detail; it was no super-rationalized system; it was a jumble of vested interests and political strings, spheres of authority and plenary powers, and ultimately a free-for-all referred to at the time as "National-Socialist war games".'[54] Professor Trevor-Roper exclaimed: 'How many people in the past years were unconsciously seduced by Nazi propaganda into believing that Nazi Germany was organized as a "totalitarian" State – totally integrated, totally mobilized, centrally controlled! . . . But in fact the totalitarianism of Germany was something quite different from this.'[55]

In Nazi Germany nothing was total except the will of Hitler; that, with its 'Führer decrees' and 'Führer orders', was what ruled 80 million people. When the Führer's intentions were laid down in black and white, the SS, as the most important instrument of the Führer dictatorship, had absolute power. In SS eyes, however, the ever-suspicious Führer had one failing – his orders did not always explain what he wanted, nor did they necessarily cover every sphere of the nation's life. Since the Reich Cabinet had ceased to sit and Hitler in his field headquarters became ever more distant from his ministers, the outcome of a Führer order was frequently the product of chance.

Moreover part of Hitler's cunning as a leader was his ability to keep the centre of political power permanently shifting among his closest collaborators, thereby preventing the emergence of unwelcome rivals. It was an unwritten law of the Führer's dictatorship that no official or legal structure should be allowed to arise which might inhibit Hitler's freedom of action. The hallmark of the National-Socialist régime was not monolithic unity but the 'anarchy of authority', in the words of Hans Frank, the disillusioned Nazi legal adviser.[56] Hitler had no wish to be tied to any hierarchical system and so he passed his orders to the largest possible number of minor authorities. A system of multiplicity, instinctive rather than deliberate, ensured that no subordinate could combine with one of his rivals to act against Hitler.

The result was a curious system of 'permanent self-frustration', as Hannah Arendt puts it;[57] by entrusting the solution of any one problem to a number of authorities simultaneously, the dictator assured his independence from his own subordinates; at the same time, however, the State became the arena of a power struggle more injurious to the efficiency of the official machine than the democratic party strife which the Nazis so much despised. The State was down-graded to a non-political administrative machine, to a façade behind which the régime's warlords carried on their struggle for power. Ulrich von Hassell, later one of the leaders of the July 20th, 1944, plot, said: 'These people have no conception of what a State is.'[58] The more intelligent of the SS leaders, such as Otto Ohlendorf, criticized Hitler because 'the strange thing is that, theoretically speaking, an absolute Führer State existed but, in particular during the war, a pluralist anarchy developed.'[59] In 1947 Ohlendorf admitted at Nuremberg: 'The Führer not only denied the State as a purpose in itself but totally destroyed it, so that it was no longer available to him as an instrument; the State was superseded by arbitrary action on the part of a multiplicity of authorities.'[60] In this 'confusion of private empires, private armies and private intelligence services'[61] there was no place for an SS monopoly. Unless they could quote a Hitler decree, the SS became one among many second-level power groups struggling for influence.

Unless the SS was carrying out a direct order from Hitler it was without the protective screen of Hitler's authority, and Himmler had to reach agreement with the other Reich authorities. The SS was frequently forced to act in the area not covered by clearly defined Führer orders, where there were no rules and victory went, not to the most orthodox National-Socialist but to whoever had the strongest private army or the greatest personal influence. This too was in accordance with the Führer's wishes; the persistent gang warfare and internal struggles of the Nazi Party spilled over into the machinery of the State – and the quarrels of his subordinates guaranteed Hitler his undisputed position both in the Party and in the State.

Like medieval feudal barons, Hitler's minions coalesced, split and came together again. They even made formal alliances among themselves; in 1936, for instance, the Sicherheitspolizei concluded a ten-point agreement with the Abwehr [Military Intelligence] which became known as the 'Ten Commandments';[62] von Ribbentrop, the Foreign Minister, accepted a number of SS commanders into his Ministry as the price of a short armistice in the battle between the SS and the Foreign Ministry;[63] Rosenberg, the Minister for the East, negotiated with SS-Gruppenführer Berger to protect himself against the intrigues of his theoretical subordinate Koch, the Reich Commissar for the Ukraine.[64]

Progress through this jungle of competing authorities was so laborious that the SS hardly had time or energy to grab the dominant position in Germany. They did, indeed, seize one position of power after another, but there were two authorities they could never overcome – The Party and The Wehrmacht. The SS had to swallow a man-hunt by the Party Labour Front and SA after the SD's secret informers;[65] they had to accept the suppression of the SD's 'Reports from the Reich';[66] they had to look on, powerless, while Frank, the Governor-General of Poland, supported by the Wehrmacht and the SA, manoeuvred SS-Obergruppenführer Krüger, the most powerful man in German-occupied Poland, out of office.[67]

Although more and more SS uniforms were to be seen among Hitler's immediate entourage, the mistrustful dictator never allowed the SS to reach the final decisive position of power in the State. Hitler left the SS leaders in no doubt that they were his minions. The police in the new Germany were just as bad as those in the old, he grumbled,[68] and when, contrary to his wishes, the SS meddled in German policy in Rumania, he shouted that he would 'smoke out the black plague!'[69] Himmler, the Reichsführer-SS, was always in a cold panic when summoned by his Chief, and Hitler seldom treated him other than as an industrious, but not particularly intelligent, pupil. Hitler never regarded him as his successor and in March 1945, he gave his reasons – Himmler would be rejected by the Party and, in addition, he was unacceptable because of his lack of artistic feeling.[70]

One of the rules of this free-for-all, of course, was that no one was likely to oppose the SS unless he knew that he had the bigger battalions on his side. In Adolf Hitler's Reich, however, there was one helpless group of human beings completely without protection – the Jews. They were easy meat for the SS concentration camps and crematoria; none of the Party bosses would stand up for them. So the one place where the SS State was to be seen, the only place where it really existed, was the secluded world of the concentration camps. The inmates of Himmler's camps really were slaves, victims of an inexorable process. And yet the history of the destruction of the Jews shows that some men who wore the brown shirt, some of the older Nazis, prominent figures in the SS and founder members of the Third Reich, managed to defy Himmler's death machine.

Ex-Gauleiter Kube, the Commissar General in White Ruthenia, for instance, accused police officers of anti-Jewish excesses, took under his protection Jews being transported to Minsk for extermination, and conducted a one-man campaign against the SS and SD until Soviet partisans blew him up with a bomb.[71] SS-Obergruppenführer Dr Werner Best sabotaged Himmler's Jew-murder programme and enabled thousands of Danish Jews to escape to neutral Sweden.[72] Felix Kersten the masseur, Himmler's personal physician, 'my only friend, my Buddha',[73] used his capacity to relieve his master of his stomach pains to save thousands of Jewish lives, first the Jews of Finland, then thousands of others who were permitted to emigrate to Sweden.[74] Finally an assortment of Italian generals, Balkan politicians and French collaborators wove a web of deception and lies round hundreds of thousands of European Jews and blocked Eichmann's executioners for long enough to get them to safety.

Werner Best's attitude alone shows that the SS-State theory does not hold water. The SS was never a monolithic organization; of all the manifestations of the Third Reich the SS was the most random and the most self-contradictory. There was hardly an informer who was not at loggerheads with another of his ilk, hardly a practical political problem upon which any two senior SS leaders thought alike. In Nuremberg SS-Oberführer [Senior Colonel] Reinecke lamented that the SS had been 'infiltrated by persons and organizations completely alien to the character of the SS.'[75]

The SS secret files show the internal conflict only too clearly. Himmler, for instance, accused SS-Gruppenführer Reeder of sabotaging the SS policy of Germanization in Belgium;[76] the Nuremberg Waffen-SS Garrison Commander refused to work with the Allgemeine SS or the SD;[77] an SS-Untersturmführer collected evidence against SS-Gruppenführer Berger,[78] while Berger was accusing other SS commanders of working for the Catholic Church.[79] Ohlendorf ridiculed Himmler's 'blood and soil' fantasies;[80] the RSHA [Reichssicherheitshauptamt – Reich Security Department] and the WVHA (Wirtschafts- und Verwaltungshauptamt – SS Economic and Administrative Department] quarrelled over whether Jews should be kept as slave labour or murdered;[81] the Gestapo shot down Soviet deserters whom the SD wished to use as a Russian counter-revolutionary army.[82] Even non-members of the order contributed to the internal conflicts within the SS; Dr Richard Korherr, a devout Catholic, was appointed Himmler's Inspector of Statistics;[83] Hans Hohberg, an accountant, became the power behind the throne in the SS economic concerns;[84] Kammler, a civil servant from the Works Department of the Air Ministry, rose rapidly to the rank of SS General as builder of the famous concentration camps.[85]

In fact the SS world was a bizarre nonsensical affair, devoid of all logic. The theories hitherto advanced to explain the SS phenomenon have been equally bizarre, though superficially logical. In fact, history shows that the SS was anything but an organization constructed and directed on some diabolically efficient system; it was a product of accident and automatism. The real history of the SS is a story of idealists and criminals, of place-seekers and romantics: it is the history of the most fantastic association of men imaginable.

2

THE FORMATION OF THE SS

THE history of the SS, like that of the National-Socialist Movement, starts in the turbulent post-war spring of 1919 when the Free Corps and the Reichswehr had driven the Red 'Soldiers and Workers Councils' out of Bavaria.

An unwitting midwife at the birth of the National-Socialist Movement was the Munich historian, Karl Alexander von Müller. He was in close touch with the young nationalist officers who were calling the tune in Munich at the time and at a soldiers' rally he was impressed by a man who seemed to have an extraordinarily compelling power of oratory. He says: 'Below locks of hair hanging down in a most unmilitary fashion, I saw a pale thin face with a close-cropped moustache and strikingly large light-blue eyes with a cold fanatical stare.'[1] Müller nudged his school-friend Mayr, who was sitting next to him: 'Do you know you have got a "natural" orator among your pupils?'

Captain Karl Mayr was head of Abteilung Ib/P (Press and propaganda) in Reichswehr Group Headquarters No 4 (Bavaria). He knew the man: 'That's Hitler from the List Regiment. You, Hitler, come here a moment.' Müller remembers that Hitler 'did as he was told, moving awkwardly, half defiant, half embarrassed.' The scene typifies Adolf Hitler's dependence upon the officers of the Bavarian Reichswehr and the sense of inferiority which the future Führer of the Great German Reich took years to overcome.

Mayr was quick to recognize Corporal Hitler's propagandist ability. In July 1919 Mayr's section in the Bavarian War Ministry drew up a confidential list of their contact men in individual units: the list included one 'Hittler, Adolf'.[2] Mayr found Hitler only too ready to use his oratory wherever the ideological front was threatened.

The corporal gradually proved himself so useful that Mayr dropped his parade-ground manner, and began to address his letters politely 'Dear Herr Hitler'.[3] Hitler was a frequent visitor to the War Ministry and ranked as a member of Mayr's political staff. One day in the demobilization camp at Lechfeld it looked as if the officers were losing control of their men; Hitler moved in at once and restored the situation. Another contact man, Lorenz Frank, reported on August 23rd, 1919: 'Hitler particularly is a born demagogue; at a meeting his fanaticism and popular appeal compel his audience to listen to him.'[4]

Mayr decided to use his discovery for greater things. One of his duties was to watch political parties in Bavaria; in September 1919 he accordingly dispatched Hitler to a meeting of the German Workers Party (Deutsche Arbeiter Partei – DAP)[5] – a collection of nationalist sectarians who, in addition to hatred of the Jews and the Republic, preached an emotional lower-middle-class Socialism using such phrases as 'breaking the yoke of the usurer'. Hitler soon became the star speaker at the DAP meetings and had little difficulty in shouting down the more discreet among his competitors in the beer cellars. In January 1920, the party, then sixty-four strong, elected him Head of Propaganda and accepted the party programme which he drew up. It later re-named itself National-Socialist German Workers Party (NSDAP).[6]

At this point Mayr was retired, and his place was taken by a little snub-nosed man with a crew cut whose battered, florid face gave evidence of unbounded energy. This was Captain Ernst Röhm, who, more than any other one man, was responsible for launching Hitler, now demobilized, into German politics. Röhm was a curious mixture of military reformer and Bavarian crook, an irrepressible conspirator, a homosexual, coarse and uncouth; nevertheless his comrades regarded him as a real soldier and he had a remarkable degree of moral courage.

Röhm was a contradictory character – a staunch Bavarian monarchist, ex-Company Commander in No 10 Bavarian Infantry Regiment, 'The Kings' with Ludwig III as its Colonel-in-Chief; when the monarchy fell in 1918 Röhm had been ready to 'honour his oath unto death'.[7] On the other hand he now regarded Bavaria as an 'orderly corner' in which the nationalists could gather their strength for the assault on that revolutionary tower of Babel, Berlin.

The 1919 Munich *condottieri* consisted primarily of the extremists from a generation of disillusioned embittered officers who, with the war lost and the monarchy fallen, found themselves condemned to a drab, humdrum existence. They had lost their social status and, so they said, their honour as well; they were vainly searching for a new form of society to which their experiences at the front had seemed to point the way. So democracy and the 'November Republic', which was weak and precarious anyway, became the target for the officers wrath and were held responsible for all their miseries. Germany's military men were determined to regain their social position and to restore to their country the capacity to defend itself, which the victors of 1918 had removed.

Chance came to their assistance. For a short while, and primarily in Bavaria, the struggle against the Communists and the Spartacists placed the officers in power; on the fall of the Red Republic no one counted who could not boast a uniform. Until constitutional government was restored, Bavarian politics were dominated by the officers, to some extent opposed by the Social Democrats and to some extent supported by the right-wing Catholic Bavarian Peoples Party. Captain Mayr kept watch on the political parties; Dr Roth was in charge of the judiciary; Lieutenant Ernst Pöhner became Police President of Munich;[8] Röhm, then thirty-two, was initially Chief of Staff to the Munich Garrison Commander, then head of Section Ib (Arms and Equipment) on the staff of Colonel Ritter von Epp's Infantry Brigade and finally was given the most delicate task imaginable for a German officer at the time, the formation and equipment of the Bavarian Home Guard [Einwohnerwehr].[9]

The Versailles Treaty had placed strict limits on the strength and equipment of the Reichswehr. Germany was allowed seven infantry and two cavalry divisions[10] but there were no reserves for use in emergency. The officers could see only one way out – formation of a second ('black') Reichswehr. Röhm conceived this reserve as a sort of national militia, a 'citizen army with its rifles in the cupboard', in Konrad Heiden's words. He found a resourceful ally in Escherich, a forestry official and member of the Bavarian Peoples Party. Together they formed the most powerful militia Germany has ever known – the Bavarian Home Guard.[11]

Röhm worked tirelessly collecting weapons and forming secret ammunition dumps; the Allies became suspicious but he covered his tracks well. In Munich alone he amassed 169 light and 11 heavy guns, 760 machine guns, 21,351 rifles, carbines and revolvers, 300,000 hand-grenades and 8,000,000 rounds of ammunition;[12] when the Army was expanded in the mid-1930s, one-third of the additional weapons required by the Wehrmacht came from Röhm's secret arsenals.[13]

In the summer of 1921, however, the Bavarian Home Guard was brought abruptly to an end. The Berlin Central Government kept its promise to the Allies and insisted upon the disbandment of the Munich defence formations.[14] Röhm had lost his main ally, and was left with nothing but a little collection of extreme right-wing defence organizations, remnants of the Free Corps leading a useless shadowy existence, playing at soldiers and pursuing their blood feuds. Although they despised democracy, the officers suddenly realized that the masses were indispensable and that they had no following to give them political weight; Bogislaw von Selchow's poem was coming true:

Ich hasse	I hate
die Masse,	The crowd
die kleine,	The little men
gemeine,	The mean men
den Nacken gebeugt,	Who bow their heads
die isst und schläft und Kinder zeugt.	And eat, sleep and beget children
Ich hasse	I hate
die Masse,	The crowd
die lahme,	The impotent crowd
die zahme	The pliable crowd
die heut' an mich glaubt	Which believes in me today
und die mir morgen mein Herzblut raubt.	And tomorrow will tear my heart out.[15]

Röhm, however, thought he knew a man who could draw the crowd. He had met Hitler of the NSDAP at a meeting of a Munich Nationalist circle known as the 'Iron Fist'.[16] Röhm saw in Hitler the demagogue he required to mobilize mass support for his secret army. In July 1921

Hitler became first President of the NSDAP[17] and Röhm's mind was made up – with Hitler he would march to power. The Austrian agitator went the rounds of the beer cellars, stirring up feeling among the lower-middle class and the victims of inflation against the 'November criminals'. Meanwhile Röhm formed the first mobile squads to protect his orator. Men of No 19 Trench Mortar Company under Captain Streck were employed to beat up any disturbers of the peace at NSDAP meetings.[18] From this military body developed the Party's strong-arm organization, which turned into the 'Gymnastics and Sport' Section and finally gave birth to the most characteristic of all the National-Socialist Movement's formations, the SA [Sturmabteilung – Storm Detachment].[19]

Röhm had selected his first recruits and he now began to look for SA commanders. He found them among the wreckage of No 2 Naval Brigade commanded by the ultra-conservative Captain Ehrhardt. The organization had been scattered to the four winds after the failure of the attempt to install Dr Kapp as Chancellor in March 1920[20] and some of the fugitives had taken refuge in Munich, calling themselves the 'Consul Organization'.[21] Ehrhardt, a crusty sea captain and an eccentric character totally unsuited to conspiratorial ways, initially refused to have anything to do with Hitler, saying: 'Good God, what will the fool do next?'[22] Röhm, however, pointed out to him that his officers must have some organization to command and Ehrhardt eventually agreed. He lent Röhm some of his best men; Lieutenant Johan Ulrich Klintzsch took over the training and coordination of the SA;[23] Lieutenant-Commander Hoffmann became Chief-of-Staff[24] and Lieutenant-Commander Manfred Freiherr von Killinger, though still wanted for his part in the assassination of Erzberger, joined them later.[25] The 'Ehrhardt Brigade' simply turned into 'Sturmabteilung Hitler'; even the sailors' battle song required little alteration:

Hakenkreuz am Stahlhelm	The Swastika on our helmet
Schwarzweissrotes Band,	Black-white-red armband
Sturmabteilung Hitler	Storm Detachment Hitler
Werden wir genannt.	Is our name.[26]

On August 3rd, 1921, according to the proclamation constituting the SA, these men undertook to serve the NSDAP 'as an iron organization' and to 'render willing obedience to its leader'.[27] But it was soon made clear to Hitler that, as far as the SA was concerned, he was an outsider. He did not call the tune: the men who gave the orders were Röhm's and Ehrhardt's officers.

Hitler regarded the SA as an instrument of political propaganda, a force to stick up election posters, use its knuckle-dusters in meeting-hall fights and impress the discipline-loving Germans by propaganda marches. In the eyes of its leaders, however, the SA was a genuine military force[28] and, in fact, it figured as a regular formation in the Reichswehr's mobilization plans; No 7 Pioneer Battalion and No 19 Infantry Regiment of the Bavarian Reichswehr were responsible for the military training of the SA; the Munich SA regiment, at a strength of 1,150 in 1923, included an artillery company and cavalry platoons and used Army ranks such as corporal and bombardier.[29]

As a counterweight to the Ehrhardt officers, Hitler recruited Captain Hermann Göring, a wearer of the *Pour-le-Mérite* [the German equivalent of the Victoria Cross], and placed him at the head of the SA; early in 1923 Göring formed an SA Headquarters[30] on the lines of a divisional staff with infantry and artillery commanders.[31] Hitler sensed instinctively that within the Party a force was taking shape which would look elsewhere for its orders. There were a number of danger signals; the NSDAP, together with other extreme right-wing groups, had affiliated itself to the Arbeitsgemeinschaft der vaterländischen Kampfverbände [Working Association of Patriotic Fighting Formations] whose military commander was Lieutenant-Colonel (Retired) Kriebel; he said flatly that: 'The politicians must keep their mouths shut.'[32] News-sheet No 2 from SA headquarters stated that local group leaders [Ortsgruppenführer] could 'best serve' their commander by assuming the role of 'tub-thumper'.[33] An instruction from Hoffmann, the Chief-of-Staff, stated that the SA was 'a specialist organization within the National-Socialist Movement to be dealt with as a separate force by local groups and Party headquarters';[34] this made ominous reading for Hitler.

Here were the first signs of the conflict which was later to plague the Movement right up to Röhm's death – the murderous strife between the SA and the political leadership. Hitler was quick to see the danger, so, to free himself from the pressure of unruly SA officers, he surrounded himself with a praetorian guard.

What later proved to be the germ of the SS appeared in March 1923; a few of the 'old fighters' swore to protect Hitler from all internal and external enemies if necessary at the risk of their lives; they called themselves the Stabswache [headquarters guard].[35] The black uniform later adopted by the SS was seen for the first time; to distinguish themselves from the SA the 'headquarters guard' wore field-grey overcoats and jackets, black ski-caps with a silver Death's-Head button, and black-bordered swastika armbands.[36]

This bodyguard did not last long. Two months later Ehrhardt broke with Hitler and recalled his men from the SA.[37] Hitler thereupon formed a new bodyguard to which he gave the name 'Stosstrupp Adolf Hitler' [Assault Squad].[38] Its leaders were an SA man named Julius Schreck and a diminutive man called Joseph Berchtold who ran a stationery business and was Number Two in the NSDAP Treasury; its normal meeting-place was the Torbräu in Munich, near the Isartor.[39] Here, in the skittle alley, the Assault Squad's first assignments were discussed. Though all were members of the Party, the men of the Assault Squad came from a social background very different from that of the followers of Ehrhardt and Röhm; they were mostly labourers from the lower-middle or working classes of Munich and the few officers among them carried ranks no higher than second lieutenants on the reserve.

Ulrich Graf, for instance, Hitler's first and leading bodyguard, was a butcher who had made quite a name for himself as an amateur boxer.[40] Emil Maurice, Hitler's bosom companion, was a watchmaker who had been convicted for embezzlement;[41] Christian Weber had been a groom and was now earning a pittance in the Blaue Bock in Munich.[42] The bond which held them all together was their great task of guarding the lives of Hitler and the other National-Socialist leaders. Hitler merely had to say the word and they would wade in with their 'indiarubbers' and 'matchboxes' (as they called their rubber truncheons and pistols)[43] to protect their Führer from tiresome opponents. Even in 1942 Hitler would still talk of the 'men who were ready for revolution and knew that some day things would come to hard knocks.'[44]

That day came in November 1923. The head of the Government in Bavaria was Gustave Ritter von Kahr, the Commissar General, a Bavarian separatist and monarchist; the Reichswehr commander was Major General Otto Hermann Lossow. Both were at such loggerheads with Berlin that Bavaria seemed likely to secede from the Reich at any moment. For years all the forces opposed to democracy and progress had been collecting in that 'orderly corner', the Bavarian military State, and now they were girding their loins for the decisive blow. Hitler thought that he could make good use of this turn in Bavarian politics.

Von Kahr had summoned a meeting of all the Bavarian dignitaries in the Munich Bürgerbräukeller in the Rosenheimer Strasse for the evening of November 8th,[45] and Hitler decided to use this occasion for his own coup. He suspected that Kahr intended to announce Bavaria's independence and was determined to force Kahr to overreach himself and march on Berlin to depose the 'November Republic'.[46] Hitler hastily alerted his allies and persuaded them to support his surprise action;[47] they included the ex-Quartermaster-General, Ludendorff, who was hurriedly brought into line;[48] he arrived for the putsch totally unaware that he was cast for the star role. Hitler collected the fifty men of his Assault Squad and he was ready; he put on a black overcoat, pinned to it his Iron Cross First Class and set off.[49] By 8 PM he was at the entrance to the Bürgerbräukeller, waiting for his moment.[50]

Three-quarters of an hour later Berchtold, the Assault Squad commander, brought along a machine gun and set it up at the entrance.[51] Hitler and his bodyguard thereupon forced their way into the crowded hall; drawing a revolver Hitler fired into the air and then jumped on to a table[52] shouting: 'The national revolution has begun. The hall is surrounded by six hundred heavily armed men and no one may leave. The Bavarian Government and the Reich Government have been deposed and a provisional Reich Government will be formed.'[53] Bavaria's surprised officers and politicians allowed this apparent madman to proceed and declared themselves ready to come to terms with Hitler.[54] The next day, however, Kahr and Lossow disowned him and mobilized against him.[55] As if paralysed, Hitler remained in the Bürgerbräukeller waiting for good news which did not come. There was only one favourable report and this finally drove Hitler on to the streets; Röhm with his defence organization, 'Reichskriegsflagge', had forced his way into the War Ministry and was holding it in face of increasing military and police pressure.[56]

About midday on November 9th Hitler and his followers and allies marched off, eight abreast, down the narrow Residenzstrasse[57] to relieve Röhm in the War Ministry. On the Odeonsplatz they were faced by about a hundred police in position on the steps of the Feldherrnhalle, barring the procession's way.[58] When the putschists continued to move on, Hitler and Ludendorff marching in step, a second police unit moved in.[59] Ulrich Graf, Hitler's bodyguard, rushed up to the muzzles of the police rifles, shouting: 'Don't shoot! It is His Excellency Ludendorff and Hitler!'[60] The police opened fire; sixteen National-Socialists, including five members of the Assault Squad, and three policemen, were killed; practically all the leaders of the Nazi Movement were arrested.[61] Berchtold, the leader of the Assault Squad, and Göring, Commander of the SA, though severely wounded, escaped to Austria.[62]

Hitler's act of lunacy wrecked the NSDAP. The Party Organization, the SA and the Assault Squad were banned, leaving only a collection of Nazis quarrelling among themselves; initially they tried to take refuge under Ludendorff's banner but later split into an increasing number of small groups and cliques.[63] The only man who still worked away was

Röhm; he had been cashiered from the Army and released on probation after a short period under arrest;[64] he believed that he could continue as before and, while still in prison in Landsberg, Hitler nominated him head of the SA, now an illegal organization.[65]

Röhm soon realized, however, that the Bavarian Government had no intention of lifting the ban on the SA. Assisted by Ritter von Epp, Röhm's former master, Kahr had brought all the defence formations under control, combining them in a 'Notbann' [Emergency Formation].[66] Röhm thereupon formed a new defence organization from the remnants of the SA and placed it under the patronage of General Ludendorff. It was called 'Frontbann'.[67]

The formation of the Frontbann brought Röhm and Hitler their first recruits from outside Bavaria. Until the November putsch Hitler's Movement had hardly penetrated outside the Munich city limits, but now the survivors of the old Free Corps and the leaderless North German National-Socialists streamed into the Frontbann.[68] Röhm was joined by a series of ruthless desperadoes, the Free Corps officers, nationalist extremists who later made thuggery the hallmark of the SA; such were Captain von Heydebreck and Graf Helldorff.[69] There was also Lieutenant Edmund Heines, a roughneck highly qualified in all sorts of vice. (Röhm, who was always interested in male relationships, says in his memoirs that Heines 'approached him for the first time'.[70])

At their peak as an armed force Hitler's SA had numbered at the most 2,000 men;[71] Röhm's Frontbann now had 30,000.[72] In his Landsberg cell Hitler became somewhat uneasy at the growth of Röhm's army; Röhm had been heard to say 'I am still a soldier and nothing but a soldier,'[73] and he was still insisting upon the autonomy of the defence organizations. 'The political and defence movements are entirely independent one of another,' he wrote to Ludendorff.'[74] When, in December 1924, Hitler was released[75] and charged Röhm with the reconstitution of the SA, the two clashed openly. Hitler was determined never to have an independent SA on the lines of the Ehrhardt Brigade; Röhm, however, insisted that the Party bosses had no business giving orders to the soldiers and that Hitler was no more than the rabble-rouser for the defence formations.[76] A memorandum from Röhm gave the ex-corporal to understand that: 'Party politics will not be tolerated either in the Frontbann or in the SA'; it ended with the blunt statement: 'I categorically refuse to allow the SA to become involved in Party matters; equally I categorically refuse to allow SA commanders to accept instructions from Party political leaders.'[77]

Röhm did not realize that Hitler had already made up his mind; he was not going to let the SA revive until he could be sure that there would be no outsiders in SA uniform to dictate to him. So Hitler split with Röhm, leaving him no choice by bidding him farewell on April 30th, 1925: 'In memory of glorious and difficult days which we have survived together. With heartfelt thanks for your comradeship and in the hope that you will not refuse me your personal friendship in future.'[78] Barely a month later Hitler gave some indication of his plans; his Secretariat announced: 'Herr Hitler has no intention of setting up a new defence formation. That he once did so was due to the activities of a certain gentleman who left him in the lurch. All he needs today are men to keep order at meetings, as in the days before 1923.'[79] The birth of the SS was now not far off. Hitler was determined to have a force which, wherever he might be, would guarantee his authority in the Party and would be prepared to carry out his orders without question and at all times. This the old SA under Röhm and Ehrhardt had not been prepared to do, and so the SS was now to undertake it. In 1942 Hitler said: 'I told myself then that I needed a bodyguard, even a very restricted one, but made up of men who would be enlisted unconditionally, ready even to march against their own brothers. Rather a mere twenty men to a city (on condition that one could count on them absolutely) than an unreliable mass.'[80]

(The Party at large, and later the Third Reich as a whole, was given an entirely different version of the formation of the SS. As the SA was still banned, the story ran, when the Party was reformed in February 1925, a protective organization had to be constituted against the increasing terrorism of its political opponents.[81] This statement concealed the facts that Hitler deliberately postponed reconstitution of the SA, that the ban on the SA did not extend to all German Länder [States], and that, primarily in North and West Germany, the SA increased considerably in size but refused to subordinate itself to the Munich party leader, who was still a controversial figure.[82])

Hitler now set about forming his own bodyguard. In April 1925 he ordered Julius Schreck, who had been a member of the Assault Squad and was now his chauffeur, to form a new headquarters guard. A fortnight later this headquarters guard was re-christened 'Schutzstaffel' (SS).[83] Schreck's first men were recruited from the same source as the headquarters guard and the Assault Squad – the Torbräu beer cellar near the Isartor, Munich. Initially, there were only eight men,[84] almost all from the Adolf Hitler Assault Squad. They wore the old Assault Squad uniform, unchanged except that the field-grey tunic had given way to the brown shirt* (now the official Party uniform) with a black tie.[85]

* The brown shirt had become the official Party uniform by accident. A certain SA commander named Rossbach had been in Austria and there received a large

Schreck now set about forming SS units in other cities. On September 21st, 1925, he sent out 'Circular No 1' urging all local Party groups to set up an SS.[87] They were to be small, efficient, élite groups, at the most a commander and ten men; Berlin alone was allowed two commanders and twenty men.[88] Schreck was insistent that, in accordance with the Nazi élite theory, only specially selected men should enter the SS. SS headquarters only accepted applicants between twenty-three and thirty-five years of age; they had to name two sponsors, be registered by the police as residents of five years' standing, and be 'strong and healthy'.[89]

The SS 'guidelines' stated: 'Habitual drunkards, gossip-mongers and other delinquents will not be considered.'[90] In November 1925 Schreck discovered from the *Völkischer Beobachter* that in Munich-Neuhausen a Party member named Daub had formed 15 ex-SA men into an SS unit and was styling himself SS commander;[91] on November 27th Schreck protested to Party headquarters: 'This new formation is no more than the old SA rechristened SS. SS headquarters therefore requests the Party leadership to do what it can to bring to the notice of these gentlemen that the name SS may not be used by these detachments. The SS is an organization laboriously built up upon sound foundations and its image must not be tarnished by imitation copies.'[92]

Schreck worked hard to collect 'the best and most reliable Party members to protect the Movement and work selflessly and tirelessly for it'; he listed the tasks of the SS as 'Protection of meetings in their area, recruitment of subscribers and advertisers for the *Völkischer Beobachter*, and recruitment of Party members.'[93] Alois Rosenwink, a section head and the real organizer of SS headquarters said with typical Nazi bombast: 'We carry the Death's Head on our black cap as a warning to our enemies and an indication to our Führer that we will sacrifice our lives for his concept.'[94]

The first success stories began to arrive in Munich. In Dresden SS men forestalled an attempt by fifty Communists to break up a Nazi meeting;[99] from Saxony 'in the Marble Palace, Chemnitz, the combined SS of Dresden, Plauen, Zwickau and Chemnitz gave the Communists a fearful beating-up, throwing some of them out of the windows, since when no Communist has dared to disturb our meetings.'[96] By Christmas 1925 SS headquarters could record that 'We have available a properly constituted defence organization of about a thousand men.'[97] Shortly thereafter the number of genuine SS men had sunk to about

consignment of brown shirts, originally intended for German troops in East Africa; Rossbach took them back to Germany in 1924. With the brown shirt the SA wore a brown tie, the SS a black one.[86]

200.[98] Nevertheless as the first nation-wide Nazi organization, the SS was now firmly established.

In April 1926 Berchtold, the old leader of the Assault Squad, returned from exile in Austria and took over command of the SS from Schreck.[99] As the men of November 1923 returned, Hitler publicly proclaimed the SS as his élite organization; at the second Party Rally in Weimar on July 4th, 1926 he handed to the SS the 'blood banner', the flag which had led the procession down the Residenzstrasse on November 9th, 1923.[100] Now that the SS was established and growing, Hitler could once more try his luck with the SA. He knew only too well that he must have some mass formation as his link to the people, that in a Germany ruled by Party armies and political processions he must have his own army to hoist him into power.

The non-Bavarian SA leaders, however, were still suspicious of Hitler, who after all was still only an Austrian, and he had to find someone to act as his contact man with the numerous scattered SA groups. He chose Captain Franz Pfeffer von Salomon, a North German Free Corps commander.[101] Goebbels' diary of July 27th, 1926, records: 'With the Chief at midday. Serious discussion. Pfeffer becomes Reich SA leader.'[102] From Hitler's point of view the position was serious, for as the contact man from the North German National-Socialist leaders, Pfeffer had to be given a piace in the party hierarchy – he was to be a watchdog as well.

Hitler had to give Pfeffer considerable power. With effect from November, 1st, 1926 he was entitled 'Supreme SA leader' [Oberste SA Führer – OSAF] and placed in command of all SA in Germany; although he was bound to follow the basic directives of Hitler as party leader, he was allowed to build up the SA organization as he saw fit.[103] In Hitler's view, however, the alliance with the North German National-Socialists was worth some concessions over the power of the SS. So the SS was also placed under Pfeffer, its commander, Berchtold, being given only a small crumb of comfort in being permitted to call himself Reichsführer-SS [Reich SS leader].[104] Berchtold soon became discouraged, fearing that his little élite force would be entirely subordinated to the SA and the Party functionaries – exactly what he had been put into office to prevent; his predecessor, Schreck, had been voted down by the members of SS headquarters as too easy-going and likely to become a tool of crafty Party bureaucrats such as Philip Bouhler and Franz Xaver Schwarz.[105] Ernst Wagner wrote to Hitler saying that Schreck had had to go because he 'had insufficient command and organizing ability, nor did he carry sufficient weight to ensure that the SS remained the Movement's élite force.'[106]

So the more dynamic Berchtold had been appointed but even he was now finding it difficult to keep the Party organizers at bay. One of his instructions ran: 'Neither the headquarters of the local group nor of the Gau [Nazi Party territorial district] is to interfere in the internal organizational problems of the local SS.'[107] Another order stated: 'The SS is a completely independent organization within the Movement.'[108] But Berchtold did not gain his point versus the Party functionaries; here was the first indication of that latent strife between the SS aristocrats and the Party bosses which was to rage right up to the end of the Third Reich. (At an internal Party meeting on May 11th, 1926, for instance, Wagner, a member of the SS, shouted that 'The bosses must be smoked out'; Bouhler and Schwarz thereupon forbade him entry into SS headquarters. Berchtold, the Reichsführer, was compelled to put the ban in writing; Wagner protested to Hitler indignantly: 'Berchtold told me that he had been compelled to do so by Bouhler and Schwarz.'[109])

When in addition to these vexations the SA was allowed to increase its strength once more, Berchtold resigned. In March 1927 his deputy, Erhard Heiden, was appointed Reichsführer-SS[110] but he too found it difficult to compete with the growing size and influence of the SA; Pfeffer, for instance, forbade the SS to form units in towns where the SA was still below strength.[111]

In each locality [Gemeinde] the SS was not allowed to exceed ten per cent of the strength of the SA,[112] so by 1928 it had only reached the miserable figure of 280 men.[113] The SS élite frequently had to allow themselves to be ordered about by SA commanders and do the chores, such as delivering orders of the day, distributing propaganda material and selling the *Völkischer Beobachter*.[114] The scale of their achievements can be judged by the following report from the year 1926: 'During October the SS recruited throughout the Reich: 249 new members for the NSDAP, 54 new readers for the *Völkischer Beobachter*, 169 new readers for the *Stürmer*, 82 new readers for the *Nationalsozialist*, 140 new readers for the *Südwestdeutscher Beobachter*, 475 new readers for the *Westdeutscher Beobachter*, 189 new readers for the remaining National-Socialist newspapers. In addition 2,000 copies of the *Illustrierte Beobachter* were sold.' The report was headed sarcastically: 'So this is what we do!'[115]

This force, which in Heiden's words was 'perhaps super-efficient but certainly arrogant', was held together only by its belief in its own selectivity.[116] Its slogan was: 'The aristocracy keeps its mouth shut.'[117] It became a silent appendage to the SA marching columns, but it kept alive its élite concept by ever stricter conditions of entry and ever more severe service regulations. 'Order No 1' for instance of September 13th, 1927, from the Reichsführer, Erhard Heiden, laid down that: 'The SS will never take part in discussions at members' meetings. SS men will attend discussion evenings for the purpose of political instruction only; no SS man will smoke during the address and no one will be allowed to leave the room. The SS man and SS commander will remain silent and will never become involved in matters (concerning the local political leadership and SA) which do not concern him.'[118] Orders laid down that before entering a meeting each unit was to parade 'sized in two ranks'; dress and passes were to be checked; the SS man was always to carry his NSDAP membership book, his SS pass and the SS song-book.[119] Special attention was paid to the contents of Order No 8 forbidding the carrying of arms; Hitler had decided to seize power by ostensibly legal methods and part of his scheme was that the Party must officially keep itself aloof from all defence organizations and illegal military bodies. Before going on duty, SS commanders had to search men of their unit for arms and confiscate any weapons found.[120]

Even their political opponents were impressed by the iron discipline of the SS. In a secret report of May 7th, 1929 Munich police headquarters noted: 'Strict discipline is demanded from SS men. Even the smallest infraction of regulations set out in the current SS orders is punished by a fine, temporary withdrawal of the right to wear the armband, or suspension from duty. Particular stress is laid upon bearing and turn-out.'[121] Their strict rules were supposed to demonstrate that the SS formed a Party aristocracy. 'The SS man is the most exemplary Party member conceivable' an SS instruction stated.[122] The SS song, sung at the end of every SS meeting, showed the organization's fanatical belief in its mission:

Wenn alle untreu werden	When all are disloyal
So bleiben wir doch treu	Then we remain loyal
Dass immer noch auf Erden	So that always upon this earth
Fur Euch ein Fähnlein sei	There may be a banner in front of you.[123]

'The SA is the infantry of the line, the SS the Guards. There has always been a guard; the Persians had one, the Greeks, Caesar and Napoleon, Frederick the Great, right up to the world war; the SS will be the imperial guard of the new Germany.'[124] These words were spoken by the man who was determined to make the SS the masters of the Reich. From this point the story of the SS becomes his story, the history of their deeds his history, the list of their crimes his crimes. On January 6th, 1929, Hitler placed him at the head of the SS as the new Reichsführer: his name was Heinrich Himmler.[125]

3

HEINRICH HIMMLER

As the train rumbled steadily northwards, the passenger looked increasingly bored. Albert Krebs, the first National-Socialist Gauleiter [the senior Nazi Party representative in a Gau] of Hamburg, had been listening for hours to the chatter of the man opposite, who had boarded the train with him at Elberfeld.[1]

The man was of medium height, well built with a rather puffy, commonplace, face. The small, slightly receding chin betrayed a certain weakness, but the blue-grey eyes behind the pince-nez seemed to indicate considerable strength of will. His somewhat blunt manner, too, hardly seemed to accord with his small, well-manicured, almost feminine hands.

At the time – spring 1929 – Gauleiter Krebs took no particular notice of these inconsistencies in his fellow-passenger's outward appearance. He was merely noting with increasing distaste what the new Reichsführer-SS, Heinrich Himmler, had to say about the political situation. Himmler was lecturing him: in politics, he said, people's private affairs were what mattered; for instance, it was particularly important to know how a certain SA commander, Conn, had come by his curious name – it sounded rather like the Jewish name Cohen; Gauleiter Lohse had been a bank official and so his possible dependence upon Jewish capital should be investigated. Krebs shook his head.[2] Even thirty years later Krebs could still remember Himmler's disquisition as 'terrifying', 'a remarkable mixture of martial bombast, lower-middle-class beer-hall gossip and the impassioned prophesyings of a non-conformist preacher.'[3]

Himmler was only twenty-nine and was on his first inspection trip to the SS; Krebs wrote him off as a loud-mouthed, dubious and somewhat provincial henchman of Adolf Hitler; many National-Socialists who had tried to preserve some freedom of judgement thought the same way.

Later, instead of this picture of the preacher and beer-hall gossip, the man was painted as a sinister diabolical figure. As Himmler's power increased, the figure of the Reichsführer-SS appeared more unreal, ghostly and inhuman to the Germans. Himmler soon became a depersonalized abstraction, the inanimate embodiment of the National-Socialist police state, a monster divorced from all humanity, waiting only to annihilate any dissentients. No detail of his private life revealed what sort of a man the Reichsführer-SS was – we still do not really know today.

Those who knew him in the flesh were incapable of giving an intelligible description of Himmler as a man. Any coherent picture contained so many discordant features that his contemporaries and biographers have presented him in a number of different lights. There is Himmler the hangman, Himmler the good companion, Himmler the fanatical racial ideologist, Himmler the incorruptible apostle of rectitude, Himmler the willing tool of his Führer; finally there is a pensive Himmler deliberating with the German Resistance.

General Friedrich Hossbach, Hitler's ex-Military Assistant, said: 'This man, Hitler's evil spirit, cold, calculating and ambitious, was undoubtedly the most purposeful and most unscrupulous figure in the Third Reich.'[4] General Guderian says, 'He seemed like a man from another planet.'[5] Burckhardt, the Swiss, League of Nations High Commissioner in Danzig, wrote: 'What made him sinister was his capacity to concentrate upon little things, his pettifogging conscientiousness and his inhuman methodology; he had a touch of the robot.'[6] Looking at a photograph of Himmler, Alfred Rosenberg, the Nazi ideologist, was struck by the fact that 'I had never been able to look Heinrich Himmler straight in the eye. His eyes were always hooded, blinking behind his pince-nez. Now, however, I could see them gazing at me from the photograph and I thought I could detect one thing in them – malice.'[7] General Walter Dornberger, on the other hand, who was in charge of the V2 programme, thought him 'like an intelligent schoolmaster, certainly not a man of violence'; Himmler, he said, had 'the rare gift of listening attentively' and his manner was 'quiet and unemotional – a man without nerves.'[8]

Count Bernadotte, who negotiated with Himmler in 1945, found him surprising: 'Certainly there was nothing diabolical in his appearance.' According to Bernadotte he had been extremely affable and was always ready with a joke when conversation threatened to flag.[9] Many diplomats described him as a man of sober judgement; both German and foreign resistance movements at one time thought that Himmler was the only National-Socialist leader who could be used to bring Hitler down.

Trevor-Roper says: 'In this monster there were many curious qualities which have made him, to some, an incredible, enigmatical figure.'[10]

Himmler's biographers eventually contrived a theory to give some sort of explanation to the existence of so many differing characters in one man. The key to the Himmler riddle, they said, lay in his boyhood and youth; he was the lonely son of a middle-class family, over-shadowed by a pedantic father and an unsympathetic mother; in the post-war period he had wandered about, unrecognized by society, until the National-Socialist Movement gave him the security which his home had failed to provide.[11]

This makes a plausible theory and is typical of the present-day tendency to invent some psychoanalytical explanation for the inexplicable. Unfortunately it is not true. Himmler came from the most normal of Bavarian middle-class families; he had two brothers, Gebhard, born in 1898, two years before Heinrich, and Ernst, born in 1905;[12] there was nothing particular to upset the family relationship. As Himmler rose in the ranks of the SS and became increasingly imbued with a sense of mission, family harmony did suffer to a degree; his wife Margarete, a nervous and plaintive individual, did not fit into the family – 'I always have to take a deep breath when I think of your parents,' she once said.[13] Nevertheless, the Reichsführer never broke with his family. When his mother died, although unwell himself, Himmler kept watch at her bedside for a whole night; at her funeral he linked hands across the coffin with his two brothers,[14] saying in his somewhat pompous manner: 'We will always stay together.'[15]

Himmler was the self-appointed family mentor. In 1921, when still a student, he wrote to: 'Dearest Mummy'[16] – 'Daddy should not work so hard; during the week he should go for a walk more often to ensure that he does not overwork.' To his brothers he adopted the attitude of a pedantic schoolmaster. 'Little Ernst', although only five years his junior, was told on November 14th, 1920: 'I am very pleased with your good report. But do not rest on your laurels. Moreover, I expect you to do well in history. Do not become unbalanced. Be a good, brave boy and do not vex Daddy and Mummy.'[17]

Himmler's brother Gebhard had an even worse time. He had the misfortune to become engaged to Paula Stölzle, the daughter of a Weilheim banker, and Heinrich did not approve. He was quick to put his objections on paper, writing to Paula on April 18th, 1923: 'If your union is to be a happy one for the two of you and salutary for our people, the very foundation of which must be healthy, clean-living families, you will have to be ridden on a tight rein and with the utmost severity. Since your own code of behaviour is not a strict one and your future husband is too kind-hearted, someone else must perform this function. I feel it my duty to do so.'[18] Determination to ensure that twentieth-century women adopted the same code of morals as the heroines of the old German sagas was one of Himmler's obsessions; he regarded any extra-marital relations as an offence against his code of purity; accordingly he instructed Max Blüml, a Munich detective agency, to investigate Paula's past.[19] Blüml reported on March 14th, 1924.[20] But Himmler had already instituted other inquiries; on March 12th he wrote to an official named Rössner; 'May I request you to inform me by return of all you know about Fräulein Stölzle and particularly about her relationship with your colleague, Daffner?'[21] Brother Gebhard capitulated and broke off the engagement.[22]

The incident shows that Himmler, unlike most other Nazi leaders, had been brought up in the security of a true middle-class civil-servant milieu. Hitler had his nightmare memories of a Vienna workhouse; Joseph Goebbels was the son of a works foreman; Alfred Rosenberg was an embittered émigré Balt; but Himmler was a true offspring of middle-class officialdom, simply the second son of Gebhard Himmler, a private tutor.

Heinrich was born on October 7th, 1900 on the second floor of 2 Hildegardstrasse, Munich.[23] His social position was already assured, for one of the great figures of the Bavarian Kingdom, Prince Heinrich of Wittelsbach, who had been old Himmler's pupil, was godfather to the baby.[24] On being informed in an obsequious letter that it weighed 7 lb 3 oz, the Prince gave permission for it to be named after him.[25] With such a name and such a godfather, Heinrich was clearly destined for the ranks of the loyal citizenry.

While at school it never crossed Heinrich's mind to question the authority of his parents or the order of society of his time.[26] From his father he learnt that the ancient Germans had been good people, and the foundation was laid for that romantic interpretation of history characteristic of the late Wagnerian era when the world was peopled by Germanic heroes and glorious women – so easily transformable into the Nordic German master race to meet the requirements of the Nazi régime. Himmler quickly learned to treat those around him with proper respect. While at school he kept an impeccable diary in which anyone he met was invariably given his correct title.[27]

For anyone who had a prince of the Royal House as his godfather, the natural career was that of an officer, and here lies a key to Himmler's character; he was always dreaming of leading his troops to victory, but could never quite make the picture come true. First he wanted to join the Navy,[28] but he had weak eyes and the Navy would not accept men who wore glasses. He then decided on the Army. On June 26th, 1917 his father wrote: 'My son Heinrich earnestly desires to become a career infantry officer.'[29] Himmler could hardly wait to get into the war. When his brother Gebhard entered the Landsturm in 1915, Heinrich wrote: 'Oh how I wish to be as old as that and so able to go to the front.'[30] He transcribed the news bulletins from general headquarters word for word and reproached the people of Landshut, where his family had moved, with lack of enthusiasm for the war.[31]

Heinrich was so persistent that his father asked some friends at court to allow the young man to enter the Army early,[32] and the friends pulled the necessary strings. About the same time Heinrich had his last present from his royal godfather, who had meanwhile been killed in action. Himmler's father received a letter from the court informing him that: 'The J.N. Oberndörffer Bank, 18 Salvatorstrasse, Munich, has been instructed to send you 1,000 5% German War Loan. Please accept this sum as a gift for your son Heinrich from his late godfather, Weiland, his Royal Highness Prince Heinrich.'[33]

In late 1917 Himmler joined 11 Bavarian Infantry Regiment, the 'Von der Tann'.[34] But his military career ended before it had really begun. Shortly before his death Himmler told Count Bernadotte that he had 'gone to war' with his men[35] and other sources refer to his participation in a battle on the Western Front;[36] but in fact Himmler was never more than a cadet and never reached the Front. The war went too quickly for him; he spent six months in Regensburg doing basic infantry training; from June 15th to September 15th, 1918, he attended a cadets' course in Freising; from September 15th to October 1st, 1918, he did a machine-gun course with No 17 Machine Gun Company in Bayreuth.[37] Two months later he was demobilized from No 4 Company of the Reserve Battalion of 11 Infantry Regiment.[38]

In the turbulent post-war period it seemed for a while that Himmler would be able to continue his military career. In February 1919 Kurt Eisner, Bavaria's left-wing Socialist Minister-President, was murdered by an officer,[39] whereupon the Communists and their revolutionary supporters set up a red republic.[40] The constitutional Social Democratic Government of Bavaria fled to Bamberg and was compelled, much against its will, to raise troops; they consisted primarily of ex-soldiers and volunteers and called themselves Free Corps.[41]

Berlin set the Reichswehr on the move, and in April 1919 the Free Corps prepared to march on Munich.[42] Himmler joined a small Free Corps commanded by Lieutenant Lautenbacher[43] but once more he missed the battle. The unit never entered Munich[44] and Himmler remained a barrack-square soldier. But he did not give up. On June 17th,

1919, he wrote to the depot of 11 Infantry Regiment asking for his military papers, 'since I am transferring to the Reichswehr in a few days' time.'[45]

Nothing came of this, however, for his father had meanwhile decided that, being no longer protected by the King and in view of the rising inflation, it was high time that Heinrich qualified in some more secure profession than that of war; he wanted him to become a farmer.[46] Heinrich agreed: next to soldiering farming had always interested him. As a boy he had kept a large collection of plants,[47] and he developed a strange addiction to garden herbs. (Later this was to provide an added burden for the inmates of the concentration camps; each camp had to produce a collection of every conceivable type of herb, since Himmler considered them far more efficacious than medicines in curing diseases.[48])

But with farming also ill luck continued to dog him. He went to a farm near Ingolstadt to learn the business but had hardly begun when he was laid low by a typhus epidemic.[49] A certain Dr Grünstadt decided: 'Must interrupt for a year and study.'[50] So on October 18th, 1919 Himmler enrolled as a student of agriculture at the Technical High School, Munich University.[51] It would hardly have been surprising had he emerged from these misfortunes in a state of depression and become a 'lone wolf', the unwanted outsider on the fringe of society, as the Himmler legend would have it, but not at all – in Munich he entered upon a gay period of his career which presents many problems to the biographers.

He was friendly, helpful, studious and something of a bore. He appeared at fancy-dress parties as 'Abdul Hamid, the Sultan of Turkey'. He had an unfortunate love affair with a girl named Maja Loritz; he developed a passion for sweetmeats.[52] No one would have suspected that here was the later mass murderer.

Nevertheless he was still fascinated by politics and soldiering. A receipt of May 16th, 1920 shows that he enrolled in the Munich Home Guard [Einwohnerwehr] receiving from No 21 Rifle Brigade '1 rifle and 50 rounds, 1 steel helmet, 2 ammunition pouches, 1 haversack (old type).[53] December 1st, 1921 was a great day in his life – the Reichswehr informed him that he could henceforth call himself 'Fähnrich' [Ensign].[54] Together with other nationalist students and officers he was preparing a plot to liberate Eisner's murderer, Count Arco-Valley. When the Count's sentence of death was commuted to life imprisonment the conspirators abandoned their plan, but Himmler was not downcast, simply noting in his diary: 'Well then, some other time.'[55]

He had far more serious worries. In November 1919 he had joined a students' association named 'Apollo'[56] and was now cudgelling his brains over the problem of reconciling his new existence with his strict Catholic family upbringing and the weakness of his stomach – the Church forbade duelling and his doctor prohibited the customary drinking in the beer cellars. The beer problem was quickly solved; he managed to obtain special dispensation from the fraternity, excusing him from beer-drinking.[57] The members of 'Apollo', however, did not take Himmler very seriously and at the next elections for membership he was dropped.[58] He also had difficulty in finding a duelling partner – most of his fellow students evidently considered him unworthy. Not until his last term, in June 1922, was an opponent found to give Himmler the facial scars which the future Reichsführer-SS considered any true Teutonic student must be able to display.[59]

The Church's ban on duelling was a much more agonizing problem than the beer. The Himmlers had always been loyal and devout Catholics; a cousin, August Wilhelm Patin, was even a Canon of Munich Cathedral.[60] Himmler was a practising Catholic and Sunday Mass was more than an outward ritual for him; it was a spiritual experience. He always noted in his diary when he went to Church, frequently saying: 'I like being in this church.'[61] When he learnt that a girl whom he was shyly courting went to Communion daily, he commented: 'This was the greatest joy which I have experienced these past eight days.'[62]

His entry into the students' fraternity cast a shadow over Himmler's relationship with the Church. There was no sudden break but his separation from the Church gradually became more definite. Personally averse to duelling, Himmler initially tried to follow the Church's dictates but eventually the urge to conform to his social environment (a heritage from his parents) overcame his religious scruples. On December 15th, 1919 he noted 'I believe that I have come into conflict with my religion,'[63] but he continued: 'Come what may, I shall always love God, shall pray to Him and shall remain faithful to the Catholic Church and shall defend it even if I should be expelled from it.'[64] (Yet this was the man who later compelled tens of thousands of SS men to leave the Church and advocated a public execution of the Pope.)[65]

His relationship to the Church left him worried but unshaken. He was more interested in worldly matters, more concerned with the gay society of Munich, meals in Frau Loritz's house and a student's sexual problems than with religion and politics.

Anna Loritz, widow of a professional singer, was a distant relative of the Himmlers. She kept a boarding-house at 9 Jägerstrasse, Munich. Himmler fell in love with her daughter, Maria, known as Maja, but found that his rival, Hans Knipp, who later became a leather merchant in Stuttgart, stood higher in her affections.[66] The whole Himmler family would sometimes meet in the Loritz house. Knipp recalled that 'there were always great greetings in the Loritz house when the five Himmlers arrived. The Himmler family knew that the food was always good at Auntie Loritz's.'[67] Himmler enjoyed the parties in the Loritz home. While he was still in Landshut, Robert Kistler, a regimental friend, had written to him: 'Are you taking dancing lessons?'[68] and in Munich he immediately took lessons in the hope of improving his standing with Maja. By January 1920 he had already learnt 'the Boston'.[69] With his friend Ludwig, nicknamed 'Lu', he was a regular attendant at Munich festivities.[70] Every detail went down in his diary; he describes one of the Loritz parties: 'The room decked out as a harem, lanterns, a tent near the oven in the corner for Lu and myself . . . Frau Loritz served enormously much food, first cocoa, which I spilled over my pants.'[71] So occupied was he with his social life that the National-Socialist Party Rally, held in Munich at about this time, passed him by.[72] The American historians, Werner Angress and Bradley Smith, describe him as: 'a young man who thought in conventional terms, cherished Bavarian middle-class values and who seems to have been eminently good-natured, colourless and normal.'[73]

He was full of good works. During the Christmas vacation he read to a blind man, fetched a cake for an old pauper woman and took part in a charity play for the poor children of Vienna; he rushed from one meeting to another,[74] for he was a member of numerous societies – cultural, farming, humanist, rifle-shooting, ex-servicemen, mountain-climbing, touring, gymnastics, regimental old comrades.[75] A member of so many societies had little difficulty in adapting himself to his environment. His political ideas were mere reflections of the views and prejudices of the society in which he moved – normal middle-class nationalist ideas with no trace of National-Socialist ideological fanaticism or of its spectral creed.

In fact at this period Himmler was a typical Bavarian conservative. He borrowed a top hat and frock coat to attend the funeral of ex-King Ludwig III; he was proud of being a Bavarian. At the elections for Asta, the student government at the University, he voted for the Nationalists.[76] Even his comments on the Jews at this stage were moderate. When he heard of the murder of Rathenau, the Foreign Minister, he noted: 'I am glad' but nevertheless considered him 'an able man'.[77] He referred good-humouredly to Wolfgang Hallgarten, with whom he had been at school, as 'a Jewish louse';[78] when he met the Jewish cabaret artist, Inge Barco, in the Reichsadler Bar, he found her 'a girl who deserves respect', although she had been turned out of home for having an affair with a student.[79]

Only on one point do his diaries show the aggressive spirit characteristic of the later Himmler: he could not accept the fact that his military career was over. When Maja Loritz refused her gauche suitor, soldiering and war seemed to him the surest way to escape from the pangs of love. On November 28th, 1919 he noted: 'If I only could face dangers now, could risk my life, could fight, it would be a relief to me.'[80] On November 22nd, 1921, the style of the latter-day Himmler showed through for the first time; he wrote: 'If there is another campaign in the East I will go along. The East is most important for us. The West will die easily. In the East we must fight and colonize.'[81] From time to time his longing for war and a military career would get the better of him: on February 19th, 1922, he wrote: 'If only there would be fighting again, war, departing troops!'[82] And on June 11th: 'Perhaps I will join up in one way or another. For basically I am a soldier. But first I am going to take my exams.'[83]

In July 1922 Himmler told his parents: 'So far I think all is going reasonably well with my exams.'[84] But then there entered Heinrich Himmler's life the man with whom his association was to end in such bloody and dramatic circumstances – Captain Ernst Röhm – and he offered the unrequited lover some prospect of satisfying his military ambitions.

It is impossible to establish with any accuracy when the two men first met. Their paths had crossed on several occasions: in late 1918 Röhm was serving on the staff of 12 Bavarian Infantry Division located in Landshut, Himmler's home town;[85] then he had been Armaments and Equipment Officer of 21 Rifle Brigade in Munich,[86] the unit from which Himmler had received his weapons in May 1920; now in 1922 Röhm was acting as secret quartermaster to the quasi-legal defence organizations accepted by the Reichswehr as a type of militia. Himmler met Röhm in January 1922 in the Arzberger Keller, Munich, at a meeting of one of these formations; he noted: 'Captain Röhm and Major Angerer [Himmler's late Company Commander] were also there; very friendly. Röhm pessimistic as to Bolshevism.'[87] Himmler was impressed by Röhm; he became the barrack-square cadet once more, unable to forget that Röhm stood several rungs higher on the military ladder; whenever Himmler met Röhm, he instinctively tended to click his heels. They were an ill-assorted pair – the much-decorated First World War company commander and the frustrated warrior, the homosexual freebooter and the prim son of a middle-class family. Yet Röhm knew how to rouse the young man's enthusiasm – Himmler was prepared to stake his all for Röhm.

Himmler passed his examination on August 5th, 1922[88] and took a job as agricultural assistant at a chemical factory in Schleissheim;[89] immediately thereafter, on Röhm's advice, he joined a nationalist organization called 'Reichsflagge'.[90] He was glad to be entitled at last to wear uniform again, even if only the gaiters and light grey windcheater of the 'Reichsflagge'. He was only too ready to shoulder his rifle on Saturday evenings and train with others of his ilk for the street fighting which the imminent civil war would bring.

He soon had a chance to give practical expression to his admiration for Röhm. At the end of August 1923 he gave up his job in Schleissheim and returned to Munich;[91] shortly thereafter Hitler's November putsch gave him his first opportunity of appearing in the forefront of the nationalist Movement. After considerable internal intrigue Reichsflagge had been rechristened 'Reichskriegsflagge' and placed itself under the leadership of Röhm and Hitler.[92] Röhm had long been a member of Hitler's Party and he knew how to persuade his friends to join the NSDAP; Himmler did so.[93] But this did not mean that he was a Nazi; he saw Röhm, not Hitler, as the coming man; for him the flag of the monarchy, not the swastika, was the standard of the future.

On the evening of November 8th, 1923 Himmler appeared at a meeting of the Reichskriegsflagge in the Löwenbräukeller, Munich, carrying the Imperial war flag; during the meeting the news arrived that Hitler, brandishing his revolver, had at last persuaded Bavaria's leading politicians and military personalities assembled in the Bürgerbräukeller to strike against the Berlin 'November Criminals'.[94] Röhm has described the scene, saying that in their enthusiasm 'people leapt on to chairs and embraced each other, many were weeping for joy and emotion. The Reichswehr soldiers tore the yellow cockades from their caps. At last! Those were the words of relief which burst from every throat.'[95] Röhm handed Himmler the old Reich war flag to which the unit had just sworn its oath, and called his men out on to the streets. A few minutes later they were formed up in column and moved off in step towards the Bürgerbräukeller where Hitler was discussing the 'National Revolution' with the great men of Bavaria, Ritter von Kahr the Bavarian Nationalist Commissar General, and General von Lossow, the Reichswehr Commander in Bavaria. When it reached the Briennerstrasse, Röhm's column was stopped by a messenger from the Bürgerbräukeller with an order to occupy the War Ministry in the Schönfeldstrasse, which contained the headquarters of

Wehrkreis [Military District] VII (Bavaria).[96] Röhm did as he was told and barely an hour later he was in possession of the War Ministry.[97] He had 400 men; the muzzles of their machine guns poked menacingly out of the windows,[98] for even Röhm was gradually beginning to realize that something had gone wrong – after their initial surprise Bavaria's politicians and generals were striking back.

Early on the morning of November 9th the intruders in the War Ministry were left in no doubt that things had indeed gone wrong; the noise of approaching tanks was heard; Reichswehr and police units moved forward and cordoned off each house, brought machine guns and artillery into position and waited for the order to fire.[99] An ominous silence ensued. On the Ludwigstrasse, where friend and foe were separated by a barbed-wire entanglement, Himmler still clutched the Reich war flag. Hitler's lunatic miscalculation had brought together a curious concourse of men – future friends and enemies, future murderers and victims; next to Himmler stood Röhm, the future head of the SA, who eleven years later was to be struck down by the SS myrmidons of the man now carrying his standard; next to Röhm was Count du Moulin-Eckardt, the future SA Intelligence Chief, who was to end in one of Himmler's concentration camps.[100] Opposite them, on the other side of the barbed wire, was Reichswehr Lieutenant Hermann Höfle, Röhm's ex-aide and a secret member of Reichskriegsflagge, who in the summer of 1934 was to warn his old chief of impending danger and later be a thorn in Himmler's flesh as a Waffen-SS General.[101]

Today's enemies are tomorrow's friends, today's comrades tomorrow's murderers; von Kahr and Röhm, the enemies of 1923, met a similar fate at the hands of the SS thugs on June 30th, 1934.[102] The only actors on the 1923 stage whom the SS allowed to survive were those who tried to mediate between Kahr and the putschists – Röhm's former commander, Ritter von Epp and Hörauf, later an SA commander.[103] But their attempt at mediation failed. Röhm had to capitulate to the Reichswehr and the police, handing over his weapons; the men of Reichskriegsflagge were only allowed through the cordon when disarmed.[104] Hitler's and Röhm's movement had apparently collapsed. Röhm was imprisoned in Stadelheim.[105]

So Himmler was alone again – no uniform, no idol, no creed. He was facing a crisis; he had lost his job and in spite of numerous applications could not find another. Maja Loritz had definitely turned him down and politics had proved a disappointment. His only consolation was the worship of his female admirers, who seriously thought that Himmler had done something historic by carrying the flag on November 9th, 1923. One of them wrote emotionally: 'Troops of the Reichskriegsflagge in front of the War Ministry. Heinrich Himmler at their head carrying the flag; one could see how secure the flag felt in his hands and how proud he was of it. I go up to him incapable of speaking a word but ringing in my ears is:

> Be proud I carry the flag
> Have no cares I carry the flag
> Love me I carry the flag.'[106]

This letter from an unknown admirer was forwarded to Himmler by his friend 'Maria R.' (probably Mariele Rauschmeier) with a note: 'This letter is for my friend Heinrich. Let it be a small indication of our fervent gratitude and faithful memory of that deed which gave us a few moments when we learnt to hope once more.'[107]

In spite of the failure of the beer-cellar putsch, Himmler decided to stay in politics. When the NSDAP was banned, the Movement split into two warring 'Völkisch' groups:[108] Himmler joined the National-Socialist Freedom Movement headed by General Ludendorff.[109] Another member was Gregor Strasser,[110] a chemist from Landshut and a passing acquaintance of Himmler's; he was an aggressive, energetic, shrewd National-Socialist, regarded as the real brains of the Movement, and he soon recognized Himmler's organizing ability; he began to make use of him forthwith.

In May 1924 there were to be elections for the Reichstag and the enemies of the Republic decided to seize the opportunity to use democracy's weapons and virtues – to bring democracy down. Strasser wished to cash in on the nation-wide publicity evoked by the Hitler putsch to get his Nazis into the Reichstag at last. Bavaria thought of little else but its first election campaign, and a feature of it was a Swedish motor-cycle carrying a heavily muffled propagandist who rushed from one Lower Bavarian village to another spreading Gregor Strasser's message.

With his motor-cycle Himmler beat all records of National-Socialist demagogy. He raged against Jews and Freemasons; he whipped up the peasants against the capitalists; he painted a picture of a world peopled only by noble peasants; he thundered against Bolshevism; he decried democracy and all forms of rational policy.[111] He travelled indefatigably; in one week his diary shows: 'February 23rd, 1924, speeches in Eggmuhl, Lanwaid and Birnbach. February 24th, discussions in Kelheim and Saal followed by "individual enlightenment". February 25th, one and a half hour's lecture in Rohr.'[112] On August 22nd, 1924 he told his friend Kistler: 'I have a terrible amount to do; I have to direct and build up the organization in the whole of Lower Bavaria – and that in every sense.'[113] His industry was rewarded, for Strasser's movement captured nearly two million votes and entered the Reichstag with thirty-two deputies.[114] But this success brought no joy to Himmler; he was beginning to wonder whether the Movement he had joined really offered prospects for the future. In a letter to Kistler he referred to 'the unselfish efforts we Völkische are making, efforts which will apparently never bear fruit in the immediate future,' adding that he felt he was supporting 'a potentially lost cause'.[115]

A weak character like Himmler was discouraged by the quarrelling between the Völkische and the National-Socialists and by the intrigues between the supporters and opponents of Hitler. He just stood bewildered, a member of the extremist right-wing gang, searching for an idol who would once more give him something to conform to. He was ready to be a slave but could not find a master. He was determined to believe in something but did not know what. He was longing to play some role in history and could already see himself as a martyr, writing:

> Although they may pierce you
> Fight, resist, stand by
> You yourself may perish
> But keep the banner high.
> Others may win victory
> When you're laid to rest
> And shall gain that glory
> To which you aspired.[116]

The problem was – what was this banner to be, what was the sacred cause it was worth dying for? Himmler knew only too well that he was no saviour, was not born to greatness. His self-confidence was always sapped by a nagging doubt; he could never quite convince himself that he was cut out to be a commanding figure. Faithfully he recorded in his diary what he thought of himself and decided that he lacked self-assurance, talked too much and was inclined to make too many silly jokes: 'What a miserable creature is man,' he wrote on November 7th, 1919,[117] and on January 29th, 1922: 'I am a phrasemonger and chatterbox and without energy. Got nothing done . . . they think of me as a gay fellow who is amusing and takes care of everything: "Heini will see to it".'[118] He knew better.

He was so unsure of himself that he seriously toyed with the idea of leaving Germany. He learnt Russian and thought of settling and farming somewhere in the East; on another occasion his future seemed to him to lie in Turkey or Peru; between 1919 and 1924 his diary contains no fewer than fourteen references to plans for emigrating.[119] Yet this insecure and superstitious being became convinced that he was destined for some terrible fate. (Years later he wrote to his wife: 'We soldiers of fortune are doomed to remain lonely outlaws,' to which she replied: 'Don't always look on the black side; let the future take care of itself.'[120] A few days later she was even more explicit: 'Here you are again saying that this New Year is going to be horrible. Have you joined the astrologers and become convinced that Mars is in the ascendant and that therefore there will be horror upon horror? Do please stop it.'[121]) He did not master his self-torturing doubts until he came into the orbit of the man who at once became his demi-god – Adolf Hitler. Hitler was released from Landsberg prison in December 1924.[122] He at once set about reforming the proscribed and divided NSDAP and within a year had swept away all that Himmler had found distasteful in the Völkisch camp. On February 27th, 1925 he united under his leadership the main body of Bavaria's Völkisch and National-Socialist Parties to form a new NSDAP; two months later he founded the SS, and by the end of 1926 he had eliminated all his Party rivals and could form his own Party army, the SA.[123] With his instinct for subordinating himself to someone, Himmler sensed that he had found his idol. In August 1925 he received his membership card for the reconstituted Nazi Party;[124] shortly thereafter he was installed in a sparsely furnished room near St Martin's church in Landshut as secretary to Gregor Strasser, at a salary of 120 marks a month.[125] Strasser, who was in charge of Party propaganda in Lower Bavaria, had plenty for his amanuensis to do. Himmler maintained contact with the most remote local Nazi groups: for the Nazi backwoodsmen he and his motor-cycle became the outward and visible sign of the Nazi Party. Soon he was nominated local organizer for Lower Bavaria.[126]

It had been held that, like Goebbels, Himmler was an ideological disciple of Strasser, who later opposed Hitler. In fact Himmler always considered himself a Party headquarters employee rather than a follower of Strasser.[127] When Strasser moved to Berlin and became the North German counterweight to Hitler, Himmler moved closer to his Leader. It is not known when the two first met, but Himmler never overcame his shyness when in personal contact with the 'greatest brain of all times', as he called Hitler.

While still in Strasser's office in Landshut, Himmler developed a schoolboyish adulation for his Führer. A friend of Himmler's told the writer Willi Frischauer that on the wall of his office was a picture of Hitler with which Himmler would hold murmured conversations.[128] Even when speaking to Hitler on the telephone Himmler would click his heels; on one occasion during the war his masseur, Felix Kersten, took a call from Hitler and Himmler could hardly contain himself at his good fortune: 'Herr Kersten, do you know whom you have been talking to? You have heard the voice of the Führer. What luck! Put that in a letter to your wife straight away! How happy she will be that you should have had such a unique opportunity.'[129]

The 'time of struggle' when he was at Hitler's side was the high spot of Himmler's career. Even in 1945 he could still enthuse over it: 'Those were glorious days. We members of the Movement were in constant danger of our lives, but we were not afraid. Adolf Hitler led us and held us together. They were the most wonderful years of my life.'[130] He was always rushing about on his motor-cycle in the service of his Führer, riddled with inhibitions, burning with ambition, plagued by stomach pains which often brought him near to fainting. 'It is incredible what you do,' one of his Berlin female admirers told him at the end of 1927: 'You ask too much of yourself and your stomach pays you back. Not surprising, since your stomach's right.'[131] His future wife wrote to him in desperation: 'So you're on the road again; I was only thinking today that your life is one long rush.'[132]

Hitler gave him his deserts and Himmler rose in the Party hierarchy. In 1925 he became Deputy Gauleiter of Upper Bavaria-Swabia, in the same year Deputy Reich Propaganda Chief, in 1927 Deputy Reichsführer-SS.[133] In the course of a few years the diffident, aimless student developed into a fanatical disciple of Hitler, appreciated by his Führer for his outstanding organizing ability. But good organization alone did not satisfy Himmler; he wished to be the trainer and teacher of those around him; he saw himself leading Party and people back to the true springs of life.

His long stay in the Lower Bavarian farm country had left him strangely obsessed with the philosophy of 'blood and soil'. From his earliest days his romantic historical notions had led him to regard the peasantry as the mainspring of the nation. 'The yeoman on his own acre,' he opined, 'is the backbone of the German people's strength and character.'[134] Later he maintained that by 'origin, blood and character' he was a peasant himself.[135] He imagined all great men to be sons of peasants, and he referred to his favourite hero, Heinrich I, 'The Fowler' (876–936), King of Saxony and conqueror of the Slavs, as a 'noble peasant of his people'.[136] In his post-student period, he was already under the spell of popular propaganda and he drew a picture for himself of a society built around the peasantry. An undated memorandum by Himmler envisages the farmers' school as the core of the 'back-to-the-land' State; its teachers and pupils were to present the 'true picture of the German character' and be the forerunners of the new society.[137]

The teachers in this school, and for the peasant population of which he dreamed, were to be 'masters' and 'companions', both male and female. The men must have qualities of leadership and be conscious of this world's 'lies and frauds'; the schoolmistresses must be 'lively, clean-living women, with true maternal instincts, free from the diseases of today's degenerate city women, strong and gracious, leaving the last word to the man in the everyday things of life.' This spring of life for Himmler's peasantry was to be 'decorated with homely taste' and be open at all times to 'German citizens, poets and artists', thus forming a 'spiritual and cultural centre' where the intellectual workers could 'create, free from the intellectual currents of delusion.' Here was clearly the origin of the National-Socialist and SS sociological Utopia. 'But value will be placed upon character, rather than knowledge,' Himmler went on; the products of his school were to be 'men of healthy bodies, strong nerves and strong wills' who 'in permanent and close contact with their school would rise to be leaders of the people.'

Himmler even found friends prepared to take steps to put this nonsense into practice. They bought a farm in Lower Bavaria and made it available to Himmler. He hoped that there might be 'a further set of generous people with the means and the will to set up a foundation.' But he was disappointed;[138] the peasant school remained a figment of the imagination. Nevertheless, Himmler did not abandon his idea of the peasants' Utopia; his father, after all, had been a tutor, and he thought he had discovered in himself a genius for teaching; he thought he had been born to be the great educator, ever ready to draw the useful lesson from events and circumstances.

Those around him were continually subjected to lectures on the doings of their ancestors in this case or that; he could always quote some historical example to illustrate the present and enlighten his contemporaries. Even during the war he longed for peace 'when people could be educated again.' Kersten, his masseur and perhaps most intimate friend, seriously thought that in his heart of hearts Himmler would have preferred to educate rather than exterminate the subject peoples of the East.[139] Himmler drew a conclusion even from the failure of his peasant school project but it was an unrealistic partisan conclusion. For the first time he had first-hand knowledge of the economic straits in which the farming population was placed – but his resultant reasoning was crazy.

Himmler, the peasant mystic, was oblivious to the fact that German agriculture was passing through a structural crisis dating from the abolition of Bismarck's protectionist policy, if not earlier; he was equally oblivious to the pressing necessity for rationalization and the elimination of unproductive smallholdings. His picture was quite different; he saw a multi-coloured web of evil labelled 'International Jewry'. The countryman's 'worst enemy', he wrote in 1924, was 'international Jewish capital' because it 'set the townsman against the countryman'. This was how it was done: 'By speculation and playing the markets, the Jews ensure that production prices are low and consumer prices high. The farmer is supposed to earn little, the townsman to pay much. The Jews and their hangers-on grab the middleman's inflated profits.'[140] Up to the putsch of November 1923 the Jews pictured in Himmler's diaries had, at least, been individuals; now, however, the Jew became a stereotyped generalized caricature and every 'non-Aryan' a partisan of the supposed worldwide menace of Jewry. From this point, the Jews in Himmler's scheme of things became simply a target for collective vilification. The future Reichsführer-SS had found his enemy.

In this same memorandum Himmler referred to another equally indispensable arch-enemy – the Slavs. The German peasantry, he argued, could only be proved and strengthened in battle against the Slavs, since the only future lay in the East. 'Particularly in the East,' he said, 'there are, today, great masses of land available for purchase; they are now held by the great estates. The sons of farmers and farmworkers must be settled there to prevent the second and third sons of the German farmer being forced into the town, as has been the case hitherto. The countryman can only regain decisive influence in Germany by widespread re-settlement.' This re-settlement, moreover, was a factor in German nationalist policy: 'Increase of our peasant population is the only effective defence against the influx of the Slav working-class masses from the East. As six hundred years ago, the German peasant's destiny must be to preserve and increase the German people's patrimony in their holy mother earth in battle against the Slav race.'[141]

In this memorandum Heinrich Himmler had unconsciously formulated two of the central points of the later SS programme, theories which lay at the root of the Third Reich's anti-Jewish and anti-Slav policies. Battle against the Slav 'sub-human' and against 'international Jewry' became an *idée fixe*. The programme, of course, still lacked its fanatical overtones, its pseudo-religious frenzy but, in the case of Himmler, here is definitely the point at which the development of political fantasy began.

At this stage, of course, the Nazi Party was in no position to offer Himmler any hope of putting his peasant theories into practice. He accordingly joined a group known as the 'Artamans', which seemed to be prepared to do something serious about the back-to-the-land idea.

The Artamans originated from the Völkisch wing of the German Youth Movement. They were nationalist idealists obsessed with the notion of the owner-settler. Most of them did not belong to the NSDAP (although their leader Georg Kenstler did); they were a collection of youths who swore by 'blood and soil' and suffered from an anti-Slav complex; one of the points in their programme was to force Polish farm-workers in the eastern provinces to return to Poland.[142]

In 1924 the first Artaman group set off for an estate in Saxony to do what they thought was their duty both to the economy and to the nation (Himmler's dream of an estate in Lower Bavaria was undoubtedly inspired by the Artamans); 2,000 youths rushed off to farms in East Germany and formed themselves up to defend Germany against the Slavs.[143] Himmler was fast becoming one of the leaders of the movement; he was made 'Gauführer' of Bavaria[144] and maintained contact with other Artaman groups in Germany (including one in Brandenburg, a member of which was a certain Rudolf Höss,[145] later to become one of Himmler's most sinister minions as commandant of Auschwitz).

In the ranks of the Artamans, Himmler met a man who gave an ideological veneer to his own ideas on peasant policy and incorporated them into a body of racial doctrine, that of the superiority of the Nordic race. This was Richard Walther Darré, an Argentine German, born in 1895, educated at King's College School, Wimbledon, ex-official in the Prussian Ministry of Agriculture and future Nazi Party agrarian expert; Himmler was five years his junior, and Darré took him under his wing.[146] He taught Himmler what he had been preaching for years; the agricultural problem was not primarily one of economics but one 'of the blood'. According to Darré the peasantry had 'always formed the only reliable basis for our people from the point of view of blood';[147] it was therefore the duty of the State to expand this peasant basis, and this must be done by settlement schemes, raising the birthrate and curbing the drift to the towns. It was imperative, so Darré said, 'to bind the best blood among our people irrevocably and as quickly as possible to the soil.'[148] The best source of blood, according to Darré, was that mythical concept with which the Völkisch Youth Movement was already wrestling – the Nordic Race. Darré claimed to have discovered that historically the world had been fashioned by 'men with Nordic blood in their veins'. 'We know', he went on, 'that almost all great empires in the history of the world and all the greatest cultures have been founded and maintained by men of Nordic blood. We know also that these great empires and cultures have fallen into ruins because the men of Nordic blood who had constructed them, did not keep their blood pure.'[149]

The practical present-day consequences of this theory were that all influences inimical to the Nordic blood myth must be held at bay, all international humanist organizations must be suppressed – and these ranged from Freemasonry, endowed by National-Socialist propagandists with the attributes of a dominant world power, to Christianity, which preached reconciliation between peoples and among men. Fascinated, Himmler saw opening up before him a world whose existence he had dimly suspected but which he had never been able to visualize clearly. Darré, with his doctrine of blood and soil, opened Himmler's eyes, and what he saw was wonderful – the Völkisch élite of the future, the lords of the new Germanic tribes, the men of his SS Order.

The Artamans disappeared into the quicksands of history; the idealism of the Youth Movement yielded to the egoism of the great eastern landowners who were quick to turn the townee dreamers to good use.[150] But for a long time Himmler did not forget his debt to Darré and the Artamans. Later he recruited Darré into the SS, and put him in charge of his new 'Rasse und Siedlungsamt' [Race and Re-Settlement Office],[151] which Darré used as a stepping stone to the Reich Ministry of Agriculture. Himmler himself now began to teach this 'blood and soil' mythology to his own organization, the Lower Bavarian SS. The peasant theorist in SS uniform caught the eye of the senior Party members and Himmler saw before him the possibility of becoming head of the entire SS. Even so, he was still uncertain whether his future lay on the land or with the SS. He thought he had found someone with whom to share his life as a peasant settler.

In 1926, to escape a sudden shower, he dashed into the foyer of a hotel in Bad Reichenhall and almost ran into a lady to whom he swept off his dripping hat with such gallantry that she was soaked.[152] When Himmler looked up in embarrassment, he saw before him the Germanic goddess of his dreams – blonde and blue-eyed, like one of the Valkyries. She was Margarete Boden, daughter of a German landowner in Goncerzewo, West Prussia.[153] She had worked as a nurse during the First World War, and then moved to Berlin where, after a short-lived marriage, she had used her father's money to found a private clinic.[154]

Himmler fell in love at first sight, but his parents were less than pleased with their son's choice. Marga, as she was called, was eight years older than Heinrich and, to make matters worse, a Protestant *and* divorced.[155] Himmler hesitated for a long time before producing Marga to his parents. He said to his brother Gebhard, 'I would rather clear a hall of a thousand Communists single-handed,'[156] but the parents eventually gave way and abandoned the two to their illusions. Heinrich and Marga were married on July 3rd, 1928[157] and planned to set up on a farm together. Marga sold her private clinic, and with the proceeds the two bought a piece of land at Waldtrudering near Munich, on which they built a small wooden house – three up and two down. Heinrich insisted upon putting up a chicken-house himself, for they planned to run a large chicken farm.[158]

Months before they were married Marga wrote: 'Darling, I think so often of that little bit of land which we shall eventually own,' and then continued in the bantering style she initially used to Himmler: 'Darling, I believe the wicked husband always has to worry about the savings, for you know that the bad wife always spends all the money she's got.'[159] They collected fifty laying hens[160] but the farming project failed owing to lack of money and the calls of Heinrich's Party career. As an NSDAP employee Himmler earned 200 marks a month[161] but this proved inadequate to run a chicken farm. On May 6th, 1929, Marga wrote to her husband: 'The hens are laying frightfully badly – two eggs a day. I worry so much about what we're going to live on and how we're going to save for Whitsun. Something's always going wrong. I save so hard, but the money's like everything else.'[162] Money was a continual worry; another letter said: 'You have not written; that's naughty. Now the money won't come tomorrow morning and so Berta [the maid] won't be able to get your shoes.'[163]

In addition to their financial troubles the marriage now began to break up – far more rapidly than either of them had thought possible. Marga was cold, nervous and anything but cheerful; she irked her sensitive husband so much that he began to stay away from home more often. After the birth of their only child, a daughter named Gudrun,[164] the Himmlers lived apart.

Vainly Marga hoped that one day National-Socialist politics would allow her husband to return to her: 'When the elections are over, then we could at least have a few years of peace. And you, you will be with me all the time.'[165] In another letter: 'You naughty soldier of fortune; you must come to this part of the world sometimes.'[166] And again: 'Even if you're only coming for two days, at least you're coming.'[167] Gradually, however, Marga realized that she had lost him. 'Sometimes it makes me sad that I just have to sit at home here all the time. Only today I was thinking how we could celebrate your birthday. My dear, let's go to some exhibition together. We've never done that.'[168] And in another letter: 'Things are not good with me. What is going to become of me. One is continually wondering that. Oh my dear, what is going to become of me?'[169]

Heinrich Himmler did not know what *was* going to become of her. He was under the spell of the Führer, who on January 6th, 1929 had called him to be head of the SS in which he was member No 168.[170] Now he could show what he had learned from Strasser and Walther Darré. The SS was waiting, Himmler thought, only for the master's hand to turn it into an order of chivalry, the élite of National-Socialism. In fact, the new Reichsführer-SS soon found out that ideological purism was not what his Führer demanded of him. Hitler wanted no order of faithful Germanic knights, but a blindly obedient bodyguard as an instrument of his personal power. The National-Socialist Party had reached a cross-roads. The economic crisis of the late 1920s was driving an increasing number of embittered Germans into the Nazi camp, both reinforcing and endangering Hitler's position as Party Leader. That position had to be safeguarded in face of all opposition: the most murderous chapter in the history of German Party politics was about to open.

4

FROM BODYGUARD TO PARTY POLICE FORCE

DURING the Nazi 'struggle period', Ludolf Haase, the local Nazi leader for Hanover South, wrote a memorandum to Party head-quarters in which he suggested that the NSDAP had disintegrated after the November 1923 putsch because the Party had no corps of leaders, and the leaders had no instrument of power. What the reconstituted Party needed was: 'A National-Socialist Order within the Party,' a secret society, ready at all times to provide the leadership with guards and henchmen. It should be a secret Order within the Party to hold the movement together in an iron grip. The men of this Order would 'cleanse the organization including, if necessary, affiliated formations and authorities'; at the same time 'by observation, etc' they should obtain 'the indispensable knowledge concerning the enemy's plans, actions and circumstances'. Within the 'general ruck of the NSDAP' the future National-Socialist Order must form an organization 'to provide the instrument which a senior leader must have, if he is successfully to pursue any popular power policy.'[1]

This was a prophetic description of the basic SS concept which was later to throw its shadow over the whole Party. But Haase's memorandum produced no action from Party headquarters; it was pigeon-holed, and its author forgotten.

In January 1929, however, in an annexe to the Party headquarters building (50 Schellingstrasse, Munich) a man arrived who thought the same way as Haase and in whose personal files Haase's memorandum was later found. This was Heinrich Himmler, the new Reichsführer-SS, and he had every intention of forming his own organization 'within the general ruck of the NSDAP'. Initially, however, he fared little better than Haase. The Party greeted his ambitions with pitying condescension.

Many regarded Himmler as an eccentric. People said that he was a fanatic who had produced this curious élite concept by applying his professional knowledge of animal breeding to the official racial doctrine of the Party. Moreover, his exorbitant ambition was out of all proportion to the minute size of the Party organization for which he was responsible. The strength of the SS at the time was 280 men; it was under Franz Pfeffer von Salomon, the 'SA Supreme Commander' [OSAF] who regarded it with little favour, and it had difficulty in making headway against the view current in the NSDAP that it was a sort of canvassing organization for the Party Press.

But Himmler was undeterred by the Party's scorn. He drew up an ambitious expansion programme envisaging a rapid numerical increase in the SS and official acceptance of its status as an élite. In April 1929 he submitted to Hitler and von Salomon a draft of regulations which, in effect, constituted the Order of the SS.[2] Henceforth no one was to be accepted into the SS who did not satisfy the strictest selection conditions; Darré, the 'blood and soil' mystic, was of course behind it and his only criterion was race, his ideal human being the romanticized picture of the Nordic warrior hero.

In a wartime speech Himmler said: 'We went about it like a nursery gardener trying to reproduce a good old strain which has been adulterated and debased; we started from the principles of plant selection and then proceeded, quite unashamedly, to weed out the men whom we did not think we could use for the build-up of the SS.'[3] Had such lofty principles been strictly applied, Himmler would have had to dismiss the best part of half his SS, for they were mostly simple middle-class citizens, bearing little resemblance to Walther Darré's picture of glorious Germanic man. But Himmler had no intention of carrying out so self-destructive an exercise. His orders stated that the new regulations did not apply to old SS members who had served in the First World War.[4] He tightened his selection programme only by degrees: 'I started with a minimum height requirement of 5 ft 8 ins,'[5] adding with the pride of the visionary: 'I knew that men of a certain height must somewhere possess the blood I desired.'[6]

Every applicant had to submit a photograph, at which Himmler would gaze through a magnifying glass until he was convinced that the man possessed what, in his vocabulary of racial purity, was termed 'good blood'.[7] He once told his officers: 'I used to think: are there any definite indications of foreign blood in this man – prominent cheekbones, for instance, which might cause people to say "he has a Mongolian or Slav look about him"? Why did I do that? Let me draw your attention to the lessons of experience. Think of the types who were members of the soldiers' councils in 1918 and 1919.'[8]

This remark shows that Himmler's insistence on biological criteria, primarily that of 'good blood', did not stem solely from racist fantasy. He was also appealing to the ideas and emotions of the ex-officers and Free Corps commanders for whom the 'soldiers' councils' epitomized their own degradation. At the end of the war left-wing soldier extremists had torn off their officers' badges of rank, and the officers had never recovered from this traumatic experience; but on the other side of the coin, the soldiers' councils had found these same officers unwilling to lift a finger to protect their imperial supreme commander against revolution. Himmler had only been a cadet at the time, and so had no personal experience of the soldiers' councils – what Röhm called 'this ignoble capitulation to the red mob';[9] nevertheless, he would frequently remind ex-officers of that unhappy period; 'every one of you who was an officer at the time has personal experience of a large number of these people. You will therefore be able to confirm that, in general, they were people who somehow looked odd to Germans, who had some peculiar feature showing that there was foreign blood somewhere.'[10]

Such arguments were well calculated to appeal to the emotions of the section of society from which Himmler drew his first SS men. They were a lonely collection of ex-soldiers, academics whose careers had been ruined by inflation, and unemployed professional men; after drifting through the Free Corps and the Nationalist Defence Formations, they were now looking for a new form of community existence and Himmler's notion of a racial élite fascinated them. He could promise them a home and release from the constrictions imposed by life as an uprooted member of a society whose social prestige had vanished.

Hitherto the word 'élite' had had a social connotation; entry into the élite postulated possessions, education and good breeding, but the lost generation which had grown up at the front found that door closed; the difficulties of re-adaptation and their romanticized 'soldier-of-fortune' theories had driven them into society's no-man's-land. Instead of the social élite, Himmler now held out to them the prospect of a quite different élite – a racial aristocracy, an ideological nobility. The notion of the 'good blood' élite was propounded in sufficiently broad and nebulous terms to offer a refuge to all this lost collection of humanity – provided they satisfied Himmler. They were soon presenting themselves in droves.

The original founders of the SS had come from lower-middle-class suburbia, men like Ulrich Graf, who worked in a butcher's shop, and Josef Berchtold, who kept a small stationery business. Now men from another level of society were flooding into the SS – the lost souls of the middle and upper-middle classes. The SS attracted these newcomers by its philosophy of 'hardness' and its attitude of bellicosity *per se*, basically unconnected with ideology. The newcomers' background was obvious; they were the left-overs from the Free Corps, people whom Ernst von Salomon, the Free Corps minstrel and one of Rathenau's murderers, referred to in 1930 as 'the men whom war will never let go, who will always have war in their blood.'[11]

The men of the Free Corps were an example, only too typically German, of a generation which despised culture and civilization. They had looked to the world war they had longed for as the means of sweeping away all the evils of bourgeois hypocrisy and complacency; they had hoped to 'lose their selves', in the words of their British idol, T. E. Lawrence.[12] The war was now over but, to their annoyance, bourgeois society was still in existence. The men who had survived the trenches hoped that they had fought the war to end all wars, but the generation which had grown up during the war still hoped that the bourgeois world they despised could be brought down by force.

Contempt for the pre-war world turned into loathing for the post-war order of society; to the wartime generation, force and savagery were justified, even in peacetime, in order to destroy the ill-gotten gains of bourgeois civilization; to make matters worse, among them were poets, the beauty of whose language inhibited clear thinking. Perhaps the greatest mouthpiece of this lost generation was Ernst Jünger, who had risen to the rank of captain and won the *Pour-le-Mérite*; he proclaimed that for all time war would remain 'like a rocky mountain within us, from which we shall stride down into the valley below to seek the promised land. And so long as the wheel of life turns within us, this war will always be the axle around which it revolves. The war may be at an end, its battlefields deserted and condemned as torture chambers and Calvaries, but in its acolytes its spirit lives on; it will never allow them to leave its service.'[13]

In the confused post-war period in Germany there was plenty of opportunity for life to revolve around the axle of war. The State needed fighting men to defend itself against Communist insurrection and Polish insurgents; the wartime generation was only too glad to take up arms once more; had not Jünger told them: 'What can be more sacred than the fighting man?' But these new-type soldiers were very different from the old. They called their units Free Corps to emphasize that they had entered Government service voluntarily – and that equally voluntarily they could leave it again. Their loyalty was not to the Government, but to whatever flag they happened to be following and to the particular commander in whose unit they served.

This collection of bellicose political adventurers who constituted the Free Corps of 1919 and 1920 can hardly be paralleled in German military history. Second lieutenants commanded units calling themselves regiments; orders from far-distant headquarters were obeyed or disobeyed as the recipients thought fit. They were soldiers of fortune and proud to admit it. Like the old soldiers of fortune, their unit was their home, their fellow-soldiers their family. There were 70,000 of them and, like the old mercenaries, they were possessed with an 'insatiable restlessness, a determination to burn themselves out; they felt the primeval male urge permanently to court danger. As soldiers of fortune, they accepted the disdain of the corpulent sedentary bourgeoisie and returned it in full measure round their camp fires and in their quarters, in battle or on the march. They denied both the ideas and the values of that other respectable half of the world.'[14]

These men were ripe material for a doctrine of uninhibited use of force. The traditions and norms of the old-style military discipline had been swept away and their place was taken by a drum-head court-martial system, euphemistically termed 'judicial self-help'. Anyone the Free Corps thought guilty they shot. Human life, either their own or that of others, counted little; their watchword, like that of the later Waffen-SS, was to deal out or to accept death.[15] In 1930 Ernst von Salomon extolled the Free Corps for their 'ruthless action against armed or unarmed enemy masses, their limitless contempt for the so-called sanctity of life and their marked disinclination to take prisoners under any circumstances.'[16] Ten years later these were the hallmarks of Himmler's soldiers.

When the Free Corps came to an end, the use of force infected politics like a cancer, the victims being the democrats and the republicans; terror was the watchword of the nationalist parties and defence formations. Even so, however, the men of the Free Corps were still without a home. Some of them took refuge in the SA, where they rose to senior positions. But meanwhile, driven by the economic depression, countless thousands of unemployed were streaming into the SA and the ex-Free Corps men began to realize that the SA was no home either. The SA men recruited from the queues of the labour exchanges were simply rebelling against the circumstances of the time; they were merely expecting Adolf Hitler to give them jobs so that they could return to their wives and children. The men of the Free Corps, on the other hand, although they might wear brown shirts, despised the bourgeois world to which even the toughest SA thug in his heart of hearts wished to return.[17]

Himmler's élitist Order offered these men a real home. From 1929 onwards men of the Free Corps began to stream into the SS. They came in two waves; first appeared the veterans who had neither wished nor been able to reintegrate themselves into society. They included some well-known names: Erich von dem Bach-Zelewski, a Reichswehr officer from Pomerania, who had had to resign from his Infantry Regiment for indulging in National-Socialist intrigue; from 1931 he was the SS organizer in the Austrian frontier zone.[18] Then there was Friedrich Karl Freiherr von Eberstein, a First World War lieutenant who became aide to Graf Helldorf when a Free Corps commander; he later took over the SS in Saxony.[19] Finally there was Udo von Woyrsch, another First World War lieutenant and an officer of the Frontier Protection Service; he organized the SS in Silesia.[20]

The economic crisis produced a second wave of applicants for the SS. This time they were men who had managed to get a foot in the door of everyday life, but had lost their positions in the pitiless competition of a free economy. The spur which drove them into SS uniform was bankruptcy. Friedrich-Wilhelm Krüger, for instance, a colonel's son and ex-lieutenant in Lutzow's Free Corps, had been a freelance salesman;[21] Karl Wolff, the son of a country solicitor and ex-lieutenant in the Grand Duke of Hesse's Regiment of Lifeguards, had run an advertising agency;[22] Dr Carl-Albrecht Oberg, a doctor's son and ex-lieutenant on the Western Front, had been director of a banana import firm.[23]

With so many dynamic ex-Free Corps men entering the SS, Himmler could snap his fingers at the Party's objections to his expansion campaign. He travelled tirelessly through Germany recruiting his élite. When he announced in Hamburg that he intended to raise an SS unit of 500 men, Krebs, the Gauleiter, objected that Hamburg could hardly produce 500 National-Socialists in all; Himmler replied haughtily that the circumstances were unimportant and all that mattered was to get the men.[24]

Röhm, his former guide and counsellor, had meanwhile quarrelled with Hitler and gone off as German military instructor to Bolivia. On January 29th, 1930 Himmler wrote to him that: 'The SS is growing and by the end of this quarter should have reached 2,000';[25] he added that his Standartenführer [Colonels] were 'splendid fellows' and that 'as each month passed, service regulations and conditions of entry were being tightened.'[26] SS numbers rose steadily; in January 1929 there were 280 SS men, in December 1929 1,000, and, in December 1930, 2,727.[27] The SS grew so rapidly that Himmler finally felt himself strong enough to tap a source hitherto closed to SS recruiting – the SA.

Ever since the Frontbann period under Röhm, the SA had included certain ex-members of the Free Corps who were now only too anxious to transfer to the SS. However, Pfeffer, the head of the SA, took care that none of his subordinates should go over to Himmler; late in 1926 he had laid down that the SS was to act only in closest accord with SA Headquarters.[28] As a matter of principle the SS was forbidden to act on its own; when SA and SS were used together, the SS was always placed under the SA commander.[29] Pfeffer was particularly careful to keep control of SS recruiting, insisting on being consulted for fear lest the SS 'siphon off all potential commanders and thereby involuntarily strangle the development of the SA.'[30]

But Himmler was undeterred by Pfeffer's restrictions. He began quietly to sing the praises of his SS Order among the SA, and succeeded in weaning many of them away. This did not pass unnoticed by the SA commanders; early in 1931 Stennes, the SA commander in East Germany, wrote to Röhm: 'It is most serious that these newly formed SS units should be carrying on their recruiting by underhand means and, in addition, trying to break up the SA.'[31] In Berlin the indignant SA produced anonymous leaflets protesting against 'the build-up, at the expense of the SA, of our civilian bosses' bodyguard, the SS'.[32]

In an attempt to restrain the growing enmity between his two Party armies Hitler handed Himmler his first great success; late in 1930 he made the SS independent of the SA. Though still formally under the command of the OSAF, SS independence of the SA as a whole was confirmed. Hitler laid down that 'No SA commander is entitled to give orders to the SS.'[33] To underline its independence, the SS was now given its own uniform, black instead of the SA brown – black cap, black tie, black breeches and black-bordered swastika armband. A black stripe, two inches above the left cuff, carried an Arabic numeral indicating the number of the SS Sturm [an SS formation equivalent to a company].[34]

The SS had won its first war of independence. More important still,

Hitler permitted it to adopt a new organization. It had originally been formed on a 'ten-man' system – the SS unit in any one locality was limited to a commander and ten men. This was now abolished and instead a new structure appeared with ranks and units exactly modelled upon those of the SA. The smallest SS unit was now to be the 'Schar' of eight men under a 'Scharführer' [Corporal]. Three 'Scharen' formed a 'Trupp' of twenty to sixty men under a 'Truppführer' [Sergeant], equivalent to a military platoon. Three 'Trupps' formed a 'Sturm', the most important SS unit; it consisted of 70–120 men, was commanded by a 'Sturmführer' [Captain] and corresponded to a company. Three 'Stürme' made up a 'Sturmbann' of 250–600 men, commanded by a 'Sturmbannführer [Major] and corresponding to a battalion. Three or four 'Sturmbanne' formed a 'Standarte' of 1,000–3,000 men under a 'Standartenführer' [Colonel] corresponding to a regiment. Several 'Standarten' formed an 'Untergruppe' (later 'Abschnitt' – Region) similar to a brigade and commanded by an 'Oberführer' [Senior Colonel]. Later several 'Untergruppen' or 'Abschnitte' formed a 'Gruppe' or 'Oberabschnitt' [Major Region], a unit corresponding to a division and commanded by a 'Gruppenführer' [Major-General].[35]

This new SS army, of course, existed only on paper; Himmler still lacked the men to give real body to his organization, but here Hitler gave the SS an opportunity of showing their self-assurance. He forbade the SS to canvass the SA for recruits in future but, on the other hand, he ordered the SA to make men available for newly formed SS units – up to 50 per cent of the proposed SS unit in any one locality. The provision that they should send only 'selected personnel' to the SS was particularly distasteful to the SA; moreover the SS Sturmbannführer concerned was authorized to reject unsuitable SA men.[36]

The SA leaders tried to convince themselves that at least any further SS interference in their affairs would now be stopped. August Schneidhuber, Pfeffer's Deputy, stated hopefully that: 'The SA is now entitled to forbid SS commanders and men to canvass within our ranks, even when off duty.'[37] But Schneidhuber was wrong. He had clearly missed the vital sentence in Hitler's order of November 7th, 1930, the real reason for the sudden agreement to so striking an increase in the SS. This sentence ran: 'The task of the SS is primarily to carry out police duties within the Party.'[38] Haase's dream had come true – a secret Order now stood sentinel within the Party.

Just at this moment Adolf Hitler had good reason to call upon his bodyguard to be the maid of all work. According to the Party grapevine his position was shakier than ever. The National-Socialist Movement was degenerating into an arena for intrigue and dissimulation, murder and political long knives. The SS was intended by Hitler to hold the Party firmly together and to beat down any insubordination, and there was a great deal of insubordination in the NSDAP – it had never been a homogeneous party.

The Party, after all, had started as a lower-middle-class pan-German society; it had then been given a doctrinal top-dressing of nationalistic socialism originating in the Sudetenland; shortly thereafter it had been debased into a political appendage of the Bavarian defence formations and a nest of warring politicians from the Völkisch camp; later it had become the proving-ground for a Völkisch Socialism with a proletarian twist, a refuge for the SA rabble and an inviting field for reactionary party leaders and captains of industry. So heterogeneous a party could have no real unity; it lived on activism, noise and agitation for agitation's sake. It was held together only by its hatred of progress and democracy and its determination to capture the State at all costs. Hardly an article of the NSDAP creed was undisputed by its members, hardly one of its senior functionaries was approved of by any other.

Hermann Esser, one of Hitler's closest associates, thought the North German Völkisch Party 'an association of visionaries, worshippers of Wotan',[39] Goebbels, who was a Rhinelander, proposed that 'the petty-bourgeois Adolf Hitler' should be expelled from the Party;[40] at almost every Party rally someone demanded that Julius Streicher, the Jew-baiter, should have his membership card withdrawn.[41] Goebbels stated that 'The future belongs to the dictatorship of the Socialist ideal within the State,' and then had to admit that the sentence came from *Red Flag*, not the National-Socialist Press.[42] Gregor Strasser demanded an alliance with the Soviet Union, because Moscow would be an ally in the fight against the 'Versailles Peace Settlement', and found himself in head-on collision with the anti-Soviet crusader Alfred Rosenberg, in whose view the Party was liable to fall prey to the Red enemy.[43] Not all Nazis were united even about the persecution of the Jews; every shade of anti-Semitism was to be found within the Party. Even Goebbels said: 'The Jewish question is more complicated than one thinks. It may well be that the capitalist Jew is not the same thing as the bolshevist Jew.'[44]

The Party was so divided that a full-time investigation and arbitration committee had to be set up under ex-Major Walter Buch, the SA Commander, Nuremberg, to deal with petty disputes between members.[45]

Hitler, however, knew how to use these intrigues to strengthen his own position. He had a flair for mediation between conflicting points of view and so was able not only to hold the Party cliques together, but to work his way to the top at the same time. Increasingly he emerged as the only man capable of keeping the Party intact but in fact he took every opportunity to fan the flames – the more violent the quarrels, the more acceptable did the arbitrator from Munich appear. Before being executed at Nuremberg, Rosenberg admitted: 'Hitler deliberately allowed opposing groups to exist within the Party in order that he might then play the role of arbiter and leader.'[46] When the Party was reformed in February 1925, Hitler's authority hardly extended beyond the borders of Bavaria, but he made good use of every crisis and every difference of opinion; internal Party differences were his ladder to the leadership.

Initially Hitler made little progress with the Völkisch and National-Socialist groups of North and West Germany, because three men stood in his way; Gregor Strasser, the Landshut chemist and a gifted organizer, Strasser's eccentric doctrinaire brother Otto, and Joseph Goebbels, his propaganda chief. These three controlled the National-Socialist organization in the north. Ideologically they were at variance with Hitler; he was steering a cautious course between restoration of the monarchy and revolution, while they believed in Völkisch Socialism, nationalization of industry and a Russo-German proletarian alliance.[47] In February 1926, however, Hitler got the better of them; at a meeting in Bamberg packed with his supporters, he had his opponents' social revolutionary programme put to the vote and carried the day.[48] Goebbels at once went over to Hitler; even Gregor Strasser concluded a half-hearted truce and entered the Munich Party headquarters as Reich organizer.[49]

Only Otto Strasser continued to conduct open warfare against Hitler from Berlin. He was editor of the *Berliner Arbeiter Zeitung*, the most influential National-Socialist newspaper in the North, and head of a group of intellectuals who were trying to give National-Socialism a definite left-wing bias; Berlin became the main centre of internal opposition.[50] But then a third party took a hand in the game – the Berlin SA marched.

Their leader was a giant of a man named Kurt Daluege. He was a Berlin sanitary engineer, had been a member of the Free Corps which had liberated Annaberg in Upper Silesia from Polish insurgents in 1921, and was considered one of the most pugnacious rough-necks in Berlin;[51] his limited intelligence had earned him the nickname 'Dummi-Dummi' ['Thicky'] in the Berlin underworld. After the 1923 putsch, he had joined the Frontbann, Röhm's substitute SA, and later formed the first Berlin SA unit, using Free Corps veterans, work-shy toughs and the gymnastic sections of the Völkisch groups.[52] Early in

1926 his unit was 500 strong, more than the whole Berlin membership of the NSDAP.[53]

The SA men made good use of their numerical superiority. They thought that the Berlin Gauführer, a civil servant named Ernst Schlange, one of Otto Strasser's men, was too weak; they accordingly demanded his resignation and put forward their own candidate, the ex-Frontbann Commander, Hauenstein.[54] The change was to take place on August 25th, 1926. When Strasser defended Schlange at a combined meeting of National-Socialist and SA leaders, Hauenstein boxed his ears and the SA went away happy.[55] The change of régime seemed complete.

Hitler now weighed in, however, and once more showed his gift for playing off warring factions against each other. In November 1926, he dispatched the renegade Goebbels to Berlin as the new Gauleiter.[56] Goebbels had every reason to stick rigidly to Hitler's line, for he had no other standing in Berlin – the Strasser camp considered him a detestable traitor and in the eyes of the Berlin SA his name was coupled with ignominious defeat. Hitler's scheme was to involve the emergent SA in the internal Party game. The SA's natural rival was Gregor Strasser's 'political organization', abbreviated PO and referred to by the SA as 'P Zero.'[57] Hitler calculated that the Party sleuths and the SA would neutralize each other, leaving him still in overall control of the NSDAP.

But this was not Hitler's only reason for pushing the SA into the forefront; it was certainly not the most important. He regarded the SA as the force which would bring him to power and only the history of the SA, the history of Hitler's hopes for it and disappointments with it, can really explain why, finally, it was the SS which emerged as the decisive instrument of the Führer dictatorship. In Hitler's eyes the SA was the organization which would give to his political ideas the essential backing of force; the SA marching columns were intended to conduct 'a sort of permanent electoral campaign using terrorist methods' (as the historian Wolfgang Sauer puts it), and so weaken the already somewhat feeble resistance of his democratic opponents.[58]

Like Hitler, Pfeffer von Salomon, the head of the SA, was an enthusiast for marching columns. Both believed that the tramp of marching feet, and the well-drilled advance of a body of disciplined men in columns of four, exerted a compelling psychological fascination over the masses. Von Pfeffer gave perhaps the most revealing description of National-Socialist methods of mass hypnosis: 'The sight of a large number of men, disciplined and coordinated both mentally and physically, with a patent or potential will to fight to the limit, makes the greatest impression upon every German; the language of the message which it carries to his heart is more convincing and compelling than any writing, speech or logic.'[59] In Pfeffer's eyes, the essential was 'an impression of might, the might of the marching column and the might of the cause for which they march. The Germans are emotionally susceptible and the inherent might of any cause will make them believe in its justice. When whole bodies of men are to be seen deliberately staking life and limb for a cause, that cause must be great and good.'[60]

Pfeffer was an ex-Army captain and so in his eyes ex-officers were the best drill sergeants for his marching columns. They knew their drill books and the majority of SA men, who had been in the Army already, knew the words of command; so Pfeffer placed a number of ex-officers at the head of his army. In 1928 he created seven Oberführer [Brigadiers] commands, all under ex-regular officers;[61] Captain (Police–retired) Walther Stennes became SA-Oberführer East (Berlin), Major (Retired) Paul Dincklage SA-Oberführer North (Hannover), Lieutenant-Colonel (Retired) Curt von Ulrich SA-Oberführer West (Kassel), Commander (Navy–Retired) Manfred Freiherr von Killinger SA-Oberführer Centre (Dresden), Major (Retired), August Schneidhuber SA-Oberführer South (Munich), Lieutenant (Retired) Viktor Lutze SA-Oberführer Ruhr (Elberfeld); Captain (Retired) Hermann Reschny was held ready to take over in Austria (Vienna).[62]

Early in 1929, Pfeffer wound his ex-officers even tighter into his organization; he appointed Stennes, Dincklage, Ulrich and Schneidhuber as his deputies and Ulrich additionally as Inspector General of SA training.[63] The cadre of the Party army was now ready to accept the mass of recruits which streamed into the SA when the economic crisis broke in autumn 1929. The increasing misery of the unemployed produced a dramatic expansion of the SA; by 1930 its strength was fluctuating between 60,000 and 100,000.[64]

Expansion increased the SA's self-confidence and its commanders were less and less prepared to accept orders from the political functionaries. The SA was making itself largely independent of the political organization and Hitler became suspicious. His suspicions deepened as messages began to arrive from Berlin showing that his crafty balance-of-power game was in danger. Economic distress was producing growing criticism that Hitler's policy was insufficiently revolutionary; Otto Strasser's intellectuals and the SA commanders were drawing closer together; even Hitler's watchdog, Goebbels, was beginning to waver.[65]

Before the two groups could really coalesce, however, Hitler stamped out the threatened conflagration. On May 21st, 1930 he appeared, unannounced, in Berlin and lured Strasser into an ideological argument which ended in deliberate disagreement. Hitler then disowned Otto Strasser, used Goebbels to expel all Strasser supporters from the Party, and capped his triumph with the receipt of a telegram of devotion from Gregor Strasser.[66] He thought that he had silenced the Berlin opposition; the SS began to shadow its leaders, Hitler setting increasing store on the detective instincts of Kurt Daluege, who had meanwhile left the SA and by spring 1929 had risen to be head of the Berlin SS.[67]

Daluege was now so strong that he was largely independent of the Reichsführer-SS in Munich. He was only too well aware that the Party internecine strife had placed him in a key position and he more or less refused to do business with anyone other than Hitler and the OSAF.[68] On Hitler's instructions he watched every move by the Berlin SA leaders. Not far from the Sports Palace, where the Berlin SA foregathered, he set up what one of his staff called 'a meeting place for specially reliable SS men and those who aspired to be so. Only comparatively few Berliners knew of the existence of this SS headquarters and those who did were ignorant of its true purpose – and even at this stage that purpose was far wider than mere command of the Berlin SS.'[69]

One of Daluege's retainers was his old friend Herbert Packebusch, a carpenter's son who had been a faithful follower of Daluege ever since the Free Corps days; as a commander of Sturm No 21 he had a desk in Berlin SA Headquarters and faithfully recorded everything he noticed.[70] Unfortunately he noticed practically nothing. He did not perceive that an SA leaders' conspiracy was forming round Stennes, Pfeffer's deputy, or that the SA was planning nothing less than the deposition of the Munich Party leader. Otto Strasser had not been unseated for nothing; the Berlin SA was still under the spell of his revolutionary Socialist harangues.

Mere economics drove the SA leaders into opposition against their political rivals and against Hitler. The unemployed were streaming into the SA, attracted both by its extremist slogans and by its standard of cooking; SA funds were gradually running out.[71] Stennes reported to Munich:[72] 'In some Berlin Standarten 67 per cent of the men are unemployed. There is a Sturm in Breslau which cannot parade for inspection – at least not in frost or snow – because it has no footwear.' By this time (the end of 1930) there were already 3,000,000 unemployed in Germany.[73]

Alongside the unemployed, criminal elements infiltrated into the SA and, as a result, the perennial underground struggle between the SA and the Red Front took on a gang-warfare character reminiscent of Chicago.

Fighting raged round the bars and speak-easies and the nicknames used showed the type of men involved; one SA Sturm in Neukölln, for instance, called itself 'The Pimps Brigade' and another in Wedding, 'The Robbers'; an SA commander known for his street-clearing ability was nicknamed 'Rubberleg' and his henchmen 'King of the Boozers', 'Revolver Snout' and 'The Bulletmiller'.[74] The SA commanders, unwilling to lose their new recruits, were clamouring for more money, for the line between Nazis and Communists was thin indeed; but the Gauleiter, who had the money, kept the purse-strings tight. The politicals had no intention of pandering to the SA's urge for expenditure.[75]

This miserliness gave rise to a nasty suspicion on the part of the SA – suppose the Party leadership was deliberately keeping the SA small; worse still – suppose that the Party leaders were finding the SA an obstacle to their climb to power and respectability. Inflammatory cries were to be heard, such as: 'Adolf is betraying us, the proletariat.'[76] Anonymous pamphlets decrying the Party leaders began to appear: 'We, the proletarian section of the Movement, are of course delighted! We are quite happy to starve in order that our dear "leaders" can enjoy themselves on their salaries of 2,000–5,000 marks a month. We were also overjoyed to hear that at the Berlin Motor Show our Adolf Hitler had spent 40,000 marks on a large new Mercedes.'[77]

The rumour went round Berlin that, to assist his projected coalition with the German Nationalists, Hitler was proposing gradually to cut down the SA. Stennes, the senior SA commander in eastern Germany, accordingly decided to take the bull by the horns. He had been assured of support from Pfeffer's other deputies and so his demands to Munich were stiff – authorization for SA commanders to enter Parliament, reduction of the influence of the Gauleiter, the SA to be paid for keeping order at Party demonstrations.[78] Stennes had chosen his moment cleverly; in September 1930 new Reichstag elections were due and, for the first time, the NSDAP had an opportunity of cashing in on the discontent of the unemployed and the have-nots. The SA therefore occupied a key position in the electoral campaign.

So a delegation from the Berlin SA went to Munich to lay their demands before the Party leaders, but Hitler refused to see them.[79] Shortly thereafter the new list of Nazi candidates for the Reichstag elections was published, and it was found that Stennes and another Berlin SA leader had again been excluded. Indignation exploded; at the end of August the Berlin SA commanders resigned and their men went on strike during the electoral campaign.[80] Goebbels, for instance, had planned an election demonstration in the Sports Palace but the SA refused to keep order; in the middle of the proceedings the SA chuckers-out withdrew, leaving the Nazi speakers to be heckled by their opponents.[81] As they went they recited in chorus:

Wenn mich die Reichstagsgeister rufen	When the Reichstag gentlemen call me
Ich folge nicht	I do not obey
Tapeten muss ich suchen	I look on the posters
Beim lampenlicht.	By lamplight
Ich sitz' auf meine Kiste,	I sit on my backside
Maltriere mein Gehirn,	And cudgel my brain
Studier' die Professorenliste	And look through the list of professors
Ob Hakenkreuz oder weiche Birn'.	Whether swastika man or nincompoop.[82]

The SA men then moved off to the Wittenbergplatz and conducted an anti-Goebbels demonstration. The *Münchner Post* reported:[83] 'There were loud cries of "Let Dr Goebbels come out and give an account of himself" '; others threatened to march to the Sports Palace and take the whole 'Goebbels rabble' apart. Goebbels hurriedly called in the Berlin SS. Daluege's men took over maintenance of order in the Sports Palace and posted guards at the Berlin Gau headquarters (10 Hedemannstrasse). Goebbels feared an SA attack at any moment[84] and during the night of August 30th it came. Stennes' men moved in, clubbed down the SS guards at Gau headquarters and broke up the furniture.[85] In desperation the Gauleiter had to ask the despised State Police to intervene and a police detachment arrested twenty-five SA men and took them away.[86] Goebbels rushed off to Munich by train to report the catastrophe to his Führer.[87] Though near a nervous breakdown, Hitler kept his head.

The next day an agitated Hitler presented himself to Stennes and begged him not to leave the Party. The Leader trailed from one bar to another, urging the SA to continue to trust him.[88] On the evening of September 1st, 1930, reconciliation was celebrated in the Berlin Ex-Servicemen's Building, when Hitler promised to meet the more important of Stennes' demands and the contestants parted peaceably.[89]

Nevertheless for the first time the SS had stood up for their Führer against their SA comrades and Hitler now decided on ruthless use of the SS as an internal Party police force. A warning that Stennes might strike again at any moment came from Dr Leonardo Conti, Senior Medical Officer at Stennes' headquarters, later an SS-Obergruppenführer and the Reich Health Leader.[90] On September 8th, 1930, Conti reported:

'Under his [Stennes'] leadership, the SA is turning into a force owing no real allegiance to the Movement or its ideals. Stennes himself takes no stock of National-Socialist ideology and deliberately refuses to study it; he is capable of letting his troops loose at any moment.'[91]

Hitler had long since realized that his position was in deadly danger. He dismissed Pfeffer from his post as head of the SA (Pfeffer was only too ready to go) and announced that he himself would take over as Supreme Commander of the SA.[92] He then remembered his old friend Röhm's parting words: 'You have only to give me the word – "Be at the Siegestor at 6 AM on such and such a day with your men" – and I shall be there.'[93] Hitler recalled Röhm from Bolivia.

Before the summons to return as Chief-of-Staff of the SA had even reached Röhm, however, Hitler had staged a scene which foreshadowed things to come. This was the point at which he introduced the Party to the cult of the charismatic Führer. Every SA man had to swear blind, eternal loyalty to the man who claimed to unite in his own person the Party and its leadership. On September 3rd, 1930, Wagner, acting Chief-of-Staff of the SA, informed all OSAF deputies that they must swear an unconditional oath of allegiance to the person of the Party leader and Supreme Commander of the SA, Adolf Hitler.[94] Every member of the SA had to swear 'to carry out all orders assiduously and conscientiously, in the knowledge that my commanders will never demand from me anything unlawful,'[95] – and, according to the official statement, those commanders were to be appointed by Hitler in person.

The Führer, Adolf Hitler, had now assumed sole authority within the National-Socialist Party and he had installed the SS as his Party police. They were needed sooner than they thought, for National-Socialists still existed who refused to be blinded by the Führer cult.

Conti's forecast came true and Stennes prepared to strike once more. Hitler and Röhm had ordered more rigid centralization of the SA, a measure which met with immediate resistance from Stennes and his people.[96] This time, however, Daluege's friend Packebusch was paying attention; Daluege admitted later that Packebusch kept him continuously informed of Stennes' preparations.[97] Whatever was planned in SA Headquarters East, Daluege was always able to take the necessary counter-measures. Packebusch now reported that Stennes was planning a major coup against the Munich leaders and was only waiting for the right moment. It came during the night of March 31st, 1931.

Early on the morning of April 1st Daluege reported to Röhm: 'I have just (3.45 AM) received a telephone call from the aide to a certain Standartenführer to the effect that between midnight and 3 o'clock a highly secret meeting of Berlin SA commanders was held under the chairmanship of Jahn, aide to Gruppenführer East. Jahn informed the meeting that, at a conference to be held in Weimar at midday on April 1st, Stennes, the Gruppenführer East, was to be dismissed by our Führer, Adolf Hitler. It was made quite clear that Hitler's orders would not be obeyed. During the meeting all the commanders present declared themselves in favour of Stennes and against Hitler.'[98]

Once more SS men went into action against SA men and once more they had to yield to force of numbers. Stennes' supporters occupied the offices of the Gau headquarters and the National-Socialist newspaper *Der Angriff*.[99] The revolt spread quickly through northern and eastern Germany. In a matter of hours Hitler's writ no longer ran beyond the Elbe. The majority of senior SA commanders in Brandenburg, Silesia, Pomerania and Mecklenburg joined the battle against Hitler[100] – Wetzel, Veltiens, Jahn, Pustrow, Lustig, Kremser[101] – all the important names were there. The only absentee was Manfred von Killinger, supposedly a close friend of Stennes;[102] elsewhere in Germany too some senior commanders refused to support him.[103]

For a short moment the Democrats, depressed by Hitler's electoral success, could rejoice over the spectacle of Nazi leaders sacking each other. Stennes dismissed Goebbels from the post of Gauleiter and Goebbels replied by releasing SA men from their oath of loyalty to Stennes; the East German SA 'took over' the Party and the Party promptly expelled them.[104] But the Stennes putsch rapidly lost momentum; the fire went out of the revolt as soon as the SA coffers were empty and Hitler then began to pick up the pieces. Paul Schulz, an ex-Lieutenant from Stettin, one of the heroes of the black Reichswehr period and a follower of Gregor Strasser,[105] was brought in to reconstitute the SA Group East and Hermann Göring combed the SA for Stennes supporters.[106]

Hitler let the entire Party know that he owed his victory over Stennes solely to the vigilance of his SS. The new SA Gruppenführer East was an SS man, Untersturmführer Friedrich-Wilhelm Krüger;[107] in a letter to Daluege Hitler produced the sentence which, in one form or another, the SS carried on their caps right up to the end: 'SS-Mann, deine Ehre heisst Treue.' (SS man, thy loyalty is thine honour).[108] The SS was now firmly in the saddle. Wherever Hitler saw his authority imperilled, whenever brown-shirted non-conformists revolted against the Führer cult, the SS was always at hand. At an SS leaders' conference Himmler shouted exultantly: 'We are not loved everywhere; when we have done our duty we may be stood in the corner; we should expect no thanks. But our Führer knows the value of the SS. We are his favourite and most valuable organization because we have never let him down.'[109]

Himmler's new instructions were designed to ensure that the SS could act rapidly and silently on Hitler's orders. SS units in any one locality were divided into sections of three to five men, each responsible for a street or area of the town; the section had to meet half an hour before the unit's time of parade to allow the section leader to check that all his members were present and to fetch any absentees.[110] Unauthorized absence was severely punished. SS regulations stated: 'Punishment for the first unauthorized absence will be a reprimand in writing from the SS commander; for the second unauthorized absence the man will be warned in writing that he may be expelled from the SS and will be reprimanded in front of the entire unit; punishment for a third unauthorized absence will be expulsion from the SS.'[111]

Unit commanders had to ensure that their men were mobile and ready for duty at all times. They had to make efforts to increase the numbers of motor-cycles and bicycles held by their unit, arrange long-distance rides and practise the transmission of messages over distances of twenty to thirty miles.[112]

At the same time a veil of secrecy descended over the activities of the SS. No one, not even a member of the Party or an SA man, was allowed to know what the SS was doing; Himmler's Order began to withdraw into a twilight of mystery. One of Daluege's orders laid down that: 'even in face of unjustified criticism, SS men and SS commanders are strictly forbidden to converse with SA men and commanders or with civilian members of the Party other than as necessary for the purposes of duty. Should criticism be voiced in a small gathering, members of the SS will immediately and silently leave the room with the curt comment that the SS carries out Adolf Hitler's orders.'[113]

Wagner, the Acting Chief-of-Staff of the SA, issued an order explaining to the Party why the SS was necessarily a law unto itself: 'The SS is a protective organization, the duty of which is first to carry out police duties within the Movement, and secondly to ensure that no breaches of official regulations or laws are committed by members of the Movement. If it is to do its duty, the SS must be completely independent, in other words independent both of the political leadership and of SA headquarters.'[114] With this sort of blanket cover the SS was free to devote all its energy to the task which it had always placed first, investigation of anti-Hitler factions and Party enemies.

As early as 1925 the SS had begun collecting confidential information on the private affairs of controversial Party members. The earliest of these SS reports carries the date September 24th, 1925; it is headed 'U to

Party headquarters' and was forwarded by Schreck, the founder of the SS. It runs: 'At yesterday's evening meeting of the local group in Neubiberg, a certain gentleman named Herzer gave the following information: "In the spring of this year, the *Völkischer Kurier* carried an article accusing Esser [Hermann Esser – a friend of Hitler] of accepting 30,000 marks from a Jew named Landauer. Since this statement has so far not been denied, I had to assume, and still do, that it is true. This is all the more likely, moreover, since Esser was at one time a Communist." '[115]

Such reports were initially the product of chance but later a regular system was established. Local SS units had to submit reports to SS headquarters on opposition groups such as the Reichsbanner and the Communist Party, on Freemasons and prominent Jews and on all political events.[116] Most of them were fit only for the wastepaper basket and only with the arrival of Himmler was some order brought into SS information activities. In June 1931 Himmler ordered: 'Our enemies' efforts to bolshevize Germany are increasing. Our information and Intelligence service must aim to discover, and then to suppress, our Jewish and Freemason enemies; this is the most important task of the SS today.'[117] In all SS Abschnitte [Districts] Himmler set up secret Intelligence sections to keep a watch on the enemies of the Party, both internal and external.[118]

Himmler reported all sorts of things to the Führer. On October 10th, 1931, for instance: 'In certain towns the Communist Party has been expelling some of its Antifa League men [Communist activists] in order to infiltrate them as spies into SS formations.' 'Captain Ehrhardt, Commander of the officially disbanded Viking Corps, has recently become very active once more. In close cooperation with Government circles and under nationalist cover, he is preparing to form a Free Corps; to judge from the manner in which it is being recruited and in view of Captain Ehrhardt's former attitude, its object must be to destroy the NSDAP.'[119]

A few months earlier an ex-lieutenant from the Navy, Reinhard Heydrich, had joined the Party and the SS. With his help Himmler proceeded to build up a so-called Ic Service [Intelligence Service] which later developed into National-Socialism's greatest informer organization – the Sicherheitsdienst [SS Security Service – SD].[120]

Sturmführer Heydrich proved to be so gifted a collector of Intelligence that the SS rapidly turned into the Party's main Secret Service. Hitler came to regard his personal security as dependent solely upon the SS. On January 25th, 1932 he nominated Himmler head of security in the Brown House, the Party headquarters at 45 Briennerstrasse, Munich (the former Barlow Palace).[121] An order issued by SA Headquarters stated: 'Control of the security service throughout Party Headquarters (The Brown House and adjacent building) is hereby transferred to the Reichsführer-SS. The SA Oberführer of the Munich/Upper Bavaria Untergruppe [Sub-Group] and the SS-Standartenführer of No 1 SS-Standarte, Munich will forward to the Reichsführer-SS a list of the SA and SS men selected.'[122] The order continued that Himmler was now responsible for measures to 'repel Marxist/Communist attacks and prevent police interference'.[123] Himmler had hardly completed his preparations before the Brown House was shaken by a murder story – and the clues led not to the headquarters of the Party's enemies, but to the offices of the Brown House itself.

In its own way this affair was further proof that Hitler's one-man leadership was still by no means undisputed inside the Party. The Stennes upheaval had raised the problem of the extent to which Hitler could ride roughshod over the views of his SA commanders; the new scandal posed the question whether Hitler was strong enough to disregard the Party's remaining moral scruples. The background to the whole business was that in Ernst Röhm, the new Chief-of-Staff of the SA, Hitler was keeping a man who was running the SA through a ring of blatant homosexuals and turning the National-Socialist revolutionary army into a perverts' playground.

Röhm had never made any secret of his tendencies saying 'I admit straight away that I do not belong to the goody-goodies, and have no desire to do so.' Any attempt by the State 'to regulate human instincts by law or divert them into other channels' he countered with a quotation from Richard Wagner: 'Folly, folly, everywhere folly.'[124] He rejected with scorn protests by leading National-Socialists. He told the Berlin Doctor Heinsoth, for instance: 'I am quarrelling violently with that blockheaded moralist, Alfred Rosenberg. His articles are aimed primarily at me since I have never made any mystery of my views. That is obvious since in my case "people" have had to get used to these criminal goings-on in National-Socialist circles.'[125]

Röhm's abnormal leanings had been common knowledge since he had taken a Berlin gigolo, Hermann Siegesmund, to court for theft of a suitcase.[126] On the evening of January 13th, 1925 Röhm had invited Siegesmund to a glass of beer in the Berlin Marienkasino followed by the usual sequel to such an encounter. Siegesmund stated in evidence: 'While we were still sitting fully clothed in the room of the hotel, Herr Röhm took a cigarette case from his pocket; I noticed that a slip of paper fell out and I picked it up. About half an hour later I left the hotel room because Herr Röhm expected me to take part in a form of sexual intercourse which was abhorrent to me and to which I would not agree. Out in the street I found that the slip of paper which I had taken while up in the room was a luggage ticket belonging to Herr Röhm.'[127] Siegesmund collected the suitcase, which proved to contain a bundle of compromising letters.

Hitler knew all about Röhm's tendencies but insisted that they were his own affair. When Röhm took on his job as Chief-of-Staff of the SA, Hitler, who was still officially head of the SA, issued a parting order that the SA was 'not a girls' finishing school, but a tough fighting formation'. Complaints about peoples' private habits he rejected 'indignantly and on principle' as 'supposition' and 'entirely private matters'.[128]

Röhm's amorous adventures, however, were anything but 'an entirely private matter'. He used the SA for ends other than the purely political. SA contact men kept their Chief-of-Staff supplied with suitable partners and at the first sign of infidelity on the part of a Röhm favourite, he would be bludgeoned down by one of the SA mobile squads.[129] The head pimp was a shop assistant named Peter Granninger, who had been one of Röhm's partners since 1928 and was now given cover in the SA Intelligence Section.[130] For a monthly salary of 200 marks he kept Röhm supplied with new friends, his main hunting ground being Gisela High School, Munich; from this school he recruited no fewer than eleven boys, whom he first tried out and then took to Röhm.[131] Meanwhile some of Röhm's more dubious friends had occupied senior SA positions left vacant as a result of the Stennes revolt.

The general meeting-point for the Granninger circle and the SA homosexuals was Röhm's reserved table in the Bratwurstglöckl, Munich. The proprietor, Karl Zehnter, was a homosexual himself whom Granninger had 'assisted' at his home.[132] Another homosexual and long-standing habitué of Röhm's table was the new Berlin Commander, Edmund Heines;[133] he had even been expelled from the SA in 1927 for homosexual practices. Karl Ernst, the new SA Chief-of-Staff, Berlin, had been a partner of Captain Rohrbein, ex-Frontbann, who had also frequently been seen with Röhm in Berlin homosexual dives such as the Kleist-Kasino and Silhouette.[134] This ring of perverted SA commanders seemed unbreakable. When asked about the goings-on in Röhm's circle, Hitler took refuge in the excuse that the Chief-of-Staff was not a proven homosexual; if anyone could give him cast-iron proof, he would draw the necessary conclusions.

Röhm and his highly organized squad of informers generally succeeded in covering their tracks. In March 1932, however, Röhm's letters began to leak, several being published in the Social-Democrat

Münchner Post.[135] Röhm's friends panicked. Any more-or-less normal SA commander was suspected of having filched the letters and passed them to some anti-Hitler National-Socialist like Dr Helmut Klotz, an ex-Reichstag Deputy.[136] Röhm was so agitated that he dispatched his confidant, the adventurer journalist Georg Bell, on a curious expedition for a National-Socialist. Bell was being paid 300 marks by the Social Democrats for information about the Nazis;[137] he was now sent to ex-Major Karl Mayr, the man who, together with Röhm, had 'discovered' Hitler in 1919 and had since gone over to the Social Democrats.[138] Mayr was now one of the leaders of the Reichsbanner which was loyal to the Republic and determined, even at this late hour, to prevent the Nazis' rise to power. Bell met Meyr in the Reichsbanner offices in Magdeburg and transmitted to him Röhm's demand for a guarantee that no more of his letters would be published in the Social-Democrat newspapers.[139] 'Mayr knew all about it,' Bell said later, adding that Röhm 'told me that it was true that these swine wished to bring us down.'[140] Whoever the 'swine' may have been who had leaked Röhm's letters to the Press, his National-Socialist enemies now determined to solve the problem after their own fashion. When Hitler once more refused to dismiss Röhm, Buch, the Senior Nazi judge and apostle of National-Socialist rectitude, formed a plan to murder the SA Chief-of-Staff together with four of his principal associates.

Buch proceeded with caution. His mind turned to an old friend from the early Party days with whom he had built up the NSDAP in Baden – Emil Traugott Danzeisen, an ex-SA-Standartenführer, now running a bandage factory.[141] Buch told Danzeisen that there was treachery abroad in the Party: Standartenführer Uhl had given the police full information about the SA informer network; moreover a 'German Nationalist' clique was forming around Röhm's cronies, the Counts du Moulin-Eckart and Spreti; this gang was determined to seize power and, in addition, was ruining the Party by their homosexual practices.[142] Danzeisen got the message and had little difficulty in thinking of one or two toughs whose line was murder. He formed a murder squad headed by Karl Horn, a bankrupt architect.[143] To secure his alibi Danzeisen moved to Austria, whence he issued orders in writing, using the pseudonym 'Wieland II'. On March 16th, 1932 Horn received his detailed orders as follows: 'Facts; Count du M who works in Room 50 is a para 175 man [paragraph 175 of the criminal code dealt with homosexual offences]. As such he has great influence with his superior R. An old story. Both are being blackmailed by a Herr Bell from Grottenmühl-am-Chiemsee. Stabsführer Uhl, who lives in the same house, to be dealt with similarly.[144] Horn proposed that an SA bandsman named Grinsch with eight men should lie in wait for Bell, slug him with a hammer and string him up with a swastika pinned on him. Then it would be Röhm's turn. Danzeisen's orders to Grinsch ended: 'Do your duty; don't forget the Chief-of-Staff. Heil and good luck. W.II.'[145] Horn then received another order: 'Room 50 drives a large Opel 10/50. It is parked every day in front of the house. Wheel nuts.'[146] The occupant of Room 50 in the Brown House was Karl Leonhardt Graf du Moulin-Eckart, head of the SA Intelligence Service, and he went to work every day by car; this message therefore meant that Horn was to liquidate him by engineering a road accident. When Horn, however, began observing the Brown House, he suddenly had his doubts. Instead of loosening a wheel of the Opel, he presented himself to du Moulin and told him everything. The Count, who in any case was not a homosexual,[147] had an idea. Supposing Horn would assist to unravel the murder plot right back to its real organizers? Horn said he would.[148]

Horn then laid a trap. He found Buch's private number in Munich-Solln and called him up. 'Horn here, Karlsruhe. I must speak to you urgently.'

Buch: 'Come to the Holzkirchner station at 4.15 today.'

Horn: 'But I don't know you.'

Buch: 'I shall be wearing brown shorts, brown shirt, brown jacket, grey overcoat, grey hat and I shall wear the overcoat open.'[149]

When they met at the station, however, Buch was clearly sharper than Horn had thought and obviously saw through Horn's game, telling him that the matter had been settled, since the information about du Moulin had proved to be inexact. He asked Horn to send a telegram forthwith to Danzeisen as follows: 'Helen's engagement broken off.'[150] The next day Horn received proof in the shape of three revolver shots that Buch had not, in fact, abandoned his plans. Horn was fired on as he was about to enter Danzeisen's house in Munich-Laim about 11 PM.[151] It was easy to guess who had fired them. Count Spreti, Röhm's aide, knew only too well; that morning Buch had observed Horn leaving the Chief-of-Staff's room in the Brown House. SA Headquarters thereupon took Horn under their protection.[152]

At this point Himmler put his oar in. Being in charge of security at the Brown House, he felt he should protect Röhm against Buch's people. On March 24th, 1932 Horn learnt that (in his words) Himmler had 'had up Major B [Buch] and asked him to explain himself, as a result of which the whole matter is finally at an end.'[153] But Röhm was not so sure. He and Bell flew to Berlin to see what their political opponents thought. On April 1st Röhm met Mayr and asked him for evidence against Paul Schulz, who was in charge of SA reorganization and whom Röhm wrongly thought to be behind the murder plot.[154] A week later Bell wandered through the editorial office of the Social-Democrat newspaper *Vorwärts* and once more told the whole story.[155] Friedrich Stampfer, the editor, noted: 'They were, in fact, running away because they thought that they would be executed by their own people. He [Bell] was instructed to tell us of the plan so that, in the event of his death, the world should know who was responsible.'[156]

Himmler now reappears in the story once more, this time in Röhm's Berlin hideout, but what role he played is not clear. In any case he succeeded in persuading Röhm to return to Munich.[157] He could not, of course, prevent the Party scandal from coming out into the open; the two SA counts, du Moulin and Spreti, had lost their nerve and gone to the police, accusing Buch and his associates. In October 1932 Danzeisen was sentenced to six months' imprisonment for instigation to murder; Buch and the Horn gang went scot-free.[158]

The Danzeisen case and the subsequent action for libel brought by the Party against the *Münchner Post* uncovered an incredible sink of iniquity. The whole situation could not have been more ironical – the SA perverts had had to appeal for help to Mayr, the champion of democracy, in order to save themselves from the murderous intentions of one of their own judges. Martin Bormann, Buch's son-in-law and confidant, was incensed; 'this beats the band', he wrote, 'one of the leading members of the Party reviles another leading member as his bitterest enemy and insults our Party leaders, calling them swine.'[159] The greater the stench rising from the brown-shirted morass, however, the more desirable Himmler's Order became in the eyes of the Party. On October 5th, 1932 Bormann wrote to Rudolf Hess, Hitler's personal assistant: 'Look at the SS. After all they know Himmler and they know his capabilities.'[160]

Outside the Party too, people began to realize that in the 50,000 men of the SS[161] there existed an uncompromising army of puritans ready to cry halt to the wild, dissolute mob of SA homosexuals. They remembered that Himmler had said to his SS commanders on June 13th, 1931: 'Perhaps it will be months or perhaps only days before the decision comes. We shall stand where our Führer stations us.'[162] The SS had not long to wait; January 30th, 1933 was not far off. The scene was set for the Night of the Long Knives but it was not yet clear who would be wielding them – the SA or the SS.

5

SEIZURE OF POWER

FOR Heinrich Himmler the Third Reich opened in disappointment. On January 30th, 1933 the 'National Revolution' took charge of Germany; bustle and dynamism became the order of the day. But no one summoned the Reichsführer-SS to assume any key post; the SA was let loose, dominating the streets and terrorizing the dissentients; Adolf Hitler's lieutenants moved into official positions. But Himmler and his SS were not among the major participants in the new régime.

Many indeed thought that Himmler was among the 'also-rans' in the National-Socialist assumption of power. Germany's new Chancellor had refused his faithful Heinrich any important assignment in the new Third Reich. Himmler had risked his health, tearing about on his motor-cycle in wind and rain, his SS had secured Hitler's position in the Party – but his master had clearly forgotten him. Göring, Goebbels, Frick and the rest had all been rewarded with the spoils of office, but Himmler, the colourless assiduous factotum, was ignored.

Even on March 9th, 1933, when the SA and SS overwhelmed the legal Bavarian Government led by the right-wing Catholic Dr Heinrich Held, Himmler played no major part. The putsch was led by Röhm's old divisional commander, Franz Ritter von Epp, whom SS men ridiculed as 'the mother-goddess general' because of his religious views.[1] And it was this reactionary general, rather than Himmler, whom Hitler installed as Reichsstatthalter [State Governor] of Bavaria.[2] Himmler was still left with no position of any importance; he was only allowed to advance one small step, becoming Acting Police President of Munich.[3]

Even more vexatious was the fact that in far-off Prussia, under the protection of Göring, who was initially Minister of the Interior and later Minister-President, Gruppenführer Kurt Daluege, Himmler's bitterest rival, rose to the highest offices of State. Göring cordially loathed the prim, servile 'Reichs-Heini' and was only too ready to play off Himmler against his theoretical subordinate, the ambitious Daluege. He included Daluege in the Government as State Commissar without Portfolio, he placed him at the head of the Prussian Ordnungspolizei, nominated him Ministerial Director, and even promoted him to Lieutenant-General of Police.[4] Daluege lost no time in working out that he was the youngest general since Napoleon[5] and now saw no reason why he should take orders from the Reichsführer-SS. The last ties between Daluege and Himmler were severed.

To bring the renegade Daluege to heel, Himmler dispatched to Berlin his best man, Reinhard Heydrich (who had meanwhile been promoted SS-Standartenführer[6]) with orders to set up a secret information service and keep Himmler continuously posted on Daluege's manoeuvres. Heydrich packed his bags and went off to Berlin with his wife, Lina, who was pregnant. He rented a house in the city's West End, and set about getting in touch with Göring's pseudo-Napoleon.[7]

The pompous Daluege, however, would not allow this tiresome visitor from Munich to get farther than his outer office; Heydrich was told that the General could not receive the Standartenführer, since he was otherwise engaged.[8] Heydrich tried other avenues but was invariably rebuffed. When he persisted, Göring's Gestapo threatened to take proceedings against him. Lina Heydrich recalled: 'My husband knew that Göring had an arrest warrant out for him.'[9] Heydrich realized that his mission was doomed to failure and departed. His wife waited until the birth of her first child (a boy) and then also returned to Munich.[10]

Himmler and Heydrich now knew that power was not going to fall into their hands for the asking. The Third Reich bore not the remotest resemblance to the totalitarian State pictured by the theoreticians. Since January 30th, 1933 the German State machine had been overlaid by a thick tangled web of rivalries and competing authorities: anyone wishing to amass power in Adolf Hitler's Germany had to fight his way though this web.

Like many others, Himmler's picture of a National-Socialist takeover had been a very hazy one before the event. The majority had simply assumed that in some way National-Socialists would take over the machinery of Government of the Weimar Republic and do away with democracy, Hitler being responsible for all details and the provision of wise counsel. Anyone who thought more deeply considered that the National-Socialist Movement and the State must be completely fused – inevitably, since the Nazi leaders would be occupying all important positions in the State. Anything inhibiting development of the national energy, the Nazis thought, would be swallowed up in this great entity; all other interests must give way to the totalitarian State. Goebbels declared: 'The aim of the National Revolution must be a totalitarian State, which will permeate all aspects of public life.'[11] Hitler proclaimed the 'establishment of the totality of the State.'[12] Frick foresaw 'a strong Government, unhampered by individual persons, groups, classes, privileges, parties or parliaments.'[13]

But the actual situation after January 30th, 1933 was very different. Instead of the democratic parties there appeared the heterogeneous cliques of the National-Socialist Party State; instead of the Reichstag with its unstable majorities, there appeared a new form of parliamentary life – the struggle for authority between the satraps and vested interests of National-Socialism.

With the advent of the Nazis the State came under the control of a Party which, though apparently monolithic, was in fact the most contradictory in the history of German party politics. Held together only by the charismatic leadership of Hitler, a peculiar collection of factions and splinter groups milled around – a faithful reflection of German society in the aftermath of defeat, inflation, unemployment and the disintegration of democracy.

According to the American historian, Robert L. Koehl, Hitler's party was divided into four groups; around the Party leader was ranged a 'group of old fighters', the 'hard core' of Nazism',[14] the fanatical survivors of the old Party days; closely allied to them was a second group of extreme right-wing individualists, mostly doctrinaire racists who had joined the Party between 1925 and 1929, when the Nazis were still socially unacceptable. The third group was what Koehl called a 'combination of Völkisch nationalism and petty-bourgeois Socialism', formed in the years of economic depression (1930–33) when shopkeepers, professional workers and farmers were all attracted by the dynamism of the 'National Revolution'. Finally the fourth group consisted of solid citizens who had turned to the 'Party of National Revival', loyalists from the Army, the bureaucracy and the business world, who seriously believed that, with Hitler as their demagogue, they could recreate their pre-war world.[15]

Even when in opposition, so heterogeneous a Party had had difficulty in finding a common denominator; after January 30th, 1933, however, the internal diversity of the Party became reflected in the State. The much-trumpeted totalitarian State degenerated into a farce, particularly since the peculiar circumstances of Hitler's takeover forced him initially to include bourgeois right-wing politicians and Conservative officials in his Government.

National-Socialist shadow organizations grew up alongside the traditional offices of State. Practically every authority had its brown-shirted watchdog; the Foreign Ministry, for example, had its counterpart in the external offices of the NSDAP, later paralleled by the so-called Ribbentrop Bureau;[16] Kerrl, as Reich Commissar for the Administration of Justice in Prussia, and Frank as Reich Commissar for Justice, were ambitious rivals to the Reich Ministry of Justice;[17] Wagner, the ex-

Chief-of-Staff of the SA, as Reich Commissar for the Economy, kept an eye on the Reich Ministry of Economics.[18] Superimposed upon and overlapping this dual structure were new political satrapies created by the leaders of the Nazi groups and cliques. New States sprang up within the State. Baldur von Schirach, the Reich Youth Leader, wanted what he called a 'Youth State within the State';[19] Lasch, the SA Gruppenführer in Thuringia, demanded the formation of an SA State as the purest expression of National-Socialist ideology;[20] Himmler dreamed of an SS State and Konstantin Hierl, ex-Colonel and later Reich Labour Leader, thought up a special form of Defence State.[21]

These swashbucklers did not bother about theory; they simply grabbed every official position they could lay their hands on. Göring, who was anyway Prussian Minister President and Reich Minister for Air, lopped the Forestry Section off the Ministry of Agriculture and proclaimed himself Reich Forester.[22] Goebbels, the Minister of Propaganda – an office created for him – set up his own Reich Chamber of Culture, encroaching upon the preserves of Bernhard Rust.[23]

Hitler's viceroys spent their time building up their private empires and laying claim to their neighbours' prerogatives. Robert Ley, for instance, chief organizer of the Nazi Political Office and head of the German Labour Front, wished to turn his staff into a National-Socialist Order;[24] Himmler, however, insisted that the SS was the true élite and destined to be the Nazi Order.[25] Then Rosenberg, the Party ideologist, laid claim to the National-Socialist Order, maintaining that his own organization, the Office for National-Socialist Ideological Training, provided the best foundation.[26] Finally there was Röhm, the Chief-of-Staff of the SA, who considered that the ideal of a National-Socialist Order had already been achieved in the form of his SA with its alleged unit socialism.[27]

Over and above this layer of personal intrigue lay a third level of conflict, striking deep into the roots of the National-Socialist State. This brought out into the open the controversy between State and Party, together with a new version of the old clash between the Reich and the Länder. Under Dr Wilhelm Frick the Reich Ministry of the Interior now included National-Socialists who took Hitler's dictum about the totalitarian State in deadly earnest. They produced a blueprint of an all-embracing State machine on the Prussian model and wished to restrict the Party to pure propaganda functions.[28] But the Party bureaucracy would have none of it, nor of Frick's proposed reform visualizing complete centralization of the administration under the Reich Ministry of the Interior; any administrative streamlining, after all, was bound to cut through that jungle of authorities and prerogatives which allowed the

Gauleiters to act like feudal barons. Led by Göring, moreover, the proposed reform was sabotaged by the largest German State – Prussia. Göring foresaw that his administration would be increasingly subjected to the authority of the Reich Ministry and therefore hived off sections of the Prussian Administration, placing them under his personal orders – to all intents and purposes out of reach of Frick's reformers.[29]

So this was what Adolf Hitler's totalitarian State with the strong Government unhampered by groups, classes and parties, looked like in practice. In this jungle of a governmental system, in Professor Trevor-Roper's words 'as incalculable . . . as any Oriental Sultanate,'[30] what place was there for Himmler's SS? In spring 1933, after the failure of Heydrich's mission, the Reichsführer himself can hardly have known the answer.

He could do nothing other than wait for his moment, nothing other than continue to do what he had always done – guard the life of his demi-god, Adolf Hitler, and safeguard his predominant position in the Party. He pursued his self-appointed task with his usual conscientiousness. Being Police President in the 'Capital of the Movement', Himmler had plenty of opportunity to prove to his Führer how wrong he had been to treat the best-behaved of all his followers so scurvily in the distribution of the spoils of office. Himmler was not averse to publicity and he kept his name in the headlines by numerous prophecies of gloom.

In mid-March Himmler arrested Count Arco-Valley, the murderer of Eisner and the man whom, as a student, he had plotted to liberate from prison. According to Himmler the reason was that the Count had 'on his own admission planned a coup against the Reich Chancellor, Adolf Hitler.'[31] A fortnight later Himmler gave further proof of his vigilance; this time he had 'discovered a planned hand-grenade attack on the Reich Chancellor.' Three Soviet agents, he announced, had 'placed three hand-grenades near the Richard Wagner memorial where Adolf Hitler's car was bound to pass.'[32] The ubiquitous Police President then warned his Führer and the populace against further terrible dangers: 'Through information from Switzerland we have, for several days, been aware that attacks on the Reich Chancellor, Adolf Hitler, and on leading personalities of the new State, have been planned by the Communists.'[33]

Himmler's assassination claptrap touched Hitler on a particularly sensitive spot. Ever since February 27th, 1933, when, according to the Nazi version of the story, the lunatic Dutchman, van der Lubbe, had set fire to the Reichstag, Hitler had been terrified of plots and explosions; he had convinced himself that assassins were continually slinking around. Hardly a meeting of the Cabinet went by without the Führer tilting at this windmill. 'The effect upon the public of a successful attack on me would be fearful,' he declared in Cabinet on March 7th;[34] a week later the Cabinet minutes recorded: 'The Chancellor indicated that a time limit should be set for the surrender of explosives. During recent years 150 tons of explosive had been stolen, of which only 15 tons had so far been recovered.'[35] Nothing could convince him that adequate precautions were being taken for his personal safety. His imaginary assassins appeared in every conceivable guise – for instance: 'One day a perfectly innocent-looking fellow will install himself in an attic somewhere in the Wilhelmstrasse. He will look like a retired schoolmaster. A perfectly ordinary citizen, horn-rimmed spectacles, ill-shaven, with a little beard. No one will ever be allowed to see his shabby little room. There he will quietly install some weapon and will gaze through his telescopic sight at the balcony of the Reich Chancellery hour after hour and day after day with sinister pertinacity – and then one day he'll pull the trigger!'[36]

Even in his office Hitler did not feel secure. At Cabinet meetings he sat with three members of his Party (Göring, Goebbels, Frick) facing a majority of bourgeois ministers;[37] the sentries on the Reich Chancellery were provided by the Reichswehr and it was by no means impossible that the Generals might one day decide to mount a putsch against him. So who more suitable to assist than the faithful Himmler, who was so obviously preoccupied with his Führer's security? Hitler ordered SS headquarters to form a 'Headquarters Guard' (the third in the history of the SS) for his personal protection. As Commander, Hitler and Himmler selected a hefty Bavarian, SS-Gruppenführer Josef (Sepp) Dietrich.[38]

Dietrich collected 120 SS men, most of whom had carried out similar functions in the Brown House. They formed around Hitler a triple cordon any visitor must pass through before he could reach the Chancellor.[39] At the Nuremberg Party Rally of September 1933, Hitler christened the unit 'Leibstandarte-SS Adolf Hitler' [Adolf Hitler's Bodyguard].[40] Unwittingly he had laid the foundation of a second Wehrmacht.

The example of the Leibstandarte inspired Himmler to form further similar units known as SS-Sonderkommandos [Special Detachments] and later Politische Bereitschaften [Political Alarm Squads].[41] Pseudo-police units appeared in many German Länder to protect Germany's new masters and terrorize political opponents. Himmler's force made its first appearance in the summer of 1933; in Ellwangen and Reutlingen the SS formed Politische Bereitschaften (800 strong in 1934)[42] to harry the Democrats on behalf of the Württemberg Political Police;[43] in

Dresden, Sonderkommando 3 was formed of volunteers from the Hessian SS; similar units were to be found in Munich and Arolsen.[44] At one stroke Himmler had succeeded in gaining a foothold in the police machine outside Bavaria. Since he could provide the most highly disciplined force in the Party, the Police Chiefs of many German Länder, still new and unsure of themselves, went to him for advice and support. Himmler's grandfather, Konrad Himmler, had been Commissioner of the Munich Gendarmerie[45] and his grandson now realized that his future lay with the police – only through the police machine could he hope to secure a place in the National-Socialist hierarchy.

Meanwhile Himmler had also advanced in Bavaria. On April 1st, 1933 he was placed in charge of the entire Bavarian Political Police together with a special section of the Bavarian Ministry of the Interior, and assumed the title Political Police Commander.[46] He soon gave practical proof of his concept of National-Socialist police work. With cold bureaucratic attention to detail, he hounded the Nazis' political enemies; he put a stop to the wilder excesses of the local SA leaders who had been venting their wrath on their less well-armed rivals; he forbade the arrest of Catholic priests unless personally authorized by him.[47] But at the same time he brought system into the political terror. Around a couple of old stone huts in the precincts of a disused powder factory near Dachau, Himmler set up a camp in which arrested Communists and Social Democrats were held.[48] The Germans learnt a new expression – 'Concentration Camp': it became the watchword of Heinrich Himmler's police.

Hardly a soul realized the significance of Himmler's concentration camp; the police chiefs of the new Germany were mesmerized by the bureaucratic efficiency and superlative organization of Himmler's machine. For the first time people sensed that Himmler was the coming Police Chief of all Germany. He was already drafting plans for an integrated nation-wide police force, since in his doctrinaire manner he found the existing police force 'a complete shambles. A police force in which the best sections had become demoralized, in which the officer had had his sabre removed and the man was given only a rubber truncheon, a police force infested with ex-criminals and Marxists.'[49]

Himmler was determined to abolish the democratic State's established police force, saying: 'I wish in the end to create a real Reich police force from these sixteen disparate Länder Forces; for a nation-wide police force is the strongest lynch-pin which a State can have.'[50] In summer 1933 he told Dr Werner Best, head of the Police Division in the Hesse State Ministry, that the police must be removed from the authority of the local Party barons but that it must be done carefully and patiently.[51] He then asked Best whether he would like to assist in the formation of a Reich police force, and Best volunteered;[52] he was one of the few police officials whom Himmler kept in reserve, pending the extension of his power to Berlin. Himmler's *alter ego*, Heydrich, was meanwhile keeping a list of candidates for the proposed Reich police force; its attraction increased when it was found to include many officials of the old school, such as the Munich detective quartet, Flach, Müller, Meisinger and Huber.[53]

There was, however, one apparently insuperable obstacle to Himmler's ambitions: more than half the total area of Germany was closed to him. Göring, as Minister-President of Prussia, was quite prepared to use his own police force against the intruder from Munich. Göring and Himmler shared the same ambition – both wished to control the Third Reich's police machine, but Göring had one advantage over his rival – he already controlled the Prussian police, and they must inevitably form the core of any nation-wide police structure.

Göring had laid hands on the police as soon as he took over in Prussia. He created his own bodyguard, known as the 'Special Duty Police Squad' under a Major Wecke, chairman of a National-Socialist Association of Police Officials;[54] he dismissed from the police all opponents of the régime, 1,457 in all.[55] The focal point of Göring's system of control was an unobtrusive section, Abteilung IA, in Berlin Police headquarters; even under the Weimar Republic and in spite of the official ban on an all-German secret police, it had been a kind of political-police Intelligence centre for the whole Reich;[56] it was now to give birth to Prussia's fearsome political police.

As head of Abteilung IA, Göring appointed Dr Rudolf Diels, a civil servant from the political-police branch of the Prussian Ministry of the Interior.[57] He was a *bon viveur* but proved to be an outstandingly subtle official, always ready with new proposals to satisfy Göring's childishly naïve acquisitive tendencies. Diels was no Nazi, but he promised Göring, to whom he later became related (in 1943 he married Ilse Göring, widow of Göring's younger brother, Karl), that he would construct an instrument of power such as had never been seen in Prussian history. He recruited more and more criminal police officers and the strength of Abteilung IA rose from 60 to 250.[58] Göring passed the necessary laws, gradually divorcing Diels' police from the State administration; he set up a Prussian central political Intelligence agency[59] and gave it independent executive authority;[60] he exempted the new organization, later to be known as Geheime Staatspolizei [Secret State Police] from Paragraph 14 of the Prussian Administrative Police Law[61] which laid down that the police should act only 'within the framework of current laws' – in other words observing basic human rights.[62] The political police office was, moreover, physically divorced from the remainder of the police force, moving away from police headquarters in the Alexanderplatz; a new 'special section for suppression of Bolshevism' occupied the ex-Communist 'Karl-Liebknecht' house,[63] while the main body of Diels' organization moved to a disused Arts and Crafts School in Prinz-Albrecht-Strasse, not far from Göring's office in the Leipzigerstrasse.[64] At the end of April Göring signed a law giving Diels' office the title: 'Geheimes Staatspolizeiamt' [Secret State Police Office] and constituting it an independent Land Police Authority responsible only to the Minister President, Göring.[65] An unknown post-office official, faced with designing a franking stamp, invented an abbreviation for this new institution – Gestapa.[66] Popular slang turned it into the most sinister word in the German language over a period of twelve years – Gestapo [Geheime Staatspolizei].

Even though buttressed by this new police machine, however, Göring's position was not unassailable. A rival was on the move; Göring was left in no doubt on this score in spring 1933 when he proclaimed the SA an auxiliary police force[67] and launched both it and the police into a major 'Gleichschaltung' and terror campaign against the last islands of democratic resistance. He called for 'the severest methods to drive out anti-State organizations, including, if necessary, ruthless use of armed force';[68] he told the SA: 'in this case I have no obligation to abide by the law; my job is simply to annihilate and exterminate – nothing more!'[69] As time went on, his expressions became more violent and his voice more hoarse; the fight against Communism, he screamed, could not be conducted solely by police methods; 'I will carry on this fight to the death with those people down there, the brownshirts! I will make clear to the people that the people must defend itself.'[70]

But when the men in the brown shirts, the SA, went into action against these imaginary enemies of the State, Göring was appalled by the violence of the forces he had let loose. All the SA's basest instincts, all its pent-up social discontent, all that inflammatory orators and propagandists had been dinning into it for years, was given free rein – and Prussia turned into a terrorists' witch's cauldron. Mobile squads of SA swept through the streets of the towns, the worst thugs being in Berlin. Section Ic of SA Headquarters, Berlin–Brandenburg, for instance, drove so-called enemies of the State in front of it, dragged them into huts, shelters, cellars and other out-of-the-way places, beat them up and tortured them.[71] In Berlin alone the SA set up fifty impromptu concentration camps.[72] In the General-Pape-Strasse, in the Kant-strasse, in the Hedemannstrasse, in the Fürstenfeldstrasse – in all of these there were bunkers where the SA maltreated their prisoners. This state of affairs was not confined to Berlin; terror reigned in the provinces too; tales of horror came from Sonnenburg, Bornim, Königswusterhausen and Kemna.[73] Göring realized that he had lost control of the SA, but unhappily he was surrounded by SA men – many of Prussia's Police Presidents wore SA uniform[74] and, in addition, so-called SA advisers were attached to all Regierungspräsidenten [Government Presidents].[75] There could be no doubt that Göring's authority in Germany's largest state was being undermined.

Diels kept urging his master to come out into the open against the SA but Göring was hesitant. Diels, however, had long since begun to take action on his own; information from the Berlin Herrenklub had put him on the track of the SA torturers.[76] Heller, one of his staff, soon reported that there was a secret SA torture chamber on the fourth floor of 10 Hedemannstrasse, the headquarters of the Berlin SA Gau. Diels thereupon collected some men of the Police Emergency Duty Battalion and surrounded the place with machine guns. After a long drawn-out palaver, he persuaded the SA to hand over their prisoners;[77] 'The victims whom we found,' he wrote, 'were half dead from starvation. In order to extort confessions from them, they had been kept standing for days in narrow cupboards. "Interrogation" consisted simply of beating up, a dozen or so thugs being employed in fifteen-minute shifts to belabour their victims with iron bars, rubber truncheons and whips. When we entered, these living skeletons were lying in rows on filthy straw with festering wounds.'[78]

Diels continued his campaign. He mobilized his Secret Police and began to smoke out one SA shelter after another. Only half-heartedly supported by Göring, he made it his business to deal with the SA thugs and was himself frequently in danger of being beaten up by the SA underworld. By the end of May there were no more impromptu SA concentration camps in Prussia.[79] But Diels still continued; he joined forces with a group of courageous lawyers from the Prussian Ministry of Justice led by Werner von Haacke and Dr Joel, to hunt out the SA gangsters and bring them to court.[80]

As the struggle against the SA increased in severity Diels began to sense that he was conducting too single-handed a war – the hotter the battle against the SA, the greater the opportunity for Heinrich Himmler's people to infiltrate unobtrusively into Göring's Prussian preserve. Diels began to suspect that the SS was the greater menace to Göring's position in Prussia. 'There was longer-range planning,' he said, 'and greater logic behind the SS moves than behind those of the happy-go-lucky SA.'[81] He had good reason to know; he had crossed swords with the SS on several occasions.

The SS had never forgiven Diels for robbing them of a prisoner who had become almost a symbol of their efficiency – Captain Walther Stennes, the SA mutineer of 1931; his death had seemed a foregone conclusion.[82] Diels, however, had persuaded Göring to take an interest in Stennes and demand that he be handed over to the Gestapo prison.[83] Stennes, after all, was involved in one of Göring's setbacks of the pre-Nazi period; in 1931 Göring, who had once commanded the SA, had been only too anxious to regain his position and had intrigued with Stennes against the SA leadership;[84] he had promised the Berlin SA that he would plead their cause in Munich.

Even at that time Stennes felt that the main enemy was Himmler's SS. On October 10th, 1931 his newspaper the *Wahrheiten der Woche* reported: 'Göring declared spontaneously that he would henceforth do all in his power to bring these goings-on to an end. He assured us, moreover, that . . . he would not shrink from relieving the Reichs-Führer-SS Himmler of his post.'[85] Even after this, the SA opposition still considered Göring to be one of Himmler's enemies; after the Stennes putsch, the *Wahrheiten der Woche* reported: Göring was genuinely determined to push this matter through, but had not the power to do so.'[86] He was now willing to make amends for his 1931 failure and he ordered Diels to rescue Stennes from the SS.[87] In the autumn of 1933, assisted by Stennes' wife and a German training officer attached to the Chinese Army, Diels managed to slip him across the Dutch frontier.[88] Stennes ended up as commander of Chiang Kai-shek's bodyguard.[89]

But such victories over the SS were rare. In most cases Diels was worsted. He never cracked Columbia House, the SS torture chamber in Berlin,[90] and the illegal SS concentration camp, Papenburg, another objective in his anti-beating-up campaign, was closed down only by an order from Hitler. An interview with Diels left the dictator so incensed that he ordered the camp, together with its unruly complement of SS men, to be 'ruthlessly shot to pieces' by army artillery.[91]

Diels was particularly irritated by the undeniable fact that SS members had a foot in both Göring's and Himmler's camps. How long, he wondered, would they remain loyal to Göring's Prussia? SS-Gruppenführer Daluege, the Chief of the Prussian Police, might have personal reasons for keeping aloof from Himmler's circus, but behind him stood men who were finding their way blocked by Göring-nominated officials. Diels was particularly suspicious of the sallow-faced Arthur

Nebe, one of the few Nazis in the Gestapo, and of his *éminence grise*, an official named Hans-Bernd Gisevius.[92]

Nebe's ambition was well known; he was Executive Head of the Gestapo and Liebermann von Sonnenberg, a Criminal Police commissioner, prophesied: 'He will either become a really great man one day or be hanged.'[93] Nebe's favourite story was that which attributed to him the remark: 'There are no such things as principles, only circumstances.'[94] A literary friend objected: 'Herr Nebe, what sort of a quotation is that! That was said by Balzac's Vautrin, the prisoner from the Bagno,' to which Nebe is said to have retorted: 'But you will remember that that prisoner later became Police Chief of Paris.'[95]

Nebe now found Diels blocking his way to promotion and Gisevius, a deserter from the German Nationalist camp,[96] added fuel to the fire; Nebe was State-educated and Diels had everything he had not – education, upper-middle-class background, self-assurance in society and a nonchalance which occasionally took even Göring aback. Göring once said to him: 'I warn you, Diels, you're trying to sit on both sides of the fence'; Diels merely chuckled: 'Herr Minister President, the Head of the Secret Police has to sit on all sides of the fence at once.'[97]

Nebe took this 'lack of character', as he described it, as an indication that Diels was in reality a disguised Communist, a suspicion which Gisevius took care to foster. 'I could very well venture combat with Diels, the unstable playboy,' he wrote.[98] Nebe and Gisevius collected incriminating evidence against Diels and even persuaded the gullible Daluege to believe in their Communist story.[99] Nevertheless Daluege, Himmler's rival, with a flash of perspicacity said to Nebe and Gisevius: 'You're jumping out of the frying-pan into the fire.'[100] Little did he know that Nebe, and presumably also Gisevius, had been playing with fire for a long time. Himmler was informed of every move made by his adversary Göring. In early October he considered Göring's position so weak that he advanced to the assault of the Prussian fortress.

SS headquarters requested Hitler's permission to move the SD and SS offices from Munich to Berlin;[101] at the same time, led by Herbert Packebusch, Daluege's old crony, SS men entered Diels' apartment. His wife was locked into the bedroom and Packebusch then broke open Diels' desk.[102] Frau Diels, however, managed to get her husband on the telephone in time, and in a few minutes Diels, with a squad of police from the Tiergarten Division, arrived at his home in the Potsdamer Strasse. Packebusch looked up as if he had seen a ghost, but before he could grab his revolver, the police had seized him and led him off.[103]

Diels' triumph, however, was short-lived. Daluege appeared in order to explain Packebusch's 'indiscipline' to Göring; there had been considerable suspicion, he said, that Diels was intriguing against the Berlin SS.[104] Göring began to wonder about his Chief of Police, who seemed to him altogether too inscrutable and he released Packebusch from arrest.[105] Diels saw the drift; Göring was unwilling to act too forcibly against the SS. When, a fortnight later he learnt that, on Göring's instructions, police and SS had searched his office, he panicked. He fled to Karlsbad in Bohemia and awaited his moment.[106] Meanwhile, however, Göring had survived the SS assault. Hitler refused to sanction transfer of the SS offices from Munich to Berlin, though as a small crumb of comfort the Reichsführer was allowed to install an SD outpost in the capital.[107]

Accordingly a certain Dr Hermann Behrends set up an office in the Eichenallee, Berlin; he was an old friend of Heydrich, son of an innkeeper in Kiel where Heydrich had often stayed as a naval lieutenant.[108] Behrends formed SD Oberabschnitt [Region] East, while another of Heydrich's confidants, SS-Hauptsturmführer Heinz Jost, was appointed Himmler's representative with the Gestapa.

Himmler could make no further inroads into Göring's empire, however. Göring recalled Diels saying: 'Himmler and Heydrich shall never come to Berlin.'[109] So Himmler had to stage a reconciliation with Göring and placate his enemy Diels. From November 9th, 1933 Diels was accorded the honour of appearing in the uniform of an SS-Standartenführer. In his personal file, however, his SS masters noted what they really thought of this remarkable recruit to the SS – he was slippery as an eel, insincere and self-seeking.[110]

So Himmler's second assault on Göring's police empire had failed. Now, however, he found an unexpected ally in the shape of Dr Wilhelm Frick's Ministry of the Interior. After the Reichstag elections of November 12th, 1933 Frick had decided to abolish the last remnants of the German Länder's sovereign rights. The Länder were to be left merely as administrative units under a Government centrally directed from Berlin.[111] Nicolai, an ex-Regierungspräsident and Medicus, a civil servant, the leading centralizers in the Ministry of the Interior, drew up a constitution under which the centre would have authority to issue instructions to the Länder Governments.[112] And the thorniest problem in this reform was that of authority over the police. Hitherto police authority had rested with the Governments of the sixteen German Länder; they alone were in charge of the police and they controlled police organization, duties and administrative law. The Reich Minister of the Interior was allowed to exercise only general supervision, although he could bring some influence to bear through the allocation of grants to the Länder police.[113]

The main feature of the draft submitted by Frick's centralizers was the transfer to the Reich Government of the sovereign rights of the Länder, including, of course, police authority. In other words the Reich Minister was claiming control over all German police forces. Henceforth no police regulations were to be issued, no changes of location planned, no promotions or appointments (to Major and upwards) made, without prior agreement from the Reich Minister of the Interior.[114] Frick's reformers were in fact trying to put into practice the programme Himmler had outlined to Dr Best – to remove command of the police from the local barons. But there was one local baron who had no intention of yielding to the Ministry of the Interior.

Though no one outside the Ministry knew of the Nicolai/Medicus plan, Göring was too quick for the centralizers. On November 30th, 1933 he issued a law raising the Prussian Secret Police to the status of an independent branch in the internal administration; matters hitherto dealt with by the Prussian Ministry of the Interior were transferred to the Gestapo, and it was placed directly under the Minister-President. Göring nominated an inspector to supervise the Gestapo on his behalf and to be responsible for appointing the head of the Gestapo.[115] At one stroke, before it had even been put in legal form, Göring had dealt a deadly blow to the Reich reform. As far as the police were concerned, the largest German Land had escaped Frick's clutches.

In face of Göring, Frick was powerless; he had no private army and as he had once been a follower of Gregor Strasser his standing with Hitler was low. So the Ministry of the Interior centralizers turned to the man who had already announced that he was going to remove control of the police from the local barons. Heinrich Himmler looked to them like a saviour; he was in control of the internal Party police; his Politische Bereitschaften already existed in many German Länder, and he had long been preaching the formation of a centralized police force.

Frick's officials were now in league with Himmler's police centralizers against Prussian separatism – undoubtedly not without Hitler's agreement.[116] With the connivance of the Ministry of the Interior, Himmler took over command of the political police in one Land after another – November 1933: Hamburg, Lübeck and Mecklenburg-Schwerin; December 1933: Anhalt, Baden, Bremen, Hesse, Thuringia and Württemberg; January 1934: Brunswick, Oldenburg and Saxony.[117] When, in January 1934, Frick submitted to the Reichstag yes-men his 'Law for the Reconstruction of the Reich',[118] Himmler was already in control of the political police in all German Länder except Prussia and

Schaumburg-Lippe. Göring, of course, did not submit. On the contrary he prepared to strike back.

On February 19th, 1934, Frick issued a decree to all Reichsstatthalter stating that he had 'direct command authority over all Land police forces in the German Reich.'[119] On March 9th Göring countered with a decree of his own; he himself took over direction of the Prussian police, making the head of the police section in the Prussian Ministry of the Interior directly responsible to him for all police matters.[120] Once more Göring had disarmed his adversary.

Drug addict though he was, Göring had played his cards well; his opponents were downcast and in despair. At this juncture, however, Göring realized that he was fighting a lost cause. He thought he could see signs of a threat to his authority far more deadily than the pressure of Frick and Himmler. The terror foreshadowed by events in Prussia in the spring of 1933 now spilled over into Germany as a whole. The tramp of the brown-shirted columns, with their thundering drums and blaring trumpets, echoed louder and louder; the battle-cry of four million SA men with nothing to do, hungry for power and thirsting for revolution, was heard everywhere.

Göring sensed that the time had come to make peace with Frick and Himmler. At the end of March he opened negotiations with the Reich Ministry of the Interior,[121] haggling for the best price for a takeover by the Central Government of the Prussian Ministries. Apart from the Minister-President's office, only the Prussian Finance Ministry remained independent; internal affairs were transferred to the Reich Ministry of the Interior whither Daluege was posted and placed in command of the entire uniformed police of the Reich.[122] As far as the political police were concerned, Göring had to accept a somewhat disadvantageous compromise; although he avoided complete acceptance of the Reich Ministry of the Interior's authority, he had to allow Himmler the post of Inspector of the Gestapo. Heydrich became head of the Gestapo and Nebe took over the Prussian Criminal Police Office.[123]

Himmler had reached a turning point in his career. For the first time the SS was now in charge of the German police. But this was no time for rejoicing; the pact between Himmler and Göring proved inconclusive and the shotgun marriage was followed by a bloody honeymoon. On April 10th, 1934 Göring inducted the new masters of Prinz-Albrecht-Strasse with the words: 'No point in tripping over every corpse.'[124] He sent Diels to safety as Regierungspräsident in Cologne.[125] Hardly had he done so, however, than the Gestapo began to receive messages which admitted of only one conclusion: Adolf Hitler's State was sliding toward the severest crisis in its short history.

The reports painted a picture of seething discontent in the SA; its ill-assorted corps of leaders was agreed upon only one thing – they disliked the entire trend of 'Adolf's' policy ever since his assumption of power on January 30th, 1933.

6

THE RÖHM PUTSCH

IN the bars frequented by the SA anti-Hitler sentiment was rife. As before the Stennes putsch of 1931, the word was going round: 'Adolf is betraying us.' Even the lowliest SA leader sensed that since the advent of the National-Socialist State the SA, the much-trumpeted National-Socialist revolutionary army, had become a foreign body.

For years the Party leaders had been instilling revolutionary ardour into the SA, preparing it for the great day of the seizure of power; but when that day arrived, peacefully and (ostensibly) constitutionally, the party did not know what to do with the SA. Eventually it had been given the innocent task of 'toughening' German youth and, allied to the Reichswehr, turning itself into the great National-Socialist People's Army.

Ever since the SA was formed, its Chief-of-Staff, Ernst Röhm, had regarded it as the seed of a new German army. 'I am the new army's Scharnhorst,' he would brag[1] – to conceal the fact that he still smarted under the arrogance and distaste with which the regular officers treated him. President von Hindenburg had refused to shake his hand; to the old Field-Marshal he was an object of suspicion as both a homosexual and military rebel.[2] As a company commander in the trenches of the Western Front, Röhm had seen that the old Prussian barrack-square system was no longer adequate to meet the realities of modern war. Dimly he felt that: 'We've got to produce something new, don't you see? A new discipline. A new principle of organization. The generals are a lot of old fogies. They never have a new idea.'[3] He thought he had that idea – a militia, the people's army, his SA. The SA had only to be made militarily competent, to be trained for modern revolutionary war, and then the moment would come when it would take over from the Reichswehr and he, Ernst Röhm, the reformer, would emerge as the leader of the new Germany's new Wehrmacht.

The cadres for the new people's army were already available. Röhm had under his command a force of 500,000 men, numerically five times the size of the Reichswehr; the Party army was organized in five SA-Obergruppen (corresponding to armies) and eighteen Gruppen (corresponding to Corps).[4] He had an operational staff in which all important positions were held by ex-officers.[5] Röhm had copied the military even down to the smallest detail; SA units had 'orderly officers'; SA standing orders followed the lines of Army Regulations; the SA Standarten carried the numbers of the old Imperial Army regiments.[6]

The more firmly SA headquarters became established in command of its vast brown-shirted army, the more did the Reichswehr cast covetous eyes upon Röhm's military acquisitions. The professional soldiers regarded the SA as the ideal source of potential recruits against the day when the Reichswehr, freed from the fetters of the Versailles armaments restrictions, would reintroduce universal military service. Hitler's order brought the two forces together.[7] But instead of the 'old fogy' he had anticipated, Röhm found a counter-schemer standing in his way – and he was one of the most progressive and unscrupulous officers in the Reichswehr.

Major-General Walter von Reichenau was a sporting artilleryman in charge of the Ministeramt [Ministerial Office] of the Reichswehr Ministry; in spite of the monocle in his right eye, he ridiculed many of the ideas sacred to the Prussian-German military tradition. Many of his conservative fellow-officers regarded him as a showman and a careerist; some even thought that he was a Nazi because, together with his Minister, Colonel-General Werner von Blomberg, he had been the first senior Reichswehr officer in whom Hitler had confided before 1933.[8] Nevertheless from the outset General von Reichenau had a plan clear in his mind; the valuable military potential of the SA must be brought under the Reichswehr umbrella and Röhm's ambitions, which were a danger to the Army, must be neutralized.[9] The only way to ensure that Röhm would play his game was to meet the SA man halfway.

Reichenau's proposal was to broaden the national defence base by introducing a militia element and in this context the SA could play an important part. There were serious gaps in the Reichswehr's defensive dispositions, particularly in the east. A so-called 'Frontier Protection Service East' was therefore to be formed, planned as a type of militia; here, Reichenau explained, was the place for the SA army. In addition, assisted by the Reichswehr, the SA should undertake pre-military training of all organizations outside the armed forces.[10]

In May 1933 SA and Reichswehr concluded an agreement whereby the SA, the SS and the nationalist ex-soldiers association 'Stahlhelm' were brought under the Reichswehr Ministry.[11] Obergruppenführer Friedrich-Wilhelm Krüger became SA Director of Training; with the assistance of a training staff from the Reichswehr, he was to train 250,000 SA men a year for subsequent entry into the Reichswehr.[12] Simultaneously Röhm was to absorb into the SA the right-wing defence formations, primarily the numerically strong and disciplined Stahlhelm.[13] As regards the latter, however, Reichenau had a special card up his sleeve.

The General urged Theodor Duesterberg, the Stahlhelm leader, to send as many of his men as possible into the SA. Reichenau's plan was that if a million or so men from the Stahlhelm entered the SA as a body, the Röhm section would then be outnumbered; if, in addition, the more important posts in the training organization and the Frontier Protection Service were occupied by Reichswehr personnel, Röhm would have been out-manoeuvred.[14] On the surface the plan started auspiciously. The key positions in Krüger's organization and in the Frontier Protection Service East were occupied by serving or retired officers.[15] But the Stahlhelm invasion went wrong. Röhm parried cleverly, dividing the SA into three groups of differing size, in the most important of which – the so-called active SA – he placed all his own 500,000 men and only 314,000 from the Stahlhelm.[16]

Röhm could now lay claim to a following of 4,500,000[17] and he promptly went over to the counter-offensive. He demanded greater influence and genuine command positions in the Frontier Protection Service East; worse still – he demanded control of the East German armaments depots, the thorniest problem of all in the eyes of the Reichswehr.[18] Röhm was in fact challenging the firm determination of the German generals never to allow any organization other than the Reichswehr to constitute the nation's armed force. The Reichswehr Ministry accordingly decided to have no further truck with Röhm's militia ideas. From December 1933 it refused to recognize the possibility of any basis for national defence other than universal military service.[19]

But Röhm was not to be deterred. On December 1st, 1933 he had been made Reich Minister without Portfolio[20] and he now allowed the SA Obergruppen to form armed 'headquarters guards'.[21] He even brought the outside world into the game; at the Geneva Disarmament Conference France had been prepared to allow Germany an increased militia army and so Röhm initiated discussions on his own account with the French Military Attaché in Berlin.[22] In early February 1934 he presented the Reichswehr with his demands in writing;[23] the memorandum was so sharply worded that, speaking at a Commander-in-Chief's Conference, Blomberg could only conclude that Röhm was claiming the entire national defence field as an 'SA domain', leaving the Reichswehr with training functions only.[24]

Colonel-General von Blomberg thereupon called for a ruling from Hitler, thus facing the Chancellor with the decision which he had hitherto managed to avoid.[25] Basically, Hitler was attracted by Röhm's ideas; he knew, however, that without the military experts he could never carry out his foreign-policy programme. Nevertheless, nothing was more painful to Hitler than to confront his friend Röhm with a flat 'No'. He therefore tried a compromise; on February 28th, 1934 he invited the Reichswehr and SA leaders to the marble-pillared lecture hall of the Reichswehr Ministry, where he implored them in a 'moving, gripping' speech to keep the peace.[26] In his presence Blomberg and Röhm had to conclude an agreement whereby the Reichswehr was recognized as the sole bearer of arms in the Third Reich and the SA was given sole responsibility for pre- and post-military training.[27] A state luncheon was then held in Röhm's headquarters in the Standartenstrasse when the SA and Reichswehr leaders ostentatiously shook hands.[28]

Hardly had the officers left the room, however, than Röhm bellowed: 'What that ridiculous corporal says means nothing to us . . . I have not the slightest intention of keeping this agreement. Hitler is a traitor and at the very least must go on leave . . . If we can't get there with him, we'll get there without him.'[29] At Röhm's table sat an SA-Obergruppenführer who listened transfixed to this tipsy tirade against his revered Führer: Viktor Lutze, Lieutenant (Retired) and Commander of SA Obergruppe [Region] Hannover, felt that high treason was in the air.[30] He hurried off to do what he could to stop it.

Early in March 1934 he presented himself to Rudolf Hess, the 'Führer's Deputy', and accused Röhm of making monstrous anti-Hitler speeches; but Hess did not know what to do,[31] so Lutze went further. He travelled to Berchtesgaden where he had an interview with Hitler, telling him of the discontent with the leadership of the Third Reich now rife in the SA. But Hitler gave him short shrift, merely saying: 'We must let the matter develop.'[32] Since Hitler was evidently unwilling to take action against his friend Röhm, Lutze confided in yet a third person; during an exercise in Braunfels he showed General von Reichenau a letter which he had written to Röhm, warning him against his anti-Reichswehr campaign.[33] Reichenau thanked him for this valuable information and, as soon as he was out of earshot, remarked sarcastically: 'That Lutze is harmless. He'll be the Chief-of-Staff.'[34]

Lutze did not know that for some days von Reichenau had been negotiating with an SS-Brigadeführer [Brigadier] who had very precise ideas on a radical solution of the Röhm problem. Reinhard

Heydrich, head of the Gestapa and SD, was determined to liquidate the entire Röhm clique. It had taken time to win Himmler over to his plan. The Reichsführer-SS was hesitant, perhaps due to a gloomy presentiment that the decision to liquidate Röhm would open a Pandora's Box, whose deadly contents would never again leave the SS and SA in peace.

As if oppressed by some presentiment of forthcoming developments, Himmler had held himself aloof from Röhm's enemies.[35] He could not forget the years when, as a mere cadet, he had been thrown together with Captain Röhm. In the early months of the National-Socialist era, Himmler had been a constant member of Röhm's immediate retinue. Together they had made inflammatory speeches; together they had dined in Röhm's Berlin apartment.[36] They had planned crime together – Heydrich and SA-Standartenführer Uhl had both been responsible for dispatching the SA flying squad which had slipped across to Austria on April 3rd, 1933 and murdered Georg Bell, Röhm's renegade confidant, in an inn near Durchholzen.[37] On Röhm's last birthday (November 28th, 1933) Himmler had wished him 'all that true loyalty as a soldier and a friend can offer. It was and is our greatest pride still to be one of your most faithful followers.'[38] Himmler and Röhm together were godfathers to Heydrich's first child.[39] Even after the February 28th explosion and Röhm's anti-Hitler tirade in the Standartenstrasse, Himmler had tried to protect Röhm from over-hasty action on the part of Hitler and the Reichswehr.[40]

In spring 1934, however, Himmler's sense of opportunism proved stronger than his much-vaunted loyalty to Röhm; the new alliance with Göring seemed more important than his relations with his former master. Upon that alliance, after all, depended the capture by the SS of the Prussian Gestapo – whence the train of thought led direct to Heydrich's assassination plan: without Göring he would not get the Gestapo; unless he broke with Röhm he would get no cooperation from Göring. And of all the National-Socialist potentates Göring had most to fear from Röhm's SA. With his network of SA police presidents and SA advisers to the Regierungspräsidenten, Röhm was a threat to Göring's authority in Prussia; moreover he was also a threat to Göring's ultimate aim – to be Commander-in-Chief of the Wehrmacht.[41]

Himmler therefore changed course. This came all the easier in that the imprudent Röhm had now fallen out with practically every power group in the régime. Everyone had some interest in seeing the Röhm gang go under; everyone could draw some profit from the break-up of the SA. The Reichswehr and Göring would be rid of a tiresome rival;

the Party organization men and the guardians of morality would be rid of a vicious, depraved mischief-maker; the SS would finally free themselves from the last ties to the SA.

So Reinhard Heydrich's deadly game began – and deadly it had to be. In a Party like the NSDAP, which had grown up in the days of the Free Corps and the drumhead court-martial, and had itself brought crime into politics, there was no answer to insoluble internal differences other than that of force. Georg Bell once remarked: 'For us there is nothing very tragic in running a man round the corner. That procedure is inherent in our organization. We call it self-defence; you call it murder. On moral grounds I find nothing extraordinary in doing away with a man if it is in the interests of the Party.'[42] (His SA murderers were later to demonstrate to him how right he had been.)

Applying the argument to Röhm's case, this meant that only through his death could the lords of the régime guarantee their security against the SA. He was the most notorious homosexual in the country; he was one of Hitler's few old friends; he knew more Party secrets than anyone else. So neither a formal dismissal nor a faked trial could satisfy the Nazi leaders. Röhm had to die.

Heydrich set to work at the end of April 1934. Himmler toured SS units, priming them to strike against their SA comrades;[43] meanwhile, Heydrich set the trap which was to topple Röhm from his pedestal. His first requirement was some cast-iron case to justify action against the SA leaders. Heydrich spent May collecting material to convince Hitler and the Reichswehr of Röhm's supposedly highly treasonable activities.[44]

He did not lack for sources. SS-Untersturmführer Friedrich Wilhelm Krüger was now wearing the uniform of an SA-Obergruppenführer and, as Director of Training, had 'mobilization representatives' with SA-Obergruppen and Gruppen; his Intelligence network provided some incriminating material.[45] Friedrich Graf von der Schulenburg, a First World War General and an enthusiastic supporter of the SS, was an honorary SA commander; he was also in the game.[46] Heydrich even made use of Lieutenant-General Wilhelm Adam, Commander of the 7th Division, Munich; though an anti-Nazi of the Schleicher school, he provided SS-Gruppenführer Schmauser with information on the SA.[47] Any information derogatory to the SA, and anyone willing to help bring Röhm down, was welcome.

But the results were meagre in the extreme. Apart from one or two reports of SA arms dumps in Berlin, Munich and Silesia,[48] Heydrich's informers had nothing to offer except bloodthirsty revolutionary wafflings by certain SA commanders – quite inadequate to support an accusation of high treason. In fact there were certain indications that nothing was further from the SA's thoughts than a plot against Hitler. Early in May Colonel von Rabenau, the Garrison Commander, Breslau, rated the likelihood of an SA rising as low;[49] when Heines, the SA Commander in Silesia, learnt from Göring that, contrary to his fears, the Reichswehr had no intention of taking any action against the SA, he promptly sent half his 'Headquarters Guard' on leave.[50]

Rather than plotting against the régime, Röhm felt it his duty to urge the police and the Reichswehr to act against its enemies. He dispatched SA-Brigadeführer Jüttner to the Reichswehr Ministry with a warning against the anti-régime intrigues of the ex-Chancellor, General Kurt von Schleicher[51] – whom the official story of the so-called putsch turned into one of Röhm's accomplices! When the writer Ernst von Salomon made some sarcastic remarks about Himmler, the one-armed Hans Peter von Heydebreck, an SA Commander, shouted: 'I live for my Führer. The thought of him is the one thing which keeps me going. If I could no longer believe in my Führer, I would rather die.'[52] A few days later his idol had him shot. But even when facing the firing squad Heydebreck called out: 'Long live the Führer! Heil Hitler!'[53]

The SA was not, in fact, thinking high treason. It was not plotting a putsch or other act of insubordination. It simply wanted to force Hitler into according it that position in the State and among the military which had so long been denied it. But the tactics Röhm employed to achieve this end were dangerous. He did not believe that Hitler could do other than gradually conform to the wishes of the SA and so he initiated a carefully calculated war of nerves on Hitler. He travelled from one SA Gruppe to another; he made rumbustious speeches announcing the 'second National-Socialist revolution'.[54] He believed that his Brownshirts' mass marches must eventually soften Hitler up. Röhm was oblivious to the fact that such goings-on inevitably made even the most unsuspecting of Germans apprehensive lest the SA army was preparing to seize power in Germany. Equally inevitably the military began to regard Röhm as a deadly enemy – and so became ready to participate in Heydrich's game. Captain (Navy) Conrad Patzig, Head of Counter-Espionage in the Reichswehr Ministry, considered it 'simply hair-raising' that 'such unstable characters' should make 'criminal plans' to elbow the Reichswehr out of its rightful place.[55] From this it was only a step to the cry 'away with the SA!' The majority of officers thought like the Garrison Commander Breslau, who said quite openly that, although the SA was not planning a putsch, it was high time that that 'Augean Stable' was cleaned up.[56]

Von Reichenau, the Reichswehr Ministry's chief political strategist, was equally uncompromising. He had found Heydrich a congenial partner and was often to be seen in the Gestapa; he provided barracks, weapons and transport for the great coup.[57] After all, as early as 1932, he had told Captain Felix Steiner (later to become the Waffen-SS General): 'I tell you they [the SA] will eat out of our hand one day.'[58]

Heydrich's execution squads were now getting ready to fulfil the General's prophecy – after their own fashion.

Early in June SS-Oberführer Theodor Eicke, Commandant of the Dachau Concentration Camp, held large-scale exercises when his troops practised surprise action against Munich Lechfeld and Bad Wiessee – in fact the plan of action against Röhm's SA.[59] Almost simultaneously the Munich SS formations took their precautions: SS-Untersturmführer Max Müller of SS Motor Sturm No 3 was ordered to prepare his unit for rapid action and await a code word; on D-day it was to assemble at the Turk Barracks in Munich near the headquarters of the Bavarian Political Police.[60] The headquarters of SD-Oberabschnitt South at No 10 Leopoldstrasse was placed on preparatory alert.[61]

From all directions Heydrich mobilized his forces; he reckoned upon four areas of violent resistance: Bavaria, Berlin, Silesia and Saxony.[62] The net closed ever tighter around the unsuspecting SA and the indefatigable Heydrich now opened phase two of his preparations. Who were to be the victims? His minions were ordered to track down Röhm's closest friends and draw up a list of candidates for execution.

As early as the end of April, Eicke had prepared a so-called nationwide list of 'unwanted persons' to be liquidated on D-day.[63] Naturally it consisted almost exclusively of SA leaders. Shortly thereafter, however, Heydrich had a new idea; if a clean-up was the order of the day, the more dangerous enemies of the régime might as well be liquidated at the same time. His death list grew longer and longer as the weeks went by; practically every SD-Oberabschnitt had a register of candidates for the firing squad, to which the SS and Gestapo were continually adding.[64] SS-Obersturmführer [Lieutenant] Ilges of the SD Hauptamt [Department] who kept the list, told an acquaintance: 'Do you know the meaning of the word bloodlust? I feel as if I was going to wade in blood.'[65]

Drafting death lists became a grisly sport for those in the know. Everyone had his own list; Göring drew one up;[66] Wagner, the Gauleiter of Bavaria, drew one up;[67] the SS, the SD and the Gestapo competed in their choice of candidates. Soon they were quarrelling over whether this man or that really merited shooting. Werner Best, Head of the Bavarian SD, wished to take the 'decent, loyal' SA-Obergruppenführer Schneidhuber off the list, whereas Heydrich thought him 'just as dangerous as the rest'.[68] Göring crossed out the name of his former Gestapo Chief, Diels, when it appeared on someone else's list.[69]

At this point the Gestapo received information which threatened to cut across all Heydrich's plans. Hitler and Röhm had unexpectedly agreed to postpone solution of the SA/Reichswehr problem; on June 4th the two had met for four hours and agreed to send the SA on a month's leave from July 1st.[70] Moreover on June 8th, 1934 the *Völkischer Beobachter* published an SA headquarters press office communiqué which made people prick up their ears. On the advice of his doctor, the communiqué stated, Röhm, the Chief-of-Staff, had had to take several weeks' sick leave (an iodine course in Bad Wiessee). Then followed a curious sentence: 'In order to avoid any misinterpretation of this announcement, the Chief-of-Staff would have it known that on recovery of his health he will continue to carry out in full the duties of his office.'[71]

The Reichswehr breathed a sigh of relief; it seemed to the Generals that Röhm had lost a battle. Captain Hermann Höfle, Röhm's old 'struggle period' companion, now at the Staff College, wrote to him 'the prevailing view in influential Army circles' was that 'the first Press announcement (of Röhm's illness) was the clearest proof that the Chief-of-Staff's position was shaky. Subsequent statements would not be able to remove this impression.'[72]

The Army was relieved but Heydrich was appalled. This new development left him short of time, for an SA on leave could hardly be accused of preparing a *coup d'état*. Ernst, Commander of the Berlin SA, was already thinking of taking a cruise to the Canaries;[73] Gruppenführer Georg von Detten, Head of the Political Office in SA headquarters, was preparing to go off on holiday to Bad Wildungen[74] – so what would remain of the much-feared SA putsch? Heydrich had to act quickly if he was not to be too late for his SA drama. The plans were ready; the murder squads had been formed; Hitler's reaction was the only remaining uncertainty – and he had now agreed to disagree with Röhm.

Hitler had always recoiled from a head-on collision with the SA. He had long been playing a double game, a reflection of weakness rather than rational thinking; on the one hand he whipped up his brown-shirted army, primarily as a counter-weight to the Reichswehr; on the other, he toyed with the idea of disbanding the SA altogether. But he did not feel strong enough simply to invite the SA to commit suicide. He had hardly the courage to resist the more outrageous of Röhm's demands. In the anterooms of the Reich Chancellery a despairing voice had been heard from his office shouting: 'No, no, I cannot do that. You are asking too much.'[75] He frequently took refuge in the hope that other people would solve this tiresome problem for him. On occasions he would agree to one of Röhm's demands, and send him off to the Reich Minister of Finance in the knowledge that the hard-headed Schwerin von Krosigk would be man enough to demolish Röhm's plans with technical budgetary arguments.[76] On one occasion Hitler thought that he could get rid of the SA through a disarmament agreement. When Anthony Eden, the Lord Privy Seal, visited Berlin on February 21st, 1934, Hitler proposed that, in return for armaments concessions by the Western Powers, he should demobilize two-thirds of the SA and submit the remaining third to League of Nations inspection.[77]

Now, however, Hitler was faced with three men, Heydrich, Himmler and Göring, who had a plan and knew exactly how to solve the SA problem. Hitler agreed, though not without hesitation. He was still only half-convinced when a spectacular speech rocked him back on his heels. On June 17th Franz von Papen, a Centre Party renegade and Hitler's Vice-Chancellor, ascended the rostrum of Marburg University and declaimed against 'all the self-seeking characterlessness, untruthfulness, vulgarity and arrogance hiding under the cloak of the German Revolution'.[78] Applauded by the students, Papen proceeded: '... confusion between vitality and brutality. No nation can live in a state of permanent revolution from below ... terroristic methods in a field of law ... decision whether the new German Reich is to be a Christian State or lose its way in sectarianism and semi-religious materialism.'[79]

The speech evoked a 'roar of applause' (Papen's words)[80] throughout the country, leaving the Nazi rulers in no doubt that a conservative opposition had survived the Gleichschaltung steamroller and was still in existence. Although the Propaganda Ministry immediately banned publication of Papen's speech,[81] its repercussions were clear enough. An uncomfortable suspicion began to grow in Hitler's mind; what would happen if the SA and the bourgeois malcontents joined forces? Gestapo observers had already detected the first indications of a connexion between the two.

The links all seemed to point to the SA showpiece prince, SA-Gruppenführer Prince August Wilhelm of Prussia, the ex-Kaiser's son, nicknamed Auwi. In practice he had a foot in both camps; the Papen circle, which looked for the restoration of the monarchy, regarded him as the natural candidate for Reich Regent when Field-Marshal von Hindenburg, the eighty-six-year-old President, finally died.[82] The Prince was also tipped as a winner by Werner von Alvensleben, a shady tycoon masquerading as Director of the ultra-conservative 'League for the Protection of Culture'. In the pre-1933 days he had arranged the contacts between Schleicher and Hitler and he had a photograph of Hitler with the inscription: 'To my most faithful friend'.[83] After June 30th, 1934 he was to learn from the *Völkischer Beobachter* that he was 'an obscure Berlin personality to whom Adolf Hitler had the greatest aversion'.[84]

Von Alvensleben told everybody, whether he wished to hear it or not, that: 'Auwi would be the next Kaiser'. One day in May 1934 Martin Sommerfeldt, Head of Göring's Press Department, was dining with a conservative politician, von Gleichen-Russwurm, when Alvensleben came up looking important and conspiratorial. Gleichen remarked sarcastically that Alvensleben presumably had the new Cabinet list in his pocket. Alvensleben nodded and, bending over the table, whispered: 'Reich Chancellor – Adolf Hitler; Vice-Chancellor – Kurt von Schleicher; Reichswehr – Ernst Röhm; Reich Regent – Prince August Wilhelm of Prussia.' When he was gone, Sommerfeldt asked what truth there was in this gossip. Gleichen replied: 'Fifty-fifty.'[85]

Hitler undoubtedly knew that this sort of talk was going round. He realized that the showdown with the opposition must come at the latest when Hindenburg died. His bourgeois opponents all had their eyes on the presidency which, in their view, must be occuped by a Hohenzollern Prince as figurehead for a monarchist restoration; with the support of the Reichswehr he would be able to bring National-Socialist dynamism under control. Hitler clearly had to strike first. So he took a sudden decision to visit Hindenburg on his estate at Neudeck, East Prussia. He wished personally to check the old man's state of health, so that he could judge how much elbow-room he had; he too had an ambitious plan which was dependent upon Hindenburg's death. From the outset Hitler had been determined to make himself Dictator of Germany. As long as Hindenburg was alive, however, that goal was out of reach; both the Field-Marshal's prestige and the fact that the Reichswehr generals were sworn to him by oath blocked Hitler's way to total power. Once Hindenburg was dead, however, the road would lie open; Hitler could then combine the offices of Chancellor and President into a new dictatorial office, 'Führer and Reich Chancellor' – provided, and only provided, that the Reichswehr would go along. The Reichswehr must say yes; Hitler's plan stood or fell by the Reichswehr.

As if to remind him of the key role played by the Generals, when the Chancellor arrived at Neudeck on June 21st, 1934 in sweltering heat, the first person who met him on the steps was the Reichswehr Minister, Colonel-General Werner von Blomberg.[86] As soon as he heard of the uproar caused by Papen's speech, Hindenburg had summoned Blomberg and, at the meeting which now followed, he left most of the talking to him.[87] Blomberg's theme was that re-establishment of peace at home was an urgent necessity; radical revolutionaries were out of place in the new Germany.[88] Hitler grasped the point. If he wished to have the Reichswehr on his side for his post-Hindenburg régime, he must sacrifice the Reichswehr's rival, Röhm's SA. According to Sir John Wheeler-Bennett, during the flight back to Berlin Hitler decided upon the action which, by the irony of history, is known as the Röhm putsch – but was in fact the Hitler régime's putsch against Röhm.[89]

The next day Viktor Lutze in Hannover was called to the telephone to find Hitler on the line.[90] He was ordered to report to the Reich Chancellery forthwith. Lutze noted in his diary that on arrival 'the Führer received me at once. He led me into his study and, taking me by the hand, swore me to secrecy until the whole matter was settled.' Hitler then explained what 'the whole matter' was; Röhm must be removed, since numerous SA commanders' conferences had been held under his chairmanship at which the decision had been taken to arm the SA and let it loose against the Reichswehr in order to liberate him, the Führer, from the military whose prisoner he was supposed to be. Lutze's diary continues: 'The Führer said that he had always known that I would be no party to such matters. Henceforth I was to accept no orders from Munich and take instructions only from him.'[91]

By June 25th at the latest, von Blomberg knew that Hitler was determined to relieve the Army of the SA threat. Hitler told him that he intended to call all SA commanders to a meeting at Bad Wiessee where Röhm was taking his cure, that he would arrest them himself and 'square accounts' with them.[92] Two days later Sepp Dietrich, the Commander of the Leibstandarte, appeared in the Reichswehr Ministry and asked the head of the Army Organization Section to make weapons available for a 'secret and most important mission ordered by the Führer'. Blomberg had known what this secret mission was ever since June 25th.[93]

When the so-called Röhm putsch took place, Dietrich was to be responsible for the main action. With two companies of the Leibstandarte he was to move to Southern Bavaria, where he was to join with Eicke's units from the Dachau Concentration Camp and move against Wiessee to take Röhm's more important followers by surprise.[94] The Leibstandarte, however, was short of transport and practically unarmed. Dietrich and the army agreed that the two companies should move by rail to a country station near Landsberg am Lech, whence army transport would take them to Bad Wiessee; they were also to draw additional equipment from Reichswehr barracks.[95]

Reichenau, Heydrich and Himmler discussed the final details of the combined Reichswehr/SS campaign against Röhm. Preparatory moves began. On June 22nd Himmler summoned to Berlin Freiherr von Eberstein, Commander of SS-Oberabschnitt Centre, and revealed to him that Röhm was planning a *coup d'état*. Eberstein was to maintain contact with Wehrkreis [Military District] commanders, place his men on 'unobtrusive alert' and concentrate them in barracks when the alarm was given.[96] On June 23rd Colonel Fromm, Head of the Allgemeine Heeresamt [General Army Office – AHA] informed his officers that a Röhm putsch was imminent; the SS was on the side of the Reichswehr and was to be given such weapons as it required.[97] On June 24th the Commander-in-Chief of the Army, General Freiherr von Fritsch, warned all Wehrkreis commanders to take precautions against a threatened SA putsch and quietly to concentrate their troops.[98] On June 27th Himmler summoned all SD-Oberabschnitt commanders, ordering them to shadow SA leaders and to report forthwith to SD Headquarters any suspicious move on the part of the SA.[99]

So the regiments and the Standarten were in position, the alarm bells were ringing in the barracks and the officers of the Reichswehr Ministry[100] kept loaded revolvers in their desks; yet – in spite of it all there was still an air of unreality and phantasmagoria about Heydrich's and Himmler's operation. Hardly anyone really believed that the SA was planning a putsch. The greatest sceptics were the officers of the Reichswehr.

After the end of the 'Thousand-Year Reich', when everyone was clearing themselves of responsibility for the bloodbath, the soldiers found that the risk of a Röhm putsch had been enormous. General Siegfried Westphal knew that 'rumours were rife of an intended putsch by Röhm';[101] 'from personal experience' Lieutenant-General Fretter-Pico considered that there was 'still every justification today for believing in the imminence of a Röhm putsch';[102] even Colonel-General Halder 'knew' that Röhm had 'worked out a plan for an SA putsch against the Reichswehr'.[103]

At the time, however, the soldiers thought quite differently. Even in 1958 Colonel Gotthard Heinrici, a section head in the AHA at the time, could still remember that two or three days before the Röhm drama none of his fellow officers really feared that a putsch was imminent; no reports of SA preparations ever reached him.[104] He continued: 'When someone placed a rifle by my desk so that, if necessary, I could defend myself (against the SA), I said: "Boys don't make fools of yourselves." ' Colonel Fromm, the Head of the AHA, merely remarked laconically: 'Insufficient determination in the SA.'[105] The story of the SA planning a putsch seemed so improbable to General Ewald von Kleist, the Wehrkreis commander in Silesia, that he spontaneously took a step which nearly ruined the plans of Reichenau and Heydrich. On receiving a flood of alarming reports about the SA's revolutionary intentions, Kleist summoned Heines, Head of the SA in Silesia, and asked him point-blank what anti-military game he was up to. Heines gave him his word of honour that the SA had never even dreamt of taking action against the Reichswehr. The General suddenly began to wonder whether 'We – the Reichswehr and the SA were being pitted against each other by a third party; I was thinking of Himmler.' He went to Berlin and told General von Fritsch of his suspicions. Fritsch summoned Reichenau, who was entirely unruffled; he gazed at the two Generals through his eyeglass and said: 'That may be, but it's too late now.'[106]

To silence the sceptics such as Heinrici and von Kleist, however, Heydrich now unleashed an avalanche of rumours, false reports and doctored documents, calculated to remove all doubts. Every Reichswehr officer was to be made to believe in the putsch. Sepp Dietrich showed the Reichswehr Ministry what purported to be SA headquarters' firing-squad list; it showed that Röhm intended to liquidate all senior Wehrmacht officers starting with Generals Beck and von Fritsch;[107] other SS representatives submitted to Wehrkreis and Garrison commanders SA lists showing that the dismissal of practically all senior officers had been decided upon.[108] An SA Obergruppenführer presented himself to Colonel Franz Halder, Chief of Staff Wehrkreis VI (Münster), and asked for information on Halder's official business, saying that SA headquarters would shortly be taking over the Reichswehr. Halder refused and made inquiries of the Reichswehr Ministry. The whole affair seemed odd to him; his SA visitor had not given his name and had departed hurriedly. He never reappeared. Halder suspected that the ostensible Obergruppenführer was not in fact an SA man at all, but an *agent provocateur* sent by interested parties.[109] Another of Heydrich's tricks was the distribution of orders purporting to come from Röhm and in most cases taken at their face value by the Reichswehr. Whenever one of these forgeries was discovered by some SA commander, the SS managed to lie their way out.

One day Karl Ernst, Commander of the SA Gruppe Berlin-Brandenburg, poured out his heart to SS-Gruppenführer Daluege, who after all had originally been an SA man. The craziest rumours were going round in Berlin, he said, of the imminence of an SA putsch; he asked Daluege to arrange an interview for him with Frick, the Minister of the Interior, so that he might protest against this slander on the SA. Daluege, who was then a Director of the Ministry, saw to it that Frick's door remained firmly closed. Instead he went to the Reichswehr Ministry and told the Deputy Head of Counter-Espionage that he had just been speaking to an SA leader who had been present at a conference on preparations for an SA putsch; the SA man had had second thoughts and now wished to warn the Reichswehr against this imminent danger.[110]

General von Reichenau faithfully backed up Heydrich's document gambit. One day Patzig, the Head of Counter-Espionage, found that an order to the SA to arm, purportedly signed by Röhm, had been spirited on to his desk; he could only conclude that the SA was planning a surprise attack on the Reichswehr and so he took the document to von Reichenau, who put on an expression of indignation and cried: 'Now it is high time!'[111]

But Heydrich's false reports were not aimed at the Reichswehr officers alone; there is much to show that Hitler was also their target. He could hardly avoid seeing them, since Blomberg never let a meeting with the Chancellor go by without complaining that the SA was arming. Hitler was, and remained, the Achilles' heel of the anti-Röhm clique. He had, indeed, given his agreement to the proposed action, but now he repeatedly gave signs of hesitation. Perhaps it was some last spark of loyalty towards his oldest 'struggle period companion'; perhaps he was unwilling to deprive himself of a counterweight to the Reichswehr and an important factor in the régime's balance of power. Whatever the reason, from time to time Adolf Hitler relapsed into sullen indecision.

As late as June 28th the officers of Wehrkreis Headquarters VII (Bavaria) were not sure whether Hitler was on the side of the Reichswehr or the SA.[112] Had they known of Hitler's conversation with Ritter von Krausser, an SA-Obergruppenführer and one of Röhm's deputies, they would have been even less sure. Shortly before his execution Krausser told SA-Gruppenführer Karl Schreyer, who was also under arrest, of a conversation he had had with Hitler on June 29th. Schreyer records it as follows: 'Hitler had assured him [Krausser] that he would use the occasion of the SA Leaders' Conference in Wiessee to talk matters out with Röhm and all the Gruppenführer and remove all differences and misunderstandings. He realized, and regretted, that he had neglected the old SA men. Hitler had been most conciliatory in his references to his faithful fellow soldier, Ernst Röhm, who, he said, would remain at his post.'[113]

So during the vital days immediately preceding the bloodbath, Hitler had given three differing versions of the fate awaiting Röhm. He had told Blomberg that he would arrest Röhm and 'square accounts with him'; he had told Lutze that Röhm would be dismissed; to von Krausser he had forecast reconciliation. Such vacillation on the part of the

Führer did not suit Himmler, Göring and Heydrich at all. Before the opening of the final scene, Hitler's hand had to be removed from the levers of power.

Here chance came to the conspirators' assistance. Early on June 28th Hitler, accompanied by Göring, left by air to attend the wedding of Josef Terboven, the Gauleiter of Westphalia.[114] The *National-Socialistische Korrespondenz* later reported that Hitler had gone to Western Germany 'to give an outward impression of complete calm and avoid warning the traitors.'[115] The majority of historians have accepted this story, believing that Hitler made this journey to allow Röhm's enemies to get to work less obtrusively.[116]

It does not, so far, seem to have occurred to anybody that this supposed deception manoeuvre on Hitler's part ran completely counter to the tactics of the anti-Röhm campaign. He had no interest in covering up the quarrel with Röhm. On the contrary – Röhm was to be challenged in a spectacular campaign using maximum publicity, in order to prepare the public for the forthcoming bloodbath. On June 25th in a speech over all German radio networks Rudolf Hess threatened: 'Woe to him who breaks faith in the belief that he can serve the revolution by revolt! Adolf Hitler is the revolution's great strategist. Woe to him who plants his flat feet among the fine threads of the Führer's strategic plans, thinking to force the pace. He is an enemy of the revolution.'[117] On June 25th Reichenau had Captain Ernst Röhm expelled from the German Officers Association for unbecoming behaviour[118] – in Wheeler-Bennett's words 'a measure which smacked of the handing over of a victim by the Holy Office to the civil arm for execution.'[119] On the same day Göring thundered: 'Anyone who erodes this confidence [in Hitler] is guilty of high treason. Anyone who wishes to destroy this confidence is a destroyer of Germany. Anyone who offends against this confidence will pay with his head.'[120]

The challenge to Röhm could not have been clearer. So what could be the point of this deception manoeuvre which Hitler's journey to West Germany was supposed to be? In fact the stage managers of the Röhm drama were only too glad to see the vacillating Chancellor leave Berlin – dependent henceforth on their messages, their suppositions and their rumours. Röhm's rival, Lutze, who was present at Terboven's wedding, said with a sudden flash of perspicacity: 'I had a feeling that it suited certain circles to aggravate and accelerate "the affair" just at this moment when the Führer was absent from Berlin and could therefore neither see nor hear things for himself, but was dependent upon the telephone.'[121]

Hitler had hardly reached the wedding reception in Essen when he was called urgently to the telephone; Himmler was on the line from Berlin.[122] The cast was well distributed. Himmler had remained in Berlin and was now reading to Hitler increasingly ominous reports of SA machinations; meanwhile, at Hitler's side, the faithful Göring stood ready to confirm the least detail of Himmler's reports. Hitler was so incensed that he left the wedding breakfast and returned to his suite in the Kaiserhof Hotel, Essen. Shortly thereafter he summoned his closest collaborators, among them Göring and Lutze.[123] Lutze's diary continues: 'Here in the hotel room the telephone was going almost uninterruptedly. The Führer was deep in thought but was apparently clear that he would now have to take action.'[124] Another confidant of the conspirators now took a hand in Hitler's discussion; Paul (nicknamed Pilli) Körner, Göring's factotum and a Secretary in the Prussian State Ministry, had just arrived by air from Berlin with further news from Himmler.[125] Throughout Germany, apparently, the SA was arming for revolt.

Suddenly Hitler got up and proclaimed: 'I've had enough. I shall make an example of them.'[126] The final decision had been taken. Hitler ordered Göring and Körner to return to Berlin and be ready to act on receipt of a code word which Hitler would issue – and to act not only against the SA but also against the bourgeois opposition. Göring lost no time; early on June 29th, back in Berlin, he alerted the Leibstandarte 'Adolf Hitler' and the Prussian Police unit 'General Göring'.[127]

Göring now drafted a letter, which was handed under seal to Heydrich. Heydrich passed it to SS-Untersturmführer Ernst Müller of the SD Hauptamt, instructing him to give it to the commander of SS-Oberabschnitt South-East.[128] The purport of this letter was that the Chancellor had declared a state of emergency and given Göring, as Minister-President, plenary powers in Prussia; he, Göring, now delegated all executive authority in the province of Silesia to the commander of SS-Oberabschnitt South-East, SS-Gruppenführer Udo von Woyrsch. Göring then ordered von Woyrsch to arrest certain SA leaders, to disarm all SA 'Headquarters Guards', to occupy Breslau police headquarters and get in touch with the commander of the Land Police.[129]

Meanwhile, in the Kaiserhof Hotel, Essen, Hitler was thinking how he could take the SA leaders by surprise. Eventually he fell back on his original plan as explained to von Blomberg – to lure them to Bad Wiessee and arrest them there. On the evening of June 28th Hitler put through a call to Bad Wiessee and told Röhm that SA men had insulted a foreign diplomat in the Rhineland; this could not go on, he said, and they must have a discussion. Then he gave his instructions; all SA-Obergruppenführer, Gruppenführer and Inspectors were to present themselves at Röhm's holiday resort for a discussion with the Führer at 11 AM on Saturday, June 30th, 1934.[130]

Hitler then waited for his opponent to react. But on June 29th, Röhm was entirely carefree; he went for long walks in Bad Wiessee with his aide, Bergmann; he expressed pleasure at the prospect of a discussion with Hitler and he greeted old friends as they arrived at the Hanselbauer Pension.[131] Meanwhile the other side was acting. The Commander-in-Chief of the Army issued a general alert.[132] SS headquarters called their units into barracks and armed them.[133] Hitler, who was inspecting a voluntary labour service camp, sent a radio message to the Reichswehr Ministry at 3 PM, ordering Sepp Dietrich to come to the Hotel Dreesen in Bad Godesberg, whither he had now moved.[134]

Dietrich arrived about 8 PM. Hitler was in conference with fifteen Nazi functionaries, including Lutze, Goebbels and the three of the Führer's aides, Bruckner, Schaub and Schreck.[135] Shortly thereafter Dietrich had to leave the glass of beer he had ordered in the hotel lounge and present himself to his Führer.[136] Hitler's order was a short one: 'Fly to Munich and call me from there.'[137] Dietrich flew to Munich with two Criminal Police officers – destination: the Brown House.[138] Shortly before midnight he once more reported to Hitler by telephone and was given a new order: proceed to Kaufering, a small railway station near Landsberg am Lech, there take over two companies of the Leibstandarte and move to Bad Wiessee.[139]

About the same time (between midnight and 1 AM) the Leibstandarte in the ex-Cadet College, Berlin-Lichterfeld was alerted by a call from the Reichswehr Ministry.[140] The duty officer hunted 220 men out of bed and shortly thereafter two companies were on their way to Kaufering by train.[141] Sepp Dietrich was on the way by road and the Leibstandarte units were already assembled when two messages put Hitler in a towering rage and made him alter his plans.[142]

The first was from Himmler in Berlin: the Berlin SA had completed its putsch preparations and action was planned for the next day, June 30th; the SA had been alerted for 4 PM and, as Hitler later told the Reichstag, 'sharp at 5 PM action was to begin with the surprise occupation of the Government buildings.'[143] Hitler in Bad Godesberg did not know that most of the Berlin SA had long since gone on leave. Even on July 13th he apparently still believed that, instead of journeying to Bad Wiessee, Karl Ernst, Head of the Berlin SA, had 'remained behind in Berlin to conduct the action in person';[144] In fact Ernst left

Berlin with his wife on June 29th en route to Bremen to board a ship for Tenerife.[145]

The second report bore little better relation to the truth. It was from Adolf Wagner, the Gauleiter and Minister of the Interior, Bavaria – in Munich the SA had come out on to the streets and were demonstrating against the Führer and the Reichswehr.[146]

Late on the evening of June 29th certain Munich SA units had marched through the Isar quarter with the cry 'The Reichswehr is against us.' Handwritten leaflets of unknown authorship had lured them out of the bars and, in addition, they were aware of the alert measures taken by the Reichswehr.[147] When Obergruppenführer August Schneidhuber, head of the Munich and Upper Bavarian SA, and Gruppenführer Wilhelm Schmid heard that their units were on the march, they intervened and ordered them back home.[148] Schmid laid hands on two copies of the anonymous orders; all he knew about them was that neither he nor Schneidhuber had either drafted them or issued them.[149]

Colonel Küchler, Chief-of-Staff in the Munich Wehrkreis headquarters, heard that an SA column was on the move towards the Oberwiesenfeld airfield. He summoned Major Hans Doerr, his transport officer, and ordered him to go out in mufti and discover what was happening.[150] Doerr drove off about 1 AM on June 30th and soon met an SA unit about 300 strong. At Oberwiesenfeld, however, he found no one. On the Königsplatz he observed another group of SA whose commanders were sending their men home with the words: 'Go quietly home and wait for the decision of your Führer. Whatever may happen, whether Adolf Hitler sends you on leave or whether he forbids you to wear uniform or not, we stand unreservedly behind him.'[151]

In face of these two midnight messages from Berlin and Munich, Hitler, whose information was abysmally poor, panicked. Now he really knew, he thought: the traitors had dropped the mask and Röhm had come out in his true colours. Now he was determined to exterminate this 'nest of traitors'. Obsessed with these illusions, he took a sudden decision which left his entourage gasping; off to Munich at once, off to Bad Wiessee at once.[152] At 2 AM shaken, fatigued and quivering with agitation, he stumped across the Bonn airfield at Hangelar and clambered with his following into a three-engined Ju 52.[153] He slumped down into the front seat of the cabin, gazing silently out into the misty night sky. Gradually the mist gave way to the pale pink of a new day, the most murderous day of pre-war German history. Germany was headed for an orgy of blood, brutality and barbarism. Lutze thought of Röhm and hummed to himself:

Morgenrot, Morgenrot,	Red of the morning, red of the morning
Leuchtest uns zu frühem Tod.	Thou lightest us to early death.
Gestern noch auf stolzem Rossen,	Yesterday mounted on a proud steed,
Heute durch die Brust geschossen	Today a bullet through the breast.[154]

As soon as the aircraft landed at Oberwiesenfeld, Munich, Hitler leapt out, stalking through the assembled Party and SA dignitaries as if in a trance. He stopped for moment in front of two Reichswehr officers whom he had ordered up by radio, saying: 'This is the blackest day of my life. But I shall go to Bad Wiessee and pass severe judgement. Tell that to General Adam.'[155] He then drove to the Bavarian Ministry of the Interior.

Shortly after 4 AM Gruppenführer Schmid was woken by the telephone. The Ministry of the Interior informed him that Hitler was awaiting him.[156] 'Before he went,' his wife stated, 'he searched desperately round the bedroom for two white leaflets saying: "They might prove that I have had nothing to do with the entire business".' But the sheets had disappeared.[157] Schmid had little chance of explaining himself to Hitler, however; the Chancellor had hardly set eyes on him when he rushed up, tore off his badges of rank, cursed him for a traitor and screamed: 'You are under arrest and will be shot.' Schmid was led off to Stadelheim Prison; he was only a few minutes behind Obergruppenführer Schneidhuber.[158] Leaving Gauleiter Wagner to dispatch squads of SS and Bavarian Political Police to arrest named SA leaders and prominent opponents of National-Socialism,[159] Hitler rushed off to Bad Wiessee with two escort cars.

By now it was 6.30 AM.[160] The SA leaders were still sleeping in the Hanselbauer Pension. The landlady murmured something about being honoured by so illustrious a visitor, but Hitler and his men stormed past her and took up positions at the bedroom doors, revolvers in hand.[161] Lutze remained behind for a moment and thumbed through the visitors list to see where the victims were. He arrived just in time to witness the arrest of Röhm.[162]

Lutze's diary records that he met Hitler 'at Röhm's door. A detective had knocked, calling out that something urgent had arrived. There was a pause before the door opened and it was then pushed wide. The Führer stood in the doorway, revolver in hand. He called Röhm a traitor, which Röhm energetically denied; he then told him to get dressed since he was under arrest. The detectives remained behind.'[163]

Hitler hurried on. He banged on the opposite door from which, shortly afterwards, appeared Obergruppenführer Edmund Heines; a male sleeping partner could be seen behind him. In a sudden access of rage against National-Socialist homosexuals, Goebbels later described the scene as 'revolting – almost nauseating'.[164] Hitler rushed off to the next room while Lutze went into Heines' room and searched the wardrobe for weapons. Heines shouted 'Lutze, I've done nothing. Can't you help me?' In some embarrassment Hitler's man turned to him saying: 'I can do nothing . . . I can do nothing.'[165] The entire 'nest of conspirators' had soon been cleared. The arrested SA men were marched down and locked in the cellar of the Pension, guarded by two detectives; they were soon on the way to Stadelheim.[166] Before Hitler could leave, however, a lorry arrived from which emerged, fully armed, Röhm's 'Headquarters Guard' summoned from Munich.[167] The situation was critical; Standartenführer Julius Uhl, the Headquarters Guard commander, was languishing in the Pension cellar and his men were in an ugly mood.

Hitler went forward, barked out an order and then turned on his usual charm. The SA men did as they were told and allowed their Führer to order them back to Munich. They drove off northwards.[168] But on leaving Bad Wiessee they had second thoughts. The lorry stopped and Röhm's Headquarters Guard took up what Bruckner, Hitler's aide, described as an 'ambiguous position'.[169] They looked so menacing that Hitler thought it better to leave Bad Wiessee in a southerly direction and return to Munich by a wide detour via Rottach-Egern and Tegernsee.[170] At about this time Dr Robert Koch, the Governor of Stadelheim Prison, strolled in through the main entrance.[171] He found on his desk a report to the effect that senior SA commanders had been arriving uninterruptedly since 7 AM.[172] The SS had surrounded the main station and Political Police officials held up every SA leader as he arrived; some they let go and some they arrested – more often the latter.[173]

When SA Brigadeführer Max Jüttner arrived at the station to meet his chief, Ritter von Krausser, off the overnight train from Berlin, he found him being escorted by two plain-clothes men, clearly police officials. Krausser told Jüttner that he had just been arrested. Krausser's chauffeur, Vollmer, tried to get his master away and was also arrested.[174] One after another the SA leaders were taken off to Stadelheim – Manfred von Killinger, Hans Peter von Heydebreck, Hans Hayn,

Georg von Detten, Hans Joachim von Falkenhausen[175] – the list included practically every well-known SA name.

Anyone who escaped the Political Police, however, and dutifully took the road to Bad Wiessee, was stopped on the way by a wildly gesticulating figure. Hitler told each SA leader that he had a new Chief, Viktor Lutze.[176] He shouted: 'I have just come from Wiessee, where I have arrested Röhm. He and Schleicher had planned a putsch against me and the leaders of the State. All SA leaders involved will be shot.' He ordered those he met to follow his car and hold themselves ready for a conference in the Brown House.[177]

At 10 AM Hitler reached Party headquarters in the Briennerstrasse; it had meanwhile been cordoned off by the Reichswehr. He gave Goebbels the go-ahead; the Propaganda Minister rushed to the telephone and put through to Göring the agreed code word: 'Kolibri'.[178] Now, at last, Heydrich and Himmler really could let the SS loose, and terror stormed through the Reich. SD-Oberabschnitt commanders opened the sealed envelopes containing their secret orders and then sent the murder squads on their way.

Bavaria provided the first SS victims. Ritten von Kahr, who had checkmated Hitler's 1923 putsch, was carried off by SS men[179] and his mutilated body was found later on Dachau Heath; he had apparently been killed with a pick-axe. Father Bernhard Stempfle, who knew too many of Hitler's secrets, ended with three bullets through his heart and a broken spine.[180]

SS men searched for the Munich doctor, Ludwig Schmitt, who had worked with Otto Strasser, one of Hitler's main enemies. They failed to find him because, unknown to them, one of the Stadelheim warders had hidden him in a woodshed.[181] Failing to find the right man, they laid hands on the wrong one, a music critic named Dr Wilhelm Eduard Schmid; he lived in a different street, he spelt his name differently, and he was a doctor of philosophy, not medicine – all the same the SS carted him away. His family knew no more until Dachau Concentration Camp delivered them a coffin which they were forbidden to open.[182]

From this point on, the most fanatical apostle of political terror was Adolf Hitler. The Reichsstatthalter, Ritter von Epp, presented himself to demand court-martial procedure for his former subordinate, Röhm; Hitler stormed at him saying that Röhm's treachery was proven and that he had forfeited his life. Von Epp was so taken aback by Hitler's bloodthirsty outburst that, as he left, he gazed tongue-tied at his aide, Prince zu Ysenburg and murmured: 'Crazy!'[183] The SA commanders who had not been arrested were equally taken aback, when at 11.30

Hitler swung open the door of the Brown House Council Chamber and approached them.[184]

Describing the scene, Gruppenführer Schreyer recalled that as he opened his mouth to speak 'a gob of foam shot out of his mouth such as I have never seen before or since. In a voice frequently choked with emotion, he described what had happened: Röhm and his followers had been guilty of the greatest act of disloyalty in world history. Röhm, to whom he had always been faithful through every difficulty, possible or impossible, had committed high treason against him; Röhm had planned to arrest and kill him in order to hand Germany over to her enemies. The principal figure on the other side had been François-Poncet [the French Ambassador]; he had given Röhm, who was always in financial difficulties, a bribe of 12,000,000 marks.' Then came the decisive piece of news: 'Exemplary punishment would be meted out to Röhm and his conspirators; he would have them all shot; the first group – Röhm, Schneidhuber, Schmid, Heines, Hayn, Heydebreck and Count Spreti – would be shot that very evening. He had already given the order.'[185] This information was in fact somewhat premature. Röhm was not shot 'that evening' and Hitler had not given the order to execute the others on the list. He was waiting for his executioner, Sepp Dietrich. The Leibstandarte commander did not appear until 12.30 AM.[186]

Hitler received him in a bad temper, and wanted to know where he had been all this time. Dietrich had his excuses. The roads to Bad Wiessee were wet and the tyres of the Reichswehr lorries carrying his men were worn; in addition he had had to take on petrol at the artillery barracks in Landsberg. The Führer's order to turn back to Munich had therefore only reached him between Bad Tölz and Bad Wiessee.[187] Where were the troops now, Hitler asked. Dietrich replied that they were on the Munich Karolinerplatz. Hitler thereupon ordered him to install his two companies in the Pioneer Barracks and report back again as soon as possible.[188]

Dietrich returned at 2.30 PM. He was kept waiting for three hours in the Brown House outer office while loud, but unintelligible, discussion was audible through the double doors of the meeting room.[189] Hitler and his immediate associates were debating the fate of the SA leaders. This was the great moment for Buch, the Party Judge, who clearly wished to make good his failure to murder the Röhm gang in 1932. Rudolf Hess and Max Amann, the Party publisher, competed for the pleasure of carrying out the murders, Hess shouting: 'My Führer, the duty to shoot Röhm is mine.'[190] The new SA Chief-of-Staff, Lutze, sat there dumbfounded, listening to the others' murderous talk. He had never imagined that a clean-up of the SA would be like this. When Hitler asked him who should be shot, Lutze was evasive, saying that he did not know who was to blame or who were Röhm's accomplices and could not quote any names. He then silently left the room.[191] About 5 PM the door opened and Buch's son-in-law, Martin Bormann, came out. He took Dietrich in to Hitler who said: 'Go back to the barracks; select an officer and six men and have the SA leaders shot for high treason.'[192] Bormann then handed Dietrich a list of prisoners sent over to the Brown House that morning by Koch, the Prison Governor; it gave the names of all the SA leaders incarcerated in Stadelheim.[193] Hitler had ticked six names in green pencil; August Schneidhuber, SA-Obergruppenführer and Police President of Munich (Cell 504); Wilhelm Schmid, SA-Gruppenführer Munich (Cell 497); Hans Peter von Heydebreck, SA-Gruppenführer Stettin (Cell 502); Hans Hayn, SA-Gruppenführer Dresden (Cell 503); Hans Joachim Graf von Spreti-Weilbach, SA-Standartenführer Munich (Cell 501) and Edmund Heines SA-Obergruppenführer and Police President Breslau (Cell 483).[194]

Röhm's name had not been ticked. Hitler drove out to Oberwiesenfeld airfield on his way back to Berlin; he was accompanied by von Epp and on the way Prince zu Ysenburg heard him say: 'I have pardoned Röhm because of his services and Krausser because of his decorations.'[195] Perhaps Hitler could not yet quite bring himself to murder his old friend.

Sepp Dietrich had no such scruples. He just took the list of the condemned, sent SS-Gruppenführer Prince zu Waldeck and Pyrmont on ahead to Stadelheim to select a suitable execution spot[196] and himself looked out 'six good shots to ensure that nothing messy happened'.[197] At 6 PM he presented himself to the Prison Governor and requested him to hand over the condemned men.[198] But Koch was a prudent official and he had covered himself. Warned by Prince zu Waldeck's visit, he had alerted the Bavarian Ministry of Justice. The Minister, Dr Hans Frank, was already on the road, so Koch played for time.[199]

He pointed out to the simple-minded Dietrich that his list carried no signature and argued so stubbornly that Dietrich went back to the Brown House for fresh instructions. The only high-level official he could find was Wagner, the Minister of the Interior, who wrote on Dietrich's list:

> By command of the Führer the men whom SS-Gruppenführer Dietrich indicates are to be handed over to him.
>
> Adolf Wagner, State Minister[200]

Meanwhile Frank, the National-Socialist legal expert, had arrived in Stadelheim and had made one or two half-hearted attempts to stop the murders.[201] He called Rudolf Hess, but Hess refused to become involved and insisted that the Führer's order be carried out.[202] Frank thought that at least the proper procedure should be observed and so informed Schneidhuber that he had been condemned to death; Schneidhuber, however reacted so forcefully and incredulously that Frank brought the interview to an end.[203] So Dietrich was now free to do his duty.

Koch ordered the six SA leaders to be led out into the prison courtyard, each guarded by two policemen.[204] Seeing Dietrich approach, Schneidhuber shouted: 'Sepp, my friend, what on earth's happening? We are completely innocent!'[205] In Dietrich's surly, bucolic face not a muscle moved. He clicked his heels and announced: 'You have been condemned to death by the Führer, Heil Hitler!' One after another the SA leaders were led out and into the courtyard.[206] They were received by an SS officer with the words: 'The Führer and Reich Chancellor has condemned you to death. The sentence will be carried out forthwith.' The courtyard's walls echoed to the crack of the rifles.[207]

Even Dietrich's nerve gave way before the end and he left before all six had been shot. He said later: 'Before it was Schneidhuber's turn, I was off. I had had enough.'[208] He waited until midday next day, when he entrained his men for Berlin. He then flew back to the capital,[209] where since 10 AM on June 30th the Göring-Himmler version of this German Saint Bartholomew's Night had been in progress.

As soon as Goebbels had telephoned through the code word 'Kolibri', the mechanism of terror had begun to operate in Göring's kingdom. The news was brought to Franz von Papen, the Vice-Chancellor, when Major Bodenschatz, Göring's aide, invited him to appear at the office of the Prussian Minister-President in the Leipziger Platz. Papen records: 'Göring was in his study with Himmler. He told me that he himself had been given powers to deal with the insurgents in the capital.' Von Papen felt that, as Vice-Chancellor, he had been bypassed and he protested. While the two were arguing, Himmler went out into the anteroom where Fritz-Gunther von Tschirschky, Papen's assistant was waiting. Himmler went to a telephone and Tschirschky heard him say: 'You can go ahead now.' The hunt for enemies of the régime was on.[210]

Police cars and lorries full of SS men roared through the streets. The Tiergarten quarter, where the most important SA Headquarters were, was cordoned off. Such SA commanders as were found on duty allowed themselves to be carted off without demur.[211] At the same time SS and police surrounded the Vice-Chancellor's office, shot von Bose,

Papen's Press Officer, and arrested certain other members of his staff.[212] The 'reactionary' enemy of the State was to be put in his place.

Meanwhile in the Lichterfeld Barracks the Leibstandarte had been placed on general alert. The Battalion Commander, SS-Sturmbannführer Wagner, was ordered by SS headquarters to prepare a number of Einsatzkommandos [Action Commandos].[213] To command the more important of these, Wagner detailed Hauptsturmführer Kurt Gildisch, who was known to be prepared to carry out any order.[214] Gildisch paraded eighteen men of his company and moved off with them. He reported to Heydrich. There were eight men already waiting in the ante-room, some in mufti and some in SS uniform.[215]

Shortly thereafter Heydrich emerged from his office and snapped out words he was to repeat very often that day: 'Putsch by Röhm – state of emergency – order from the Führer – immediate action.' He then withdrew into his office and summoned each of the waiting men individually. The Gestapo plain-clothes men were each given a list of names of victims. One Gestapo official, together with Gildisch's men, was to arrest so-called enemies of the State. Gildisch himself was given a special mission: 'You will be responsible for the Klausener Case; you will shoot him personally. Go forthwith to the Reich Ministry of Transport.' As an afterthought Heydrich asked whether Gildisch knew Klausener; when Gildisch said that he did not, Heydrich simply raised his hand in the Hitler salute, said 'Heil Hitler' and Gildisch was dismissed.[216]

On the way to the Ministry of Transport in the Wilhelmstrasse Gildisch mulled over methods of shooting his victim. On his belt he carried a 9-mm 'Parabellum' service pistol, but concealed in his right trouser pocket was a loaded 7.65-mm Mauser. This was the weapon he planned to use for his surprise attack.[217] One wonders whether this was all that Gildisch was thinking, and the answer is that it was. Dr Erich Klausener was a Director in the Reich Ministry of Transport, President of Catholic Action and ex-Head of the Police Section in the Prussian Ministry of the Interior, yet not for one moment did Gildisch wonder what crime Klausener might have committed to deserve to be shot without trial and without the slightest opportunity to defend himself.[218]

It was now 1 PM and Klausener was just coming out of his office to wash his hands when he saw the steel-helmeted SS man in front of him. He went back into his office and asked Gildisch in. When the latter told him that he was under arrest, Klausener turned and went to a cupboard to get his jacket. Gildisch thereupon drew his automatic and shot Klausener through the head; he fell to the floor dead. Gildisch seized the desk telephone and dialled Heydrich's number. The unnaturally high-pitched voice from the Prinz-Albrecht-Strasse ordered him to fake a suicide, so he placed the Mauser near Klausener's limp right hand and put a double guard on the door. As far as the Third Reich was concerned, the Klausener Case was settled.[219]

Gildisch was back with Heydrich by 1.15 and only then did he learn whom he had shot – 'a dangerous Catholic leader'. He was forthwith dispatched on another mission – to fly to Bremen, arrest Karl Ernst, Head of the Berlin SA, and bring him to the Lichterfeld Barracks. Gildisch was responsible for a number of other victims that day, including the SA Medical Officer, Standartenführer, Dr Erwin Villain.[220]

Gildisch with his eighteen thugs, however, was nothing out of the ordinary on June 30th, 1934. Everywhere in Göring's Prussia, the SS robots were hunting down supposed enemies of the State. They did not think; they simply obeyed. They did not grumble; they simply acted. Without a word they carried out the duty assigned to them. Himmler's human automata asked no questions. All they wanted to know were the names of their victims.

Escape necessitated bold and instant action. Gottfried Treviranus, for instance, a retired Minister of the Reich, heard Himmler's minions ringing his doorbell; though dressed only for tennis, he climbed his garden wall and fled abroad.[221] Captain Ehrhardt, Hitler's reluctant ally in 1923, withdrew into the woods of his own estate, taking a couple of shotguns with him and, as soon as the Gestapo had left his house, got some friends to smuggle him across into Austria.[222]

Major-General Ferdinand von Bredow, Reichenau's predecessor in the Reichswehr Ministry, was suspected by the Nazis of having written *Diary of a Reichswehr General* which had appeared in émigré circles in Paris. Since he was in obvious danger, a foreign military attaché invited him to spend the night in his embassy, but Bredow refused. A few hours later a Gestapo car delivered his body to the Lichterfeld Barracks: he had been shot through the head.[223] The SS thirst for blood increased hourly. They soon ceased to be content with the official victims, the mutineers and enemies of the State, and turned over to a campaign of personal vengeance. Erich von dem Bach-Zelewski, an SS-Oberabschnitt Commander, sent two SS men to deal with his rival, the SS Cavalry leader, Anton Freiherr von Hohberg und Buchwald; they shot him down from behind in his own smoking-room on his estate. When his seventeen-year-old son rushed in, one of them said casually: 'We have just shot your father' – and calmly went away.[224]

The settlement of private SS scores was particularly savage in Silesia.

There the Oberabschnitt Commander, Udo von Woyrsch, lost control of his men. SA-Sturmbannführer Engels, Acting Police President of Breslau, was driven out into the woods by SS men and killed with a shotgun.[225] Sembach, who had been a member of SS headquarters Silesia, was drowned in a reservoir near Brieg and his murderer was then murdered in his turn.[226] Vengeance for anything was the order of the day; Dr Förster, a lawyer from Hirschberg, was killed because he had taken part in legal proceedings against National-Socialists;[227] Kamphausen, the Waldenburg Municipal Engineer, was murdered for being uncooperative over the issue of building licences.[228] Many of Göring's and Himmler's actions were governed by personal spite. For instance they hunted down Gregor Strasser because, more than any other National-Socialist leader, he had seen through them both. Until 1932, when he had split with Hitler on a tactical disagreement, he had been ranked second in the Party; he had once described 'the Himmlers and Anhimmlers' (a pun meaning 'Hitler's adorers')[229] as the greatest threat to the Führer and the Movement; of Göring he had said: 'Göring is a brutal egoist who does not give a damn about Germany as long as he can amount to something.'[230]

For Himmler and Göring such a man was all the more dangerous in that they could not discount the possibility of a reconciliation between him and Hitler one day. They knew that Hitler had toyed with the idea of appointing Strasser Minister of the Interior.[231] There had already been danger signals; Hitler and Strasser had had a conciliatory talk; on June 23rd Hitler had invested Strasser with the Golden Party Badge carrying the membership Number 9.[232] So if June 30th, 1934 was to mean anything for Göring and Himmler, Gregor Strasser had to die. In the early afternoon he was arrested by two Gestapo men and a couple of hours later an SS man shot him from behind in Cell 16 in the Gestapo prison. His death was officially announced as 'suicide'.[233]

Meanwhile, where was the fearful SA mutiny? Where were the masterminds behind the 'greatest act of disloyalty in world history' which Hitler had announced to the SA survivors in the Brown House? The masterminds were in fact enjoying a sunny weekend. They were at home; they were preparing to go on leave. General Kurt von Schleicher was sitting at his desk in his house in the Griebnitzstrasse, Neu-Babelsberg; his cook, Marie Guntel, ushered two men into his study and one of them asked whether the man at the desk was the General. Marie Guntel later stated in evidence: 'On hearing the question he [von Schleicher] looked up and said "Yes." At that very instant the shots rang out.' The General's wife, who was in the room listening to the radio, ran towards him – and was shot down too.[234]

But in the murdered man's papers the Gestapo found nothing to indicate any collusion by Schleicher with either Röhm or Strasser or François-Poncet. He had not met Röhm since June 1933; as far as François-Poncet was concerned he has said that Schleicher 'at no time said anything indicating . . . that he was involved in any sort of plot . . . Whenever he uttered Röhm's name it was with contempt and disgust.'[235] The tale of a Schleicher-Röhm putsch was so improbable that even the Reich Propaganda Ministry did not believe it. That afternoon the Ministry held a Press conference and a journalist asked whether General von Schleicher's death was in any way connected with the action against Röhm's SA. The Ministry's spokesman answered: 'That is not the case.'[236]

Göring and Himmler were uneasy, wondering whether the Reichswehr would strike, now that its most prominent political general had, for no good reason, been shot down by the SS murderers. But not at all. General von Reichenau was not the man to allow a complete scheme to be upset by one tiresome corpse. That afternoon he dictated a communiqué: 'In recent weeks it has been established that the ex-Reichswehr Minister, General (Retired) von Schleicher has maintained treasonable relationships with foreign powers and with SA leadership circles inimical to the State. It has therefore been proved that both in word and deed he had been acting against the State and its leaders. This meant that in connexion with the general purge now in progress, his arrest was essential. When police officers came to arrest him, General (Retired) von Schleicher offered armed resistance. There was an exchange of shots as a result of which both he and his wife, who placed herself in the line of fire, were mortally wounded.'[237]

As a result of the murder of von Schleicher, however, a rift appeared between the executioners. Göring said later that he had intended only to arrest the General but the Gestapo squad had arrived before his policemen and had forthwith carried out the murder.[238] In fact Göring now felt that it was time to check this orgy of blood. The news from the country made it clear that the SS units were becoming increasingly violent and his policemen were losing control; at the same time he had no wish to spoil the picture of bonhomie and conservatism which he liked to present to the nation.

One of the first to realize that the rift existed was von Papen, the Vice-Chancellor. On attempting to leave Göring's office in the Leipziger-Platz, he was stopped at the door by two SS guards. Bodenschatz, Göring's aide, stormed past, shouting: 'We'll see who is in command here, Ministerpresident Göring or the SS!'[239] The victims soon realized that they could turn the disagreement between Göring and

Himmler to good account. SA-Gruppenführer Siegfried Kasche, who was clearly facing death, held forth to Göring at such length that the latter released him;[240] Göring also took von Bülow, an Under-Secretary in the Foreign Ministry, off the list;[241] in the same way he saved the ex-Crown Prince, who was also in some danger.[242]

Göring soon dropped the role of jovial saviour, however, when Hitler returned from Munich[243] at 10 PM bringing the news that Röhm was not to die. Hitler had given his word to Ritter von Epp. Göring and Himmler were appalled: the slaughter would be meaningless to them if Röhm lived. As early as the evening of June 29th Himmler had told Frau von Ribbentrop: 'Röhm is as good as dead';[244] and thus it had to be. Hitler may well suddenly have thought that it might be in his own interests to save Röhm from Göring and Himmler; he had no wish to see his two henchmen become over-powerful. On June 30th, 1934 Hitler was not yet the totalitarian dictator (that he would only become through the succession to Hindenburg and the elimination of the Wehrmacht as a power factor as a result of the Blomberg-Fritsch crisis). If Röhm disappeared altogether, the delicate balance-of-power system, upon which Hitler's leadership depended, would be upset.

Hitler now began to play a highly sophisticated game. He had been entirely unmoved by the shooting of the most important SA leaders in Stadelheim; he had used the word 'exterminate' continuously. Back in Berlin, however, he assumed the role of the moderate, thoughtful Führer, who did not necessarily approve all that his subordinates did. He told the Cabinet that he took responsibility for the shooting of the 'traitors – even though the measure of their guilt had not been proved in every case and certain of the summary shootings had not been ordered by him personally.'[245] He told Jüttner that he had wished to have a legal investigation, but had been overtaken by events.[246]

Out of loyalty the SA survivors, led by Viktor Lutze, the new Chief-of-Staff, took their Führer at his word. In fact Hitler brought off a psychological masterstroke; the more the survivors raged against Himmler and Göring, the more shining an example of rectitude did Adolf Hitler become. 'There is no question about the shootings ordered by the Führer. They are not a subject of discussion,' Lutze wrote.[247] He genuinely believed that Hitler had ordered the shooting of only seven SA leaders and 'subsequently recognized' ten further murders committed without his permission.[248]

Whatever Hitler's purpose may have been in playing the man of moderation, Himmler and Göring now brought pressure on him to sacrifice Röhm. Even during the night June 30th–July 1st they had begun to argue – and Hitler had always been one to fight on the side of the big battalions. That night anyone whose life depended upon a promise from Hitler found that he had miscalculated. Lieutenant (Retired) Paul Schulz, who had reorganized the SA after the Stennes putsch and was a friend of Gregor Strasser, was one of them. He was running for his life through the woods near Potsdam, covered in blood, gasping, stumbling over tree roots, getting up and running again.[249]

The crazy logic of June 30th had turned Schulz, one of Röhm's bitterest enemies, into one of his accomplices. The Gestapo was after him. Later he described what happened: he had been arrested at dinner by 'five young toughs in plain clothes, some without collars and ties, but with pistols at the ready.' An hour later he was incarcerated in Room 10 in the Gestapa.[250] Three men had then pushed him into a grey convertible and the death ride began. They roared towards Potsdam, looking for some quiet spot where an 'escaper' could be shot. But it was Saturday evening and every road was brightly lit by the headlights of the approaching cars, so they had to go on.

They took the Leipzig road and at last they found a suitable spot. Schulz was made to get out and turn his back on one of the escort. He made a dash for it and, although he was hit, the range was too great for the bullet to kill him. With considerable presence of mind he pretended to be dead and his escort went back to the car to get a sheet in which to wrap the supposed corpse. Schulz's account goes on: 'At that instant I jumped up and ran as fast as I could into the wood, keeping an eye on my murderers over my shoulder. They stood staring, as if transfixed.[251]

Schulz ran on. His back was hurting from the bullet which grazed his spine 'but, to my relief, I noticed that I was not bleeding from the mouth.' On and on he ran, determined not to faint and after the first few hundred yards he doubled back. He reached a village named Seddin, but there he saw cars with searchlights lighting every inch of the road. He dived behind a hedge – where his followers later discovered the trail of blood.[252] He crept to a stream, the Nuthe, where he hid in the reeds. By the light of the moon he washed off the blood and began to think how he could escape his pursuers.

Then a name occurred to him; he knew a certain retired Rear-Admiral named Lübbert, who had only recently moved to Berlin and consequently was hardly known to the police; this was where he would hide. The plan worked. The Admiral took the fugitive in, while a vast posse of police and SS searched the neighbourhood of Potsdam, urging people to look for Schulz and, if necessary, to kill him. Schulz knew that he must 'work quicker than those who were trying to kill me'.[253]

He had a friend who had access to Hitler, and he now alerted him. Via a contact man, who was not allowed to know where Schulz was hiding, a pencilled note was smuggled through; the address given was misleading: 'In a cornfield.'[254] The friend rushed off to Hitler, who promised that Schulz's life should be spared and that he had nothing to fear. Another friend appeared in the hideout with the message: 'You are under the Führer's protection. Hitler has said "The past is forgiven; Schulz is under my personal protection."'[255] But Schulz knew Hitler too well to trust him completely. For some days he refused to give away his hiding place and his friends took some time to persuade him to leave it. He had not been far wrong; as the days went by Hitler's promise became increasingly fragile and eventually Schulz had to settle for banishment from Germany – all that remained of Hitler's great promises.[256]

Like Paul Schulz, the last surviving SA leader was soon to find what Adolf Hitler's word was worth. On the morning of July 1st Hitler was still determined to save the life of his old friend Röhm, but by midday Göring and Himmler had won and SS-Brigadeführer Theodor Eicke was ordered to shoot him.[257] Hitler still hoped that Röhm would relieve him of the necessity to issue the final order and Eicke was instructed to give Röhm a chance to commit suicide. Eicke loaded a pistol with one bullet, summoned his deputy, SS-Sturmbannführer Michael Lippert, and drove out to Stadelheim. With them was SS-Gruppenführer Schmauser, the SS Liaison Officer with the Reichswehr.[258]

At 3 PM the trio presented themselves to Koch, the Prison Governor. Once more he made difficulties; he was not prepared to hand Röhm over simply on a verbal order, and he muttered something about the usual channels. He followed his usual procedure in such cases and alerted Frank, the Minister of Justice. When, speaking over the telephone the Minister seemed to be taking Koch's side. Eicke snatched the receiver out of his hand and roared into it that the case had nothing to do with the Minister; he, Eicke, had an order from the Führer and that was enough.[259] Koch gave way. He summoned a warder named Lechler and ordered him to take Eicke, Lippert and Schmauser to cell 474 in the new prison block.[260] Röhm was squatting on an iron bedstead, stripped to the waist and sweating profusely. He looked up as the door grated and Eicke came into the cell. Eicke said: 'You have forfeited your life. The Führer gives you one more chance to draw the conclusions.'[261] He then laid the pistol on the table together with the latest edition of the *Völkischer Beobachter* carrying the banner headline: 'Röhm arrested and dismissed – far-reaching purge in the

SA.'[262] As he went out Eicke remarked that Röhm had ten minutes, by which time all must be over. The door closed.

The three SS men waited for a quarter of an hour in the narrow passage outside the cell. No sound came from within. Eicke looked at his watch. He and Lippert drew their revolvers. Eicke pushed open the door and shouted: 'Chief-of-Staff, get ready!' Looking sideways, he saw the revolver in Lippert's hand quivering and he hissed: 'Aim slowly and calmly.' There were two shots. Röhm fell to the ground, gasping: 'My Führer, my Führer,' to which Eicke replied: 'You should have thought of that earlier; it's too late now.' Röhm was still breathing; one of the two SS men (it is not clear which) shot him once more through the chest. Ernst Röhm, founder of the SA, Hitler's only friend and the rival of the Reichswehr, was dead. He died at 6 PM on July 1st, 1934.[263]

The death of Röhm was the signal for a resumption of shooting. SA-Gruppenführer Karl Schreyer was in Columbia House, the second largest SS torture chamber. He heard the bangings of cell doors, the staccato commands and the echo of the shots getting closer and closer. Dawn was breaking on July 2nd but the shooting still went on; from his cell, Schreyer could count the victims; SA-Oberführer von Falkenhausen at 2 AM, Gruppenführer von Detten at 2.30, and at 3 AM Ritter von Krausser, the man to whom Hitler had granted a pardon.[264]

Half an hour later it was Schreyer's turn. The cell door swung open and an SS-Truppführer straddled the doorway; behind him were two SS men with fixed bayonets. 'Schreyer out!' the NCO shouted. 'You will now be shot on the Führer's orders.' Schreyer said: 'I demand a preliminary investigation.' The SS man replied: 'That would be nice for you, you traitor. You will be taken out and shot. Put your head under the tap like the others, so that you look fresh and make a good impression.'[265]

A little later they returned to fetch Schreyer but then he was taken back to his cell once more; he was to be taken to Lichterfeld to be shot but the car had not yet arrived. It came a few minutes later; Schreyer describes what then happened: 'I was led down the stairs. A small sports car stood before the door of the prison; two men got in and I was preparing to follow them when a large Mercedes roared up and a Standartenführer from the Leibstandarte jumped out, signalling violently and shouting: "Stop! Stop!" He then told us: "Nothing more is to happen; the Führer has given Hindenburg his word that the shooting is now finally over." '[266]

It was exactly 4 AM on July 2nd, 1934. The Third Reich's first mass murder had happened. Eighty-three men had been done to death[267] – without trial, without a chance to defend themselves, victims of a brutal

Party and gang intrigue. Hitler stated: 'In this hour, I was the supreme judge of the German people.'[268] The Cabinet hastened to give legal coverage to these crimes. On July 3rd the Ministers passed a law submitted by Adolf Hitler; it consisted of the single sentence : 'The measures taken on June 30th and July 1st and 2nd to suppress treasonable activities, are legally considered to have been taken in emergency defence of the State.'[269]

In the Reichswehr barracks there was jubilation; champagne glasses clinked in the officers' messes. When the last SA leaders had been shot, General von Reichenau telegraphed to Patzig, his head of counter-espionage, in erratic English: '*All catched.*'[270] Major-General von Witzleben rubbed his hands saying: 'What a pity. I ought to have been there.'[271] Blomberg, the Defence Minister, issued an order of the day praising the 'soldierly decision' and 'exemplary courage' with which the Führer 'had attacked and crushed the traitors and murderers'.[272] The only discordant voice was that of Captain (Retired) Erwin Planck, previously a Secretary in the Reich Chancellery; he warned General von Fritsch: 'If you look on without lifting a finger, you will meet the same fate sooner or later.'[273]

It was a prophetic remark; von Fritsch fell as the result of a similar intrigue; von Witzleben ended on a meat hook, condemned by the People's Court. Even Lieutenant Schenk Graf von Stauffenberg, who reaped the bitter fruit of youthful enthusiasm in 1944, regarded June 30th, 1934 as no more than the 'lancing of a boil'.[274] But Blomberg soon found his officers' jubilation to be somewhat sinister. Colonel Heinrici observed that Blomberg's notes for a speech to section heads in the Reichswehr Ministry included: 'Troops have not adopted the attitude which one has a right to expect. Unseemly to rejoice over the victims and talk in the mess.'[275]

Blomberg had already realized that the Reichswehr were not the victors of June 30th. Heinrich Himmler's SS had conquered all along the line; they were now free of SA tutelage and their power within the Party was assured. As early as June 9th Party headquarters had announced that the SD was the sole political intelligence organization of the NSDAP;[276] on July 20th Hitler decreed: 'In view of the great services rendered by the SS, particularly in connexion with the events of June 30th, 1934, I hereby promote the SS to the status of independent organization within the framework of the NSDAP.'[277] Hitler also permitted the SS to form armed units,[278] thereby invalidating the Reichswehr's hallowed concept – the whole reason for its feud with the SA – the claim to be the sole bearer of arms within the State. June 30th, 1934 marked a decisive phase in the history of the Third Reich. The SA murders accelerated Hitler's move towards a one-man dictatorship founded on terror; they were the basis of the Göring–Himmler axis, the decisive factor in Nazi gang warfare up to the outbreak of war;[279] they foreshadowed a development which was to be seen in the future in all its frightfulness; the SS had shown that it was prepared to carry out any, literally any, order from Adolf Hitler. At the same time, however, these murders opened a deep rift within the structure of the Party – the deadly enmity between SS and SA.

Thousands of SA men never forgot this day of shame and humiliation when the SA was, in fact, demoted to the status of a prisoner of the SS. Nothing could have been more symbolic than the fact that on Hitler's orders Lutze had to charge SS-Gruppenführer Daluege, of all people, with purging and reorganizing the entire East German SA.[280]

All sections of any political significance in SA Headquarters (the political office and the ministerial office) were abolished and Lutze was forced to issue a decree: 'I charge SS-Gruppenführer Daluege with the execution of this disbandment, including responsibility for all property belonging to SA Supreme Headquarters (office furniture and equipment, cars, etc).'[281]

Not until early August was the SA master in its own house once more. It was then allowed to carry out its own purge. SA-Gruppenführer Böchenhauer formed a special SA court, with investigation commissions accredited to each Gruppe; its task was to discover so-called accomplices of Röhm and, in the words of Hitler's order of August 9th, 1934, to investigate 'all circumstances by which SA leaders have rendered themselves unworthy of membership of the SA corps of leaders, such as mode of life, immorality, place-seeking materialism, embezzlement, drunkenness, snobbery and debauchery.'[282] This inquisition got to work but the nature of its inquiries soon changed; instead of an organization for hunting out Röhm's accomplices it found itself turning into a collecting centre for reports on SS behaviour on and after June 30th.

A stream of complaints testified to SA indignation, rage, hatred and revulsion. Sturmführer Hermann Baecke, who had belonged to the SA since 1925, stated: 'I have, after all, always fought for justice and honesty; now I am threatened with arrest. We, the longstanding SA men, are now no longer thought worthy to be called an élite, although for years we have battled with the Communists and the Reichsbanner, been spat upon, had our clothes torn off us by the police and been thrown out of our jobs; and now we have reached the stage where we are being threatened all over again.'[283] On July 28th, the Commander of SA Standarte 168 reported: 'I issued strict orders to my people to comply with the orders of the SS under all circumstances. The treatment of the older SA men by the SS, many of whom were mere boys, was shattering.'[284]

Scharführer Felten of Offenbach reported indignantly: 'My men complain to me of the behaviour of SS patrols passing up and down the Kaiserstrasse . . . an SS probationer passed me on a bicycle calling out, "Can't you salute – you've not woken up yet!" When I ordered him to get off his bicycle, he took no notice and rode off as quickly as he could. Had he got off, I would have made it clear to the young fellow in no uncertain terms how to behave to a wartime comrade of Adolf Hitler, longstanding Party member and an SA man entitled to the badge of honour.'[285]

The SS had earned itself the undying hatred of the SA. The two Nazi Party armies were never to be reconciled. From now on SA and SS were embattled against one another in a silent, unseen war. During the night of August 17th–18th, 1935, Viktor Lutze threw down the challenge and declared war on the SS. He was in the restaurant of the Preussenhof Hotel, Stettin, with twenty of his SA comrades, three SS Commanders and innumerable glasses of beer.[286]

'One of these days,' Lutze shouted 'the unjust and arbitrary action of June 30th will be avenged. The German is a fair-minded being and this violation of justice will one day rebound upon those responsible and their end will be a bitter one.' SS-Standartenführer Robert Schulz of SD-Oberabschnitt North could barely conceal his rage and he hissed back: 'Unfortunately we did not exterminate them root and branch. We were far too indulgent. Some people who escaped and are still in the SA, knew perfectly well what Röhm was up to.'

Lutze threw back that the SS were in no position to play the moralist, for they were living in a glass house themselves. The three SS men flew into a rage but Lutze rode through their protest shouting: 'Who was always urging Röhm to live it up? Who was always swearing loyalty to him? Was it some old SA commander or any SA commander at all? Shall I tell you who it was?' (The subsequent report to Berlin from SD-Oberabschnitt North stated: 'If Standartenführer Schulz had not once more intervened at this point, we should have had the painful experience of hearing Lutze say: "The Reichsführer-SS!" ') But Lutze was not to be stopped; he went on: 'Who has been up to their necks in what Röhm was supposed to have done. Was it the SA? These bestialities were not the SA's work or, at least, not the SA alone; the other side was much worse. Shall I give you names? I can produce names straight away!'

Schulz interjected hurriedly: 'Chief-of-Staff, it's nearly two o'clock.

We'd better go to bed.' He summoned the waiter and called for the bill. The party broke up. Viktor Lutze swayed out but he had the last word and it was loud enough for everyone to hear: 'I shall go on saying this, even if I am dismissed tomorrow and sent to a concentration camp.'[287]

7

THE ORDER OF THE SS

A NUMBER of officers, industrialists, scholars and landowners in Munich suddenly received an invitation to an address by the Reichsführer-SS: they attended, some curious, some hesitant and some suspicious. In recent months Germany's upper classes had become used to hearing the Nazi leaders revile them as decadent and Jew-ridden, but on this occasion no word of criticism came from Himmler. Instead of the anticipated offensive, the head of the SS called upon his audience to 'assist in directing into the SS all the various currents of tradition'.

Every state, he argued, required an élite. In National-Socialist Germany that élite was the SS, but it could only fulfil this function if 'its members brought to the social requirements of the present day the genuine military tradition, the distinctive outlook, bearing and breeding of the German nobility, and the creative efficiency of the industrialist, on a basis of racial selection.' One of the audience later told Felix Kersten, Himmler's masseur, that the address had 'evoked general astonishment'. This was an unusual line for a Nazi to take, and as a result practically the entire audience joined the SS.[1]

This incident, which occurred in Year One of the National-Socialist era, showed that Himmler had no lack of ability in presenting his SS to the outside world. More than any other National-Socialist organization the SS reputedly stood on a higher level than that of the plebeian brown-shirted foot-soldiers. Walter Schellenberg later recalled that 'the better type of people' preferred to join the SS rather than one of the other Party formations;[2] in 1946 Dr Grober, the Catholic Archbishop of Freiburg, admitted that 'we in Freiburg considered the SS to be the most respectable of the Party organizations.'[3]

Many Germans could see nothing wrong in the SS claim to be an élite;

every period had had its élite and in the long run no State, whether democracy or dictatorship, could do without one; looking at the Anglo-Saxon democratic 'establishments' and the Soviet system's party hierarchy, the Germans were convinced that the more firmly a régime was based on a governing social class, the more crisis-proof it would be.

The Weimar Republic had just demonstrated the fate awaiting a State in which selectivity was not recognized. The SS élitist propaganda therefore sounded attractive, particularly when Himmler presented it in the conservative romanticist terms so dear to Germans. Even in 1934 Hitler's biographer Konrad Heiden, who was certainly no Nazi, thought that in contrast to the 'revolutionary SA' the SS stood for conservatism.[4] Even the murders of June 30th, 1934 did not affect the respect in which Himmler's Order was held by the man in the street. Relief at the disappearance of the SA informer, who had ruled the streets since the Nazi seizure of power, was more potent than the traditional sense of right and wrong.

'Liberation of our people from the rule of second-raters is a prize worth considerable sacrifice,' announced the *Frankfurter Zeitung*,[5] echoing the thoughts of practically every German. The murders of the régime's bourgeois opponents and the slaughter of the SA leaders were forgotten. The nation lived in hope that the ordinary citizen's peace and quiet would never again be disturbed by the brown-shirted thugs. The Germans did not yet recognize the 'devil's masquerade';[6] they did not yet realize that on the road to absolute dictatorship maintenance of law and order can conceal an assault on civil liberties and historical necessity can be used as cover for the 'plausible crime'.

Moreover this so-called crime of necessity of summer 1934 masqueraded in the costume dearest to the German heart, a uniform – and a becoming one too. Discreetly suppressing the plebeian brown, the SS was now arrayed from head to foot in black – black cap with black chinstrap and silver Death's-Head, black tunic over a brown shirt with black leather buttons and black tie, black Sam Browne belt, black breeches and black jackboots.[7]

The designers of this uniform had left no stone unturned to tickle the imagination of the hierarchically-minded Germans, introducing all sorts of mysterious marks and badges. An 'old fighter' wore an aluminium chevron on his right forearm, a member of the notorious Sicherheitsdienst a diamond enclosing the letters 'SD'. The shoulder tabs had subtle distinctions. Officers of the Hauptsturmführer and below carried six parallel silvered threads on the shoulder tab; from Sturmbannführer to Standartenführer three plaited silver threads and from Oberführer upwards three double-plaited silver threads. The collar patches were even more complicated; senior officers carried the badges of their rank on both collar patches – for a Standartenführer one oak leaf, for an Oberführer two oak leaves, for a Brigadeführer two oak leaves and a star, for a Gruppenführer three oak leaves, for an Obergruppenführer three oak leaves and a star, and finally for the Reichsführer three oak leaves enclosed in an oak-leaf wreath.[8]

All this external flummery was intended to demonstrate that in the SS an élite was forming, an Imperial Guard of strict puritans, guardians of the welfare of the State; the purpose was to symbolize their spirit of obedience, which in Himmler's words 'hesitates not for a single instant, but executes unquestioningly any order coming from the Führer.'[9]

To admit such members of the upper classes as were willing to conform, Himmler opened the doors of his SS wide. The primary requirements in the SS, particularly in the special branches such as the SD, the Totenkopfverbände [Death's-Head Formations] and the Verfügungstruppe [General Service SS Troops], were money and officer material, and they could come only from one source – the old-established ruling-class élite – the nobility, the world of commerce and the financiers. Himmler threw himself so wholeheartedly into the business of creating a reserve of personnel for the various branches of his growing empire that initially he hardly perceived that he was contradicting himself. For years the Imperial Guard of National-Socialism had preached the law of selection on racial and biological grounds; now, however, the SS began to lure into its ranks sections of the population possessing qualities which appeared in no dictionary of Nazi racial philosophy – prestige, money and an aptitude for command born of generations spent in positions of authority.

From the social point of view the SS picture now changed radically; men of an entirely new class of society streamed in. The original SS had consisted primarily of ex-Free Corps men, intellectuals whose careers had been cut short by the economic crisis, and the lower-middle-class Party veterans. Of this pre-1933 SS only a tiny band of leaders remained, though admittedly they occupied the decisive posts right up to the end of the Third Reich. By the outbreak of World War II, however, ninety per cent of the old SS had been pensioned off.[10]

Only ten per cent of the old hands survived the influx of newcomers which poured into Himmler's organization from March 1933 onwards (they were greeted with suspicion by the veterans who referred to them as 'March Violets'). The first arrivals were from the aristocracy. Even before the Nazi seizure of power certain great names had been added to the SS list; they included the hereditary Grand Duke of Mecklenburg, the hereditary Prince zu Waldeck und Pyrmont, Prince Christof and

Prince Wilhelm of Hesse, Count Bassewitz-Behr and von Pfeil-Burghauss, Reichsfreiherr von Tüngen and Freiherren von Geyr, von Reitzenstein and von Malsen-Ponickau.[11]

In spring 1933 came a further infusion of blue blood. Prinz von Hohenzollern-Emden of the House of Sigmaringen and Count von der Schulenburg joined the SS; its seniority list began to resemble a series of pages from the Almanach de Gotha. Hardly one of the famous names in Prussian/German military history was missing; they were all there – von Daniels, Count von Rödern, Count Strachwitz, Freiherr von der Goltz, von der Planitz, von Keudell, von Alvensleben, von Podbielski, von Treuenfeld, von Nathusius, and so on and so on.[12] Many of the senior SS posts were occupied by the nobility (in 1938 18.7 per cent of SS-Obergruppenführer, 9.8 per cent of SS-Gruppenführer, 14.3 per cent of SS-Brigadeführer, 8.8 per cent of SS-Oberführer and 8.4 per cent of SS-Standartenführer[13] were from this social group).

After the aristocracy came the sons of the upper middle class. In contrast to their predecessors they were men of the twentieth century, mostly intellectuals who had completed their academic training (the majority in law); emotionally and intellectually the vast majority were products of the German Youth Movement. Almost all of them drifted into the SD, giving it a legalistic and intellectual atmosphere foreign both to the front-line-soldier Socialism of the SS veterans and the vulgar lower-middle-class National-Socialism of the early days. Men like Walter Schellenberg, Reinhard Höhn, Franz Six and Otto Ohlendorf were all university-trained with an educated upper-middle-class background; they were typical of the hard-boiled SS technocrats, the 'social engineers' who provided the Führer dictatorship with the necessary veneer of legality and organization; they were astute realists with no ideology other than that of power, but they were also spiritually rootless and uninhibited by any of the generally accepted norms of conduct.

Allied to the SD intellectuals was a group of young upper-middle-class economists, who manned the staffs of the SS economic enterprises. They were barely distinguishable from the technocrats to be found today in the management of West German industry. They were even less interested in SS ideology than their SD counterparts; in Himmler's economic undertakings they saw simply the prospect of an exceptionally secure career. The personal file of Standartenführer Dr Walter Salpeter, one of the up-and-coming men in the SS economic empire, contains a report by his superiors to the effect that he would do well 'to temper his ambition with National-Socialist ideology';[14] the comment was equally applicable to the majority of these people.

A further group of newcomers came from the middle-class section of the Reichswehr officer corps, bringing further shades of difference into the personnel pattern of an already heterogeneous SS. These officers mostly joined the Verfügungstruppe (VT) which had been formed in 1934. They very soon overshadowed the original SS soldiers, who were mostly sergeant-major types like Sepp Dietrich. It is difficult to generalize on the subject of these new professional officers; Paul Hausser, for instance, the Inspector of the VT, had been a Reichswehr Lieutenant-General and a leader of the Stahlhelm; he was a dyed-in-the-wool monarchist and so naturally gave the VT a marked conservative twist;[15] on the other hand reformers like Major Felix Steiner from East Prussia and the ex-Air Force Lieutenant Wilhelm Bittrich looked upon the VT as a suitable field for military experimentation.[16]

The farming community also provided its SS men. The rank and file of the Totenkopfverbände, which provided the guards for the concentration camps, were mostly drawn from the younger generation of the peasantry who could see no future on the land. The more intelligent farmers' sons, on the other hand, could try their luck in the SS Cadet Schools in Bad Tölz and Braunschweig; they offered what the Reichswehr did not – an officer's career for those without educational qualifications.[17]

As if the SS was not heterogeneous enough already, Himmler now produced a new form of SS membership, the honorary commander. Influential officials, Party functionaries, scientists and diplomats were given SS ranks and the right to wear the corresponding SS uniform; these honorary commanders were mostly carried on the strength of the Reichsführer's staff; they did not have to do a single hour's duty and had no powers of command. Himmler clearly hoped that such honorary titles would make the SS socially acceptable and influence the recipients in its favour – a fantastic notion believed in by no one except Himmler, the post-1945 de-Nazifiers and one or two historians.[18]

The fact that an anti-Nazi diplomat like Ernst Freiherr von Weizsäcker, the Permanent Secretary in the Foreign Ministry, carried the rank of an SS-Brigadeführer,[19] and that a bitter enemy of Hitler such as Gauleiter Forster that of an SS-Obergruppenführer,[20] has led certain of the less perspicacious historians to see a concealed member of Himmler's State and Party fifth column in everyone who wore the black uniform. In fact the honorary commanders were no more supporters of Himmler than was Signora Ciano, the wife of the Italian Foreign Minister,[21] on whom Himmler also bestowed honorary SS membership.

The honorary rank of SS-Oberführer did not prevent Rudolf Diels, the Regierungspräsident of Cologne, from resisting any interference by the Gestapo in his internal administration;[22] in 1943 Himmler even attempted disciplinary action against another honorary commander, the military administrator SS-Gruppenführer Eggert Reeder, who openly refused to allow the SS to interfere in his business in any way.[23] SS uniform covered a number of curiosities: Konrad Henlein, the Sudeten German Party Leader, was made an SS-Gruppenführer because the SD had failed to unseat him;[24] Martin Bormann, another SS honorary commander, put many spokes in the wheel of the Inland-SD [Internal Affairs Section of the SD].[25]

Nevertheless Himmler continued to canvass for new recruits for his empire. At times he even incorporated entire organizations into the SS if he thought that they would give him the entrée to established society. He already had a foot in the door of rural society, for instance – via the Equestrian Association.

Himmler was determined to capture this stronghold of German conservatism. Some of the Equestrian Associations did indeed join the SA, but by far the greater number reinsured via the SS; all the Equestrian Associations in the main breeding areas – East Prussia, Holstein, Oldenburg, Hanover and Westphalia – put on SS uniform.[26] Himmler owed many social successes to his SS horsemen; in 1937 SS riders won all the German horse championships.[27]

Himmler had to pay dearly for these victories. He had promised the Equestrian Associations that he would accept any of their members into the SS regardless of their political views.[28] This led to grumbling on the part of the SS 'old fighters' who said that, in spite of their SS uniform, the horsemen were still reactionary German nationalists. *Das Schwarze Korps*, the SS newspaper, adopted a menacing tone towards these newcomers: 'In the first place, they must cultivate the National-Socialist spirit. In other words all those . . . qualities which the SS has cultivated over the years since its formation and by which it has proved itself – loyalty to the Führer, readiness to obey, and discipline.'[29] The majority of the SS riders knuckled under but a few had other ideas; in 1933 eleven of them refused to take the SS oath and were dispatched to a concentration camp.[30] Anton Freiherr von Hohberg und Buchwald, the leading SS horseman in East Prussia, was shot by SS men on July 2nd, 1934 for giving away SS secrets to the Reichswehr;[31] ten years later Himmler had the head of his remount office, SS-Sturmbannführer Hans-Viktor Graf von Salviati, another show-ring rider, executed for plotting against Hitler.[32]

The pact with the Equestrian Associations had given Himmler the entrée to rural society. It was followed by an alliance with the leaders of the semi-monarchist ex-servicemen's association 'Kyffhäuser' and this allowed him to tap the reservoir of ex-soldiers. The Central Council and local leaders of Kyffhäuser joined the SS as a body.[33] But when the 'old fighters' saw General Wilhelm Reinhard, who was still loyal to the Kaiser, joining the SS at the head of the Kyffhaüser leaders,[34] they felt they could understand Himmler no longer; for Reinhard was one of those reactionary military men stigmatized by the *Schwarze Korps* in 1935 as typifying that 'middle-class nationalist arrogance which excludes the worker from society and must give him the impression that he is regarded as a third-class citizen.'[35]

The height of irony was reached when the ultra-conservative General Rüdiger Graf von der Goltz, a friend of Reinhard's who had fought with him in the Kapp Putsch of 1920, was accepted as an SS-Obergruppenführer just after being reviled by the *Schwarze Korps* as the worst type of reactionary.[36] Even as late as 1941 Franz Xaver Schwarz, the Reich Party Treasurer and an SS man of long standing, could not bear to see a monarchist like Reinhard in SS uniform; he said: 'I regret that such a man should be an SS-Gruppenführer, should wear this fine uniform and yet basically remain exactly his old self.[37]

The SS veterans reacted similarly to the survivors of Ehrhardt's Naval Brigade, whom Himmler also lured into the SS. They thought back to SS Order No 53 of October 10th, 1931 when Himmler had warned against Ehrhardt's sinister machinations, saying that he was 'trying to disrupt the NSDAP' by infiltrating his supporters into Party organizations.[38] Now Himmler wished to accept the Ehrhardt Brigade into the SS as a body. Details of the arrangement had already been worked out when the headstrong Captain torpedoed the whole project by making the strangest speech ever delivered by an SS candidate.

The Brigade was drawn up for its last parade with a number of Nazi dignitaries present. In his farewell address Ehrhardt shouted: 'Men of my Brigade, you know that only rather late in the day and after numerous and prolonged battles have we declared ourselves ready to join a formation of the new Reich. And I welcome that. For only in battle does one learn to know one's enemy and respect or despise him. And thus we shall continue in future.' The Nazi leaders were so put out that Himmler abandoned the Ehrhardt Brigade and only individual members joined the SS; they included Hartmuth Plaas, Ehrhardt's ex-aide, who became an SS-Sturmbannführer but in 1944 landed in a concentration camp as an accomplice of the July 20th plot.[39]

New recruits for the SS, however, were not the only objects of Himmler's canvassing; he was equally short of money for the increasingly expensive SS formations. Germany's captains of industry and managerial class, however, were only too ready to support the Reichsführer.

They formed themselves into a club known as the 'Friends of the Reichsführer-SS', whose members, for a variety of reasons, thought it best to be on Heinrich Himmler's side. The club included opportunists such as Dr Heinrich Bütesfisch from the Board of IG Farben, convinced Nazis like the Propaganda Ministry Secretary Dr Werner Naumann, worried businessmen such as Friedrich Flick and disguised anti-Nazis such as Hans Walz, a Director of Robert Bosch; but they all had one thing in common – they gave money to the SS.[40]

The 'Friends' were an offshoot of the 'Planning Committee for Economic Problems' formed by Wilhelm Keppler, Hitler's Economic Adviser, in summer 1932; the committee was intended to give expert advice to Germany's future masters and it included prominent economists and financiers, among them Schacht, the President of the Reichsbank, Albert Vögler, Chairman of Vereinigte Stahlwerke and Kurt Freiherr von Schröder, a Cologne banker.[41] The economic advice idea came to nothing, but Keppler's young assistant, SS-Hauptsturmführer Fritz Kranefuss, persuaded Himmler to take an interest in the Club and it came under the Reichsführer's wing from mid-1934.[42]

Schacht and Vögler resigned[43] but in their place many firms joined the 'Friends of the Reichsführer-SS'. Practically every major concern lived in the hope that by sending a member of their Board to the 'Friends' meetings and paying contributions to the SS, they might protect their own interests from Nazi encroachment. The membership list of the 'Friends' read like an extract from the business register. It included representatives from: the Deutsche Bank, the Dresdner Bank, the Commerz und Privat Bank, the Reichsbank and the J.H. Stein Bank, Norddeutscher Lloyd and Hamburg-America Shipping Companies, German-American Petroleum and Continental Oil Companies, the Dr August Oetker Food Production Company and great concerns such as IG Farben, the Mitteldeutsche Stahlwerke, Siemens-Schuckert, Portland Cement, Rheinmetall-Borsig and the Reichswerke 'Hermann Göring'.[44]

Kranefuss, the Secretary of the 'Friends', called regular meetings at which senior SS leaders were always present. Initially the club met twice a year, at the Party Rally in Nuremberg and the oath-taking ceremony for the Verfügungstruppe in Munich; later, however, members met monthly at the 'Haus der Flieger' in Berlin.[45] From 1936 onwards Himmler required regular financial contributions from all these gentlemen. He pointed out to Schröder, the 'Friends' banker, that money should be made available 'for the cultural, social and charitable activities of the SS'[46] and the banker rushed off to do his bidding.[47]

The firms concerned agreed and shortly thereafter contributions began to flow into General Account S in the J.H. Stein Bank in which Schröder was a member of the Board. Total annual contributions were 1,000,000 marks. These were paid into a special SS Account R at the Dresdner Bank on which Karl Wolff, Himmler's senior aide, was authorized to draw cheques.[48] Himmler gave proof of his gratitude. A shower of SS titles descended on the members of the 'Friends'; of the thirty-two non-SS members fifteen were nominated honorary SS commanders.[49]

To those averse to wearing the Death's-Head uniform, the SS offered an even less onerous and cheaper form of membership. The rapacious SS was the only Party formation permitted by Hitler to run its own finances and recruit 'sponsoring members' [Fördernde Mitglieder – FM].[50] They were merely sympathizers who gave financial support to the SS but did not join it. They did not have to take an oath to Hitler and were not subject to SS orders.[51] Every SS-Standarte had a sponsoring members' organization and it was the duty of each SS man to recruit at least one member. On March 1st, 1933 Kurt Wittje, an SS Commander, explained: 'The sponsoring members' organization is the only sure source of SS income and must constitute the guarantee for further expansion of the SS economy.'[52] After the seizure of power, the SS laid even greater emphasis on its propaganda to sponsoring members, calculating that many Germans would rather join this amorphous organization than any other Party formation. The letters FM protected the wearer from many Nazi impositions; moreover a sponsoring member did not necessarily have to belong to the Party and could fix the amount of his financial contribution himself; the minimum was one mark per year.[53]

In addition Himmler developed other gimmicks to attract members. He designed a silver FM badge, not obtainable on the open market; it consisted of an oval containing the swastika, the runic double-S and the letters FM. He started an FM periodical which reached a circulation of 365,000 by the outbreak of war; to every citizen interested in becoming a sponsoring member, he dispatched the motto:

Es ist eine Ehre, SS-Mann zu sein,	It is an honour to be an SS man
Es ist eine Ehre, Förderndes Mitglied zu sein;	It is an honour to be an honorary member;
Tue jeder weiter seine Pflicht,	Let each continue to do his duty
Wir SS-Männer und ihr Fördernder Mitglieder,	We SS men and their honorary members
Jeder an seiner Stelle;	Each in his appointed place
Und Deutschland wird wieder gross werden.	And Germany will be great once more.[54]

The propaganda drive was unexpectedly successful. Soon Himmler's shadowy army of sponsoring members outnumbered the active SS and money came pouring into the empty SS coffers; in 1932 there were 13,217 honorary members contributing 17,000 marks, in 1933 167,272 members contributing 357,000 marks and in 1934 342,492 members contributing 581,000 marks.[55]

Nevertheless there could be no real solidarity in an SS composed of such heterogeneous elements. The SS veterans suddenly saw in SS uniform men who clearly did not know the ABC of National-Socialism. The SS idea had become all things to all men. Schwarz, the Party Treasurer, no longer liked wearing his SS uniform because, according to Gruppenführer Berger, 'Too many people were in SS uniform and, still worse, many SS commanders had neither moral nor actual right to it.'[56] The uniform and badges of rank by no means meant that a man was an SS member at heart. Heinrich Müller, for instance, the future Head of the Gestapo, wore the 'old fighter' chevron on his sleeve,[57] but on January 4th, 1937 the Munich/Upper Bavaria Party Headquarters labelled him 'ambitious and self-seeking', 'no Party Comrade', a man who had 'never worked actively within the Party' and therefore 'had rendered no services to the National Revival'.[58]

The Reichssicherheitshauptamt [Central Security Department – RSHA] personnel section noted that Dr Heinrich Bütefisch was an ex-Freemason and 'the complete businessman'. His 'whole mentality was geared to international cooperation; he therefore naturally looked upon his firm as a state within the State, with its own rules and privileges.'[59] An SS internal report dated August 1937 stated that Oberführer Freiherr von Schröder, the banker, had been connected with the Rhineland separatists, was a friend of Konrad Adenauer and therefore was 'certainly no activist in the SS sense'.[60]

Himmler himself gradually began to see the danger threatening the internal unity of the SS. In 1937 he admitted that 'numbers presented a danger' since a vast number of men had entered the SS 'who were neither sincere nor idealistic'.[61] Himmler thought that he had overcome this danger but in fact it persisted to the very end of the SS.

In mid-1933, however, he called a temporary halt to SS recruiting: 'I said, "No one else will be accepted" and then from 1933 to 1935 we combed all the useless material out from among the newcomers.'[62] In these two years 60,000 SS men were expelled.[63] The primary victims of Himmler's clean-up were the patent opportunists, alcoholics, homosexuals and men of uncertain Aryan background; even some of the old thugs went by the board – they may have been good enough to clout down opponents during the 'struggle period' but now they did not fit into the Praetorian Guard picture. In addition Himmler would no longer tolerate the professional unemployed, saying: 'A man who, without valid reason, changes his job for the third time, we shall expel. We have no use for loafers.'[64]

Himmler dealt particularly severely with homosexuality, which he regarded as a personal insult. In his eyes it was a crime worthy of death and no SS homosexual escaped his wrath – not even 'old fighters' like Gruppenführer Kurt Wittje, the first head of the SS-Hauptamt [SS Head Department].[65] On May 22nd, 1935 the *Schwarze Korps* reported that Wittje had been relieved of his post 'because of illness'; Himmler said in a speech that he had released Wittje 'to his regret' and 'with a heavy heart' and that he hoped Wittje 'would be fully available again in the foreseeable future'.[66] The SA commanders, with the SS homilies about Röhm's homosexuality still ringing in their ears, knew what Wittje's real disease was. Lutze, the Head of the SA, remarked sneeringly: 'It has taken time enough and pressure from all sides to get rid of Wittje.'[67] In 1937 Himmler insisted that every SS homosexual be expelled and handed over to the courts; after serving his prison sentence 'he will be sent on my instructions to a concentration camp and shot while attempting to escape.'[68]

The discovery of any drop of non-Aryan blood in SS veins invariably excited Himmler. From June 1st, 1935, every SS commander from the rank of Sturmführer upwards had to show proof that neither he nor his wife had Jewish ancestors; from October 1st, 1935 the requirement was extended to include Oberscharführer and Hauptscharführer [Warrant Officers] and shortly thereafter every SS man.[69] Everyone had to be able to produce an 'Aryan' family tree going back, in the case of other ranks to 1800 and in the case of officers or officer cadets to 1750;[70] the SS men, including even old wartime comrades of Himmler, spread far and wide searching, often for years, through Church registers and other old documents. If Himmler detected any trace of Jewish origin in a man's family tree, he acted ruthlessly – at least in so far as the lower ranks were concerned. Anyone who found that he had a drop of Jewish blood in his veins had to report to his superior officer forthwith and request release from the SS; if he did not, the SS Court took action and decreed expulsion.[71]

Himmler was much more lenient, however, in the case of the senior ranks. The wife of a certain Obersturmführer M (as he is referred to in the SS files) had a Jewish grandparent; M was allowed to remain in the SS provided his wife agreed to have no more children and he undertook not to send his sons into the SS.[72] As time went on Himmler's caution increased with the rank of the evil-doer. Gruppenführer Walter

Krüger was treated even better than Obersturmführer M. During the war Krüger's daughter became engaged to SS-Sturmbannführer Klingenberg; it was then suddenly discovered that on Frau Krüger's side there was, in Himmler's words, 'a full-Jewish ancestor in 1711'. Klingenberg was forbidden to marry the daughter but Krüger's son was allowed to join the Leibstandarte.[73]

Nevertheless the expulsion of 60,000 men could not in itself guarantee the SS the necessary internal solidarity. Himmler realized that what the SS lacked was a corps spirit to hold it together; it must also have rigid organization, stricter conditions of entry and a code of honour to which every SS man would feel himself bound. Hitherto the SS had been no more than an organization; now it was to become an Order. Himmler had discovered from history an example on which he proposed to model his Order – the Jesuits. It was no accident that Karl Ernst, the murdered SA leader, had frequently ridiculed him as the 'Black Jesuit'; even Hitler referred to the Head of the SS as 'my Ignatius Loyola'.[74] In the Jesuits Himmler had found what he regarded as the central feature of any Order's mentality – the doctrine of obedience and the cult of organization. Schellenberg confirms that Himmler had built up the SS organization 'on the principles of the Order of Jesuits'.[75]

The similarity between the two was in fact astounding; each was an Order conferring enormous privileges on its members, subject to no temporal jurisdiction, protected by the strictest conditions of entry and held together by an oath of absolute blind obedience to its lord and master – Pope or Führer. The history of the two organizations showed equally remarkable parallels; in the seventeenth century the Jesuits founded their own state among the Paraguay Indians – it recognized no temporal sovereignty; during the Second World War the SS dreamed of an SS State outside the borders of the Greater German Reich – the SS State of Burgundy with its own Government, Army, Administration and Legation in Berlin.[76] Even the crises which each faced were similar. There were always enemies of the Jesuits within the Catholic Church and enemies of the SS within the Party. The Jesuits debated whether they should be the sword of the counter-reformation or an example of monastic piety; the SS never made up its mind whether to be National-Socialism's ideological leavening or the régime's policeman.

The higher organization of the SS Order was also reminiscent of that of the Jesuits. Ignatius Loyola (1491–1566), the founder of the Jesuits, organized a kind of Government of his Order with a General at its head, advised by four assistants.[77] Himmler followed the same system when he set about organizing a central command structure for the SS. In place of the Jesuit General's four assistants, the Reichsführer-SS was assisted by a number of Hauptämter [Departments]; first came the Private Office under Brigadeführer Karl Wolff, the highest SS operational staff, re-named 'Personal Staff Reichsführer-SS' in 1936 and raised to Hauptamt status in 1939; next came the SD-Hauptamt under Gruppenführer Reinhard Heydrich, the directing organization for the Security Service; third come the 'Rasse- und Siedlungshauptamt' [Race and Re-settlement Office – RuSHA] under Obergruppenführer Walther Darré, who was also Reich Minister of Agriculture (it was the guardian of the ideological and racial purity of all SS members); fourth came the head of the SS-Gericht [SS Court], Brigadeführer Paul Scharfe, responsible for special SS jurisdiction – also raised to Hauptamt status in 1939; finally, there was the SS-Hauptamt under Wittje's successor, August Heissmeyer, the administrative centre for all SS units with the exception of the SD.[78]

The latter, the SS-Hauptamt, later developed into an over-organized colossus, dealing not only with the old SS (re-named 'Allgemeine SS' in mid-1934 to distinguish it from the special formations)[79] but also with the Totenkopfverbände and the Verfügungstruppe. When the SS-Hauptamt additionally became responsible for the Cavalry Standarten and the entire financial administration of the SS, it was reorganized.

By 1942, four new Hauptämter had come into being, three of them taking over certain responsibilities from the SS-Hauptamt which, in its reduced form, was placed under Gruppenführer Gottlob Berger.[80] The new offices were: the Führungshauptamt [Operational Department] under Gruppenführer Hans Jüttner, the headquarters of the Waffen-SS; the Personalhauptamt [Personnel Department] under Gruppenführer Maximilian van Herff, dealing with all SS Commanders' personal details and with appointments in the Allgemeine SS; the Wirtschaft- und Verwaltungschauptamt [Economic and Administrative Department – WVHA] under Gruppenführer Oswald Pohl, dealing with all SS economic undertakings and the administration of the concentration camps; finally, also of Hauptamt status, there was the 'Office of SS-Obergruppenführer Heissmeyer', the controlling authority for the political education institutions.[81]

These central authorities supervised the closely coordinated structure – Oberabschnitte, Abschnitte, Standarten, Sturmbanne and Stürme – which comprised the Great SS army. Hauptamt representatives were continually checking the discipline and efficiency of SS units. The emissaries of the Reichsführer-SS arrived unannounced: during interviews, frequently of a highly embarrassing nature, they inquired into individual commanders' knowledge of regulations, checked unit diaries and reported on the energy and enthusiasm of even the most senior officers.[82]

Gruppenführer Zech of the SS-Hauptamt, for instance, commented adversely: 'On my inspections I have noted that in almost every case Sturmbannführer and Standartenführer do not attend their troops' normal duty periods with sufficient frequency.' He continued that the official diaries must 'show exactly what the SS commander has done with and for his troops each day' and 'must be written up exactly as the regulations lay down.'[83] SS units frequently regarded the arrival of one of these spies from Berlin with unconcealed apprehension, as an office note by Zech shows: 'The word supervise should not be used. Our commanders do not supervise our Stürme; they inspect them.'[84]

Himmler was now free to turn to a further point in his programme. Instead of the heterogeneous types of mankind now composing the SS he wished to concentrate on the standardized SS man, the nordicized master-race type who, in Himmler's scheme of things, was to be typical of the SS. The RuSHA was ordered to work out new and stricter conditions for acceptance into the SS.[85] Hauptsturmführer Professor Bruno K. Schultz submitted a set of criteria to the RuSHA Racial Commission, before which all SS applicants had to appear for their final acceptance test.[86]

The Professor listed his criteria under three headings – racial appearance, physical condition and general bearing (there was no mention of intellectual attainments). Since Himmler was a believer in the theory developed by the National-Socialist demographic policy experts that the master race must consist solely of blond, blue-eyed Nordic beings and the SS must gradually be purged of representatives of other races, Schultz angled his scale of values on the Nordic type of mankind. He listed five racial groupings: 'pure Nordic', 'predominantly Nordic or Phalic', harmonious bastard with 'slight Alpine, Dinaric or Mediterranean characteristics', bastards of predominantly East-Baltic or Alpine origin, and bastards of extra-European origin.[87]

Only men falling into the first three categories were considered worthy of acceptance into the SS. Even this involved some concession on Himmler's part, for he considered that in a few years all important posts in the State should be held only by blond men and in a maximum of 120 years the entire German people should once more be pure-blooded Nordic Germans in appearance.[88] Nevertheless even racial background was not everything. Schultz drew up a list of nine headings as a guide for the physical examination of SS candidates to ensure that they were well-proportioned, for the Reichsführer had an aversion to 'people who might be tall but were in some way disproportioned.'[89]

With the fastidious precision of the expert poultry breeder Himmler insisted that the SS man must be 'of well-proportioned build; for instance there must be no disproportion between the lower leg and the thigh or between the legs and the body; otherwise an exceptional bodily effort is required to carry out long marches.'[90]

Schultz therefore only accepted applicants who fell into the first four categories of his nine-point schedule ('ideal stature', 'excellent', 'very good', 'good'); the bottom three categories were rejected but those in categories five and six were given another chance. In spite of their 'inadequate' physique they were allowed to prove by their bearing that they were true Nordic men. Himmler laid down: 'The point is that in his attitude to discipline the man should not behave like an underling, that his gait, his hands, everything, should correspond to the ideal which we set ourselves.'[91]

Once the candidate had successfully surmounted the hurdle of the racial commission, he entered upon a phase of prolonged examination and testing. Here again Himmler had copied the Jesuits; just as the Jesuit novices had to undergo two years of severe tests and exercises before taking the three vows of poverty, chastity and obedience and entering the ranks of the scholastics, so the SS candidate had to undergo manifold tests before he was allowed to swear the 'kith and kin oath' [Sippeneid] and call himself an SS man.

The various phases of the SS novitiate were geared to the great festivals of the National-Socialist calendar. On November 9th, the anniversary of the Munich Beer Cellar Putsch, the SS candidate, aged eighteen, was accepted as an applicant and allowed to wear an SS uniform without collar patches. On January 30th, the day of the Nazi seizure of power, the candidate became a cadet and was given a provisional SS pass. The culminating point was April 20th, Hitler's birthday, when the cadet received his collar patches and his permanent SS pass and when he swore his oath to his Führer:

Ich schwöre Dir, Adolf Hitler,	I swear to thee Adolf Hitler,
Als Führer und Kanzler des Deutschen Reiches	As Führer and Chancellor of the German Reich
Treue und Tapferkeit.	Loyalty and Bravery.
Ich gelobe Dir und den von Dir bestimmten Vorgesetzten	I vow to thee and to the superiors whom thou shalt appoint
Gehorsam bis in den Tod,	Obedience unto death
So wahr mir Gott helfe.	So help me God.[92]

The oath-taking ceremony was intended to give the newcomer a taste of that mystic bond uniting the charismatic Führer with his black-uniformed acolytes. Special ceremony attended the oath-swearing by the Verfügungstruppe; unlike the Allgemeine-SS, the VT took the oath at 10 PM every November 9th in Hitler's presence and at the National-Socialist shrine in Munich. Emil Helfferich, a member of the 'Friends of the Reichsführer-SS', still remembers with emotion 'the midnight oath-taking ceremony before the Feldherrnhalle in Munich. Splendid young men, serious of face, exemplary in bearing and turnout. An élite. Tears came to my eyes, when, by the light of the torches, thousands of voices repeated the oath in chorus. It was like a prayer'.[93]

For the Allgemeine-SS candidate, even this did not end the test. Between the oath-taking ceremony on April 20th and entry into service on October 1st, he had to obtain the Reich Sport Badge and learn the SS catechism[94] which, with its interplay of question and answer, was intended to initiate the candidate further into the SS Hitler cult. For instance: 'Why do we believe in Germany and the Führer?' Answer: 'Because we believe in God, we believe in Germany which He created in His world and in the Führer, Adolf Hitler, whom He has sent us.' Question: 'Whom must we primarily serve?' Answer: 'Our people and our Führer, Adolf Hitler.' Question: 'Why do you obey?' Answer: 'From inner conviction, from belief in Germany, in the Führer, in the Movement and in the SS, and from loyalty.'[95]

Ideology thus having been dinned into him, the SS candidate next completed his term in the Labour Service and the Wehrmacht, finally returning to the SS as a 'Vollanwärter' (full candidate). If his Wehrmacht report was good, he might be finally accepted into the Order within a month.[96] When November 9th came round once more, however, there was a further ceremony at which the new SS man had to swear yet one more oath. This time he bound himself and his future family to obey the marriage law issued by the Reichsführer-SS on December 31st, 1931 prescribing that SS members might marry 'solely if the necessary conditions of race and healthy stock were fulfilled' and only after approval by the RuSHA or the Reichsführer-SS.[97]

Now the young member of the Order received his SS dagger and was finally admitted into this bizarre exclusive brotherhood in which the fanaticism of the religious sect, the rites and customs of a feudal age and the romantic cult of Germanism blended oddly with contemporary political and economic management and cold-blooded power politics. Himmler could now proceed to the final phase of his plan for the training of his SS-type master men – the inculcation of a corps spirit. Here he clearly followed the example of the Prussian officer corps; every order from Himmler, every little service detail was designed to instil into the SS man the conviction that he belonged to an élite and that the SS was different from all other Party organizations. Himmler intended that special prestige should attach to his Order, comparable to that of the medieval orders of chivalry.

Scharfe, the Head of the SS Legal Service, explained why the SS was an organization apart, even within the Party: 'Compared to the ordinary member of the Party, the SS man naturally occupies a special place, primarily because it is his duty to protect the Movement and its Führer, if necessary at the sacrifice of his life. This special position ... of course means that the SS man must be dealt with in a special way.'[98] From this, Scharfe drew the conclusion that no State court, not even a Party court, had the right to judge an SS man; this was the sole prerogative of SS Judges and SS superior officers.[99]

So a special SS jurisdiction came into being applicable to the SD, the Verfügungstruppe, the Totenkopfverbände, the SS Cadet Schools and practically every SS leader down to the rank of Sturmbannführer. The SS was no longer answerable to the normal courts; centuries of European legal history were pushed aside; the SS man had his own code which he defended jealously and of which the dagger was the symbol. After the Röhm affair the SS was removed from the jurisdiction of the SA Courts of Honour and in November 1935 Himmler laid down: 'Every SS man has the right and the duty to defend his honour by force of arms.'[100] So the duel, that hallmark of aristocratic arrogance, was resurrected.

Subject to the agreement of the Reichsführer, every SS man was henceforth entitled to challenge another to a duel. In his usual precise headmasterish manner Himmler laid down the details in an order. The injured party, he prescribed, must 'within 3–24 hours, Sundays and holidays excepted, initiate steps to demonstrate that he intends to obtain clarification or satisfaction.' If he fails to obtain satisfaction or should satisfaction be refused him, he should warn his opponent 'that he will revert to the incident through his representative (his second), from whom the opponent will hear further'. A second should 'where possible, be of equivalent rank to the party challenged', should 'in principle appear in uniform', was to issue his principal's challenge to a duel and agree upon the weapons to be used. Written communication by the second was 'only permissible in exceptional cases' and must 'invariably be made by registered letter'.[101]

In Himmler's view, under the special SS code of honour suicide was also permissible. Even here the procedure was laid down in pedantic, bureaucratic detail. An illustration is the case of Obersturmführer Johannes Buchhold, who was condemned to death for maltreating his subordinates; on June 22nd, 1943 Hauptsturmführer Bleyl recorded:

'I informed Buchhold of the Reichsführer's instruction that a revolver be placed in his cell for a period of six hours, an indication that he was thereby being given an opportunity himself to expiate the crime he had committed. I handed Obersturmführer Buchhold a 0.8 revolver, loaded with one round, cocked and with the safety catch off; I then departed. The criminal was forced to acknowledge the Reichsführer's clemency in writing: 'I confirm that the above record of hearing is correct and append my signature, *Buchhold, SS-Obersturmführer*.'

Next a note by the Reichsführer: 'The body is to be delivered to the relatives. By his death Buchhold has expiated his crime. The relatives are to be provided for as if B. had fallen in action.'[102]

In Himmler's eyes, however, this special jurisdiction valid for every SS man, carried with it a threat to good order and military discipline – it could act as a leveller down or equalizer. In the SS the honourable estate which the Prussian tradition had reserved to the officer was extended to cover the most lowly ranks. To counteract this pseudo-democratization, Himmler was forced to re-emphasize the hierarchical structure of the SS.[103]

So through the body of his organization Himmler drew a horizontal dividing line, separating the Priests and High Priests of the Order from the lay brothers. From the Freemasons, of whom he had an almost superstitious dread, Himmler learnt that imposing insignia and ranks endowed the hierarchy of an Order with power and mystery. So in his counter-Freemasonry, he introduced three insignia.

Irrespective of rank, proven SS men were allowed to wear a silver Death's-Head signet ring. Initially the ring was intended for 'old fighters' and was bestowed only on SS men with a membership number below 10,000. Gradually, however, the circle was widened and by 1939 practically every SS commander who had held a senior position for three years was a wearer of the ring.[104]

Himmler proceeded more cautiously with the dagger, the sign of the SS Corps of Leaders; it became one of the most important adornments of neo-German knighthood. The dagger was granted only to SS men of the rank of Untersturmführer [Second Lieutenant] and upwards. Moreover, unlike the Death's-Head ring, the grant was governed by no prescribed rule but was dependent exclusively upon the Reichsführer's will and pleasure. Only the young nobles of the Order, the graduates of the Cadet Schools, were given the dagger automatically on passing their final examination.[105] The dagger was intended to show those whom the Grand Master considered a member of the Order's hierarchy; the higher the rank, the greater the proportion of dagger-wearers; by the end of the war the dagger was carried by 362 out of 621 Standartenführer,

230 out of 276 Oberführer, 88 out of 96 Gruppenführer, 91 out of 92 Obergruppenführer and by every one of the four Oberstgruppenführer.[106]

These niceties of differentiation, however, still left Himmler's mysticism unsatisfied. From his books on ancient romantic history he had learnt that King Arthur assembled about the Round Table his twelve bravest and most noble knights, with whom he defended the Celtic creed and liberties against the invading Anglo-Saxons.[107] Here was clearly a lesson for the SS. The tale of King Arthur must have impressed Himmler, for he never allowed more than twelve guests to sit at his table. And as King Arthur had once chosen his bravest twelve, so now Himmler appointed his twelve best Obergruppenführer to be the senior dignitaries of his Order.[108]

For the chosen few Himmler invented yet a further mark of distinction. In 1937 Professor Karl Diebitsch, Head of the SS office in Munich dealing with artistic matters, was ordered by the Reichsführer to design coats of arms for the more important SS leaders.[109] The Professor set about his task with scientific zeal but he had hardly begun when yet another Himmler invention appeared on the scene – the excavation of old Germanic relics. The researchers scattered far and wide digging up raw material for Deibitsch's armorial bearings.[110]

On July 17th, 1937 Gruppenführer Pohl, one of the chosen few, was informed by 'Ancestral Heritage' [Ahnenerbe] that: 'We take as our starting point the ancient coats of arms of Germanic man; these form the basic design. They are the symbol of the Germanic tribe and its forebears. To establish a connexion with the ancient Germanic tribal signs demands the most careful research.'[111]

In Wewelsburg Castle Himmler found a Valhalla where he could set up his Round Table and place his knights' coats of arms in a worthy setting. In Himmler's Camelot the chosen few would assemble around the Reichsführer's oaken table in a 100-foot by 145-foot dining-hall, sitting in high-backed pig-skin chairs, each carrying the name of its owner knight inscribed on a small silver plate.[112] They would meet regularly for hours of conference and meditation, reminiscent of a spiritual session. Each of the chosen few had his own quarters in the Castle, decorated in differing historical styles and dedicated to some historical personality.[113]

The Lord of the Castle, described by the Armaments Minister Albert Speer as 'half schoolmaster, half crank',[114] had already thought out the final ceremony for his knights. Beneath the dining-hall lay a stone crypt; its wall, five feet thick, enclosed the holy of holies of the Order – the realm of the dead.[115]

A flight of steps in the middle of the crypt led down into a well-like cavity; in the centre of the cavity there was a stone stoop and around the walls were twelve stone pedestals. In the event of an Obergruppenführer's death, his arms were to be burnt in the stoop and an urn containing the ashes placed upon one of the pedestals. The four vents in the ceiling were so arranged that, during the burning ceremony, the smoke would ascend to the roof in a single column.[116]

Himmler intended Wewelsburg to be the setting in which he and his Obergruppenführer would work out the ideology of his Order – and the setting was a good one. Wewelsburg, named after one of its early owners, the robber knight Wewel von Büren,[117] was one of the few mountain fortresses of Westphalia and had once been a retreat of the Bishops of Paderborn, near which town it lies. In the time of the Huns it had formed a focus of Saxon resistance and in the seventeenth century had been rebuilt in massive triangular form[118] – exactly the place to capture the imagination of a man like Himmler, who lived as much in the past as in the present.

The story goes that Himmler had once heard the saying that a Westphalian castle would be the sole survivor of the next assault from the East and had therefore searched the province for this castle until he lighted upon Wewelsburg.[119]

The facts are somewhat more prosaic; the Landrat [Local Council] of Büren District, which was responsible for maintenance of the Castle, was only too glad to make it over to Himmler.[120] On July 27th, 1934 the building became Himmler's property for a nominal annual rent of 1 mark. Shortly thereafter Himmler informed Schmitt, the Reich Minister of Economics: 'I propose to develop Wewelsburg . . . as a Reich SS leaders' school and request the highest possible Reich grant to meet the building costs.'[121] Within his personal staff he set up a Wewelsburg Office under Standartenführer Siegfried Albert Taubert, who became 'Fortress Commandant' in 1937;[122] the SS Architect, Hermann Bartels,[123] was in charge of the rebuilding and the work was carried out by a detachment of the Labour Service under a staff of SS experts.

In the southern wing of the fortress, above the dining-hall, were the Reichsführer's private apartments including a hall for his extensive collection of weapons, a library ultimately containing 12,000 books, a meeting-hall and a courtroom for the highest SS Court. In the same wing were the guest rooms for Hitler who, however, never appeared in Wewelsburg – a fact which, perhaps, gave rise to the village rumour that one day Adolf Hitler would be buried there.[124]

By the end of the war his castle had cost Himmler 13,000,000 marks.[125]

The castle and its contrived rituals, however, were more than a mere historical charade for Himmler; he thought that ideologically history (or his version of history) might be both a bond and a driving force for the SS. Wewelsburg was not the only SS castle; in 1937 Himmler said: 'It is my aim that, if possible, the area of every Standarte should include a similar cultural centre of German greatness and German history which should be restored and put into a condition worthy of a cultured people.'[126]

In 1936 he founded a 'Society for the Promotion and Preservation of German Cultural Monuments'.[127] It was supposed to take care of historical buildings but unfortunately from Himmler's favourite periods – the early Germanic, the early medieval pagan era and the epoch of the German colonizing mission in the East under the Teutonic Knights – all they could find were documents. The association deliberately gave priority, however, to the old castles of the Teutonic Knights or such places as Sachsenhain bei Verden on the Aller, the site of the memorial to 4,500 pagan Saxons massacred in 782 by Charlemagne (referred to by Himmler as 'Charles the Frank').[128] This was the type of ancient monument which fitted into the SS anti-Christian and anti-Slav symbolism. Himmler commented: 'These things interest us because they are of the highest importance in the ideological and political struggle.'[129]

In an SS recruited from all walks of life and classes of society, Himmler looked to romanticized history, Germanic legend and paganism to provide the integrating factor; this was the background to the 'Monuments Society' and many of his other creations. Pride of place among these inventions was taken by the 'King Heinrich I Memorial Foundation'[130] for, as a German King of the Saxon dynasty and conqueror of the Slavs, Heinrich I (875–936) was a particular hero for Himmler, epitomizing his hatred of the Poles. On July 2nd, 1936, the thousandth anniversary of the King's death, Himmler visited his tomb (which was empty at that time) in Quedlingburg Cathedral and swore to pursue and to complete the Saxon king's mission in the East.[131] A year later he had the bones of Heinrich I carried into the cathedral in solemn procession.[132] According to Himmler, the tomb was to be 'a sacred spot to which we Germans make pilgrimage to do honour to King Heinrich'.[133] On each anniversary of the King's death, at the stroke of midnight in the cold crypt of the cathedral, Himmler would commune silently with his namesake.[134]

Himmler was continually entering into contact with the great men of the past. He believed he had the power to call up spirits and hold regular meetings with them, though only, as he told Kersten, with the spirits of men who had been dead for hundreds of years.[135] When he was half-asleep, Himmler used to say, the spirit of King Heinrich would appear and give him valuable advice; he often began with the words: 'In this case King Heinrich would have acted as follows.' He became so obsessed by his hero that he gradually came to regard himself as a reincarnation of the King.[136]

The reason for all this occultism, however, was no mere love of history for its own sake. Contact with the past was supposed to instil into the SS Order the realization that they were members of a select band, to lay the foundations of a historical determinism, marking out the SS man as the latest scion of a long line of Germanic nobility. Himmler's 'basic features of the SS' laid down that the SS was on the march 'in accordance with immutable laws as a National-Socialist Order of men of Nordic stamp and as the oath-bound community of their clans'; it continued: 'We would wish to be, not only the men who fought of old, but the forebears of later generations essential to ensure the eternal existence of the Germanic people of Germany.'[137]

This cult of ancestors and Germanic tribes was clearly intended by Himmler to lend the SS that ideological unity which it lacked – for even the well-reasoned mysticism of the SS Order could not conceal the fact that the SS did not possess that which distinguishes a genuine Order from the world around it – a coherent doctrine.

As far as the principles of an ideology were concerned, the SS had no more to offer than the other Nazi formations – fanatical belief in Hitler, exaggerated nationalism and racist fantasy. Himmler and Darré, the two former Artamans, had indeed introduced into the SS a few of their own special ideas, such as the peasant settlement policy; but these articles of the SS creed, which the RuSHA was intended to put into practice, remained a dead letter – at least until 1940. The demand for peasant resettlement had long since proved to be a Utopia preached by reactionary eccentrics oblivious of the realities of modern industrial society. Even in the Third Reich the requirement for men on the land was falling year by year.[138]

The fact was that the SS did not possess any distinctive ideology. The RuSHA Education Officers were always complaining of the Verfügungstruppe's lack of interest in ideology and even the Allgemeine-SS tended to yawn. Educational evenings were among the worst-attended SS gatherings. Gruppenführer Zech reported that even SS commanders often found it more important to be present at the Wehrmacht's beer evenings than to attend the SS educational courses.[139] In January 1939 Standartenführer Dr Cäsar, Head of the SS Educational Office, complained that racial policy instruction was making little impact on SS men – 'Boredom with these subjects is gradually becoming noticeable among the men and so instruction has been extended to cover the basic concepts of National-Socialist ideology.' But even this did not 'meet requirements'.[140]

Responsibility for education was accordingly removed from the RuSHA and given to the SS Hauptamt, which instituted a new policy, playing down ideology and 'placing increasing emphasis on historical themes'.[141] Bowdlerized history, coloured with ideology, was the substitute used to fill the vacuum left by the absence of any original SS idea.

Further to reinforce the SS Corps spirit, Himmler instituted a curious pseudo-Germanic custom drawn from history. The SS was to differentiate itself from the outside world by a deliberate policy of neo-paganism. The schoolmaster in Himmler floated uppermost, and he pried into the most intimate details of the lives of his SS men; their love life, their family life and their religion were all subject to the prior approval of the Reichsführer; in his eyes the SS was more than an association of men; it was an 'Order of Germanic clans'.

In an instruction issued as early as 1936 he laid down that 'the SS man is expected to marry, preferably between the ages of 25 and 30, and found a family.'[142] The Reichsführer-SS marriage law of 1931, to which every SS man was bound by oath, gave Himmler the power to veto unsuitable SS brides.

The SS man and his fiancée had to complete an RuSHA questionnaire, undergo a health examination by an SS doctor, provide proof of Aryan origin and submit photographs of themselves in bathing costumes. The RuSHA then decided whether both parties to the proposed marriage were worthy to be entered in the SS 'clan book'; in the case of SS leaders Himmler made the decision himself.[143]

Even the marriage ceremony was governed by SS rules. Church services were taboo and, instead, after civil marriage in the Register Office, at which only immediate relatives were present, 'marriage vow ceremonies' were conducted by the local unit commander. The couple exchanged rings and received bread and salt from the SS.[144] All Himmler's rules for married life were designed to divorce his SS men from the Christian church. A man could only be promoted Commander if he turned his back on the church and declared himself 'a believer in God'; no priest was allowed to be present at an SS christening or a death-bed.[145]

The local SS leader functioned as the priest; instead of baptism came carefully graduated presents from the Reichsführer, produced by the SS-owned factory at Allach near Munich – for the first child a silver beaker, a silver spoon and a blue silk shawl; for every fourth child a birthday candlestick inscribed 'You are only a link in the clan's endless chain.'[146]

Christmas, the Germans' favourite festival, faced Himmler with problems of theory. In 1936 he had thundered: 'We will . . . lower a barrier to ensure that *Gemütlichkeit*, which has so often proved deadly to the German people, is banished from our ranks.'[147] But the SS wives continued to long for the splendour of the Christian Christmas. Himmler therefore invented a substitute – the Feast of Midsummer. Every year the Allach Factory disgorged on SS families a stream of 'midsummer candlesticks' and 'midsummer plates'. Himmler ruminated: 'It is the wives; when the Church myth is taken away from them, they want something else to take its place and gladden the hearts of the children.'[148]

The ideological hullabaloo about Christmas showed how far the SS ideology was divorced from reality. In fact Himmler's neo-pagan customs remained primarily a paper exercise. Even the marriage rules, which the men had sworn to obey, remained the subject of so much controversy that many SS men disregarded them. In 1937, 307 SS men were expelled for contravention of the marriage Order.[149] From year to year discontent in the SS increased and Himmler was forced continuously to reduce the punishment laid down for contravention of the marriage rules. An SS-Hauptamt order of July 3rd, 1935 laid down that any man deliberately disregarding the marriage rules would be expelled from the SS.[150] A further order on June 23rd, 1937, however, stated that no SS man need necessarily be expelled for this reason, provided he and his wife subsequently satisfied the SS racial regulations.[151] Finally, on November 1st, 1940 Himmler issued an instruction that all SS men expelled for breaking the marriage rules should be re-accepted into the Order, provided they themselves were racially satisfactory.[152]

Equally Himmler never succeeded in implementing his anti-Church programme. Two-thirds of the Allgemeine-SS remained in the Church – 54·2 per cent Evangelicals and 23·7 per cent Catholics. Himmler's 'believers in God' were in the majority only in the armed SS units – 53·6 per cent in the Verfügungstruppe and 69 per cent in the Totenkopfverbände.[153] The war, however, drove the 'believers' onto the defensive even in the Waffen-SS. Catholic chaplains appeared from time to time among the SS troops[154] and the 'Germanic volunteers' were allowed to go to church;[155] in some units (those of Obergruppenführer Bittrich, for instance) notices of church services were even posted in the offices.[156]

Even more disappointing to Himmler must have been the evident reluctance of the SS wives to raise large families. The SS birthrate hardly differed from that of the nation as a whole; instead of Himmler's much trumpeted four-child family, statistics of December 31st, 1939 showed an average of 1·1 children for the 115,650 married SS men; SS officers were only marginally better with an average of 1·41.[157] Even Himmler's breeding establishment, formed in 1936 and known as 'Lebensborn', with its cheap private maternity homes, failed to raise the SS birthrate. Although all the 3,500 full-time SS leaders were forced to join and contribute a defined proportion of their pay (5–8 per cent), by 1939 only 8,000 SS men were members – 8,000 out of a total of 238,159 members of the Allgemeine-SS.[158] An additional – in fact the main – attraction of Lebensborn was that unmarried mothers could give birth to their children in its homes. Dr Ebner, the Head of Lebensborn, boasted: 'Lebensborn is in fact the only organization in a position to guarantee the complete secrecy of a confinement.' The Reichsführer, he said, had 'ordered every SS man to adopt a protective attitude to the future mother of good blood.'[159] The majority of SS men, however, disregarded even this broad hint that in the interest of 'good blood' all barriers of normal convention might be broken. Of 12,081 children of married SS leaders between the ages of 20 and 50, only 135 were born out of wedlock.[160]

Clearly uniformity was not to be imposed upon so bewilderingly heterogeneous an organization as the SS merely by Himmler's neo-German rites. The anti-Church propaganda, moreover, did the SS more harm than good; it deterred many from joining. The aristocracy began to turn away from the SS and seek their traditional place in the Wehrmacht.[161] Sponsoring members' contributions fell from 581,000 marks in 1934 to 400,000 marks in 1936;[162] Pohl, the SS Treasurer, stated flatly: 'The sponsoring member organization . . . has passed its peak.'[163] Full-time leaders began leaving the SS in increasing numbers – 44 in 1938 alone.[164] On December 31st, 1938 Schmitt, the Head of the Personnel Office, stated: 'The fact that full-time leaders are drifting off to industry constitutes a great danger', and noted that departures included 'some of our best leaders'. Particularly in Oberabschnitt Danube, he went on, many leaders had 'used their position in the SS as a springboard to obtain a better job in industry.'[165]

In addition the Personnel Chancellery calculated that of the medium-level leaders (Commanders of Standarten and Sturmbannen, Abschnitt Staff Officers and desk-holders in the higher-level staffs) 273 would shortly have to be relieved for inefficiency and replaced by new men. The Personnel Chancellery went on: 'Of 513 full-time leaders now serving in the most important positions, it seems that in all probability only 128 (ie, 26 per cent) are really fitted for their present employment and suitable for promotion to the higher posts.'[166]

This faced Himmler with a dilemma which he was never to solve. The increasing size of his empire and the shortage of officer material meant that the recruitment of new personnel was imperative; the increased difficulty of recruiting, however, meant that he was forced to accept men bearing little relation to the SS image of the perfect Nordic man.

The recruiters' difficulties would have been even greater had not the SS, in spite of its abstruse Germanic cult, offered a certain intellectual attraction to the more active brains. For the SS did possess one characteristic, and one only, differentiating it from the Party and the outer world – its own special mode of life. The hallmark of the true SS man was neither the firmness of character nor the National-Socialist fanaticism demanded by Himmler's bizarre Order; in the words of Schwerin von Krozigk, the ex-Reich Finance Minister, 'unlike the Party, the aim of which is political, the SS is devoted to cultivation of a certain character.'[167]

This was simply further proof that the SS had inherited the old Free Corps mentality of which Ernst Jünger, its great prophet had once written: 'The important point is not what we fight for but how we fight.'[168] One of Jünger's disciples, Dr Werner Best, the one-time Gestapo official and SS-Obergruppenführer, extracted from Jünger's philosophy a notion later hallowed as one of the dominant characteristics of the SS leader – the concept of 'heroic realism'.[169] In 1930 Best elaborated: 'The fight itself is essential and permanent; the aims of that fight are temporary and changeable. There can therefore be no question of success in our fight . . . the yardstick of the new code of morality, therefore, is not its content – not "what" but "how".'[170] Such an ethic, with no specific aim, opened the door to concentration upon achievement for achievement's sake and this became the focal point of the SS mentality described by Himmler with classic simplicity: 'The word "impossible" must never be heard in the SS.'[171] The 'worship of achievement for achievement's sake', as Hans Buchheim puts it,[172] attracted even non-Nazis, men who basically found the SS heroism claptrap repulsive. The call to energy and efficiency, the ceaseless challenge to action and trial, launched SS men into a primitive competitive struggle in which all normally accepted rules of conduct were forgotten. In 1930 Best still believed in the 'good fight' and a 'heroic code of morals'; his fighter was an independent personality, a true subjectivist responsible only to himself. The heroic SS fighter, however, was subject to orders from above and became a prisoner of an ethic linked to no purpose, an ethic which, ostensibly for purposes of political necessity, could suddenly order the commission of crimes and present them as goals of human technological efficiency. Buchheim says: 'If a man is concerned not with what he is fighting for but only with how he fights, he is conditioned to heroic action in a criminal cause. Although such a heroic fighter imagines that he must rely on himself alone . . . he can be swept up into the service of an organization claiming totalitarian authority – and he will perceive that this had happened either not at all or too late.'[173]

Werner Best perceived it too late. The romantic ideal of heroic realism collapsed when Best found himself at Reinhard Heydrich's side building up the Third Reich's police and terror machine. Long before this, the SS had begun to turn itself into the most effective of all the tools at the disposal of the Führer dictatorship.

8

HEYDRICH AND THE GESTAPO

IN the summer of 1932 Rudolf Jordan, Gauleiter of Halle-Merseburg, gave Nazi Party headquarters a fright. The Gauleiter spied strangers; according to his information a representative of the Jewish world enemy had infiltrated into Adolf Hitler's immediate entourage.

On June 6th, 1932 Jordan wrote to Gregor Strasser, the Nazi Organization Chief: 'It has come to my ears that in the Reich Leadership, there is a member named Heydrich whose father reputedly lives in Halle. There are grounds for suspecting that Bruno Heydrich of Halle, said to be the father, is a Jew. It would perhaps be wise for the Personnel Department to check this matter.' To his letter Jordan attached an extract from Hugo Riemann's *Musiker-Lexikon* in which the horrified Party functionaries read: 'Heydrich Bruno, alias Süss, born February 23rd, 1865 in Leuben, Saxony.'[1]

Strasser called for the personnel files. They showed that from October 1st, 1931 a certain SS-Sturmbannführer Reinhard Heydrich had in fact been occupying a position in SS headquarters; he was in charge of a small but top-secret organization known as the 'Sicherheitsdienst Reichsführer-SS' [SS Security Service – SD].[2] Could it be, Strasser wondered, that Heinrich Himmler had entrusted to a Jew the security of Germany's most violently anti-Semitic party?

Strasser summoned Dr Achim Gercke, the Party's leading genealogist, and ordered him to trace the suspect's family tree. A fortnight later the doctor produced the results of his researches in a 'Submission concerning the racial origin of Lieutenant (Navy, Retired) Reinhard Heydrich.'[3] The conclusion was that: 'The attached ancestry list shows that Lieutenant Heydrich is of German origin and free from any taint of Jewish or coloured blood . . . all the information given is based upon original sources, the reliability of which has been checked.'

Gercke's memorandum was dated June 22nd, 1932; it went on to explain that the rumour about Heydrich's Jewish ancestry had arisen because 'Lieutenant Heydrich's grandmother, Ernestine Wilhelmina Heydrich, *née* Lindner, had been married twice, her second husband being a locksmith's assistant named Gustav Robert Süss; having a large family by her first husband, Reinhold Heydrich, she frequently called herself Süss-Heydrich, In this connexion it should be noted that the second husband, Süss, was equally not of Jewish origin.'

Gercke continued: 'This second marriage of Bruno Heydrich's mother led to a false assumption, given currency by a note in the 1916 edition of *Reimann's Musiker-Lexikon* reading "Heydrich alias Süss". At the request of the Heydrich family this erroneous note was expunged in later editions of the *Lexikon*.'[4]

The genealogists believed that they had now cleared up the Heydrich affair but in fact it was still in its infancy. The higher Reinhard Heydrich, 'the Third Reich's evil young God of death',[5] climbed on the National-Socialist ladder, the more persistent became the rumour that the number two SS man was of Jewish origin.

The tenacity with which many historians, even today, still cling to this 'Jewish ancestry' theory, is no more than a reflection of the urge to discover some well-guarded secret concealed behind the classically Nordic features of Reinhard Heydrich; they feel that there must be a monster hidden somewhere, some ineradicable stain which placed Himmler's *alter ego* and head of his Security Police under hypnotic pressure and turned him into the most pitiless champion of National-Socialist doctrine, 'the most fanatical of racialists' in Gerald Reitlinger's words.[6]

Somewhere, they thought, this fine figure of a man, 'one of the greatest criminals of history',[7] must have a chink in the armour and what more plausible than this supposed blot on his ancestry? For a National-Socialist, after all, it was suicidal, the equivalent of a deadly sin. So Reitlinger promptly discovered in Heydrich a 'pathological Jewish self-hate' as the key to an understanding of this supposed fanatic;[8] H. G. Adler in his *Theresienstadt 1941–1945* considered that the Third Reich offered Heydrich 'unlimited power enabling him, by murdering every Jew within reach, to exorcize the hated Jewish spot within him.'[9]

Even Himmler secretly believed the theory, saying that Heydrich was 'an unhappy man, completely divided against himself, as often happened with those of mixed race.'[10] Carl Burckhardt, the League of Nations Commissioner, found the same thing, saying that he could detect a dual personality in Heydrich's face: 'I said to myself: two people are looking at me simultaneously.'[11]

Burckhardt tells a story of Heydrich regaled to him by SS men. One day, when under the influence of drink, Heydrich staggered into his brilliantly lit bathroom and came up against his reflection in the great wall mirror. He snatched his revolver from the holster and fired twice at the mirror shouting: 'At last I've got you, scum!' Burckhardt's comment is: 'The man with the split personality had shot at his reflection because at last he had met his other half – but he had met him only in the mirror and could never get rid of him; that other half was to accompany him to the end.'[12]

But however detailed the biographers' picture of the 'blond beast' as Heydrich was sometimes called even by the SS, the ultimate conclusion must be that it is perfectly possible to have a great deal to do with a man and yet not know him. For Reinhard Heydrich was not the Saint-Just of the National-Socialist Revolution; he was no racial fanatic, he was not even what Freund called: 'A professional criminal of Lucifer stature.'[13]

It is, of course, attractive to compare Himmler and Heydrich with their terrorist counterparts of the French Revolution, Robespierre and Saint-Just. As far as crime is concerned, the head of the SD was far ahead of his French predecessor, but he had none of Saint-Just's doctrinaire revolutionary fanaticism or perverted idealism. In fact Himmler and Heydrich were two archetypes of the twentieth century raised to the *n*th degree – the ideologist and the technologist. They frequently invoked history and they twisted it to their own purposes but basically Himmler and Heydrich were anti-historical figures, radical merciless rebels against tradition, morality and all humanitarian rules of conduct.

Heydrich's deity was power for its own sake; he was an incarnation of the technology of government by brute force, linked with that distrust of his lords and masters which earned him the nickname 'Mr Suspicion'[14] but he did not hate. The connecting link between Saint-Just and the victims of the guillotine had been hatred, but Heydrich did not hate the Jews; in his scheme of things, they were simply the subjects for technical planning procedure, faceless objects for a 'mopping-up action' on the ghastly scale ordered by the leaders of his State. With Heydrich hatred was an expression of personal spite. Grand Admiral Raeder, for instance, who had had him cashiered from the Navy, was an object of his undying thirst for revenge; Heydrich rejected all attempts at reconciliation by his former fellow-officers.[15] Ideological hatred, on the other hand, was foreign to him, for he despised all ideologies, the National-Socialist included. Heydrich had a passion for all forms of sport; he was a fencer, a horseman, a pilot, a skier and modern pentathlon competitor; he was also SS Inspector for physical training; on occasions he would even protect Jewish sportsmen – for instance, he helped Paul Sommer, the German fencing-master, to emigrate to America and provided Kantor of the Polish Olympic team with money and papers.[16]

Heydrich obviously had none of that blind faith in Hitler which was the elixir of life to Himmler, the stimulant enabling the small-timer to grow to supernatural size. Heydrich could quite well visualize a Germany without Hitler but not a Germany without Heydrich. Those who knew him well are still convinced that, had he been alive on July 20th, 1944, he might well have been found on the side of Stauffenberg – two of his fencing friends can remember him saying to them in Bad-Kreuznach in 1941 that he would be the first to do away with Hitler if 'the old man makes a mess of things'.[17]

Right to the end he remained a technician of power and an apostle of expediency. When, as Reich protector of Bohemia and Moravia, he was struck down by the Czech parachutists' hand-grenade on May 27th, 1942, the Czech conspirators were aiming not at a brutal overlord but at the sophisticated SS rationalist whose flexible stick-and-carrot policy constituted such a danger to their positon that they could see no solution other than his liquidation.

Such a craftsman of pragmatism was, of course, infuriated by Himmler's interminable ideological ramblings. To his wife Lina, Heydrich would frequently unburden himself of his wrath with the Reichsführer and his racial fantasies. One evening, when he had drunk too much, he yelled: 'Just look at his face, his nose – typically Jewish. A real Jewish lout!'[18] Lina Heydrich egged him on, for she cordially loathed the entire Himmler family, particularly the 'Madame Reichsführer'. Even after the war Lina ridiculed Marga Himmler: 'Size 50 knickers. That's all there was to her . . . that narrow-minded, humourless blonde female, always worrying about protocol; she ruled her husband and could twist him round her little finger – at least until 1936.'[19]

Lina Heydrich had good reason to know how strong Marga Himmler's influence was. Urged on by his wife, Himmler demanded that Heydrich should divorce Lina, whom he regarded as impossible and ungovernable. But Lina Heydrich proved stronger than the jaundiced Frau Himmler. At one of Göring's garden parties she struck back. As chance would have it, Himmler was presiding at Frau Heydrich's table. She tells the story: 'They were moments of tragi-comedy. I put on my most mournful expression and sat stock still. Himmler asked: "Why are you so quiet?" To which I replied: "Do you find that surprising?" Then we danced. Himmler danced badly. Then he said "Well, Frau Heydrich, everything will be all right." You see, that was typical of Himmler; on paper he ordered us to divorce, but when face to face with me, his courage left him. The matter was never referred to again.'[20]

Heydrich's vexation, however, was all the greater when he realized how dependent he was upon Himmler with his pernickety mysticism about the SS Order. Although intellectually the superior of his Chief, Heydrich never forgot to treat his Reichsführer 'as a Prussian second lieutenant behaves to a senior general.'[21] Kersten noted: 'Heydrich behaves . . . with quite inexplicable servility. He addresses Himmler as "Herr Reichsführer" – a thing absolutely forbidden throughout the SS – instead of simply "Reichsführer". Heydrich's side of the conversation between them goes like this: "Certainly, Herr Reichsführer; if that is the Herr Reichsführer's wish, I will have the necessary arrangements made at once and report back to the Herr Reichsführer." ' To Lina, however, he would rage: 'Himmler is always manoeuvring and trimming his sails; he won't take responsibility.'[22]

Himmler rather dreaded his senior staff officer's appearance with some proposition. Kersten says: 'Sometimes I had the impression that after one of these expositions Himmler was quite overwhelmed.' Heydrich's reports, Kersten goes on, were 'masterpieces of exposition; a short sketch of the person or subject, then his arguments perceptively built up to the decisive trump card, which he played last of all, then his conclusion which Himmler could hardly resist.'[23]

Sometimes the intimidated Reichsführer plucked up his courage again – once Heydrich was gone. Then he would seize the telephone and tell Heydrich that he must first discuss with Hitler the measures already agreed.[24] Shortly thereafter Himmler would issue a different order, camouflaged for the benefit of Heydrich as an order from the Führer. On one occasion Himmler had the courage to lose his temper; he screamed at Heydrich, stuttering: 'You, you . . . and your logic. We never hear about anything but your logic. Everything I propose, you batter down with your logic. I am fed up with you and your cold, rational criticism.' Heydrich drew back and gave way at once. Himmler was pacified once more.[25]

Himmler always kept suspicious watch on possible rivals, but he never regarded Heydrich as potentially dangerous. He had detected in Heydrich characteristics which, though admirable in a secret policeman, were hardly calculated to further more exalted political ambitions. He was irritable, power-hungry, always ready to pounce: he was glacial, incapable of friendship or even loyalty. Heydrich's restlessness, his versatile, though superficial, intelligence, his tendency to be a know-all, his urge to be top dog in everything, whether in the SD, the fencing room or over the bottle, could not conceal the fact that within him there was a vacuum in which both ideologies and human beings sank without trace.

Though he avoided making declared enemies, he equally had no friends; his only real bond with his wife was his insatiable sexual appetite. Wherever he appeared, men drew back. Even his fencing partners, though appreciating his skill, avoided him.[26]

Even today quite a number of ex-members of Himmler's staff can still be found to sing their Reichsführer's praises as a kind and thoughtful man, but there has never been a word from any friend of Heydrich, 'the man with the iron heart' as Hitler called him.[27] Sepp Dietrich's coarse expression upon hearing of Heydrich's death echoed the thoughts of many SS men: 'Thank God that sow's gone to the butcher.'[28]

Even the Berlin prostitutes were not invariably pleased to see him. He always took an aide with him when he went night-clubbing, and there were frequent scenes when the ladies appeared to prefer the aide to the man with the sinister wolf's eyes.[29] Few realized that behind Heydrich's arrogant exterior lay a sensitivity springing from the inferiority complex of the cashiered naval officer and the actor's susceptibility to criticism, inherited from his parents. Brutality was not a basic feature of his character; when Burckhardt once visited Heydrich he said feelingly: 'Abroad people take us for bloodhounds, don't they? It is almost too hard for the individual, but we must be hard as granite.'[30]

So unstable a being, alternating between aggressiveness and a longing for recognition, was cut out to be Himmler's second-in-command; he would be no threat to the Reichsführer's supremacy. Both knew that neither could do without the other – for reasons of self-preservation. Without Himmler and his firm position in the Nazi hierarchy as head of the SS, the restlessly ambitious Heydrich would find his rise to power blocked; without Heydrich, his lightning intellect and his dynamism,

Himmler would never hack his way through the spider's web of Nazi potentates.

Initially it seemed that the partnership between these two men would be a very one-sided affair. In June 1931, when Himmler received young Heydrich while convalescing at his home in Waldtrudering[31] and engaged him for the SD, he had clearly been a broken man who had lost the profession which he longed for – that of an officer.

Reinhard Tristan Eugen Heydrich was born on March 7th, 1904 in Halle on the Saale.[32] His early career was no different from that of many middle-class young men in republican post-war Germany. He was the son of an opera singer and an actress, went to the Reform Gymnasium [High School] in Halle[33] and, at the age of sixteen joined General Maerker's Free Corps – primarily to escape the poverty of his home, which had been hit by the war and inflation.[34] When he returned, he knew what he wanted to be – an officer. Like Himmler, his first choice was the Navy since in post-war disarmed Germany the best chance of satisfying his urge for self-expression and adventure was to be found at sea.

In 1922 Heydrich reported to Kiel as a naval cadet. In July 1923, as part of his training, he was posted to the training cruiser *Berlin*[35] and so met the man who later described him as 'the cleverest brute of them all,' Wilhelm Canaris, then First Officer of the *Berlin*. From the outset the little fastidious captain found this lanky cadet with the Mongol eyes somewhat sinister, though he admired his mathematical ability and navigational skill.[36]

Canaris' wife Erika, however, daughter of Carl Friedrich Waag, a manufacturer from Pforzheim, was artistic and she found Heydrich's violin playing delightful.[37] Aronson, Heydrich's Jewish biographer says: 'Heydrich's playing was mellow and delicate, his finger-work was first-class and he showed outstanding feeling as a violinist.' When playing Heydrich could 'weep for prolonged periods. This was the other side of the coin – cynicism and cruelty combined with soft sentimentality.'[38]

In 1924 Canaris was posted to the Naval Staff in Berlin.[39] Heydrich meanwhile continued a normal uneventful naval career; early in 1926 he was promoted Oberfähnrich [Midshipman] and later that year Sub-Lieutenant; he attended the Naval Signal School, became signals officer of the fleet flagship *Schleswig-Holstein* and occupied various positions in the signals division of the Baltic Naval Station.[40] In 1928, by which time Heydrich had been promoted Lieutenant[41] and had also passed an examination in Russian, he was regarded as a talented naval officer;

admittedly he was unpopular with his brother officers and was teased as a 'nannygoat' because of his falsetto voice; among the sailors he was reckoned one of the most unpopular officers because of his harsh, overbearing manner.[42]

Nevertheless he seemed to have an assured career in front of him, but at this point an amorous adventure brought it to an abrupt end. The starting point was an evening canoeing expedition near Kiel in late summer 1930;[43] as the boat carrying Heydrich and Mohr glided peacefully along, they saw another boat capsize. In it were two girls; Heydrich and Mohr dived into the water and rescued the ladies; one of them was a blonde nineteen-year-old schoolgirl beauty, Lina Mathilde von Osten, daughter of a schoolmaster on the Baltic Island of Fehmarn.[44] As a result of this adventure Heydrich and Lina struck up a friendship which culminated on December 9th, 1930 in engagement – much against the will of Lina's father.[45]

But Heydrich was a pathological womanizer and Lina was only one more addition to his collection of young ladies. Another soon appeared with a prior claim – a student at the Kolonialschule in Rendsburg, daughter of a director of IG-Farben. Heydrich rejected her coldly, but her father had connexions with Admiral Erich Raeder, the Head of the Navy, and Heydrich's superiors were soon pointing out to him that he would have to give up Lina von Osten; when he refused, Raeder set the wheels of naval justice in motion.[46]

Early in 1931 a court of honour, consisting of four naval officers, met and examined Lieutenant Heydrich for weeks[47]; the President and First Member of the court was Captain Gustav Kleikamp, commander of the Baltic station and Heydrich's ex-instructor at the Naval Signal School; he says that he 'discussed the case as put forward by Heydrich thoroughly and in detail.'[48] Heydrich, however, answered his old instructor with such arrogance that the court of honour reprimanded him for insubordination.

What primarily turned the court against Heydrich was his blatant attempt to shift the blame on to the girl; he accused her of lying and protested his own complete innocence. This was incompatible with the code of honour of a great Navy. Vice-Admiral Kleikamp stated subsequently: 'In view of Heydrich's inexcusable behaviour, in particular the striking lack of candour in his presentation of his case, the court of honour was moved to raise the question whether the retention of such an officer in the Navy was possible; the decision on this matter, however, was left open.'[49]

Raeder, a stickler for naval propriety, answered this question in the negative and threw Heydrich out of the Navy. Judgement was pronounced at the end of April 1931: 'Dismissal for impropriety.'[50] Rumour has it that Heydrich later told the 'other girl', who was expecting a child by him, that he could not marry a girl who had given herself to him beforehand.[51]

As a result of Raeder's decision, Heydrich descended from the security of the ultra-conservative Navy into the army of the unemployed millions who were besieging Germany's labour exchanges. He revolted against the fate which he had brought upon himself. The openings seemed few; he could have become a sailing instructor, like many other ex-naval officers, and there seemed a possibility of a post with a yacht club,[52] but – as far as any form of naval uniform was concerned, even that of the merchant navy, there were no prospects. To heal his wounded pride, Heydrich had to satisfy himself with a second-rate uniform – that of the Naval SA,[53] but this did not mean that he had developed political leanings; Lina Heydrich said: 'He was just a professional naval officer; he was wedded to his naval career. His only other interest was sport. He knew nothing about politics – and had never shown any great interest in them.'[54]

But Lina knew her politics (Höttl describes her as 'a typical example of the evil, ambitious woman in a novel');[55] she was a Hitler enthusiast and was convinced that her future husband should look to the Nazi Party for a career. Heydrich's sister Elizabeth came to the rescue. She remembered that his godmother had a son who was a senior SA leader in Munich and was about to become one of the influential personalities in the SS. 'Little Karl,' alias Friedrich Karl Freiherr von Eberstein, she was sure, would help 'Reini' – and he did.[56]

Eberstein fortunately did not know the difference between a signals officer and an Intelligence officer; Heydrich was therefore summoned to Waltrudering to meet Himmler, who was then looking for a counter-espionage man for his Security Service. Heydrich entered Himmler's house – and his life – on June 14th, 1931.[57] Himmler gave him twenty minutes to draw up the outline of a future SS counter-espionage service[58] – and this was the real genesis of the SD. Himmler accepted Heydrich's plan and on October 5th, 1931 Party headquarters Hamburg received the following message from Munich: 'Party Member Reinhard Heydrich, Hamburg, Membership No 544916, will, with effect from October of this year, be carried on the strength of Party Headquarters as a member of the staff of the Reichsführer-SS.'[59] Heydrich was given the rank of Sturmführer[60] and set to work.

Early in 1931 on Hitler's instructions, Himmler had commenced the formation of a Security Service to protect Nazi leaders. His first step had been to form within SS headquarters an 'Ic' section – in Army general staff terminology Section Ic dealt with enemy Intelligence. Even after Heydrich's appointment Himmler himself remained titular Head of Section Ic but he left the actual work to Heydrich.[61]

Armed only with a couple of Himmler's files, Heydrich moved into a room in the Brown House[62] and embarked upon the career for which he was better fitted than any other National-Socialist, that of totalitarian secret policeman. In late August 1931 he appeared at a meeting of SS leaders in the Brown House in the capacity of future Head of the Secret Service, and he painted a horrifying picture of a Party riddled with innumerable spies in the pay of the opposition parties and the police. His conclusion was that the Nazi Party must be ruthlessly purged of all agents and saboteurs.[63] Shortly thereafter an order was issued to all SS units: 'With immediate effect every Abschnitt will set up an Ic desk to deal with all Intelligence activities within the Abschnitt. Subsequently an Ic desk is also envisaged for every SS-Standarte.'[64]

No sooner had Heydrich placed his men in SS units than he moved himself out of the Brown House, whose inmates were becoming over-curious. With three staff officers, he transferred to a two-roomed apartment at 23 Türkenstrasse, Munich,[65] where he inaugurated a curious system obviously based upon detective and spy novels; no more than two people were ever allowed to be present at any discussion – Heydrich and one other.[66] Early in 1932 he had built up his staff sufficiently to seek new horizons. Occasional contact with his spies and informers was not enough.

In April 1932 he toured Germany in order to see how his scattered staff might be concentrated into one organization.[67] Just at this moment, however, the defenders of the Republic forced him to juggle with its title; the Reich Government banned both the SA and SS; Ic was forced to re-name itself Presse- und Informationsdienst [Press and Information Service – PID].[68]

Nevertheless Heydrich was so encouraged by his tour, that he now set up a great organization, later to be known as 'Sicherheitsdienst' (SD). He withdrew counter-espionage personnel and informers from SS units, concentrating them under his own authority;[69] he had thus formed the first specialized SS organization. Although it had its own separate establishment, the new organization remained a unit of the SS but, at the same time, was an SS within the SS. Heydrich set up his own territorial organization, paralleling the SS-Oberabschnitte and Abschnitte. Its job was to track down anti-Party elements within the NSDAP and keep a watch on opposition parties.[70] Every report, every observation, every little personal detail was meticulously entered in

Heydrich's card-index in the new SD headquarters at 4 Zuccalistrasse, Munich.[71]

But Heydrich's ambition did not end there. Observation of the Party's enemies was not enough for him – other Party and SA counter-espionage services were already doing that. He was determined that the SD's work should be so outstanding that all Party rivals would be eliminated, leaving it as the sole Intelligence service of the entire Nazi Party. Even this was not enough for the SS; when Adolf Hitler seized power in Berlin, Heydrich hoped that the SD would emerge from the shadows and form the new police force of the new Reich.

In astonishment verging on perplexity, Himmler, the small-timer, watched his secret-service chief drive on with merciless energy. All the self-torturing melancholy of the cashiered naval officer was gone; Heydrich drove his men with the missionary fervour of the newly converted – imperious, impatient, issuing a stream of orders in his staccato, strikingly high-pitched voice. Himmler rewarded all this industry with the requisite promotions and Heydrich climbed the ladder quickly; August 10th, 1931 Shurmführer, December 1st, 1931 Hauptsturmführer, July 19th, 1932 formal appointment as Head of the SD, July 29th, 1932 Standartenführer, March 21st, 1933 Oberführer.[72] Himmler sensed instinctively that chance had given him a 'born Intelligence officer', 'a living card-index, a brain which held all the threads and wove them all together', as Kersten puts it.[73] Heydrich was ideally equipped to be head of a Secret Service – he was hard, he was unsentimental, his thirst for information was apparently insatiable and his contempt for his fellow-men was enough to make the flesh creep.

It was no accident that Heydrich's favourite sport was fencing. The watching and parrying, the lightning reaction to unforeseen situations, were second nature to him. Schellenberg found in him 'the ever-watchful instincts of a predatory animal, always alert to danger and ready to act swiftly and ruthlessly.'[74] He had an uncanny knack, almost a sixth sense, of putting his finger on the point, however intricate the situation. Himmler's files of reports from other sources often carried notes in Heydrich's angular writing: 'Don't believe it' or 'Simply a rumour'; when Himmler asked him whether he had investigated the report in question, he would reply: 'Not yet,' but that the comment was simply his feeling – and he was usually right.[75]

Himmler added: 'He possessed an infallible nose for men . . . he saw the ways which friend or foe would take with a clarity which was absolutely amazing. His colleagues hardly dared to lie to him.'[76] Heydrich seemed to have been born to become Head of the Secret Service in a totalitarian State. Obersturmbannführer Höttl of the SD believed that Heydrich was the first 'to make Himmler aware of the potentialities of his position as Reichsführer-SS'; the idea of turning the SS into the Third Reich's Police Force originated with Heydrich.[77]

Heydrich's vision was of a close-knit system of supervision, covering every facet of the national life and guaranteeing the total dominance of the Nazi Party; the instrument was to be none other than the Reichsführer's SD, and its Director none other than Reinhard Tristan Eugen Heydrich. He sketched out a Political Police Force which differed from its predecessors in one decisive aspect: previous police systems had been satisfied to catch enemies of the State *in flagrante delicto*; they acted when some definite danger could be detected; Heydrich's police, on the other hand, were to track down the enemy before even his thinking, let alone his actions, savoured of resistance.

The power of the police as conceived by Heydrich was limitless, embracing every aspect of the nation's life. The police force was no longer to be a defensive organization, it was to pass to the attack – not only that; it was to be the 'educator' of the people, the omnipotent purifier cleansing the nation of all non-conformist ideas. According to Hauptsturmführer Alfred Schweder of the SD, the mission of the police was to 'raise to the highest level the activity of our people's innate forces by correcting and directing their thoughts in a single direction, in the process eliminating from the national thinking all foreign, and therefore destructive, tendencies.'[78] Heydrich's concept, of course, postulated disregard of all traditional legal restraint on police activity. In Werner Best's view the police should be ubiquitous 'in order to suppress and avert any disturbance of governmental order in the Third Reich, even though an infringement of law and order may not, or not yet, have taken place.'[79]

In other words Heydrich wished the police to be omnipotent, subject only to the 'overall mission of the German Police'[80] – which was the ruthless protection of Adolf Hitler's Führer dictatorship. Obviously, however, so free a hand could not be given to a Police Force brought up under the Weimar Republic to respect the law and the constitution; still less could it be given to an administration for which, despite lip service to National-Socialism, the Prussian norms of law and order still remained valid.

Heydrich knew what had to be done; in the first place the SD must occupy the key positions in the new Political Police; secondly, the specialized Police Force must then be divorced from all connexion with the internal administration; finally, the entire Police Force must be merged into the SS to form a State Protection Corps. This plan contained the germ of an even more far-reaching and more revolutionary project – the formation of a purely SS administration, combining the Police, the SS and the official bureaucracy into one coordinated whole.

Himmler was intoxicated by Heydrich's vision. Some of the 'old fighters' such as SS-Gruppenführer August Heissmeyer, sounded the warning that if it became too closely connected to the police, the SS Order would be hampered in its educational mission by a heavy load of unpopularity.[81] In 1946 Seyss-Inquart said: 'The SS idea foundered because Himmler misused the organization as an executive authority.'[82] But nothing could now deter the Reichsführer from his dream of becoming Germany's supreme policeman. In Bavaria a testing ground was already available for Heydrich to put his ideas into practice.

Himmler and his sleuths already had a foot in the police door as a result of the National-Socialist coup in Bavaria on March 9th, 1933; Himmler moved into Police headquarters as Acting Police President and Heydrich took over the political desk in Abteilung VI.[83] A week later the two SS men took a further major stride forward. Himmler was nominated political adviser to the Bavarian Ministry of the Interior and given command of the Bavarian Political Police; he hastened to summon Heydrich as his executive deputy.[84]

The two now used Bavaria as the testing ground for the procedure they were to follow throughout the Reich a few years later. Himmler created in the Ministry of the Interior an office known as 'Political Police Commander, Bavaria,' while Heydrich began to build up a Bavarian Political Police Force, manning it with personnel from his SD.[85] Heydrich's primary object was to make the Political Police, hitherto part of the overall police machine, independent of the Bavarian administration, and so he now cut all administrative connexions with the Bavarian Government. The Political Police moved out of Munich Police headquarters and was given the status of an independent authority.[86]

Heydrich concentrated into one organization the political sections of Police headquarters [Polizeidirektionen] and Police offices [Polizeiämter], together with the political police desks in the Bezirke [Districts] and municipalities; all headed up to a single office – that of the Political Police commander, who was authorized to call upon the uniformed police of Bavaria for executive duties as occasion demanded.[87] In accordance with the theories of Heydrich and Himmler, the authority of the Political Police commander was even further extended to include certain preserves of the judiciary; Himmler was placed in charge of the concentration camps which Adolf Wagner, the rabid Nazi Minister of the Interior in Bavaria, had set up to relieve the normal prisons, overflowing with political prisoners.[88]

Meanwhile, the emergency decree 'For the Protection of People and State' issued by the Reich President, empowered the police to consign citizens to 'preventive custody' in a concentration camp on mere suspicion of anti-State activity;[89] as he was already in control of the concentration camps, this gave Himmler undreamed-of power and nothing could now stop his fanatical campaign for political purity. On paper he was still the subordinate of Wagner, the Gauleiter and Minister of the Interior, but his dual function as Reichsführer-SS and Political Police Commander enabled him to evade the authority of his nominal superior. Wagner, as Minister of the Interior, could give orders to Himmler in his capacity as Political Police Commander but not in his capacity as Head of the SS, for as head of a Party formation, Himmler was superior to Wagner, a mere Gauleiter; conversely, within the Party, Röhm, as Chief-of-Staff of the SA, which frequently obstructed the work of the political police, was superior to the Reichsführer-SS and could therefore give him orders; within Bavaria, however, Röhm could not give orders to the Political Police Commander. Himmler and Heydrich made good use of their well-nigh completely independent position. Dachau became a household word, signifying a barbaric efficiency which incensed even convinced Nazis; in Bavaria the two SS men were still filling their camps with prisoners when the first great wave of terror produced by the National-Socialist Revolution had long since died away. Himmler later recalled: 'In 1933, under pressure from the Ministry, we released a large number of prisoners from preventive custody in Prussia and other German Länder. In Bavaria, however, I did not give way and did not release my prisoners.'[90]

Ritter von Epp, the Reichsstatthalter of Bavaria, was disturbed by the frequent 'abuse of the imposition of protective custody'; he suggested to Wagner on March 20th, 1934 that such arbitrary action might 'undermine confidence in the law'. But Wagner would have none of it. On April 14th von Epp noted that 'every sentence' of Wagner's reply was 'questionable and refutable' and that it contained a series of 'inaccuracies, distortions, misrepresentations and falsifications'.[91]

Even Frick, the lethargic Reich Minister of the Interior, entered the lists, criticizing Himmler's crude methods and his passion for placing people under arrest. On January 30th, 1935 he wrote: 'I have on several previous occasions drawn attention to the comparatively large number of persons in protective custody in Bavaria; I have had no satisfactory explanation from the Bavarian Political Police, nor have I seen signs of any serious effort to reduce the number of prisoners . . . I cannot allow such a situation to pass without comment; according to the latest figures, the number of persons in protective custody in Bavaria is several hundreds higher than the combined total in all other German Länder, Prussia included.' But Himmler ignored these admonitions from Berlin; Frick's letter simply evoked the bleak comment: 'The prisoners will remain.'[92]

But Himmler and Heydrich soon found Bavaria too small for them; they cast covetous eyes on the rest of the Reich, where in the sixteen other German Länder the police were without a master or, at least, without a single guiding hand. Time was pressing, for in Prussia Göring had already set up a Political Police in the form of the Gestapo, organized similarly to Himmler's and Heydrich's machine – divorced from the administration, responsible only to one man, and independent of State and Party.

The power struggle between the National-Socialist potentates, however, brought Himmler and Heydrich a quicker victory than either had expected. Frick, a weak man but intent on reforming the Reich on centralist principles, found his way blocked by Göring's Prussian separatism and could see no other solution but to call in Himmler – he and Frick at least agreed on one point: both wanted a centralized Reich Police Force. Frick allowed Himmler to take over one Land police force after another. Prussia held out to the end. (The story of the fall of that fortress, as a by-product of preparation for action against Röhm, has been told in Chapter 5.)

So by the end of April 1934 Himmler and Heydrich had laid hands on the Prussian police. Himmler became Deputy Chief and Inspector of the Gestapo, the Prussian equivalent of the Bavarian Political Police; as deputy to the Deputy, Heydrich took over control of the Gestapo.[93] At the same time they contrived to broaden the basis of their power within the Party. The Party leadership recognized the SD as the sole Party information service, the Führer's Deputy decreeing on June 9th, 1934 that thenceforth: 'Apart from the Sicherheitsdienst RFSS there will be no Party Intelligence or counter-espionage service, not even in the form of an internal Intelligence organization for foreign policy purposes.'[94]

But the SD's victory came too soon. Heydrich had somehow lost faith in his own creature. His experience with the Bavarian Political Police had destroyed his dream of the SD as the basis of a new police force. The old-school police officials had shown themselves superior in every respect to the young upstarts of the SD. Heydrich must have sensed this early on, for only a few days before the National-Socialist seizure of power, he had cut adrift from the SD. In January 27th, 1933 he resigned as Head of the SD and was appointed to the staff of the Reichsführer-SS as 'Standartenführer specially employed'.[95] For nine months, the SD machine ran on without Heydrich.[96]

The past and future Head of the SD was realist enough to know that, from the point of view of numbers alone, his organization was in no position to form the cadre of a new police force. In autumn 1933 the SD totalled only 100 members; SD-Oberabschnitt South-West (Stuttgart), for instance, consisted only of five men.[97] Moreover Heydrich doubted whether the SD had any future as an independent organization. His wife told Aronson, the Jewish historian, that her husband had once said: 'Now we have no further need of the Party. It has served its purpose and opened the way to power. Now the SS must penetrate the police and, with them, form a new organization.'[98]

Here then was the objective. On Himmler's instructions Heydrich, from his desk as Head of the Gestapo, now set about combining all the Länder Police Forces in Germany under the SS umbrella; his object was to turn their experienced police functionaries into loyal servants of the régime, available for any task allotted by the Führer dictatorship; of Nazism they need possess only the thinnest veneer. For Heydrich, the pragmatist, technical ability was more important than ideological purism – and he found that technical ability among a group of Munich criminal police officers who made no secret of the fact that the new-style SD was abhorrent to them.

Senior Inspector Reinhard Flesch and his colleagues, including Heinrich Müller, Franz Josef Huber and Josef Meisinger, worked in Abteilungen II and VI of the Bavarian Political Police, expecting to be displaced at any moment, by the SD upstarts. 'Heini' Müller took a strong line saying: 'Just let them come. We'll look after them!'[99] But, in fact, the old professionals had good reason to fear that their new masters might sack them because, with the exception of Meisinger, they had all been anti-Nazis before 1933. Meisinger was an 'old fighter' who had marched to the Feldherrnhalle on November 9th, 1923,[100] but every other member of the Flesch group was a supporter of some democratic party, in most cases the Bavarian People's Party.

This applied even to Müller, the thickset bullnecked criminal-police inspector with the yokel's face. Born in 1900, he had been a sergeant pilot on the Western Front and a member of Munich Police headquarters from the end of 1919. While still only an assistant in the central office, he had had to deal, as his first case, with the murders of hostages during the Red Republic period in Bavaria, and as a result had become a fanatical anti-Communist.[101] During the Weimar Republic he had been in charge of the anti-Communist desk in the political section of Police headquarters; even the headquarters of the Munich/Upper Bavaria Nazi Party Gau, where the ambitious Müller was detested, was forced to 'admit categorically' that Müller was a 'most violent opponent' of Communism 'who at times would disregard legal rules and regulations'.[102]

Nevertheless the Gau headquarters' opinion of Müller continued: 'It is, however, equally clear that, had it been his job, Müller would have acted similarly against the right wing. Being incredibly ambitious . . . he would be bent on recognition from his superiors under any system.'[103] Munich Party headquarters doubted whether a man like Müller had any professional future in the new Germany; he was a 'regulation' policeman and an assiduous churchgoer, who contributed no more than 40 pfennig to the Eintopfspende (a Nazi device to raise money); to make matters worse Dischner, the Bavarian People's Party publisher, was his father-in-law.[104] He was hardly the type of police official likely to be acceptable to the Nazis.

On January 4th, 1937 the Munich Gau headquarters described Müller's character as follows: 'He acts ruthlessly, uses his elbows and seizes every opportunity to display his efficiency; he is quite prepared to deck himself out in borrowed plumage.'[105] The head of the local Nazi group in Munich-Pasing confirmed: 'We can hardly imagine him as a member of the Party.'[106] Heydrich, however, was both sufficiently imaginative and sufficiently hard-headed to take on a technician such as this – the same applied to the other members of the Flesch group. He even accepted Huber, who was loathed by the Party as the leading anti-Nazi in Police headquarters.

Heydrich summoned Huber and produced the schedule of dismissals. Without a word, in oppressive silence he ran a finger down the list. Suddenly he looked up: 'Which Huber are you?' Huber explained. A short conversation followed. When Huber left the room, Heydrich knew that he, like all the other good brave citizens of Munich Police headquarters, would now work even more unscrupulously and dutifully for the régime whose advent they had resisted.[107]

A Munich Party headquarters internal memorandum, dated March 9th, 1937 found it incomprehensible that 'so odious an opponent of the Movement' as Müller should now be one of the régime's guardians; he had always 'tried to curry favour with his superiors by particularly vigilant persecution of National-Socialists'; he had once referred to the great Führer, Adolf Hitler, as an 'immigrant unemployed housepainter' and 'an Austrian draft-dodger'.[108]

Müller and his ilk were only too ready to repay Heydrich's tolerance with 'an unconditional readiness to serve'. Instead of being sacked, the Munich criminal police officers found themselves unexpectedly promoted – they were accepted into the SD as a body.[109] Heydrich's cold calculation, however, threw up one unfortunate by-product, hardly noticed at the time; SS-Untersturmführer Müller, Flesch, Huber and the rest were quite prepared to sew the SD diamond on their sleeves but, right up to the end of the Third Reich, they retained their allergy to the SD and this was a contributory factor in its failure to gain control of the Gestapo.

Heinrich Müller and his gang were not the only professionals recruited by Heydrich. In Berlin a similar group was to be found, headed by Oberregierungsrat [senior civil servant] Arthur Nebe; he was as expert a policeman and as great an opportunist as the Bavarian Müller.

Nebe, born in 1894, was the son of a Berlin schoolteacher; he had served as a Lieutenant in the Engineers and had been with the Berlin Criminal Police since 1920. Later he was promoted SS-Gruppenführer but was then involved in the July 20th, 1944 plot and executed as a member of the resistance. At that time Ernst Kaltenbrunner, Heydrich's successor, wrote a character sketch of Nebe not unlike that given to Müller by the Munich Party headquarters: 'A two-faced character with an unhealthy degree of ambition . . . Nebe would ruthlessly push aside anything which stood in his path to promotion.'[110] Kaltenbrunner was no doubt influenced by his hatred of the 'traitors' of July 20th but nevertheless his picture of Nebe was basically not far wrong; on many occasions Nebe proved himself only too willing to adopt the prevailing attitude of cynicism.[111]

He was a suspicious inscrutable being, employed alternately in the drugs and theft sections of the Berlin police, who had been drawn to the Nazi Party in 1931[112] because, like many police officers at the time, he found their plans for the police tempting; National-Socialism offered what the Weimar Republic had refused to the police – more money and technical equipment, coordination of the fight against crime, protection from attacks by the press and increased use of preventive detention. The death-throes of the Republic encouraged the more far-sighted to commit themselves further. Nebe became a sponsoring member of the SS, joined the SA and accepted a transfer to the Gestapo, where he became head of the Executive (Abteilung III) in the Gestapa.[113]

This he was soon to regret, for he became involved in the sniping campaign between the Himmler–Heydrich team and Rudolf Diels, Göring's protégé and first Head of the Gestapa.[114] As already related (Chapter 5) Diels and Nebe disliked each other; Nebe passed to Heydrich incriminating material on Röhm, hoping thereby to work his way out of the Gestapa[115] – a hope only partially fulfilled.

In addition to these two teams of professional police officers from Munich and Berlin, Heydrich now collected a third group of educated experts, officials and lawyers from all over Germany, including the man who became Heydrich's closest collaborator and ultimately his enemy, the ex-District Judge from Hesse, Dr Werner Best.

Karl Rudolf Werner Best, born in 1903 in Darmstadt, was the son of a Post Office official. After studying law at Freiburg, Frankfurt and Giessen Universities, he entered the legal profession.[116] He was a supporter of the authoritarian State, an ardent nationalist, a disciple of Ernst Jünger and a romantic exponent of the Free Corps mentality, which (in his own words) regarded war as 'a necessary and natural form of the whole scheme of existence'.[117] In 1930 he published an article which read like a blueprint for a State founded on the 'law of the people'. He called for 'passionate support of the State as the highest expression of the urge for power, transcending all individual interests'; clearly he did not accept the ideal of a liberal State founded on the rule of law, nor did he concede to the law any overall validity.[118]

In Best's eyes, therefore, the word 'legality' did not imply that, all men being equal before the law, the ordinary citizen could obtain redress against the all-pervading power of the State; Best considered the law merely as a weapon to be used in the struggle for power, a 'codification of the outcome of a preceding phase of struggle – accession of power on one side, loss of power on the other'. He continued: 'The goal of each individual authority within the State is to assure its dominance over the others; as a result all of them . . . seek to identify themselves with "the State". The State inevitably tends to maximize its authority; the more complete its predominance, the more perfect the State.'[119]

In Best's case these were no empty words. In mid-1931, when the spectre of Communist revolution was still abroad in Germany, Best attended a meeting of certain Nazis in a farmhouse named 'Boxheim' near Worms and expounded both verbally and in writing his thoughts on a National-Socialist counter-revolution; they soon became notorious as the 'Boxheim Documents'. He proposed, for instance, that after 'the disappearance of the old high-level State authorities and after the suppression of the commune', the SA and local defence formations should 'seize power in the leaderless State' and ruthlessly impose 'the strictest discipline upon the population'; those carrying arms should be executed 'without trial and on the spot'.[120] A renegade Nazi gave Best's plans away to the police, who acted forthwith; Best was forbidden to practise in Hesse but, in October 1931, the Leipzig High Court decided not to proceed further against him 'on grounds of lack of evidence'.[121] The National-Socialist seizure of power, however, gave Best, the police state theoretician, a place in the police; his friend, Dr Heinrich Müller, was nominated Reich Commissar in Hesse and asked Best to take over the police force there. Naturally he accepted.

As Police President of Hesse, however, Best soon fell foul of Sprenger, the Gauleiter, who disliked his critical realist attitude to the Party's requirements, and in autumn 1933 Best was sacked.[122] Meanwhile, however, he had joined the SS and, on losing his job in Hesse, was placed in charge of the SD-Oberabschnitte South and South-West;[123] his name was therefore on Heydrich's list and in late 1934, when the latter set about expanding the Gestapa, Best was summoned. Little did Heydrich think that he was engaging his most persistent 'wet blanket' – as he put it.[124] For in spite of all his theoretical longings for the national authoritarian State, in his heart of hearts Best was still a lawyer; a tiny remnant of the barrister's mental approach still remained. Moreover he was too firmly cast in the official mould and his thinking was too factual to enable him to compete with the unscrupulous opportunism characteristic of the rising generation of legally-trained SD functionaries such as Walter Schellenberg.

But these shades of difference between the Nazi police officials were still in the distant future. Heydrich and his new staff were now laying the foundations for the future machine of tyranny, the instrument whose name alone made millions of Germans shudder – the Gestapo.

Heydrich deliberately played upon the horror evoked by the name. Only a reputation for omniscience and pitiless action could make the Gestapo the Führer dictatorship's great deterrent weapon and stifle all possible opposition to the régime. Heydrich once said that the Gestapo was regarded with a mixture of 'fear and horror'[125] – betraying the secret satisfaction of a man who had reached his goal.

The foundations of the Gestapo were laid by Göring as Premier of Prussia. He had hived off from the Kripo [Kriminalpolizei – Criminal Police] its specifically political sections, together with the Political Police which dealt with high treason, and the counter-espionage police [Abwehrpolizei] which dealt with treason. These were all amalgamated into a new organization known as the Secret State Police [Geheime Staatspolizei – Gestapo].[126] Political police tasks had originally been the responsibility of the Prussian LKPA [Landeskriminalpolizeiamt – Land Criminal Police Office] which maintained a so-called 'Ia Abteilung' in each police headquarters, the one in Berlin functioning as a sort of Intelligence centre for the political police as a whole. As part of the police, the Landeskriminalpolizeistellen [Land Criminal Police Offices] came under the jurisdiction of the Oberpräsidenten [Provincial Prefects] and Regierungspräsidenten [Government Presidents].[127]

All this Göring altered radically. In April 1933 the Geheime Staatspolizeiamt [Secret State Police Office], known as the Gestapa, took the place of the LKPA and all branches of the Political Police were brought under a single authority; the true Political Police, the core of the Gestapo, became Abteilung III in the Gestapa and the counter-espionage police became Abteilung IV; to these were added Abteilung I (Organization and Administration) and Abteilung II (Legal).[128]

On the middle levels similar changes were made. In the provinces the LKPA offices [Stellen] were replaced by Gestapo Stellen which – and here was the decisive point – were responsible to the Regierungspräsidenten on paper only. From the end of 1933 the Gestapo claimed to be an autonomous authority independent of the internal administration and responsible only to the Prussian Minister-President. A sentence in the Prussian Gestapo law of November 30th, 1933 stated in so many words that the head of a Gestapo Stelle might conform to the 'wishes' of the Regierungspräsident but only 'in so far as this does not conflict with existing directives and instructions' – from the Gestapa.[129]

The internal administration was, in effect, deprived of any say in political police matters and from April 1st, 1934 the State Police Authorities were forbidden to maintain political sections.[130] When, in addition, it is remembered that the emergency ordinance 'For Protection of People and State' issued by the Reich President on February 28th, 1933 had suspended all basic legal rights and empowered the police to make house searches, carry out arrests, confiscate property, tap telephones and open letters – all without a Court Order[131] – a more powerful police than Göring's Gestapo can hardly be imagined.

But this did not satisfy the secret-police perfectionist, Heydrich. He spent his time painting the dangers to the régime in the most glaring colours. In fact he followed the procedure which a dictatorship's Chief of Police invariably adopts when he wishes to initiate build-up of his terror machine – he creates an enemy of the State.

As Head of the Gestapo, Heydrich suddenly emerged from his anonymity and sounded the alarm to the world at large. In a speech early in 1935 he upbraided his Party comrades for failure to understand that, although 'the enemy organizations had been smashed', the enemy had by no means been annihilated; the régime's enemies had 'coordinated' themselves and must now be 'sought out in their new positions'. 'The enemy motive forces,' he explained, 'will always be the same – world Jewry, world Freemasonry and the clergy who are to a large extent political'; more dangerous, however, than this 'visible' enemy was the undercover enemy: 'He works outside the law. His objective is the destruction of the leadership's unity, both in Party and State ... the ramifications of this network are enormous.'[132]

The build-up of the control machinery could now begin. The Gestapa

Sections [Abteilungen] were expanded into three divisions [Hauptabteilungen] and the general staff of terror took over.

The new arrivals set out to draw Göring's police net ever tighter round the population. If, however, action against the 'enemies of the State' was to be intensified, the Gestapo had to know who these enemies were. Göring had often left his officials wondering, but in general terms 'enemy of the State' had seemed to be synonymous with 'Communist' or 'Marxist'. The new masters of the Prinz-Albrecht-Strasse, however, left no one in any doubt.

'An enemy of the State is anyone who consciously opposes the People, the Party and the State, their ideological tenets or their political actions' – said SS-Hauptsturmführer Alfred Schweder;[133] in an internal memorandum Wendzio, an ex-Criminal Police official, described the enemies of the State in terms more comprehensible to the simpler Gestapo intellects: 'In detail the term covers: Communism, Marxism, Jewry, political activities by the Churches, Freemasonry, political malcontents (grousers), national opposition, reaction, the "Black Front" (Strasser, Prague), industrial saboteurs, habitual criminals, abortionists and homosexuals (offences from the demographic point of view against the strength and defence capacity of the people, risk of espionage in the case of homosexuals), treason and high treason.' According to Wendzio, this conglomeration of evil-doers had a single 'goal' in common; their efforts were directed against 'the spiritual and racial patrimony of the German people'.[134]

A highly developed system of lists and card indexes kept track of every conceivable opponent of the régime. The Gestapa in Berlin and its out-stations in the provinces kept a so-called 'A' card index, wherein 'dangerous' enemies of the State (in the Gestapo sense of the word) were divided into three groups:

Group A1, distinguished by a red tab on the left of the card, consisted of opponents of the régime who were to be arrested as soon as unobtrusive preparations for general mobilization were initiated.

Group A2 (Blue Tabs) listed persons to be arrested on a public announcement of mobilization.

Group A3 (Green Tabs) consisted of persons who were not security risks but who, in Heydrich's words 'in times of stress . . . must be regarded as so dangerous politically that their apprehension or close supervision must be considered'.[135]

Yet another system of coloured tabs enabled the Gestapo to draw even finer distinctions between their victims. Enemies of the State were further classified by a second tab on the right of the card – dark red for a Communist, light red for a 'Marxist', brown for an 'assassin' and violet for a 'grumbler'. Cards were checked twice yearly on April 1st and October 1st to ensure that the classifications still held good.[136]

So detailed a system for keeping 'enemies of the State' under observation naturally necessitated continuous expansion of the authority and activities of the Secret Police. The Gestapa was formed from Abteilung Ia in Berlin Police Headquarters which had a staff of 35, but by early 1935 it had reached a strength of 607 officials and employees; in 1933 the Gestapo's annual budget was around 1,000,000 marks but by 1937 it had reached 40,000,000 marks.[137]

The Gestapo 'Stellen' [local offices] in each Regierungsbezirk [Government administrative district] and the 'Leitstellen' [regional offices], formed in 1937 at the headquarters of each Oberpräsident or Land Government, increased in size.[138] The counter-espionage police began to encroach upon the preserves of the military counter-espionage service. Gradually, the frontier control service came under the Gestapo's wing. The Frontier Commissariats, hitherto under the LKPA, were attached to the Gestapo and given the status of 'out-station' to the local Gestapo Stelle.[139] Later the Gestapo created its own frontier police which in fact had nothing to do with frontier control but carried out purely secret-police functions. Its task was to apprehend enemies of the régime on the frontier and track down persons suspected of treason: for this reason it came under Desk [Referat] G of Hauptabteilung III of the Gestapa, in other words the counter-espionage police.[140]

An iron curtain descended on the frontiers of Hitler Germany. A carefully calculated tracking system was supposed to guarantee that no fugitive could escape the Gestapo's all-seeing eye. Various types of search warrant were instituted – local warrants (for action by the local police and municipal authorities) and State Police warrants. Again colours were used to differentiate between the criminals – brick-red for escaped prisoners and white with red stripes for deportees.[141] Eight letters were used to signify the object of the search:

A Arrest
B Arrest, if no fixed address
C Report place of residence
D For deportation
E Search for missing persons
F Recover lost papers
G Unobtrusive observation
V Professional criminal – arrest[142]

The greater the power of the police, the easier it became for the Gestapo to keep track of people. In later years, for instance, stateless persons due for deportation were consigned to a concentration camp by the Gestapa pending completion of the formalities. Everything, of course, had to be done in proper form; a minute from Best, dated July 26th, 1937, for instance, states: 'The acceptance of the stateless person into the concentration camp designated by me will take place through the Land Police Authority, under the provisions of Gestapa Form No 240. On acceptance of the deportee, the concentration camp will forward to me the top copy of Gestapa Form No 240, together with the index card Gestapa No 98 carrying a photograph of the deportee.' Only when some other country had signified willingness to accept the deportee was he allowed to leave the concentration camp. Best laid down: 'Before passing him across the frontier, the Frontier Police Authority will obtain from the stateless person a statement in duplicate recognizing that, should he return, he runs the risk of detention in a concentration camp.'[143]

The authority to issue warrants for preventive arrest, and consign men to concentration camps placed a murderous weapon in the hands of the Gestapo. It undermined the rule of law in Germany and all the machinery of judge, solicitor and defence counsel was unable to prevent men suddenly disappearing behind the barbed wire of the concentration camps.

The highest authority for the issue of preventive arrest warrants was the Gestapa; unhampered by any legal system, it had the power to consign initially every Prussian, and later every German, to a concentration camp for an unspecified period. Lower-level Gestapo offices could also place men under preventive arrest, but only for a period of seven days. If the order was not confirmed by the Gestapa, the prisoner had to be released on the eighth day.[144] As soon as Heydrich took over the Gestapo, however, the number of concentration-camp prisoners rose; in 1935–6 alone over 7,000 'Marxists' were arrested[145] on grounds explained by Dr Best as follows: 'Any attempt to gain recognition for, or even to uphold, different political ideas will be ruthlessly dealt with as the symptom of a disease which threatens the healthy unity of the indivisible national organism, regardless of the subjective wishes of its supporters.'[146]

However, the more menacing the growth of the Gestapo's power became, the more numerous its enemies grew. The lawyers and the bureaucrats combined to halt, or at least to retard, the Gestapo's victorious progress – and they were aiming at nothing less than the removal of the Gestapo's favourite weapon, the concentration camp. Certain courageous lawyers uncovered crimes and abuses in the concentration camps and publicized them in the hope of persuading the more moderate Nazi leaders to disband these torture factories.[147]

As early as summer 1933, when Heydrich and Himmler were setting up their trial system of terror in Bavaria, individual lawyers had begun to play a carefully concealed game. The Public Prosecutor's office of State Court II, Munich, was alerted to numerous unexplained cases of death in Dachau concentration camp; on June 2nd, 1933, in a memorandum to the Bavarian Ministry of Justice, it stated that 'the proceedings regarding the events in Dachau Concentration Camp are to be pursued with all determination'.[148] On several occasions the Public Prosecutor's office recorded its findings on murders in Dachau. In the second fortnight of May 1933 it inquired into the deaths of four Dachau prisoners (Schloss, Hausmann, Strauss and Nefzger) and found that they had been tortured to death by the camp guards. At the end of September 1933 the office insisted on a post-mortem examination of the body of Hugo Handschuch, another prisoner who had died in Dachau; conclusion – 'haemorrhage originating from blows with a blunt instrument. Evidence of guilt on the part of third parties.' In late October 1933 the same office attempted to clear up the supposed suicides of two further prisoners, Wilhelm Franz and Dr Delwin Katz; judgement – 'the autopsy gave grounds for a well-founded suspicion that in the case of both corpses force by an outside hand had been applied . . . strangulation and throttling'.[149]

The Public Prosecutor's office, Munich II, then requested authority from the Ministry of Justice to check the legitimacy of the arrangements in Dachau and filed cases for incitement to murder against SS-Oberführer Hilmar Wäkkerle, the Camp Commandant, Dr Nuernbergk, the Camp Medical Officer and Mutzbauer, the Head of the Camp Office.[150] Himmler was obliged to sack the Camp Commandant.[151] Himmler and Heydrich, however, reacted all the more violently against any attempt by the Public Prosecutor's office to investigate other cases. They persuaded Wagner, the Minister of the Interior, to propose to the Cabinet that in the case of concentration-camp crimes investigation should be refused 'for reasons of State policy'.[152]

The majority of the Bavarian Cabinet, however, rejected Wagner's proposal, so Himmler now raised another obstacle between the Public Prosecutor and the Concentration Camp. He persuaded Hans Frank, the Minister of Justice, to issue an instruction to all Public Prosecutors 'to refrain for the time being from making an application for the opening of preliminary investigations'.[153]

The Public Prosecutor, however, persisted. On July 12th, 1934 he requested the Bavarian Political Police 'in consultation with the Commandant of Dachau Concentration Camp, to clarify further the facts of the case and attempt to discover the persons suspected as the culprits'. Heydrich's Political Police commented acidly: 'The latest application by the Public Prosecutor, Munich II, for production of evidence shows what far-fetched means are employed to saddle the Dachau Concentration Camp with alleged crimes.'[154] The camp staff hastened to cover their tracks and on September 27th, 1934 Wintersberger, the Public Prosecutor, was forced to suspend proceedings.[155]

Himmler now thought up a clever manoeuvre to tie the hands of the Public Prosecutors. The leading light of the anti-Dachau group was Dr Walther Steppe, the senior State Attorney; he was a convinced National-Socialist and Himmler persuaded him to join the SS, feeding him the story that, as an SS-Hauptsturmführer, he would be better placed to deal with the abuses in Dachau. So from critic of the Political Police, Steppe turned into its functionary – one year later he was its Deputy Chief.[156]

In Prussia too, brave men were found to take up the cudgels against concentration-camp crime. Diels, the first Head of the Gestapo, disbanded numerous 'unofficial' concentration camps, the majority run by the SA. He planned to use the Minister's authority to suppress political crime and persuaded two National-Socialists in the Ministry of Justice, Werner von Haacke and Gunther Joel, to support him. Within the Prussian Ministry of Justice these two set up a central Public Prosecutor's Office which, though primarily occupied in dealing with the SA gangsters, from time to time contrived to attack criminals in the Gestapo and the SS.[157]

Von Haacke scored the first major success of his campaign in a battle with the Stettin Gestapo Office. SS-Sturmführer Joachim Hoffmann, the Head of the Office, maintained a concentration camp in the Vulkan Shipyard, Stettin-Bredow, where men were bestially tortured (in Gestapo slang 'Vulkanized'). Haacke succeeded in arresting Hoffmann and recalls that he found standing before him, 'a fanatical, sadistic intellectual with an absence of feeling such as I had never experienced before. I have only known one other man whose character, even his manner and his gestures, immediately reminded me of Hoffmann – and that man was Heydrich.'[158] On April 6th, 1934 No 2 High Court Stettin condemned Hoffmann to thirteen years' hard labour; his assistants also received prison sentences.[159]

Encouraged by this success, other members of the legal profession began to resist the SS torturers. Dr Walther Schaeffer, the Public Prosecutor of Breslau, showed particular courage; after the June 30th blood bath, he arrested twenty SS men, including two Standartenführer, as suspected murderers and was only forced to release them after prolonged argument with Roland Freisler, the Permanent Secretary in the Ministry of Justice.[160] The departure of Diels, however, and Göring's defection to the Himmler–Heydrich camp left the lawyers without protection, half-hearted though it had frequently been. At a sitting of the Prussian Staatsrat [State Council] in November 1934, Göring fulminated: 'There are still State Attorneys who specialize in dragging senior members of the Party off to prison, but we will bring their dirty work to an end.'[161]

Nevertheless some lawyers still refused to be intimidated. Early in 1935 Dr Walther, the State Attorney of Saxony, laid a charge of serious maltreatment of prisoners against an SA man, the Head of the Hohnstein concentration camp; the Gestapo was also involved and Walther prepared a separate case against Erich Vogel, the Gestapo official responsible. The concentration-camp thugs were duly condemned to several years imprisonment, but then Mutschmann, the Gauleiter of Saxony, brought pressure to bear on the Court and demanded their release. This brought a protest from Dr Franz Gürtner the Reich Minister of Justice: 'However bitter the struggle, there can be no explanation or excuse for such cruelties; they are reminiscent of oriental sadism.' The Court confirmed its sentence but the Nazis soon had their revenge. The two Court assessors were expelled from the Party and the State Attorney was requested to leave the SA. Then Hitler, the supreme judge, intervened – he pardoned the accused and quashed the case against Vogel.[162]

At heart, Gürtner, the Minister of Justice, was still a liberal nationalist and such arbitrary action turned his mind towards a desperate, even foolhardy, plan; the only method, he thought, of curbing the despotism of the Führer dictatorship and the Gestapo would be to produce an abridged form of the legal code in National-Socialist style, thus preserving the essential minimum of legal norms, by which even Hitler and his minions would be bound.[163] Gürtner found an ally in the new Reich Commissar for Justice, Dr Hans Frank, the most extreme of all the National-Socialist guardians of the law. Frank's object was a fundamental de-liberalization of the entire legal code, which he then proposed to base upon a new, somewhat hazy, notion – the protection of the so-called 'popular values'. Nevertheless Frank was opposed to arbitrary action by an omnipotent police force. Unfortunately not until he was under sentence at Nuremberg did he perceive 'the horrifying thing about Adolf Hitler' – 'that in his struggle period he had himself enjoyed the protection of the law but later, as a statesman, had shown contempt for the law and the legal profession.'[164] Even on June 30th, 1934 Frank had found in the Stadelheim Prison that the hands of justice were tied by the Führer dictatorship; his experience at that time sowed within him the seeds of doubt which caused him, when Governor General of Poland in 1942, to lead the most sustained public attack on Heinrich Himmler's police despotism ever made in the greater German Reich.

In late 1933, Frank and Gürtner set up an 'Official Criminal Law Commission' [Amtliche Strafrechtskommission] to work out a new punishment code. Frank contributed the National-Socialist slogans, which the assiduous Roland Freisler dressed up in paragraphs; meanwhile Gürtner and his amanuensis Dohnanyi, who later became a Clerk of the High Court and was eventually executed in connexion with the July 20th, 1944 plot, sought means of preventing Hitler and the Gestapo from treating the law in too cavalier a fashion.[165] In the process, however, Gürtner managed to persuade Frank to support him in his major objective – the abolition of the concentration camps.

In summer 1934 Frank and Gürtner plucked up their courage 'to attack Hitler direct' (Frank's words). A meeting was held in the Cabinet room of the Reich Chancellery with Hitler and Himmler present and the two lawyers put forward their arguments against the concentration-camp system.[166] In his memoirs Frank says: 'I proposed that the earliest possible terminal date should be set for the entire system and that an immediate halt should be called to further arrests; I further proposed that the cases of all persons still under arrest, together with all complaints of ill-treatment, should be examined under the law, in other words by the normal courts. Dr Gürtner supported me energetically but he and I were alone.' Hitler rejected the proposal, saying that it was 'premature' to abolish the concentration camps. Even Frank's new punishment code he later pigeon-holed.[167]

Gürtner, however, continued to search for methods of restricting the power of the Gestapo and the injustices of the preventive detention system. He amassed a wealth of evidence on unadmitted cases of death in the concentration camps and eventually demanded that persons under preventive detention be accorded the right to demand legal aid from a qualified attorney. But Himmler would have none of it, merely noting: 'The concentration camps are conscientiously run and special measures are not therefore considered necessary.' He knew, of course, that he would invariably be supported by Hitler; on November

6th, 1935 he wrote to Gürtner: 'On November 1st I transmitted to the Führer and Reich Chancellor the request submitted to us that lawyers should be permitted to intervene in protective custody cases. The Führer has prohibited the consultation of lawyers and has asked me to inform you accordingly.'[168]

Gürtner was weak and over-cautious and so inevitably he failed in face of the inflexible determination of Himmler and Heydrich. Moreover many of the lawyers brought up in the nineteenth-century school of legal positivism showed themselves incapable of thinking more deeply; in the euphoria of the Nazi Führer cult they soon allowed themselves to become no more than dutiful underlings. So the opposition was doomed to failure.

The tone of the legal profession was not set by courageous champions of the law such as Schaeffer, nor by cautious defenders of the established system such as Gürtner; the tone was set by time-serving legal doctrinaires such as Carl Schmitt, who hoped 'to do away with the restrictions of precedent and the compulsion to base judgements upon findings of fact' and turn the legal profession 'into creative collaboration of the Führer's will.'[169] The *Juristische Wochenschrift* [Legal Weekly] of 1934[170] cried: 'Away with the pettifogging yoke of positivist law.' And Germany's judges began, with increasing lack of scruple, to underpin the might of the Gestapo. On May 2nd, 1935 the Prussian Administrative High Court decided that the actions of the Gestapa could not be contested in the Administrative Courts; the only recourse was registration of a disciplinary complaint with the Head of the Gestapa.[171] On October 7th, 1935 the Hamburg Administrative Court laid down that 'in the National-Socialist State, the legislature, the administration and the judiciary cannot be legally opposed . . . the judiciary cannot, therefore, invoke another point of view and disavow action by the State taken as a political measure.'[172]

From his desk in the Gestapa, Best observed with pleasure the agility with which the judiciary was attempting to adapt itself; he forwarded the judgements of the Courts to all Gestapo Stellen for information and delectation.[173] Step by step the majority of the judges moved closer to Best's cynical definition of police action: 'In so far as the police are acting in accordance with the rules laid down by their superiors – right up to the highest level – they can never be acting "lawlessly" or "contrary to the law". Provided the police are carrying out the will of the Leadership, they are acting legally.'[174]

As Minister of Justice Gürtner was indignant: 'It is enough to drive one to despair!' He told Dr Sahm, the Burgomeister of Berlin, that he hardly dared go to a reception now, since foreign journalists were always asking him about conditions in the concentration camps. Sahm asked what Frick, the Minister of the Interior, was doing about it. Gürtner waved him away saying: 'Göring and Heydrich carry a hundred times more weight than Frick.'[175] Gürtner knew only too well that Frick, the timorous Nazi conservative, was trying desperately to get rid of the miracle man whom he had once called in to help him against Göring. Frick was in fact repenting bitterly that he had handed over a unified Reich Police Force to so dangerous a man as Himmler.

All Frick's efforts would have been in vain had he not been joined by two senior bureaucrats who, though supporters of the régime, refused to accept the Gestapo's claim to increasingly wide authority over the administration. Ironically the leaders of the anti-Gestapo cabal were two men ostensibly closely connected with the SS – Eggert Reeder, the Regierungspräsident of Aachen, a sponsoring member and later an SS-Gruppenführer,[176] and his counterpart in Cologne, SS-Standartenführer Rudolf Diels,[177] Göring's ex-protégé, who had contributed more than any other official to the increase of the Gestapo's authority.

Frick and the two Regierungspräsidenten played their cards well in their efforts to curb the Gestapo's influence, at least outside Berlin. The Gestapo law of November 30th, 1933 had deprived the Oberpräsidenten and Regierungspräsidenten of all authority over the Gestapo Stellen;[178] the object at this stage, therefore, was to recapture some control over the Gestapa's outposts in the country as a whole. Frick opened the campaign on July 16th, 1934 with a circular addressed to all Oberpräsidenten and Regierungspräsidenten;[179] it contained a singular sentence to the effect that 'there was general agreement' that the independence of the Gestapo was 'only a transitory phase necessitated by the tense political situation resulting from the Röhm revolt.' Frick went on to lay down that there must be 'the closest collaboration between the Gestapo and the Administration to ensure that Oberpräsidenten and Regierungspräsidenten are kept continuously informed of the activities of the Gestapo Stellen.'[180] In other words, Frick was subordinating the Gestapo to the Administration.

From Aachen Reeder wrote promptly to the Minister of the Interior in August 1934, saying that the Regierungspräsident must 'assume actual undisputed political responsibility for his District' and therefore 'inevitably the Head of the Gestapo Stelle is one of my subordinates.'[181] Diels was even more explicit; on November 4th, 1934 he wrote to Göring: 'The separation of the political police from the remainder of the Administration must, in the long run, lead to difficulties of which you, Herr Ministerpräsident, are no doubt aware. To this "erosion" of the internal administration are added all the difficulties associated with the predominance of the Party over the State. . . the notion of political reliability must finally be done away with . . . this notion is at the root of the shameful lack of confidence which is hampering the work of the State Administration.'[182]

East Prussia's Oberpräsident, the fanatical anti-SS Gauleiter, Erich Koch, also complained about the Gestapo's sleuths, and called for assistance from Frick. On September 23rd, 1935, referring to the situation in Königsberg, Frick wrote to Himmler: 'I consider the present relationship between the Oberpräsident and the head of the Gestapo Stelle to be impossible in the long term and highly injurious to the authority of the State.' Himmler replied characteristically: 'The Führer has decided that no change should be made in the position of the Königsberg Gestapo.'[183]

The bureaucrats, however, brought such pressure to bear on the police machine that Himmler and Heydrich eventually declared themselves ready to negotiate a new Gestapo law with the Ministry of the Interior. After months of haggling the law was issued on February 10th, 1936. In effect it confirmed the existing situation; nevertheless in paragraph 5 it said: 'Gestapo Stellen are, at the same time, *subordinate* to the relevant Regierungspräsident, will conform to his instructions and will keep him informed of all political police matters.'[184]

To offset their concessions to the Administration, Himmler and Heydrich now demanded that the Ministry of the Interior fulfil its promise to put through legislation establishing a Reich Police Force. Basically the question had long since been decided. After their capture of the Gestapo in April 1934, Himmler and Heydrich had set up within the Gestapa a 'Central Bureau – Land Political Police Commanders',[185] which in practice coordinated the work of the Land police authorities with that of the Gestapo. In fact Himmler was already commanding the political police throughout the Reich and the only question remaining was the form in which he would exercise authority over the entire German Police Force, including its non-political elements.

Their partial success over the Gestapo law, however, had made the Ministry of the Interior officials bellicose and they now prepared a further line of resistance against the two SS men. They began toying with the idea of placing the unified police force under the Minister of the Interior and playing off against Himmler, whom they regarded as too powerful already, his Berlin rival, SS-Obergruppenführer and Police Lieutenant-General Kurt Daluege. As early as May 1933, when commanding the Prussian Land Police, Daluege had worked out plans envisaging what in local jargon was called 'Reichification' of the political police.[186] The idea suited Frick and henceforth he regarded Daluege as the future German police chief. When the Prussian Ministry of the Interior was absorbed into the Reich Ministry, Frick took on the pliable Daluege as head of the new police department. Himmler's rise to power in the summer of 1934 did not of course help Frick's plans for Daluege; nevertheless he asked his Ministry's legal experts to draw up a command organization for the new Reich Police Force, as far as possible excluding Himmler.

Frick's concept of the police command organization was this: the entire police force of the Reich to be concentrated under the Reich Ministry of the Interior; Himmler, as Inspector of the Gestapo to take over the police department within the Ministry as the subordinate of the Minister and with Police General Daluege as permanent deputy. According to Hans-Joachim Neufeldt, Frick's object clearly was 'to relegate Himmler to a purely political and protocol role, while exercising actual command of the entire police force through Daluege.'[187]

Himmler rejected Frick's proposals. On June 9th, 1936, speaking in the name of his Reichsführer, Heydrich demanded overriding authority; Himmler, he said, must be given ministerial rank, be on a level with the Commander-in-Chief of the armed forces, be entitled 'Reichsführer-SS and Chief of the German Police' and be subordinate to the Minister of the Interior only 'in his personal capacity' – in other words not at all. Himmler was therefore demanding undisputed control of the police machine. In a fury Frick sought an interview with Hitler but the Führer calmed the indignant Minister down; Himmler, he said, would not be given ministerial rank; he would only be invited to Cabinet discussions as a 'State Secretary'. Nevertheless, the Minister of the Interior returned a broken man – Hitler had given him to understand that Himmler's appointment as Head of the Police was a foregone conclusion.[188]

The Minister could now only manoeuvre in retreat. He objected that a Party office (Reichsführer-SS) should not be combined with a Governmental office (Chief of the German Police). In the draft of the law he added the words 'within the Reich Ministry of the Interior' after Himmler's title in four places. He clung tenaciously to his demand that Daluege should be Himmler's permanent deputy.[189] Himmler withdrew a fraction of an inch. He abandoned his demand for Ministerial rank; he allowed himself to become the 'personal and direct' subordinate of the Minister of the Interior – an almost meaningless term in the topsy-turvy Nazi phraseology; he accepted Daluege as his permanent deputy but only 'in the case of his [Himmler's] absence'.[190]

Hardly was the ink dry on Hitler's decree of June 17th, 1936, nominating a Chief of the German Police, than Himmler showed what his interpretation of his new authority was. He not only demanded authority over the entire Police Department, but he also grabbed certain other important spheres of activity within the Ministry of the Interior – legal matters concerning the press and the carrying of arms, arms traffic, passports, personnel questions concerning all officials of the Police Department including Police Presidents and Police Directors.[191]

Frick's candidate, Daluege, was left at the post. He ranked only as number three, with both Himmler and Heydrich above him, for, as in Bavaria, Himmler allotted the key role to Heydrich. As Chief of the German Police, Himmler set up beneath him two Hauptabteilungen entitled Hauptämter [Departments]:

Hauptamt Sicherheitspolizei [Security Police] under SS-Gruppenführer Reinhard Heydrich. It included the Gestapo and the Criminal Police.

Hauptamt Ordnungspolizei [Regular Police] under SS-Obergruppenführer and Police General Kurt Daluege. It included the Schutzpolizei [Urban Constabulary] the Gendarmerie [Rural Constabulary] and the Gemeindepolizei [Municipal Police].[192]

The entire police force of Hitler's Germany was now in Himmler's grip. Now he and Heydrich could initiate Phase Two of their great plan – the fusion of SS and Police into the Third Reich's State Protection Corps.

9

THE SD

On January 27th, 1937 the Prussian Landeskriminalpolizeiamt [Land Criminal Police Office – LKPA], the Headquarters of all Kripo Offices in Germany, was on stand-by alert. The LKPA teleprinters tapped out a message telling all Kripo Leitstellen and Stellen throughout the Reich what headquarters considered to be the most urgent task in the anti-criminal campaign.

The Alexanderplatz Headquarters required 'speedy transmission of a list of all criminals in your district, who in the opinion of the Criminal Police must be regarded as professional and habitual criminals or as habitual offenders against morality and who are at liberty.'[1] The Kripo Stellen were ordered to draw up lists allocating a number to each known criminal. The order continued: 'When the time comes, only the list number of the professional criminals concerned will be telegraphically transmitted.'[2]

A month later all was ready. On February 23rd the Chief of the German Police issued an instruction to the Prussian LKPA that on March 9th 'some 2,000 professional and habitual criminals or dangerous offenders against morality will be taken into preventive police custody.' Once more the LKPA teleprinters tapped out the orders and on March 9th the great manhunt duly began throughout Germany. The Criminal Police swarmed out and 2,000 prisoners were delivered to Sachsenhausen, Sachsenburg, Lichtenburg and Dachau concentration camps.[3]

This action directed from the LKPA ushered in the most controversial non-political measure in the history of the Third Reich's police – the preventive method of crime suppression. Heydrich's Sicherheitspolizei, which now included the Criminal Police, labelled whole categories of persons 'anti-social malefactors' [Volksschädling] and placed them under preventive arrest regardless of legal considerations.

The initiative had come from the Kripo: they had long been urging severe preventive measures to control the habitual criminal[4] and Sicherheitspolizei Headquarters seized on the idea. By virtue of paragraph 42 of the Reich Criminal Code, the Courts were now authorized to order preventive arrest in the interests of public security;[5] but in the eyes of the Sicherheitspolizei the Courts were overscrupulous in the use of their new-found authority, their decisions too 'liberalistic', too 'regulation'.[6]

The Sicherheitspolizei therefore now claimed for themselves the right to place a so-called professional criminal under preventive arrest – and in the Third Reich that meant the concentration camp. As their reason they maintained that a court could only judge how dangerous a criminal was in the light of a single act of crime; the police, on the other hand, possessed knowledge of all the internal and external circumstances affecting the criminal and so could form a broader judgement.[7]

There was a difficulty here: legally the police had no authority to place a criminal under preventive arrest; the procedure was embodied in no law,[8] but the Sicherheitspolizei found a way out. Best, the SD's legal expert, later gave a lecture on the subject and his argument ran as follows: a legal basis for this police procedure did exist since, in accordance with the Völkisch concept of law, both the authorities and individual members of the public were representatives of the people and they 'must work together for the maintenance of law and order in accordance with rules laid down by the leadership for the attainment of the people's aims.' Even in a case of arrest those representatives were working together, the police being the active partner and 'the criminal who is taken into preventive custody being the passive.'[9] More cold-blooded and cynical use of semantics can hardly be imagined – the criminal was assisting the police by allowing himself to be arrested and incarcerated in a concentration camp! Use of preventive arrest for the suppression of crime, however, meant that the normal system of justice was deprived of its right to conduct an unprejudiced examination of each individual case. So a process began in which 'the community was treated like a nursery garden where the ill-grown shoot has to be "pricked out" and "rooted out" at regular intervals.'[10] Crime in Germany had not noticeably increased at the time,[11] but nevertheless the Sicherheitspolizei prescribed a seasonal quota of arrests. The Chief of the German Police, or his immediate subordinate the Chief of the Sicherheitspolizei, simply decided when a new intake of criminals was due for the concentration camps.[12]

This system of preventive arrest was but a further illustration of the power Heydrich now possessed. Since Himmler's nomination in June 1936 as Chief of the German Police and his own appointment as Head of the Sicherheitspolizei, Heydrich had commanded an instrument of tyranny unparalleled in German history.

In the grasping hands of Himmler and Heydrich the words 'Security Police' took on a new meaning. In legal parlance 'Security Police' had hitherto been used to describe the police as a whole with its two main groupings, the Administrative Police (eg, Traffic Police and Industrial Police) and the Executive Police; the latter was divided into four branches, the Kripo [Criminal Police] the Schupo [Urban Constabulary], the Political Police and the Gendarmerie.[13] Himmler, however, hived off from the Executive Police its politically significant branches, the Political Police and the Criminal Police, and formed the Sicherheitspolizei [Security Police – Sipo] under Heydrich. The remainder of the Executive Police and the Administrative Police he left to his SS rival, Kurt Daluege; they were merged to form the new Ordnungspolizei [Regular Police – Orpo].[14]

Parallel to Daluege's Hauptamt Ordnungspolizei and subordinate to the 'Reichsführer-SS and Chief of the German Police', Heydrich formed the Hauptamt Sicherheitspolizei, which ranked as a ministerial authority under the Reich Ministry of the Interior. However, since Hauptamt Sicherheitspolizei had no legal authority to make arrests or order interrogations, it had to rely upon two existing police organizations – the Gestapo and the Prussian LKPA; as supreme Land authority the Gestapa administered the Secret State Police in Prussia and as supreme Reich authority it administered the Political Police in all other German Länder (Political Police terminology in the other Länder had been brought into line with that of Prussia on October 1st, 1936); the Prussian LKPA, which had directed the Kripo in the other Länder, was now officially re-named Reichskriminalpolizeiamt [Reich Criminal Police Office – RKPA] and became a supreme Reich Authority responsible for the entire German Criminal Police Force.[15]

The Gestapo and the RKPA remained part of Hauptamt Sicherheitspolizei, as so-called 'Reich Specialist Headquarters'; Abteilung I (Administration and Legal) of the Gestapa, however, was hived off and became a ministerial authority directly under the Ministry of the Interior.[16] Hauptamt Sicherheitspolizei therefore consisted eventually of the Administration and Legal Department, under Dr Werner Best, the Political Police under Heinrich Müller, the Counter-Espionage Police under Dr Werner Best, and the Criminal Police under Arthur Nebe.[17]

Here was a vast concentration of power. The Sicherheitspolizei was continually extending its control over different spheres of the nation's life and gradually it created an area within which the rule of law did not exist and into which no other official institution or legal authority was able to penetrate. On paper Hauptamt Sicherheitspolizei was a Ministry of the Interior authority and Heydrich a subordinate of the Minister;[18] in practice, however, Heydrich gave Frick no insight into what he was doing – the fact that his more important offices were far removed from the Ministry was not accidental.

Heydrich worked tirelessly to screen his machine from prying eyes. His quick-witted lawyers could always produce some sophism to convince the gullible citizenry that arbitrary police action was a more exalted form of law. The ever-inventive Best, for instance, declared that in relation to police work legal rules were unnecessary since Hitler's will 'created law and altered existing law'.[19] Professor Reinhard Höhn of the SD went one better. He proposed to abolish the concept both of the State and the individual as persons in law; the State, he said, was not an end in itself but merely a means of attaining the people's goal as laid down by the Führer.[20]

If, however, the concept of State and individual as persons under law was abolished, the citizen had no further redress against arbitrary action by the police. No Sicherheitspolizei measure could be contested in law, neither before the administrative courts nor by an action for compensation for damages, nor by a private libel suit, and certainly not by criminal proceedings for deprivation of liberty. Only one recourse was open to the citizen and it was a dangerous procedure – a disciplinary complaint to the Head of the Sicherheitspolizei.[21]

The law thus being powerless, Heydrich was in effect able to decide for himself how far his power over the defenceless citizenry should extend. His power to order preventive arrest and send men to concentration camps made him absolute master of life and liberty.[22] The Minister of the Interior's decree of April 12th, 1934, laying down the principles for preventive arrest, did indeed state that 'protective custody shall not be used as punishment for criminal offences or offences which ... are reprehensible'; these were to be 'dealt with by the courts' alone.[23] The Sipo, however, took it upon itself to amend and increase sentences passed by the courts.

When prisoners were released from the normal jails on conclusion of sentence, Heydrich's men were waiting at the gates and any who fell into the following categories were automatically consigned to concentration camps: persons condemned for treasonable activities; Communist officials; anyone condemned by a 'People's Court'; and members of the banned International Bible Research Association (whose pacifist pronouncements were regarded by the Sipo as incitement to refusal of military service).[24]

According to the whim of Heydrich and his minions politically suspect persons could either be handed over to the courts or dispatched to a concentration camp. In most cases their destination was the latter, for preventive arrest, as opposed to police arrest, was subject to no examination by the courts. On February 26th, 1937 Heydrich instructed the Gestapa: 'I desire that in future no use should be made of the power to order police arrest, so as to avoid the necessity for subsequent examination by the courts of measures taken by the police. Imposition of police arrest ... is superfluous since in all these cases the possibility of imposition of preventive arrest is open.'[25]

But Heydrich did not confine himself solely to political cases. The 'enemy of the State' became an increasingly all-embracing notion. Where political criteria did not fit the bill, criminal police considerations came into the picture and the 'enemy of the State' turned into the 'anti-social malefactor'.[26] Using the preventive method of crime suppression as a cover, the Sicherheitspolizei began to sweep up into their net those groups on the fringe of society who, by one method or another, had contrived to evade the totalitarian grip of the régime.

The circle of those liable to preventive detention was drawn wider and wider and the notion of the 'anti-social malefactor' became increasingly imprecise.

Three ill-defined groups of potential concentration-camp inmates emerged: 'Professional and habitual criminals' – these were people who had been sentenced to a minimum of six months' imprisonment or hard labour on three occasions; 'anti-socials' – these were beggars, tramps, gipsies, nomads, prostitutes, homosexuals, grumblers, drunkards, brawlers, traffic offenders, psychopaths, lunatics and swindlers; 'the work-shy' – these were men who, according to Himmler, 'could be proved to have refused without adequate reason employment offered to them on two occasions.'[27] Anywhere and at any time the Sicherheitspolizei could decide who belonged to these categories and who, therefore, was destined for the concentration camp. Never before in Germany had men been at the mercy of such liberty of decision on the part of the police.

Nevertheless the apparently monolithic Sicherheitspolizei concealed certain internal weaknesses and tensions. Heydrich's rapid rise to power had aroused the jealousy of the more powerful SS leaders; the heads of the SS Hauptämter were offended by his domineering manner and even the mistrustful Himmler sometimes had to take emergency action to slow his subordinate's headlong progress.

In Adolf Hitler's Germany precedence belonged to the man who could cut the broadest swathe through the jungle of intrigue over prerogatives and spheres of authority. The battle for authority took the place of the old parliamentary squabbles; political power was measured in terms of areas of jurisdiction, numbers of subordinates and powers of command; mere rank and theoretical position in the hierarchy meant little. In this jungle, however, Heydrich's dominance was not yet complete. He could issue warrants for preventive arrest but he did not control the concentration camps. He accordingly suggested to Himmler that he should take over administration of the camps, probably calculating that if he could combine the police and the camps under his own hand, his power really would be total.

The concentration camp was the centrepiece of Himmler's police State; it was the silent ubiquitous threat hanging over every German. With its electrified barbed wire and its wooden watch-towers, it lent sinister reality to the SS-run system of police control. The very name was intended to cast a spell over every German, to stifle every movement of opposition. Eugen Kogon says: 'Their main purpose was the elimination of every trace of actual or potential opposition to Nazi rule. Segregation, debasement, humiliation, extermination – these were the effective forms of terror.'[28]

The SS masters of the concentration-camp world deliberately refused to allow the camps to become centres of political re-education. The more gullible National-Socialists may genuinely have believed that the purpose of the camps was to re-educate political opponents and, after a probationary period, release them again; in practice, however, the camps were planned from the outset as instruments of terror for the maintenance of the régime. Until, with the war, they became war production factories manned by armies of slaves, the purpose of the camps was to frighten and to deter. The torture sheds of Dachau, Buchenwald and Sachsenhausen were intended to demonstrate to the Germans the fate awaiting those who opposed the Führer.

'Forget your wives, children and families. Here you will die like dogs,' was Karl Fritzsch's greeting to every new batch of arrivals in his concentration camp.[29] Stories which filtered through the barbed wire and were passed on by the grapevine – of the Buchenwald 'Cowstall' arranged for nape-of-the-neck shooting, of the Dachau 'Dog Kennel' where prisoners could only lie wedged together on their sides, or of the rigged accidents in the Mauthausen quarries[30] – simply increased the terror and panic which the words 'concentration camp' induced in Hitler's Germany. If Heydrich was to be sole master of his machine of terror, however, he could not allow so powerful a tool of the Führer dictatorship to remain outside the Sicherheitspolizei for long. He was continually urging Himmler to place the camps under his Hauptamt, and shortly after the Gestapo law of February 10th, 1936 an instruction was issued placing the concentration-camp administration under the Gestapo;[31] in his authoritative book published in 1938 Helmut Schlierbach says: 'The political police in Prussia and the concentration camps were directly administered by the Gestapo through the Inspector.'[32] As in the Diels period in the early 1930s the Gestapo once more appeared to have become masters of the concentration camps.[33]

But in fact Himmler had no intention of handing over the camps to Heydrich and the 1936 instruction remained a dead letter.[34] Himmler retained control of the concentration-camp system himself; they belonged to the SS as a whole. Heydrich was faced with a repetition of the events of March 1933; at that time Dachau had come under Himmler's command in his capacity as Political Police Commander Bavaria;[35] when, however, Heydrich as his deputy placed the administration of the camp under the Bavarian Political Police, Himmler barred his way with a man who refused to allow the newcomer to interfere.

This was Theodor Eicke, a failed police officer and an ex-Paymaster whom Himmler had rescued from a psychiatric clinic in Würzburg where he had been confined as a 'dangerous lunatic' by his arch-enemy

Gauleiter Bürckel. 'Papa Eicke' was eternally grateful and consequently a pliant tool of his Reichsführer.[36]

His pleasant-sounding nickname was misleading. Eicke was an Alsatian with a grudge of explosive proportions against society, the legacy of a career which had failed at every stage: in 1919 shortage of cash had forced him to terminate his studies at the Ilmenau Technical College; in 1920 he became a police informer in Ilmenau but was dismissed without notice; he then attended the police school in Cottbus but was refused employment; he joined the Schutzpolizei in Weimar but was dismissed without notice after a fortnight; he applied for a job at police headquarters in Sorau but was refused.[37] For a man like this there was only one hope left – the National-Socialist revolution and a career in the SS. At the end of June 1933 Himmler promoted him SS-Oberführer and found him employment for which he was totally suited – commandant of Dachau.[38]

Here Eicke found men of his own stamp, failures in life nursing grudges which they worked off on the prisoners. Benedikt Kautsky, who was in Dachau, described the camp staff as drawn from the stupidest and most indolent section of the population who, when unemployment ended, saw no way of avoiding doing a decent job of work other than joining the SS.[39] Under Eicke's experienced direction anyone who still retained a shred of decency and humanity was very soon brutalized.

Later Eicke complained that on arrival in Dachau he found 'a corrupt guard detachment of barely 120 men' and that in addition SS Oberabschnitt South had sent him men 'who for some reason or another the people in Munich wished to get rid of.' He continued: 'We were generally regarded as a necessary evil which unfortunately cost money.'[40] Eicke put his house in order with barbaric discipline. He drew up a set of camp orders threatening any prisoner who refused to obey with 'being shot on the spot or subsequently hanged for mutiny'; he inspired his guard personnel with virulent hatred for the 'enemies of the State'.[41]

Höss, later the commandant of Auschwitz, once heard Eicke proclaim that pity for enemies of the State was unworthy of an SS man; there was no room for weaklings in his unit and they would do well to lock themselves up in monasteries as soon as possible; he had a use only for hard, determined men who would carry out any order ruthlessly; they did not wear the Death's-Head badge for nothing.[42] Himmler was so delighted with Eicke's Regiment in Dachau that he decided to put the ex-Paymaster in charge of all the concentration camps. After June 30th, 1934 (when Eicke murdered Röhm), Himmler gave him extraordinary powers; he became head of all concentration-camp guard units, the

Totenkopfverbände (Death's-Head Formations – TV), and Inspector of Concentration Camps.[43]

Heydrich strove vainly to break Eicke's grip on the camps, but found himself hamstrung. Though theoretically a member of the SS-Hauptamt as 'Inspector of Concentration Camps and Commander of SS Guard Formations', Eicke was Himmler's personal subordinate.[44]

Heydrich quietly collected evidence on the catastrophic conditions in the camps. Eicke had meanwhile concentrated the smaller scattered camps into four – Dachau, Sachsenhausen, Buchenwald and Lichtenburg; in 1937, when the lowest figure of concentration-camp prisoners was recorded, 4,833 TV men were keeping watch over some 10,000 prisoners.[45] Reports of ill-treatment of prisoners continued to come in; Broszat states: 'The main forms of punishment were regular beatings, close arrest, hard labour, making detention conditions worse by prohibiting prisoners from writing or receiving letters, as well as tying prisoners to trees – a form of punishment originally introduced by Eicke in Dachau . . . Even in this period there were instances of prisoners being maltreated and killed by SS guards.'[46]

Heydrich's lawyers began to criticize the treatment meted out to prisoners in Eicke's camps – not of course for reasons of humanity but as a move in the struggle for power within the SS. In October 1935 the Gestapo issued concentration-camp regulations requiring commandants to inform the regional public prosecutors forthwith whenever unassailable medical reasons could not be given as the cause of a prisoner's death.[47] The camps, however, took little notice, for Eicke was urging them to treat prisoners with the utmost severity and ruthlessness. Any trace of pity, he said, would be taken by the 'enemies of the State as a sign of weakness which they would not fail to exploit'.[48]

Heydrich kept an ever-sharper watch on Eicke's camps. The Political Sections, the outposts in enemy territory, increased in size; they were staffed by Gestapo or Kripo officials who noted everything that happened within the camp, conducted the interrogation of prisoners and kept the prisoners' card index. Heydrich's emissaries were responsible to the relevant Gestapo or Kripo Stelle, and according to Kautsky, even at a later date 'invariably constituted a State within a State, feared not only by the prisoners but by the camp staff.'[49]

Eicke sensed danger and alerted his protector Himmler. On August 10th, 1936 he wrote: 'Rumours are going around in the Gestapo that in the autumn the SS Totenkopfverbände will be removed from my command and placed under the SS Oberabschnitte. These rumours originate in Dr Best's office.'[50] Even worse was to come; 'SS-Standartenführer Dr Best of the Gestapa has stated on various occasions that the situation in the concentration camps is disgusting and that it is high time the camps were returned to the command of the Gestapa.'[51]

Eicke kept a suspicious eye on Heydrich's manoeuvres and prepared himself for battle. In February 1937 he did in fact forbid mishandling of prisoners, saying 'Although as a National-Socialist I naturally sympathize with such action, I cannot and must not tolerate such behaviour; otherwise we shall run the risk of being reported by the Reich Ministry of the Interior as unfit to deal with prisoners.'[52] He was continually warning his troops to be on their guard against the enemy in their own ranks, saying 'Once more we are struggling for recognition and acknowledgement of our existence.'[53]

Eicke need not in fact have worried, for Himmler had no intention of handing the concentration camps over to Heydrich, who was too powerful already. Eicke and his empire continued to constitute a tiresome gap in Heydrich's web.

In the police sector also Heydrich found his way blocked by one of those minefields of intrigue which did more damage to the structure of the Third Reich than all the underground work of the resistance. With Heydrich's connivance Himmler had relegated Daluege to third place in the police hierarchy but now Heydrich found Police General Daluege laying claim to command of the police.

The Chief of the Ordnungspolizei was admittedly too weak and too lethargic to declare open war on his rival Heydrich. Nevertheless he had at his disposal a police force with an *esprit de corps* comparable only to that of the old Prussian Army; Prussia's green-uniformed Schutzpolizei had once been the pride of Weimar Germany and even under the Third Reich they retained this prestige – in the early stages at least. Of the original total of 150,000 men one-third went off to the new Wehrmacht, while the remainder formed the Ordnungspolizei.[54] The new régime had many attractions to offer the police – ostensible law and order, smart new uniforms and better prospects of promotion instead of hazardous political street battles and low pay. Even in face of 'Gleichschaltung' the Ordnungspolizei retained a will of its own and refused to submit to complete incorporation into the SS as had the Gestapo and Kripo.[55]

Foremost among the opponents of Heydrich's plan were the civilian bureaucrats in Hauptamt Orpo. They all originated from the old bureaucracy of the Ministry of the Interior and Werner Bracht, for instance, head of the 'Administration and Legal' office in Hauptamt Orpo and a senior civil servant [Ministerial Director] was even more vehement than Daluege in his opposition to Heydrich's attempts to establish his hegemony.[56]

Year by year Heydrich became more strident in his demands that 'all matters of political significance are the responsibility of the Sicherheitspolizei', as he once wrote to Daluege.[57] Bracht would have none of it, saying 'In that case the policeman would eventually become simply an executive "bobby" employed on odd jobs, without any worthwhile powers of command and used merely to carry out other people's orders.'[58] Bracht and Heydrich were soon deep in a sort of trench warfare; every question of authority was bitterly disputed. Although in 1936 a clear delineation had been made between Orpo and Sipo, there were still some Orpo outposts in enemy territory. Daluege's office, for instance, dealt with all organizational questions concerning local police administration, was responsible for the Criminal Police budget and handled all accommodation problems for both Kripo and Gestapo.[59]

The sector of the front on which the most bitter battles were fought was that of control over the Kriminalpolizei. One of the numerous monstrosities of the National-Socialist régime was the fact that it created new structures while leaving the façade of the old still standing: on the higher level, for instance, the Kriminalpolizei had merged with the Gestapo to form the Sicherheitspolizei, but on the middle and lower levels the old administrative chains of command still held good. As a result the Kripo Stellen out in the country received their technical instruction from Nebe's RKPA and to that extent were organs of the Sicherheitspolizei; at the same time, however, they were part of the official police administration and therefore the Police President, the head of that administration, was automatically responsible for them; as the Police Presidents came under Hauptamt Orpo, the Kripo Stellen were also indirectly organs of the Ordnungspolizei.[60]

The battle between the two Hauptämter spilled over into provincial police headquarters. Heydrich demanded that here also authority should be divided, writing to Daluege: 'The division of the head offices into two branches means that provincial police headquarters must be similarly divided.'[61] Daluege would have none of it and Bracht, his strategist, gave undercover encouragement to any Police President prepared to be anti-Sipo.

Heydrich accordingly launched a counter-attack. After discussion with Himmler he appointed to each Wehrkreis [Military district] an 'Inspekteur der Sicherheitspolizei' [Security Police Inspector – IdS] whose job was to force through on the middle and lower levels the merger between Kripo and Gestapo.[62] The IdS developed into dangerous opponents of the Police Presidents who remained under the Orpo. Suddenly the Kripo Stellen had two masters and they obeyed the one who seemed the stronger – generally the Sipo Inspector.

SS-Brigadeführer Karl Pflomm, for instance, the Police President of Dresden, complained: 'Since their [the Inspectors'] arrival there has been so much interference with my activities as Police President that to some extent my authority is affected. I do not feel justified in remaining in my present position if my responsibilities as Police President are continually being whittled away.'[63]

Undermining the position of Police Presidents, however, was not the only purpose of Heydrich's inspectors; they were also intended to eliminate another weakness in the Heydrich empire – lack of coordination between Kripo and Gestapo.

Nebe's Kriminalpolizei surrendered only too willingly to the lure of increased police authority; all the old legal scruples rooted in the Weimar system were forgotten. The Kripo had always been kept short of funds and Heydrich now offered it an undreamed-of opportunity – a higher-powered system of crime suppression, uninhibited by considerations of publicity or legality. In Heydrich's office serious consideration was given to the abolition of public prosecutors and the transfer to the police of the initiation and conduct of legal proceedings. The abuse of the preventive arrest system had already shown how far the men of the RKPA had become infected with Sipo ideas. Nevertheless between RKPA headquarters in the Wedersche Markt and Sipo headquarters in the Prinz-Albrecht-Strasse there remained a gulf which no SS uniform could bridge.[64]

Arthur Nebe's servile attitude in face of Heydrich and his National-Socialist tirades later proved to be the deliberate sacrifice of a professional police officer determined at all costs to prevent the Kripo from becoming a dependency of the Gestapo. Nebe accepted the blame. He did at least enable non-Nazis such as his deputy Werner, and the head of the Kripo executive Hans Lobbe, together with anti-Nazis such as Gerhard Nauck, the head of the Vice Squad, to keep the RKPA largely free of Gestapo influence.[65]

The heads of the Gestapo looked with envy and suspicion on the doings of their Kripo counterparts, duly noting every fault and every failure – and well they might. Heinrich Müller and his Bavarian brigade had been recruited by Heydrich and now they were working with the blind fanaticism of the converted, but the bitter realization was beginning to grow that they were involved in repellent business. An internal Gestapo report of 1937 bears witness to the feelings of Müller, Huber and Meisinger; the report, the author of which is unknown, compares the work of the Gestapo and Kripo, saying: 'The Gestapo profession is not popular with the man in the street and is frequently the target of direct attacks in the Press'; the Kripo, on the other hand, was said to have 'full understanding and recognition from the public'.[66]

Müller seized every opportunity to taunt his 'friend Arthur' with inefficiency. Both were of the same rank – Reichskriminaldirektor – and they fought a bitter battle, Nebe knowing that Müller had Heydrich's ear and was urging that the Kripo adopt Gestapo methods in the fight against crime.

Heydrich, the perfectionist in surveillance, could therefore feel fully confident only in the Gestapo, but that had nothing like enough manpower to keep track of every suspicious movement among a nation of 80 million. Best of the Gestapo said after the war that 'with the few officials, who were always busy, anything like that could not be carried out.'[67] The gaps in Heydrich's system of control were shown up by a vice ring story from Bavaria where, for three years, a gang of political adventurers, alcoholics and psychopaths managed to throw dust in the eyes of all the senior officials.

The leader of the group was Emil Traugott Danzeisen, who played a part in the 1932 plot to murder Röhm.[68] As a longstanding enemy of Röhm, he had clearly hoped that when Röhm was finally murdered he would receive his due reward. When the orders and titles failed to appear, Danzeisen felt that he had been let down by the Party leadership, and determined to take his revenge after his own fashion.

He collected a circle of kindred spirits, 'old fighters' who for various reasons had a grudge against the Party; some of them had even marched in the Munich putsch but had then fallen foul of the law and were therefore out of favour with the Party. They included Albert Ampletzer, the standard-bearer in the Hitler putsch of 1923; he had numerous convictions against him, the latest being for embezzlement of 16,000 marks from the Munich Boxing Club; another was Erich Gruhl, an employee of Munich Party Headquarters, on whom the Gestapo had reported: 'A serious psychopathic case, only kept going by narcotics.'[69]

Late in 1934 this distinguished company set up an organization designed to manoeuvre its members into lucrative posts and, at the same time, to create an Intelligence organization which would make the Party shake in its shoes. Denzeisen had a splendid idea – it would henceforth be called 'Sicherheitsdienst', in the confident expectation that, in the new Germany, no doors would remain closed to an SD man.

'SD Danzeisen' soon became a power in the land in Munich; no one cared to disobey the orders of this secret security service. Danzeisen soon had no fewer than sixty-nine informers with contacts ranging from the staff of SS-Oberabschnitt South to the political Abteilung in Munich Police Headquarters and reaching even into the Brown House.[70] A whole group of officials and employees in these Headquarters dutifully collected information on important personalities and offices; Danzeisen even had contact men in the Bavarian Labour Office and the Labour Exchanges at Pfarrkirchen, Deggendorf, Weissenburg, Schweinfurt and Bamberg.[71]

The *éminence grise* of the Labour Office was Danzeisen's closest collaborator, ex-SA-Oberführer Hans Kallenbach. The Gestapo reported on him later: 'He was generally regarded in the office as the man who had the *entrée* even to the Führer. Anyone who wished to get anywhere fell in behind Kallenbach.'[72] Any of Bavaria's longstanding Nazis who obtained employment through Kallenbach were naturally willing to sign up as his contact men. Kallenbach let it be known that his job was to find positions for 'old fighters'. Even the Deputy President of the Labour Office thought that Kallenbach had been commissioned by the Party to find posts for the older Nazis throughout Germany.[73]

When, however, Danzeisen began to use the material provided by his contact men to blackmail senior Nazi functionaries, including the Munich Police President, the Gestapo pricked up its ears. In the spring of 1937 they uncovered the pseudo-SD's network. Even then, however, Danzeisen's friends in Police Headquarters continued to believe that they had in fact been in the service of the real SD.[74]

Heydrich was realist enough to recognize that there were gaps in his system of surveillance and control. He would not achieve his object with the Gestapo alone and so the second front must be opened. This was the moment to send into action the other organization also responsible to Reinhard Heydrich – the SD.

The SD had long been in eclipse. The National-Socialist seizure of power had taken place without any noteworthy assistance from it; in autumn 1933 it included a mere 100 full-time personnel and 100 part-timers and was used only for low-level odd jobs.[75] It had played no distinguished part in Himmler's capture of the police machine in the Länder. In fact the SD had been disregarded for so long that many SS men hardly knew what purpose the 'Sicherheitsdienst Reichsführer-SS' was supposed to serve.

SS-Scharführer Adolf Eichmann of the Dachau Guard Unit joined the SD because he thought it was Himmler's escort, saying to himself: 'One gets around; one sits in the car and merely has to keep a lookout'; he was soon to be 'greatly disappointed'.[76] Otto Ohlendorf thought the SD was an information service; he said: 'The first disappointment was to find that there was no such thing as an SD information organization.'[77]

The Party bosses did not find the SD men particularly impressive. In autumn 1933, for instance, Strenger, the Gauleiter of Hesse, dismissed Dr Best from the post of Police Chief.[78] Dietrich Klagges, the National-Socialist Minister-President of Brunswick, administered an even more humiliating snub to the SD; during the summer of 1933 the SD was intriguing against Klagges and two other SS leaders who were rivals of Himmler, the Minister of Justice, Alpers, and the Police Chief, Jeckeln; the object was to drive Klagges and his supporters from power but Klagges arraigned the SD before the Supreme Party Court. Himmler hoisted the white flag at once. The Head of the Brunswick SD was expelled from the SS and sent to a concentration camp; his most important contact man was dismissed and the director of the SD office indicted before a Party Court. Simultaneously Himmler was forced to grant senior SS Rank to the SD's enemies; Alpers, who was an SS man, was promoted to Standartenführer; Klagges, who was not an SS man, was made a Gruppenführer.[79]

The SD's prestige was temporarily so low that the Party had to give it a shot in the arm. In late 1933 Martin Bormann, presumably at Himmler's behest, issued a circular to all Gauleiter denying the rumour that the SD was to be disbanded.[80] The post-war historians, however, painted a very different picture. In their view the SD was always a sinister uncanny organization, a ubiquitous secret society, a messenger of terror 'even in the ranks of the Nazi Party itself.'[81]

During the early years of the National-Socialist régime, the SD resembled a society of hyper-intelligent youth leaders rather than a serious Secret Service. Even at this stage, however, it had one important function; it was in fact the only centrally directed organization available for use by the Party leadership.

During the lean years of the so-called 'struggle period' the Party had held together, though with some difficulty; after the seizure of power on January 30th, 1933, however, it practically fell apart. The Party élite laid hands on official positions in Berlin, while the middle- and lower-level Party barons fell upon their booty out in the country and set up their little feudal empires. In the jungle of warring Party cliques the SD was the only independent organization available to the Party leadership which was not a target for the local Party bosses' thirst for power. Frequently in collaboration with the police, the SD kept watch on the intrigues of the new lords and lordlings and began to construct a fine-spun network of surveillance and observation.[82]

The leading sleuths in this spy system could quote a directive from the Party leadership instructing them to report on and expose opposition elements within the Party. The leadership in fact kept urging the SD to be more vigilant; in June 1934 Rudolf Hess proclaimed the SD to be the sole Party counter-espionage service.[83]

The romance of a secret service and the SD's declared opposition to the 'little Hitlers' attracted a group of young National-Socialist intellectuals whose object was both professional advancement and 'the improvement of National-Socialism' – in the words of Gunter d'Alquen, one of the SD's most versatile brains. The SD soon became the refuge for National-Socialism's most intelligent men. They were flotsam from the wreckage left by the social disintegration which had overtaken the German middle class in the early 1930s; they were the rearguard of a bourgeoisie which had lost its faith in the pre-war standards of values. These young men, born in the 1900–12 period, took their cue from the Völkisch wing of the German Youth Movement. They had matured in an atmosphere of disgust with the tottering democracy of Weimar and believed that in place of the 'decadent' republic a better, specifically German, régime must be installed, superior to its Western counterparts.[84]

Three factors held them together: the disintegration of the bourgeoisie, the traumatic experience of Versailles, and the hallucination that only by the strictest discipline and personal self-sacrifice could the Fatherland once again be raised to its old position of power. Patriotic speeches by their professors reinforced the youngsters' blind devotion to their country. Many of them were law students and the doctrine then holding sway in the legal faculties of the German universities placed State power high in the scheme of values. As early as 1892 Bergbohm, the legal expert, had laid down that however villainous a law might be, it was binding on the legal profession if produced in proper form;[85] the young students thus grew up in a tradition of legal positivism.

These youngsters developed into legal automata, who considered that they could have no higher duty than to ensure, by a watertight system of laws and ordinances, that the demands of the State were met. For them the State was a deity to which every kind of sacrifice must be made. The law had only one function – to provide the State with the legal means to fulfil its intentions without let or hindrance.

The question was: 'What sort of State did they wish to serve?' Dictatorship met youth's demand for a leader because it gave responsibility to a man of flesh and blood instead of to a faceless assembly;[86] to the Völkisch sons of the bourgeoisie nothing could be more natural than that this dictatorship should be National-Socialist. The bourgeoisie's sociological catastrophe simply increased these youngsters' readiness to accept dictatorship. Then the economic crises of the 1930s left them rootless and in revolt against the capitalist system, as their fathers had been before them.

The reaction against international banks and businesses instilled into these young intellectuals a poison which many, all too many, regarded as the antidote to all economic ills – anti-Semitism. In the minds of the National-Socialist youngsters, anti-Semitism and the dogma of State omnipotence combined to produce a dynamic based on no doctrine, a technology of power serving one, and only one, supreme source of energy – the State, or more specifically the charismatic Führer. Having lost their roots in society, they gradually discarded the moral standards of the old bourgeois community. Domination, power for its own sake, became a new ethical norm, a duty to be performed by a self-elected élite which had long since outgrown the plebeian National-Socialism of the Party veterans.

In these young men's view, however, the Third Reich's Order should be 'level-headed', the one-man dictatorship should answer to some rational concept, the National-Socialist revolution should not violate the basic principles of human reasoning. But what these young intellectuals frequently saw in practice was crude lust for power, ideological blather by the Party bosses or opportunists and the megalomania of the eager Party beavers. They had never imagined that the Third Reich would be like this. Then they heard that in the SD an organization existed which had set itself the task of exposing abuses and correcting false tendencies in the State. It seemed to be fairly influential since behind the SD stood Heinrich Himmler, the coming man. The SD offered many malcontents hope and escape. One of them was a certain Otto Ohlendorf, son of a Hannoverian farmer, born in 1907, trained as a lawyer and economist and a 1925-vintage Party member.[87]

He was a member of the Institute for World Economics in Kiel where, together with his friend and teacher, Jens Peter Jessen, the Professor of Economics, he had spent months resisting what seemed to him a prostitution of National-Socialism – collectivist State socialist tendencies in the Party. He resisted so fiercely that he landed in prison under interrogation by the Gestapo.[88] In a letter to his wife he lamented: 'Something inside me has been shattered. I no longer possess the old, carefree assurance with which I fought for our National-Socialism.'[89] As a National-Socialist Ohlendorf was finished; the Party would have no more of his critical public speeches.

In desperation he turned to his friend Jessen, who advised him to go and see a certain Professor Reinhard Höhn who was in charge of a coordinating Abteilung in the SD Hauptamt, 102 Wilhelmstrasse, Berlin, and had a vacant post for an Economics Adviser.[90] Ohlendorf went and was astonished; Höhn told him that the SD needed critical intellects like his. Otto Ohlendorf signed up.[91]

Alongside him other National-Socialist intellectuals flooded into the SD. It already possessed a hard core of young men and experienced investigators like Dr Best, the SS Leader from Hesse, and Dr Herbert Mehlhorn, a lawyer from Saxony;[92] now there appeared an even younger cross-section of National-Socialist academics. In October 1933, Gunter d'Alquen arrived, a racy journalist, lately on the staff of the *Völkischer Beobachter*, who had had enough of the dull uniformity imposed by the National-Socialist Press;[93] shortly thereafter Dr Hermann Behrends appeared, a lawyer from Wilhelmshaven and an old friend of Heydrich;[94] meanwhile Professor Höhn was gradually collecting around him a circle of promising National-Socialists, mostly his own acquaintances.

One contact led to another. Having levered his pupil Ohlendorf into the SD, Jessen himself fell under the spell of Höhn, the Professor of Political Science. Though Jessen did not answer the call in person,[95] Höhn was able to win over one of his colleagues, Dr Franz Six, another Professor of Political Science;[96] he in turn persuaded one of his pupils, Dr Helmut Knochen, who really wanted to become a professor of literature, to join the SD.[97] The star turn of the SD intellectual brigade was an ambitious young man from Saarbrücken named Walter Schellenberg born in 1910 and qualified in law and political science; while still a student at Bonn University he had done some spy work for the SD[98] and Heydrich, who was a good judge of men, sensed that here was a brain which he could twist to his own purposes.

The appearance of an SD élite composed of nimble intellectuals relieved Heydrich of one threat to the expansion of his police state machine. Hitherto the Gestapo had necessarily occupied a key position in his system and he was therefore in danger of becoming over-dependent upon it, and on its atmosphere of officialdom. All the lip-service paid to National-Socialism by the Gestapo officials could not conceal the fact that, though its methods might be new, remnants of the Prussian-German administrative tradition were still present. Even Best, the Gestapo's legal expert, had proved to be an exponent of the old official attitude and had resisted Heydrich's attempts to substitute revolutionary dynamism for the routine of the trained civil servant.[99]

The first differences between Heydrich and Best had already appeared; with his legal training Best's approach savoured too much of official impersonal objectivity to suit Heydrich. The widening gulf between the two men was first demonstrated by an innocent notice on a wall. Some of his staff had painted one of Best's own slogans on a plaque and fixed it to the wall of his office: 'In the long run factual work gets the better of any enemy.' On seeing it when visiting Best's office one day, Heydrich reacted acidly: 'That may be good enough for the civil servants who come here in the course of business. But for real life that bureaucratic principle is nonsense.'[100]

Gestapo appointments also produced friction. Heydrich wished to staff the senior posts with yes-men who had no legal training and were bound by no rules; Best, on the other hand, maintained that only legally trained men should be considered. Unfortunately Heydrich's opinion of lawyers was similar to that of his Führer, who said: 'I shall not rest until every German realizes that it is a disgrace to be a lawyer.'[101]

Here were the signs of a conflict and, for Heydrich, the obvious method of solving it was to step up the activity of the SD. Early in 1935 he initiated a manoeuvre which has given the historians a lot of trouble; almost overnight, the SD became a dual-purpose organization. As a *Party formation* it was the parent organization for all members of the Sicherheitspolizei, the instrument through which the entire corps of Sipo officials was to be incorporated into the SS. As an *Intelligence organization*[102] it was to be what Schellenberg described as 'the versatile instrument for use against all opposition circles and in all spheres of life, the people's sense of touch and feel.'

By this master-stroke Heydrich freed himself from the pressure of the stiff-necked Gestapo officials. Best and the professionals such as Müller and Huber, though on paper members of the SD in its capacity as a Party formation, were divorced from the real SD – what other explanation can there be for the later ludicrous situation when Best and Müller, though ostensibly SD leaders, were doing their utmost to prevent the SD from prying into the affairs of the Gestapo? In its capacity as an intelligence organization, however, Heydrich now gave the SD a completely free hand; in his scheme of things the SD was destined to be the 'Intelligence Service' of the Great German Reich.[103]

The existing structure of the SD surveillance machine was expanded and improved. New sections and new senior posts sprang up in the Sicherheitshauptamt in the Wilhelmstrasse, where SS-Standartenführer Siegfried Taubert ran the staff in Heydrich's name, Heydrich himself remaining in the Prinz-Albrecht-Strasse nearby.[104]

The organization alone lends substance to the statement by Shlomo Aronson, Heydrich's biographer, that the young SD men were 'fascinated by the idea of dealing with secret Intelligence and espionage affairs' and so were caught up in a sort of James Bond world.[105] They took their cue from the detective story and the adventure novel rather than from books on the development of National-Socialism, and one of the results was a ludicrous over-estimation of the British Secret Service. Heydrich, who was a great reader of detective stories, had somewhere discovered that the Chief of the 'Intelligence Service' was mysteriously referred to as 'C' and he now began to imitate this habit. The mysterious 'C' began to appear in the SD files – 'C has ordered . . .' or 'the decision concerns C personally'; a rubber stamp was even made – 'Submit to C'.[106] It was all intended to enhance the magic of the almost invisible 'Chief'.

The mysterious signs denoting the individual offices, branches, divisions, etc, further illustrated this naïve pleasure in playing Secret-Service games. The SD Hauptamt was divided into three Ämter [Offices] designated by Roman numerals – I for Organization, II 'Combating of Opposition', III for Foreign Countries;[107] subdivisions were distinguished by Arabic numerals, increasing in number with each step down the ladder – for instance I1 indicated the Zentralabteilung [Co-ordinating Section] 'Organization and Supervision' within Amt I I11 was ordinating Section] 'Organization and Supervision' within Amt II11 was teilung 'Appointments' and I1111 the Desk concerned.[108]

With few exceptions the heads of all the more important Zentralabteilungen and Hauptabteilungen were academics holding a degree; the Zentralabteilung 'Organization' was under Wilhelm Albert, who held an engineering degree,[109] Hauptabteilung 'Staff Duties' under Dr Herbert Mehlhorn, a lawyer and economist,[110] the Zentralabteilung 'Idealogical Combating of Opposition' under Professor Franz Six,[111] the Zentralabteilung 'Reports on Spheres of German Life' under Professor Reinhard Höhn,[112] and the Zentralabteilung 'Counter-Espionage – Enemy Intelligence Services' under SS-Oberführer Heinz Jost.[113]

This then was the General Staff of the 'Intelligence Service'. From it the threads ran to the staffs of the seven SD-Oberabschnitte; territorially these were geared, not to the Wehrkreise [Military Districts] like the Oberabschnitte of the Allgemeine-SS, but to the Länder.[114] Under each Oberabschnitt were two or three Unterabschnitte and these led on down to SD-Aussenstellen [Out-Stations] each responsible for a Landkreis [Rural District or major town]. These last were the most important cells in the SD Intelligence Organization.[115]

The work of the Aussenstellen can be illustrated by the directive issued in spring 1937 by SD-Oberabschnitt 'North-West': 'The Head of every Aussenstelle must, under all circumstances, try to engage one or more contact men in each locality in his district; every contact man should in turn have his informer network. To take an example: suppose that Aussenstelle D is responsible for 32 Landgemeinde [parishes]. The Head of the Aussenstelle must have a contact man in each parish to represent SD interests in the area. The task of the contact man is to ensure that his area is covered by a network of informers'. And a little later: 'The informers should never know that they are working for the SD. It would also be a good idea to provide the contact men with message pads and get them to submit a telegraphic daily report written in indelible pencil. A contact man will soon lose interest if the Head of his Aussenstelle requires him to produce long-winded reports. Most people do not take to their pens easily.'[116]

In the cities the Aussenstellen were geared to the local Nazi Party Group and distributed accordingly; in the Universities and High Schools the contact men formed so-called 'SD Working Associations'.[117] According to Oberabschnitt 'North-West' anyone could be a contact man who 'had the necessary general knowledge and could think logically and practically'; 'suitable people' for these posts were said to be 'teachers, local group leaders, SS and SA leaders, local peasant leaders, veterinary surgeons and, if necessary, retired officials.'[118]

Only a comparatively small proportion of the SD's great informer army actually belonged to the Party or the SS. After the war one of the SD leaders, Heinz Höppner, estimated that of the full-time members of the SD only ten per cent came from the Allgemeine SS and only ten per cent of the part-time assistants were SS men.[119] At times outright opponents of the régime were used by the SD to supply information on anti-Nazi tendencies.

The antennae of the Intelligence machine penetrated into every sphere of German society. The SD's collaborators were not solely small-time informers and spies; they included perfectly respectable magistrates, businessmen, artists and scientists. The headquarters was staffed by young academics of all disciplines; similarly in the Aussenstellen an intellectual élite worked as 'reporters'. In 1938, for instance, SD-Abschnitt Koblenz had twenty-four part-time workers, among them four with academic degrees; of eleven named contact men in the Abschnitt, four were local government officials, four were police officials, one a doctor, one a teacher and one a veterinary surgeon.[120]

These Secret-Service intellectuals showed a curious maidenly aversion to the word 'spy'. Schlierbach, the theorist on police work who was closely connected with the SD, wrote that it would be 'unworthy of the National-Socialist State to make use of spies and agents';[121] a confidential Sipo Service Instruction contained the sentence: 'Employment of professional agents is not permitted.'[122] The staff of the SD Hauptamt had an almost superstitious horror of coming into physical contact with informers. Adolf Eichmann recalled: 'We knew none of them and conversely the contact man hardly ever entered the headquarters.'[123] Only at a later stage, when the intellectuals had long since lost their scruples, did Walter Schellenberg put some order into the contact system; from then on every headquarters knew its contact men.

The Wilhelmstrasse maintained a file on every individual contact man. It was divided into two sub-files; sub-file A, also known as the 'Placement File', contained, among other things, the man's code name, a short curriculum vitae, which did not reveal the name, the outcome of the SD's internal vetting, the man's declaration of engagement, information about his special qualifications and a record of his place in the SD network. Sub-file B, the 'Control File', contained information on the individual missions allotted to the contact man, an estimate of the value of his reports, ranging from 1 (excellent) to 5 (completely useless) together with an account of all expenses incurred. In neither sub-file was the name of the contact man given. This was only to be found in two places: in the contact-man card index, used to locate the files, and in the central card index maintained by each SD office.[124]

The density of the SD's surveillance network increased year by year; its strands gripped the country ever tighter. By 1937 the SD numbered 3,000 full-time members with an invisible army of 50,000 informers.[125]

But what was the object of it all? Who was the SD supposed to watch? What was it supposed to unearth? Here was the great question. During the 'struggle period' the SD's task had been simple; it was to eliminate opponents within the National-Socialist ranks and discover the intentions of Nazism's opponents. This was a plausible story so long as the enemy controlled the police machine. After January 30th, 1933, however, the Party itself took over the police; the enemy, whoever he might be, could therefore now be dealt with through the resources of the police.

Initially the SD had been content to act as a sort of auxiliary police force. On July 4th, 1934 Himmler declared it to be 'the sole political counter-espionage service of the Gestapo';[126] six months later he directed: 'The SD will discover the enemies of the National-Socialist concept and will initiate counter-measures through the official police authorities.' Executive action was therefore excluded.[127] But the SD was to proud to assume the rule of mere informer for the Gestapo and so it thought up a new task for itself; it was to be a thought police, the instrument of National-Socialist thought control.

Himmler spelled out the new terms of reference: 'The SD is the

Party's great ideological information service, and ultimately that of the State also. The SD is concerned only with the great ideological questions.' As the guardian of ideological purity the SD had now pre-empted for itself a new field of activity which, according to Himmler, included: 'Communism, Jewry, Freemasonry, ultramontanism, the activity of politically-minded religious persuasions and reactionaries.'[128] In practice this was only another way of expressing the old 'struggle period' task – 'combating of opposition', as the SD called it.

'C' put his intelligence machine into action. The SD watchers probed the community for irregularities. No opportunity was missed of reporting upon discordant tendencies among the population. The Wilhelmstrasse teleprinters ceaselessly tapped out orders and telegrams called out the Einsatzkommandos [Action Commandos].

Wherever he went the German seemed to be shadowed by the SD. On January 26th, 1938 SS-Obersturmführer Grillenberger reported from the KdF [Kraft durch Freude – the Nazi holiday organization] ship *Der Deutsche* which was on an Italian cruise: 'One of the holidaymakers, Fritz Schwanebeck, born March 30th, 1901, resident Mückenberg-Ferrosiedlung, makes a bad impression; when the national anthem was sung he adopted a sloppy attitude, evidencing a complete lack of interest. Sixty holidaymakers arrived late at the passport office. The general attitude was criticized at the final roll-call. Violations of currency regulations.'[129]

When so-called elections were in the offing the SD was very busy. They were at work well before polling day, as an order by Aussenstelle Erfurt (dated April 4th, 1938) shows; this prescribed that 'all persons in your area who may confidently be expected to vote "No" at the forthcoming election are to be reported to the SD.' If the names of dissidents were available, special voting papers were prepared for the suspects; a figure was typed on the voting slip using a machine without a ribbon and the same figure entered against the name on the voting list. On May 7th, 1938 Unterabschnitt Koblenz reported that by this method it had been possible 'to discover the persons who had voted "No" or spoiled their papers. Skimmed milk was used to bring out the figures.'[130]

The mountain of notes and reports in the SD-Hauptamt grew as the years went by. Any movement made by a suspect was noted; Rudolf Kircher, for instance, the editor of the *Frankfurter Zeitung*, was something of a non-conformist and so Abteilung II 112 began collecting his articles of the Weimar period, noting: 'Very informative regarding Kircher's real political views.'[131] In a report from Palestine Schwarz van Bergk, the star Nazi journalist, had the misfortune to suggest that even

Jews might fight and die for their cause. Oberscharführer Hagen, Professor Six's amanuensis, found that: 'In my view it is inexcusable that a journalist should openly admit, in a National-Socialist newspaper to boot, that certain happenings within the Jewish community in Palestine should be passed over in silence for propaganda reasons.'[132]

Whenever opportunity offered the SD spared no effort to prove that unwanted non-Nazis were of Jewish origin. Professors Ernst and Heinrich Seraphim, for instance, both of whom came from Poland, had refuted the rumour current in the Party that they were of Jewish origin; the SD, however, spied a chance 'to prove the assertion that Seraphim is of Jewish origin on the basis of the facts as set out herein.' But they proceeded cautiously. An SD man named Augsburg was instructed to urge the German association in Poland to find a student willing to trace Seraphim's family tree. But again caution: 'In conversation with II 112 SS-Sturmbannführer Six approved the procedure proposed by Augsburg. Care was to be taken, however, that the source of these instructions should not become known.'[133]

However, the fact that his shadowy army was silently extending its grip over the whole country was not enough for Heydrich. Totalitarian thought control postulated noise, the thunder of ideological slogans, the shouting of ideological drill-sergeants and schoolmarms. So Heydrich called to his assistance the most extraordinary and most widely feared organ of the National-Socialist Press – Gunter d'Alquen's weekly *Das Schwarze Korps* [The Black Corps].

D'Alquen was the son of a wool merchant in Essen. He had revolted against the solid German nationalism of his home and become one of the earliest Hitler Youth leaders. He had very soon found out what work for the Party Press entailed. He had started with the miserable *Bremer Nationalsozialistische Zeitung* – where copy arrived in longhand, the telephone was always being cut off for lack of funds and the type-setting machines were decrepit; he had then moved on to the internal policy desk of the *Völkischer Beobachter* which he found equally sterile. D'Alquen sometimes wondered whether it was possible to be a National-Socialist and a journalist at the same time.[134]

The first steps on the ladder to fame were not a success. Early in 1934 Max Amann, the Party publisher, offered him the editorship of the Berlin *Angriff* and asked him to draw up an editorial programme. D'Alquen tells the story: 'And then I committed a stupidity – perhaps the greatest of my life; I told the truth. I voiced the opinion that a constructive opposition was absolutely necessary if the State was not to die of hardening of the arteries.' The impudent young man was forthwith sacked by the Party.[135]

A month or so later, in the sleeping-car of a train on the way to a meeting of the Silesian SS frontier district, d'Alquen met Wittje, the head of the SS Hauptamt, and told him the story of his lost job. 'My dear Gunter,' Wittje replied, 'I will speak to Heinrich. After all the SA and every twopenny-halfpenny society has its newspaper; why not the SS?' A few days later Wittje had an interview with Himmler, who had already heard arguments on the same lines from Max Amann. Himmler already knew what the newspaper should be called – *Das Schwarze Korps*. Wittje's initiative, moreover, bore fruit; Gunter d'Alquen was given the job of 'Head Leader-Writer of the special SS Newspaper'.[136]

The pedantic Himmler insisted upon reading the 24-year-old Hauptsturmführer a long lecture on the business of producing a newspaper; d'Alquen's reaction was: 'He simply had no idea.' They could not even agree upon the paper's title; d'Alquen proposed *Die Bewegung* [The Movement] but Himmler would not change his mind. D'Alquen did not give way until two days before the appearance of the first issue, and then had to sit up day and night with the Party draughtsman, Hans Schweitzer-Mjölnir, designing the paper's heading. Meanwhile SS headquarters had concluded an agreement with the Party's publishing firm, Franz Eher, guaranteeing a 40,000-copy run.[137]

On March 6th, 1935 appeared the first number of the 'Newspaper of the NSDAP's SS – the organ of SS headquarters', as the sub-title had it. D'Alquen began with a staff of only six located at 88 Zimmerstrasse, Berlin, but he soon contrived to increase the circulation of the *Schwarze Korps*; it appeared on Thursdays, initially (in 1935) in 16 pages, rising later to 20. In 1937 it sold 189,317 copies but circulation later rose to 500,000 and during the war it was running at 750,000.[138]

The success of d'Alquen's paper lay in the fact that it both shocked and fascinated the regimented Germans. Its hate campaigns against churches and Jews, its poison-pen attacks on the bourgeoisie and officialdom and its ceaseless vilification of non-conformist Germans broke all bounds of decency. Nevertheless many people could detect an undertone of a different strain; the *Schwarze Korps* was popularly known as 'the only opposition newspaper', for in its pages was mirrored all the schizophrenia of the SD intellectuals as they strove to be both radical and intelligent National-Socialists. What they could not be in the hard world of official political life they tried to be on paper; they wanted to oppose – and to expose – the inflated Party bosses, corruption within the Party and the brown-shirted place-seekers.

On January 21st, 1937 the *Schwarze Korps* proclaimed: 'After every revolution comes the danger of stagnation. History proves it. We

National-Socialists have studied history ... in order to draw lessons therefrom concerning our political structure. Hence the necessity, which many will find surprising, for a new form of opposition.'[139] The paper frequently did not mince its words; it observed, for instance, that 'National-Socialists have had to be placed in posts for which they are neither physically nor mentally equipped';[140] it inveighed against Party 'profiteers of the revolution' who 'brand anyone who does not possess a membership card as a second-class citizen, as a detestable individual and probably, if he is a poor man, as a Marxist.'[141]

When, in summer 1935, the Munich Nazis went round breaking the windows of Jewish businesses in a sort of trial run for the 1938 'Kristallnacht', the *Schwarze Korps* castigated these 'criminal machinations' saying: 'The Jewish question is one of our people's most burning problems; it will not be solved by terror on the streets. As for healthy popular sentiment, a competent magistrate has no need to base his judgement upon so elastic a concept.'[142] It even had a word to say to its own police, warning them to be more careful in their use of the words 'enemy of the State' – 'over-savage persecution can do more harm than good ... one day precise figures should be given for the number of cases based on denunciation and personal spite.'[143]

A paper which was clearly so critical of conditions in the Third Reich gained the confidence of its readers and d'Alquen encouraged them. On February 18th, 1937 he wrote: 'From the outset the reader may feel confident that not only do we wish to be read but that we ourselves also take trouble to read – to read the mood, the opinions, the experiences of our people.'[144]

This particular sentence gave Heydrich the idea of including the *Schwarze Korps* in his system of surveillance. It could be the mouthpiece of his thought-control system and also a channel of continuous up-to-date information on the habits and thoughts of the populace. Heydrich and d'Alquen quickly reached agreement. The SD Hauptamt fed into the *Schwarze Korps* the information produced by its Intelligence machine; the newspaper's editorial office forwarded a high proportion of its reader mail to the Wilhemstrasse for evaluation. Correspondence between the Hauptamt and the editor's office became so voluminous that d'Alquen even had printed slips prepared, such as: 'Attached letter from one of your readers is forwarded to you with the request that you express an opinion, take note and return. With thanks for your trouble. Heil Hitler.'[145]

As an instance of how the system worked – on June 7th, 1938 a Berliner named Paul Koch wrote to the *Schwarze Korps* reporting that a butcher, Gustav Shiewek, of 37 Stralsunder Strasse, invariably 'handed his customers their purchases wrapped in a paper carrying an advertisement for a Jewish business.' Koch continued: 'Could the man not be assisted by being given a reproof in the form of a thick ear?' On June 21st the *Schwarze Korps* forwarded the letter to 'SD Reichsführer-SS for the attention of Dr Six.' The letter made its way to Abteilung II 112 which forwarded it a fortnight later to SD Oberabschnitt East 'with a request for further recommendations.' On July 8th, 1938 the SD Hauptampt wrote back to the *Schwarze Korps*: 'For information Paul Koch's letter has been forwarded to the relevant Gestapo Stelle. Further information on conclusion of investigations.'[146]

The *Schwarze Korps* was soon being produced in the closest collaboration with the SD. The SD Hauptamt acted as a vast information library of secrets, always on hand to assist the leader-writers in obtaining their information.[147] The more important articles were discussed beforehand. After a conference with Rolf d'Alquen, Gunter's younger brother and Number Three in the *Schwarze Korps* editorial office, Oberscharführer Hagen noted: 'With reference to articles on the situation of German Jewry, it was agreed that no special initiative would be taken and the present line would be maintained pending final agreement with the Ministry of Economics on funds to be made available for Jewish emigrants.'[148]

The SD became all the more willing to give away its secrets as it began to realize that publicity represented a coercive method of thought control, capable of compensating for the SD's lack of executive powers. The suggestive effect upon the ordinary citizen of the *Schwarze Korps*' lurid polemics was often more disturbing than the potential but invisible threat of the Gestapo; conversely the SD information gave the newspaper an air of sinister omniscience.

The *Schwarze Korps*, for instance, took the ultra-conservative Reich Union of German Officers aback by publishing anti-Nazi extracts from the confidential minutes of one of their meetings.[149] The publicist Wilhelm Stapel was put in his place by publication of one of his private letters containing the sentence that a conservative could only support Hitler 'with a shudder'.[150] A certain Werner Grund of Zwickau wrote to Chamberlain thanking him for his efforts for world peace; he found Chamberlain's answer, not in his letterbox but in the columns of the *Schwarze Korps*;[151] Dr Wolfgang Denk, an attorney from Leipzig was publicly attacked for writing a confidential memorandum defending a woman who had been sent to a concentration camp.[152]

At times the paper would openly admit that it had denounced people or provided the necessary material. In summer 1944 for instance, it reported: 'We are pleased to record that the Wiesbaden Court has given short shrift to an anti-social malefactor denounced by the *Schwarze Korps*; he was sentenced to four years hard labour and four years loss of rights.'[153]

Cooperation between the SD and the *Schwarze Korps* would have been more profitable had Heydrich observed the elementary rule, valid even under the National-Socialist Reich, that some limits must be set to a partnership between Press and Secret Service. D'Alquen, who at heart was a restless demagogue, refused to allow his paper to become subject to every tactical shift on the part of SD headquarters. The *Schwarze Korps*' scurrilous attacks frequently cut across the interests of the SD – still the most controversial of the SS organizations.

In course of time the sparks began to fly between the two partners. D'Alquen refused to submit his articles for prior censorship by the SD; he refused to hand over Heinar Schilling, one of his reporters, whom the SD suspected; he protested against the mis-use of *Schwarze Korps* Press cards as cover for SD Secret-Service operations.[154] Heydrich's people, on the other hand, warned that the *Schwarze Korps* was overdoing its attacks on actual or supposed enemies of the régime and was making less and less use of SD material. As a result the paper ran into increasing difficulties.[155]

Relations between the two later reached such an all-time low that Heydrich was forced to appoint a liaison officer, SS-Sturmbannführer von Kielpinski, to try and improve the situation.[156] D'Alquen exploded: 'I am sick and tired of being treated as an outsider by SD men, who after all are supposed to be working with us.'[157] In reply Ohlendorf summarized the SD's complaint against the *Schwarze Korps*; its articles, he said, 'were full of false assumptions and equally false generalizations'; 'in their incredibly libellous form' they were 'certainly not calculated to influence those to whom they were addressed'; on the contrary 'their style and tone caused decent National-Socialists to rally to the support of those whom the articles (rightly) attacked.'[158]

Ohlendorf concluded that cooperation was only possible if 'the *Schwarze Korps* refrains from attacking people unless the facts of the case have been established beyond doubt and the SD is available to do this'; he continued that 'problems of fact should first be discussed with us in order to make use of our knowledge and material.'[159] The *Schwarze Korps*, however, refused to accept the SD's claim to authority.

Heydrich had long since realized that the SD would not achieve its object through the *Schwarze Korps* publicity. The old question raised its head once more: what was the real job of the SD? The urgency of this question increased with the ominous approach of a head-on collision between Heydrich's two engines of domination, the SD and the Gestapo.

10

THE RSHA

REINHARD HEYDRICH scented danger. The SD and the Gestapo planned as two interlocking parts of his machine of tyranny, were threatening to neutralize each other. Each was extending its sweep of power, each was striving for control over the nation; Adolf Hitler's Greater Germany was too small for them both. This was the inevitable result of the failure, when reconstructing the SD in 1935, to allot to it a logical field of activity clearly differentiated from that of the Gestapo. Their researches covered the same area, and the SD was always coming across the trail of its Gestapo rivals. Abteilung IIA (Marxism) of the Gestapo, for instance, was hunting the same Communist resistance men as Abteilung II 121 (left-wing movements) of the SD Hauptamt.[1]

In an attempt to curtail the battle between the two, on July 1st, 1937 Heydrich issued a decree setting out their functions. The theme was: 'Let there be no rivalry; neither is senior or junior to the other; they are mutually complementary and duplication of work must be avoided.' The Gestapo was allotted Marxism, treason and émigrés; the SD were to be responsible for science, Germanism and folk-lore, art, education, Party and State, constitution and administration, foreign countries, Freemasonry and miscellaneous societies.[2]

A sufficient area of friction still remained, however, since both were still responsible for: 'churches, sects, other religious and ideological associations, pacifism, Jews, right-wing movements, other anti-State groups (the Schwarze Front, the Bundische Jugend, etc), economics and the Press.' Even here some division of responsibility was attempted; the SD was to deal with 'all general and basic questions', the Gestapo with 'all individual cases in which secret police measures enter into consideration'.[3]

The length of the SD's list of responsibilities, however, could not conceal the fact that it was under increasing threat from the Gestapo of relegation to the ideological field only, and this it refused to stomach,

The SD Hauptamt central office produced well-argued theses pointing out acidly that pride of place belonged to the SD. The Gestapo, the argument ran, had come into being to meet a legal and administrative requirement of the State; the Third Reich, however, needed 'a more potent guarantee of the State's security, springing from and vitalized by the will of a political movement' – and this was the SD's speciality.

The memorandum containing this sentence was entitled 'The Independent Status of the SD.' The unknown author laid down the principle that the Gestapo's task was to suppress 'anti-State manifestations,' the SD dealing with 'anti-social manifestations ... anti-State action is a legal phenomenon and is present whenever it can be proved that a person, or an action, contravenes a law protecting the State.' On the other hand, 'the peculiar characteristic of anti-social manifestations is that, in general, they are not amenable to criminal law; nevertheless the manifestations of anti-social action frequently constitute a far greater danger to the people, and therefore also to the State, than direct anti-State manifestations.'[4]

This exercise in self-inflation, however, did not solve the SD's problem of finding new fields of activity. Eventually the Wilhelmstrasse did find two unexplored areas but they carried with them the seeds of further conflict and intrigue; they were: espionage in foreign countries and investigation of 'spheres of life'.

From the outset espionage had enthralled the young men of the SD. Its secret foreign Intelligence service had, however, been a product of chance, a by-product of pursuit of the régime's enemies beyond the Reich frontiers. One of these enemies was Otto Strasser, the leader of the Schwarze Front, located in Prague, whence he conducted a Quixotic campaign against his former Party leader Hitler.[5]

Strasser's 'black radio' seemed particularly dangerous to the SD leaders, for it broadcast anti-Hitler speeches into the totalitarian thought-controlled Reich. The SD discovered that the transmitter was operated by an engineer named Rudolf Formis, lately senior technician of Radio Stuttgart. Heydrich was convinced that Formis must be disposed of. On January 10th, 1935 he summoned his factotum, an ex-mechanic and SS-Untersturmführer named Alfred Naujocks, and ordered him to bring Formis to Berlin.[6] Naujocks drew up a plan of campaign.

The SD had established that Strasser's transmitter must be located some fifteen to twenty miles south-east of Prague. Naujocks arranged papers for himself in the name of Hans Müller, a trader; then, together with his girlfriend, Edith Kasbach, a Berlin gym-instructress, he drove across the frontier in a Mercedes. He found what he was looking for; the 'black' transmitter was located in a place called Dobris, in a room of the Zahori Hotel.[7] Naujocks and his girlfriend took Room 4, close to that of Formis.[8] He made a wax impression of the key to Formis' room and telegraphed to the SD Hauptamt: 'Found.' Then he waited for orders. A couple of days later he prepared for action.

On January 23rd at 9.30 PM, Naujocks looked at his watch; he took a torch and swung it out of his hotel window. At the signal another SD man, Werner Goetsch, climbed the wall by a rope and jumped into the room.[9] Both were convinced that Formis was not in the hotel; they slunk along the corridor and stopped at his door. When they put the skeleton key in the lock, however, they realized that their man was inside. Naujocks took a quick decision; he knocked. A voice called: 'What do you want?' Naujocks mumbled something to the effect that they had forgotten to put out Herr Formis' soap.

Formis opened the door and immediately the two SD men burst into the room and overpowered him. Formis attempted to draw a revolver. One of the intruders fired and Rudolf Formis fell dead. Naujocks and Goetsch just had time to lay a phosphorus charge on the transmitter and ignite it; then they fled as the hotel staff came running up.[10]

Back in Berlin Heydrich was furious at the clumsy gangster-film methods which passed for Secret-Service work among SD men such as Naujocks. Nevertheless during the next two years the SD remained a refuge for inexperienced amateurs who drove the Secret-Service professionals to distraction. In spite of this, the SD penetrated further and further into the jungle of the German secret services. The SD's Aussenstellen near the frontier insisted upon collecting reports from abroad; certain SD leaders set up informer networks run by acquaintances resident in foreign countries.[11]

The SD's espionage work was under the direction of the totally inexperienced SS-Oberführer Heinz Jost and his Zentralabteilung III 2 (Enemy Intelligence Services); other sections of the headquarters, however, also felt impelled to take a hand in the game. For instance the SD's Jewish Abteilung maintained its own Intelligence network in the Middle East, collecting information on the Arab–Jew conflict in Palestine.[12] The main collecting centre here was the office of Dr Reichert, the German News Agency's correspondent in Tel Aviv; he had informers in both camps: on the Arab side the Nationalist leader Ibrahim Chanti, editor of the newspaper *Al Difah*, and on the Jewish the Zionist leader Feivel Polkes, one of the commanders of the Jewish Secret Army, 'Haganah'.[13]

A note in one of the SD Hauptamt files says: 'Provided adequate support is forthcoming, Dr Reichert has undertaken to work only with the SD on the more difficult cases; he will transmit all material of intelligence importance either via Herr von Ritgen of the German News Agency under code sign H or to the addressees indicated by Oberscharführer Hagen.' Reichert's information service registered one or two successes. (In 1937 he laid hands on a letter from the ex-Prime Minister Stanley Baldwin alluding to a secret Anglo-Turkish treaty; the Italian Secret Service offered £150,000 for it.[14])

But the further the SD penetrated into the Secret-Service undergrowth, the more it came into collision with Military Intelligence under Admiral Wilhelm Canaris. He was a diplomatic officer and so far had contrived to maintain cautiously good relations with his ex-midshipman, Heydrich; they were wrecked, however, by the SD's expansion.

During the early years (1932–4) when the Abwehr [Military Intelligence] was run by Captain Patzig, it had frequently clashed with the Gestapo; then the Wehrmacht leaders had thought that in Canaris they had found the ideal officer to rub along with Heydrich.[15] Canaris, born in 1887, was, after all, a naval captain and ex-U-boat commander; he had been an outspoken opponent of the Weimar Republic and had the reputation of being on good personal terms with Heydrich. Canaris and Heydrich could reminisce about their time on board the training cruiser *Berlin*; Canaris' wife, Erika, had long missed Heydrich's violin-playing at her musical evenings. Even after his appointment as head of the Abwehr in January 1934, Canaris had kept in close contact with Heydrich.[16-18]

On official matters Canaris and Heydrich initially reached a working arrangement. On December 21st, 1936 Canaris and Best, the head of the Abwehrpolizei, signed an agreement (known as 'the Ten Commandments') laying down the spheres of the Abwehr and Gestapo respectively. The Abwehr was to deal with espionage abroad and counter-espionage at home; the Gestapo was to be responsible for 'investigation of culpable actions under para 163 of the State Police Ordinance (Treason) and the necessary follow-up action.' Canaris had therefore conceded a certain technical preponderance to the Gestapo. In peacetime, moreover, the Abwehr had no military police and so the Gestapo had to be called in as executive agents even in cases dealt with by the military. At the same time, however, the Canaris–Best agreement gave a certain precedence to the requirements of Military Intelligence, for it included the following: 'in dealing with individual cases the interests of the Secret Intelligence Service and of counter-espionage take precedence over executive action by the Abwehrpolizei.' The Gestapo was bound 'at the request of the relevant Wehrmacht Abwehr office to refrain from proceeding with their measures until, in the judgement of the Wehrmacht Abwehr office, neither Military Intelligence nor counter-espionage has any further interest in the case.'[19]

The Abwehr's privileged position was now imperilled by the expansion of the SD, who began to meddle in the network of foreign secret services and upset the Abwehr's plans. Even on such subjects as other countries' economic potential and armaments industries the collisions between Abwehr and SD became increasingly violent.[20] A breach between Canaris and Heydrich was obviously coming; it was accelerated by an affair which, for the first time, showed Canaris how totally lacking in scruple the SD dilettantes were.

Late in 1936 Heydrich received information via SD channels that an opposition group was forming in the Soviet Union, whose object was to bring Stalin down by force; the leader of the group was said to be Marshal Tukachevsky, Deputy Commissar for War of the Soviet Union. Heydrich had a fantastic idea: suppose it were possible to feed this information to Stalin, giving it verisimilitude by means of one or two forged documents. It might then be possible at one stroke to annihilate the entire Soviet Army leadership – and to do so with the assistance of Stalin and the Soviet Secret Police.[21]

Heydrich already had an outline plan. In the immediate post-war period relationships between the Reichswehr and the Red Army had been close; there ought, therefore, to be documents, notes and letters bearing the signatures of the Soviet generals now suspected of conspiring against Stalin. If these old papers were given a new look by the addition of a few sentences, they could be made to give the impression that Soviet generals were in league with German officers against the Kremlin. Heydrich summoned Naujocks, who was in charge of a false papers and passports factory in the Delbruckstrasse, Berlin, and let him into the secret. SS-Standartenführer Hermann Behrends, the SD Commander East, was also informed confidentially and the forgers got to work.[22]

SS-Hauptsturmführer Erich Jahnke, one of the few professional Secret Service men in the SD, sounded a warning. He did not believe that the Tukachevsky story was genuine; it could all well be a trick by the Soviet Secret Service. The reason for his suspicion was that the story originated from a certain Russian exile living in Paris who was working both for the SD *and* for the Soviet Secret Service.[23] But Heydrich thought he knew better: he placed the tiresome Jahnke under house arrest. The false papers took only four days to prepare and Heydrich then obtained Hitler's agreement to pass them across to the Soviets.[24]

Behrends took the documents to Prague and, through various contacts, persuaded Beneš, the Czechoslovak President, to advise Moscow of their existence. The Soviets reacted and immediately sent a special delegate to Berlin to negotiate with Heydrich. According to Schellenberg, Moscow paid a sum of 3,000,000 roubles for them – but in notes which unfortunately proved to be as good forgeries as the documents themselves.[25]

On June 11th, 1937 the Soviet news agency *Tass* reported that Marshal Tukachevsky and seven Red Army generals had been condemned to death by a special tribunal because 'the accused had maintained treasonable relationships with leading military circles of a foreign power which was pursuing a policy hostile to the Soviet Union. The accused were working for this Power's espionage service.'[26] The execution of Tukachevsky and his companions heralded the bloodiest political purge in the history of Stalin's Russia. In a single year almost half the entire officer corps – 35,000 officers – was eliminated; 90 per cent of the Soviet generals and 80 per cent of the colonels were liquidated or cashiered – 3 out of 5 marshals, 13 out of 15 Army commanders, 57 out of 85 corps commanders, 110 of 195 divisional commanders and 220 out of 406 brigade commanders.[27]

A few months later the Ausland-SD submitted to Heydrich a secret report entitled 'Political Situation in the Red Army'. It contained this: 'The new arrivals will inevitably take time to overcome the effects of so far-reaching a purge in the higher ranks of the Soviet Army. The new commanders are inadequately trained and prematurely promoted; it is difficult to underestimate their efficiency.'[28] Heydrich was jubilant. He went round telling a story repeated by all the SS memoir writers from Walter Schellenberg to Wilhelm Höttl, publicized in the film *Canaris* and believed even by Winston Churchill and Nikita Khruschev[29] – that the SD had lopped the head off the dreaded Soviet Army.

At about this time a certain War Ministry staff officer stopped Lieutenant-Colonel Karl Spalcke in the corridor and asked whether he had heard that Heydrich was boasting of having brought down Tukachevsky. Spalcke, who had the Russian desk in the Abteilung 'Foreign Armies' (T 3), simply laughed saying: 'Pure bragging by Heydrich.'[30] He was at the time the only man who suspected the truth for, in fact, Tukachevsky was not brought down by Heydrich and the SD. In 1937 Spalcke could not substantiate his suspicions but today the proof is there that Heydrich was no more than a small, unimportant pawn in a Soviet Secret Service game.

The fact was that in Stalin's opinion Tukachevsky had become overpowerful and a threat to his personal dictatorship; Stalin had decided to put an end to the Marshal long before Heydrich started his document gambit; he had been preparing his blow against the military ever since late 1936. In December 1936 Yezhov, the Head of the Russian Secret Police, set up an 'Administration for Special Tasks' known as the 'Special Bureau' and this undertook the initial investigations against Tukachevsky.[31] Shortly thereafter Yezhov had General Vitaliy Putna, one of Tukachevsky's closest collaborators, arrested.[32] On January 27th, 1937 the first reference to the Marshal as a friend of the 'traitor' Putna was made at the fake trial of Karl Radek, the right-wing deviationist.[33] On March 3rd, in a speech to the Central Committee of the Communist Party, Stalin referred to the enormous damage 'which a handful of spies in the ranks of the Red Army could do to the country.'[34] On May 11th Tukachevsky was dismissed as Deputy Commissar for War and put in cold storage as Commander of the remote Volga Military District.[35] Three weeks later he was arrested.[36]

Comparison of this sequence of events with the accounts of the SS memoir-writer shows how small was the SD contribution to the Tukachevsky affair. Höttl of the SD says that 'the systematic work of forgery' began on Heydrich's instructions in April 1937[37] – by which time, Putna, Tukachevsky's friend, had already been publicly denounced and Stalin had spoken of the 'handful of spies' in the Red Army. Schellenberg states that the forged documents were handed over to the Soviets in mid-May 1937[38] – Tukachevsky had already been dismissed on May 11th.

Any attempt to ascribe to the SD some major hand in the liquidation of Tukachevsky presupposes that the Soviet Secret Service was working through several channels simultaneously. In any case it may reasonably be assumed that Yezhov's Special Bureau would have looked for incriminating material in Germany, a country with which Tukachevsky had Service relations. In the post-war period he had frequently visited Germany; he had been a guest of the Reichswehr at their manoeuvres and he had shaken Hindenburg's hand.[39] What more natural source of incriminating material for Yezhov than the National-Socialist régime, which had never approved of military collaboration with the Bolshevist 'world enemy'? The Soviets, however, obviously had to conceal their interest in this incriminating evidence and, for this purpose, Skoblin, a double agent with the panache of an ex-civil war general, was exactly the right man to lure Heydrich into a game which the omniscient 'C' never perceived.

One regularly repeated feature of the Tukachevsky story is, however, totally untrue – that Heydrich asked his opposite number Canaris for the Reichswehr's correspondence with the Soviet Army and, when the

Admiral refused, obtained it by breaking into a Wehrmacht office.[40] Spalcke, the Russian expert, confirms that Canaris knew nothing of Heydrich's plans up to the time of Tukachevsky's death. When Spalcke reported to the Admiral on the Tukachevsky affair, the latter was completely unsuspecting.[41]

Canaris used to go riding with Heydrich in the mornings and was, no doubt, informed of the SD's stroke of genius on one of these occasions. The news must have shaken him for it revealed to him the existence of a world of crooks, capable of dragging the whole Reich down to ruin. Abshagen, Canaris' biographer, considers that the Tukachevsky affair was the turning point in the Admiral's attitude both to Heydrich and to the régime.[42] Barely a year later Canaris had become determined that the entire leadership both of the Sicherheitspolizei and the SD must go.

Here then were the first signs of conflict between the Wehrmacht and the SD/SS. The SD's second new field of activity, however, aroused the suspicion of an authority far more dangerous to it than the Wehrmacht – the Party. The Ausland-SD had already broken the letter of the law contained in the Canaris–Best Agreement; now the work of the Inland-SD violated the spirit of an unwritten agreement subordinating the SD to the Party – Rudolf Hess had declared the SD to be the sole Intelligence and counter-espionage organization of the National-Socialist Party.[43]

This unique position had been granted to the SD only on the understanding that it would not interfere in internal Party affairs. The SD, so the formula ran, was an enemy Intelligence organization – in other words its job was to uncover opposition within the Party but not to concern itself with internal Party questions.[44]

Himmler and Heydrich had issued strict instructions forbidding any SD man to take part in internal Party discussions in any way. Reporting of Party matters was forbidden; any unauthorized reports were to be forwarded at once, and unprocessed, to the Party Chancellery.[45] The Party, and especially the Gauleiter, kept jealous watch to ensure that the SD did not develop into an organization of Party snoopers.

Since the reconstruction of the SD, however, there were two men working in the Wilhelmstrasse in whose eyes this – maintenance of a watch on the Party – was exactly what the SD was for. In the view of Professor Reinhard Höhn, Head of Zentralabteilung II 2 in the SD Hauptamt, and of Otto Ohlendorf, his staff director, the SD was the National-Socialist dictatorship's corrective, the voice of criticism.[46]

At their very first meeting in May 1936, Höhn had told Ohlendorf that, since public criticism was no longer allowed, it was the task of the

SD 'to inform the leading organizations of the Party and State about National-Socialist developments and especially wrong developments, wrong tendencies, etc.'[47] The professor found a willing pupil in Ohlendorf; he was an 'old fighter' and had long been searching for an opportunity of countering what seemed to him a catastrophic trend in National-Socialism. Ohlendorf was a fastidious creature, regarded by many Party members as typical of the neurotic sharp-tongued intellectual know-all;[48] he maintained that two mortal dangers threatened the health of National-Socialism from within – collectivist tendencies in economic and social policy and absolutist tendencies in constitutional policy. The former he loosely described as 'Bolshevism'; he regarded Robert Ley, the Head of the Labour Front, and SS-Obergruppenführer Walther Darré, the peasant ideologist, as its protagonists. The opposite tendency he labelled 'Fascism', categorizing as its supporters all who preached a National-Socialist form of imperial authority untrammelled by rules and institutions – Carl Schmitt, the Professor of Law, for instance.[49]

Ohlendorf and Höhn seriously believed that through the SD they could influence the development of National-Socialism. Höhn had already made the first organizational preparations. Even before Ohlendorf joined, Zentralabteilung II 2 had transferred its attention from anti-opposition action to a new concept – that of so-called 'spheres of life' observation.[50] Höhn declared that it was the SD's job to investigate opinion in all spheres of the national life and to discover the reaction of the population to measures taken by the Government and Party organizations, only thus could the leadership of the State know whether the people were in tune with its policy – it was a sort of National-Socialist version of the Gallup poll.[51]

Höhn opened his 'spheres of life' reporting campaign in an area familiar to the political economist – the High Schools and Universities. But the results he achieved were moderate. When Ohlendorf joined the SD, he found that Höhn's office consisted of 'about twenty young people without any office help, any registration, without any means at all.'[52] Ohlendorf took over the Hauptabteilung 'Economics' and rapidly built up a staff of expert economists from all parts of the country; they collected reports on the economic situation and subjected the overall results to critical analysis.[53] The main purpose of their work was summarized by Ohlendorf in a memorandum entitled 'The Economy in the National-Socialist State.'

The rearmament of the Reich, Ohlendorf said, was leading to 'unparalleled strains' in the economy, for instance 'expansion of big businesses and contraction of others, elimination of private initiative in numerous fields and its replacement by major purchasing and distribution organizations with all their disadvantages, such as interference with the prices and wages structure.' It was therefore now the 'task of the political and economic leaders to recognize the limits which these stresses and strains must not exceed if the purpose of the economy as a whole is not to be prejudiced . . . through its system of reporting on the situation, the climate of opinion and abuses, the SD has here a task of quite extraordinary importance.'[54]

Höhn was so pleased with the sober factual reports from Ohlendorf's section that, in April 1937, he appointed him director of the entire staff of Zentralabteilung II 2.[55]

Ohlendorf expanded his reporting system, hitherto confined to the economy, to cover all facets of the national life. Soon hardly a sphere of activity remained uncovered by Ohlendorf's and Höhn's office. Three large-scale staffs sprang up in the Wilhelmstrasse charged with investigating the true state of the nation: Hauptabteilung II 2 1 – Culture, Science, Education, the Community; Hauptabteilung II 2 2 – Law and Administration, Party and State, High Schools and students; Hauptabteilung II 2 3 – All Aspects of the Economy.[56]

The deeper Ohlendorf's investigators delved, however, the more critical their reports became. The SD reporters did not mince their words, referring for instance to increase of the power of big business, unchecked deficit spending by the State, collectivist tendencies in the Labour Front, denigration of the middle class, arrogance and megalomania in the Party. Earlier than they had foreseen, the investigators were at loggerheads with the Party hierarchy. The party functionaries soon realized that they were being subjected to examination by the SD. A process began later referred to by Ohlendorf as 'a continuous struggle, defeats, victories and again defeats for the SD and for me.'[57]

In summer 1936, however, Höhn put a foot seriously wrong and the SD's enemies seized on the opportunity to out-manoeuvre him. He had been intriguing against Professor Walther Frank, the leading National-Socialist historian, in an attempt to infiltrate SS experts into key positions in the writing of German history.[58] With the assistance of Julius Streicher, who loathed the SD, Frank struck back. He discovered certain earlier anti-Nazi remarks by Höhn as for instance: 'It was primarily Hitler with his National-Socialist Movement who created an anti-intellectual current of opinion'; such remarks rang so ominously in National-Socialist ears that, according to Lammers, the Head of the Reich Chancellery, even Hitler expressed 'the most serious doubts regarding Professor Höhn.'[59] Himmler and Heydrich were forced to relieve Höhn of his office; he was dismissed from the SD and disappeared to Sweden for a few months to escape the threat of expulsion from the Party.[60]

Hardly had Höhn disappeared, however, than Ohlendorf came under fire. Initially Himmler had been pleased with Ohlendorf's detailed reports.[61] As the Party's suspicions increased, however, the ever-cautious and opportunist Reichsführer kept his distance; moreover he began to dislike the doctrinaire manner of 'Nazism's Knight of the Holy Grail', as he called Ohlendorf.

Rudolf Brandt, Himmler's secretary, lamented: 'He [Ohlendorf] doesn't know how to cope with the Reichsführer. Really to get into contact with him he ought to bring him a rune stone from time to time and chat with the Reichsführer about his Germanic ideals. Instead of that he's very cold and superior in his manner as he goes into some matter of which the Reichsführer has little knowledge; he makes the gloomiest prophecies with a deadly serious face.'[62]

Himmler even did something which he was normally at pains to avoid – he bypassed Heydrich, summoned Ohlendorf and reprimanded him.[63] Ohlendorf was given to understand that the SD's 'spheres of life' investigations were illegal and would never be countenanced by the Party; the SD was only authorized to deal with enemy Intelligence and everything else was contrary to SS interests. Heydrich followed suit. Ohlendorf was relieved as staff director of Abteilung II 2 and relegated to his original sphere, economics.[64] On September 4th, 1937 Heydrich issued a decree: 'Situation reports on spheres of life can have only one purpose – to report the progress made by National-Socialist ideology in the individual spheres of life and to indicate the resistance encountered and, if necessary, from whom; cultural, material or other matters affecting the life of the community will only be reported from this viewpoint.'[65]

Under these circumstances Ohlendorf had no further wish to remain in the SD and he asked Heydrich to be allowed to resign. Heydrich refused;[66] he did not wish to deprive himself of Ohlendorf's expertise, nor of a possible tool for the expansion of his power. Himmler, also, in spite of his fear of Party criticism, clung to Ohlendorf.

Not until spring 1938 was Ohlendorf able to work his passage out of the SD Hauptamt. Hitherto he had only been a part-time Standartenführer in the SD; now he was permitted to join the 'Reich Group Commerce', one of the Nazi economic pressure organizations, where he became managing director.[67] He did not completely sever his connexions with the SD, however; he continued to work part-time (some two hours a day) in his old Hauptabteilung in the Wilhelmstrasse.[68]

Ohlendorf's was not an isolated case. Messages from all parts of the

SD network poured into the Wilhelmstrasse, all expressing anxiety for the future. The Ohlendorf crisis had once more emphasized the fact that the SD's future was as opaque as ever. Schellenberg noted: 'An increasing volume of "reports from the front" [a term peculiar to the SD referring to the lower levels of the Intelligence organization supposed to be in direct contact with the enemy] refer to growing uncertainty regarding the SD's future; psychologically the effect of this is catastrophic. Simultaneously a wave of resignations by full-timers has started.'[69]

Himmler and Heydrich found themselves faced with the necessity ultimately to produce some fundamental clarification in the status of the SD. Even before Ohlendorf's resignation a mammoth scandal had shown how insecure their machine of tyranny was. This scandal could be laid at the Gestapo's door and it bade fair to break both Heydrich's power and the partnership between him and Himmler.

The background to this affair went back as far as May 1936 – in the office of the examining magistrate, Berlin Police Court, Police headquarters. Ernst, an assistant judge, was examining an old habitué of the Berlin courts and prisons, a labourer named Otto Schmidt with a record of many previous convictions.[70] Schmidt's card showed: Otto Schmidt, aged 29; 1921–2 three convictions for theft, sentenced to two weeks, three weeks and 30 days imprisonment respectively; 1924, four months imprisonment for theft; 1927, one month for embezzlement; 1928, four months for blackmail and in the same year six months for blackmail and extortion; 1929, two weeks for fraud.[71] In 1935 Schmidt had been arrested by the Criminal Police on suspicion of further blackmail. At his first interrogation by Justus, a clerk of the court, he had admitted a couple of minor acts of blackmail but denied anything larger.[72] So Schmidt finally landed in the office of the interrogating magistrate. Ernst succeeded in loosening his tongue. He suddenly became voluble, chattering about having blackmailed a lot of people – 'hundreds' – with well-known personalities among them. The majority had been homosexuals whom he had caught *in flagrante delicto*. He gave names. They included Rüdiger Graf von der Goltz, the lawyer son of the Baltic Free Corps commander, SS-Standartenführer Graf von Wedel, the Police President of Potsdam, Funk, the Reich Minister of Economics and also a 'General' Fritsch.[73] Ernst pricked up his ears: which Fritsch? But Schmidt was saying no more.

A very ordinary case of blackmail had suddenly turned into a homosexual case with every sort of political implication; such affairs were the responsibility of the 'Reich Coordinating Office for the Suppression of Homosexuality' located in the Gestapa and directed by Kriminalrat

[Criminal Counsellor] Josef Meisinger. So the Schmidt files were sent across to the Prinz-Albrecht-Strasse. Meisinger read the files and he too caught his breath at the name Fritsch. Could this, he wondered, be the Commander-in-Chief of the Wehrmacht, Colonel-General Werner Freiherr von Fritsch, the secret hope of the conservative opposition in Germany and the declared enemy of all attempts by the SS to use the Verfügungstruppe to break the Wehrmacht's monopoly as an armed force? Meisinger summoned Schmidt from prison and had him interrogated by Hausser, a captain in the Schutzpolizei.[74]

On July 8th or 9th, 1936 Hausser confronted Schmidt with a collection of photographs assembled by Meisinger, from which Schmidt, who was all for making a name for himself, picked out the man with the most honourable title.[75] Meisinger, who was hardly an exponent of the niceties of police work, had entered beneath each photograph the name and official title of the person concerned. When Schmidt read: 'Colonel-General Freiherr von Fritsch, Commander-in-Chief of the Army', he gestured saying: 'That's him.'[76] Then he recorded a statement: 'One evening in November 1933 he had observed in the vestibule of the Wannsee Station Berlin a man dressed in dark overcoat with brown fur collar, dark hat, white scarf, and wearing a monocle. The man had left the station with a youth of no fixed address named Martin Weingärtner and had gone into the unlit private railway road. There he, Schmidt, had observed a homosexual act between the two.'[77] After a time, Schmidt went on, the man had returned and gone to the Ring Station on the Potsdamerplatz nearby; there he, Schmidt, had confronted the man, presenting himself as 'Kriminalkommissar Kröger'.[78] The man had said that he was General von Fritsch and had shown him an identity card. The name 'von Fritsch' was easily legible on the top right-hand corner of the card. Negotiations on the blackmail money then began; the man had said that he did not wish to be unfair – a couple of thousand marks meant nothing to him; unfortunately he had only 100 marks on him. Together they had gone to Lichterfelde where the man had disappeared into No 21, Ferdinand-Strasse. Ten minutes later he returned and pressed 500 marks into Schmidt's hand, promising a further thousand for the following day. Schmidt had collected this money and been promised yet a further thousand marks. These he had received in mid-January 1934 in the second-class waiting room of the Lichterfelde-Ost Underground station; on this occasion he had been accompanied by a friend named Heiter, whom he had presented as his chief. He, Schmidt, had given Heiter 500 marks.[79]

So much for Otto Schmidt's statement in early July 1936. Meisinger was triumphant; chance had placed in his hands a deadly weapon against von Fritsch, the Commander-in-Chief of the Army, and with it he, Josef Meisinger would rid the SS of one of their most dangerous enemies. Meisinger pursued the case. In August Schmidt was interrogated once more, this time by Löffner, another Criminal Police official, and he embroidered his story; on August 20th Heiter, his accomplice, corroborated the tale.[80] Meisinger now had no doubts; Schmidt's von Fritsch was the abominable Colonel-General von Fritsch.

Meisinger forthwith reported his happy discovery to his superiors and Himmler went off at once to tell his Führer. In the Reich Chancellery, however, he met with a disappointment. Hitler cast a cursory glance over the eight-page record of the interrogation and ordered him to burn 'this muck'.[81] Von Fritsch, the military technician, whom Hitler had once said that he 'loved',[82] was far too useful to Hitler the rearmament fanatic to be sacrificed over such a trifle.

Unfortunately for Himmler he had shown the dictator the Fritsch file just at the moment when, in the words of the Chancellor's military aide, Colonel Friedrich Hossbach, Hitler was treating the Commander-in-Chief of the Army 'with respectful discretion', allowing him in general a free hand and refraining from direct criticism of the Army leadership.[83] Himmler received one of those snubs which Hitler was then reserving for anyone who dared to criticize the Wehrmacht and even more its generals. He had, after all, once said to Admiral Boehm 'Then someone from the Party may come to me and say "All right, my Führer, but General So-and-So both speaks and works against you." Then I shall say "I don't believe it." And if the man then says "But I can show you proof my Führer," then I shall tear the bumf up, for my faith in the Wehrmacht is unshakeable.'[84]

So Himmler and Heydrich had to tear up their 'bumf'. Heydrich had the Fritsch file destroyed – but not before he had carefully taken extracts.[85] Presumably he expected to be able to use them one day when playing for high stakes. That day came quicker than he had hoped, for in the meantime a scene had been enacted in the Reich Chancellery which must be reckoned as one of the decisive turning points in the history of the National-Socialist régime. On the afternoon of November 5th, 1937 it had been borne in on Hitler that von Fritsch and Field-Marshal Werner von Blomberg, the Defence Minister, were hesitant to follow him in his increasingly reckless adventurist policy and were likely to prove a restraining influence.[86]

Hitler had assembled six of his closest collaborators – Göring, Raeder, the Commander-in-Chief of the Navy, and Freiherr von Neurath, the Foreign Minister, in addition to von Fritsch, von Blomberg, and Hossbach; he had revealed to them future plans which he regarded as so important that, as Hossbach recorded in the minutes, they were to be regarded 'as a political testament'. They amounted to this: by 1943 at the latest Germany must have expanded her 'Lebensraum' by force, Austria and Czechoslovakia must be under German control.[87] Blomberg and Fritsch raised objections, though of course only on technical military grounds; the Czechoslovak frontier defences, they said, presented a most difficult problem; even if Italy and France were at war, the presence of a strong French army on the German western frontier must be assumed. War could not be waged unless British and French neutrality could be guaranteed.[88] Hossbach noted 'At times the discussion became extremely heated, primarily during an argument between Blomberg and Fritsch on the one side and Göring on the other, Hitler mostly adopting the role of attentive listener.'[89]

Hitler had heard enough to form an opinion. If this was the attitude of his military men the warlike phase of National-Socialist foreign policy would get off to a bad start. Hitler's relations with his leading military advisers cooled abruptly – suddenly Meisinger's Fritsch file was a matter of interest once more. Possibly the decision to reopen the case came from Hitler himself but this seems unlikely; there was someone else with far more interest in letting the Gestapo thugs loose on the Commander-in-Chief of the Army – Göring; during the scene in the Reich Chancellery von Fritsch had accused him of dilettantism; although he had the rank of Colonel-General, he invariably felt himself ridiculed in professional military circles – and on paper he was still head of the Prussian Gestapo. In autumn 1941 Meisinger told Fritz Wiedemann, Hitler's former political aide, that the order to reconstitute the Fritsch file had come to him from Göring.[90] The only obscure factor is the timing.

The Gestapo's interest in the Fritsch case must have been reawakened immediately after the Fritsch–Göring argument in the Reich Chancellery, for when Fritsch left for a trip to Egypt on November 10th, 1937 he was already being shadowed by two Gestapo agents whose brief was to confirm whether the General visited homosexual dives.[91] In mid-January 1938 Meisinger set his policemen going again, subjecting Schmidt's evidence to yet another cross-check.[92] Inspector Fehling of Meisinger's staff in fact came near the truth; on January 15th he discovered that a certain Captain (retired) von Frisch lived next door to 21 Ferdinand-Strasse where Schmidt's victim was supposed to have disappeared – this trail was so hot that he promptly lost it again![93]

Göring's definitive order to reconstruct the Fritsch file, however, only came later – when von Helldorf, the Berlin Police President, came to him with a revelation highly embarrassing to the military and so offered him the possibility of satisfying his life's ambition – to become Reich Minister of War.

Field-Marshal von Blomberg had been a widower since 1932 – with two sons and three daughters. On January 12th, 1938 he had married Erna Gruhn, a shorthand typist in the Reich Egg Marketing Board.[94] The wedding had been a small one with Hitler and Göring as witnesses and the happy couple had forthwith set off on their honeymoon.[95] Shortly afterwards Curt Hellmuth Müller, head of the Reich Identification Office in the RKPA received a batch of lewd photographs sent over by his colleague Gerhard Nauck of the 'Morality Crimes' desk. Müller's secretary, Burkert, drew his special attention to certain of the photographs and Müller examined them more closely.[96]

Müller recalls: 'I noticed that someone had inked in names on the photographs of the two naked bodies and so I called Nauck and asked him whether he was interested in knowing who they were. He thought that at the moment this was not necessary. I was sure, however, that I had read the name of the woman somewhere but could not think who it might be.' So he searched in his fingerprint index 'and lo and behold the woman concerned appeared two or three times in our register.'[97] He went to Mesch, the head of the domicile registration office, to find out who the woman might be. From a steel tray Mesch drew a registration card – it was that of Blomberg's wife.[98]

Müller hurried off to his chief, Arthur Nebe, who exclaimed: 'Good God, Müller, and this woman has kissed the Führer's hand!'[99] Nebe proceeded cautiously and took Helldorf, the Police President, into his confidence. On the morning of January 23rd, Helldorf appeared in the office of General Wilhelm Keitel, the head of the Wehrmacht office in the Reich Ministry of War and Blomberg's closest confidant.[100] He asked the General to confirm whether the lady referred to on the index card was the new Frau von Blomberg. Keitel, however, said that he was in no position to do so, since he had never seen the lady. He called the Minister's office but Blomberg was not at home. Then Keitel had a fatal idea; he advised Helldorf to go and see Göring; he, after all, had been a witness at the wedding and must therefore know Blomberg's new wife.[101]

So from that moment on the evening of January 23rd, 1938 when Helldorf let him into the secret of the Blomberg case, Göring held a decisive trump card in his hand. He realized at once that the scandal would lead to Blomberg's dismissal. Who would then move into the Bendlerstrasse? None other than Göring's rival, Colonel-General von Fritsch. And that Göring was determined to prevent under all circumstances.

Göring had to wait twenty-four hours before he could strike, for

Hitler was not expected back from the Berghof in Bavaria before the evening of January 24th.[102] Hitler had hardly reached the Reich Chancellery, however, when Göring arrived, lamenting to Hossbach that he always had to be the bearer of bad news. He gave Hossbach an indication of what the bad news was; it had something to do with Blomberg, the Minister of War. He said not a word about the Commander-in-Chief of the Army.[103] Göring seems to have mentioned the Fritsch case only at his meeting with Hitler and then merely in passing. When Göring had left, Hossbach found his Führer 'in a great state of agitation but neither anxious nor depressed'.[104]

Göring must therefore have ordered Meisinger to reconstitute the Fritsch file during the night January 24th–25th. When he visited the Reich Chancellery on the evening of the 24th he had not got it with him but by the next morning it was on Hitler's desk.[105] It therefore seems a reasonable assumption that it took shape during that night. (Gestapo officials invariably state that the work of reconstituting the file took place 'at high pressure and at night'.[106]) A telephone call from Schaub, Hitler's aide, to Hossbach at 2.15 AM on January 25th ordering him to come to the Chancellery forthwith, also fits into the picture.[107] Presumably Meisinger's Fritsch file had just arrived.

The Hitler whom Hossbach met a few hours later was almost unrecognizable. There was no doubt that the double Blomberg–Fritsch affair had hit the dictator hard; it had perhaps shaken a lifetime of naïve trust in the Prussian/German military man. Wiedemann, Hitler's aide, says: 'Throughout the whole four years during which I served him, I have never seen him so downcast. He paced slowly up and down in his room, bent and with his hands behind his back, mumbling that if a German Field-Marshal could do something like this, then anything in the world was possible.'[108] General von Rundstedt found Hitler 'in a fearful state of excitement such as I had never seen before. Something had cracked in him; he had lost all confidence in men.'[109]

Was it all play-acting? Initially, certainly not. Soon, however, Hitler's predatory instinct asserted itself; here was an opportunity with one blow to deprive the Wehrmacht top level of its authority and to place himself at the head of the Army. Henceforth no soldier would be able to stop his career of foreign policy adventure.

So Hitler now changed front and played off Göring against the military. When the courageous Hossbach continued to protest Fritsch's innocence Hitler commissioned his henchman to check the truth of Schmidt's statement. Twice Göring drove over to the Prinz-Albrecht-Strasse and obtained confirmation of what he and Hitler wished to hear – that Schmidt stuck to his evidence.[110] Hossbach then took the initiative. Contrary to Hitler's express order, during the night of January 25th–26th he went to Fritsch and told him what was brewing. Von Fritsch seemed paralysed, shouting 'It's a stinking lie!'[111] – nothing more.

This was the moment which proved that, when its great crisis came, the men in charge of the Wehrmacht were obsessed by a sense of discipline and blinded by the Führer cult; their motto might well have been the adage of the French Marshal MacMahon: 'Of all people in the world the generals are those who have the least courage to act.'[112] This applied with special force to Fritsch; his contemporaries have wrongly labelled him as a secret opponent of Hitler but in fact, perhaps more than any other general, he had fallen under the spell of the Führer. Right to the end he could not understand what his Führer had done to him, could not see the abyss into which he would have fallen had his fellow generals not dragged him back. He now simply resigned himself to his destiny. His destiny? – it was that of Germany. Later he wrote of Hitler: 'This man is Germany's destiny for good or ill and this destiny will go to the end of the road; if it leads us into the abyss he will take us all with him – there is nothing to be done about it.'[113]

Nevertheless military men were still to be found who were not prepared to abandon themselves to their fate with such supine resignation. Once more Hossbach stood up for his Commander-in-Chief. He argued with Hitler at such length that the latter eventually agreed to receive von Fritsch.[114] On the evening of January 26th the Colonel-General was summoned to the Reich Chancellery. Fritsch hastened to his Führer, hoping eventually to see 'the pig', and was at once confronted with Schmidt who had also been summoned. Schmidt said at once: 'That's him.' Von Fritsch gave his word of honour 'I do not know this gentleman.'[115] Meanwhile Hossbach was waiting in the little dining-room of the Reich Chancellery; he says: 'After waiting alone for a long time I suddenly heard footsteps pounding from the library to the little dining-room; the door swung open; Göring rushed in, both hands up to his face, howling at the top of his voice; he threw himself on the sofa shrieking over and over again 'He did it, he did it!'[116]

Hitler declared that even the Colonel-General's word of honour did not satisfy him.[117] Now Göring saw his moment. He took Wiedemann, Hitler's aide, aside and said: 'Listen – you might talk to the Führer. Tell him to give me the Army as well. I am ready to give up the Four-Year Plan.'[118] But one intermediary was not enough for Göring. On hearing that Keitel had been summoned to Hitler at 1 PM on January 27th he called and asked him to look round. He asked who Blomberg's successor would be. Keitel replied: 'There can be no question of anyone other than you, for you, as C-in-C of the Luftwaffe, would not serve under another Army General.' Göring could of course only applaud such delicacy of feeling,[119] but he apparently recruited yet a third member of the team – Blomberg; he too regarded Göring as his natural successor.[120]

But Hitler had no intention of allowing Göring to ruin his own plans; in his inimitable way he produced three different reasons for refusing Göring's candidature. To his aide Wiedemann he said: 'No question of it. That fellow Göring does not understand how to carry out even a Luftwaffe inspection. I know more about it myself.'[121] He told Keitel: 'There could be no question of it; he had given him [Göring] the Four-Year Plan; he must retain the Luftwaffe because no better man could be found and as his [Hitler's] successor he must play his proper part in State business.'[122] Blomberg later recalled that Hitler made 'one or two unpleasant remarks about Göring; he was too easy-going – the word "idle" may even have been used – and in any case there was no question of him.'[123]

At this point – 4 PM on January 27th, 1938 – the disgraced Minister for War was seized with hatred for the military caste which had always shown its aversion to Hitler's protégé and now, in accordance with its stiff-necked code of honour, refused any gesture of sympathy to a fallen Field-Marshal. Blomberg was bent on revenge; he would ensure that the military bitterly regretted their insulting behaviour. And take his revenge he did; at his farewell visit to Hitler he suggested that the Führer and Reich Chancellor should himself take over the post of Reich Minister of War.[124] Hitler concealed his feeling of triumph. At about the same time General Alfred Jodl, Head of the 'National Defence' Section in the Reich Ministry of War, was writing in his diary: 'One has the impression that this is a fateful moment for the German people. How great is the unconscious influence a woman can exert on the fate of a people and hence of the world!'[125]

Hitler had taken his decision. The next day Keitel was told that Hitler himself would take over the War Ministry, transformed into an 'Oberkommando der Wehrmacht' [High Command of the Armed Forces – OKW]; 'I was to remain his Chief-of-Staff; I must not and could not leave him in the lurch in this situation.'[126] On February 4th, 1938, the nation heard the news that all the sceptics regarding Hitler's policy had been removed: von Blomberg and von Fritsch had retired, Freiherr von Neurath, the Foreign Minister, had been replaced by the outsider Joachim von Ribbentrop, sixteen generals had been retired, forty-four others posted, the War Ministry had been disbanded and renamed OKW.[127] The Propaganda Ministry's slogan for this German version of the Tukachevsky affair was: 'Concentration of powers.'[128] The road to catastrophe was now open. Adolf Hitler was untrammelled Dictator of Germany.

The case of Fritsch, however, remained to be solved. A few days before his compulsory retirement Hitler had worked out a most convenient plan: Fritsch was to hand in his resignation, nothing was to be said on either side and there were to be no legal proceedings.[129] The Commander-in-Chief of the Army, however, refused to accept, so Hitler had a new idea: the case should be decided by a special court,[130] but now the military and legal professions took a hand and weighed in on the side of the General. On January 27th Dr Heinrich Rosenberg, head of the Wehrmacht Legal Section in the War Ministry, said that a special court for Fritsch was out of the question; an officer was entitled to a military court and, in fact, paragraph 11 of the Military Legal Code laid down that for officers of the rank of Lieutenant-General and above the President and members of the court should be appointed by the Führer. Keitel was horrified; he did not relish the idea of putting such proposals to Hitler. Hesitantly he replied: 'You must bear in mind that these men are children of the revolution and their standards are different from ours.'[131]

Nevertheless Rosenberg gained his point, for he was supported by the Reich Minister of Justice.[132] At last Gürtner saw a chance of calling a halt to the growing power of the Himmler–Heydrich machine. He hoped that Fritsch's case could be used to prove that if the police alone could condemn a man, the Reich was heading for a situation in which arbitrary action could replace the rule of law.[133] Hitler himself had summoned Gürtner and asked for his opinion. The Minister of Justice pored over twenty-two files of court proceedings, seven Gestapo files and two additional records of interrogations.[134] Then he reached his decision, though he expressed it in the cautious terms characteristic of National-Socialist bureaucracy; he wrote to Hitler: 'I must not and cannot pronounce judgement on guilt or innocence; irrespective of the status of the person concerned, his rank or his position, this must remain a matter for the judgement of the court.'[135]

The Dictator now had no alternative but to agree to the convening of a court martial. He nominated a Supreme Commander's Court consisting of the Commanders-in-Chief of the Army, Navy and Luftwaffe together with the Presidents of the two Divisions of the Supreme Military Court; he charged two Judge Advocates, Biron and Dr Carl Sack, with the preliminary investigations.[136] At the same time Hitler introduced one or two safety devices into the legal machine: Göring was nominated President of the Court and the Gestapo was authorized to conduct a parallel investigation.[137] The struggle between SS and Army had begun.

At first the Gestapo seemed to be in the lead. Before Sack, the official investigator, had even started work, von Fritsch suddenly and on his own initiative appeared in the Prinz-Albrecht-Strasse and submitted himself to a Gestapo interrogation.[138] Fritsch's friends were thunderstruck. For years the Army had dinned into every recruit, however junior, that the Gestapo had no right to arrest a soldier nor even summon him for interrogation; for years the Wehrmacht had insisted upon the principle that its territory was forbidden ground to any Gestapo official, however high his rank – and now here was the Commander-in-Chief of the Army losing his nerve, disregarding the restrictions which he himself had laid down and allowing himself to be interrogated by the Gestapo.

Fritsch went to the Gestapo not once but twice. On January 27th SS-Oberführer Werner Best interrogated him in the presence of Kriminalrat Franz Josef Huber; on January 28th Best confronted him with Schmidt, the witness for the prosecution.[139] The Fritsch interrogations were among the longest in the history of the Gestapo. But Best was a lawyer by profession and he was assailed by a curious feeling of unease. Admittedly Fritsch gave an irresolute impression; he was obviously nervous and became hopelessly entangled in an attempt to explain away the origin of the homosexual story by various nonsensical tales about two so-called NSV [National-Socialistische Verein – a Nazi association] youths whom he had once put up in his apartment.[140] Best was also disgusted by Fritsch's prolonged arguments with Schmidt.

Nevertheless Best could not bring himself to believe Schmidt's story. After all many of his other so-called revelations had proved to be figments of the imagination. Finally Best's doubts got the better of him, and he poured them out to Himmler who, however, waved him away, saying: 'There is such a thing as honour among thieves.' In other words – even a crook would not lie in so delicate a situation.[141] So Schmidt's statements were checked yet once more but this time the Gestapo must have realized that they had been hoaxed.

Hans-Bernd Gisevius, Nebe's confidant, maintains that Nebe told him on the evening of January 30th 'that the "case" of Fritsch was a matter of mistaken identities. Heydrich and Himmler knew this but had taken every imaginable measure to cover up the fact.'[142] Schellenberg also confirms that 'when Heydrich began to have doubts, the files were already on Hitler's desk.'[143]

An iron curtain of silence descended on the Prinz-Albrecht-Strasse. Not a word was spoken or indication given which might lead the other side to suspect the truth of the Fritsch case. The Gestapo initiated a bold diversionary manoeuvre, as if they were still convinced of Fritsch's guilt. Heydrich's minions swarmed into the barracks and interrogated any soldier who had ever acted as batman to von Fritsch.[144] The General's ex-aides were also interrogated. Even the mothers of the two youngsters whom Fritsch had once fed and housed were plagued by the Gestapo.[145]

Nevertheless the Police Chiefs were now nervous – so nervous that it was noticeable to the outside world. Himmler's confidence in his talented head of the Sipo and SD was shaken; Heydrich lamented that he would probably be put to the sword.[146] General Jodl noted in his diary: 'Himmler must be depressed that senior Wehrmacht officers are casting unheard-of aspersions on him.'[147] Every day messages arrived in the Prinz-Albrecht-Strasse giving Himmler and Heydrich to think that the Army officers were closing their ranks and toying with the idea of breaking the Sicherheitspolizei's grip. For Heydrich, credence was lent to these messages by the fact that Admiral Canaris had now become one of his bitterest opponents.[148]

One day Schellenberg received a cry of alarm from his master. Heydrich ordered him to provide himself at once with a revolver and ammunition and report to his office. Schellenberg found 'C' very uneasy: together they went to the Gestapo mess. Hours passed, Heydrich becoming increasingly nervous. Suddenly he looked at the clock and said: 'If they don't start marching from Potsdam during the next hour and a half, the danger will have passed.' It was Schellenberg's first intimation that Heydrich had seriously thought that the Potsdam Wehrmacht garrison might take action against the Gestapo headquarters in the Prinz-Albrecht-Strasse.[149]

Certain officers had actually been considering plans of this nature but the generals recoiled and contented themselves with pathetic gestures. Beck, the Chief of the General Staff, was slow to grasp the deeper implications of the Fritsch affair;[150] the new Commander-in-Chief, Colonel-General Walter von Brauchitsch, protested against Gestapo intrusions into the barracks;[151] Fritsch challenged Himmler to a duel, but General von Rundstedt, his second, never delivered the challenge and kept it at home as a souvenir.[152] The battle against the SS was relentlessly pursued only by Colonel Hossbach and Canaris, the Head of the Abwehr; their staunchest allies were Rüdiger Graf von der Goltz, Fritsch's defence counsel, and Sack, the official attorney. Gradually their investigators succeeded in penetrating the Gestapo's secret.

Sack and von der Goltz set out to disprove Schmidt's statements. They were able to show that von Fritsch had never possessed the identity card referred to by Schmidt and had never lived in the neighbourhood of the Ferdinand-Strasse; moreover, the General had never been a smoker (as was Schmidt's Fritsch) and did not possess an overcoat with a fur collar.[153] Gradually, however, it began to dawn on Fritsch's defenders that the incident described by Schmidt must actually have happened. Schmidt's description of the locality was clearly correct.

Then von der Goltz had an idea: he searched through the telephone book for the name Fritsch or something similar. And there he found it: 'von Frisch, Captain retired' – and he lived at number 20 Ferdinand-Strasse! Sack and his assistant hurried to that address and the riddle was solved.[154] Everything fitted: Captain von Frisch admitted the incident at the Wannsee Station; he had an overcoat with a fur collar; he was a heavy smoker – and finally he produced the receipt for the blackmail money drawn on his account.[155] Von der Goltz drove at once to his principal and without even greeting him blurted out: 'General, you can rest assured; the real Fritsch has been found; the case has been cleared up without question.' But the ex-C-in-C was doubtful: 'Even that won't satisfy the Führer. He will not wish to believe anything like that.'[156] Fritsch's fatalistic assumption was almost borne out in practice. The Gestapo laid hands on the Captain and seemed to have every intention of causing him to disappear, for Frisch was the repository of a secret which, for the Gestapo, could be mortal: he knew (and had told Sack so) that Inspector Fehling of the Gestapo had visited him as early as January 15th, 1938 and had checked his bank statements.[157] Von Fritsch's friends, however, were alive to the possibilities. Sack intervened and insisted that the Captain be released by the Gestapo.[158]

On March 10th the Supreme Commander's Court, sitting in the Berlin Preussenhaus, opened the main proceedings against Werner Freiherr von Fritsch.[159] Though the real accused was the Gestapo, the start of the case was, from Fritsch's point of view, unpromising. After only a few hours the proceedings were suspended, Hitler having summoned the Commanders-in-Chief of the Services to the Reich Chancellery. Confidentially von Fritsch was given the reason; Adolf Hitler had ordered the move into Austria.[160] A week later the trial was resumed.[161] Schmidt, the Gestapo's witness made every effort to stick to his story, but then Göring, the President, intervened; although, more than anyone other than the Gestapo, he had made great play with the Fritsch case, with a couple of powerful outbursts of rhetoric he now drove Schmidt into such a corner that the blackmailer confessed everything.[162] On March 18th, 1938 judgement was given: 'In the case against Colonel-General (retired) Werner Freiherr von Fritsch, the Supreme Commander's Court has pronounced as follows on the basis of the main hearing: the main hearing has proved that Colonel-General (retired) Freiherr von Fritsch is innocent on all counts.'[163]

Himmler and Heydrich went to ground. Surely, they thought, the Wehrmacht must strike now; surely the soldiers would play their trump card. But the Wehrmacht kept its mouth shut. Only Hossbach and Canaris produced a 'draft of demands' which the Army should put to Hitler. Canaris dictated it:

> (a) Public reinstatement of Colonel-General Freiherr von Fritsch in the most impressive manner possible; the true reason for the General's retirement to be given wide publicity.
> (b) Considerable changes in senior Gestapo appointments.
> In the first instance the following to be considered:
> Himmler, Heydrich, Jost (of the SD), Best, Meisinger, Fehling and others.[164]

Once more the generals drew back. Beck studied the Canaris–Hossbach paper and pigeon-holed it.[165] Politically the Blomberg–Fritsch crisis had broken the Wehrmacht's back. Moreover Hitler made a gesture to the military. He summoned an assemblage of generals and rehabilitated von Fritsch, though without re-appointing him to his office, merely nominating him Commander of the 12th Artillery Regiment;[166] with this regiment Fritsch, the fatalist, the 'target' as he called himself, fell in action near Warsaw on September 22nd, 1939.[167] Himmler, on the other hand, had Schmidt, the blackmailer, shot.[168] He arraigned Inspector Fehling before a disciplinary Court and transferred him to an inconspicuous post.[169] Kriminalkommissar Eberhard Schiele, one of the experts working on the Fritsch case, was dismissed from the Gestapo[170] and even Meisinger was deprived of his 'office for the suppression of homosexuality'; in 1939 Himmler sent him off to German-occupied Poland.[171]

Himmler took some time to forget the Fritsch setback. He remained extremely susceptible to Wehrmacht accusations that he was campaigning against the Generals. When SS-Gruppenführer Streckenbach was inquiring into the case of a certain SS Commander accused by the Wehrmacht, Himmler said: 'Examine everything; omit nothing so that people cannot go on accusing me of disrespectful behaviour towards the Wehrmacht.'[172] Even to the SS-Verfügungstruppe Himmler thought it advisable to deny any complicity in the Fritsch case. In a speech to VT Commanders he said that he had been the victim of incompetent officials. Hausser, the VT Inspector, commented: 'We gave him that much.'[173]

The Reichsführer was clearly in some trepidation and kept anxious watch to ensure that neither the police nor the SS voiced criticisms of the Wehrmacht. Anti-military comments were forbidden even at secret SS Commanders' conferences. In January 1939, when SS-Brigadeführer Leo Petri submitted notes for an address to be made at a Gruppenführer conference in Berlin containing sly allusions to the Blomberg–Fritsch crisis, Himmler's green pencil was used with every indication of ill-humour; he noted on the draft: 'must not be put in this way', and made numerous mollifying corrections.[174]

Heydrich also felt that his position had been affected; Lina Heydrich says that her husband lived under severe nervous strain at this period.[175] Heydrich realized a fact which has escaped the majority of historians: the police machine had not gained in strength as a result of the Blomberg–Fritsch affair. The case had of course set the seal upon the final transition to the total dictatorship of Adolf Hitler. In the relative positions of police and Wehrmacht, however, nothing had changed: the new Army leaders showed the same reserve and hostility towards the SS as their predecessors.

If anything, the conflict had sharpened. Although Military Intelligence was officially forbidden to report on political matters, Heydrich's enemy, Canaris, and even more Lt-Col Hans Oster, Head of the coordinating Abteilung in the OKW Ausland Abwehr [Foreign Intelligence], allowed their organization to extend their activities into this field; moreover they were continually assisting enemies of the régime to escape the clutches of the Gestapo and SD.[176] Even Hitler's yes-man, General Keitel, the head of OKW, considered one of his primary tasks to be the prevention of SS and Police interference in military matters. One day Halder, successor as Chief of the General Staff to Beck, who had been dismissed shortly after the Fritsch crisis, reproached Keitel for invariably giving way to Hitler; tears came into Keitel's eyes and he retorted: 'Halder, I do it only for your sake after all. Do try and understand me.'[177]

Heydrich knew only too well that his authority was unlikely to be accepted unquestioningly. He must therefore subject his machine to even stricter centralized control and eliminate all sources of friction within his empire. The Gestapo's loss of prestige in spring 1938 and the SD's crisis of confidence led him to develop a plan for merging the two halves of his surveillance system into one coordinated whole – in short he proposed combination of the SD and Gestapo into a Reich Security Service.[178]

The impulse was given by Himmler. In summer 1938 he stepped up the tempo of his great project – the merger of SS and police into 'a consolidated State Protection Corps of the National-Socialist Reich', in the words of a Himmler decree of June 23rd, 1938.[179] Himmler visualized a two-stage merger: members of the Ordnungspolizei were to join the Allgemeine SS, even forming combined SS/Police units in the major cities; members of the Sicherheitspolizei, on the other hand, were to join the Party Organization, the SD.[180] Himmler had already worked out (at least on paper) a detailed system for this personnel merger, the object being to bind the SS and Police indissolubly together. In autumn 1936 Commanders of SD-Oberabschnitte were nominated 'Inspectors of the Sicherheitspolizei and SD' [IdS], in order to promote the gradual fusion of Gestapo, Kripo and SD.[181] In late 1937 Commanders of SS-Oberabschnitte were nominated 'Höhere SS- und Polizeiführer' [Senior SS and Police Commanders – HSSPF]; in the event of mobilization they were to assume direction of all SS, Ordnungspolizei and Sicherheitspolizei units in their Wehrkreis [military district].[182]

Himmler's plan for a State Protection Corps, however, threatened to undermine the independent status of the SD. The proposal that Sipo personnel should join the SD as the Party organization implied a new influx of men into the SD and they necessarily originated primarily from the Gestapo; as far as their official activities were concerned they were the SD's competitors in intelligence. In addition police officials now came flooding into the SD and, although they did not hold even junior SS ranks, they were now given rank corresponding to their status in the Police Force; for instance, a 'Kriminalobersekretär' became an SS-Untersturmführer, a 'Kriminalrat' at SS-Hauptsturmführer and a 'Regierungsdirektor' an SS-Standartenführer.[183] The old SD men therefore saw the day approaching when they would be swamped by newly nominated 'rank-parity' officials from the Gestapo. The potential numbers of ex-Gestapo candidates were enormous; in mid-1936 only 244 out of 607 Gestapo officials belonged to the SS and by the outbreak of war only 3,000 out of 20,000.[184]

The majority of the older SD men, moreover, were in no position to compete, for the members of the Sipo and SD were drawn from different backgrounds. The Sicherheitspolizei consisted primarily of the traditional police officials and administrative law experts; the SD Intelligence organization, on the other hand, was a bustling, heterogeneous collection of men, thrown up by the arbitrary SS career regulations – a further reflection of the fact that the SD was a Party organization and the Sicherheitspolizei a State institution.

Heydrich now decided to put an end to this disparity. He proposed to amalgamate the SD's Intelligence organization with the Sicherheitspolizei and, at the same time, to give the SD official status; this would eliminate two major disadvantages from the SD point of view: its dependence on the Party and the lack of an official career structure with assured pension facilities.[185] The arguments over the SD's 'spheres of life' activity had already shown that politically the SD was entirely dependent upon Party good-will.

The SD's permanent shortage of funds was a further and even more aggravating proof of its dependence on the Party; every year it had to send a begging letter to the Party Treasurer. In 1936, for instance, Oswald Pohl wrote to Franz Xaver Schwarz, the Party Treasurer:[186] 'Please do not be taken aback by this request; SS headquarters funds are completely exhausted. Savings and reserves have been completely expended. The safes are empty. In recent months the financial situation has frequently been worse than catastrophic. During the last four months liquid funds available to the SS have averaged 3,000 marks!!!'[187] From time to time Schwarz went on strike, reproaching the SD with asking for more money than all the Party Members' contributions put together (in 1934 it was demanding 700,960 marks per month). Continuous SS promotion did not move Schwarz to loosen the purse strings. The Führer's Deputy and Party Headquarters frequently had to intervene to tide the SD over its difficulties.[188]

Heydrich was determined to rescue the SD from the position of suppliant. Late in 1938 he commissioned Schellenberg to examine the problem of merging SD and Sipo,[189] salient points of the proposed reform being: 'The SD to become a State Organization independent of the Party – its budget to be borne by the Reich.' Time was pressing, for the rumour was rife throughout the country that the SD's days were numbered. On April 4th, 1939 Schellenberg wrote: 'These rumours have built up until there is now general talk of the SD's disbandment or its absorption by the Sicherheitspolizei; the inevitable conclusion drawn is that all SD members who are without a career recognized by the internal administration, in particular those without full legal training, will lose their means of livelihood.'[190]

These rumours were no figment of the imagination. At one moment Himmler had, in fact, toyed with the idea of disbanding the entire SD Intelligence organization.[191] He was only prevented from doing so by considerations of power policy; his position within the Party rested upon the fact that the SD was the sole Party Intelligence organization. If he abolished the SD, some other Party power group might set up a new Intelligence organization – and it would be independent of the Reichsführer-SS.

The way was therefore open for Schellenberg to proceed to design a new super-organization. To Himmler's conception of a State Protection Corps – the SS plus the Police, he now added the notion of a Reich Security Service – the SD plus the Sicherheitspolizei. He therefore proposed amalgamation of the SD Hauptamt (a Party organization) with the Hauptamt Sicherheitspolizei (a State institution) to form a Reichssicherheitshauptamt. In each Wehrkreis it would maintain Security Service Inspectors in charge of Security Service Abschnitte, thus bringing all Sicherheitspolizei and SD units under one authority. Nevertheless – and here was the decisive point – the SD was not to be absorbed into the Sicherheitspolizei but was to retain its 'specialized' character.[192]

Schellenberg's proposal, in fact, amounted to this: the SD would have all the advantages of becoming a State organization, independent of the Party; members of the SD and of the Sicherheitspolizei would have equal status, but at the same time the SD would remain closed to the ex-Gestapo civil servants. Schellenberg's nightmare was the prospect of SD freedom of action being hampered by administrative lawyers. Like his master Heydrich, he was fanatically opposed to the lawyer's normative habits of thought. Though a lawyer himself, he had an almost pathological mistrust of administrative lawyers; in his view they lacked that unthinking tractability which must be characteristic of the new master-men; the type of functionary envisaged by the SD must be uninhibited by laws laid down by society or the State; they must be prepared to carry out unquestioningly every whim of the Dictator, including even the most criminal order from Adolf Hitler. In Schellenberg's view the new machine must 'put aside all inhibiting or traditional notions – it must at last possess that flexibility which the government of a state must have if it is to administer a country smoothly in accordance with the directives which the Führer sees fit to issue.'[193] An old-style lawyer like Werner Best, however, was incapable of such flexibility; in his view the administrative lawyer must continue to occupy a key position and so he revolted against the 'de-officialization' of the police envisaged by Heydrich and Schellenberg. He therefore proposed new career regulations, under which the SD man would be a servant of the State and full legal training a condition of employment.[194]

Between Schellenberg and Best a sniping war developed and it was not confined to the four walls of the Prinz-Albrecht-Strasse. In April 1939 Best published an article in the periodical *Deutsches Recht* clearly aimed at Heydrich's anti-legal advisers.[195] In the Third Reich, Best said, the lawyer's calling must be envisaged as 'that of a monitor within the structure of society, a man who has mastered the technique of giving and executing orders in civil life and who possesses such knowledge of the tasks both of the leadership and of the community that he is in a position to carry out his monitoring function in every sphere. Within the present-day structure of society the legal profession is therefore the "most political" profession in existence.'[196]

Heydrich was so furious over Best's article that he immediately commissioned Schellenberg to draft a retort[197] and the latter set to work with his usual acumen. He criticized Best's article as 'a question of personal taste'. On April 25th, 1939 he commented: 'This implies nothing less than a perpetuation of the arrogance shown towards the leadership by the expert on forms of words and it is this which leads to the present criticisms. It must also lead to perpetuation of the disadvantages associated with a period which we thought was past ... highly doubtful whether this is the moment to defend the "lawyers" ... failure to prove innocence . . . presumption.'[198]

Best continued to demand, however, that if he became a member of the Sicherheitspolizei, the SD man must be subject to the normal rules of State Administration. He continued to insist that senior officials must have had some legal training, drawing from Heydrich the remark: 'Oh, you and your assessors' kindergarten!'[199] All this arguing, however, proved unnecessary, for Schellenberg's ambitious project foundered on the rock of Himmler's timidity. He was not confident of his ability to defend the proposal for a Reich Security Service against the Party's objections. A tentative inquiry from Rudolf Hess had convinced him that the Party leadership would never permit combination of a Party organization with a State institution to form a new official superauthority.[200] The Party was still keeping jealous watch to ensure that no State authority, although manned by the most ardent of National-Socialists, should have any insight into Party matters.

In its final form the Reichssicherheitshauptamt (RSHA) was no more than a feeble compromise. An organization with this title did, indeed, come into existence on September 27th, 1939 but it was never allowed to use the name in public; the instructions laid down that the letterheading 'Reichssicherheitshauptamt' was not to be used in correspondence with other authorities.[201]

The RSHA, in fact, led a shadowy existence; officially no one was supposed to know of it. It remained an organization valid for internal purposes only; the only title appearing on the surface was that of 'Chief of the Sicherheitspolizei and SD' (CSSD).[202]

Even the dream of combining the SD with the Sicherheitspolizei came to nothing. Party and State refused to mix.

The RSHA 'Ämter' were formed from the Abteilungen of the SD Hauptamt and Hauptamt Sicherheitspolizei, but even these 'Ämter' led a comparatively independent existence, some being Party institutions and others State authorities. Amt I (Administration and Legal) was formed from the Legal and Organization sections of both Hauptämter; its Head was Dr Werner Best; it was a State authority.[203] Amt II (Ideological Investigation) was formed from Zentralabteilungen I 3 and II 1 of the SD Hauptamt; its Head was Professor Franz Six; it was a Party organization.[204] Amt III (Spheres of German Life or Inland-SD) was formed from Zentralabteilung II 2 of the SD Hauptamt; its Head was Otto Ohlendorf; it was a Party organization.[205] Amt IV (Suppression of Opposition) was formed from Abteilungen II and III of the Gestapa and Zentralabteilung III 2 of the SD Hauptamt; its Head was Heinrich Müller; it was a State authority.[206] Amt V (Suppression of Crime) was identical with the RKPA and the Kripo office in Hauptamt Sicherheitspolizei; its Head was Arthur Nebe; it was a State authority.[207] Amt VI (Foreign Intelligence Service or Ausland-SD) was formed from SD Amt III of the SD Hauptamt; its Head was Heinz Jost; it was a Party office.[208] (After Best's departure in 1940 the RSHA Ämter were reorganized once more; Best's Amt I was split into two new Ämter – I (Personnel) and II (Organization, Administration and Legal), the original Amt II becoming a new Amt VII.)

The SD was in fact still dependent upon Party good-will. Apart from certain SD offices incorporated into RSHA Ämter I and IV (and therefore financed by the State), the idea of making the SD budget official misfired;[209] even the Inland SD continued to work in the semi-official capacity to which it had been relegated ever since embarking upon its 'spheres of life' investigations. The Inland-SD in fact became a mere façade, maintained in being solely to ensure that no one else in the Party should have the bright idea of setting up an Intelligence organization. Even the SD-Hauptamt officially remained in being as a Party organization[210] although it had, in fact, long since been disbanded. Ohlendorf gave the reason: 'As the Reichsführer-SS did not intend to develop the "spheres of life" Intelligence service, since he had had so much difficulty with it ... the solution of an external façade was sufficient.'[211]

The SD would have sunk into complete insignificance had not Ohlendorf and his people gone on striving to expand their sphere of activity, frequently in opposition to Himmler's declared policies. This naturally led to fresh conflicts with the Party and eventually, in 1944, Himmler threw the SD to the Party wolves. Henceforth it had only two real functions – to carry on espionage abroad, and to form the parent organization for the leaders of the Einsatzgruppen [Action Groups] and Sonderkommandos [Special Detachments] which carried political terror and genocide into Adolf Hitler's new Europe during the Second World War.

The man who had laid the foundations of this fearful machine of tyranny, however, was not involved in the issue of orders for organized terror. Werner Best had realized that, peculiar though his concept of the legal profession was, there was no place for it in the SS world. He seized the first opportunity to resign from the Sicherheitspolizei. In May 1940 he asked Heydrich to release him to go to the front – in the Wehrmacht.[212] Heydrich was only too relieved to be rid of his millstone. He told Best: 'Whenever I had a good idea, I risked finding you standing in my way and proving to me, with your legalistic arguments, that it could not be done or should be done some other way.'[213]

The two parted amicably but, as time went on, Heydrich's aversion to the RSHA renegade grew. Aversion turned to hatred. Wherever Best appeared, Heydrich put obstacles in his path. In a letter to Heydrich, Best lamented: 'I once promised your wife, who has always been very sensitive to atmosphere, that I would be a true friend to you. But you do not want a friend. You want a subordinate.'[214] Heydrich never answered the letter.[215] He rejected all approaches by his former legal adviser, writing to Daluege, the Head of the Orpo: 'In my office, the lawyer . . . is not allowed so-called power of decision on all matters . . . but is merely an adviser and an assistant . . . this, as you know, was in essence the reason for my disagreement with Dr Best.'[216]

Best, the lawyer, had resigned from the Sicherheitspolizei. It was almost symbolic. Even under Best's control, the rights of the people had been curtailed, the liberal notion of individual liberty had disappeared, but some vestiges of normality and certain salient points of what is normally meant by the word 'law' had remained. Even these were now no longer valid; Heydrich's juggernaut had no braking system any more. The period of war and mass murder was at hand.

11

THE SS AND FOREIGN POLICY

ON Tuesday, August 22nd, 1939 the military élite of the Reich, the Commanders-in-Chief, Chiefs-of-Staff and Commanding Generals of the Wehrmacht, were summoned to the Berghof to hear from Hitler's own lips a momentous decision – the decision to go to war.

Hitler's opening words were: 'I have called you together in order to give you a picture of the political situation so that you may have some insight into the individual factors upon which my irrevocable decision to act is based.'[1] His monologue continued for hours; from it the military gathered that never had the situation been so favourable to Germany – England was 'most seriously threatened', the position of France had 'equally worsened', Soviet Russia was prepared to sign a non-aggression pact with Germany. Hitler concluded: 'No one knows how long I shall live. Therefore better to have the showdown now.'[2]

From minute to minute, Hitler's bellicose frenzy increased; his eyes bulged and he screamed: 'Close your hearts to pity! Act brutally! Eighty million people must obtain what is their right.'[3] Suddenly he recovered himself, and announced calmly that next day he would lay down the date for the attack on Poland.[4] War was to come by hook or by crook – 'I shall give a propagandist reason for starting the war – never mind whether it is plausible or not. The victor will not be asked afterwards whether he told the truth. In starting and waging a war, it is not right that matters but victory.'[5]

As the military dispersed, none of them knew that the men who were to create Hitler's 'propagandist reason for starting the war' were already standing by. Hitler had selected Heinrich Himmler for this task: the operation links him for all time with the blood and tears of the Second World War.

The only man in the Berghof with any inkling of Hitler's plans was Halder, the Chief-of-Staff of the Army. On August 17th, 1939 he had noted somewhat cryptically in his diary: 'Canaris . . . Abteilung I. Himmler–Heydrich, Obersalzberg. 150 Polish uniforms with accoutrements . . . Upper Silesia.'[6] This recorded that via Admiral Canaris, the Head of the Abwehr, Halder had heard of a conference held by Hitler in the Obersalzberg; the Dictator had discussed with Himmler and Heydrich an incident planned to take place in Upper Silesia, the props for which were 150 Polish uniforms. Such was the overture to a drama which eventually cost the lives of 55,000,000 men.[7]

The idea came from Heydrich. During the Sudeten crisis of 1938 he had proposed that the Reich should create a pretext for the move into Czechoslovakia by faked frontier incidents.[8] Only the Western Powers' capitulation in face of Hitler's threats and the subsequent Munich Conference had prevented the plan from being carried out. The forthcoming showdown with Poland now tempted Heydrich to produce his plan afresh. By early August he had worked out how the world could be made to believe that Germany had been provoked into war by Poland.

Heydrich's plan was that during the night preceding the German attack, SD detachments dressed as Polish soldiers and guerillas should engineer incidents along the German-Polish frontier. The pseudo-Poles were to occupy the German radio station at Gleiwitz for a few moments and shout, in Polish, one or two anti-German slogans into the microphone;[9] they were also to attack the Forestry Station at Pitschen, north of Kreuzburg[10] and destroy the German Customs building at Hochlinden between Gleiwitz and Ratibor.[11]

The most horrifying feature of Heydrich's plan was the fact that, to lend realism to the SD's war game, actual blood was to be shed. The journalists of the world's Press had to be convinced, and so bodies must be found on the battlefield. Heydrich commented: 'Actual proof of Polish attack is essential both for the foreign Press and for German propaganda.'[12] But where to get the bodies? Heydrich, the cynic, knew the answer to that too. The 'fallen' were to come from the concentration camps; for the greater glory of the Third Reich, certain concentration-camp prisoners were to be given lethal injections on D-day and then made ready to play their part on the Upper Silesian stage. In the repulsive Gestapo jargon, they were referred to as 'canned goods'.[13]

Early in August Himmler and Heydrich submitted their plan to the Führer and he leapt at it. The SD Hauptamt teleprinters were soon tapping out orders to SS-Standarten 23 and 45 stationed in the Gleiwitz-Beuthen-Oppeln area, instructing them to dispatch to 102 Wilhelmstrasse, Berlin, men with knowledge of the Polish language for employment on a secret mission.[14] At about the same time SS-Oberführer Dr Herbert Mehlhorn was ordered to report to the Chief of the Sicherheitspolizei and SD. Heydrich initiated him into the secret and commissioned him to prepare the incident in the Hochlinden area.[15] The next visitor to come heel-clicking into Heydrich's office was SS-Sturmbannführer Alfred Naujocks, Heydrich's old crony from the early SD days; he was placed in charge of the attack on the Gleiwitz transmitter.

Heydrich explained that 'merely for the sake of appearance, we must place the blame for forthcoming events on other shoulders'; Naujocks took the point at once. Heydrich ordered him to take six men, go to the Gleiwitz area, reconnoitre the ground, and wait for the code word 'Grandmama dead'.[16] He warned: 'First: you are not to get in touch with any German authority in Gleiwitz about this business. Second: none of your men will carry any form of identity papers which might indicate membership of the SS, the SD or the Police, or the possession of German nationality.'[17]

This took place on August 10th. Naujocks selected five men from his office, obtained a Polish-speaker for the proposed anti-German announcements, and set off for Gleiwitz with his men.[18] They took rooms in two hotels,[19] and Naujocks set about reconnoitring the position of the transmitter. It was situated outside the town on the minor road to Tarnowitz and proved to be surrounded by six-foot-high wire netting; the general area of the station and the two attached blocks of living quarters were practically unguarded.[20]

Meanwhile Heydrich had collected the other key figures in the business and discussed final details with them. The various roles were distributed: Polish uniforms to be obtained by SS-Brigadeführer Heinz Jost, Head of the Ausland-SD; the attack on the Pitschen Forestry Station to be led by SS-Oberführer Dr Otto Rasch; SS-Oberführer Dr Mehlhorn to clear the Wehrmacht from the Hochlinden area and coordinate the attack/defence game; the attackers consisted of a detachment dressed in Polish uniform which was to move against Hochlinden from the south (ie, from the direction of Poland) under SS-Obersturmbannführer Ottfried Hellwig; SS-Standartenführer Dr Hans Trummler commanded the Frontier Police and the Hochlinden 'defenders'; finally SS-Oberführer Heinrich Müller, the Head of the Gestapo, was to convey the 'canned goods' from the concentration camps to the various battlefields.[21]

By mid-August preparations were so far advanced that Himmler and Heydrich could report to Hitler once more. An order from the Führer gave the SD the run of the Wehrmacht's secret clothing stores. On August 17th, 1939 the diary of Amtsgruppe Abwehr in OKW noted: 'The Führer has given Admiral Canaris, the Head of the Amtsgruppe, the following instructions: Hold ready 250 Polish uniforms for an operation under the Reichsführer-SS Himmler.' Captain Dingler, Counter-Espionage Officer of VIII Corps Headquarters in Breslau, was instructed to hand the uniforms over to representatives of the SD; Canaris' office provided Polish weapons and paybooks.[22] Jost, who was in charge of this side of the business, assembled all the material in the SD School at Bernau, where the men detailed by the Upper Silesian Standarten began practising night attacks and Polish words of command.[23]

The majority of the men training at Bernau were given Polish uniforms with a rifle and thirty rounds per man; the SS men detailed for the attacks on the Forestry Station and Customs House, however, were dressed as guerillas. Hauptscharführer Josef Grzimek, one of the Bernau men, later said 'for these men clothing consisted of green shirts, long trousers and civilian jackets of varying colours. On their heads they wore civilian caps and hats'.[24]

By August 20th all was ready. Mehlhorn collected all his men in the lecture hall of the SD School and issued detailed orders for the top-secret 'Frontier Mission'.[25] Then they moved off in closed trucks to their assembly areas. Grzimek reported: 'Before moving off, we were strictly forbidden to look out of the vehicles, to speak to anyone, or to engage in any form of conversation.'[26] Two days later, reports reaching Heydrich showed that action might be required at any moment. On August 23rd Hitler decided that the Polish campaign would start at 4.30 AM on August 26th.[27]

Heydrich would have been somewhat less sure of himself had he known that exactly at this moment the régime's opponents in the Abwehr were engaged in compiling a record of Hitler's August 22nd speech to the generals; in addition to certain verbatim quotations it contained the apocryphal, though basically correct, statement that the Dictator intended to use one or two companies of troops to make simulated attacks on the German frontier in Upper Silesia. These so-called minutes reached Hermann Maas, the opposition Youth Leader, and he, via Louis Lochner, head of the Associated Press office in Berlin, passed them to the British Embassy. As early as the afternoon of August 25th, 1939, therefore, the British Government was aware that Hitler was preparing to start war against Poland by means of simulated frontier incidents.[28]

Danger threatened Heydrich's operation from another quarter, however, and of this Hitler was totally oblivious when, at about 3.0 PM on August 25th, he issued the final order to start war against Poland next morning.[29] Heydrich seized the telephone and gave his final instructions; Naujocks was told not to leave his hotel and to be ready for the executive order at any moment; Mehlhorn was instructed to dispatch Hellwig's detachment to the frontier; Müller set in motion his lorries carrying the dead prisoners.[30]

Then something happened on which Heydrich had not reckoned at all – Hitler called off the war. In late afternoon two messages reached the Reich Chancellery which gave the Dictator pause; the Italian Ambassador transmitted the news that the Duce felt unable to participate in this war-like adventure; London reported that England had just concluded a mutual assistance agreement with Poland. Hitler summoned Colonel-General Keitel and ordered him: 'Stop everything at once; get Brauchitsch [C-in-C Army] immediately; I need time for negotiations.'[31]

Keitel rushed off to the telephone – it was now 6.30 PM – and informed the Commander-in-Chief of the Army: 'Operation White, which has already started, will be halted at 8.30 PM owing to changed political circumstances.' The war machine had already begun to roll and was only brought to a standstill with the greatest difficulty.[32] Heydrich followed suit. Orders sped to Upper Silesia ordering the frontier action to be halted forthwith but Mehlhorn could no longer contact Hellwig's men for they had long since crossed into Poland. Hellwig's detachment duly attacked the Hochlinden Customs post and opened fire, which was promptly answered from the German side; fighting was only brought to an end by Müller's intervention.[33]

Mehlhorn and Hellwig could never subsequently agree who was responsible for this bloody incident. Hellwig had clearly taken Mehlhorn's warning as the definitive order to act; the ever-suspicious Heydrich, however, regarded the incident as more than a mere misunderstanding. In fact it was surprising that Heydrich had allotted Mehlhorn such a key role in the operation. Mehlhorn was an attorney from Chemnitz, one of the oldest and cleverest members of the SD staff, but regarded in the SD-Hauptamt as a 'scruples merchant' – one of the old-style intellectuals opposed to the complete lack of principle or scruple shown by Heydrich and his people. He had been head of the 'Staff Duties' division in the SD-Hauptamt but, as an opponent of Heydrich, had been relieved in 1937 and sent off to the Reich Ministry of the Interior, whence he had been dispatched on a study trip to America and Japan. Nevertheless in Heydrich's schizophrenic mind Mehlhorn was worth including in the SD's war game as a guarantee that the action would be carried out cautiously and circumspectly. When, however, Heydrich heard that Mehlhorn had referred to the entire operation as an 'historical crime' and when the August 25th misfire threatened to affect his prestige, he jettisoned Mehlhorn. He was relieved by Müller, dismissed from the SD and never allowed to enter the SD Hauptamt again; in fact Heydrich feared him more than any other of his subordinates, and he was never further promoted. Hellwig too was dismissed, and Standartenführer Trummler, hitherto in charge of the 'defence', took over his part in the scenario.[34]

Everything went better second time round. On August 31st Hitler issued his new and final date for the attack: September 1st at 4.45 AM.[35] Heydrich immediately alerted his secret army on the German-Polish frontier once again; about 4 PM the telephone rang in Naujocks' hotel room in Gleiwitz and a high-pitched metallic voice said: 'Call back.' That was all. Naujocks called Heydrich's office in the Prinz-Albrecht-Strasse Berlin and the same high-pitched voice told him: 'Grandmama dead'.[36] Naujocks collected his men and arranged that they should leave for the radio station at 7.45 PM.[37] At a villa in Oppeln Müller started up his trucks. He had to hurry to get the corpses to the scene of action in time. He had one 'piece of canned goods' ready for

Naujocks and it must be lying at the gate of the Gleiwitz transmitter by 8.20.[38]

Meanwhile Naujocks and his team were roaring down the Tarnowitz road towards the transmitting station. Shortly before 8 PM one of the engineers, named Foitzik, saw five men enter the station engine room and go up the stairs to the broadcasting room. Foitzik was about to ask what they wanted when he found himself staring into the muzzle of a revolver. Naujocks greeted the remainder of the station personnel with 'Hands up!'[39] He then gave a signal and his men began to make a noise. Telling the story later, Naujocks said: 'We fired our pistols in the broadcasting room. We loosed off a couple of warning shots into the ceiling in order to make a bit of a shindy and frighten people.'[40]

The station staff were handcuffed and carted off to the cellar. Naujocks continued: 'We then had a feverish search before we could get our broadcast through.' For a moment the intruders were at a loss, for they did not know how to interrupt the broadcast already in progress in order to put their political diatribe on the air. Finally they discovered the so-called storm microphone, normally used by the announcers to inform listeners of interference with the programme in the event of a storm. Naujocks pulled out his Polish manuscripts and a few minutes later thousands of German listeners heard a confused babble of voices, obviously speaking Polish, interspersed with one or two shots. The broadcast lasted four minutes and then Naujocks withdrew with his men.[41] When he reached the road he found the body of one of the concentration-camp prisoners laid out in front of the gate. Two of the Naujocks team had collected the corpse from Müller. Naujocks gave him a passing glance and then signalled for home.[42]

Similar scenes were enacted at the other places. As Josef Grzimek came stumbling out of the Hochlinden Customs House, which his detachment had meanwhile devastated, he fell over something in the dark. He records: 'I bent down and saw several men lying motionless on the ground; they were wearing Polish uniforms and . . . their heads were shaved. I knelt down because I thought they might be some of our people. When I tried to pick one of them up, I found that he was completely rigid.'[43] But Himmler did not worry his head over one or two dead concentration-camp prisoners. He had provided his Führer with what the latter required to initiate the Second World War – Polish provocation. Though Adolf Hitler's soldiers and tanks had long since moved into Poland, the Press of the Third Reich hastened to register well-orchestrated indignation, to report to the world the monstrous happenings on the frontiers of greater Germany. 'Polish insurgents cross the German frontier' was the *Völkischer Beobachter* headline on

September 1st, 1939; the paper continued that the Gleiwitz crime was 'clearly the signal for a general attack on German territory by Polish guerrillas'.[44] Another paper had apparently discovered that 'detachments of the Sicherheitspolizei on frontier duty had opposed the intruders. Fierce fighting is continuing'.[45]

The leaders of the Third Reich took up the story with enthusiasm. In his September 1st speech to the Reichstag announcing the outbreak of the Second World War, Hitler declared that there had been fourteen frontier incidents the previous night – three of them serious;[46] von Ribbentrop told the French Ambassador that the Polish Army had entered Reich territory at three points.[47] Even Göring, who had had his doubts about Hitler's war policy, 'after some hesitation' told Birger Dahlerus, the Swedish mediator, that: 'War had broken out because the Poles had attacked the Gleiwitz Radio Station.'[48]

To support the lamentations of the Press and the potentates, Gestapo Müller had to return to the scene of action, though in a different role. He and his Kripo colleague, Arthur Nebe, appeared with a murder squad to establish the facts of the Polish onslaught in proper Criminal-Police form.[49] To impress neutral visitors, Nebe even had an elaborate scale model of the frontier incident constructed; it could be seen by all visitors to the RKPA; on pressing a button, concealed bulbs lit up and camouflaged model machine guns chattered. When such shows were given, Heydrich would stand by murmuring: 'Yes, yes. That's how the war started.'[50]

The SD's war game on the German-Polish frontier showed that the SS was well on the way to establishing for itself a key position in the Third Reich's expansionist policy. The fact that the road to foreign-policy adventure should be opened by shots from SS men was little less than a portent. Those shots were the signal for Hitler's Germany to set forth towards the new horizons opened up by a policy of limitless conquest. But Gleiwitz was only a stage in Himmler's great plan; he was determined that, one day, he would dictate the course of German foreign policy. A man like Himmler, obsessed with the world mission of the Germanic master race, could have no object other than to open the door to world-wide expansion for his master men – and this implied that, one day, the SS must be the deciding factor in German power-policy and German foreign policy.

Nevertheless Himmler had to proceed with caution. He was not yet strong enough to impose his will on the other rival power groups struggling in the jungle of the Third Reich's hierarchy. His power was, of course, enormous. Next to the Wehrmacht he controlled the most powerful machine in the State – the Police; he commanded 258,456 SS men,[51] including four regiments of armed Verfügungstruppe;[52] he was in charge of the only political Secret Service in the Reich. On that level, however, on which the Dictator allowed his senior henchmen a free hand, his power was not enough to enable Himmler to dictate the political line. The power of the SS was overriding only when it was acting on express instructions from the Führer; when acting in its own interests it paled into impotence.

The struggle for control of foreign policy showed how small was the prospect of the SS carrying the day in the jungle warfare of National-Socialist authorities and cliques. Even in the early days of the régime, the ambitious SS foreign-policy experts had become bogged in the morass of intrigue peculiar to National-Socialism; worse still in 1933–4 they had plunged the régime into its worst foreign-policy crisis so far, hinging on the murder of Dollfuss.

At the time the Austrian Anschluss had been first on the list of new German foreign-policy demands. There were no fewer than five contestants for control of German policy in Austria; the Foreign Ministry under the professional diplomat, Freiherr von Neurath; the External Policy Office of the NSDAP under Alfred Rosenberg; the so called 'Ribbentrop bureau', a Party-run organization under Hitler's adviser, Joachim von Ribbentrop, whom the Foreign Ministry regarded as an outsider; the Foreign Organization of the NSDAP under Gauleiter Wilhelm Bohle; and finally the headquarters of the Austrian Nazi Party, in exile in Munich under Theo Habicht whom Hitler had nominated Inspector for Austria. In the autumn of 1933, however, the SS accidentally became involved in the Austrian problem and so plunged, as the sixth contestant, into this tangle of warring groups.

In summer 1933 Dollfuss, the authoritarian right-wing Catholic Chancellor of Austria, had banned the Austrian Nazi Party.[53] Dollfuss' police were tough and so thousands of Austrian Nazis fled to Bavaria – straight into the arms of Himmler, who was looking for new recruits for his army. The SS formed the fugitives into an 'Austrian Legion' under SS-Brigadeführer Alfred Rodenbücher; it trained at the military camp of Kloster Lechfeld and was armed by SS headquarters.[54] More important from the SS point of view, however, was the fact that the more active Nazis remaining in Austria turned to the SS. Is the Austrian Party, the political and SA leaders had been at loggerheads and so an increasing number of Austrian Nazis opted for the Reichsführer-SS. One of them was Fridolin Glass, an ex-Sergeant-Major in the Austrian Army, who had formed a Nazi group of soldiers and been dismissed from the Army when the Party was banned in the summer of 1933.[55]

The men of Glass' Nazi cell were dismissed at the same time and so he formed them into a 'Military Standarte' of six companies. Initially he placed the unit under SA-Obergruppe XI, but he soon found that neither the rules nor the mentality of the SA were to his liking, so he went to Berlin and offered his unit to the SS.[56] By spring 1934 he had won over Gruppenführer Wittje of the SS-Hauptamt to his plan to incorporate his 'Military Standarte' into the SS. Himmler agreed and Glass' unit became Standarte 89 of the Allgemeine SS.[57] Glass' action was to have devastating consequences for the Austrian Nazis. An SS investigation commission later stated that 'Glass' behaviour was regarded as treachery by SA Headquarters, Austria'.[58]

Glass, who had meanwhile been promoted SS-Sturmbannführer, had a plan to rid the Austrian Nazis of the Dollfuss régime by force, though whether he divulged this at the time to SS headquarters in Berlin is not clear. He proposed to bring the Vienna Government down by a putsch. The plan was nothing new. In summer 1933 a group of National-Socialist police officials in Vienna had plotted to eliminate the Austrian Government by force but the plan had come to nothing owing to Hitler's opposition; in October 1933 Austrian Nazi headquarters in Munich had informed the conspirators that the foreign-policy situation was not yet ripe for a putsch.[59]

Glass, however, had no intention of accepting a permanent veto from Hitler, and he worked out a new putsch plan. With 150 men of his Standarte he proposed to arrest the Vienna Government during a ministerial council in the Federal Chancellery, occupy the radio station and proclaim a new Government, whereupon the SA throughout the country would rise.[60] Habicht, the senior Austrian Nazi and Hitler's main contact for all Austrian questions, heard of Glass' project and summoned him to Munich early in June 1934. Glass was confident that part of the Vienna police force and also some Army units would support a National-Socialist putsch. Habicht gave the conspirators the green light.[61]

This brought Glass into contact with Habicht's closest collaborators – ex-Captain Dr Rudolf Weydenhammer, Director of the Austrian Nazi Office, and the Vienna SS-Sturmbannführer, Dr Otto Gustav Wächter, Habicht's Deputy in Austria. Habicht's entourage took up the putsch idea with enthusiasm;[62] they allotted responsibilities: Wächter was to be the political leader of the putsch and Glass the military; Weydenhammer was to maintain contact with the outside world.[63] On June 25th, 1934 they all met Habicht in Zürich and fixed the preliminary details. Glass was charged with preparing the action 'under all circumstances' and, even more important, with ensuring that the Vienna police and military would collaborate. Weydenhammer was to obtain the weapons and groom Dr Anton Rintelen, Dollfuss' Christian Socialist opponent and Austrian Ambassador to Rome, for the role of opposition Chancellor.[64]

Preparations gathered momentum, and developments seemed promising. Rintelen declared himself ready[65] and Lieutenant-Colonel Sinzinger, the Vienna Garrison Commander, joined the plot. He undertook to make uniforms available for Glass' men who were to enter the Federal Chancellery and arrest the Ministers.[66] When the conspirators met for a further council of war on the evening of July 16th in Habicht's apartment at 60 Kunigundenstrasse, Munich, they fixed the date of the putsch.[67] The last ministers' meeting before the summer holidays was scheduled for the afternoon of July 24th in the Federal Chancellery and this was the moment when the conspirators would strike.

Although failure would obviously have a disastrous effect on German foreign policy, they clearly cared little about what Chancellor Hitler might say of their venture. Wächter later put it on record that never for one moment had the idea entered his head that he might not be acting in accordance with Adolf Hitler's ideas. In fact Habicht had divulged the plan to his Führer and obtained Hitler's agreement[68] – but in such vague terms that Hitler was able subsequently to deny all responsibility and in 1938 even to arraign Wächter before the Supreme Party Court for having 'deliberately acted against the declared will of the Führer'.[69]

The Dictator was once more playing that double game which allowed his right hand to be ignorant of what his left hand was doing. While conniving at Habicht's intrigues against Dollfuss, he was urging von Neurath's Foreign Ministry to warn the Austrian Nazis to refrain from any ill-considered action against the Dollfuss régime. While the conspirators were meeting in the Kunigundenstrasse, Dr Reith, the German Minister in Vienna, was drafting a telegram to the Foreign Minister, informing him that Austrian National-Socialists were planning a putsch against Dollfuss.[70]

An Austrian Nazi named Hans Kohler, a post-office official in Heinfeld, had handed a memorandum to the legation with the request that it be forwarded to Hitler; it amounted to a demand for the arrest of the entire Austrian Government. The legation telegraphed: 'Herr Kohler was told by the Legation that the ideas contained in the memorandum were prejudicial to the policy of the Reich and he was requested, moreover, to prevail on his collaborators to desist from the plan. The memorandum was retained to prevent it from falling into the wrong hands. Since it cannot be ascertained here whether Herr Kohler is pursuing his plan further, in spite of the fact that he was warned against it, I suggest that appropriate steps be taken to stop this action.'[71]

The Foreign Ministry bureaucrats were just as disturbed as the minister in Vienna. The Foreign Ministry wrote forthwith to Habicht, requesting him to 'prevent any such plans that might possibly exist'.[72] It is not known whether, for the delectation of his fellow conspirators, Habicht read them the Foreign Ministry's letter. Nevertheless at the conspirators' table sat a man who was determined to cause the *coup d'état* against Dollfuss to fail; Wächter later called the result 'the most shattering experience of my life'.[73]

SA-Obergruppenführer Hermann Reschny, head of Austria's proscribed SA, could not reconcile himself to the fact that in their plans for a coup, Glass and Wächter, both SS commanders, had allotted the SA no more than a subordinate role; the SA was only to emerge when the decision had already been reached in Vienna. Reschny sensed in this a deliberate insult to the SA. It seemed to him no accident that SS men should once more relegate SA interests to second place. Back in Germany the SS had destroyed the SA's unique position; they had murdered the SA old guard. Now the SS seemed to be demanding the predominant position in Austria too. They had already filched from the Austrian SA its most powerful unit, Glass' Standarte.

Moreover Reschny could not forget that on that bloody Saturday of June 30th, 1934, a mere month before the Austrian putsch, when Röhm and his retinue had been liquidated, only chance had saved the head of the Austrian SA from the SS thugs. Could it be that he was now destined to avenge his murdered SA comrades – now that the SS was apparently girding its loins for a further expansion of its power?

By his tactics Habicht unconsciously made things easier for Reschny. He had laid down that on the day of the revolt, though they would strike in unison, the SA and SS would march separately. Wächter stated: 'Comrade Habicht told me that I was not to get in touch with the SA. The SA was separately commanded and, on receipt of the code word, would be used as a body under Obergruppenführer Reschny.'[74]

Reschny concluded from this that, should the SS putsch fail in Vienna, there would be no repercussions on the SA since the two groups were to act completely separately. Without appearing in the open himself, he cautiously fed information about the putsch plans to the Austrian security services.[75]

Reschny used two 'trusties' who had already, on several occasions, contacted the Dollfuss Government on his behalf – SA-Sturmbannführer Friedrich Hamburger, Liaison Officer to the SA-Obergruppe in Vienna, and his friend, Captain Schaller. When Schaller was tried in 1935, Wächter, basing his comments on the material brought in evidence, stated: 'In 1933 and 1934 the Austrian governmental offices were kept fully informed of everything which the Party wished to keep secret from them.'[76] After Habicht's conspiratorial council of war, Reschny summoned his two 'trusties' to Munich for an SA-Obergruppe Commanders' Conference and discussed the putsch once more in complete detail.[77]

Schaller took the point; he noted down all the details and passed them to the Federal Chancellery via a Vienna security official named Cyhlar.[78] But Reschny, apparently, wished to make doubly sure. Schaller later stated on oath that Hamburger had given him further detailed instructions to pass to the Austrian police – names and personal details of the putsch leaders, Glass, Wächter and Weydenhammer.[79] So the Austrian Secret Police knew all about the putsch. In 1935 Cyhlar stated: 'As regards Wächter, during the final months Schaller kept me continuously informed about the July putsch.'[80]

The Government was nevertheless taken by surprise: the historian Hellmuth Auerbach ascribes this to the extraordinary contortions of the Viennese spy world. 'The agent business' in Austria at the time, he says, was 'so highly developed that it cancelled itself out.'[81] Wächter was placed under observation by the Austrian State Police; wherever he went he was shadowed by two secret policemen. One thing, however, Weiser, the Vienna Police Chief, did not know – Wächter's shadows were National-Socialists and every evening he and they would get together to draft the observation report for the police.[82]

So Wächter and Glass still seemed to have a chance of bringing off their putsch. July 24th, the day of the final ministerial council in the Ballhausplatz, approached. Rintelen was holding himself in readiness in the Imperial Hotel, Vienna; the 150 SS men of 89 Standarte prepared for action; the senior conspirators hurried off to the agreed assembly points.[83] Then, on the afternoon of July 24th, Weydenhammer heard from Rintelen that the Ministers' meeting had been postponed and fixed for 11 AM the next day.[84] Rintelen wished to quit but the Nazi leaders insisted that now, at last, they must strike.[85] A fresh order was issued to the SS men detailed for the attack on the Chancellery: '89 – 12.45 PM, Gymnasium, 11 Siebensterngasse – do not approach the Siebensterngasse via the Breitegasse.'[86]

Punctually on the next day, July 25th, 1934, thirty SS men arrived at the German Gymnastic Association's great gymnasium to fit themselves out as soldiers. A lorry rumbled up bringing uniforms of the Deutschmeister Regiment obtained by the conspirators from Army stocks. Glass hurried his men along, for the changing process seemed to be taking too long[87] – the lorry full of pseudo-soldiers was due to leave for the Federal Chancellery at 12.30. Eventually it left, fifteen minutes late. Every man knew the cover story which was to gain them the entrée to Dollfuss – President Miklas had ordered them to the Chancellery for a special mission.[88]

While Glass and his men were on the way to the Ballhausplatz, Wächter, the political leader, took up position in the Tischler restaurant in the Schauflergasse near the Chancellery, ready to intervene if necessary.[89] He was only to appear later: his job was to conduct negotiations with the arrested Ministers and install the new Government. Neither Glass nor Wächter, however, knew that the putsch was, in fact, a failure before it had ever begun. It had been betrayed – and not by the SA. One of the Wächter-Glass conspirators, Johann Dobler, a District Police Inspector and ex-Economic Director in the Brown House, had lost his nerve and given away the whole thing.[90]

Before the Ministers' meeting ever began, Emil Fey, the Heimwehr [the Austrian right-wing defence formation] Minister was informed that a group of Nazi extremists was planning an attack on the Federal Chancellery.[91] Unfortunately he was an ambitious man and so, instead of alerting Dollfuss and the Army, he called his own private army, the Heimwehr, out on to the streets and sent them off on a cops-and-robbers-style hunt to track down the conspiracy.[92] When at last he bethought him of his duty, valuable minutes had been lost. He hurried into the Ministers' meeting only shortly before midday, took the Chancellor into a corner and whispered the news into his ear. Dollfuss was incredulous but determined.[93] He said to the ministers: 'Fey has just told me something but I don't yet know whether there is anything behind it. But it's perhaps better that we should interrupt the session and that every Minister goes back to his own office. I will let you all know when we can continue.'[94] The ministers left, thoroughly baffled. The only people to remain in the Chancellery were Dollfuss, Fey and Karwinsky, the Permanent Secretary in charge of security.[95]

Karwinsky ordered police reinforcements to the Ballhausplatz. Unsuspectingly he looked down into the courtyard as a lorry turned in at the gate. That will be the police, he thought: in fact it was the conspirators.[96] A few minutes later a captain rushed in and told Dollfuss that armed men had broken into the Federal Chancellery. Dollfuss hurried out of his study into the hall next door to look out of the window into the courtyard. A Criminal Police officer reported that the intruders were soldiers, to which Dollfuss replied: 'Oh? Soldiers?'[97] Hedvicek, the doorkeeper, then came pounding into the room and seized the Chancellor's arm, shouting: 'Chancellor, quick!' He knew a secret spiral staircase leading out of the building; it could be reached from a corner room near the Chancellor's study.[98]

Hedvicek and his charge had hardly reached the corner room, however, when eleven SS men led by Otto Planetta burst in from the stairway and came across to the Chancellor.[99] The intruders stood still for a moment and then all shouted hysterically: 'Hands up!' The Chancellor looked them straight in the eye saying: 'What do you want from me?' He made a gesture of impatience. Planetta drew back and pulled the trigger of his automatic. Dollfuss collapsed and fell back, blood streaming from his chest.[100]

The conspirators laid the wounded man on a sofa. After a moment Dollfuss opened his eyes and asked in puzzlement: 'Little ones, what on earth's happening? A major, a captain and several soldiers suddenly come in and shoot me.'[101] Gradually Dollfuss realized that he had not long to live; he collected the men around him and there began what Gordon Shepherd called 'a curiously placid political discussion' between Dollfuss and the rebels.[102]

Dollfuss opened with: 'I always tried to do the best I could and I always wanted peace.' An SS man retorted that the Chancellor had it in his power to bring about peace with Germany. The dying man answered: 'Children, you simply don't understand.'[103] Glumly the SS men looked down at their victim; no one said a word. At 3.45 PM Austria's Chancellor breathed his last; his final words were: 'Little ones, people have been so good to me. Why aren't the others like that? All I have wanted is peace. We have never attacked but we had to defend ourselves. The good God will forgive you.'[104]

Nevertheless the putschists did not give up. The coup against the ministerial council had failed and the arrest of all the Ministers, the essential feature of the whole action, had misfired. Only the occupation of the radio station had been successful.[105] Wächter raced off through Vienna to get help. This, he thought, was the moment when the SA must strike; now Obergruppenführer Reschny must call his cohorts out on to the streets and send them into action against the Government. Finally Wächter reached the Saint James Hotel where the leaders of the Austrian SA were assembled, and presented himself to SA Brigadeführer Turk.[106] Wächter describes the sequel: 'After I had given a short account of the situation and asked the SA to move, Turk issued in my presence an order alerting the SA Groups in Vienna and Lower Austria. In answer to my question, he declared that the SA would be on the march to the centre of the city within an hour.'[107]

But Turk was of the same mind as his master, Reschny. When Wächter rushed off to another appointment, Turk cancelled the orders and instructed the Vienna SA, which had already been alerted, to return to its billets. Not an SA man moved to assist the hard-pressed SS putschists. Shortly thereafter Turk let it be known that: 'The putsch of July 25th is an operation peculiar to SS-Standarte 89, for which the SA disowns all responsibility.'[108] The SA looked on unmoved while Austria's police and army put an end to the Vienna putschists. Planetta and six of his fellow conspirators were executed; the remainder were sentenced to long periods of imprisonment.[109]

Hitler, however, now found himself unexpectedly faced with a wave of international protest. For the first time since the formation of the Third Reich, Adolf Hitler was now regarded by the world at large as an out-and-out murderer, against whom it was the duty of any responsible statesman to mobilize all the forces of the civilized world. 'We are faced with a second Sarajevo' Hitler screamed, when urging his ex-Vice Chancellor von Papen to go as Ambassador to Vienna and use his reputation as the principal Catholic member of the régime to patch matters up.[110] Hitler made a clean sweep; Habicht was relieved of his post; the 'Austrian Legion' was disbanded and an official Party inquiry into the conspiracy was held.[111] The hardest hit by the débâcle, however, was the Reichsführer-SS, who had to swallow a severe loss of prestige. It was useless for Wächter to rage that the SA 'used traitorous methods to further their policy, which was aimed at SA predominance in Austria' and that 'anything was possible with leaders who, for their own selfish motives, could hand over their comrades to the enemy.'[112] The damage to the reputation of the SS was not to be made good so easily. Hitler's confidence was shaken and the SS had to work its passage back.

The SS had learnt one lesson – in the struggle between the National-Socialist potentates power groups were to be found prepared to achieve their ends by the use of naked force and without regard to the supposedly unifying influence of common belief in National-Socialism. The battle of cliques and power groups within the Party and, since 1933, within the State-Party machine, had become so habitual a pastime with its brown-shirted masters that even an appeal to their common interest in averting the régime's threatened self-frustration would not stop it. People were prepared to give way to a political opponent rather than renounce any shred of authority or power in favour of some rival within the Party. In 1932, for instance, Röhm had allied himself with the Social-Democratic Reichsbanner rather than compromise with his internal Party enemies; in Austria Reschny preferred to see a National-Socialist putsch fail rather than concede victory to the SS; back in Germany Lutze, the Chief-of-Staff of the SA, rather than bury the hatchet after the Röhm upheaval, dreamed of combined SA-Wehrmacht action against his *bête noire*, the SS.

In this tussle of unyielding interests, locked in a sort of trench warfare, the SS was only one force among many and could make no worthwhile breakthrough on its own. In the field of German power policy and foreign policy it could inch its way forwards only when under the protection of the sole source of power recognized on all sides – the authority of Adolf Hitler and the Party leadership installed by him. The latter was now embodied in Rudolf Hess, the 'Führer's Deputy', and it was he who eventually allowed the SS to take a hand in a secondary theatre of German foreign policy, where full rein could be given to Himmler's racial and biological hallucinations – the field of German 'Volkstum' [racial or demographic] policy.

From the earliest days the Party leaders had realized that the islands of German nationals on and beyond the frontiers could form bastions of a future German great-power policy; their manpower resources were considerable and they had increased in number as a result of the frontier rectifications decreed at Versailles. There were many links, some visible and some invisible, between the NSDAP and the 'racial Germans', primarily those in eastern and south-eastern Europe.

In 1931 Party headquarters had set up a 'Foreign Section' to deal with all persons of German nationality resident abroad. The Section [Abteilung] later became known as the 'Auslands Organization' [Foreign Organization – AO] under Gauleiter Wilhelm Bohle; in 1937 it had over 51,000 members.[113] The Organization soon became such a factor in foreign policy that von Neurath took the precaution of appointing Bohle State Secretary in the Foreign Ministry, hoping thereby to keep a tighter rein on him.[114] Bohle's organization, however, was only one among many power groups intruding into the sphere of traditional German diplomacy. Rosenberg's 'External Policy Office' dealt with German students from abroad[115] and the Verein für das Deutschtum im Ausland [Association for Germanism Abroad – VDA], officially a private organization but long since Nazified, maintained contact with 'racial Germans' throughout the world.[116]

The intrigues between these various organizations eventually became so intolerable that in 1936 Hitler charged Hess with control of all matters concerning Germans abroad. Hess, in turn, nominated Otto von Kursell, an 'old fighter', to head a 'Volksdeutsche Mittelstelle' [Reference Office for Racial Germans – VOMI]; it was responsible to the Party leadership and was intended to act as a sort of undercover headquarters coordinating the work of all governmental and Party offices concerned with questions affecting Germans resident abroad.[117] Kursell, however, lacked the authority to bring to heel all the various organizations which were locked in the battle for spheres of influence. Hess suddenly had an idea for saving the situation. The only Party formation which could help was the one whose leaders were supposed to possess discipline and organizing ability – the SS. Hess asked the Reichsführer-SS to select a man capable of bringing some order into the confusion and Himmler at last spied a chance to lay hands on some aspect of German foreign policy. He detailed SS-Obergruppenführer Werner Lorenz to take charge of the 'Germans Abroad' front.

Lorenz was one of the most personable and adroit SS leaders. Born in 1891, he had been a Cadet Officer and Air Corps pilot in the Imperial Army; he owned an estate in Danzig and had finally ended as Commander of SS-Oberabschnitt 'North-West' in Hamburg; his daughter had married the Hamburg publisher, Axel Springer. He was regarded as the SS *bon viveur*, with the manners of the old Prussian officers' mess and the air of a master of backstairs intrigue.[118] Subsequently Himmler probably regretted his choice, for Lorenz was a power-seeker and soon succumbed to the temptation to profit from the triangular battle between Party, Foreign Ministry and SS to create his own private army – and it was by no means always used to further the ambitions of the Reichsführer. In any case, from the SS point of view, a great gulf was fixed between the two men; Lorenz was a traditional nationalist and invariably treated his master's racial fantasies with condescending pity.[119] Himmler was well aware of this, but not until the outbreak of war was he able to force Lorenz out of his dominant position in German racial policy and incorporate VOMI, which had become far too independent, into his empire as a new SS Hauptamt.

Nevertheless VOMI enabled the SS to take a major step forward in the field of German racial policy and consequently also in that of foreign policy. Originally intended as a Party coordinating office, it developed into an SS centre of power, absorbing an increasing number of fields of activity and organizations concerned with racial policy.

Lorenz began in January 1937 with a small organization of only thirty men[120] but he contrived to gain control of one institution after another. In July 1938 Dr Steinacher, who headed the VDA and had become over-powerful, was dismissed and VDA business was taken over by one of Lorenz's close associates;[121] shortly thereafter VOMI took under its wing the influential 'Bund Deutscher Osten' [League of Germans in the East – BDO];[122] as the BDO was responsible for the frontier areas, VOMI was assured of a preponderant position in the leadership and financing of the German minorities in Eastern Europe.[123] The SD made good use of VOMI's manifold connexions with the German racial groups beyond the Reich frontiers and set up a network of listening and observation posts, using VOMI representatives as cover. VOMI and the SD worked closely together. The appointment of Dr Hermann Behrends, a senior SD official and close associate of Heydrich's, to be Lorenz's Deputy in VOMI was no accident.[124]

The network of SS and SD contacts began to impinge more and more perceptibly upon the official work of the Foreign Ministry. SS men began to appear in the higher ranks of the numerous cultural organizations and societies dealing with the countries of south-eastern Europe. For instance, SS-Oberführer Ewald von Massow became President of the 'German Bulgarian Society' and Lorenz took over the Chairmanship of 'Inter-State Contacts'.[125]

Himmler and Lorenz kept in specially close touch with the man to whom VOMI was theoretically subordinate. This was SS-Gruppenführer Joachim von Ribbentrop, the 'Deputy for External Political Questions on the Staff of the Führer's Deputy', to give him his official title;[126] the SS had high hopes that through Ribbentrop they might make a major breakthrough into the control of foreign policy. Relationships between Ribbentrop and the SS were so close that many people regarded the future Foreign Minister as the 'SS spokesman' on foreign policy.[127] Correspondence between Himmler and Ribbentrop was full of glowing phrases: 'You know my attitude to your SS and how I admire the way you have built it up entirely by your own efforts. I shall always regard it as a special honour to be a member of this proud corps of leaders which is of such decisive importance for the future of our great German Reich' (Ribbentrop to Himmler in July 1940).[128]

The two men had known each other since the end of 1932; at that time von Ribbentrop, demobilized as a Lieutenant in 1919, an ex-champagne merchant and married to the heiress to the Henkel champagne fortune, had made available his villa in Berlin-Dahlem for secret negotiations between Hitler and von Papen.[129] Himmler's job at the time had been to assist Hitler to evade the reporters by climbing over the back garden wall of Ribbentrop's property and then to demonstrate by his polished behaviour at table that even Nazis were fit to be included in the Government.[130]

Himmler's demonstration at least convinced his host von Ribbentrop, for shortly thereafter the latter joined the Nazi Party and asked Himmler for the favour of permission to belong to the SS. On May 30th, 1933 he was given the rank of Standartenführer and Himmler was henceforth a welcome guest in the Ribbentrop villa.[131] Ribbentrop sat at Hitler's feet and successfully worked himself into favour with the dictator, becoming his special adviser on foreign affairs; the further he advanced, the more closely did Himmler cling to the coat-tails of this dilettante upon whom fortune was clearly smiling. On Hitler's instructions Ribbentrop later set up a bureau in the Wilhelmstrasse opposite the Foreign Ministry; it created its own reporting system to cross-check the work of the Foreign Ministry, which Hitler found suspect. Himmler provided both money and personnel to assist his friend.

In 1937 SS-Oberführer Rolf von Humann-Hainhofen joined the 'Ribbentrop Office' as Director;[132] he was the forerunner of that type of SS diplomat who was to be found in increasing numbers in Ribbentrop's entourage. SS-Oberführer Rudolf Likus, Ribbentrop's old schoolfriend,[133] and SS-Standartenführer Werner Picot, who dabbled in Secret-Service affairs,[134] were among the most trusted Ribbentrop men. Ribbentrop and the SS worked so closely together that when the former was nominated Foreign Minister in February 1938, Himmler was justified in considering the appointment a major prestige victory for the SS.

As Foreign Minister Ribbentrop continued to cling to the SS; all his 'adjutants' were SS commanders[135] and he sent his son, Rudolf, into the Leibstandarte Adolf Hitler.[136] One day he had a splendid idea, which horrified the Foreign Ministry diplomats; he informed all the senior bureaucrats that he had agreed with Himmler on their acceptance as a body into the SS.[137] Everyone now had to put on SS uniform. Freiherr von Weizsäcker, the Permanent Secretary, turned into an SS-Oberführer,[138] Ernst Woermann, the Under Secretary, into an SS-Standartenführer,[139] von Dörnberg, the Chief of Protocol, into an SS-Obersturmführer.[140] According to Erich Kordt, an opponent of Hitler masquerading as an SS-Obersturmbannführer, nothing gave Ribbentrop greater pleasure than 'to appear in the office in the uniform of an SS-Gruppenführer with his great jackboots. He presumably thought that this gave him the greatest resemblance to his predecessor, Bismarck, whom he always pictured as a man who usually went about in a cuirassier's tall, uncomfortable jackboots.'[141]

The Führer's Bismarck could not have enough SS-uniformed men around him; at times he even reproached his 'Dear Himmler' for failing to make sufficient numbers of SS men available for the Foreign Ministry, writing: 'since taking over the Foreign Ministry, I have not received a single first-class staff officer from the SS; in view of the good relations between my office and the SS, together with our close personal friendship, it would be more than regrettable if the SS were conspicuous by its absence.'[142]

Ironically, however, the struggle for power within the bureaucracy brought the two partners into collision and turned them into bitter enemies. The man who had introduced the SS uniform into the Foreign Ministry would later fly into a paroxysm of rage if he ever saw any of his diplomats wearing it.[143] The fact that he wore an SS-Gruppenführer's uniform did not prevent von Ribbentrop, as Foreign Minister, from becoming involved in those intrigues which were the daily bread of the Nazi potentates. For he had become head of an authority which could not but resist SS penetration into its preserves, if it did not wish to lose to the SS the technical control of German foreign policy.

The occasion of the quarrel was a decision by Hitler pregnant with consequences for the history of the world. After the occupation of Austria the Dictator decided to expand the German sphere of influence and, regardless of the risk of war, to play up the problems of the German minority groups in Czechoslovakia and Poland, both fraught with potentialities of crisis. This, however, brought the racial problem into the forefront of German foreign policy and, in that field, the SS had already achieved a position through VOMI. The Foreign Ministry diplomats found themselves being pushed to one side by the SS racial experts.

In the Sudeten crisis engineered by Hitler in the summer of 1938 the Foreign Ministry in fact played only a secondary role. Ernst Eisenlohr, the German Minister in Prague, being opposed to Hitler's annexation policy, was deliberately left in ignorance,[144] while Lorenz, the head of VOMI, on Hitler's instructions discussed the detailed moves against the Czechoslovak Government with the Sudeten German leader, Konrad Henlein.[145] However, independently of, and sometimes in opposition to, VOMI, another SS authority now took a hand in the game – Heydrich's Ausland-SD; it was destined to become a nightmare to the Foreign Ministry for it was pursuing an entirely different aim – to bring down Henlein. The SD had managed to convince itself that Henlein was a compromiser and a weakling who did not promote the Führer's interests with sufficient energy. Certain of the Sudeten Party leaders, such as Walter Brand, Wilhelm Sebekowski and Heinrich Rutha, were regarded with suspicion by the SD as being supporters of the Catholic Authoritarian State theory; they had no wish to join Hitler's Germany; they simply hoped that the great powers would assist them to obtain improved minority status *within* Czechoslovakia.[146] In 1934 even Henlein himself had said: 'We do not hesitate to state that a fundamental difference exists between us and National-Socialism. We will never renounce the freedom of the individual.'[147] Incorporation of the Sudetenland into the Reich was supported only by a small group of National-Socialist extremists – and on them Heydrich set his sights.[148]

In late 1937 Heydrich decided to bring Henlein down by means of a Party revolt. Henlein was too quick for him, however; Heydrich's main allies consisted of a circle of politicians centred around the newspaper

Der Aufbruch and these Henlein expelled from the Party.[149] Early in the summer of 1938 Heydrich spied another chance. He had meanwhile established contact with Carl Hermann Frank, Henlein's principal Party opponent and leader of the Sudeten Nazi Party, which had been banned and absorbed into Henlein's Organization. Frank was not averse to capturing leadership of the Party, even with the assistance of the SD.[150]

Henlein must have sensed the danger, for he escaped from the SD's clutches by precipitating matters. He had, in any case, come to the conclusion that the intransigence of the Prague Government, together with the disappearance of Austria, left him no other choice than to collaborate with Germany; accordingly at the end of July 1938, he went to the German Gymnastic Festival in Breslau and there reached agreement with Hitler, who was also present.[151] The Dictator forbade the SD to intrigue further against Henlein. Henlein was therefore saved, though the price demanded was high. The SS, on the other hand, was left to draw the necessary conclusions from the changed situation – Henlein, the ex-critic of the Nazis, was given the rank of SS-Gruppenführer.[152]

The Foreign Ministry diplomats, however, had now been shown how far the SS had already penetrated into their foreign-policy preserve. Von Ribbentrop did manage to prevent Lorenz of VOMI being nominated Secretary for German minority questions,[153] but this only increased the SD's greed for diplomatic privileges. The next foreign policy crisis saw the Foreign Ministry completely outpointed by the SD. The Dictator left it to his own trusted secret service men to lay on the scenario – the destruction of the 'remainder of Czechoslovakia' in March 1939.

Hitler had worked out a sophisticated plan. The leaders of the ultra-conservative and clericalist Slovak People's Party were to be urged to declare their country's secession from the centralized Czechoslovak State; simultaneously the Czechs were to be encouraged to suppress the Slovak revolt. In the resulting upheaval Hitler would emerge as arbiter and take both countries under his control. The 'remainder of Czechoslovakia' was to form the Reich Protectorate of Bohemia and Moravia, Slovakia remaining as a theoretically independent State under the 'protection' of the Greater German Reich.

Early in 1939 SS-Gruppenführer Wilhelm Keppler, together with SS-Standartenführer Edmund Veesenmayer and a troop of SD agents, travelled to Bratislava and established contact with the Slovak politicians.[154] These secret emissaries had strict instructions from Hitler that under no circumstances were they to allow the Foreign Ministry to know the purpose of their journey.[155] Keppler and his gang arrived just in time; the Prague Government, weary of continuous friction with the semi-autonomous provincial Government of Slovakia, had just invited the Slovaks to a conference of reconciliation in the capital. The men from Berlin, however, persuaded Josef Tiso, the Slovak Minister-President, to reject the invitation from Prague and make immediate preparations for Slovak independence.[156]

At this point, one of the most prominent of the Slovak politicians threw a spanner in the works. Dr Karel Sidor, the Slovak Minister of State in the Prague Government and Commander-in-Chief of the Hlinka Guard (a sort of Slovak SA) rejected the Germans' separatist plan. This gave the remaining Slovak politicians pause. The Germans negotiated with Sidor but he refused to budge.[157] The SD therefore turned to its normal solution in such situations – criminal methods.

Alfred Naujocks, the SD troubleshooter, was ordered to Slovakia with a sabotage squad. He was to engineer incidents apparently the work of the Slovak Nationalists.[158] All was going well – the first bombs had gone off in a Bratislava chocolate factory, Prague had swallowed the German bait, deposed the Tiso Government and declared a state of emergency in Slovakia – when suddenly an amateur diplomat took a hand unscheduled in the programme.[159]

Josef Bürckel, the Gauleiter of Vienna and another SS Gruppenführer, called on Sidor, whom Prague had meanwhile nominated Minister-President of Slovakia in place of the separatist Tiso, and tried to get him to change his mind. But 'these remarkable efforts on the part of the Gauleiter' (Keppler's caustic description) failed.[160]

Back in Berlin Hitler was becoming nervous. Time was pressing. Suspecting that the Germans were playing a double game, Hacha, the Czechoslovak President, had announced his arrival for a visit to Hitler on March 14th[161] and this meant that the dictator was forced to obtain the Slovak declaration of independence not later than the evening of the 13th; without it Hitler would not obtain the capitulation which he intended to force on the Czechs. On March 11th Keppler went to Tiso once more, imploring him to agree to a split with Prague. During the night of March 12th–13th Tiso gave way.[162] Hardly had he given his agreement than an invitation to Berlin reached him from Hitler. A few hours later he was in Hitler's presence, just in time to lay Slovakia at the feet of the overlord of Central Europe before Hacha arrived.[163]

For the first time the SD had shown its mettle as the executor of Hitler's will in a matter of foreign policy. From Vienna Bürckel protested that the SD had shown themselves downright bunglers in Slovakia; if only he, Bürckel, had been given more time to negotiate with Sidor, everything would have passed off far more smoothly; but the

Führer ignored him. Even this, however, led to an internal SS quarrel; after the victory in Slovakia harsh words passed between SS commanders unable to agree upon whose the victory was. SS-Gruppenführer Bürckel deluged Hitler, Göring and Ribbentrop with memoranda about the inefficiency of SS-Gruppenführer Keppler. SS-Gruppenführer Keppler retorted that SS-Gruppenführer Bürckel had nearly caused irreparable damage to the Reich. In a letter to Himmler Keppler complained: 'I trust that you will not misunderstand me if, in pursuing this matter further, I take as little account of Bürckel's SS membership as he has done of mine; it seems to me likely that I shall have to defend myself against gross slanders.'[164]

Hitler now placed unlimited confidence in his SD. It was not therefore surprising that he allotted it the 'honour' of lighting the spark which set off the Second World War. The actions on the German–Polish frontier described earlier in this chapter were only part of the SD's war provocation; simultaneously no fewer than twelve SD commandos moved into Poland with orders to initiate 200 individual actions by the end of August, all to be ascribed to Polish extremists.[165]

The SD became increasingly prominent in affairs of foreign policy. In Hitler's field headquarters SD reports were frequently used in place of the regular Foreign Ministry diplomatic dispatches. Ribbentrop later lamented that 'Hitler, without informing me, would take immediate decisions based on false information' (from the SD).[166] There was hardly an area of foreign policy where Ribbentrop was in sole charge. In January 1939, without any consultation with the Foreign Ministry, Himmler had assisted General Oshima, the Japanese Ambassador in Berlin, to dispatch to the Soviet Union ten Russian émigrés armed with bombs to murder Stalin.[167] Similarly, during the war, the SD pursued a policy all their own; on their own initiative, for instance, and in face of the Foreign Ministry's opposition, SD representatives tried to lure Castillo, the President of Argentina, into an alliance with the Third Reich directed against the USA;[168] in Spain they attempted to bring down Franco and replace him by a Falangist leader more sympathetic to National-Socialism;[169] in Rumania, they attempted to manoeuvre the Fascist organization, the Iron Guard, into power.[170]

An even more serious threat to any further independent existence for German diplomacy was the fact that in the first hectic days of the war, Ribbentrop gave his agreement to a new proposal from the RSHA, something which the Foreign Ministry was to rue for many a long day – the inclusion of so-called Police Attachés in diplomatic missions. On October 26th, 1939 Ribbentrop agreed that the SD might make use of German Embassies and Legations as cover for their work in foreign countries; in any particular country the head of the SD Intelligence network was to be given diplomatic status and entitled Police attaché. As a *quid pro quo* the SD promised not to interfere in matters of foreign policy.[171] The Police attachés, however, soon began to criticize their Ambassador's or Minister's policy and spy upon the Mission's personnel. The Foreign Ministry could do nothing, for Ribbentrop was still set upon the closest possible collaboration with the SS and had given Himmler and Heydrich the right to install SD agents 'direct' – in other words without prior reference to the Foreign Ministry; their reports, moreover, went direct to the RSHA. These SD reports frequently contained violent criticism of German diplomats. In his memoirs Ribbentrop said: 'On one occasion, for instance, secret SD reports direct to the Führer led to the sudden order that I should recall three Heads of Mission – those in Spain, Portugal and Sweden.'[172]

Nevertheless Joachim von Ribbentrop was not a man to lie down under such an invasion of his preserves. He barricaded himself behind his prerogatives and initiated a dogged war of outposts against his erstwhile comrade Himmler. The Foreign Minister soon became a doughty exponent of internecine National-Socialist strategy.

As the opening shot in his counter-offensive Ribbentrop astutely made use of an order from the Führer. On September 3rd, 1939 Hitler had laid down that 'For the duration of the War all representatives of civil authorities or Party offices located abroad . . . will be subordinated to the German Head of Mission in the country concerned. These representatives or delegates will report to the Foreign Ministry through the Head of Mission.'[173] Ribbentrop proposed to use this Hitler ukase to bring the SD agents abroad under the control of the Foreign Ministry. Nevertheless he had to proceed with caution; so long as the SD was working on Hitler's instructions and adhering strictly to Hitler's orders, the Foreign Ministry had no hope of regaining even a minimum of authority over its work abroad. Ribbentrop had to wait until the SD made a gaffe which shook its prestige even in the Führer's headquarters. He waited.

Shortly after the Police attaché agreement of October 25th, 1939, an incident had occurred which showed how unwise it still was to voice criticism of the SD's behaviour in Hitler's presence. Ribbentrop had heard that the SD was planning one of the greatest kidnappings in Secret-Service history to take place on the German/Dutch frontier – and he was worried.

In mid-October 1939 Walter Schellenberg of the SD received instructions from Heydrich to initiate a Secret Service operation against the much-admired British Intelligence Service in Holland, at the time still a neutral country. Heydrich hoped for great things from this particular gambit – insight into the methods of the British Intelligence Service, into the degree of cooperation between the British and Dutch Secret Services, and into the German internal opposition's contacts abroad.[174] A certain German émigré in Holland named Dr Franz worked for the SD under the code number F479 and he had good contacts with the British Secret Service, in particular with Captain S. Payne Best, the 'Intelligence Service' representative in Holland; Best was particularly interested in signs of opposition to Hitler among the German generals. F479 promised to obtain information.[175]

Via Franz, the Ausland-SD (alias Amt VI of the RSHA) provided Best with carefully prepared false information. Meanwhile the RSHA began to think that it might perhaps be worthwhile to hear a few more details from the Intelligence Service representative. For this task Heydrich selected his best man, his confidant Schellenberg. The latter quickly turned himself into Captain Schemmel of the OKW Transport Section, wearer of an eyeglass and bearer of important secrets regarding internal German opposition.[176] F479 arranged a meeting and on October 21st Schemmel, monocle in eye, was sitting opposite Best (who also affected a monocle) somewhere in the Netherlands.[177]

Best took Schellenberg/Schemmel in his Buick to Arnhem, where two more Intelligence Service men were waiting, the British Major Stevens and a Dutch staff officer who called himself Copper though his real name was Klop.[178] The three foreigners found the revelations of their new German friend extremely interesting. Schellenberg presented himself as the confidant of a general who, together with other military men, was planning a *coup d'état* against Hitler.[179]

They agreed to meet again on October 30th when Schellenberg once more travelled to Holland.[180] Copper/Klop had arranged to have Schellenberg temporarily arrested in error, in order surreptitiously to examine the German's papers; the British, however, were fully confident in the SS man[181] – they even gave him a radio set for urgent communications, with the call sign ON4.[182]

Meanwhile the two British officers had given the impression of being the repositories of such valuable secrets that Heydrich had the idea of kidnapping Best and Stevens and carrying them across the Dutch frontier into Germany.[183] This was the moment chosen by Ribbentrop to tell his Führer of his anxieties over SD methods. The moment was badly chosen in any case; Adolf Hitler was in no mood to listen to criticism of his SD. He reacted with such ill humour that Ribbentrop executed one of his well-known somersaults, stammering: 'Yes, my

Führer, that has always been my opinion, but these bureaucrats and lawyers in the Foreign Ministry are so tedious.'[184]

In fact Ribbentrop withdrew just in time, for irrationality now took control of Schellenberg's Secret-Service game. As a result of an assassination attempt by a lone-wolf cabinet-maker, Stevens and Best became labelled for ever more in Hitler's mind as the central figures of a traumatic experience.

On the evening of November 8th, 1939, Martin, the Police President of Nuremberg, stopped the 'Führer Special' as it was moving out of Munich station with Hitler and Himmler on board. Martin clambered on to the train and reported that a few minutes after the Führer's traditional Bürgerbräu speech in Munich a bomb had exploded in the 'Old Fighters' ' Assembly Hall; the ceiling of the hall had fallen in, ten or twelve Party members were feared dead, and the criminal was still unknown.[185] Immediately it flashed through Hitler's mind that this was the doing of the British Secret Service and that Stevens and Best were behind it. Himmler got the point. He hurried to the telephone and alerted the RSHA. Then he dialled a number in Düsseldorf. The telephone rang in Schellenberg's room and an excited Himmler was on the other end of the line: 'This evening, just after the Führer's speech in the beer cellar, an attempt was made to assassinate him . . . the Führer had left the cellar a few minutes before . . . there's no doubt that the British Secret Service is behind it all.'[186] Himmler then passed on Hitler's order to arrest Stevens and Best forthwith and bring them to Germany. Schellenberg did as he was told. He had been ready for the operation for days: Naujocks from the SD was standing by with an armed squad and Schellenberg had agreed to meet the two British officers on the afternoon of the next day in the Dutch frontier town of Venlo.[187]

At 3.00 PM the next day, November 9th, Schellenberg installed himself in a Venlo café close to the frontier. The minutes dragged by interminably. Schellenberg looked out of the window and kept a watch on the street – the *coup* must take place before the two British officers entered the café. Then Schellenberg saw Best's Buick drive up. With a great show of geniality he went out to welcome his visitors. Best and Stevens approached.[188]

At this moment an SS convertible roared up, crashed through the frontier barrier and stopped in front of the two British officers. Submachine-guns fired and the two Englishmen drew their revolvers. Naujocks and his men jumped out of the car and overpowered them; Klop, though severely wounded, was carted along too. Schellenberg meanwhile hurried off to his own car, parked behind the café, and in a few moments all was over. The *coup* had succeeded.[189]

The next day the German propaganda machine went into top gear. The Germans were told that the Reich Security Services had succeeded in arresting the manipulators behind the abominable attempt upon the Führer's life. SS-Oberführer Walter Schellenberg received from the Führer's own hand the Iron Cross First Class for his bravery in violating international law; the Dictator even invited him to dinner in the Reich Chancellery with the heads of SS.[190] The precocious Schellenberg, however, had a disappointment in store for his master during the meal. He voiced his opinion that the attempt upon the Führer's life had not been the work of the British Secret Service and certainly not of his two prisoners, Stevens and Best; in his view only one man had the crime upon his conscience – the man under arrest, Georg Elser.[191]

Himmler intervened immediately to say that this was only Schellenberg's personal opinion.[192] In fact it was the unanimous view of the RSHA. Schellenberg had taken the precaution of studying the RKPA files and they led only to one conclusion – Elser was a lone-wolf operator.[193] During the night of November 9th Nebe, the head of the Kripo, together with the members of the Special 'Assassination Commission' (Heydrich, Gestapo Müller, Lobbes, Nebe's deputy, and explosives experts) had flown from Döberitz airfield to double-check the clues in the Bürgerbräu, Munich.[194] But Nebe discovered little which the Kripo Leitstelle Munich had not already noted.

All the indications and scraps of evidence showed that the *coup* had been prepared over a long period. The criminal had used a time-bomb with an explosive charge of no more than twenty pounds, which had been concealed in one of the wood-panelled ferro-concrete pillars of the Bürgerbräu. Soon the man responsible was cowering in front of the Gestapo's interrogation arc-lights; he had been arrested on the evening of November 8th while attempting to cross the Swiss frontier illegally. He was Georg Elser, an apprentice cabinet-maker and watch-maker from Königsbronn, aged thirty-six, a worker both by inclination and principle, who wanted no more than peace and a quiet life and so did not like Hitler's war.[195]

He described his actions in detail: 'Using a padsaw, I cut the wooden panelling of the pillar, fixed a couple of hinges and then replaced the piece of wood in the form of a little door. Later I lined this door with 2-mm thick iron plate. The plate served two purposes. In the first place in the event of anyone tapping the pillars it would conceal the existence of a cavity behind; secondly, in the event of redecoration of the hall it would prevent some accidental nail damaging the clockwork.' Then he brought along his dynamite charge connected to a timing device: 'on the evening of November 5th between 9 and 10 PM I went to the Bürgerbräu with the timing mechanism in a box. I went up into the gallery . . . and hid myself behind a pillar. There I waited until the lights were put out and the hall was shut. As a precaution I waited a further half-hour. Then I went to the pillar with the timing mechanism, opened the little door, and checked that the clockwork parts would fit into the front part of the chamber. Finally I set the two watches.'[196] It was as simple as that. But the simple truth did not satisfy the Führer of the Great German Reich; he was convinced that this was a gigantic conspiracy by the British Secret Service, a widespread net of intrigue in which all his deadly enemies had had a hand – the Jews, the British, the Freemasons and, last but not least, Otto Strasser. Himmler was in a state of panic. Where were the master-minds? When Nebe could not find them, he was dismissed and recalled to Berlin.[197] Almost in tears, Himmler lamented: 'Schellenberg, what we have to do is to find the people behind this thing. The Führer simply will not believe that Elser did it alone.'[198] On the record of the first Elser interrogation which produced the lone-wolf theory, he wrote indignantly: 'What idiot conducted this interrogation?'[199]

With the rage of desperation characteristic of the panic-stricken subordinate, Himmler descended upon the unfortunate prisoner Elser who by this time was almost beside himself. Dr Bohme, the head of the Kripo Leitstelle Munich, witnessed the scene in the Wittelsbach Palace, the Gestapo Headquarters: 'With wild curses Himmler drove his boots hard into the body of the handcuffed Elser. He then had him removed by a Gestapo official whom I do not know and taken to the lavatory leading off the head of the Gestapo Leitstelle's office where he was beaten up with a whip or some similar instrument until he howled with pain. He was then brought back at the double to Himmler, who once more kicked him and cursed him.'[200]

But Georg Elser stuck to his story. Himmler ordered another top investigator to Munich, Franz Josef Huber, head of the Vienna Gestapo. He too failed to find the master-minds. Huber called Müller in Berlin and told him of the conclusions he had reached, but the head of the Gestapo was indignant: 'Good God, how can anyone think that!'[201] One after the other, however, they came to recognize that Elser was in fact a lone wolf. Even Heydrich was forced to accept the truth.[202] Himmler alone continued to chase the phantom master-minds; on December 4th SS-Gruppenführer Karl Wolff, head of Himmler's personal staff, wrote to SS-Oberführer Zimmann: 'We are not satisfied with the single man.'[203] But a single man it remained.

Finally, Himmler had to accept from Hitler's own lips the reproach which he most feared – that of having failed. Hitler never forgave the Reichsführer-SS for withholding from him the real criminal of November 8th, 1939; these were sufficient grounds for Himmler to preserve Elser as the most valuable witness to police efficiency – he was the only man who might be able to confirm that Himmler's minions had not in fact failed.

For Himmler's rival, Ribbentrop, however, the Elser affair provided a most encouraging pointer: the power of Himmler's machine was unassailable only so long as it was carrying out Hitler's orders and wishes to the letter; if it diverged, even by only a hair's-breadth, from the Dictator's line, the SS was fair game for any criticism. The Foreign Minister waited patiently for the moment when he could prove to his Führer that the SS was not a totally reliable instrument of the Führer's will. That moment came a year later. The SD proved itself so undisciplined that Hitler flew into a rage, screaming that he would 'smoke out the black plague' if it did not toe the line.[204]

The reason for the Dictator's wrath was an attempted rising by the SD-backed Iron Guard in Rumania, the object of which was to bring down Hitler's ally, the ultra-conservative Minister-President, General Antonescu. German policy in Rumania was a particularly ludicrous illustration of the tug-of-war between Foreign Ministry and SD. For years the SD had been supporting the Iron Guard, a nationalist revolutionary party with Fascist leanings, which Himmler's and Heydrich's emissaries regarded as first cousin to the Nazi Party.[205] In September 1940, however, General Antonescu, a Balkan leader equally averse to Fascism and democracy, stepped into power just ahead of the Iron Guard.

Antonescu had good reason to be grateful to the Germans; in July 1940 he had been arrested by King Carol and had only been released as a result of representations by German diplomats.[206] Since the Iron Guard, moreover, possessed no personalities of note, the Berlin Foreign Office put its money on Antonescu as the future Dictator of Rumania.[207] This called for no great decision from Hitler, since initially Antonescu made common cause with the Iron Guard and ruled Rumania with its assistance. But the alliance between the reactionary and the revolutionaries was short-lived and two months later Horia Sima, the head of the Iron Guard, was girding his loins for revolt against Antonescu, confident of the assistance from Germany promised him by his SD advisers.

On January 21st, 1941 the Iron Guard struck in Bucharest. Almost all the capital's important open spaces and buildings fell into their hands,

Antonescu retaining control only of the Minister-President's office.[208] His situation was desperate; this was the moment when only Hitler could help. On January 22nd, via the German Legation, Antonescu inquired whether he still enjoyed Hitler's confidence. The reply flashed back from Ribbentrop: Yes; Antonescu should act as he thought fit; the Führer advised him to treat the legionaries as he, Adolf Hitler, had once dealt with the conspirators in the Röhm putsch.[209]

Antonescu struck back and put down the revolt, pursuing his enemies ruthlessly. But suddenly the SD intervened, rescuing the leaders of the Iron Guard, including its Chief, Horia Sima and fourteen Commandants; Sima was hidden in the house of the German minority leader, Andreas Schmidt.[210] When the Rumanian police abandoned their hunt for the fugitives, the SD smuggled them out of the country disguised in German uniforms and travelling in ambulances.[211]

As soon as Ribbentrop heard of the SD's Rumanian extravaganza he worked Hitler into a rage. He painted a picture of a gigantic SS conspiracy against the official foreign policy of the Reich; the head of the SD in Rumania had encouraged Horia Sima to revolt; SS-Obergruppenführer Lorenz, the Head of VOMI, had installed Schmidt as minority leader and Schmidt had provided Sima with a hiding place. According to Ribbentrop, the entire SS headquarters was involved in the plot, for Schmidt's connexions reached back to Himmler's immediate entourage; Gruppenführer Gottlob Berger, Head of the SS Hauptamt, was Schmidt's father-in-law.[212]

Ribbentrop dispatched a new German representative to Bucharest with full plenary powers; he immediately dismissed the SD Commander attached to the Embassy and ordered him back to Germany. An arrest warrant awaited him and he spent months in the Gestapo prison.[213] Such inroads had been made into the SD's prestige that Ribbentrop finally plucked up his courage to bring the sinister Police attachés to heel. In April and June 1941 he wrote three letters to Heydrich, amounting to a demand for a new working arrangement between the Foreign Ministry and the RSHA in view of continued SD interference in the field of foreign policy.[214]

Ribbentrop now revoked the October 26th, 1939 agreement, basing his case on Hitler's instruction that all German representatives abroad must act under the authority of the head of mission concerned, and demanded that, like everybody else, the Police attaché conduct his official correspondence only through the head of mission.[215] Himmler gave way. On August 9th, 1941 he concluded a new agreement with Ribbentrop, providing that all correspondence between Police attachés and the RSHA should be seen by the head of mission; in addition, the SD was not to interfere in the internal affairs of the country concerned.[216]

Whether or not the SD took such agreements seriously, this development in the power struggle clearly constituted an invitation to Ribbentrop to be more insistent in his demands upon the SS. He missed no opportunity to remind the Reichsführer-SS of the Foreign Minister's prerogatives. On one occasion Himmler was invited to Italy by the Italian Foreign Minister; Ribbentrop pointed out to him that 'applications for authorization for foreign travel by leading personalities of the State and the Party should be transmitted in writing and in good time to the Foreign Ministry'. Only if Himmler would inform him of the exact purpose of his journey to Italy, could he, as Head of the Foreign Ministry, decide whether he could recommend this journey to the Führer. He continued: 'If you are basing yourself upon the assumption that your functions within Germany give rise to some form of special authority to take action abroad, I would point out that on my side I could under no circumstances recognize any claim to authority in relation to foreign countries such as might affect the external policy of the Reich.'[217]

In south-eastern Europe, where SS contacts were particularly numerous, Ribbentrop now put a stop to any further SS foreign-policy adventures by allying himself to a force which had already, on several occasions, stood in the way of Himmler's foreign-policy ambitions – the SA. In summer 1941 he filled all Embassy and Legation posts in the Balkans with SA leaders, deliberately selecting survivors of the Röhm putsch. SA-Obergruppenführer Siegfried Kasche from Lower Saxony became Minister in Zagreb, SA-Obergruppenführer Dietrich von Jagow from Berlin Minister in Budapest, SA-Obergruppenführer Manfred Freiherr von Killinger from Central Germany Minister in Bucharest, SA-Gruppenführer Hans Ludin from Swabia Minister in Bratislava and SA-Obergruppenführer Adolf-Heinz Beckerle from Hesse Minister in Sofia.[218] None of these men had forgotten that they were once near to death at the hands of the SS.

Ribbentrop, in fact, drew a line which Himmler was never allowed to pass. When SS-Gruppenführer Werner Best joined the Foreign Service, Ribbentrop told him that from now on he must be his, Ribbentrop's, man, not Himmler's.[219]

But his erstwhile friend's pinpricks could now no longer hurt the Reichsführer-SS. He had long since realized that the longer the war went on, the less foreign policy mattered. The field of independent foreign policy was growing ever smaller; the world of neutral and independent states was shrinking. Occupation policy was taking the place of foreign policy. In the West, and even more important in the vast open spaces of the East, a new field of activity was opening. There Himmler, with his prophet's eye, saw a promised land – the world of the German master race.

12

RACIAL POLICY IN THE EAST

HEINRICH HIMMLER took every known precaution to safeguard the secrecy of his precious document. No unauthorized person was to read it; only a select few of the Third Reich's most senior officials were allowed to know of its contents. The reason was not far to seek; on its six pages were set down Himmler's most private day-dreamings – fevered ravings, but they were to dictate the fate of millions of men.

On May 28th, 1940 Himmler noted: 'The Führer directed that only a limited number of copies should be made, that it was not to be reproduced and that it was to be treated as top secret.' Only a few Nazi potentates were initiated into the mystery – one or two Gauleiters, two Ministers of the Reich, the Governor-General of Poland, the HSSPF [Höhere SS- und Polizeiführer – Senior SS and Police commanders] and the Heads of the SS Hauptämter. To the latter the file was brought by hand of officer, who waited while it was read and demanded a written acknowledgement from the reader.[1]

The document was written by Himmler and submitted to Hitler in May 1940; it was entitled: 'Some thoughts on the treatment of foreign populations in the East.'[2] This was the secret which the Reichsführer-SS was so anxious to conceal even from the most orthodox National-Socialist eyes, for it amounted, to a proposal, in Himmler's dry bureaucratic language, for the destruction of the Eastern peoples in order to make room for the German master race.

As the ultimate goal of German policy in the East, the author proposed that what had once been Poland with its numerous races (Poles, Ukrainians, White Russians, Jews, Gorals, Lemkes and Kashubs) should be 'broken up into the largest possible number of parts and fragments'. The 'racially valuable elements should be extracted from this hotchpotch' and the residue left to wither slowly away. Himmler continued:

'If these measures are consistently carried out, over the course of the next ten years the population of the Government General will necessarily be reduced to a remnant of substandard beings. It will consist of a leaderless labour force, capable of furnishing Germany with casual labourers annually, together with the manpower required for special projects.'[3] The peoples of the East were gradually to be reduced in number and driven farther eastwards; the Jews were to be 'completely eliminated by means of a major deportation operation to Africa or some colony'; 'in our area' it should be possible 'to cause the Ukrainians, the Gorals and the Lemkes to disappear as racial entities. Making allowance for the larger area involved, the same should apply . . . in the case of the Poles'.[4]

But how to destroy a racial entity? Himmler's answer was: elimination of its upper classes and 'screening' of its youth; children were to be classified in two categories: 'racially valuable' to be carried off to the Reich and Germanized, 'the remainder' were to be deliberately left to vegetate. Himmler prescribed: 'No higher education than that provided by a four-class primary school will be allowed for the non-German population of the East. The aim of this primary school should be to teach the pupil solely: how to count up to a maximum of 500, how to write his name, that it is God's command that he should be obedient to Germans, honourable, industrious and brave. I regard reading as unnecessary.'[5]

No flatter statement of National-Socialist determination to dominate can be imagined; the old German 'Drang nach Osten' was being resumed in a far more virulent form. But Himmler's memorandum carried a further implication. It was proof of the SS claim to control of German policy in the East; it was a reflection of that imperious SS demand succinctly expressed by SS-Gruppenführer Otto Hofmann of the RuSHA: 'The East belongs to the SS.'[6]

As it so happened Hitler's initial victories had in fact placed the SS in a key position in the Eastern territories; the real master in that area appeared to be Himmler. For the first time he could visualize the possibility that his long-standing dream might really come true, that his SS, his neo-German order of knighthood, might carve out a new kingdom of Teutonic knights and found a strong Teutonic State; his SS would form the breakwater damming the rising Slav tide and standing guard over fertile settlement areas filled by a German peasant population.

Ever since he became capable of coherent thought, Heinrich Himmler had been preparing himself for exactly this mission. No one, he thought, could be more ideally suited to fulfil this sacred mission, to lead the Germans eastwards and turn them back into a nation of peasants. One day he returned overjoyed from a conference in the Führer's headquarters, saying to his masseur, Felix Kersten: 'You won't understand how happy I am . . . the Führer not only listened to me . . . he went so far as to approve my proposals . . . this is the happiest day of my life.' The proposal which Himmler had laid before his Führer was his project for the construction in the East of a network of SS settlements manned by armed peasants. He continued: 'The Germans were once a farming people and must essentially become one again. The East will help to strengthen this agricultural bent inherent in the German nation – it will become the everlasting fountain of youth replenishing the lifeblood of Germany whence it will, in its turn, be continuously renewed.'[7]

Himmler had always seen himself in this role of great Germanic peasant leader. In his bizarre dream-world the romantic historical picture of medieval eastern settlements combined with his biological horror of dark-haired bullet-heads to produce the crazy notion that Germany's salvation lay in a sort of feudal peasant aristocracy settled in the East. He never tired of propagating his theory of German settlement in the East. At heart he was still the Artaman who, with his friend Walther Darré, had once tried to stem the influx of low-paid Polish workers on to the East German estates; now he was continually drumming into his SS men the necessity for Germans to recapture their roots in the soil and win new settlement areas for themselves.

Himmler and Darré, the Head of the RuSHA, had been quick to lay hands on responsibility for German settlement policy. In 1934 SS-Gruppenführer Darré had been promoted Reich Minister of Agriculture;[8] SS-Standartenführer Dr Horst Rechenbach had become Head of the Reich 'Office for Settler Selection';[9] all the leading officials of the Reich Food Organization had been made honorary SS Commanders.[10] Nevertheless the hard facts of modern industrial society torpedoed the sociological Utopia envisaged by these two reactionary enthusiasts and in the process terminated the friendship between Darré and Himmler. Darré clung to his theory of a 'blood-and-soil' aristocracy and in February 1938 Himmler dismissed him as 'too theoretical'.[11] Himmler, the opportunist, waited until his Führer's policy presented him with new settlement areas in which to install the great German Reich's new peasantry.

In March 1939 when the first foreign people, the Czechs of the 'remainder of Czechoslovakia', were incorporated into the Greater German Reich, Himmler saw a chance to revive his old plans. In June he dispatched SS-Oberführer Curt von Gottberg to Prague to set up a Real Estate Office.[12] The idea was that in the rich agricultural areas of the 'Reich Protectorate of Bohemia and Moravia', von Gottberg should dispossess Czech landowners and settle Germans on the farms thus made vacant; even Hitler was already talking of deporting six million Czechs.[13] But von Gottberg's mission was a failure. The German armament industry was relying largely on Czech industrial and labour potential and it refused to hear of any major deportation measures in the Reich's back garden. The Prague Real Estate Office had to content itself with preparations for the settlement of one or two SS families in Bohemia and Moravia.[14]

Not until the outbreak of World War II could Himmler, the anti-Slav peasant mystic, see the promised land before him. Disappointingly, entry could, initially, only be gained by the back door. Although the Dictator had summoned his most faithful disciple before the start of the Polish campaign, what he wanted from him was not the missionary zeal of the settler, but the ruthless action of the policeman.

Adolf Hitler had decided upon a solution of the 'Polish question'. In his eyes the Polish war was far more than the violent settlement of the Danzig and Polish corridor problems; now was the moment to fulfil the prophecy made years before in *Mein Kampf* 'We begin where we left off 600 years ago. We put an end to the perpetual Germanic march towards the south and west of Europe and turn our eyes towards the lands of the East. We finally put a stop to the colonial and trade policy of pre-war times and pass over to the territorial policy of the future.'[15] In the path of this 'territorial policy', however, stood a foreign people already cultivating the soil. But on this subject too Hitler knew his own mind as early as 1928; the Reich, he wrote, must 'either sterilize these racially foreign elements to ensure that its own people's blood is not continually adulterated or . . . remove them altogether and make over to its own people the land thereby released'.[16]

Translated into 1939 terms this means that the Poles were to be reduced to the level of a nation of helots, deprived of their upper class, of their existence as a nation or a State, and of their culture. The proud Polish people were to become a nation of slave labour, condemned to serve one purpose only – to work for their German masters. From the August 22nd conference in the Obersalzberg, Germany's senior soldiers knew that Hitler was set upon the destruction of Poland. Field-Marshal von Bock recalls that Hitler said that 'things would be done of which the German generals would not approve. He did not therefore wish to burden the Army with the necessary liquidations but . . . would have them carried out by the SS.'[17]

This was the reason for Hitler's summons to Himmler and this is why, for all time, the SS must remain indissolubly linked with the Polish tragedy. Hitler gave Himmler the task of forming 'Einsatzgruppen' [task forces] to follow the German troops as they advanced into Poland and liquidate Poland's upper class wherever it was to be found.

Einsatzgruppen of the Sicherheitspolizei had so far been a regular feature of every stage of National-Socialist expansionist policy. During the move into Austria Heydrich's 'Sonderkommandos' [Special detachments] had gone in with the troops;[18] Einsatzgruppen had moved into Czechoslovakia when that country was broken up.[19] The Einsatzgruppen were mobile advanced detachments of the Sicherheitspolizei and SD, and their purpose was rapid intervention in Intelligence and security police matters. Once their immediate task was ended, they turned themselves into static outposts of the two organizations on the lines of those known in the Reich as Gestapo Leitstellen and SD Abschnitte;[20] they also provided the personnel for further Einsatzgruppen.

Heydrich formed his five Einsatzgruppen for the Polish campaign at high speed; their members wore the service uniform of the SS-Verfügungstruppe with the SD diamond on the left sleeve;[21] they were allotted one to each army and each was sub-divided into four 'Einsatzkommandos' [Action Commandos] of 100–150 men; these, in turn, were sub-allotted to Army corps.[22] All the senior posts were occupied by SD commanders – Bruno Streckenbach,[23] Dr Emanuel Schaefer,[24] Dr Herbert Fischer,[25] Lothar Beuthel,[26] and Ernst Damzog.[27]

However, if Heydrich and Himmler were to carry out Hitler's order for mass liquidation of the Polish élite and to do so undisturbed by the Wehrmacht, this RSHA on wheels had to be extremely careful not to divulge its hand to the military. The Wehrmacht had numerous opportunities of controlling the Einsatzgruppen; throughout the operations zone Heydrich's units were under Army command, although they did of course receive their technical instructions from the RSHA in Berlin; moreover they were subject to Wehrmacht jurisdiction.[28] In addition, the Army Commander-in-Chief had persuaded Hitler to agree that, on conclusion of operations the military should retain plenary powers in occupied Poland.[29] Provided Germany's generals showed sufficient political acumen, these powers could considerably restrict Himmler and Heydrich in their terror campaign.

The two SS men had to trim their sails carefully. They gave the military only the bare minimum of information; in an order of September 9th, 1939, for instance, 8th Army described the task of the Einsatzgruppen as: 'suppression of all anti-Reich and anti-German elements in rear of the fighting troops, in particular counter-espionage, arrest of politically unreliable persons, confiscation of weapons, safeguarding of important counter-espionage material, etc'.[30] The necessity to camouflage the real purpose of the Einsatzgruppen made Himmler and Heydrich uneasy; they were murdering Polish aristocrats, priests and intellectuals and, in the long run, this could hardly be kept secret from the soldiery. They found themselves caught on the horns of a dilemma; either they must betray Hitler's secret or resign themselves to being labelled by the military as an undisciplined gang of murderers.

Months later Himmler and Heydrich were still bemoaning the invidious position in which Hitler had placed them. Himmler adroitly attempted to place the blame on the Führer, protesting pathetically to the generals: 'I am doing nothing which the Führer does not know about.'[31] In an office minute Heydrich later admitted that there had been serious differences of opinion with the Army in occupied Poland, because the 'directives governing police activity were exceptionally far-reaching – for instance, the liquidation of numerous Polish leading circles running into thousands of persons was ordered; such an order could not be divulged to the general run of military headquarters, still less to members of the staffs; to the uninitiated, therefore, the action of the police and SS appeared arbitrary, brutal and unauthorized'.[32]

The military soon realized what had really brought the Einsatzgruppen to Poland. On September 8th Admiral Canaris of the Abwehr reported to General von Stülpnagel, Deputy Chief-of-Staff I in Army Headquarters, that SS commanders were boasting of shooting 200 Poles a day. Executions were in most cases carried out without trial and the victims were primarily Jews, aristocrats and priests.[33] Three days later Canaris was in the Führer Special near Illnau and reported to Keitel, the Chief of OKW. He warned: 'The world will one day hold the Wehrmacht responsible for these methods since these things are taking place under its nose.' Keitel was unimpressed. He took refuge behind Hitler's primitive logic: if the Wehrmacht did not want to do 'these things' it must not complain when the Sicherheitspolizei and SS undertook the work of liquidation.[34]

The Wehrmacht resigned itself to the unworthy role of spectator. Canaris and his staff continued to amass evidence of the horrors perpetrated by the Einsatzgruppen but they need not have troubled; before the eyes of the military, Poland was subjected to a wave of terror reminiscent of the fearful days following the Nazi seizure of power in Germany. Hitler had said: 'Whatever we can find in the shape of an upper class in Poland is to be liquidated; should anything take its place, it will be placed under guard and done away with at an appropriate time';[35] the men of the Einsatzkommandos went off on their manhunt to make his words come true.

Armed with previously prepared lists, Heydrich's thugs rounded up Polish teachers, doctors, officials, priests, landowners and businessmen. On arrest they were herded into reception camps which frequently proved to be places of execution. The Torun grease factory, Muhltal near Bydgoszcz, Soldau Camp, Stutthof and Fort VII in Poznan[36] – all became synonymous with terror and death for thousands of Poles. SS-Sturmbannführer Dr Roeder, Commander of the Bydgoszcz Einsatzkommando, declared: 'It is planned to liquidate the radical elements'[37] – the word 'radical' covered any Polish nationalist; mere membership of the Westmarkenverein (an association of Polish chauvinists which demanded annexation of additional German territory and had, in fact, been of great assistance to Hitler's Polish policy) was enough for the liquidators to pronounce sentence of death.[38]

Gradually the Polish élite was decimated. In the diocese of Chelm-Pelplin two-thirds of the 690 priests were arrested and 214 executed, including almost the entire cathedral chapter of Chelm-Pelplin.[39] Roeder reported to Berlin: 'A high proportion of the Catholic clergy has been eliminated in view of their well-known radical Polish attitude.'[40] Martin Broszat, the expert on German policy in Poland, gives 'some tens of thousands' as the figure of victims for the first month of German rule.[41] On September 27th, 1939 Heydrich stated: 'Of the Polish upper classes in the occupied territories only a maximum of three per cent is still present.'[42]

The Einsatzgruppe liquidation squads worked on a cold, rational plan, but alongside them now appeared another SS organization governed not by a secret order from the Führer, but solely by hatred and thirst for revenge. Fanatical members of the German minority streamed out in their thousands, primarily in Danzig and West Prussia, unable to forget that they had recently been fair game for the Polish chauvinists.

Incensed by Hitler's 'back-to-the-Reich' propaganda and prey to a panic-stricken spy mania, when war broke out the Polish authorities and organizations had fallen upon the German minority. The Germans of Poland were martyred; an avalanche of arrest warrants descended on their heads – red for imprisonment in the local jail, pink for incarceration in an internment camp and yellow for deportation to central and eastern Poland. Every nationalist organization had its black list and took independent action against the 'Germans', the 'Hitlerites' or the 'Swabians'.[43]

Fifty thousand members of the German minority were driven from their homes in western Poland and deported to the east; thousands disappeared behind prison bars;[44] roaming bands of Poles sacked German houses and farms, murdering the inmates; thousands of

Germans were killed and others died as they ran the gauntlet of screaming, spitting mobs in the villages. The German authorities subsequently stated that by February 1st, 1940 they had discovered the bodies of 13,000 murdered Germans.[45] The figure is probably exaggerated; nevertheless, a memorandum drafted in 1954 by the Polish 'West Institute' in Poznan, mentions a figure of 'several thousands'.[46] Broszat is probably nearest to the truth; he gives a figure of 4,000–5,000 Germans murdered, together with a further 2,000 deaths directly attributable to the war.[47]

The Polish murders, however, differed from the German crimes in one important aspect; they were not the product of a coordinated plan nor were they carried out at the behest of the State; many Poles, including a number of officers, protected Germans from the wrath of the mob. The German minority, however, prepared to take revenge upon their persecutors. No sooner had the war rolled by than the German-speaking minority in each locality formed itself into a self-defence organization. Initially defence alone was the subject, for the Germans in Poland genuinely feared that they might once more be attacked by the Polish majority and this volunteer militia was intended for their protection.[48]

Soon, however, nationalistic spite became the governing factor; Albert Forster, the Gauleiter of Danzig, moved into West Prussia with his own Home Guard and a newly formed organization known as 'SS-Sturmbann Eimann', raising the tempo of the anti-Polish racial battle.[49] West Prussia soon became the scene of a pitiless anti-Polish campaign in which deliberately inflamed passions were combined with cold calculation. The Danzig racial fanatics, brought up in the revolutionary tradition of the SA, worked off years of suppressed anti-Polish feeling; they were adroitly directed by the ambitious Forster, whose aim was to present himself to his Führer as the first Eastern Gauleiter with an area 'clear of Poles'.[50]

Himmler had long regarded Forster as one of the more serious competitors for Hitler's favours and so this evidence of the Gauleiter's ambitions put him on the alert. Under no circumstances could Forster be allowed to become master of the self-defence organizations and he therefore dispatched SS-Brigadeführer Gottlob Berger, the Head of his Recruiting Office, to organize the self-defence units into a 'racial German' SS.[51]

Berger took with him a number of racial German SS leaders and they assumed command of the German self-defence organization in occupied Poland. The militia was divided into four self-defence regions, subdivided again into so-called inspectorates responsible to the relevant HSSPF.[52] In general the self-defence organization was used as an auxiliary police force; the only areas where murderous man-hunts still continued were West Prussia and later Lublin.

The head of the self-defence organization in West Prussia was SS-Oberführer Ludolf von Alvensleben; he was a fanatical National-Socialist and in his area he instituted a régime of tyranny reminiscent of that to which the democrats and republicans had been subjected by the SA thugs of the Karl Ernst school with their 'wildcat' concentration camps.[53] Von Alvensleben was master of life and death in his region. Mere denunciation by a German or a tiny tick on a list were enough for his men to appear and cart some Pole off to a cellar, a garage or a copse and murder him.

Even many Nazis gradually found the persecution of the Poles too savage for their liking. In a letter of protest to Göring, Lily Jungblut, a Party member and wife of a German landowner in the Hohensalza district, complained that 'thousands upon thousands of innocent men were being shot'.[54] Even Heydrich grumbled about 'certain intolerable and uncontrolled acts of revenge' on the part of the self-defence organization – though he was worried about discipline rather than humanity.[55]

All that mattered to Himmler, however, was the 'success' of his operation, the figures of Poles liquidated or, in the current jargon, 'subjected to special treatment'. In mid-September he dispatched a new murder squad, the 'Special Duty' Einsatzgruppe under SS-Obergruppenführer Udo von Woyrsch, to liquidate Poles and Jews in the Katowice area.[56] He had been Himmler's partner in the Röhm man-hunt and was intended to initiate a new phase of SS policy in eastern Upper Silesia – deportation of the 50,000 Jews of Danzig, West Prussia, Poznan and Upper Silesia into the interior of Poland.[57]

Von Woyrsch's Einsatzgruppe was clearly designed as a form of shock unit to strike terror and panic into the Jews of Upper Silesia and force them to move in the general direction of Cracow. No sooner had the campaign opened than Heydrich paid a visit to Army headquarters to initiate Eduard Wagner, the Deputy Chief of Staff, into the secret of the new plan. In the eastern territories now once more under German rule, he said, it was proposed to concentrate *all* Jews in ghettos in Poland for shipment abroad in due course.[58] Wagner raised no objections. Twenty-four hours later, on September 21st, Heydrich instructed the Einsatzgruppen to start deportation of Jews into the heart of Poland.[59]

Heydrich's prior warning to the Army, however, proved to be an error, for the soldiers suddenly began to kick over the traces. A military occupation régime had meanwhile been set up in conquered Poland with

Commander-in-Chief East, Colonel-General Gerd von Rundstedt at its head. Poland was divided into four military districts, each under a General to whom some trusted National-Socialist functionary was attached as head of the civil administration;[60] the military were responsible for public security and order and they were determined to fulfil the Army's solemn proclamation to the Poles: 'The Wehrmacht does not regard the civil population as enemies. All provisions of international law will be respected.'[61] But the savage terror imposed by the SS units, primarily the brutal actions of von Woyrsch's Einsatzgruppe, were now making a mockery of the Army's assurances. Fortunately officers were still to be found ready to raise their voices against the SS murderers.

On September 20th, 14th Army Operations Section reported that the troops were becoming restive 'because of the largely illegal measures taken in the Army area by Einsatzgruppe Woyrsch (mass shooting, particularly of Jews). The troops are especially incensed that, instead of fighting at the front, young men should be demonstrating their courage against defenceless civilians.'[62] Von Rundstedt thereupon declared that Woyrsch's Einsatzgruppe would no longer be tolerated in the Operations Zone. Himmler gave way and von Woyrsch had to bow to the wishes of the military. In addition, the Army demanded that anti-Jewish measures already under way should cease. Once more Himmler complied.[63] On October 1st Army headquarters informed Corps HQs in Poland: 'Order No II (reference No 288/39G dated September 21st, 1939) issued to Einsatzgruppen by the Chief of the Sicherheitspolizei should initially give rise to preparatory measures only. A fresh instruction on these lines is being issued to Einsatzgruppen by the Reichsführer-SS.'[64]

Had the Wehrmacht been determined to maintain pressure upon Himmler, it might possibly have stopped arbitrary action in the East – but Hitler knew his generals. He quickly brought military government in the East to an end, confident that his senior soldiers would heave a sigh of relief.

On October 5th Gauleiter Forster presented himself to Hitler and complained of the continuous vexation caused him by the military in West Prussia. That very day Hitler issued an order removing West Prussia from military jurisdiction and placing it under Forster.[65] This snap decision started an avalanche which ultimately swept away all military government in the East. In mid-October, with a stroke of the pen, Hitler set up a complete new system of rule in German-occupied Poland, a new maze of competing authorities and a fruitful field for intrigue among those Nazi potentates who had a finger in the Eastern pie. Danzig and West Prussia were amalgamated and incorporated into the Reich as a new Gau under Gauleiter Forster. A new Reich Gau named Wartheland (Poznan) was formed under Arthur Greiser, Forster's rival in Danzig where he was Deputy Gauleiter and President of the Senate; certain small Polish areas bordering on East Prussia were placed under another of Forster's rivals, Erich Koch, the Gauleiter of Königsberg; Upper Silesia was incorporated into Silesia under Gauleiter Josef Wagner (in 1941, it became an independent district under Gauleiter Fritz Bracht); the remainder of Poland, now isolated both from the Germans in the West and from the Russians in the East, was placed in a straitjacket, known as the 'Government-General' under Dr Hans Frank, the Nazi legal adviser who was given unusually extensive plenary powers.[66]

The military might have been expected to rise in wrath against the rape of their powers in the East, to protest against Hitler's abandonment of his promise that overriding authority was the prerogative of the Wehrmacht. But not at all. The generals were only too glad for the Dictator to relieve them of responsibility for murder; in any case Hitler had adroitly taken the precaution of painting them a horrifying picture of Poland's future. On October 17th, with Keitel present, he had outlined his policy towards Poland. The horrified military scribbled down: 'increased severity of the racial struggle permits of no legal restriction; methods used will be incompatible with our principles . . . ensure that the Polish intelligentsia cannot throw up a new leader class . . . Jews, Poles and similar trash to be cleared from the old and new Reich territories.'[67]

The military turned their backs with a shudder. How right Hitler's calculation had been was shown by the attitude of von Rundstedt: when he learned that Frank, the ultra-Nazi, was to be Governor-General, he handed in his resignation.[68] The generals were in such a hurry to bring their military government to an end that the build-up of the new administration could hardly keep pace with the military withdrawal. In Broszat's words a 'legalized vacuum of anarchy' appeared: Himmler filled it with his SS and police units.[69]

Even before the new governmental dignitaries were at their desks, an SS shadow government had already spread its net over Poland. The Einsatzgruppen transformed themselves into static Gestapo Leitstellen and SD Abschnitte, responsible in each district of the Government-General to a 'Kommandeur der Sicherheitspolizei und des SD' [Local Security Police and SD Commander – KdS]; the KdS in the five districts of Poland were under a 'Befehlshaber der Sicherheitspolizei und des SD' [Security Police and SD Commander – BdS] who, in turn, was the direct subordinate of the RSHA.[70] Parallel to this organization another police chain of command ran through occupied Poland, that of the

Ordnungspolizei. On the outbreak of war the Orpo had been mobilized and a number of Police battalions had taken part both in the Polish campaign and in many Einsatzgruppe operations. The Orpo hierarchy paralleled that of the Sicherheitspolizei; in each district of the Government-General was a Kommandeur of the Ordnungspolizei, an Orpo Befehlshaber was responsible for the Government-General as a whole and he, in turn, was responsible to Hauptamt Orpo.[71]

Real power, however, lay in the hands of the HSSPF, since they covered both chains of command. In Germany the HSSPF had existed since 1937; they were generally the commanders of SS-Oberabschnitte whom Himmler had nominated to represent him in the Wehrkreise. In theory they were to coordinate the operations of all SS and Police units in the event of mobilization; in practice they were intended by Himmler to guarantee the SS/Police integration for which he was striving. In Germany itself, however Himmler's representatives led a wretched existence; the civil administration refused to countenance the intrusion of SS functionaries who had no official place in the police hierarchy and the Reichsführer was compelled to confine his HSSPF to purely formal representative duties.[72]

However, in Greater Germany's colony, Poland, leaderless and deprived of any traditional bureaucracy, Himmler was able to give his HSSPF more power. There they were to supervise all Police and SS formations, form a counterweight to the over-powerful position of Heydrich within the SS and set up a special political police administration destined in Himmler's eyes to be the real agent of the Führer's will.[73]

For Himmler success or failure in the East might well depend upon his HSSPF; he therefore chose three hard-working, ambitious SS commanders, dynamic personalities, yet not strong enough to be dangerous to him. As HSSPF Vistula/Danzig he nominated Gruppenführer Richard Hildebrandt, an 'old fighter' regarded as an opponent of the 'Little Hitlers' (Himmler had once had to relieve him of all his SS offices for quarrelling with Gauleiter Streicher).[74] HSSPF Warthe (Poznan) was Gruppenführer Wilhelm Koppe, an energetic operator.[75] As HSSPF East (Cracow) Himmler chose one of the most unpopular SS leaders, Obergruppenführer Friedrich-Wilhelm Krüger, loathed by the SA for his treachery in the Röhm affair; he was a scandalmonger and a pedant, whose tales of supposedly deviationist comrades even Himmler found hard to stomach.[76] HSSPF in Poland were allotted a new category of subordinate not found elsewhere – the 'SS- und Polizeiführer' [SS and Police commanders – SSPF],[77] one to each district of the

Government-General. They were to guarantee SS/Police integration on the provincial level.

Himmler used the rapid expansion of the SS and Police system in the East to lay claim to the leading role in German occupation policy. Without consulting the Wehrmacht, he began to take action against remnants of the Polish armed forces and newly formed partisan groups; under cover of the anti-partisan war, the extermination campaign against the Polish upper class proceeded. Arrests of Poles continued and, from time to time, whole groups of them would be liquidated; the operation culminated in the 'special pacification action' of spring 1940, when 3,500 Poles were shot.[78]

Himmler's units now began to play the role of occupation force with such frequency that even the Wehrmacht generals reacted angrily. Although the yes-men, such as Keitel of OKW, or the fatalists, such as Rundstedt, were quite ready to renounce any political role in the East, the Army as a whole was not prepared to be elbowed out of its dominant position as occupation force. Too late the SS leaders realized that the new Commander-in-Chief East, Colonel-General Johannes Blaskowitz, 'felt himself complete master of the situation and the man who was really in command', as Brigadeführer Berger put it.[79]

The Wehrmacht's position in the Government-General was a strong one. Under a Hitler decree it was in sole command in the event of internal unrest; it was responsible for all measures connected with external defence; it was in control of the traffic and communications networks; it supervised all factories and businesses important to the war effort.[80] The Wehrmacht was therefore not prepared to allow itself to be elbowed out by some Himmler. Only a spark was needed to bring the officers' wrath to the boil and this was provided by the accelerated extermination campaign conducted by the Sicherheitspolizei and SS units. Blaskowitz launched the first, and perhaps only, Wehrmacht campaign against the SS murderers and did so, in the words of the Munich historian Helmut Krausnick, 'in a language unparalleled in German military history'.[81]

Blaskowitz collected reports on SS crimes in Poland and collated them in a memorandum dispatched to the C-in-C of the Army in mid-November 1939. By November 18th the Blaskowitz memorandum was on Hitler's desk.[82] Captain Engel, Hitler's Wehrmacht aide, summarized the contents in his diary: 'Great concern over illegal shootings, arrests and confiscations; risk to the discipline of the troops who see these things happening; local discussion with SD and Gestapo fruitless

– reference to instructions from SS headquarters; request for re-establishment of the rule of law – in particular executions only to be carried out on sentence by a court.'[83] Hitler rejected such 'childish ideas' on the part of the Army. He had never had confidence in General Blaskowitz, he raged, and now it was high time to relieve the man of his appointment.[84]

But Blaskowitz was undeterred by his Führer's explosions of rage and continued to collect evidence against the SS. Unit reports poured in from all sides. To cite a few examples – report by General Petzel, Wehrkreis Commander Warthegau, November 23rd, 1939: 'In almost all major localities, the organizations referred to (SS and Police) carry out public shootings. Selection is entirely arbitrary and the conduct of the executions in many cases disgusting. Arrests are almost invariably accompanied by looting.'[85] Report of incidents in Turck town on October 30th, 1939: 'A number of Jews were herded into the synagogue and there were made to crawl along the pews singing, while being continuously beaten with whips by SS men. They were then forced to take down their trousers so that they could be beaten on the bare buttocks. One Jew who had fouled his trousers in fear was compelled to smear his excrement over the faces of other Jews.'[86] Letter from General Ulex, C-in-C Frontier Sector South, February 2nd, 1940: 'The recent increase in the use of violence by the police shows an almost incredible lack of human and moral qualities; the word "brutish" is almost justified. The only solution I can see to this revolting situation which sullies the honour of the entire German people, is that all police formations together with all their senior commanders . . . should be dismissed in a body and the units disbanded.'[87]

Blaskowitz drew up a new list of SS crimes; it cited thirty-three incidents proved in every detail, maltreatment of Jews and Poles, rape, looting, murder.[88] On February 6th Blaskowitz summarized: 'The attitude of the troops to the SS and Police alternates between abhorrence and hatred. Every soldier feels disgusted and repelled by these crimes committed in Poland by nationals of the Reich and representatives of our State.'[89] Blaskowitz' new attack drove the SS and Police on to the defensive. Even Hitler's military disciples such as von Reichenau, joined the anti-SS ranks; in the Führer's headquarters, no Wehrmacht officer would shake the hand of an SS leader. To save his face, even Himmler had to make some gesture and therefore he ordered the Chief of the Ordnungspolizei and the Hauptamt SS-Gericht to investigate Blaskowitz' 'complaints'.[90] Frank, the Governor-General, now came to the assistance of the hard-pressed Reichsführer – an action which he was later bitterly to regret. On February 13th he presented himself to Hitler and asked for something upon which the Führer had long since decided – the dismissal of that tiresome critic, Blaskowitz.[91] Three months later Himmler was rid of his military enemy. Blaskowitz was transferred to the West and with him went the main body of the German Army located in the Government-General. They were destined for the Franco-German frontier, for May 10th, 1940, the opening of the Western campaign, was only a few weeks away.[92]

May 1940 was the month in which Himmler dictated his memorandum on 'treatment of foreign populations in the East'. The way was open; from the moonscape of the devastated Polish State Himmler could now begin to carve out his SS Order's promised land, the Utopia of the future race of German peasant-warriors.

The May memorandum marked a new phase in Himmler's eastward drive. The mass liquidator of the Polish upper class became the nurseryman of the Germanic ideal, the Chief of the German Police turned into the 'Reich Commissar for the Strengthening of Germanism' [Reichskommissar für die Festigung deutschen Volkstums – RKF]. A new SS invading army was poised for action, though with highly unwilling auxiliaries. SS re-settlement staffs set themselves up, refugee camps appeared, racial commissions drew up questionnaires – the greatest migration in German history was in course of preparation, directed by the SS in accordance with a master plan.

Soon the men whom the SS intended to use to validate their claim to be overlords of the East were on the move, the unsuspecting victims of unscrupulous power policy, summoned – lured – by the 'home-to-the-Reich' propaganda; 120,000 Germans came from the Baltic States, 136,000 from Soviet-occupied Eastern Poland, 200,000 from Rumania and thousands from Yugoslavia and Slovakia.[93] They were to be settled in the German Eastern territories. The propagandists told them that they were answering the call of their blood; in practice, however, the lords of the régime had decided upon their repatriation for a much more prosaic reason: Greater Germany's labour force was inadequate; the country of the 'people without space' had insufficient manpower to keep its industry and agriculture running at full blast.

As early as 1937 Göring, the plenipotentiary for the Four-Year Plan, had calculated that the Reich was short of 150,000 workers.[94] As Chief of Police, Himmler had thereupon been ordered by Göring to do what he could to ensure that the labour requirement was met. So within his personal staff Himmler set up a 'Four-Year Plan office' and at its head he placed an SS commander regarded as one of the leading brains among the SS technocrats.[95] This was Ulrich Greifelt, son of a Berlin chemist; he had been a member of a Free Corps, a business manager, once an anti-Nazi and was now an SS-Oberführer; he was more at home in the world of statistics, production figures and sales records than in that of ideology; only when alone would he allow himself the relaxation of a little sentimentality.[96]

By January 1939 the labour shortage had risen to more than 500,000 men[97] and at this point Greifelt explained how the labour shortage problem could be solved. His answer was repatriation of the thirty million Germans and 'racial Germans' resident abroad; they were the natural reservoir of labour which must be tapped to meet the shortage.[98] Six months later Greifelt had occasion to put his suggestion into practice. Hitler and Mussolini had agreed to eliminate a tiresome piece of grit affecting the smooth running of the Axis machine – the German-speaking population of South Tyrol; in July 1939 the two governments agreed upon the repatriation of this minority to the Reich. It was Greifelt's job to arrange their transportation.[99]

Greifelt set up a staff of twenty, known as the 'Controlling Office for Immigrants and Repatriates' located at 142 Kurfürstendamm, Berlin.[100] The first repatriates were just arriving in the Reich when Himmler found a far more important task for his planner – Greifelt was to resettle German-occupied Poland with 'racial Germans' from Eastern Europe.[101]

The loss of hundreds of thousands of German workers to the Army and the growing requirements of the armaments industry had led Hitler and Göring to adopt Greifelt's solution to the labour problem. At the end of September the Reich concluded an agreement with the Soviet Union and the Baltic States providing for transfer to the Reich of the Germans resident in that area.[102] Hitler summoned his direct subordinate, SS-Obergruppenführer Lorenz, the Head of VOMI, and charged him with control of the re-settlement operation.[103] The choice was a natural one, since all political and financial dealings with racial Germans abroad had been channelled through VOMI since 1938.

No sooner had Himmler heard of the good fortune of his friend Lorenz, however, than he hurried along to his Führer. He pointed out that so important a field as racial policy could hardly be left in the hands of a single Obergruppenführer; it was the task of the SS as a whole.[104] Hitler gave way and allowed Himmler to assume overall control of the business. By September 29th Himmler already had on his desk the draft of a secret decree from the Führer, charging him with the 'strengthening of Germanism'. It laid down three tasks for the Reichsführer-SS; 'Repatriation of persons of German race and nationality resident abroad and considered suitable for permanent return to the Reich; elimination of the injurious influence of those sections of the population of foreign origin constituting a danger to the Reich and the German community; formation of new German settlement areas by transfer of population, in particular by giving land entitlement to persons of German race or nationality returning from abroad.'[105] The decree also gave Himmler such wide plenary powers that he was, in effect, in a position to lay down the law in the East; he was authorized 'to make use of the existing authorities and institutions of the Reich, the Länder and the Gemeinde [Municipalities] as also of other public bodies and existing re-settlement associations.'[106] Providing he made full use of the overriding authority now given him, he could very soon be overlord of the conquered territories in the East.

He knew only too well, of course, that he was headed straight for a minefield of National-Socialist intrigue; a whole collection of brown-shirted would-be imperialists had turned the corpse of Poland into an arena for the exercise of neo-feudal ambitions. Himmler could not challenge the lordlings of the East all at the same time. He had to gather the reins of power as unobtrusively as he could. He could not afford to create a sensation until his new invading army was in position.

He gave himself the portentous title of Reich Commissar for the Strengthening of Germanism (RKF).[107] At the same time, however, he was careful not to set up a mammoth organization. As the General Staff of the racial offensive he selected Greifelt's 'controlling office', re-christened 'RKF Office' (in 1941, it was raised to the status of 'Stabs-hauptamt' [Staff Department].[108] He then distributed the work among several SS organizations; the RKF Office was to be responsible for planning the re-settlement of German repatriates and providing re-settlement areas by confiscation of Polish or Jewish property.[109] VOMI would transport the repatriates, accommodate them in reception camps and supervise the political leadership of individual immigrant groups;[110] the RuSHA would keep an eye on racial purity;[111] the RSHA was to deal with the requisitioning of property of 'anti-State' persons, deportation of the Poles and their so-called 're-settlement' in the Government-General.[112]

All was now ready. Lorenz and his staff had meanwhile been concluding their preparations for the repatriation of the German Balts and on October 20th the first settler ships arrived from Estonia;[113] the Balts were due to be accommodated in the Danzig area. However, if Himmler thought that his new access of power had passed unnoticed by his rivals, he was soon disillusioned. One of the Reichsführer's bitterest enemies who, to make matters worse, was entitled to wear the uniform of an SS-Gruppenführer, refused to allow the RKF to interfere in his kingdom in any way – this was Gauleiter Forster.

To ensure that all the various authorities cooperated in the repatriation exercise, it had been Himmler's intention to nominate the most senior personality in each area as his representative. Forster, however, who was in charge of the Danzig-West Prussia Gau, refused to take orders from Himmler and the latter had to nominate the HSSPF as his representative.[114] No persuasion could bring Forster to cooperate with the RKF. When VOMI personnel, assisted by the Sicherheitspolizei, began to earmark whole areas of West Prussian towns for the reception of immigrants, Forster summoned the VOMI representative and threatened him with arrest if he did not immediately order his people to stop.[115] Forster proved so inhospitable that the repatriate ships heading for Danzig were re-routed to Stettin.[116] He only changed his attitude after a couple of telephone calls from Himmler, and even then he would only allow the returning Balts the most transient accommodation in his area.[117]

Himmler was compelled to postpone settlement of the German Balts to the following year. Owing to Forster's obstruction and the inefficiency of the VOMI organizations, the repatriates' situation was so miserable that another critic of Himmler's racial policy appeared, the National-Socialist ideologist Alfred Rosenberg, who was a German Balt himself. In a letter to Himmler he complained that 'the manner in which the Balts are treated is reminiscent of the Bolshevik period.' VOMI, he went on, had turned the German Balts into 'a disorganized mob of disappointed, embittered and hopeless men.'[118] But Forster and Rosenberg were not Himmler's only rivals and opponents. Others were on the scene to dispute his authority over the settlement area upon which the whole success of his operation depended.

Gauleiter Koch of East Prussia, for instance, was also in charge of certain ex-Polish territories now incorporated in his Gau and known as 'New East Prussia'; he refused to allow his area to be used for the resettlement of the RKF's German repatriates. When Professor Konrad Meyer-Heterling, Greifelt's senior area planner, initiated a survey, Koch threatened to have him thrown out of East Prussia.[119] Others found more subtle methods of opposition. For instance Himmler set up a Central Real Estate Office to direct the requisitioning of Polish land; hardly had he done so than Göring's Four-Year Plan office organized a 'Haupttreuhandstelle Ost' [Main Trust Office for the East – HTO]. Here was the Reich's Number Two staking his claim to control of all Polish-Jewish property – precisely the land which Himmler's Central Real Estate Office wished to reserve for its settlers.[120]

Göring immediately rubbed into Himmler the fact that he was not regarded as an equal. Alerted by the formation of the HTO, Himmler promptly made representations to Göring in his capacity as head of the Four-Year Plan; Göring, however, referred him to the Head of the HTO, Max Winkler – a mere burgomaster. Only after endless discussions did Himmler reach agreement with Göring's representative: the HTO to retain control of all Polish industrial and urban property, Himmler being allowed only confiscated agricultural property in German-occupied Poland.[121]

Yet even now Himmler was not in full control of his new settlement area. He had had to concede some voice in the business to Darré, his disillusioned friend of the old Artaman days, now Minister of Agriculture.[122] Moreover, Darré now reinsured via Göring's newly constituted organization in the East. He set up his own office for the management of requisitioned Polish estates and placed it under Göring – clearly in the hope of strengthening his hand *vis-à-vis* the RKF.[123]

In face of such resistance Himmler had to manoeuvre with caution if he was to achieve his object. The National-Socialist rule of self-frustration would soon have brought the RKF to an end, had Himmler not been able to rely upon his police machine in the East – and this had work to do: as early as November 8th, 1939 HSSPF East had held a meeting in Cracow with the Commander of the Government-General's Sicherheitspolizei at which they had discussed what, in SS terminology, was euphemistically called the 'negative' aspect of racial policy – in other words, the deportation of Poles and Jews from the ex-Polish territories now 're-incorporated' in the Reich[124] (see Appendix 4).

In Lodz the Sicherheitspolizei set up a so-called 'Deportee Centre' [Umwanderungszentralstelle – UWZ] responsible for planning the deportation to the Government-General[125] of unwanted Poles and Jews from the new 'Germanized' areas. With their usual ruthlessness the Sicherheitspolizei proceeded to eject all Poles on their list and by February 1940 300,000 Poles had been 're-settled' in the Government-General. The Sipo's deportation figures climbed faster and higher – 120,000 Polish landowners deported from Warthegau, 35,000 from Danzig-West Prussia and 15,000 from Eastern Upper Silesia.[126] By the outbreak of the war against Russia a million Poles had been driven from their homes.[127] The SS re-settlement staffs were quick to introduce their 'racial German' immigrants and distribute them to the deserted Polish properties – though only after complicated checking by the RuSHA.

By mid-1941, 200,000 German repatriates had been provided with new homes.[128] Greifelt's office distributed Polish property; of Poland's 928,000 farms, comprising 245,000,000 acres, German settlers inherited in all 47,000 farms, comprising 23,000,000 acres. By the end of 1942 German settlers had been allotted some 20 per cent of the 60,000 Polish business concerns and Reich Germans 8 per cent; 51 per cent already belonged to indigenous Germans and 21 per cent were controlled by German trusts. Of the small craftsman businesses some 2,000 were transferred to German immigrants, the bulk (80 per cent) remaining with their Polish owners.[129]

The recall to the Reich of the true racial Germans and their re-settlement in the East, however, was not enough for Himmler, the racial fanatic. True to his memorandum of May 1940 he now began to extract from the Polish population every drop of German blood; racial commissions travelled round seeking out concealed members of the German race; Himmler had a 'German racial list' prepared on which was entered every inhabitant of German origin in the East. They were divided into four categories: Category 1 – Proven 'racial fighters'; Category 2 – passive 'racial Germans' who had at least a fifty per cent knowledge of the German language; Category 3 – persons of doubtful German origin; Category 4 – anti-Nazis of German origin who had taken part in measures directed against the German minority.[130]

Racial investigation, however, was not confined to persons of German origin; many Polish nationals had to pass under the microscope and if any Nordic traits were detected the 're-Germanization' mechanism was set in motion. In accordance with the crazy doctrine of racial purity and in the words of an SS memorandum entitled 'The Use of Human Material', the object was to 'recover for the German community German blood available in the East', even though it might run in Polish veins.[131] In Himmler's view no foreign race existed which did not include 'Nordic representatives' capable of Germanization. He stated that 'in course of time' even Gorals, Lemkes and Huzuls should be 'Germanized', since 'their Germanic origin or, at least, their German descent' could be established.[132]

Himmler was especially persistent in his pursuit of Polish children, regarding them as ideal candidates for Germanization. A rumour current in Poznan was that, in the early days of the war, the Poles had kidnapped German children and hidden them in orphanages. The RKF promptly issued an order for the disbandment of all Polish orphanages and the transfer of their inmates after racial examination to German children's homes. Later, children were even torn from their families and carried off to Germany.[133] On June 13th, 1941 Himmler wrote to Greiser, the Gauleiter of Warthegau: 'Racially pure children of Poles should be brought up by us in special kindergartens or children's homes. The parents can be told that this is being done for the children's health.'[134]

Six months later Himmler brought 'Lebensborn', the SS maternity organization, into the game; its homes were to be used for the reception of Polish children, later to be distributed to childless SS families. A large-scale kidnapping operation was instituted (code name Haymaking) as a result of which thousands of Polish children disappeared into Germany.[135] Those who refused to allow their children to be Germanized were subjected to severe reprisals by the Sicherheitspolizei. Brunhilde Muszynski, for instance, the German wife of a Polish officer, refused to allow her children to be brought up in Germany. The Zamosc Immigration Centre [Einwandererzentralstelle – EWZ], an RuSHA office, decreed: 'her children will be sterilized and accommodated somewhere as foster children.'[136]

Such cases, however, were rare; in general both Poles and racial Germans complied with Himmler's Germanization procedure; 100,000 pure Poles allowed themselves to be Germanized, a million men registered in categories 1 and 2 of the 'racial list', and a further two million in categories 3 and 4.[137]

The greater the success of Himmler's re-settlement and Germanization policy, however, the larger the number of his enemies grew. Josef Wagner, the Catholic Gauleiter of Silesia, expressed fears lest Himmler force the entire Polish skilled labour force to leave Upper Silesian heavy industry; his counter-measures were largely successful in reducing the severity of the deportation measures ordered by Greifelt's office.[138] Even the Economic Office of OKW appealed to Himmler to reduce the tempo of re-settlement.[139] In Danzig Forster openly ridiculed 'certain theorists' who had no conception of racial policy; the local Sipo Inspector reported that he had expressed himself 'very cynically.' It was abundantly clear that he was referring primarily to the SS.[140] In letters to the Reich Chancellery, the Government-General complained heatedly that 'the re-settlement policy was gradually becoming impossible and was no longer tolerable in view of its catastrophic consequences.' A letter of June 25th, 1940 stated that the continued influx of Polish deportees into the Government-General had led to a 'hopeless food situation'.[141]

Himmler found himself confronted by so many jealous rivals and critics that he could only hope for some miracle to give him new freedom of manoeuvre. That miracle was provided by Adolf Hitler; on June 22nd, 1941 all German radio networks announced that the Army of the Reich had set forth on its crusade against the Bolshevik world enemy.

The Russian campaign opened up for Himmler vast new territories in which to deploy his energies. That which Forster, Wagner, Koch and Göring had so far prevented, he could now do in the limitless expanses of Russia; vast new settlement areas were there for the taking. Himmler and his SS leaders were intoxicated by the prospect of the endless steppes and vast woodlands. Bemused by the continental expanse of Russia, the SS planners seized their drawing boards and drew up fantastic visions of the future – grotesque, unreal, pathological day-dreams.

As early as January 1941, at a meeting in Wewelsburg, Himmler had confided to SS-Gruppenführer Erich von dem Bach-Zelewski that the German master plan for the East necessitated the elimination of thirty million Slavs.[142] The racial experts now foregathered in Group III B of the RuSHA to plan the German Eastern empire of the future.[143]

Their dreamings were committed to paper in the shape of the 'master plan East'. The entire area as far as the line Leningrad–Lake Ladoga–Valdai Hills–Briansk and the bend of the Dnieper was to be settled by Germans; fourteen million people of other races were to be deported; fourteen million were to be allowed to remain in the settlement area but must be Germanized within a period of thirty years. The Government-General and the Baltic States were to be completely 're-populated'; 85 per cent of the twenty million Poles and 65 per cent of the West Ukrainians were to be deported to Western Siberia to make room for German immigrants. These were to arrive in several waves – 840,000 for 'immediate settlement', followed by a second wave of 1·1 million; the RuSHA plans provided for an influx of 200,000 annually over the next ten years and a total of 2·4 million Germans moved during the following two decades.[144]

But how were such comparatively small numbers to maintain themselves in the face of the numerical superiority of the other races? How were they to establish the dominant position which Himmler's Order postulated? The answer, on paper at any rate, was provided by SS-Oberführer Professor Konrad Meyer-Heterling, Senior Settlement and Area Planner and Director of the Institute for Agriculture and Agrarian Policy in the University of Berlin. On May 28th, 1942 the Professor submitted to the Reichsführer-SS a memorandum outlining the German master race's wonderland.[145] The great area of the East was to be carved up into settlement provinces ('Marks') under the supreme authority of the Reichsführer-SS; he was to be the liege lord of the East, directing the settlers to the areas provided for them and granting them fiefs of varying types – 'life fiefs', 'hereditary fiefs' and 'special status properties'.[146] Provincial 'headmen' appointed by the Reichsführer-SS were to supervise the 'Marks'; after a 25-year pioneering period their population should be 50 per cent German. The Baltic States and Poland were to be fully Germanized; besides these, Meyer-Heterling envisaged three 'Marks' – the area west of Leningrad (to be known as 'Ingermanland'), the Crimea–Kherson area (to be known as 'Gotengau') and the Memel–Narev area.[147] The German colonial empire in the East was to be protected by a system of 26 strong-points. In these areas the population was to be only 30 per cent Germanized; in Himmler's words the strong-points were to guard 'the intersections of German arteries of communication; they were to consist of small towns of about 20,000 inhabitants surrounded by a ring of German villages at a distance of 2–5 miles.'[148]

The Reichsführer was overjoyed. Here, at last, the world of his dreams was taking shape – the world of armed peasant settlers under the sole authority of Heinrich Himmler. 'Just imagine,' he said to Kersten, 'what a sublime idea! It's the greatest piece of colonization the world will ever have seen linked with a most noble and essential task, the protection of the Western world against an irruption from Asia.'[149] He was continually producing maps and plans showing the warrior-peasant settlements and explaining the layout to Kersten – here were the 30 to 40 farmhouses constituting a village – there the leader's mansion around which the village was grouped – there the SS peasant-warrior 'Sturm' to which all male inhabitants would belong. Kersten remembers Himmler saying: 'We will instil a fighting spirit such as has never been seen before; it will guarantee the indestructibility of the resulting community.'[150]

Himmler had already selected the SS leader to turn this dream world into reality – the SSPF Lublin, Brigadeführer Odilo Globocnik. Globocnik was the son of a Trieste cavalry captain, a builder by trade and a long-standing Nazi; he was one of Himmler's least educated and most hot-headed disciples; his display of unflagging enthusiasm was designed to curry favour with his Reichsführer – and for good reason; he had only been accepted into the SS as a result of Himmler's influence, after being described by Schwarz, the Party Treasurer and certainly no prude, as one of the most dubious characters ever to wear a Party badge. In 1933, when a deputy Gauleiter, he had fled to Germany after murdering a jeweller in Vienna; in 1939, by which time he had become a Gauleiter, he was dismissed for trafficking in currency.[151] He made good his lack of respectability by dog-like devotion. The SS Personnel Department noted: 'His impetuosity frequently leads him to break the rules and forget the restrictions imposed upon him by the Order.'[152]

Like Himmler, Globocnik, the future mass murderer of Jews, was captivated by the prospect of vast racial biological experiments. In the south-eastern part of Lublin District he had come across traces of early German settlements and the discovery inspired him with the notion of re-creating a German settlement area; the Polish population was to be deported and German settlements created in each district using SS and Police units; Globocnik proposed to begin with the towns of Zamosc, Tomaszow and Hrubieszow.[153]

Globocnik, of course, knew that Frank, the Governor-General, was unlikely to agree to deportations on so large a scale since they would inevitably aggravate Poland's already catastrophic economic and communications situation. Staking his luck, however, upon the rivalry between Frank and Himmler, he submitted his plan to the Reichsführer and Himmler seized upon it. A glance at the map must have shown him that Globocnik's proposed experimental area lay at the base of the elongated quadrilateral on which Himmler proposed to centre his SS resettlement policy.

This quadrilateral was bounded by Lublin, Zhitomir, Vinnitsa and Lwow, each a special centre of SS activity; Lublin was the headquarters of Globocnik, in Zhitomir Himmler had set up his command post during the first phase of the eastern campaign and had opened a settlement centre for German Ukrainians; Vinnitsa was on the edge of Transnistria where a further German settlement area was planned; Lwow, capital of Eastern Galicia, now incorporated in the Government-General, was the Headquarters of SS-Brigadeführer Wächter, who had been involved in the Dollfuss putsch.[154] The American historian Robert L. Koehl, one of the outstanding experts on SS racial policy, says: 'In this quadrilateral, straddling two different German administrative areas and the Polish–Ukrainian ethnic frontier, an SS State might have arisen some day if the Germans had been victorious in Russia.'[155]

In autumn 1941, Himmler gave Globocnik the green light,[156] obviously calculating that Frank was unlikely to resist the Lublin deportation plan. In fact, however, he touched off a violent power struggle which proved, yet again, how little influence the SS, acting alone, could exert on the Third Reich's policy.

Without informing the Government-General, Himmler paid a visit to Lublin and announced that Zamosc district would be the first major German settlement area.[157] He promptly found himself in opposition to a man who had hitherto concealed from the outer world that he had no intention of allowing the RKF to interfere in his sphere of authority – Dr Hans Frank, the Governor-General of Poland, Reich Minister without Portfolio, Reich Legal Adviser and a Party Reichsleiter (the highest-ranking Nazi functionary).

Nothing had so far given anyone reason to suspect that Frank was nursing a hatred against the SS which was now at boiling point. He was regarded as one of the most radical Nazi leaders; he had proposed to divest the legal code of all its liberal provisions; he followed Adolf Hitler with a blind, fanatical devotion, with that subservience, indeed, which frequently binds misfits and homosexuals to some virile authoritarian father-figure. Gilbert, the American psychiatrist, described Frank as 'one of the most intelligent of the "old fighters" as well as one of the most unstable emotionally.'[158] He had come to Poland determined to carry out his Führer's programme ruthlessly; his diaries contain excerpts from his speeches redolent of a diseased mania for power – 'we will hold on to the Government-General and will never give it up again[159] . . . I admit, quite openly, that this will cost the lives of several thousand Poles, primarily from the intellectual upper class[160] . . . We liquidate things in this country. We will do so in the manner which proves simplest[161] . . . Our primary object here in this area is to fulfil National-Socialism's great mission in the East. It cannot, therefore, be our object to set up here a State based on the rule of law[162] . . . Anyone suspected by us should be liquidated forthwith.'[163]

Nevertheless, Frank was too intelligent not to realize that it was impossible to rule by brutality alone. In his view if the Poles were to be mobilized in the service of the Reich, the Government-General must become a model of economic development, a German ruling class must be introduced into the country and the peoples of other races, such as the Ukrainians and the Kashubs, must be used as a counter-weight to the Poles.

Himmler's racial policy, however, wrecked Frank's plan. The Sicherheitspolizei drove into the Government-General a million Poles from the areas incorporated in the Reich, thus playing havoc with the food position in Frank's kingdom; Himmler then lured into the Warthegau 30,000 of the 90,000 racial Germans resident in the Government-General,[164] thereby ruining Frank's dream of a German ruling class; finally the RKF began to Germanize the Gorals, the Lemkes, the Kashubs and the Huzuls, the minorities whom Frank wished to use as a counterweight to the Poles. But worse was to come; SS formations and the Sicherheitspolizei initiated a pitiless campaign against actual or suspected Polish resistance fighters, driving thousands of innocent peasants into the woods or into the ranks of the partisans. SS and Police Courts passed blanket sentences of death without regard to the Government or any normal form of legal procedure.[165]

Gradually Frank began to suspect that Himmler's real purpose in dispatching his HSSPF, Friedrich-Wilhelm Krüger, to Cracow was 'to put an end to Frank' – as Gottlob Berger now openly admits.[166] Signs multiplied that an SS and Police administration, distinct from that of the Government-General, was forming and setting itself up as the real ruler in Frank's kingdom.

In impotent rage the hard-pressed Governor-General cursed and swore at the SS invaders. He dispatched a stream of protest letters to the Reich Chancellery;[167] at almost every 'cabinet meeting' in Cracow, he took occasion to demonstrate to Krüger, verbally at any rate, that he was master in the Government-General. 'I have never left anyone in any doubt that it is only possible to rule here if he who carries the responsibility carries it in full,' Frank stormed at Krüger. 'It is therefore clear that the HSSPF is my subordinate, that the police form an integral part of the Government and that the SSPF in districts are subordinate to the Governors.'[168] And on another occasion: 'No organ of the Reich is empowered to take action, directly or indirectly, in this area. Orders are issued solely by the Governor-General as the Führer's direct representative and by no one else.'[169]

But Himmler's minions were entirely unruffled by Frank's homilies. They awaited their moment and, in late autumn 1941, they thought it had come; the Sicherheitspolizei was on the trail of a corruption scandal in which Frank himself was involved.[170]

SS-Untersturmführer Lorenz Löv, Head of the Governor-General's Central Administrative Office in Warsaw, had fallen under suspicion of running a highly profitable black market in furs and other articles stored in a warehouse under his control. He was brought before SS/Police Court VI in Cracow and sentenced to life imprisonment for embezzlement by the SS judge, Dr Günther Reinecke.[171] In the process the investigators stumbled upon the fact that the Governor-General and his family were busily engaged in feathering their nest and had clearly been using official funds to purchase articles, said to be 'for representational purposes'. Frank's family was evidently particularly interested in furs.

Immediately after Löv's arrest, Frank closed down the fur warehouse and the contents were sold at bargain prices. On December 1st, 1941 Reinecke reported to Himmler: 'The Governor-General's wife procured from the warehouse a number of fur coats (at least ten) far in excess of her personal requirements. But even this by no means satisfied her need for furs! From Apfelbaum in Warsaw she ordered a moleskin jacket, a beaver coat, a musquash coat, an ermine coat, two broadtail coats, an ermine jacket, a silver fox cape, a blue fox cape and other furs. According to SS-Sturmbannführer Fassbender, the persons making these purchases on behalf of the Governor-General's wife were members of the Governor-General's office and they simply fixed the price at approximately 50 per cent of the cost price.'[172]

The Governor-General had also used his position to divert certain other articles into his own possession; according to Reinecke, the Frank family had picked up from the Jews of Warsaw rings, gold bracelets, gold fountain pens, tinned food, picnic hampers, coffee machines and groceries 'at staggeringly low prices'.[173] From his official estate at Kressendorf in Poland, Frank shipped both property and produce to Schobernhof, his private estate in Southern Germany; it included 200,000 eggs, a whole year's produce of dried fruit, sheets, blankets and furniture.[174] In November 1940, two whole convoys of foodstuffs left for Schobernhof. The first contained 150 lb of beef, 50 lb of pork, 20 geese, 50 chicken, 25 lb of salami, 30 lb of ham sausage, 25 lb of ham; the second: 175 lb of butter, 110 lb of cooking oil, 30 lb of cheese, 1,440 eggs, 50 lb of coffee beans and 12 lb of sugar.[175] Simultaneously Frank took sculptures, figures of the Madonna, angels and icons from Polish churches and dispatched them to the Schobernhof private chapel.[176] Reinecke summarized: 'This affair constitutes a case of corruption of the basest sort, all the more deplorable in that it shows that Germans are misusing their positions as senior political leaders of the Reich to enrich themselves personally by exploiting the circumstances arising from the war.'[177]

Himmler seized upon this affair to strike at Frank. One of Frank's closest collaborators, Dr Karl Lasch, the Governor of Radom, had meanwhile been brought down by the Sicherheitspolizei because of a corruption scandal,[178] so Himmler now thought that he could force his enemy to his knees. On March 5th, 1942 Frank was summoned to appear before Lammers, the Head of the Reich Chancellery; in Lammers' special train he was subjected to an inquisition; the other members of the tribunal were Bormann, the Head of the Party Chancellery, and Himmler. The Reichsführer made the speech for the prosecution. In his meticulous, pedantic manner, he detailed every one of Frank's peccadilloes, starting with his brother-in-law, Heinrich Herbst, who had suddenly assumed Swedish nationality, and ending with Frau Frank's fur coats.[179]

Frank had to do obeisance before they would let him go. The price: acceptance of Krüger as Secretary of State in his Government, agreement that Krüger should receive instructions direct from the Reichsführer-SS, and an undertaking to dismiss Zörner, the anti-SS Governor of Lublin.[180]

But Himmler's inquisition did not achieve its object. No sooner had he returned to Cracow than Frank showed that he intended to continue the battle. On March 10th, he sent an almost impertinent letter to Lammers, in effect withdrawing everything to which he had agreed in the special train. 'Today I can state,' he said, 'that among the Germans in the Government-General, there exists an impeccable official economic and social order which only the basest slander can dispute. Primarily I would wish to refute most vehemently any suggestion that an accusation of major corruption can be substantiated.'[181]

Frank then proceeded to act as if nothing had happened. He was, indeed, compelled to nominate Krüger as Secretary of State, but Zörner remained at his post.[182] Both in speeches and ordinances he resumed his attack on the SS and the Police. He had it recorded in the cabinet minutes, for instance, that the SD reports were 'the worst type of spy product, bearing no relation to objective truth and being little more than a manifestation of hatred for the work of the officials of the Government-General.'[183] When Globocnik in Lublin finally began to deport the Poles and settle Germans in their stead, all without the agreement of the Cracow Government, Frank's wrath exploded. Regardless of the consequences, he launched a campaign against Himmler unparalleled in the history of the Third Reich.

The truth had dawned on Frank – shortly before his death he said: 'Comprehension finally came to me in 1942.'[184] On June 30th, 1934 in Stadelheim prison a still, small voice had spoken; during his struggle against the continued existence of the concentration camps it had become louder; now he knew. The Führer's legal adviser began warning the Germans against the poison spread by the totalitarian State. He accepted invitations to lecture in German Universities; he peregrinated from rostrum to rostrum. Berlin, Vienna, Munich, Heidelberg – in all of them his shocked audience heard a message never before voiced in public: Away with arbitrary action by the Police and SS.

Berlin University, June 9th, 1942: 'Without law – or contrary to law – no German Reich is conceivable. A people cannot be ruled by force, a community without law is unthinkable . . . it is intolerable that the State should be able to deprive a member of the community of honour, liberty, life and property, declare him an outlaw and condemn him, without first giving him an opportunity to reply to the accusations made against him.'[185] Vienna University, July 1st, 1942: 'I shall continue to assert, with all the force at my command, that it would be bad if the Police State were to be presented as the ideal of National-Socialism. Nowadays many people say that humanity is an out-of-date notion, something incompatible with the severity of this period. That is not my opinion. The principle which every State, including our own, must follow, is that its methods must be designed to meet the historical tasks which any State must fulfil but that, in no circumstances, can a State be endangered by being humane.'[186] Munich University, July 20th, 1942:

'Even in wartime, a mode of life based on the rule of law is important for the development of our community. We must not give the impression that in our Reich the law is powerless. The law is the personal safeguard of our people . . . force alone cannot make the State strong. Brutality is never synonymous with strength . . . I say: only the man who does not fear the law is strong.'[187] Heidelberg University, July 21st, 1942: 'The Police State must never exist – never! I reject it. As a National-Socialist and leader of the German legal profession I therefore feel it my duty to protest against these continual disparagements of the law and its servants. I protest against a profession being attacked and slandered simply from spite or a permanent nagging desire to criticize.'[188]

The initiated held their breath. By his self-destructive criticism of the SS, they thought, Frank was inviting the final blow; nobody and nothing could now save a man who thus challenged Himmler. The blow fell. From the rostrum Frank proclaimed: 'Führer, protect the legal profession also!'[189] Hitler gave him his answer: he stripped Frank of all his Party offices and dismissed him as Minister of the Reich.[190] On August 24th, 1942 Frank handed in his resignation as Governor-General of Poland.[191]

But then came a curious phenomenon. Perhaps out of respect for the courage of his old comrade-in-arms, or perhaps to prevent the police machine from becoming over-powerful, Hitler allowed Frank to remain at his post in Cracow. He was there from 1942 to 1944 – in fact he remained until called to the gallows in Nuremberg. By contrast Frank's SS enemies fell by the wayside. In autumn 1943 Himmler withdrew Globocnik from the anti-Frank battle for dealings which even he found too shady;[192] Globocnik was followed by Krüger, the HSSPF, who had regarded himself as successor to the tottering Frank.[193]

Himmler had to swallow this loss of prestige, but his Führer gave him little time to ruminate upon it. Hitler had already selected him for a new task compared to which the martyrdom of Poland was no more than a feeble overture. To the Reichsführer-SS was reserved the most grisly executioner's task in recorded history – the annihilation of European Jewry.

13

THE JEWISH QUESTION

ON November 11th, 1941 Kersten, Himmler's masseur, noted in his diary: 'Today Himmler is very depressed. He has just come from the Führer's Chancellery. I gave him treatment. After much pressure and questions as to what was the matter with him he told me that the destruction of the Jews is being planned.'[1] This was the first Kersten had heard of the 'Final Solution of the Jewish Question'. 'I was horrified,' he says,[2] and he spoke up vehemently against this fearful plan. But Himmler, normally so talkative, was curiously reserved.

Shortly afterwards Kersten returned to the charge. On November 16th he noted: 'In these last few days with Himmler I have been constantly trying to return to the fate of the Jews. Contrary to all his habits he only listens to me in silence.'[3] A year later, however, on November 10th, 1942, Himmler's tongue was looser: 'Ach, Kersten, I never wanted to destroy the Jews. I had quite different ideas. But Goebbels has it all on his conscience.'[4] And he went on: 'Some years ago the Führer gave me orders to get rid of the Jews. They were to be allowed to take their fortunes and properties with them. I made a start and even punished excesses which had been committed by my people, which were reported to me. But I was inexorable on one point: the Jews had to leave Germany . . . up to the spring of 1940, Jews could still leave Germany without any trouble. Then Goebbels got the upper hand.'

'Why Goebbels?' Kersten asked.

Himmler replied: 'Goebbels' attitude was that the Jewish question could only be solved by the total extermination of the Jews. While a Jew remained alive, he would always be an enemy to National-Socialist Germany. Therefore any kindness shown them was out of place.'[5]

This conversation with Himmler, recorded by that assiduous diary-writer Kersten, does not square with the picture which many of Himmler's contemporaries and the majority of the post-war world have formed for themselves of the origins of the so-called 'Final Solution' of the Jewish problem. The annihilation of European Jewry is so closely bound up with the history of the SS that in centuries to come it will probably be the only single event which the letters SS will call to men's minds; consequently the natural (but erroneous) assumption has been made that the agents of the greatest mass crime in history were also its instigators.

After the war Rudolf Diels held that the 'Final Solution' had 'taken shape in the brains of Himmler and Heydrich' in 1942;[6] Paul Schmidt, the Foreign Ministry's ex-interpreter-in-chief, was equally convinced that 'the "Final Solution" originated from the Heydrich–Himmler–Streicher group'.[7] Even serious historians have accepted this view. Leon Poliakov, for instance, considers that Heydrich was the first highly-placed National-Socialist to plan the annihilation of the Jews and that he did so before the outbreak of war.[8] The American Henry A. Zeiger maintains that Hitler and Göring only decided upon the 'Final Solution' in 1941 as the result of a proposal from Heydrich to kill every Jew in Europe.[9]

There is no concrete proof of this theory. It springs, in fact, from the self-evident conclusion that the men who slaughtered millions of Jews in an orgy of blood and sadism can hardly have been transformed overnight from peaceful citizens into mass murderers – in other words the annihilation of the Jews was present in the hearts and minds of the SS long before the actual order was issued. Other indications, however, lead to the conclusion that the decision to murder the Jews originated elsewhere than in SS headquarters.

Hitler's decision must have been taken in early summer 1941 and no earlier document from any SS organization has been found foreshadowing the physical annihilation of European Jewry. In his famous memorandum of May 1940 on 'Treatment of foreign populations in the East,' Himmler had characterized 'the Bolshevist method of physical extermination of a people as un-Germanic and impossible' and had therefore rejected it 'from inner conviction'.[10]

One undisputed fact alone is enough to demolish the theory that Himmler was the originator of the 'Final Solution'. Hitler's decision wrecked an entirely different policy which the SS had been pursuing for years – the expulsion of the Jews from Germany, euphemistically called the 'Emigration Policy'. Pitiless this SS Jewish policy may have been, but, at least up to the outbreak of war, there was one notion it did not contain – that of physical liquidation of the Jews. The occupants of Jewish desks in SS headquarters were infuriated by the crude incitements to murder issuing from the Jew-baiting Gauleiter Julius Streicher and his weekly newspaper *Der Stürmer*. Ever since the SS had become the Führer dictatorship's primary instrument its leaders had supported a Jewish policy differing in many respects from the Party's crude anti-Semitism, though they naturally subscribed to the inhuman thesis that the Jews were a sort of racial blot and a manifestation of evil; they would have agreed with the comment by Buch, the Senior Party Judge: 'The Jew is not a human being. He is a symptom of putrefaction.'[11]

Following the economic crises of the early 1930s, anti-Semitism became even more firmly established as an SS article of faith; their livelihood gone, the sons of the farming and lower-middle classes streamed into the SS; having been taught to regard the Jew as the root of all evil, they saw in him the real cause of their economic misfortunes. These SS youngsters had inherited from their fathers an anti-Semitism tinged with socialism but in their minds it was overshadowed by a more sophisticated form of anti-Semitism – social Darwinism. The protagonists of this doctrine were believers in the laws propounded by the British biologist, Charles Darwin (1809–82) – natural selection and the struggle for existence; these they transposed into the sphere of State policy.

More than any other Nazi organization, the SS subscribed to the theory culled from Darwin and adapted to their own purposes, that a people's valuable characteristics could be increased and improved by a process of selection. The SS racial mystics recognized only one criterion of value – the Nordic Germanic race.[12] The political twist given to Darwin's biological theory presented his concept of the struggle for existence in a new light. What Darwin had regarded as a law of nature, the social Darwinists wished to impose from without through measures of coercion decreed by the authoritarian State; this culminated in the belief that the superior and stronger race had the right to eliminate racially inferior beings.

The aim of any normal civilized State's social policy was inverted. The normally accepted task of any State is to protect the weak, the handicapped and the minorities; here, however, the rule was to reinforce the 'good blood' and root out those elements of the race considered incapable of maintaining themselves. The SS looked upon nations not as formed entities but, in Buchheim's words, as 'a plantation overgrown with weeds, which must be cleared by isolating the incorrigible, cutting out the "ferment of decomposition", cultivating the worthwhile elements and allowing the sub-standard to wither.'[13]

Even the early social Darwinists had kept the notion of race in the forefront of their minds. As early as 1903 Wilhelm Schallmayer, the biologist, had proposed 'fertility selection'; in his view good racial characteristics could be cultivated by methods of racial selectivism, such as control or banning of marriages and sterilization of inferior members of society.[14] This was clearly the forerunner of Himmler's racial fantasies with his 'clan oaths', marriage permits and racial hygiene examinations. In his social-Darwinistic phraseology Himmler once said: 'Unless the blood of leadership in German veins, by which alone we stand or fall, can be increased by the admixture of good blood from elsewhere, we shall never achieve world mastery.'[15]

It was at this point that anti-Semitism springing from economic difficulties merged with social Darwinism based on racialism to produce the hatred of the Jews characteristic of the SS philosophy. The Jew became symbolic of the foreign body or inferior being against whom men of good race must hold their own. Himmler proclaimed that the anti-Jewish crusade was 'a struggle between humans and sub-humans'; it was 'a law of nature, just as men fight some disease or a healthy body fights the plague virus.'[16] The SS man was subjected to a torrent of anti-Semitic indoctrination lectures; the fact that the Jew was a foreign body was dinned into him at every turn. A standard lecture for SS units issued in 1936 contained the following: 'The Jew is a parasite. Wherever he flourishes, the people die. From the earliest times to our own day the Jew has quite literally killed and exterminated the peoples upon whom he has battened, in so far as he has been able to do so. Elimination of the Jew from our community is to be regarded as an emergency defence measure.'[17]

But how to 'eliminate' the Jews? For the Nazi anti-Semites this was the national problem upon which opinions differed. The young intellectuals, primarily those in senior SD posts, displayed unmistakable horror at the crude official Party solution – 'down with the Jews'. For some time, however, they knew only what they did *not* want. They did not want the methods advocated by the *Stürmer* and Julius Streicher; they would have none of his wild campaign of hatred and jealousy motivated by sex and economics; in the final analysis this could only let loose the basest instincts and deprive the Jews of all right to existence.

The SD intellectuals wanted to be thought radical National-Socialists, but they also wanted to be regarded as 'decent', and this type of anti-Jewish action seemed to them 'harmful anti-Semitism', in the words of a *Schwarze Korps* headline.[18] Inciting street mobs against the Jews seemed to the SD leaders to be unintelligent folly; breaking Jewish shop windows, they argued, damaged the new Germany's reputation in the world without advancing the solution of the Jewish question one inch. On June 5th, 1935 the *Schwarze Korps* proclaimed: 'The National-Socialist Movement and its State opposes these criminal machinations with all its energy. The Party will not tolerate prostitution of its sacred struggle for the good of the nation by street riots and destruction of property.'[19]

The men of the SD were too intelligent to accept the Party's crude anti-Semitic propaganda, and if they had had their way most of it would have been suppressed. Their sole object was to solve the so-called Jewish problem in a cold, rational manner. They censored much of the literature produced by the anti-Jewish Nazi fanatics. In autumn 1935, for instance, the Berlin publisher Paul Schmidt produced a leaflet, folded in the form of a caricature Jewish head, blaming the Jews for the Abyssinian war; Abteilung II 2 B of the Gestapa commented: 'The contents of the leaflet are arrant nonsense. Reinke of the Berlin Gestapo has been instructed by telephone to arrange its confiscation forthwith.'[20]

Even the *Protocols of Zion*, the stock-in-trade of every anti-Jewish propagandist, awoke no echoes in the SD though they were regarded as suitable mental fodder for the SS rank and file and references to them were retained in the Allgemeine-SS education courses; SS-Untersturmführer Edler von Mildenstein, who occupied the Jewish desk in the SD, regarded them as mere 'poppycock'.[21] On July 21st, 1938 SS-Oberscharführer Herbert Hagen, the SD's Jewish expert, referring to books produced by the Hochmut firm, wrote them off as insignificant productions, 'quite apart from the fact that reference is made to the *Protocols of Zion*'.[22] Commenting upon a brochure entitled *Der Judenspiegel* (*The Jewish Mirror*) produced by the Party's Central Press and written by Rudolfs, Hagen noted: 'This over-zealous author is determined to see the hand of Jewry in every development; he does so even where something perfectly natural has occurred which would have led to some sort of result, whether or not Jewry had had a hand in it.'[23]

In criticizing the cruder anti-Semitic outbursts, the SD memo-writers took no account of the author's Party seniority. The most notorious production from the Streicher camp, for instance, was a book for the young entitled *The Poison Pill* written by Ernst Hiemer, the editor of the *Stürmer*. It was the subject of much laudatory comment; Amman, the Party publisher, wrote: 'should be read by every German boy and girl'; Lutze, Chief of Staff of the SA: 'This is a unique book, well calculated to clarify the Jewish question'; Gauleiter Wächter: 'A guarantee that Germans will adopt a correct attitude to Jewry in future.'[24] The SD-Hauptamt, on the other hand, commented drily: 'Cannot agree with the view of most commentators; quite apart from its contents, the style of the book is by no means impeccable; in my view it is therefore unsuitable for children's education.'[25]

Unmistakable though their disquiet was, however, the SD élite gave little open expression to it until the summer of 1935 when Edler von Mildenstein, later an SS-Untersturmführer, began to formulate a Jewish policy peculiar to the SS. Born in Prague, von Mildenstein, though a qualified engineer, was at heart a globe-trotter to whom Heydrich's attention had been drawn by an article he had written for the Berlin newspaper *Der Angriff* describing a trip to Palestine and giving a reasoned view of the prospects of a Jewish state there.[26]

Von Mildenstein was no more anti-Jewish than his ham-fisted amanuensis Adolf Eichmann or Reinhard Höhn, Head of the SD Zentralabteilung; the latter, in fact, had published a book in 1929 in which he referred to anti-Semitism as a 'poisonous agitation'.[27] Von Mildenstein was friendly with a number of Zionist leaders and a regular attendant at Zionist Congresses; at one of these he had become convinced that emigration to Palestine was the only solution to the Jewish problem and he therefore established contact with the Zionists. He laboured under the delusion that their anti-Semitism could and would lead the Nazis to support emigration. Knowing that SS headquarters was largely opposed to the arbitrary and inconsistent Jewish policy pursued by the Party, he turned to the SS for help.

The Party had never been able to make up its mind how to put its anti-Semitism into practice. In *Mein Kampf* Hitler had not adumbrated any actual anti-Semitic legislation; in 1933 Achim Gercke, the Nazi racial expert, thought it 'premature from all points of view to work out plans'.[28] Alfred Rosenberg took refuge in the formula that the 'Jews must be recognized as a nation resident in Germany' but 'excluded from all positions of authority in politics, culture and industry.'[29]

SS-Standartenführer Dr Conti (later to become Reich Health Leader) even declared that the new Germany was averse to any form of racial hatred and that the Jews were 'not an inferior but a different race'.[30]

Many recent historians have formed the theory that the inconsistency of these Nazi statements was no more than cover for a centrally planned, phased and increasingly savage extermination campaign. Any attempt to read so much logic into the actions of the Third Reich, however, misses the point that the system of National-Socialist rule was inherently structureless and contradictory. These differing statements were in fact reflections of the views of the various anti-Semitic factions within the Party. There were at least three: first a 'Völkisch' group which desired to restrict Jewish influence in politics and culture but allow them almost unlimited freedom in the business world; among the leaders of this group were Dr Walther Gross, Head of the Party Racial Policy Office and Dr Bernhard Lösener, who occupied the Racial Desk in the Reich Ministry of the Interior. The second group consisted of the anti-Semitic mystics and racial theorists led by Alfred Rosenberg; the third, of the pornographic neurotic Jew-baiters such as Julius Streicher, later joined by Joseph Goebbels. The history of German Jewry's sufferings from 1933 onwards shows clearly which of the various groups was in the ascendant at the time.

During the first months after the Nazi seizure of power the régime's anti-Jewish measures were governed by the anti-Semitism of the Streicher group. The bloody attacks on the Jews of March 1933, the boycott of Jewish businesses on April 1st, the dismissals of Jewish officials, doctors and lawyers, the Aryanization of Jewish businesses and the exclusion of Jews from swimming pools, concert halls and art exhibitions – all these bore the unmistakable mark of Streicher.[31]

In 1934 the anti-Jewish terror eased. The running was taken up by somewhat more moderate anti-Semites such as Hans Frank, the Nazi head of the legal profession; he stated that the régime wished 'to introduce a certain limit on the further pursuit of its quarrel with the Jews'.[32] The Jews began to raise their heads once more; on May 9th, 1935 the *Völkischer Beobachter* reported that of the Jews who had fled from Germany, nearly 10,000 had returned.[33]

Inexorably, however, in 1935 the anti-Jewish pendulum swung back. Joseph Goebbels was now setting the pace. Speaking on June 29th, 1935 he screamed: 'We want no more Jews!' He then proceeded to fulminate against the 'stupid, absurd statements of middle-class intellectuals to the effect that the Jew is a human being'.[34] Gradually German Jewry's possibilities of existence shrank. Jewish citizens were assaulted on Berlin's Kurfürstendamm, Jews were forced to leave the Wehrmacht and the Labour Service, placards reading 'Jews not wanted' began to appear. All this culminated in the most shameful series of laws in German history, the Nuremberg Laws, classifying German Jews as a group of outcasts and declaring all intercourse between Jews and non-Jews a crime against the State.[35]

A year later, however (1936), the grip of the anti-Semites loosened once more; the grumbling anti-Jewish campaign of denigration continued but the dominant voice was now that of Göring, Head of the Four-Year Plan, and he was clearly hesitant to exclude the Jews from industry altogether (he was thought at one time to have been a member of the 'Völkisch' anti-Semitic group).

Von Mildenstein's object was to put an end to this interplay between the Party's anti-Semitic factions and solve the Jewish problem in the only way capable in his view of furnishing a reasonable and lasting settlement – Jewish emigration. There was nothing new about the idea but practical steps had invariably been blocked by the unwillingness of other countries to accept large numbers of Jews. SD headquarters' proposal, therefore, was that Germany's 503,000 Jews should be shipped off to the country which both the SS and the Zionists regarded as Jewry's home – Palestine (See Appendix 4).

But von Mildenstein's Palestine plan encountered a serious difficulty – only a minority of Germany's Jews showed any desire to go there; in 1933 only 19 per cent of Jewish emigrants from the Third Reich went to Palestine; a year later the figure had risen to the exceptional level of 38 per cent but then it fell rapidly once more – 36 per cent in 1935, 34 per cent in 1936, 16 per cent in 1937.[36] In spite of harassment, slander and terror the mass of German Jewry clung on in desperation; the *CV Zeitung*, the mouthpiece of the Central Union of German Citizens of the Jewish Persuasion, voiced the view: 'With dignity and courage we shall manage to endure in our own home country the pitiless measures taken by Germans against German Jews.'[37]

Alongside this majority, however, a small group of Zionist spokesmen was at work, and their object was to turn the minds of German Jewry away from their traditional German patriotism and direct them towards Palestine. Initially therefore they regarded the advent of National-Socialism as by no means a catastrophe; in their eyes it presented Zionism with a unique opportunity to fulfil its object, the return to a Jewish State and Jewish national consciousness. The rise of anti-Semitism in Germany exerted a curious fascination over the Zionists, for in it they saw the defeat of Westernized Jewry which, they considered, was striving to identify itself with the non-Jewish industrialized peoples. After the Nazi seizure of power the Zionist newspaper *Jüdische Rundschau* proclaimed on a note of triumph: 'An ideology has collapsed; we will not lament it but will think of the future.'[38]

Many were tempted to regard January 30th, 1933 as a favourable turning point in Jewish history – 'Jewry for the Jews' could become the watchword once more. This remark was to be found in an article entitled 'We Jews' written by a young Rabbi, Dr Joachim Prinz. (Hans Lamm, the historian of German Jewry under the Third Reich, described it as 'a curious, almost apologetic, interpretation of the anti-Semitic phenomenon'.) Prinz considered that 'there can be no further evasion of this Jewish problem; emancipation has forced the Jew to accept anonymity and deny his Jewish nationality'. But this, he continued, had not profited the Jews at all. 'Among those who nevertheless realized that a man was a Jew, this anonymity gave rise to the tensions generated by mistrust and the sense of contact with a foreigner.' What solution could there be to the Jewish tragedy other than to take the road to Palestine? Prinz continued: 'No subterfuge can save us now. In place of assimilation we desire to establish a new concept – recognition of the Jewish nation and Jewish race.'[39]

For the Jewish nationalists the prospect was tempting; under the pressure of German racialism and with its assistance the Zionist ideal might win that victory denied it in the humanitarian and democratic atmosphere of the Weimar republic. If both the Zionists and National-Socialists regarded race and nationhood as universally valid criteria, some common ground must be discoverable between the two. As early as June 13th, 1933, the *Jüdische Rundschau* had come out into the open: 'Zionism recognizes the existence of a Jewish problem and desires a far-reaching and constructive solution. For this purpose Zionism wishes to obtain the assistance of all peoples, whether pro- or anti-Jewish, because in its view, we are dealing here with a concrete rather than a sentimental problem, in the solution of which all peoples are interested.'[40]

At this point von Mildenstein stepped in. The task of the SD, he argued, was to turn the German-assimilated Jews back into 'conscious' Jews, to promote 'dissimilation' in order to awaken in the breasts of the largest possible number of Jews the urge to go to Palestine, the only country open at the time to large-scale Jewish immigration. Himmler seized on Mildenstein's plan and set him to work. Within the SD Hauptamt Mildenstein set up a Jewish desk (entitled II 112), a period of SS Jewish policy began in which, according to Hans Lamm, 'the adoption or affectation of a pro-Zionist attitude' was in order.[41]

The new SS policy made its first appearance in the columns of the *Schwarze Korps*; in place of the paper's anti-Jewish tirades references began to appear to the 'sensible, totally unsentimental Jew' of the Zionist movement. The paper forecast: 'The time cannot be far distant when Palestine will again be able to accept its sons who have been lost to it for over a thousand years. Our good wishes together with our official goodwill go with them.'[42]

Although Jewish emigration to Palestine was officially the responsibility of the Gestapo and the Reich Ministry of the Interior, the SD now began to force the pace. Between 1933 and 1937, 24,000 Jews had left for Palestine; the SD now increased its pressure upon those still willing to emigrate.[43] Von Mildenstein gave all possible support to the Zionist organization's re-training camps, where young Jews were trained for the farm work which they would have to do in Palestine's kibbutzim.[44] He kept close watch on the work of the Zionists, and maintained large-scale maps in his office showing the progress of Zionism among German Jewry.

The staff of Section II 112 in the SD Hauptamt regarded every Zionist success or failure as its own. With some pride they recorded that one of the results of the Nazi seizure of power had been 'to turn a section of

German Jewry back to Jewish nationalism'.[45] They noted with regret 'that a high proportion of ostensibly enthusiastic Zionists were only pseudo-Zionists, on whom the Zionist ideal has made no real impact'.[46] The SD's Zionist observers regarded the activities of the anti-Zionist Jews with suspicion; for instance the athletic association of the patriotic Reich League of Jewish Front-line Soldiers was said to 'dominate Jewish sport both numerically and by the results it achieves – a most unwelcome situation and further proof that the Zionist idea has not taken root among the majority of Jewish youth'.[47]

Among the observers of the Zionists was a young SS man named Adolf Eichmann. He had been born in 1906 in Solingen; his family had then moved to Upper Austria, where he had worked at the coal face, as a salesman of electrical goods, and as a commercial traveller in oil products; accidentally finding himself on the German side of the frontier, he served for a short while in the SS-Verfügungstruppe and then joined the SD. His SS superiors discovered him in a window bay of the Johannis Hall in the Wilhelmstrasse Palace (SD headquarters) occupied in sticking on the wall old seals from masonic lodges. He caught the eye by the ludicrously subservient manner with which he greeted any senior officer; his rule was to regard any SS commander as a superior being, and whenever an officer passed through the hall (and a good many did) he sprang to attention and clicked his heels.[48] Von Mildenstein could make good use of so zealous an assistant and Eichmann was asked whether he would like to work for Section II 112. He nodded stiffly; he could think of no reason why he should not work on the Jewish question though later he said: 'I would have said yes to anything to get away from sticking those seals on.'[49] Eichmann was detailed to the Jewish office.

Anti-Semitism had played no noticeable part in Eichmann's previous existence. He had had difficulty in making up his mind whether to join the SS or a masonic lodge; he did not really know what to think of the Jews. He had no more anti-Jewish prejudice than the next man – rather less, in fact; he had many Jewish acquaintances and a Jewish girlfriend; he owed his modest career in business to the good offices of Jews.[50] Nevertheless under Mildenstein's guidance he rapidly developed into an anti-Semitic expert and soon became an indispensable member of the Jewish section's staff. Von Mildenstein, however, whose unorthodox methods were disapproved of by Himmler's staff, resigned after 10 months in the SD Hauptamt and later joined the Foreign Ministry.[51]

In Section II 112 Eichmann was given the 'Zionist Organization' desk;[52] he trotted out Hebrew words and Zionist clichés so convincingly that rumour in the SD Hauptamt had it that Eichmann was an ex-Palestinian German with detailed knowledge of the country and its people.[53] In fact he had crammed himself with a few exiguous ideas by laborious nocturnal study of Theodor Herzl's *Der Judenstaat* and a Hebrew grammar.[54] Nevertheless this knowledge sufficed to give him the entrée to the Zionist organizations and parties and he soon produced a memorandum entitled *The Zionist World Organization*, issued in October 1936 as an SS pamphlet.[55] While drafting this *magnum opus* Eichmann and SS-Oberscharführer Herbert Hagen (a journalist who had succeeded von Mildenstein) realized for the first time the difficulty for which SS emigration policy was headed.

In fact the SS was faced with an ideological dilemma which it was never to resolve; on the one hand it wished to ship all Jews to Palestine; on the other, its hair stood on end at the prospect of a strong Jewish state. Eichmann's 1936 brochure contained this: 'The work of the "Zionist World Organization" carries with it a growing danger – a strong Jewish Palestine. For all time world Jewry will remain an enemy of Germany; a strong Jewish Palestine could be an important factor in its struggle.'[56] But the danger did not end there; Zionism threatened to challenge German anti-Semitism on its own ground and this it would do as soon as a Jewish state had been formed in Palestine and could take the German Jews under its protection. As Hagen saw it: 'It is axiomatic that Germany cannot approve the formation of such a monstrosity of a state; otherwise the day might come when all the stateless Jews in Germany would be given Palestinian citizenship, call themselves a minority and demand representation in the German Government.'[57]

Hagen and Eichmann were not prepared, as Ohlendorf was later, to concede minority status to the Jews;[58] they were left only with the vague hope that Britain, the mandatory power in Palestine, would never permit the formation of a Jewish state; but no one could be sure. The SD decided to place the Zionist organizations under much stricter surveillance.

Orders were issued that a sharp watch be kept upon the doings of the Zionist Union for Germany [Zionistische Vereinigung für Deutschland – ZVfD] and the Zionist Movement 'Hechaluz'. An SD internal order stated: 'The work of ZVfD Headquarters, No 10 Meinekestrasse, Berlin W, telephone number J 1 90 31, requires particularly strict vigilance.' In the case of Hechaluz, Section II 112 ordered: 'The work of the Hechaluz re-training camps and their subsidiary organizations is to be watched as closely as possible; nominal rolls of those attending the courses should be prepared. On conclusion of the courses it should be ascertained whether those attending, in so far as they are resident in the area of the Oberabschnitt, do in fact emigrate.'[59]

Mere control of the Zionists in Germany, however, did not satisfy Hagen and Eichmann. If they were really to estimate the chances of formation of a Jewish state, they had to force their way into the nerve centre of the Zionist movement.

The opportunity to do so came via an old friend of von Mildenstein. This was Otto von Bolschwingh, a Party member, an SD informer and an experienced salesman in the motor trade; he was in contact with a group of Palestinian Germans who lined their pockets by certain extra-mural intelligence activities. Among them was Dr Reichert, the German News Agency's Jerusalem correspondent.[60] Reichert, in turn, possessed contacts with one of the leaders of a secret Zionist organization, the Hagana, which (with the exception of the 'British Intelligence Service') fascinated the SD more than any other institution. Eichmann's comment on the Hagana in his 1936 brochure had been: 'All parties and formations included in the Zionist World Organization are kept under observation by a central counter-espionage and supervisory office which plays an extraordinarily important role in Jewish political life. This office is known as "Hagana" (translated – self-defence).' The Hagana was not only the Jewish settlers' military defence organization but, in addition, maintained a widespread espionage system.[61] On the headquarters staff of this secret army there was a chartered accountant named Feivel Polkes, born in Poland on September 11th, 1900, who drew considerable sums from Dr Reichert for occasional scraps of information.[62] He carried the rank of Commander in the Hagana and according to Hagen was responsible for 'running the entire self-defence organization of the Palestinian Jews'.[63]

Section II 112 evinced interest in the Hagana Commander and in February 1937 he journeyed to Berlin. On February 26th he and Eichmann met; on the first occasion Eichmann entertained him at the Traube restaurant near the zoo;[64] during the return match Polkes invited Eichmann to Palestine.[65] Polkes was, of course, no ordinary agent. His object, he explained to Eichmann, was to accelerate Jewish immigration into Palestine so that the Jews in their homeland might outnumber the Arabs; for this purpose he was already working with the British and French Secret Services and was only too willing to cooperate with Hitler's Germany.[66]

On June 17th, 1937 Eichmann's office noted: 'He [Polkes] was prepared among other things to give powerful support to German foreign policy interests in the Middle East ... on condition that German currency regulations were relaxed for Jews emigrating to Palestine.'[67] Gradually the SD realized that Polkes had not made the journey to Berlin on his own initiative – he was patently representing the immigration policy of the Hagana. Eichmann minuted: 'As a *quid pro quo* the following assurances could be given to Polkes: pressure would be exerted upon the German Jewish leaders to place an obligation upon all Jews emigrating from Germany to go to Palestine and not to go to any other country. Such a measure is completely in line with German interests and preparatory steps have already been taken by the Gestapa.'[68]

At 8.50 AM on September 26th, 1937 Eichmann and Hagen boarded a train and set off to crown these first cautious steps towards an SS-Hagana alliance.[69] Heydrich had given Eichmann permission to accept Polkes' invitation to Palestine.[70] Their cover was amateurish; Eichmann travelled as a correspondent of the *Berliner Tageblatt* and Hagen as a student.[71]

On October 2nd the *Romania* with the two SD men on board docked in Haifa, but here the Jews' Arab enemies put a spoke in the wheel of the Jews' German enemies. In late September the Arab nationalists had risen once more, forcing the Mandatory Power to declare a state of siege and close the frontiers of Palestine.[72] The meeting with Polkes had to take place in Cairo. Polkes declared himself satisfied with a monthly salary of £15 sterling and delivered his first batch of information.[73] Hagen recorded Polkes as expressing the opinion that 'in Jewish nationalist circles people were pleased with the radical German Jewish policy, since the strength of the Jewish population in Palestine would be so far increased thereby that in the foreseeable future the Jews could reckon upon numerical superiority over the Arabs in Palestine.'[74]

Eichmann rated the results of his Palestine journey as 'meagre';[75] Himmler and Heydrich, on the other hand, regarded their Zionist expert's work as so promising that six months later, after the move into Austria, they placed him in charge of the whole Jewish emigration problem. For the first time the SD was formally involved in the régime's Jewish policy. Eichmann, who had been promoted Untersturmführer in January 1938, was dispatched to Vienna as Jewish Adviser to the Inspector of the Sicherheitspolizei and SD;[76] his primary task was to promote Jewish emigration by all available methods.

Hitherto emigration had been more or less voluntary. Now, however, Eichmann brought Sicherheitspolizei pressure to bear and so harried the Jews that emigration became almost synonymous with deportation. Organization was his passion and he suddenly discovered that he was now entitled to plan and give orders. He had an idea. He wished to put an end to the crossing of wires between police, State and Party authorities, all of whom had some responsibility for Jewish emigration, and to concentrate all those concerned – both German authorities and Jewish representatives – into one organization. One office only should be responsible for the compulsory Jewish emigrants; in Eichmann's words 'it should be a conveyor belt – you put the first document followed by the other papers in at one end and out comes the passport at the other'.[77]

The conveyor belt took the form of the Central Office for Jewish Emigration, headed by Eichmann and located in an old Rothschild palace at 20–22 Prinz-Eugen-Strasse, Vienna. With him arrived a staff later to provide the ambassadors and couriers of genocide – the brothers Hans and Rolf Günther, Franz Novak, Alois and Anton Brunner, Erich Rajakovich, Stuschka, Hrosineck – all cold-blooded and indefatigable strategic planners for the expulsion of the Jews.[78]

Eichmann's new office used blackmail to give impetus to the Jewish exodus. The majority of Austria's 300,000 Jews were destitute and could not produce the minimum capital demanded by the receiving countries; the Nazi régime, on the other hand, was short of foreign currency and could provide no funds. The richer Jews were accordingly compelled to subsidize the exodus from their own resources.[79] Heydrich later explained the procedure: 'We worked it this way: through the Jewish community we extracted a certain amount of money from the rich Jews who wanted to emigrate . . . The problem was not to make the rich Jews leave but to get rid of the Jewish mob.'[80] Simultaneously Eichmann allowed the leaders of Austrian Jewry to travel abroad to obtain money for the emigration from Jewish aid organizations; in spring 1938, for instance, the American Joint Distribution Committee provided $100,000.[81]

Such methods enabled Eichmann to report record figures to Berlin. By late autumn 1938 his office had organized the emigration of 45,000 Austrian Jews; in a bare 18 months he had driven 150,000 Jews from their homes.[82] His merciless policy of compulsory emigration, however, could only succeed provided both the frontiers of the receiving countries and the coffers of the Jewish Aid Organizations remained open, and neither would do so unless the SS technocrats could keep the deportations running smoothly. The Party extremists now set out to sabotage this machinery; annoyed by the SD's intrusion into Jewish policy, they initiated a fresh anti-Jewish atrocity campaign in the summer of 1938.

The opening shots were fired by Julius Streicher's *Der Stürmer*. In increasingly strident tones the newspaper called for the exclusion of the Jews from the few positions still remaining to them in business and industry; it called on the countries of Europe to unite in the battle against the Jews and close their frontiers to 'World Enemy No 1' – the same frontiers which Eichmann was trying to keep open for his emigrants.

In vain Eichmann strove to change *Der Stürmer*'s line. At the end of May 1938 Hiemer, the editor, visited Vienna and Eichmann took him to task, explaining the SS emigration policy and giving him what he called 'a two-hour briefing'.[83] He arranged to visit Streicher in Nuremberg in order (as he noted in the file) 'to use the opportunity to bring about a different line on the part of *Der Stürmer*'.[84] His efforts were fruitless. A two-page article by Hiemer on Viennese Jewry showed Eichmann and Hagen 'how wrong we were in our opinion that we could bring about a change of heart by such methods'.[85]

On June 28th, 1938 Hagen wrote to Eichmann: 'Of all the crazy things – he [Hiemer] refers to the highly satisfactory fact that many Viennese Jews are returning to the Jewish faith and then adds the following in brackets "to a religion which recognizes the teachings of the Talmud as the supreme law! the Talmud which permits any crime against non-Jews!" When I see something like that, I tear my hair. What are they after! Perhaps *Der Stürmer* supports the radical solution – off with their heads to ensure that they cannot get the praiseworthy idea of admitting once again that they are Jews.'[86] Relations between Streicher and the SD became so bad that Heydrich ordered Eichmann to excuse himself from any further visit. Obersturmbannführer Six noted: 'C desires that for the moment Untersturmführer Eichmann should refuse any further invitation, saying that he has just gone on leave.'[87]

A few weeks later the opponents of the SS Jewish policy received a far more formidable reinforcement in the person of Goebbels, the Reich Propaganda Minister. He had long been waiting for an opportunity to lay hands on the régime's Jewish policy; his propaganda machine was already standing by to launch a new wave of anti-Semitic measures.

Goebbels' opportunity came when Polish and German anti-Jewish leaders began sniping at each other. On October 6th, 1938 the Polish Government issued a decree invalidating all Polish passports unless by the end of the month holders had had them franked with a special stamp obtainable only in Poland.[88] The Berlin Foreign Ministry at once suspected that the Warsaw Government's purpose was to rid themselves in one operation of the numerous Polish Jews resident in Germany. The reaction of the Nazi régime was typical. On October 28th Heydrich had 17,000 Polish Jews arrested, crammed into railway wagons and shipped to the Polish frontier. During the night of October 28th–29th these victims of the Third Reich's first mass deportation of Jews were driven across the frontier – against the muzzles of the Polish frontier troops' machine guns.[89]

Among those wandering between the German and Polish frontiers was a tailor from Hannover named Grunspan whose seventeen-year-old son heard of his father's plight while in Paris. On November 7th the latter bought himself a revolver and with five shots laid low Ernst vom Rath, Third Secretary in the German Embassy.[90] The murder of a German diplomat by a Jew was just what Goebbels had been waiting and hoping for. His propaganda machine began to operate. On November 8th the *Völkischer Beobachter* thundered: 'It is clear that the German people will draw its own conclusions from this new deed.'[91] In the Gaue of Kurhesse and Magdeburg-Anhalt Nazi-directed mobs were already gathering and looting Jewish shops.[92]

For Goebbels this was the moment. On November 9th each year Hitler's oldest comrades-in-arms forgathered in Munich's Old Town Hall to celebrate the Hitler Beer Cellar Putsch of 1923. Everyone of note in the Party would be there – and, Goebbels thought, one incendiary speech from him would suffice to launch the Party into the final battle against the Jews. Berlin's wits christened the sequel the 'Reichskristallnacht' [plate-glass night], a reference to the thousands of Jewish shop windows smashed that evening. It has gone down to history as a night of shame – men were officially ordered by their régime to carry out a pogrom.

In the context of the internal history of the Hitler régime, however, 'Kristallnacht' has another significance. It is a typical example of the Nazi system of rule. Like the Röhm affair and the Blomberg-Fritsch scandal, it illustrates how nonsensical, chaotic and structureless was the jungle which served as a system of government in the Führer state. An ironic and sinister sidelight on this episode is that the later mass murderers of Jews were opposed to Goebbels' *coup*. A factor in the action of November 9th, 1938, was internal Party indignation against the dominant role played by the SS in Jewish policy.[93] It was no accident that Himmler and Heydrich only heard of the action when it was well under way – under the control of the Reich Minister of Propaganda.

Goebbels had gone to Munich on November 9th with the definite purpose of inciting the 'old fighters' to initiate an anti-Jewish pogrom. Chance came to his assistance. The old Nazis had hardly sat down to dinner in the Town Hall when the news arrived that Ernst vom Rath had died of his wounds at 4.30 PM.[94] SS-Obergruppenführer Freiherr von Eberstein, the Police President of Munich, said in evidence: 'Hitler was very strongly affected by this and refused to speak as he had always done before.' Hitler and Goebbels put their heads together; they seemed to Eberstein to have a 'very serious discussion'.[95]

Undoubtedly this was the moment when the decision was taken. As Head of State Hitler could not be involved in the pogrom but Goebbels was only too willing to take control. The Dictator left the hall, whereupon Goebbels made a speech saying everything and nothing; the text has not survived but it must be reckoned as one of the masterpieces of National-Socialist demagogy. Baldur von Schirach, the Reich Youth Leader, later recalled that 'the speech was definitely of an inflammatory nature and one was free to assume from this speech that Goebbels intended to start some action'.[96] The speech was all things to all men; some took it as an instruction not to stand in the way of action against the Jews, others as an order actively to engineer a pogrom, still others as an invitation to set fire to synagogues and finally some as a command to hunt the Jews out of the city.[97]

But what had Goebbels actually said? Simply this: he, Goebbels, had informed the Führer that in certain areas anti-Jewish demonstrations had already taken place. The Führer had thereupon decided that such demonstrations were neither to be prepared nor organized by the Party; should they occur spontaneously, however, no action was to be taken to stop them.[98] This was all that Goebbels said. The 'old fighters', however, were used to reading between the lines of their leaders' speeches. The subsequent judgement of the Supreme Party Court read: 'All the Party leaders present took the verbal instructions of the Reich Propaganda Minister to mean that the Party must not outwardly appear to be the instigator of the demonstrations, though in reality it should organize and execute them.'[99]

The 'old fighters', the majority of whom were leaders of Party formations, rushed to their telephones and alert orders sped to their units all over the country. At last they could feel themselves masters of the Jewish problem; at last the Party could once more assert its right to be heard; at last the SA saw the moment approach when it could emerge from its shadowy existence and avenge itself for the Röhm affair. And the man in full control was Dr Joseph Goebbels. Tirelessly he dictated messages to the Party propaganda offices, telephones rang uninterruptedly and aides bustled in and out taking the Propaganda Minister's orders.

The official directors of National-Socialist Jewish policy, however, knew nothing of what was brewing. Göring, officially in charge of the Jewish problem, was on an overnight train to Berlin;[100] Himmler and his SS commanders were on the way to the SS recruits' oath-taking ceremony in front of the Feldherrnhalle;[101] Heydrich and his cronies were sitting in a room in the Four Seasons Hotel, Munich.[102] Werner Best, who had accompanied his master Heydrich to the traditional meeting of Nazi dignitaries, later stated that Heydrich was 'completely surprised' by Goebbels' action; 'I was with him when, only a few metres from the hotel where we were staying, a synagogue went up in flames.'[103]

Left: The Reichsführer-SS Heinrich Himmler on his appointment as Political Police Commander Bavaria
Right: Gruppenführer Heydrich, Reichsfachamtsleiter of Fencing

Reinhard Heydrich dining with Wilhelm Canaris, the head of the Abwehr

Himmler inspecting a prisoner-of-war camp

Ernst Röhm, Chief of Staff of the SS and Himmler in the funeral procession for the SS leader Seidel-Dithmarschen in 1934

Röhm and Himmler at an open-air service during a 'national' rally in Bad Harzburg in 1931

In the streets of Hamburg after the Nazi seizure of power. The placards read:
left 'I am the biggest swine in the place and cohabit only with Jews.'
right 'Being a Jewish lout, I take only German girls up to my room.'

Flemish volunteers of the Waffen-SS 'Flanders Legion' taking the oath to Hitler

A body being cremated in a concentration camp crematorium

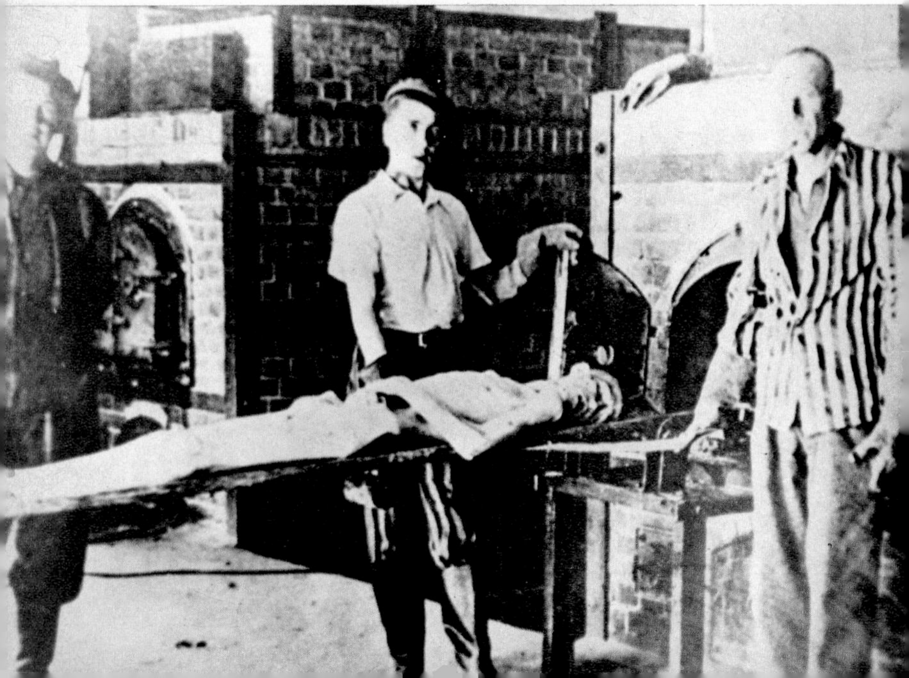

Recruiting for the Waffen-SS in Vienna

The Leibstandarte Adolf Hitler parading on January 30th, 1938, the fifth anniversary of the seizure of power

Parade of the SS on Hitler's 50th birthday

The kettledrummer of the Leibstandarte

'Ritual Festival' of the German 'People's Group' at Siebenbürgen

Himmler saluting the tomb of King Heinrich I at Quedlinburg on the thousandth anniversary of the king's death

SS horn-blowers at a 'Nordic musical festival', a feature of a 'Nordic Society' rally

SS Guard of Honour in front of the memorial in Munich to the casualties of December 9th, 1923

Sepp Dietrich, Commander of the Leibstandarte, collecting on 'National Solidarity' day

A 'traditional SS festival' with girls from the 'Faith and Beauty' organization, in honour of Italian visitors

Members of the Leibstandarte Adolf Hitler at a lecture on early German history in the Lecture Hall of the History Museum, Berlin

Education in early German history – explanation of the Germanic runes

The SS lining the streets on Hitler's birthday

Heydrich and his companions were still puzzling over the background to the assault on the synagogue when the riddle was solved by a telephone call from the Gestapo Leitstelle, Munich. At 11.15 PM the Duty Commander reported that he had just been informed by the Munich/Upper Bavaria Party Propaganda Office that Jewish pogroms had been ordered; the Gestapo was not to intervene to prevent them.[104] The Commander asked for orders but Heydrich did not know what to say. He immediately dispatched Gruppenführer Karl Wolff, the Head of the Reichsführer's Personal Staff, to find Himmler and tell him the news. It was 11.30 PM when Wolff found his master in Hitler's private apartments in the Outer Prinzregentenstrasse.[105]

No one could have appeared more astonished than Adolf Hitler. The unsuspecting Himmler later noted: 'When I questioned the Führer I had the impression that he knew nothing of these events.'[106] Nevertheless Hitler quickly recovered from his well-simulated surprise. He ordered the SS not to become involved in the action; the Gestapo was merely to secure Jewish property. Wolff passed on the order to Heydrich.[107] There is nothing to show what happened during the next few minutes – Himmler was meanwhile on the way to the Feldherrnhalle with Hitler. It may be assumed, however, that Heydrich instructed Gestapo Müller, who was still in Berlin, to alert all Gestapo offices. Heydrich himself whose information on the background to these events was extremely hazy, avoided giving detailed orders pending Himmler's return. He clearly wished to hear from his master what attitude the SS should adopt to Goebbels' coup. At 1 AM on November 10th Himmler finally arrived in the Four Seasons and issued his orders to Heydrich and the assembled Oberabschnitt Commanders of the Allgemeine SS.[108]

In an urgent teleprinter message to all Gestapo and SD offices Heydrich ordered: 'Jewish businesses and houses are not to be damaged or looted. The Police have been instructed to ensure that this order is carried out and to arrest looters.' In business quarters special care was to be taken 'that non-Jewish businesses are protected from damage under all circumstances' and 'foreign nationals, even if Jews, are not to be inconvenienced'.[109] No sooner had Himmler issued his orders, however, than fury with his enemy Goebbels became the uppermost thought in his mind. From the outset he had realized the implications of the November 9th pogrom: it was a shot across the bows of the rational SS Jewish policy; it was an attack upon the dominant position of the SS in all Jewish emigration questions; it was sabotage of the only solution of the Jewish question which the SS thought feasible. Himmler summoned Untersturmführer Luitpold Schallermeier, Wolff's personal assistant, and at 3 AM dictated to him a note for the file which he placed in a sealed envelope. Himmler pronounced: 'I presume that Goebbels in his lust for power and foolhardiness, which has struck me for some time, has sponsored this action at a time when the situation as regards foreign policy was at its worst.'[110]

Himmler was not the only SS leader to be infuriated by Goebbels' action. According to a non-political student friend, Otto Ohlendorf, later head of the Inland SD, was 'highly indignant' over the pogrom.[111] Gruppenführer Wolff admitted to the Indian politician Hafiz Khan that Germany had lost 'a moral battle';[112] von Eberstein, the Police President of Munich, forbade his SS units to have anything to do with the business and regarded the whole action as 'downright indecent'.[113] But – was this all that the SS did to register their protest? The answer is that it was – or very nearly. It never crossed the mind of any SS commander to go on strike and refuse to cooperate in an undertaking regarded as crazy by the SS Jewish experts. The SS paraded and did as it was told.

Rumour has it that Himmler did actually make a more effective gesture of protest. Popitz, the Prussian Minister of Finance, heard that Himmler had told Hitler that he was unable to obey the Führer's orders;[114] Günther Schmitt of the SS told the ex-Ambassador Ulrich von Hassell that the Reichsführer had 'disapproved of the pogrom and confined the Verfügungstruppe to barracks for two days'.[115] The only particle of truth in all this is that Himmler patiently collected evidence of the damage and looting perpetrated by Goebbels' mobs and then pointed out to the Dictator the stupidity of the entire affair, demanding the dismissal of his enemy from all his offices of State.

Once the bill of devastation had been compiled, Himmler prepared to do battle against Goebbels. On November 11th Heydrich produced preliminary totals: 815 business premises damaged, 29 warehouses demolished, 171 houses destroyed, 76 synagogues devastated and a further 191 set on fire; 36 Jews murdered, 36 severely wounded, 171 looters arrested.[116] The prudent Reichsführer-SS looked around for an ally against the mighty Propaganda Chief. He found such an ally in Göring, who also saw his own position in Jewish policy threatened by Goebbels.

As soon as the first reports of the pogrom arrived, Göring hurried to the Reich Chancellery and implored Hitler to stop the action forthwith.[117] His arguments were similar to those of Himmler – not of course of a humanitarian nature – the Head of the Four-Year Plan was interested only in material damage. 'I am sick of these demonstrations,' he said.[118] Hitler defended his Propaganda Minister but Göring pursued his campaign. When they next met he used 'very sharp words' to

Goebbels[119] and Himmler meanwhile produced yet another complaint in the hope of bringing Goebbels down. Goebbels' irresponsible pogrom, he said, had done the Reich irreparable harm abroad.[120]

The anti-Goebbels battle reached its height on November 14th. On that day Carl Burckhardt, the League of Nations Commissioner in Danzig, had requested an interview with the Minister of Propaganda; but on reaching the Ministry was told that Goebbels could only receive him later. Burckhardt soon found out why.[121] Lipski, the Polish Ambassador, told him that 'a spontaneous anti-Goebbels movement had taken place' in the Reich Cabinet; from an 'eye-witness source' Burckhardt learnt that 'the immediate dismissal of the Propaganda Minister had been demanded'.[122] On November 13th the battle was still undecided, but by the morning of the next day Hitler had opted for Goebbels. About 11 AM he drove down to Goebbels' private apartment and assured him of his continued confidence; that evening Berlin and the world learnt that Hitler had accompanied Goebbels to a play in the Schiller theatre.[123]

Burckhardt returned to Danzig puzzled. On arrival, however, he found a message to say that Himmler had called, asking him to go urgently to Berlin.[124] Himmler was still pursuing his anti-Goebbels battle and thought that capital was still to be made of the argument that damage had been done to German foreign policy. However, von Ribbentrop, the Foreign Minister, had lined up with Goebbels, assuring him that there was no question of any damage to the Reich's foreign-policy interests.[125] In this situation Burckhardt was the only man who might help, for he was known to be an energetic supporter of any Nazi leader whom he regarded as a potential restraining influence on Hitler's adventurist policy.

But when Burckhardt appeared in the Prinz-Albrecht-Strasse, Himmler had already given up the struggle. Instead of the Reichsführer-SS, Burckhardt was received by Gruppenführer Karl Wolff. His master was unfortunately sick, Wolff said; the events of the last few weeks had been a severe strain on Himmler's nerves. Nevertheless – the Reichsführer condemned the ruinous methods employed against the Jews. 'The internal situation in this country has become intolerable,' Wolff shouted; 'something must happen. Goebbels is responsible for it all; his influence upon the Führer is catastrophic. We had hoped to bring him down on the pretext of his propaganda during the Czech crisis and this time we definitely thought we were sure of success. But once more the Führer has saved him. This cannot continue; we shall have to act.'[126] As he returned to Danzig, Burckhardt was completely at sea, comforting himself with the thought that Himmler must after all be 'more astute than his appearance or his acts would lead one to think'.[127] He did not, of course, know that his invitation to Berlin was Himmler's last move in a battle already lost to Goebbels. Nevertheless Goebbels had to pay a high price for his survival. He remained in office but was forbidden to meddle further in the Jewish question. Hitler had decreed that Göring alone should carry responsibility in this field – should now 'concentrate the decisive steps under one central authority' as Göring put it in typical Nazi jargon.[128]

What this meant was increased pressure on German Jewry, complete exclusion of the Jews from industry and commerce, and above all increased emphasis on the SD's emigration policy. On January 24th, 1939 Göring issued an order to Heydrich that Jewish emigration should be promoted by all possible means. Expropriation of Jewish property and expulsion of Jews continued.[129]

Heydrich now set up in Germany a larger-scale replica of Eichmann's Austrian organization. A Reich Central Office for Jewish Emigration was created in Berlin; like its Vienna predecessor it included representatives both of the Reich Authorities and (compulsorily) of German Jewry (from the Reich Association of Jews in Germany); all were supposed to collaborate in the exodus of non-Aryans.[130] The office came under Heydrich in his capacity as Chief of the Sicherheitspolizei; he in turn nominated as Director SS-Standartenführer Heinrich Müller, Head of Abteilung II in the Gestapa.[131] New forms of pressure were brought to bear on the Jewish leaders to compel their people to emigrate.

The Reich Central Office demanded that the Jews of Berlin submit a daily list of 70 families prepared to emigrate and the Jewish representatives applied the spur; in summer 1938 they had already stated in public that 200,000 German Jews would have to go.[132] Heydrich's and Müller's offices were soon able to show record figures. In 1939 78,000 Jews left Germany compared with 40,000 in 1938.[133] Meanwhile Eichmann, who had by this time set up a further Office for Jewish Emigration in Prague, could record only 30,000 forced to emigrate from the Protectorate of Bohemia and Moravia.[134]

Heydrich's emigration experts missed no opportunity to ship Jews out of the country. They even established contact with a secret Zionist organization whose aim, like that of Eichmann and Hagen in their 1937 conversations with Feivel Polkes, was mass emigration of German Jews to Palestine. But the plan was thwarted by the British Mandatory Government. After the bloody incidents between Arabs, Jews and the Mandatory Power in autumn 1937, the British Government had adopted a policy of strict limitation of Jewish immigration into Palestine.[135]

The first regulations were issued in December 1937; in 1938 the British Government took new restrictive measures summarized in a British White Paper of May 17th, 1939, providing for the acceptance of 75,000 Jews into Palestine over the next five years. London, however, reserved the right to issue definite immigration quotas every six months covering the succeeding six months.[136] To fight England's new immigration policy, a Zionist Resistance Group was formed supported by the Hagana (of which Polkes, it will be remembered, was a member); the group was named Mossad le Aliyah Bet (Immigration Bureau); it had been formed in 1937 by Eliahu Golomb, the powerful Hagana leader.[137]

Throughout Europe Mossad set up a network of contact men to smuggle Jewish immigrants into Palestine in small ships. Its representatives combed every country of Europe for young Jews ready to accept the hard life of Palestine. Inevitably their eyes turned to the Third Reich as a priority target and Golomb's men were sufficiently hard-boiled to use even the SS as an instrument to obtain Jews for Palestine; in the words of the British journalists Jon and David Kimche, they were prepared to risk a 'pact with the devil'.

At about the time of 'Kristallnacht' two representatives of Mossad, Pino Ginzburg and Moshe Auerbach, journeyed to Adolf Hitler's Reich to offer the SS their assistance in the matter of Jewish emigration.[138] They were prepared to accelerate the Zionist re-education programme for Jews willing to emigrate, and to ship the Jews to Palestine. Emigration figures had already begun to fall and so the SD leapt at the idea and guaranteed Mossad their cooperation. Untersturmführer Hagen noted that 'receiving countries were raising increasing barriers against immigration'; on June 15th, 1939 he further recorded: 'Objects of German Jewish policy: promote emigration by all means available. Jewish immigration becoming more difficult. Promote all plans for emigration no matter whither.'[139]

The SD was prepared to show its gratitude to anyone ready to ship German Jews abroad but the SS could hardly be seen in open collusion with the Zionists. Ribbentrop's Foreign Ministry was opposed to any immigration into Palestine and the Party Foreign Organization was also intriguing against the incomprehensible SS policy which was apparently helping to build up a Jewish State. A Foreign Ministry circular issued on January 25th, 1939 to all German diplomatic missions and consulates summarized the views of the anti-Israel camp, saying that instead of promoting an 'internationally recognized increase of power' for world Jewry, the object of German policy must be continued 'fragmentation of Jewry'.[140]

The SD accordingly imposed a secret condition – under no circumstances must Palestine be given as the destination of Mossad's emigrant ships. The line-up was a curious one: the SD was now in league with the Zionists, first against the Foreign Ministry and Party radicals, and secondly against England – England had now reinforced her naval patrols off the Palestine coast and was stopping any illegal immigrant ship.

Nevertheless Pino Ginzburg moved into Zionist Headquarters in the Meinekestrasse, Berlin and began to assemble his convoys.[141] Heydrich's Emigration Office demanded that he organize 400 Jews per week for emigration and ship them to Palestine;[142] later the Office even engaged a German-Greek shipowner, but unfortunately his ships soon proved to be no better than miserable hulks.[143] Golomb, who was planning the operation from Palestine, therefore looked round for better means of transport; initially he had had to content himself with small boats carrying only 50 passengers; now he began to charter ships carrying 800 in spite of the fact that the Mossad office in Germany lacked the funds to pay for them.[144]

Despite these difficulties, in March 1939 Ginzburg managed to organize his first convoy. It consisted of 280 emigrants destined, according to the SD, for Mexico. They were joined by a further group from Vienna organized by Auerbach, and together they boarded the *Colorado* in the Yugoslav port of Susak. Off Corfu they were transhipped to the *Otrato*, another Mossad ship, and taken to Palestine.[145] Mossad's convoys now began to flow more smoothly and the number of immigrants began to rise. In summer 1939 the *Colorado* put to sea with a further 400 immigrants, followed shortly afterwards by the *Dora* from Holland with another 500.[146]

The British reacted strongly against this illegal immigration. The Admiralty stationed a destroyer flotilla off the coast of Palestine and ordered more intensive air reconnaissance; British Secret Service agents appeared in European ports to report the departure of immigrant ships.[147] On the diplomatic network Britain urged the Greek and Turkish Governments to refuse to accept refugee ships in their ports. The British Mandatory Government then proceeded to impose a 'penalty'; all quotas for Jewish immigration during the next six months were cancelled.[148] To a chorus of protest from the Opposition Malcolm MacDonald, Secretary of State for the Colonies, reported many a victory over the helpless immigrants. On July 21st, 1939 he told the Commons that British forces had arrested 3,507 illegal immigrants in two months. In June the *Astir* carrying 724 Jews was arrested. In August the Royal Navy stopped five ships carrying 297 German Jews, and shortly thereafter a further ship with 800 illegal immigrants on board.[149]

The more the British authorities reacted, however, the more forthcoming did Heydrich's Central Office become. In mid-summer he allowed Ginzburg to route his ships to Emden and Hamburg to enable emigrants to leave the country without trans-shipment; Ginzburg had already chartered four ships for October and under his new programme 10,000 Jews were to leave the country.[150]

At this point, however, Adolf Hitler's World War II terminated the uneasy partnership between SS and Zionism. The last real chance to save the Jews of Europe vanished amid the thunder of the guns and the scream of the Stukas.

The outbreak of war put an end to the SD's independent Jewish policy. The Jewish question now became the sole responsibility of the Gestapo, where officials were more prone to apply ruthless police-state standards to all political problems and to regard human beings as mere objects to be disposed of at any time by the all-embracing power of the State. The SD intellectuals of the Herbert Hagen type had at least attempted to see the Jewish question other than in black and white, to move towards a solution which, while conforming to National-Socialist dogma, bore some relation to reality. The men of the Gestapo, however, were barrack-square officials, brain-washed by Reinhard Heydrich, nurselings of the Führer cult and frequently bent on concealing their lack of National-Socialist fervour by an excess of zeal in their official duties; for them the Jewish question was simply an aspect of State security; the political leadership would decide how far they should or should not go.

The shining example of this drill-sergeant attitude of mind was Hauptsturmführer Adolf Eichmann, who was shortly to head the Gestapo version of Jewish policy. In October 1939, Gestapo Müller had relinquished his post as Director of the Reich Central Office for Jewish Emigration, proposing Eichmann as his successor.[151] Eichmann came unwillingly. 'I resisted,' he told his Israeli interrogator: 'I much preferred life in the provinces.'[152] But Eichmann would not have been Eichmann had he not dutifully clicked his heels and accepted his new assignment with alacrity. Obedience and acceptance of orders were the limits of his capabilities.

In some astonishment that the great SS-Oberführer Müller should think him worthy of notice, Eichmann rapidly climbed the Gestapo ladder. He was assigned to Amt IV (Gestapo) of the RSHA where he was given Desk IVD4 (Emigration and Evacuation). Later he was transferred to IVB4 (Jewish Affairs – Evacuation Affairs).[153] He summoned his former staffs from Vienna and Prague; he took a suite of rooms in a four-storey house at 116 Kurfürstenstrasse, Berlin; it had marble stairways and great halls – 'quite unsuitable for an office', as Eichmann said.[154] Little did he know that he had entered the headquarters of the future annihilation campaign.

The last and most grisly phase of the 'Final Solution' was of course still some way off; initially Eichmann imagined that he would be continuing his emigration policy. Gradually, however, even he perceived that extremely few Jewish applicants were reporting to the Kurfürstenstrasse – 'the general trend is listless, I must say'.[155] Nevertheless he clung to the emigration idea, for he knew of no other way to solve the Jewish problem. Then the Polish campaign seemed to him to offer an opportunity. He and SS-Brigadeführer Walter Stahlecker had already drafted a programme summarized by Eichmann in the words: 'Give the Jews land and then the whole problem is solved for them all.'[156]

The idea was to set up a Jewish reserve in the extreme eastern area of German-occupied Poland, where all Jews would be concentrated. Eichmann and Stahlecker went to Poland to look for an area of adequate size and they found it south-west of Lublin near the little town of Nisko on the San. Like a prophet viewing the promised land, Eichmann exclaimed: 'We saw a vast area; we saw the San, villages, markets and little towns – and we said to ourselves "This is it." Then we said to ourselves – "Why should we not re-settle the Poles and give the Jews a vast territory here?" '[157]

Without realizing it, Eichmann and Stahlecker had given SS Jewish policy a further inhuman twist. Gradually the concept became more pitiless and its methods less humane. Initially the Jews had been permitted to emigrate 'voluntarily', then emigration had become compulsory, now came intensive expulsion and deportation. Heydrich explained the new plan of campaign to his staff on September 21st, 1939; his orders were noted down in telegraphese: 'Jews into the towns as soon as possible; Jews out of the Reich to Poland; systematic evacuation of Jews from German areas by goods train.'[158]

In full this meant: the Jews in the ex-Polish areas annexed by Germany, together with those in German-occupied Poland, were to be concentrated in towns east of Cracow; 'councils of elders' or 'Jewish councils' were to be formed in the ghettos to be responsible later for administration of the proposed Jewish reserve.[159] In an express letter to the heads of the Einsatzgruppen responsible for concentrating the Jews in the East, Heydrich outlined the area of the proposed Jewish reserve: 'This decree does not apply to the area of Einsatzgruppe I, ie, the zone east of Cracow bounded by Polanico, Jaroslav, the new demarcation line and the former Slovak-Polish frontier. In this area, only summary registration arrangements need be made.'[160] In the centre of this area lay Nisko; this was Eichmann's future Jewish state.

Early in October the first train, carrying building materials, engineers and 4,000 settlers rounded up by the Sicherheitspolizei from the Jews of Czechoslovakia and Vienna, began to roll to Eichmann's Utopia in Nisko.[161] Then the Sicherheitspolizei set off on their great manhunt in the eastern territories. Ruthlessly the Jews were driven from their homes and hunted into the Government-General – 6,000 from Vienna and Moravska Ostrava, 87,000 from the so-called reincorporated territories.[162] Train after train carried the Jews into Eichmann's far-eastern land of dreams, there to meet an unknown fate.

Eichmann already saw himself as the future Governor of a Jewish state, lord of a Jewish settler people in the East. At this point unfortunately he was made aware of a basic principle of National-Socialist Jewish policy, which he described sadly as follows: 'Every office meddled in it; it became fashionable to have a hand in Jewish affairs.'[163] The first to 'meddle' was Hans Frank, the Governor-General. He disliked being the sole receptacle for Jewish refugees; in addition the ambitious SS Jewish policy upset the already precarious food situation in the Government-General; in fact Heydrich's and Eichmann's increasingly bold re-settlement plans threatened to destroy the economy of the country completely. So Frank rebelled against the evacuation policy. On February 12th, 1940 he went to Berlin and complained to Göring of the chaotic manner in which Jews were being shipped to the Government-General. His protest was successful. Göring ordered the transport of Jews to stop;[164] from the end of March Jews might only be dispatched to Poland with Frank's permission. And that permission was seldom given. Eichmann's dream collapsed and, on April 13th, 1940, the Jewish hutted town of Nisko was broken up.[165]

To take the place of this Jewish Paradise Lost in the East, the anti-Semitic Utopians thought up an even more fantastic plan. During the French campaign Nazi diplomats had toyed with the idea of settling all Europe's Jews on the East African island of Madagascar. The main protagonist of the plan was Franz Rademacher, a foreign service officer, Head of the Jewish Desk in the German Abteilung of the Foreign Ministry. France, he proposed, should cede Madagascar to Germany; under the peace treaty, all Frenchmen resident there should be re-settled and a 'giant ghetto for four million Jews created and placed under the Sicherheitspolizei'.[166] Eichmann seized on the idea and prepared learned theses which met with the approval of Himmler and Heydrich. He worked feverishly; with his friend Rajakovich, he travelled to the

Tropical Institute in Hamburg to discover the climatic conditions on this far-off island,[167] he dispatched Theodor Dannecke, one of his staff, to the French Ministry for the Colonies to obtain information about Madagascar.[168] He burrowed in history books and discovered that many politicians from Napoleon to Bonnet, the French Foreign Minister, had had the idea of shipping Jews to Madagascar.[169]

Talking to Dr Bernhard Lösener, a counsellor in the Reich Ministry of the Interior, he said that after the war some six million Jews would be sent to Madagascar under a five-year plan – in 'non-German shipping' of course. Lösener noted: 'The Jews were to be productively employed down there. Production and trade would be managed by German-run organizations. There would be purely German and purely Jewish businesses. The merchant bank plus the issue and transfer bank would be German. The trading bank and production organization would be Jewish.'[170]

Once more Eichmann could see himself as Governor-General of a Jewish State; his macabre dream caught the imagination even of the most senior dignitaries in the State and the SS. At a meeting with Mussolini on June 18th, 1940 Hitler declared: 'One could found a State of Israel in Madagascar.'[171] But once more Eichmann's promised land evaporated. He was soon at 'the critical point where I said to myself: no more beating about the bush; away with dreams; no good'.[172] In fact the Madagascar plan was the death spasm of the SS emigration policy, the end of an idea.

The sequel was genocide.

14

THE 'FINAL SOLUTION'

HITLER is recorded as saying to the Czechoslovak Foreign Minister, Chvalkovsky on January 21st, 1939: 'Our Jews will be destroyed';[1] nine days later he forecast that, if war came, 'the result would be, not the bolshevization of the world and therewith the victory of Jewry, but the annihilation of the Jewish race in Europe'.[2] Hitler was determined to make these statements come true; he was prepared to exterminate an entire people. We do not know exactly when he gave the order for the

'Final Solution of the Jewish Question'; no document reveals the date of this frightful decision.

There does exist, however, an order from Göring, dated July 31st, 1941, requesting Heydrich to 'send me, as soon as possible, a draft setting out details of the preliminary measures taken in the organization, technical and material fields for the achievement of the "Final Solution" which we seek.'[3] Hitler's basic order had thus been issued earlier than this. Krausnick, the historian, has summarized all that can be said with certainty concerning the genesis of the 'Final Solution' plan: 'What is certain is that the nearer Hitler's plan to overthrow Russia as the last possible enemy on the continent of Europe approached maturity, the more he became obsessed with the idea – with which he had been toying as a "final solution" for a long time – of wiping out the Jews in the territories under his control. It cannot have been later than March 1941, when he openly declared his intention of having the political commissars of the Red Army shot, that he issued his secret decree for the elimination of the Jews.'[4]

Documentary evidence exists for a sort of warning order: on March 3rd, 1941 Hitler dictated to General Alfred Jodl a general directive for the forthcoming war against the Soviet Union and this contained the first intimation that the Reichsführer-SS, Heinrich Himmler, would assume responsibility for the extermination of the Jewish/Bolshevist ruling class in the East. Jodl noted: 'The Bolshevist/Jewish intelligentsia must be eliminated as having been the "oppressor" of the people up to now.' The primary task was to liquidate 'all Bolshevist leaders or commissars,' if possible while still in the operations zone; 'the necessity for employment of organizations responsible to the Reichsführer-SS, in addition to the Field Security Police, to be examined with the Reichsführer'.[5]

The mass crime thereby announced was not, of course, openly stated. Initially Hitler referred 'only' to the annihilation of the Jewish Soviet ruling class; his directive contained not a syllable to show that in practice every Jew would be handed over to the extermination machine – following the Nazi Jew-baiters' obscure reasoning that Bolshevism was a typical manifestation of Jewry. Hitler tightened the SS murder screw only by degrees. At first only Jewish 'Bolshevist leaders' were to be exterminated but gradually the circle of victims widened; political functionaries were followed by the intelligentsia, the intelligentsia by all officials, officials by persons suspected of partisan activities – and finally the circle spread to every individual Jew.

The military knew nothing of this grisly process of inflation. As Hitler had indicated that the Reichsführer-SS would have a key role to play in the East, they were quite content to negotiate with Himmler and leave the dirty work to the SS, provided they did not infringe the Wehrmacht's prerogatives. On March 13th Major-General Eduard Wagner met Heydrich to find out how the RSHA proposed to cooperate in the East. Heydrich was only too willing to tell him: as in the Polish campaign, the Reichsführer-SS would use Einsatzgruppen of the Sicherheitspolizei and SD.[6]

The only point left undecided was the measure of control over the Einsatzgruppen to be exerted by the fighting formations. Heydrich deputed Gestapo Müller to negotiate with the Army High Command [Oberkommando des Heeres – OKH] but the uncouth Gestapo man behaved with such arrogance that discussions soon reached an impasse.[7] The military were forced, however, to reach some agreement with the police, for on March 20th Hitler assembled 200 senior Wehrmacht officers in the Reich Chancellery and explained to them that the eastern campaign would be the most barbaric of all time. 'Bolshevism is a sociological crime,' he screamed. 'We must abandon any thought of soldierly comradeship. Commissars and OGPU men are criminals and must be treated as such.'[8] Hitler's diatribe heralded the most criminal order in German military history, the notorious 'commissar order' which made it the duty of Army formation commanders to treat political and Secret-Service officers captured from the Red Army, not as soldiers, but as political criminals to be liquidated or handed over to the Sicherheitspolizei for execution. Since hardly a single general was prepared to offer active resistance to Hitler's ukase, the temptation was all the greater to leave the 'special treatment' to Himmler's police.[9]

The OKW international lawyers had just started drafting the commissar order when, on April 4th, Wagner sent Heydrich the draft of an agreement on the role of the Einsatzgruppen in the eastern campaign.[10] This showed that the Army was prepared to concede them well-nigh unrestricted activity. The draft proposed that in the Rear Army Area the Einsatzgruppen should be under orders of Armies 'for movement, rations and accommodation'; for disciplinary matters and technical instructions they would be under the RSHA. The Commander-in-Chief of an Army, however, might forbid action by the Einsatzgruppen in areas where this might have adverse effects upon operations. But from Heydrich's point of view the overriding sentence of the Wagner draft was 'The Sonderkommandos (or Einsatzgruppen) are authorized, within the framework of their task and on their own responsibility, to take executive measures affecting the civilian population.' Heydrich accepted Wagner's draft.[11] He could see the way clear for his murder squads.

Had the Army thereby given its agreement to wholesale murder of Jews by the Einsatzgruppen? The answer is that it had not. Everything goes to show that the military knew nothing of the 'Final Solution of the Jewish Question' as ordered by Hitler. Wagner set out the tasks of the Einsatzgruppen as follows: 'In the Rear Army Area: prior to the opening of operations, listing of certain concrete objects (material, archives, card indices of anti-German or anti-Government organizations, associations, groups, etc) and certain important individuals (leading émigrés, saboteurs, terrorists, etc)'; and 'in the communications zone: discovery and eradication of anti-German and anti-Government movements in so far as these do not form part of the enemy's armed forces, provision of general information to the commander of the communications zone regarding the political situation'.[12]

Here, in black and white, was an example of that curious military schizophrenia which so greatly facilitated the work of the Einsatzgruppen. The generals regarded Heydrich's shock troops as normal counter-espionage organizations designed to deal with the enemy in rear of the Front; at the same time, however, they did at least know that the Einsatzgruppen in the East had 'special tasks' of a political nature – but the military were only too glad to leave those 'special tasks' to Heydrich's people.[13]

Initially, the men of the Einsatzgruppen were similarly deceived; Heydrich thought it best to reveal the murder order to his thugs in small doses. When he summoned the RSHA Heads of Division in April 1941, he spoke only of a 'heavy task', explaining that the problem was to 'secure and pacify' the Russian area using Sicherheitspolizei and SD methods. He concluded: 'I need real men and hope that my Heads of Division will place themselves unreservedly at my disposal.'[14]

Arthur Nebe, the Head of the Kripo, stepped forward, clicked his heels and announced: 'Gruppenführer, you can count on me.' Heydrich nodded – the first Commander of an Einsatzgruppe had reported for duty before it had even been formed.[15] Nebe was later in touch with the Resistance and so his present-day friends have been at pains to explain why he thus volunteered. In his book *Wo ist Nebe?* (*Where is Nebe?*), for instance, Hans Bernd Gisevius attempts to show that Nebe only assumed command of an Einsatzgruppe after much cogitation and on the advice of the Beck-Goerdeler Resistance group.[16] Gisevius even attempts to clear his friend Nebe by saying that the 'outsize deeds of horror only occurred after he had returned' (from Russia).[17] The fact remains that Nebe's Einsatzgruppe reported the liquidation of 45,000 Jews.[18] Gisevius' arguments in fact are reminiscent of those of defence counsel during the Nuremberg War Crimes Trial which the US prosecutor, Robert Kempner, countered with the question: 'Tell me now, Mr Resistance Leader, how many Jews did you really have to liquidate in order to offend against humanity?'[19] In Nebe's case the truth was somewhat simpler – he thought that by promptly volunteering for duty in the East, he would earn himself the clasp to the Iron Cross First Class and curry favour with the unpredictable Heydrich. Initially, however, Nebe certainly did not know that 'employment in the East' was synonymous with the greatest mass murder in history.

Of the leaders of the Einsatzgruppen, Nebe was the only volunteer. Hardly one of them came of his own volition; each had cogent personal reasons for obeying Heydrich's order. Otto Ohlendorf, for instance, the Head of the Inland SD, did so because he was National-Socialism's cantankerous, argumentative 'knight of the holy grail' and had consequently fallen into disfavour with Himmler; he had twice refused to go to the East and now complied only to avoid the reproach of cowardice.[20] SS-Brigadeführer Walther Stahlecker was an opponent of Heydrich's who had transferred to the Foreign Ministry and hoped to win his way back into the RSHA by commanding an Einsatzgruppe.[21] SS-Brigadeführer Dr Otto Rasch was kicking his heels in the SD East Prussian Abschnitt, and thought that a display of zeal in the East would give him a chance of a senior appointment in the Berlin head office.[22]

Ironically enough, the only commanders actually to carry out murders of Jews in the East were the two unconventional Heads of Division in the RSHA, Nebe and Ohlendorf. Their colleagues were more expert at finding loopholes; Franz Six (Advance Commando Moscow) and Heinz Jost (Einsatzgruppe A) left their units after only a few weeks in the East;[23] the remaining Heads of Division – Heinrich Müller, Bruno Streckenbach, Walter Schellenberg and Dr Nockemann – contrived to avoid any call to SS heroism.

The middle-level commanders, the Sturmbannführer and Obersturmbannführer, were little more enthusiastic. Heydrich had selected them from all branches of the police organization and, in the majority of cases, they came from intellectual professions. The Jew-liquidators in fact were a curious collection – highly qualified academics, ministerial officials, lawyers and even a Protestant priest and an opera singer. Several availed themselves of some opportunity to leave the murder machine. Just as Six and Jost left their posts with or without the agreement of Heydrich, so some Einsatzkommando leaders such as Erwin Schulz or Karl Jäger avoided the worst consequences of the racial frenzy.[24] Even the lower levels sometimes managed to evade the murder order. SS-Oberscharführer Mathias Graf refused to take command of a sub-commando in Russia; he was arrested and returned to the Reich.[25] Professor Six testified: 'One could at any rate *try* to get posted away from an Einsatzgruppe. At least no one was shot for doing so.'[26]

Even among the rank and file, enthusiasm for Heydrich's duty in the East was so small that he had to comb all the Gestapo, Kripo and SD offices to obtain the necessary personnel. He was even compelled to scratch men out from the Ordnungspolizei and Waffen-SS; a Berlin Police battalion was disbanded and distributed by platoons to the individual Einsatzgruppen.[27]

Nevertheless, by May 1941 Heydrich had assembled some 3,000 men whom he formed into four Einsatzgruppen.[28] Stahlecker assumed command of Einsatzgruppe A which was to follow Army Group North through the Baltic States towards Leningrad; Nebe was in charge of Einsatzgruppe B attached to Army Group Centre, operating between the Baltic States and the Ukraine. Rasch commanded Einsatzgruppe C, operating in the west, north and east of Army Group South's area. Ohlendorf's Einsatzgruppe D was responsible for the southern part of Army Group South's zone between Bessarabia and the Crimea[29] (See Appendix 5).

An Einsatzgruppe was of approximately battalion strength; Einsatzgruppe A for example, consisted of 9 per cent Gestapo men, 3·5 per cent SD men, 4·1 per cent from the Kripo, 13·4 per cent from the Ordnungspolizei, 8·8 per cent foreign auxiliary police personnel and 34 per cent from the Waffen-SS; the remainder consisted of technical personnel and clerks.[30] The strength of an Einsatzgruppe varied between 990 men in Einsatzgruppe A and 500 men in Einsatzgruppe D.[31] Each Einsatzgruppe was divided into two sections – a number of Einsatzkommandos or Sonderkommandos of about 70–120 men each attached to an Army, and sub-commandos of about 20–30 men.[32]

In late May, Heydrich assembled the 120 Einsatzgruppe and Einsatzkommando leaders in the Frontier Police School at Pretsch on the Elbe near Wittenberg, to train for their annihilation campaign against the racial enemy.[33]

Slowly Heydrich increased the pressure of ideological indoctrination; RSHA instructors schooled the men in genocide, their language increasing in savagery. In mid-June Heydrich paraded the 3,000 men of the Einsatzgruppen near the little town of Duben on the Mulde. The Head of the Sicherheitspolizei and SD faced his murder brigade drawn up on three sides of a square. He made a vigorous speech, though he kept it vague, speaking only of a task which demanded 'unparalleled hardness'.[34]

Later, addressing the Einsatzgruppe commanders in the old baroque castle of Pretsch, he was more explicit. Even after the war Standartenführer Dr Walter Blume could still remember him saying that 'Judaism in the East is the source of Bolshevism and must therefore be wiped out in accordance with the Führer's aims.'[35] Years later Ohlendorf remembered that Heydrich had passed on to them a Führer order including the sentence that 'Communist functionaries and activists, Jews, gipsies, saboteurs and agents must basically be regarded as persons who, by their very existence, endanger the security of the troops and are therefore to be executed without further ado.'[36]

Did any of them revolt against this monstrous order? Did anyone refuse to obey the Dictator? Ohlendorf says that while in Pretsch, 'in the presence of all the assembled Einsatzgruppe and Sonderkommando commanders, I protested loud and clear against the order for mass execution'; nevertheless it was his duty 'to obey the orders of my Government, no matter whether I regarded them as moral or immoral'.[37]

Similarly Martin Sandberger, Commander of Sonderkommando 1A and a doctor of law, stated that, although he rejected the Führer's order, he considered it 'legal' since Hitler 'represented the supreme authority in the State'.[38] Blume argued similarly; he had wished to resist the Führer's order but 'for me an order from the Führer was the means of making war'.[39]

No one rebelled, everyone obeyed. The men of the Einsatzgruppen moved happily off to their assembly areas. On June 23rd, 1941, one day after Adolf Hitler had let loose his war on Russia, Heydrich's messengers of death set off on their most grisly adventure – 3,000 men hunting Russia's 5,000,000 Jews.[40]

The murderous impact of the Einsatzgruppen caught Russian Jewry totally unprepared. Only a few Jews in Russia, where anti-Semitism had been dormant under Stalin, realized the mortal danger represented by the German form of the disease; National-Socialist anti-Semitic atrocities had hardly been reported in the Russian Press. In some towns (in the Ukraine, for instance) the Jewish community compared Adolf Hitler's soldiers to those of the Kaiser in 1918 and welcomed the Germans as liberators. 'The Jews are remarkably ill-informed about our attitude towards them,' Sonderführer [Detachment Commander] Schröter reported from White Russia on July 12th, 1941.[41] The impact of Heydrich's murderers was all the more cruel as a result.

To gain the advantage of surprise, the Einsatzgruppen followed close behind the advancing troops, their main objectives being the Russian cities where over 90 per cent of Russian Jews were concentrated.[42] In many cases advanced detachments of the Einsatzgruppe had started their murderous task while fighting was still going on around the town. The RSHA murder commandos frequently entered alongside the German troops. Kovno, Yelgava, Riga and Reval fell to the Einsatzgruppen and the Army simultaneously; as they moved on Zhitomir the leading tanks were followed by three vehicles of Einsatzgruppe C; Einsatzkommando 4A occupied Kiev on the day the city fell (September 19th, 1941).[43]

No sooner had an Einsatzgruppe unit reached a town than a deadly stranglehold gripped the Jewish inhabitants claiming thousands upon thousands of victims day by day and hour by hour. For Heydrich's men no brutality was too base, no trick too mean, no barbarity too disgusting, if it allowed them to raise their grim tally. Report after report testified to the murderers' fanatical zeal – reports couched in cold, official language as if recording production figures for refrigerators or numbers of vermin destroyed.

Einsatzgruppe D report No 153: 'Area of the sub-commandos, primarily in smaller localities, reported cleared of Jews. During period covered by this report 3,176 Jews, 85 Partisans, 12 looters, 122 Communist functionaries shot. Total 79,276.'[44] Einsatzgruppe C report No 17: 'In accordance with RSHA instructions, liquidation of all State and Party functionaries undertaken in the above-named White Russian town. As regards Jews, orders similarly carried out.'[45] Report from Einsatzgruppe C: 'To deal with this situation [risk of epidemic] 1,107 adult Jews shot by Commando 4A and 661 Jewish adolescents by the Ukrainian militia. Up to September 6th, 1941, therefore, Sonderkommando 4A has dealt with 11,328 Jews in all.'[46]

Kill, kill, kill. Einsatzkommando 6: 'Of the remaining 30,000 approximately 10,000 were shot.'[47] Einsatzgruppe D: 'In the period covered by this report 2,010 persons were shot.'[48] Einsatzkommando 8: '... liquidated 113 Jews.'[49] Advanced detachment of Einsatzkommando 4A: '... in all 537 Jews (men, women and children) apprehended and liquidated.'[50] The news of the Einsatzgruppe horror spread like a forest fire. The further German troops penetrated into the interior of Soviet Russia, the more panic-stricken became the flight of Jews from towns in the path of the German advance. At last the Jews had been warned and the 'final solution' became more difficult to put into operation. One Einsatzkommando reported in vexation: 'Rumours from other areas regarding the shootings have made action considerably more difficult. Information regarding our action against the Jews is gradually filtering through via fugitive Jews, Russians and talkative German soldiers.'[51]

The manhunters developed numerous ingenious methods of catching their victims *en masse*; for instance: 'The Jews of the town were invited to present themselves at a certain spot for registration and subsequent accommodation in a camp. Some 34,000 reported, including women and children. After being stripped of their valuables and clothing all were killed, a task which demanded several days.'[52] In Kiev, Einsatzgruppe C reported: 'The Jewish population was invited by poster to present themselves for re-settlement. Although initially we had only counted on 5,000–6,000 Jews reporting, more than 30,000 Jews appeared; by a remarkably efficient piece of organization they were led to believe in the re-settlement story until shortly before their execution.'[53]

The cold, bureaucratic language of the reports naturally gave no indication of the atrocities attendant upon the annihilation of Russian Jewry. Even the accounts of independent eye-witnesses, however great their revulsion, cannot give a true picture of the horror – the calvaries of thousands and hundreds of thousands, the mass graves, the columns of naked women with babies in arms, the murderous scene at the edge of the grave.

In late July 1941 Major Rösler, commanding 528 Infantry Regiment, was alerted in his billet in Zhitomir by a wild fusillade of rifle fire. He went out to look and, climbing an embankment, came upon 'a picture of such barbaric horror that the effect upon anyone coming upon it unawares was both shattering and repellent'. Rösler was looking down into a pit in which were heaped innumerable bodies of Jews of all ages and both sexes; soldiers and civilians stood around staring curiously into it. He continued: 'In this grave lay, among others, an old man with a white beard clutching a cane in his left hand. Since this man, judging by his sporadic breathing, showed signs of life, I ordered one of the policemen to kill him. He smilingly replied: "I have already shot him seven times in the stomach. He can die on his own now".'[54]

Hearing of the approach of a murder commando, the Jews of one Russian village had gone into hiding; when the commando reached the village, the only person whom the SS men saw in the street was a woman with a baby in her arms. She refused to tell them where the Jews were hidden. One of the men snatched the baby from her, gripped it by the legs and smashed its head against a door. An SS man recalls: 'It went off with a bang like a bursting motor tyre. I shall never forget that sound as long as I live.' Beside herself, the woman gave away the hiding place.[55]

In Riga an SS man saw two Jews carrying a log of wood; calmly he pulled out his revolver and shot one of them, saying: 'One's enough for that job!'[56] Similarly while clearing a Latvian ghetto, an SS Commander, seeing sick Jews being carried out on litters, went from one to another with his service revolver and shot each in turn.[57]

Pitilessly the Einsatzgruppen decimated Russian Jewry. By winter 1941/42 they had reported the following figures for Jews liquidated: Einsatzgruppe A – 249,420, Einsatzgruppe B – 45,467, Einsatzgruppe C – 95,000, Einsatzgruppe D – 92,000, a total of almost half a million.[58]

The first wave of Einsatzgruppen was soon followed by a second batch of SS murderers. Behind the front a German civil administration had meanwhile been established under Alfred Rosenberg who was entitled 'Reich Minister for the Occupied Eastern Territories'; he was responsible for two Reich Commissariats known as 'Ostland' and 'Ukraine'; these were again sub-divided into 'Commissariats-General'. Within this civil administration the Reichsführer-SS occupied a key position, for a Führer decree of July 17th, 1941 had charged Himmler with 'police security in the newly occupied territories' and empowered him 'in discharging his responsibility to give instructions to the Reich Commissars'.[59] Himmler had already nominated HSSPF [Senior SS and Police commanders] as his principal representatives in Russia: Gruppenführer Hans Prützmann as HSSPF North in Riga, Gruppenführer Erich von dem Bach-Zelewski as HSSPF Centre in Minsk and Obergruppenführer Friedrich Jeckeln as HSSPF South in Kiev; in mid-1942 they were reinforced by Brigadeführer Gerret Korsemann as HSSPF Caucasus.[60]

Each of Himmler's senior representatives controlled a regiment of Ordnungspolizei and certain Waffen-SS units reinforced by half-trained 'auxiliary volunteers' from the Baltic States and the Ukraine. They were given liquidation tasks similar to those of the Einsatzgruppen – anything which the initial murder brigades had missed was to be steamrollered by the formations of the HSSPF. The latter soon started a sinister race with the Einsatzgruppen for numbers of Jews liquidated. The eventual winner turned out to be Jeckeln who, for the month of August 1941 alone, reported a total of 44,125 executions, primarily of Jews.[61]

Actual numbers of Jews killed by units under the HSSPF during the early months of the Eastern Campaign cannot be accurately established. It is known, however, that when the Einsatzgruppen and HSSPF formations suspended operations at the end of 1941 to gather strength for the following spring, 500,000 Jews had been murdered, 300,000 by the Einsatzgruppen.[62]

In spite of these 'successes' the SS murderers were now showing clear signs of exhaustion. In September, Schulz, a commando leader, had requested a posting;[63] Rasch, commanding an Einsatzgruppe, had gone on leave, never to return;[64] in November, Nebe had told his deputy,

Werner, that he was for home (Werner's comment was 'Arthur, if you can't go on, I'll release you'); Gisevius says that Nebe was 'a mere shadow of his former self, nerves on edge and depressed';[65] Nebe's driver, Köhn from the Kripo, had shot himself in horror at the anti-Jewish atrocities.[66]

A few months later even Himmler's most aggressive Eastern minion became a victim of the nightmare – von dem Bach-Zelewski was taken to the SS hospital in Hohenlychen, suffering from a nervous breakdown and congestion of the liver. Haunted by his guilt, he would pass his nights screaming, a prey to hallucinations. Dr Grawitz, the Head SS doctor, reported to Himmler: 'He is suffering particularly from hallucinations connected with the shootings of Jews which he himself carried out and with other grievous experiences in the East.'[67] When the doctor asked him why he was in such a state of fear, Bach-Zelewski growled: 'Thank God, I'm through with it. Don't you know what's happening in Russia? The entire Jewish people . . . is being exterminated there.'[68] Yet when Bach-Zelewski asked the Reichsführer whether the Jewish business in the East could not now be brought to an end, Himmler replied angrily: 'That is a Führer order. The Jews are the disseminators of Bolshevism . . . if you don't keep your nose out of the Jewish business, you'll see what'll happen to you!'[69]

Even so fanatical a devotee of the Führer's orders as Himmler must have known that, apart from a small minority of natural sadists and killers, the men of the Einsatzgruppen felt like Bach-Zelewski or Brigadeführer Eberhard Herf, Head of the SS Personnel Hauptamt, who wrote that he 'wished to get out of the East, since frankly I've had more than enough of it'.[70]

Nevertheless in the Einsatzgruppen a determined army of death had arisen, unparalleled even in the SS. Wholly dedicated to achievement, 'hardness' and camaraderie, they reached a degree of insensibility surpassed only by those soulless automata, the concentration-camp guards. Here was to be found the élite of that barbaric type of mankind, intoxicated by its own achievements, which Himmler exalted as the SS ideal; it was indeed an Order of the Death's Head, divorced from the world of ordinary mortals and from their moral standards, ready to undertake any mission ordered by its masters, and prisoner of a community claiming the sole right to decide the SS man's social and ethical standards. For years their leaders had drummed into the men now forming the Einsatzgruppen that they should yield themselves to the intoxication of power, that they should savour the élite's feeling of superiority and consider themselves a class above the mass of Party members, too superior to conform to their moral standards – they even claimed for themselves the right to turn men into subjects for biological laboratory experiments.

Both by background and training, therefore, no one could have been more eminently suited to be Jew-murderers than the men of the SS Order. Moreover the deeds demanded of them took place in the vast expanses of Russia, so far distant from their normal environment that the whole murder business seemed like a dream; those who had such a thing as a conscience could pretend, by a process of self-deception, that what occurred had never really taken place. Nevertheless – when faced individually with the thousand-fold murders they themselves had committed, all their façade of neo-German heroism collapsed. The Germanic knights shrank back into what they had always been – inflated mediocrities, carrying on their bestial handiwork with typical German self-pity, all the while thinking, with sentimental tears in their eyes, of their wives and children at home.

While mowing down their Jewish victims, the Einsatzgruppen believed that they were entitled to the sympathy of all good Aryans. 'The job is not a pretty one,' Gruppenführer Turner lamented, while proceeding with his murders in Serbia.[71] After the war Paul Blobel, leader of Einsatzkommando 4A, maintained that the real unfortunates were the liquidators themselves: 'The nervous strain was far heavier in the case of our men who carried out the executions than in that of their victims. From the psychological point of view they had a terrible time.'[72] Fritz Jacob, a Gendarmerie Commander, bewailed the fact that he had to do his Jew liquidations so far from home; his superior, Gruppenführer Querner, had to remind him of his duty to the fatherland; Jacob promised to do better: 'I thank you for your warning. We men of the new Germany must be hard with ourselves, even at the price of prolonged separation from our families.'[73]

Himmler was only too well aware of the sufferings of his little men. He seized every opportunity to encourage the men of his Einsatzgruppen – in sonorous pseudo-patriotic phraseology, calculated to make even the most cynical of his audience believe that he was participating in a mighty world plan, almost incomprehensible to human intelligence, designed to save the German people and the Nordic race.

For instance – 'Most of you will know what it means to see a hundred corpses – five hundred – a thousand – lying there. But seeing this thing through and nevertheless – apart from certain exceptions due to human infirmity – remaining decent, that is what has made us hard. This is a never-recorded and never-to-be-recorded page of glory in our history.'[74] His imagination worked overtime in the effort to prove that mass murder was no crime. Nevertheless his speeches to the SS liquidators contained an element of self-exculpation and self-justification; at a meeting of Reichsleiter and Gauleiter, Himmler declared that the 'Final Solution' had become 'the most painful question of my life'.[75]

Even to his closest collaborators, he attempted to minimize the true enormity of the Jewish massacres, using every known argument to cover up the horror of the reality. In his heart of hearts he felt himself an outcast like his minions, saw himself an object of world detestation – the daily flood of requests for mercy for individual Jews was there to prove it. 'Remember,' Himmler said to the Gauleiter, 'how many people, Party members included, send their precious plea for clemency to me or some other authority; they invariably say that all Jews are, of course, swine but that Mr So-and-so is the exception, a decent Jew who should not be touched. I have no hesitation in saying that the number of these requests and the number of differing opinions in Germany, leads one to conclude that there are more decent Jews than all the rest put together.'[76]

There was only one possible escape from this sense of isolation; he had to convince himself and his executioners in the East that they were the instruments of a great historical mission, the creators of a work surpassing all human comprehension. Himmler told Kersten: 'You oughtn't to look at things from such a limited and egotistical point of view; you have to consider the Germanic world as a whole . . . a man has to sacrifice himself.'[77] He was continually encouraging his Einsatzgruppen to fulfil their 'heavy task', continually speaking words of comfort to his unhappy executioners in the East: 'I can tell you that it is hideous and frightful for a German to have to see such things. It is so, and if we had not felt it to be hideous and frightful, we should not have been Germans. However hideous it may be, it has been necessary for us to do it and it will be necessary in many other cases.'[78]

Himmler toured the Einsatzgruppen to raise the sinking morale of his executioners. In Minsk he attended the execution of 200 Jews, but was so shocked by the disgusting scene that Wolff, the Head of his Personal Staff, barely managed to prevent him from collapsing. 'Good for him to see what he expects people to do,' Wolff commented.[79] Gradually Himmler recovered and began his pathetic 'must-see-it-through' speech. The men would no doubt have observed, he said, that he 'hated this bloody business', but everyone must do his duty, however hard it might be. He then told Nebe, the Head of the Einsatzgruppe, that a new method of killing must be found.[80] This incident heralded the birth of the gas vans.

The actual heads of the Einsatzgruppen, however, were not prepared to rely on Himmler's mealy-mouthed exhortations. The nightmare that haunted Ohlendoff, Rasch, Nebe and Stahlecker was a breakdown of discipline and a chain reaction starting from individual acts of sadism by uncontrolled Jew-murderers. Precise regulations were laid down to ensure that executions passed off rapidly and effectively before the executioners had time to realize what they were doing.[81]

In Einsatzgruppe D, Ohlendorf carried out his executions in military form. It was a macabre perversion of the military tradition, but the reasoning behind the policy was sound: the individual man of the Einsatzgruppe should have no contact with his victim; he should feel himself part of a unit acting as such and acting only on the orders of his superiors, thus eliminating any individual sense of guilt. No individual was allowed to do the shooting; moreover Ohlendorf took care to ensure that the victims remained calm up to the last minute, for any uproar carried with it the danger that the liquidators might start firing wildly into the crowd and running amok – and that prospect Ohlendorf feared more than a mass escape by the Jews. Anxiety on this score rather than any considerations of humanity caused Ohlendorf to recoil before the employment of gas vans. The gas vans, he thought, would produce 'an intolerable psychic burden' for his men, for after the execution they would have to unload the distorted bodies – frequently covered in excrement – and so the executioners would be brought face to face with what they had done – the moment of truth from which Ohlendorf wished to save them.[82]

Dr Otto Rasch, Head of Einsatzgruppe C, adopted other tactics. In his view every man of the Einsatzgruppe must partake of its collective guilt; scenes of horror witnessed in common were to form the bond of comradeship holding the unit together; collective blood guilt was to be its cement.[83] Rasch insisted that every man of his Einsatzgruppe take part in executions; the individual had to 'overcome himself'.[84] There was hardly a man in this Einsatzgruppe who did not suffer from 'the most horrible dreams', an eyewitness reported.[85] Nevertheless, the aim was achieved – the camaraderie of guilt.

Every trick of psychology was employed to ease the work of the executioners. Even terminology played its part. In the murderer's vocabulary the word murder did not appear; instead he used a picturesque selection of ostensibly innocent code words – 'special actions', 'special treatment', 'elimination', 'execution activity', 'cleansing', 're-settlement'. An unending stream of propaganda, even more intense in Russia than elsewhere, aimed to eradicate any feeling among the executioners that the Jew was a human being; he was presented as a pest or vermin.

Nevertheless for the leaders of the Einsatzgruppen even this ghastly propaganda was inadequate. The American historian Hilberg, who has made a meticulous study of the actions of the Einsatzgruppen, considers that 'psychological justifications were an essential part of the killing operations. If a proposed action could not be justified, it did not take place'.[86] The two most commonly used excuses were fear of epidemics and prevention of collaboration between the Jews and the enemy. In Balti, for instance, the Jews were liquidated for 'attacks' on German troops.[87] In Novoukrainka for 'encroachments',[88] in Kiev for 'arson' and in another town for 'a spirit of opposition'.[89]

In 1942 Himmler admitted to Mussolini: 'In Russia we had to shoot a considerable number of Jews, both men and women, since there even the women and older children were working as couriers for the partisans.' The Jews, he said, were 'everywhere primarily responsible for sabotage, espionage and resistance, as also for the formation of partisan bands'.[90]

The theory that all Jews were partisans ushered in a new annihilation programme, beginning in 1942. It was a clever idea, for murder of Jews could now take place under cover of the anti-partisan war and some of the responsibility for the greatest crime of the century therefore inevitably attached to the Wehrmacht.

On occasions the Army had used the Einsatzgruppen for military purposes such as dealing with scattered enemy units; from the outset, therefore, the commanders of the fighting formations were on good terms with Heydrich's people. Einsatzkommando 4B, for instance, reported: 'Armed forces, surprisingly, welcome hostility against Jews';[91] Einsatzgruppe A considered that relations with 4 Panzer Army were 'very close – yes, almost cordial'.[92] As a result of the Jewish panic and the partisans' early activities, the military urged the Einsatzgruppen to take more severe measures against the Jews. In September 1941 17th Army requested Einsatzkommando 4B to exterminate the Jews of Kremenchug; the reason was that Army cables in Kremenchug had been cut on three occasions by persons unknown.[93] In August XXX Corps Field Security Police requested a detachment of Einsatzkommando 10A to take action against the Jews in the Ukrainian town of Kodyma, because Captain Kramer of the Field Security Police had been told that the Jews were planning an attack on German Army units.[94]

Many (though not all) military men regarded the liquidation of Jews as nothing unusual. In an order of the day to the soldiers of 6th Army, for instance, Field-Marshal Walter von Reichenau told them that they were 'the standard-bearers of an inexorable popular concept' and so must have 'full comprehension for the necessity of this severe but justified atonement required from the Jewish sub-humans.'[95] The Army did indeed comprehend: 17th Army issued an order that when those responsible for acts of sabotage could not be traced, Jews, and particularly Jewish Komsomol members, were to be shot;[96] Einsatzgruppe A reported that by December 1941 Army Group Centre had liquidated 19,000 partisans and criminals, the majority of them Jews.[97] The Army in Russia even organized concentration camps. As a defence against partisan attacks, the Commanding General of XXX Corps decreed that hostages should be taken and held in a concentration camp. Infantry Regiment 124 maintained a concentration camp in Kutschuk Muskomja, Infantry Regiment 226 another in Warmutka and No 72 Anti-Tank Battalion yet another in Foros.[98]

The military reacted nervously to any signs of unrest among the Jews in their area. The local Commander of Dzhankoy, for instance, fearing an epidemic among the Jews in the concentration camp for which he was responsible, asked Einsatzgruppe D to liquidate all Jews in the camp; but the Einsatzgruppe was short of personnel and required much persuasion before it was prepared to help the Field Security Police to do his bidding.[99] So persistent were some of the military in their demands for additional liquidations that Sturmbannführer Lindow exclaimed indignantly that the Gestapo was not, after all, 'the Wehrmacht's hangman'.[100]

As the Russian-organized partisan war increased in intensity, the military became yet more eager to call in the Einsatzgruppen. When Halder, Chief-of-Staff of the Army, assembled Army commanders at Orscha in December 1941, they were unanimous in their praise of the Einsatzgruppen: 'These people are worth their weight in gold to us. They guarantee the security of our rear communications and so save us calling upon troops for this purpose.'[101]

The first to be used in the partisan war was Einsatzgruppe A. In late September 1941 Soviet partisans were sighted in the Leningrad area and by the end of the year most of Stahlecker's Einsatzgruppe was concentrated on the northern front for anti-partisan operations. Stahlecker himself was killed in the process early in March 1942.[102] Himmler was quick to seize the opportunity of using the partisan war as cover to step up his anti-Jewish campaign – in July 1941, after all, Hitler had said: 'This partisan war has some advantages for us; it enables us to wipe out everyone who opposes us.'[103]

Himmler camouflaged his army of executioners as a semi-military anti-partisan force, officially known as 'Anti-Partisan Formations'. The Einsatzgruppen turned themselves into static Sicherheitspolizei command posts, the Heads of Einsatzgruppen A and C becoming Befehlshaber (BdS) and the commanders of Einsatzkommandos

Kommandeure (KdS).[104] This heterogeneous army of anti-partisan units was later placed under a 'Chief of Anti-Partisan Formations' in the person of Bach-Zelewski; to them were added five regiments of Ordnungspolizei and the indigenous militia of the German-occupied eastern territories.[105] The overall strength by the end of 1942 was 14,953 Germans and 238,105 auxiliaries.[106]

Thus carefully camouflaged, the murderers returned to the attack, supported as occasion required by the Army and the Waffen-SS. Jeckeln, who had been transferred to the Northern Front as HSSPF, was the first to get going. In February and March 1942 he initiated an anti-Jew and anti-partisan operation known as 'Action Marsh Fever'. At the end of it he was able to report: 389 partisans killed, 1,274 persons shot on suspicion and 8,350 Jews liquidated.[107]

This combined operation was the forerunner of a series of murderous sweeps whereby, under cover of military necessity, Himmler continued his extermination of Jewry. No fewer than five major operations were initiated: the purpose of all of them was the annihilation of the Jewish people.[108] Simultaneously, the net was drawn tighter round those Jews who had not taken refuge with the partisans. The liquidators had driven the mass of the Jews into ghettos and concentration camps; in 'Ostland', for instance, 100,000 Jews were still alive, of whom 68,000 were in the towns.[109] A further deadly blow against them was in course of preparation.

The new extermination campaign was concentrated upon the White Russian Commissariat-General, re-christened 'White Ruthenia' by its new masters. Town after town was combed by the Police Battalions and Auxiliary Brigades; ghetto after ghetto fell to the liquidators' sub-machine-guns. The SS hierarchy, from HSSPF through BdS to KdS, could soon calculate when the last Jew in White Ruthenia would have disappeared. At exactly this moment, however, the civil administrators of the Reich Commissariat 'Ostland' developed a proprietary and protective instinct which turned even long-standing Nazis into opponents of the Thousand Year Reich's racial policy. Leading the revolt was one of the most corrupt of Party functionaries – Gauleiter Wilhelm Kube, Commissar General of White Ruthenia.

Like other Nazi colonial governors in the East, Kube based his case upon the fact that over-hasty anti-Jewish action by the SS and Police formations had ruined the country's economy. Even Stahlecker, after all, had once warned: 'The immediate removal of all Jews employed in industry is not possible, particularly not in the larger cities.'[110] The 'Final Solution' expert – in White Ruthenia, however, SS-Obersturmbannführer Dr Eduard Strauch, the KdS, continued his fanatical campaign of liquidation and the infuriated Kube found himself facing an economic breakdown in his area, for the White Russian Jews were the only craftsmen and skilled workers in the country. Even more vexing to Kube, however, was the fact that the SS commanders were descending upon the Jews without informing him beforehand. His anger had been at boiling point even before the latest offensive by the murder brigades.

On October 27th, 1941 the adjutant of No 11 Police Battalion reported to Carl, the Area Commissar in Slutsk, and told him that within the next few hours the Battalion would start liquidation of all Jews in the town.[111] Carl was horrified. He begged the Commander of the Police Battalion to leave the Jewish craftsmen alone, but the Police ignored his request. The Jews of Slutsk were exterminated. On October 30th Carl reported to Kube: 'The whole picture was worse than disgusting. With indescribable brutality, both German Police officials and, even more, the Lithuanian partisans (Auxiliary Police) herded the Jews out of their houses. Shots were to be heard all over the town and in some streets the bodies were piled high.' Carl and his staff had attempted to 'save what might be saved. On several occasions I had to drive German policemen and Lithuanian partisans out of business premises, literally revolver in hand'.[112]

Kube filed a case for undisciplined behaviour against the entire officer corps of No 11 Police Battalion.[113] Burying alive Jews who had been shot – as had happened in Slutsk – was a 'bottomless infamy', he wrote; 'law and order in White Ruthenia will not be established by such methods'.[114] Kube was a long-standing anti-Semite; in 1934 he had said: 'This plague virus must be exterminated.'[115] He would therefore not have objected to an 'orderly' annihilation of Russian Jewry and would have been quite prepared to participate, as he had done before, in the murder of Jews. Now, however, he suddenly saw thousands of Jews from Germany being deported to Minsk for killing;[116] when he saw German Jews arrive, his entire ideology collapsed – Kube the anti-Semite became Kube the protector of the Jews.

Kube discovered that among the German Jews were men who had served in the First World War and had been decorated. He compiled a list of their names and appealed to the RSHA as if the 'Final Solution of the Jewish Question' was something new to him. Heydrich retorted angrily that everything was in order; moreover 'in wartime there were far more important things to do than run around after a bunch of Jews, prepare time-wasting reports and thereby prevent my staff getting on with other and more important jobs'. He concluded: 'I find it regrettable that six and a half years after the issue of the Nuremberg Laws, I have to justify these measures.'[117]

But Kube refused to accept the situation. He placed the German Jews under his personal protection and as soon as he heard that the Sicherheitspolizei under Obersturmbannführer Strauch was preparing to take the final step, Kube hurried to see him. 'A remarkable attitude towards the Jewish question,' Strauch scoffed;[118] he had not yet realized that one of the Third Reich's first Gauleiters had turned into a protector of the Jews. The bottom was falling out of Strauch's world; he noted: 'I emphasized that it was incomprehensible to me why Germans should fall out over a few Jews. I was continually hearing myself and my men accused of barbarity and sadism whereas all I was doing was my duty.'[119] According to Strauch, Kube countered with: 'This sort of action was unworthy of a German or of the Germany of Kant and Goethe. The fact that Germany's reputation was falling all the world over was our [the SS] fault. Moreover, he said, it was quite true that my men actually took pleasure in these executions.'[120]

Kube did not confine himself, however, to public denunciation of the executioners as barbarians. He replaced the SS guards on his office building by SA men.[121] He was always on the spot if some SS man committed a crime against a Jew.[122] Wherever he could, he sabotaged the liquidation programme. March 1st, 1943, for instance, had been earmarked by Strauch for a killing operation in the Minsk ghetto; 5,000 Jews were ordered by the Sicherheitspolizei to assemble at a certain spot for 're-settlement'. The plan was betrayed by Kube. He arranged for the Jews to be warned of Strauch's real intentions, and all Jews employed in the General Commissariat Offices were told indirectly not to go into the ghetto. A furious Strauch found only a few Jews to arrest.[123] As a result riots took place and the Commissar General protested once more. Strauch reported: 'He cursed several of my men savagely, using expressions such as "filthy brute" and "you'll hear more of this." '[124]

Kube became such a thorn in Strauch's flesh that the latter alerted his superiors. Himmler complained to Rosenberg, the Minister for the East and Kube's ultimate superior, who promised to give Kube a warning.[125] But Kube refused to give way; he was reinforced in his attitude by the knowledge that Heinrich Lohse, the Reich Commissar for Ostland and therefore his immediate superior, loathed the SS as much as he did. When a further mass liquidation of Jews, camouflaged as anti-partisan operations (code word 'Major Undertaking Kottbus'), took place, Kube seized the opportunity for general criticism of the tactical methods used by SS formations. In a letter to Rosenberg he warned that the political repercussions of such operations would be 'devastating', since many of the Russians liquidated by the Police were not partisans at all but simply harmless peasants. 'If only 492 rifles are found on 4,500 enemy dead, that is, to my mind, proof that among those dead were numerous ordinary peasants,' Kube reported.[126] On June 18th, 1943, Lohse noted on Kube's report: 'What is Katyn* compared to this? Think of what would happen if the enemy found out about these things and made use of them! I suppose such propaganda would be ineffective because listeners and readers would simply refuse to believe such things.'[127]

The masters of the terror machine were at their wits' end to know how to get rid of their enemy in Minsk but finally Soviet partisans came to their aid: during the night of September 22nd, 1943 Wilhelm Kube was blown up by a bomb which his maid-servant, who was a partisan agent, had placed under his bed.[128] Himmler was radiant; Kube's death, he stated, was a blessing for the fatherland.[129]

He could afford to take it calmly, for the 'Final Solution' in Russia was drawing to a close. Much had been accomplished; of the 2·5 million Russian Jews unable to escape from the Germans, 900,000 had been liquidated.[130] It remained to erase the evidence before the Soviet armies began to drive back the German invaders; this was the task of Standartenführer Paul Blobel, commanding a special detachment known as 'Commando 1005'. He opened the mass graves and burnt the bodies on oil-soaked grids; any remaining bones were ground up in special machines.[131] The burning bodies illuminated an eerie scene, the final act of a perverted militarism unparalleled in the history of war.

Yet even before the extermination of Russian Jewry had ended, Himmler had issued the order for a new phase of mass murder. The mobile killing units were to turn into static death factories; bullets gave way to gas – the grisly era of the gas chambers had begun. The initiative had come from SS-Gruppenführer Arthur Greiser, Reichsstatthalter of Warthegau. In autumn 1941 he asked Himmler and Heydrich for an assignment of trained executioners to enable Wartheland to be 'cleared of Jews' as soon as possible. 100,000 Jews still remained in his area, he said, almost all in the Lodz ghetto, and they should be liquidated quickly.[132]

Himmler and Heydrich agreed at once and dispatched Hauptsturmführer Lange. Heydrich allotted him the most ghastly invention

* On entering the Soviet Union, German troops found the mass graves of some 10,000 Polish Officers at Katyn, near Smolensk; they had been murdered by the Russians in 1940.

at his disposal – the gas vans already used in Russia. By the end of the year Lange had set up near Lodz the first murder factory in human history. In the woods of Kulmhof (Chelmno), forty miles north-west of Lodz, he found an old, isolated mansion, ideally suited for his bestial task. In December 1941 Commander Lange set to work with three gas vans.[133]

In a steady stream the Jews were brought from Lodz to Kulmhof Station and carted off to the mansion; there they were made to strip and climb into a closed van, supposedly to go to the showers. But their journey was to death, not to a bath hut. As soon as the doors of the van were closed behind them, the exhaust gases were diverted into the van by a concealed pipe, killing the inmates. Meanwhile a special detachment of selected Jews stood ready to heave the dead into the waiting mass grave and to remove their last valuables. Such service earned many Jews the privilege of existing for a few weeks longer in the cellars of the mansion, waiting for the next convoy of unfortunates.[134] The system was a primitive one, however, and the liquidators often had trouble with it; the gassing did not always work. The RSHA service instructions said that all should be over in fifteen minutes, but often it lasted for hours. Sometimes a few of the victims were still alive when the doors of the death van were re-opened.[135]

Reports of the mass horrors in Kulmhof must have reached Müller in Gestapo Headquarters, for one day he summoned SS-Sturmbannführer Adolf Eichmann, his Jewish expert, and said to him: 'Go down there. I'd like to know what goes on.' Eichmann arrived at Lange's mansion and saw the Jews being driven into the death vans and carted off to the mass grave. Later he told his story: 'I followed the van and then came the most horrifying sight I've ever seen in my life. The van drew up alongside a long pit, the doors were opened and the bodies thrown out; the limbs were still supple, as if they were still alive. They were thrown into the pit. I saw a civilian pulling out teeth with a pair of pliers and then I took off. I rushed to my car and departed and said no more. I was through. I had had it. A white-coated doctor said I ought to look through the peephole and see what went on inside the vans. I refused. I couldn't. I couldn't speak. I had to get away. Frightful, I tell you. An inferno. Can't do it. I can't do it. That's what I told him [Müller].'[136]

The horrors of Kulmhof heralded a macabre competition between the technicians of murder and the gas specialists. The success of Lange's installation was the signal for the opening of a new chapter in the Final Solution, a new chapter of racial frenzy – the mass annihilation of Polish

Jewry, the largest group of Jewish people whom the Second World War had brought under the shadow of the swastika.

A 1931 Polish census had shown a total of 3,000,000 Jews, of whom 2,300,000 were in the German-occupied areas.[137] During the first months of the Nazi occupation, almost all had been forced into ghettos designated by Heydrich and initially intended as collecting points for the planned Jewish emigration; since the initiation of the Final Solution, however, they had turned into the anterooms of death. 'We must annihilate the Jews wherever we find them,' Hans Frank, Poland's Governor-General, shouted at his staff. 'We cannot shoot these Jews, we cannot poison them, but we can undertake operations which will somehow lead to successful annihilation in connexion with ... major measures.'[138]

The 'major measures' had already been thought out by Heinrich Himmler. He intended to solve the problem after his own fashion and the Kulmhof experiments had shown him the way: on the territory of what had once been Poland, both in the Government-General and in the so-called incorporated territories, a chain of death factories was to be set up, designed to eliminate every Jew in Poland and, indeed, in Europe. Chance had made available to him the necessary highly specialized executioners; even before Greiser had asked for assistance in the liquidation of 'his' Jews, another murder operation had just ended; it was known as 'Euthanasia' and had succeeded in killing 100,000 men who were either mentally handicapped or, in the Nazi phrase, 'unfit to live'.[139]

The Reichsführer-SS and Chief of the German Police had loaned to operation 'Euthanasia' a number of SS commanders and Criminal Police Officials, and they had proved to be experts in killing their victims with gas. Their leader was a self-opinionated ogre, Kriminaloberkommissar [Criminal Police Inspector] Christian Wirth; in the Führer's Chancellery, the headquarters of the euthanasia plan, he was regarded as head executioner.[140] In the death factories of the euthanasia project Wirth had been working with carbon monoxide gas which killed quickly and silently. When, early in 1942, Himmler asked Dr Ernst Grawitz, the SS Medical Officer-in-Chief, how one could most quickly liquidate one million Polish Jews, the Doctor referred him to Wirth, who was then out of a job.[141] Himmler summoned the gas expert and ordered him to continue his work in Poland. Shortly thereafter Wirth reported to Odilo Globocnik, the SSPF Lublin, whom Himmler had commissioned to liquidate the Jews ('Operation Reinhard').[142] Wirth set to work.

Wirth, the specialist, regarded Lange as a mere bungling amateur.

Instead of the Kulmhof-type mobile gas chambers he constructed static chambers into which he piped exhaust gases from diesel engines. The death chambers masqueraded as 'inhalation and bath rooms'. An observer noted that the system of death chambers looked somewhat like 'a sort of bath house' with 'geraniums, then a little stairway and then, on each side, three rooms 16 feet × 16 feet × 6 feet with wooden doors like a garage. The rear wall was formed by large wooden folding doors. As a "thoughtful little witticism" a Star of David was painted on the roof.'[143] Around these murder installations Wirth constructed the normal trappings of National-Socialist concentration camps – huts, parade grounds, barbed wire and more barbed wire. A chain of these extermination camps soon extended along the river Bug, all, with the exception of the Lublin camp, under SS-Brigadeführer Globocnik. One after another the death factories sprang up. The first of Wirth's installations opened on March 17th, 1942 – Belzec Camp on the Lublin-Lwow railway; it was equipped with six gas chambers and could deal with 15,000 men a day.[144] It was followed in April by Sobibor Camp, near the frontier of the Ukraine Reich Commissariat; its maximum output was 20,000 persons a day.[145] Three months later Treblinka appeared, seventy-five miles north-east of Warsaw; this was Wirth's largest camp, equipped with thirty gas chambers and capable of dealing with 25,000 men a day.[146] Finally in autumn 1942 a set of gas chambers was added to the existing Lublin Concentration Camp, known after the war as Maidanek.[147] Wirth was now in technical control of all SS extermination installations on Polish territory.[148] He was continually raising the death figures, testimony to a ghastly efficiency which earned him the title of uncrowned king of Poland's Jew liquidators.

Meanwhile in the eerie extermination-camp world competitors appeared with their eyes on Wirth's position. Competition came primarily from Auschwitz in Upper Silesia, the largest concentration camp in the German-occupied East and also designated as an extermination factory; there the staff was determined to discover new methods to topple the gas expert, Wirth, from his lonely pedestal. The Commander of the Auschwitz protective custody camp put his Treblinka rival in the shade by discovering a new killing agent, entirely compatible with the theory that murdering Jews was equivalent to pest control; this was the prussic acid gas, Zyklon B, sold on the market as an anti-vermin substance by Degesch [Deutsche Gesellschaft für Schädlingsbekämpfung GmbH – German Pest Control Company Limited].[149] Zyklon B was better than Wirth's gas in that the operator, provided he was protected by a gas mask, had only to open the tin and scatter the contents – and in a few minutes the victims were dead. Wirth's process took much longer.[150]

A number of SS leaders got together to topple Wirth from his throne. In August 1942 SS-Obersturmführer Kurt Gerstein, who was in the prussic-acid trade, together with Rolf Günther, Eichmann's No 2, appeared in Belzec Camp to put Wirth's methods to the test. Gerstein later wrote up his experiences:[151]

> The train arrives; 200 Ukrainians fling open the doors and hunt the people out of the trucks with ox-hide whips. Instructions come through the loudspeaker: strip completely, including artificial limbs, spectacles, etc. Then the women and girls go off to the barber, who, with two or three strokes of his shears, cuts off all their hair and stuffs it into a potato sack. Then the procession starts, an extremely pretty girl in the lead. So they move down the alleyway, all naked, men, women and children, artificial limbs gone ... They mount the steps, hesitate, and enter the death chambers. The majority say not a word. One Jewess, aged about forty, eyes blazing, calls down upon the murderers the blood which is being shed here. She gets five or six strokes of the whip across the face and disappears into the chamber like the rest. The chambers fill up, packed tight – that's Wirth's order. People are treading on each other's toes ... at last I understand why the whole set-up is known as the Heckenholt system. Heckenholt is a little technician who drives the diesel motor and also constructed the installations. The victims are to be killed by the diesel's exhaust gases.'

The start of the motor, however, was Wirth's most humiliating moment; the engine refused to fire. Gerstein took out a stop-watch and measured the extent of Wirth's defeat in seconds, in minutes, in hours. 'Wirth arrives. He is clearly extremely embarrassed that this should happen just on the day when I'm here. Yes, indeed! I can see the whole thing! And I wait. My stop-watch ticks faithfully on – 50 minutes 7 seconds and still the diesel won't start! The men in the gas chambers are waiting. In vain! One can hear them sobbing and weeping ... Wirth strikes Heckenholt's Ukrainian assistant twelve or thirteen times across the face with his riding crop. After 2 hours and 49 minutes – measured exactly on the stop-watch – the diesel starts ... a further 25 minutes pass. Correct – many are dead. One can look through the peephole when the electric light in the gas chambers is on for a moment. A few are still alive after 28 minutes. Finally after 32 minutes they're all dead. Men of the labour detachment open the wooden doors from the other side. Jammed in the chambers, the dead are still standing there like marble pillars. There's no room for them to fall or even bend over.'[152]

The Zyklon B enthusiasts such as Günther had seen enough and Wirth had lost his leading position as a technician of murder. From this moment a state of war existed between Auschwitz and Wirth's camps. The pest-control method was eventually introduced into Auschwitz and no one was happier than Rudolf Höss, the Commandant. In his autobiography he says: 'I must admit that the gassing process had a calming effect upon me. I always had a horror of the shootings, thinking of the number of people, the women and children. I was relieved that we were all to be spared these blood-baths.'[153]

High-pressure extermination of Polish Jewry could now begin. Himmler gave the green light. The Ordnungspolizei, foreign auxiliaries and the German-organized Jewish Law and Order Service drove the Jews from the ghettos to the six extermination camps. On July 19th, 1942 Himmler wrote to Obergruppenführer Krüger, HSSPF East in Cracow: 'I command that the re-settlement of the entire Jewish population of the Government-General shall have been carried out and completed by December 31st, 1942.'[154] The miserable processions of victims were already on the way to the murder factories and one ghetto after another was already being emptied when, once again, an outside authority threatened to bring the mills of death to a halt. For the second time in the short history of German occupation of Poland, the Wehrmacht rose in wrath against the lunacy of the Final Solution.

Unlike their comrades in Russia, many of whom had been unnerved by the partisan war, the German Army in Poland set out to protect the Jews, come what might. They deployed an argument calculated to impress even the racial fanatics – the closing phase of the Final Solution would deprive the Wehrmacht of the Jewish labour essential to keep the armaments industry in the East functioning. The objection had already been foreseen by Heydrich. On October 4th, 1941 he had stated that there was a risk 'that primarily on economic grounds many a claim will be made that the Jews are an indispensable labour force and that no one will make any effort to obtain alternative labour to take the place of the Jews.'[155] General Curt Freiherr von Gienanth, C-in-C of the Polish Wehrkreis, and Colonel Freter, the Head of the Warsaw Armaments Commission, were determined to do exactly what Heydrich had anticipated.

They were under no illusion that the so-called 're-settlement' of the Jews was, in fact, cover for a murder campaign; Globocnik, after all, had said: 'This entire matter is one of the most secret things with which we have to deal at the present time.'[156] In July Captain Friedrich Wilhelm Hassler asked Colonel Freter whether it was true that the Jews were to be liquidated. Freter said nothing, but Hassler persisted: 'What is happening here is legally a crime and from a Christian point of view, a sin. One day there will be a reckoning.' Freter pointed out to him that he had three alternatives: he could express his opinion openly but must then reckon that his life would be forfeit; he could report sick; or he could stay with him, Freter, and help the Armaments Commission to do what it could for the Jews. Captain Hassler stayed.[157]

Krüger, the HSSPF, realizing what the military were up to, got a jump ahead of them. He agreed with the OKW Armaments Inspectorate that they might temporarily retain their Jewish labour force but that the Jews employed in factories or camps must be quartered in barracks under SS command.[158] This, Krüger hoped, would gradually deprive the military of any authority over the Jews. Even these modest concessions, however, were too much for Himmler, who was continually urging Krüger not to give an inch to the Wehrmacht. He also brought pressure to bear against the military in another quarter, urging OKW to order the soldiers in the Government-General to pipe down.[159]

As so often happened in the case of political disagreements, Field-Marshal Keitel of OKW let his officers down. While the Armaments Commission in the Government-General was struggling tenaciously for every Jew, on September 5th, 1942 Keitel issued an order that all Jewish labour was forthwith to be replaced by Poles.[160] Von Gienanth angrily turned against the yes-man in the Führer's headquarters. On September 18th he dispatched a memorandum to the OKW Operations Staff setting out his view, supported by statistics, that 'immediate removal of the Jews would lead to a considerable reduction of Germany's war efforts; supplies to the front and to the troops in the Government-General would be held up – at least for the time being.'[161]

Gienanth continued: 'It is requested that Jews working in industry be exempted from evacuation till then [completion of certain important production tasks].'[162]

For better or for worse Keitel was forced to show Gienanth's memorandum to Himmler. His reaction was one of fury against the military saboteurs of his new annihilation programme. On October 2nd he thundered: 'I have ordered that ruthless steps be taken against all those who think that they can use the interests of war industry to cloak their real intention to protect the Jews and their own business affairs.'[163] The intimidated Keitel hardly waited for Himmler's reaction but, via his staff, cracked down on the rebels in Poland. General von Gienanth was relieved at once.[164] On October 10th a teleprinter message from the OKW operations staff reiterated the decision: 'OKW is in entire agreement with the principle laid down by the Reichsführer-SS that all Jews employed by the armed forces in auxiliary military services and in the war industries are to be replaced immediately by Aryan workers.'[165]

So the Wehrmacht had capitulated. Between October 13th and 15th, 1942, the Communications Zone commander in the Government-General was ordered to dismiss his Jewish labour. As a result, in the words of the historian Hanns von Krannhals, 'All Jews in the Government-General were delivered into the hands of the SS.'[166] The murderers could now go on their way unhindered. Hour by hour, day by day, week by week, the SS and their local auxiliaries drove Jews into the gas chambers, beating, tormenting, insulting and torturing.

The death factories in the East ground remorselessly on, every hour and every victim adding to the list of German crime. Even today the figures from the murder factories stagger the imagination; in Kulmhof 152,000 Jews died, in Belzec 600,000, in Sobibor 250,000, in Treblinka 700,000, in Maidanek 200,000, and in Auschwitz over 1,000,000[167]. Hundreds of thousands of Jews were overwhelmed by a murderous wave of unbridled sadism. Gomerski, the Sobibor executioner, used an iron water pot to batter in the skulls of Jews who had fallen sick during the journey;[168] children's heads were smashed against barrack walls; these savages in SS uniform were capable of every form of infamy in their 'extramural activities'.[169]

A prisoner named Max Kasner was a disposer of bodies in Auschwitz. One day he was ordered to the courtyard of one of the blocks: 'On the left were lying some 70 dead women, real good-lookers too – even in death. All their breasts were cut off and from all the fleshy parts, such as the thigh all the meat was removed with great, deep incisions. The courtyard sloped steeply and the drain became blocked with blood; we were wading in blood way above our ankles.'[170] Every day came reports of guards firing on children. Professor Ludwik Hirszfeld of Warsaw saw 'a little girl trying to slip past the guard. The sentry called, slowly he took his rifle from his shoulder. The child was clasping his boots and begging for mercy. The sentry laughed and said: "You needn't die but you won't do any more smuggling". Then he shot the child through the feet. Both had to be amputated later.'[171]

In the evenings Oberscharführer Oswald Kaduk, the Auschwitz Rapportführer [NCO in charge], would hunt a number of prisoners into the bath house and there make them jump, stark naked, over a walking stick which he held about two feet six inches high. Anyone who stumbled was directed to the left and then taken off to be gassed. If too many prisoners managed to do the jump, Kaduk would beat them till they fell.[172] Lederer, one of the prisoners, described 'another of Kaduk's specialities: at the so-called louse inspections, any prisoner on whom a louse was found was made to lie on the floor and a pole, used for carrying the food containers, was placed across his throat; Kaduk would then place a foot on either end and rock from side to side until the prisoner was dead.'[173]

Kurt Franz, Commandant of Treblinka, regularly set Bari, his savage Saint Bernard, on to prisoners. Jews were hung head downwards from a gallows and mangled by the dog. Franz maintained an execution spot camouflaged as a hospital; attached to it was a grave 25 feet × 10 feet in which a fire was kept burning continuously. Every day Franz would hold three roll calls and on each occasion select ten Jews to be liquidated by him personally. Jakubowicz, one of the prisoners, reported that he 'drove them into the hospital with a whip and shot them there. It was an automatic procedure – shoot and into the grave – shoot and into the grave.'[174]

Oberscharführer Wilhelm Boger of the Auschwitz Political Section invented the most notorious torture known to Europe's largest extermination camp; after the war Oberscharführer Perry Broad described it as follows: 'Two tables were placed side by side about a yard apart. The victim was made to sit on the floor, draw up his knees and place his hands in front of them. His wrists were then tied together. A large pole was then slipped between his elbows and knees and its ends placed upon the tables. He was now hanging helpless between the tables, head downwards. He was then beaten upon the buttocks and the soles of his bare feet. The blows were so violent that the victims almost described a full circle. Whenever the buttocks were in the right position another blow would descend with all Boger's force. If the screams became too ear-splitting, the sadist would put a gas-mask on him . . . after about fifteen minutes, the victim's convulsions would cease. He could not speak. His trousers were dark red and blood was dripping on the floor. Finally his head hung down motionless; he had fainted. But this did not shake Boger at all. With a knowing grin he would take a flask of smelling salts from his pocket and hold it to the prisoner's nose. After a few minutes, the man would regain consciousness.'[175]

As a result of such bestialities, the post-war world has been misled into the belief that sadism was at the root of the mass-extermination phenomenon. The executioners are depicted as dehumanized beings, a horde of monsters whose only pleasure was destruction and murder. This is too simple a picture. Dr Ella Lingens-Reiner, who was a prisoner in Auschwitz, testified: 'I know hardly a single SS man who could not say that he had saved someone's life. There were few sadists. No more than five or ten per cent were criminals by nature. The others were perfectly normal men, fully alive to good and evil. They all knew what was going on.'[176]

The shattering revelations, during the West German War Crimes trials, of the torments imposed upon their victims by the mass exterminators threatened to obscure a truth propounded as early as 1944 by Hannah Arendt, the German-American sociologist; she submitted that the mass extermination organization was manned 'neither by fanatics nor by natural murderers nor by sadists. It was manned solely and exclusively by normal human beings of the type of Heinrich Himmler.'[177] The fact that brutes and sadists made use of the extermination machine does not mean that they were typical of it. The most diverse characters have always been attracted by crimes of this nature – witness the guillotine during the French Revolution and the fanatical purges of the Soviet OGPU.

The sensational fact, the really horrifying feature, of the annihilation of the Jews was that thousands of respectable fathers of families made murder their official business and yet, when off duty, still regarded themselves as ordinary law-abiding citizens who were incapable even of thinking of straying from the strict path of virtue. Sadism was only one facet of mass extermination and one disapproved of by SS headquarters. Himmler's maxim was that mass extermination must be carried out coolly and cleanly; even while obeying the official order to commit murder, the SS man must remain 'decent'.

Briefing Sturmbannführer Franke-Gricksch, Himmler said: 'The SS commander must be hard but he must not become hardened. If, during your work, you come across cases in which some commander exceeds his duty or shows signs that his sense of restraint is becoming blurred, intervene at once. Anyone who finds it necessary to dull his senses, or forgets himself in face of the enemy who is handed over to him, shows that he is no true SS commander.'[178] Himmler even issued definite instructions forbidding his minions to torment their victims; an order of August 1935 laid down: 'Any independent, individual action against the Jews by any member of the SS is most strictly forbidden';[179] the concentration-camp guards had to sign a declaration every three months, acknowledging their duty to refrain from maltreating prisoners.[180]

In autumn 1942 the Hauptamt SS-Gericht [SS Legal Department] posed the hypothetical question of how unauthorized shootings of Jews should be dealt with. Himmler's answer was: 'If the motive is purely political there should be no punishment unless such is necessary for the maintenance of discipline. If the motive is selfish, sadistic or sexual, judicial punishment should be imposed for murder or manslaughter as the case may be.'[181]

On occasions he actually had SS sadists punished. In June 1943 an SS

Untersturmführer was condemned to death for bestial ill-treatment of innumerable Jews. On June 9th, 1943 the Supreme SS and Police Court pronounced judgement: 'He succumbed to the temptation to commit atrocities unworthy of a German or an SS commander. These excesses cannot be justified by saying, as does the accused, that they are a just recompense for the damage done by the Jews to the German people. Necessary though the annihilation of our people's worst enemy may be, it is not in the German manner to use Bolshevist methods to do so. And the methods adopted by the accused border upon those of Bolshevism.'[182]

When sadism was combined with corruption, then Himmler let the hounds of justice loose, for he regarded both as crimes against the SS – sadism undermined its discipline and corruption destroyed its ideology. The temporary clean-up which Konrad Morgen, the SS Judge, was allowed to conduct among the SS liquidators was a good illustration of Himmler's Jekyll-and-Hyde character; the Reichsführer's dual personality was suddenly exposed – the lower-middle-class citizen with his strict moral upbringing clashed with the automaton, the fanatical agent of the Führer's commands. It was an absurd spectacle; one or two 'unauthorized' murders of Jews were investigated – by a whole squad of SS legal experts – inside the extermination camps where thousands were being murdered daily!

Dr Konrad Morgen was the son of a railwayman, born in 1910 in Frankfurt-am-Main. His professional legal career had ended when he refused to accept a judgement by his provincial magistrate, but he had then been appointed to the SS/Police Court in Cracow as Assistant Judge to deal primarily with cases of corruption. After quarrelling with Krüger, the HSSPF, he had been posted to the SS 'Viking' Division as a punishment. In 1943 he was transferred to the RKPA but forbidden to deal with political cases.[183] There he stumbled across a case of widespread corruption in the concentration camps.

One day the RKPA group 'Financial Crimes Office', to which Morgen belonged, received a call for assistance from Kassel, where SS Police Court XXII was located. The Court, which was responsible for Buchenwald concentration camp, wished to clear up an old corruption case with ramifications extending into the camp itself.[184] Emil Holtschmidt, a young Criminal Police officer, had been keeping a watch on Bornschein, the local Nazi Group leader in Weimar; he was a provisions merchant who had run various profitable rackets in partnership with Karl Koch, the Commandant of Buchenwald. When Holtschmidt became over-inquisitive, Bornschein joined the Waffen-SS and got himself posted to the headquarters staff of Buchenwald.[185] The SS/Police Court took up the case but could do nothing, since such Courts had jurisdiction over the Waffen-SS (to which the concentration-camp guard units theoretically belonged) only in the capacity of a sort of court-martial; within the camp itself, however, so-called legal officers were in charge and they were responsible not to the Hauptamt SS-Gericht but to the highest legal authority concerned with the concentration camps, Obergruppenführer Oswald Pohl, Head of the SS Wirtschaftsverwaltungshauptamt [Economic and Administrative Department – WVHA].[186]

The SS/Police Court Kassel now brought the RKPA into the game. It asked for Criminal Police assistance against the Koch gang, specifying as a condition, however, that the selected RKPA official must carry officer rank in the Waffen-SS – no one else would have the smallest prospect of penetrating into Buchenwald concentration camp.[187] Morgen, being an Obersturmführer in the Waffen-SS, was allotted the job and went to Weimar where he installed himself in the Elephant Hotel and initiated unobtrusive investigations. He soon succeeded in convicting Bornschein.[188] Then, however, he found himself uncovering the murkiest secrets of Buchenwald Camp. Though not officially authorized to do so, he checked Koch's accounts in Weimar banks and intercepted letters between Koch (who had meanwhile been appointed Commandant of the Lublin extermination camp) and his wife Ilse, who had remained in Buchenwald.[189] The deeper he delved, the more clearly he perceived that a network of corruption existed with ramifications extending into the other concentration camps.

From corruption the case developed into one of multiple murder, for Morgen discovered that Koch had not only been blackmailing rich Jews who had landed in his concentration camp after the 1938 Kristallnacht, but had also been causing awkward witnesses among the prisoners to disappear. Morgen determined to bring to justice the entire blackmail and murder gang centred around Koch. When, however, he submitted the results of his researches to Nebe, his Kripo master was appalled by the over-enthusiasm of his sleuth. Nebe foresaw frightful consequences from Morgen's campaign and was unwilling to take responsibility. Morgen, however, hot on the trail of his prey, chased from one SS leader to another. He explained the case in detail to Gestapo Müller, who sent him to the Head of the RSHA. The latter passed him on to the Head of the Hauptamt SS-Gericht who could think of only one solution – Himmler.[190]

Morgen proceeded to the Reichsführer's Field Headquarters but could not get in touch with Himmler. With one of Himmler's personal staff, to whom he told the whole story, he drafted an innocently worded telegram; provided it was delivered, Himmler's agreement seemed certain. The telegram was delivered.[191] No one can say what caused Himmler to give the go-ahead for action against the Koch gang. Perhaps it was his permanent mistrust of Obergruppenführer Pohl and his corrupt hangers-on, or he may have underestimated the chain reaction which the Koch case was bound to produce. The fact remains that, for a short instant, Himmler (in his lower-middle-class role) could congratulate himself on putting his house in order.

Morgen seized his chance. He ordered Koch to Buchenwald and subjected him to so severe an interrogation that the ex-king of the camp finally broke down and confessed everything. The case for the prosecution became longer and longer; it included murder of two prisoners, Krämer and Peix, embezzlement and actions detrimental to the war effort.[192] Morgen also got his hooks on Koch's accomplices – Sommer a sadist in charge of one of the barrack blocks, Dr Waldemar Hoven, the camp doctor, Hauptscharführer Blanck and last, but not least, the 'Queen of the Camp', Ilse Koch. The indictment included murder, manslaughter, and assault with intent to murder.[193]

But Morgen and his assistants were not prepared to be satisfied merely with the elimination of the Koch gang. On his initiative the Kassel SS/Police Court had been turned into a 'special' court with the right to investigate all crimes in concentration camps.[194] Morgen had discovered new clues and they led eastwards, straight into the top-secret extermination camps. He unearthed what he was not supposed to unearth, the million-fold murders of Jews in the death factories of the East. In Lublin and in Auschwitz he suddenly stumbled across the gas chambers and realized that he had been hunting one or two cases of murder in places where millions were being slaughtered.[195] But how did he react to his discovery? The answer he gives today shows that he also suffered from his Reichsführer's schizophrenia. There were at the time, he would have us believe, three types of murder: the officially decreed murders of Jews 'against which nothing could be done because the orders issued from the Führer's Chancellery within the framework of the "Final Solution" and were given by Hitler himself'; the euthenasia killings, which were equally official; finally 'arbitrary killings' of prisoners.[196] Only against the third category of murders did he set the SS judicial machine in motion.

In practically every concentration camp Morgen and the RKPA installed Commissions of Inquiry to investigate cases of corruption and 'arbitrary killings'.[197] Pohl's minions, however, put up fierce resistance to the entry of the investigators; looking for sadists in a concentration camp was a dangerous business, for the camp staff reacted savagely, sometimes even with murder. One of the Oranienburg prisoners named Rothe, who was an RKPA informer, was only saved in the nick of time[198] from a public execution arranged by the camp staff as a warning to other prisoners not to collaborate with Morgen.[199] In another camp a hut containing RKPA files was burnt down and in Auschwitz Hauptscharführer Gerhard Palitsch, whom Morgen had dispatched to investigate the doings of Höss, the Camp Commandant, vanished into a punishment cell.[200]

Nevertheless Morgen registered numerous successes. 800 cases of corruption and murder were dealt with and 200 resulted in sentences.[201] Well-known names from the sinister concentration-camp aristocracy figured on Morgen's list: Karl Koch, Commandant of Buchenwald and Lublin – two death sentences for murder – executed;[202] Hermann Florstedt, Commandant of Lublin – condemned to death for murder and executed;[203] Hermann Hackmann, in charge of protective custody in Lublin – condemned to death for murder but eventually posted to a penal unit;[204] Hans Loritz, Commandant of Oranienburg – proceedings initiated on suspicion of arbitrary killings;[205] Adam Grünewald, Commandant of 'sHertogenbosch – sentenced for maltreatment of prisoners and posted to a penal unit;[206] Karl Künstler, Commandant of Flossenburg – dismissed for drunkenness and debauchery;[207] Alex Piorkowski, Commandant of Dachau – accused of murder but not sentenced;[208] Maximilian Grabner, Head of the Political Section in Auschwitz – accused of murder but not sentenced.[209]

The deeper the men of RKPA delved into the secrets of the concentration-camp world, however, the more uneasy did Himmler become. As early as mid-April 1944 he ordered Morgen to confine himself to the Koch case; all other investigations were to be stopped.[210] The order illustrated the conflict of principle between Himmler the mass liquidator and Himmler the apostle of rectitude. He ordered that Pohl should personally supervise Koch's execution; the other miscreants, however, must report their crimes voluntarily; anyone who came forward of his own free will could be sure of clemency.[211] Himmler withdrew into his world of illusion. At a meeting of SS-Gruppenführer as early as 1943 he had said: 'All in all we can say that we have completed this painful task (the annihilation of the Jews) out of love for our people. In our own selves, in our souls and in our character we have suffered no damage therefrom.'[212]

It was no accident that Himmler closed down Morgen's campaign just at the moment when investigations were starting against Höss, the Commandant of Auschwitz. Rudolf Höss was an outstanding exponent of the hygienic mass-murder system, the clinically clean automatic process; he was the ideal SS man, for whose 'purity' Himmler had been so concerned when he authorized this short period of house-cleaning. The system and the rhythm of mass extermination were dictated not by the sadists such as Boger or Kaduk but by men like Rudolf Höss – worthy family men brought up in the belief that anti-Semitism was a form of pest control, harnessed into an impersonal mechanical system working with the precision of militarized industry and relieving the individual of any sense of personal responsibility.

Martin Broszat, the historian, describes mass extermination as 'the work of ambitious, strait-laced philistines, men obsessed with a sense of duty, faithful servants of the powers-that-be; they had been brought up in a spirit of soulless conformity; they were incapable of criticism and devoid of imagination; so in all good faith and with a clear conscience, they persuaded themselves, and allowed themselves to be persuaded, that the "liquidation" of men in hundreds of thousands was a service to their people and their country.'[213] The machine of extermination was served by modern production-line employees whom Hannah Arendt, for want of a more precise sociological expression, calls 'John Citizen'.[214] They were sinister illustrations of the gulf which existed between public and private morality; refusal to admit of any connexion between their official duties and their private existence, together with an ineradicable self-righteousness, prevented them regarding themselves as murderers.

On the contrary – from their grotesquely exaggerated sense of righteousness in the fulfilment of their civic duty sprang the notion that basically in the midst of all this murder they were men of compassion who had every sympathy with those who must die, with the 'existing and the perishing' – Höss's hypocritical description of mass murder.[215] 'Nothing is more difficult,' Höss said, 'than to have to make one's way through this business cold, unsympathetic and without pity.'[216]

Like the men of the Einsatzgruppen, the death-camp technicians entrenched themselves behind a spurious self-pity which enabled them seriously to believe that in fact they were tragic figures. Höss, for instance, says: 'There was no escape for me. I had to carry on the process of extermination, of mass murder, to live with it, to be an unemotional spectator of something at which my whole soul revolted.'[217] In emotional terms he continued that, if some particular incident had moved him, 'I could not go home to my family. I would get on a horse and let the fresh air blow away the picture of frightfulness; alternatively at night time I often went through the stable and found peace among my beloved animals.'[218]

No sooner, however, had a dent been made in their armour of philistine self-righteousness, than these men relapsed into whimpering sentimentality and, as a rule, took refuge in alcohol. In his cups even so barbaric a Jew-exterminator as Globocnik admitted to a friend: 'My heart's no longer in it but I am so deeply involved in these things that I have no alternative but to ride to victory with Hitler or go under.'[219] At the graveside of his children, who had died of diphtheria, Hermann Höfle, Globocnik's minion who had been responsible for the deportation of more than 200,000 Jews, sobbed: 'This is Heaven's punishment for all my misdeeds.'[220]

Through all these burgeoning doubts, however, one sheet-anchor remained to them – they had received an order. Höss says: 'I had no second thoughts at the time; I had received an order and had to carry it out. When the Führer himself had ordered the "final solution" of the Jewish question, a long-standing National-Socialist could have no second thoughts, still less an SS officer. "*Führer, befiehl, wir folgen*" [Führer, command – we follow thee] was for us no empty phrase, no mere slogan. We took it with deadly seriousness.'[221] The official order was their idol, their justification and their final refuge. When Gilbert, the American psychologist, later asked Höss if he had ever considered whether the Jews whom he murdered had deserved their fate 'he tried patiently to explain that there was something unrealistic about such a question because he had been living in an entirely different world. "Don't you see, we SS men were not supposed to think about these things; it never even occurred to us".'[222]

When, however, the order was no longer unequivocal, when it contradicted, indeed condemned, what had hitherto been an article of faith, what was to happen then? The mass murderers were then abandoned, lost in a maze from which there was no exit. Exactly this occurred during the final stage of the extermination programme; before Polish Jewry had been completely annihilated an SS authority appeared bent on reducing the tempo of extermination and preserving the Jews as slave labour for Greater Germany's war effort.

This was the headquarters of the SS economic enterprises, the WVHA, under Oswald Pohl, a newcomer to the world of concentration and extermination camps. Originally the camps had been under the authority of Theodor Eicke, the Inspector of Concentration Camps, who on paper came under the SS-Hauptamt; when Eicke transferred to the Waffen-SS, his successor Richard Glücks was placed under the SS-Führungshauptamt [Waffen-SS Headquarters].[223] In 1942 Himmler reorganized the concentration-camp command system yet again; Glücks and his staff were transferred to Pohl's WVHA, where the Inspector of Concentration Camps became Head of Amtsgruppe [Division] D.[224]

This transfer into the realm of the managerial and production enthusiasts gave the concentration-camp system a new twist. Hitherto the camps had aimed solely at the punishment and extermination of so-called enemies of the State and the race; the theorists of the WVHA, however, could see no purpose in them other than to provide armies of slaves for the SS business empire. On April 30th, 1942 Pohl wrote to Himmler that the increased armaments requirements necessitated 'mobilization of all prisoner labour' and required 'measures involving gradual transformation of the concentration camps from their previous purely political form into an organization capable of meeting our economic requirements.'[225]

Hitherto prisoners had been treated with unrelenting brutality, the object being to get rid of them; now preservation and maintenance became the order of the day. Glücks ordered prisoners to be sent out to work and 'in this connexion it is axiomatic that it is forbidden to strike, kick or even touch a prisoner.'[226] Himmler added that the prisoners' work output must be raised 'by reasonable (if necessary, improved) food and clothing; prisoners must be encouraged to take interest in the economic enterprise concerned; cooperative prisoners should be held up as an example to the listless majority.'[227] The German Excavation and Quarrying Co Ltd, a WVHA concern producing building materials, instituted courses to train skilled prisoner labour. To attract prisoners who showed interest, promises of lucrative employment were made, including prospects of special accommodation or even release from the camp and continued employment as civilian workers.[228] Some of the SS concerns seriously planned to house considerable numbers of released prisoners in housing estates near their firms.[229]

Simultaneously, however, the WVHA increased the severity of the prisoners' working conditions; Pohl's slaves had to work an average of eleven hours a day, undernourished and frequently wretchedly clothed. The WVHA's army of involuntary workers appeared in all sectors of SS and private industry. Of the 600,000 prisoners in WVHA camps in December 1944, 250,000 were working in privately owned armament firms, 170,000 in firms directly under the Ministry of Armaments and Munitions, 15,000 in building firms, 12,000 for firms constructing a new Führer Headquarters in Thuringia, 50,000 for firms under Amtsgruppe C of the WVHA and 130,000 in agriculture and the distributive trades.[230]

Earlier than he had foreseen, Himmler found himself faced with the ideological and practical consequences of this change of policy, and they threatened his Final Solution programme. The WVHA pragmatists cast greedy eyes on the mass of Jewish death candidates. German Armaments Works Ltd, the controlling organization for all wood- and metal-working concerns within the concentration camps, was already putting out its feelers for Polish Jewry's surviving labour force.[231]

By the end of 1942 three-quarters of Polish Jewry had been murdered, leaving 700,000 alive.[232] These men were languishing in the innumerable labour camps maintained by the SSPF in the Government-General and at regular intervals they furnished their quota to the death factories. The WVHA business tycoons, however, soon brought the Polish camps under their control. In March 1943 Pohl's experts formed Eastern Industries Ltd to exploit Jewish labour and take over such businesses as still survived within the ghettos. A number of ex-Jewish concerns came under its control – the peat-cutting industry in Dorohueza, the brush factory in Lublin, the armaments works in Radom-Blizyn and the tannery in Trawniki.[233]

The Final Solution fanatics, however, found this desire for Jewish labour highly disturbing, for it threatened to jeopardize their work of extermination. SSPF Warsaw summarized their feelings: on seeing a WVHA man arrive he explained: 'Eastern Industries! I only have to hear the word "industry" to be nauseated.'[234] The technicians of murder in fact bore their WVHA colleagues so much ill-will that they dealt Eastern Industries a mortal blow. Hardly had the concern got going than they deprived it of all its Jewish labour. On November 3rd, 1943 'Eastern Industries' Jews were summoned to the gas chambers.[235] Obersturmführer Dr Max Horn, Deputy Director of Eastern Industries, lamented: 'As a result of the withdrawal of Jewish labour all our work of organization and expansion has become totally valueless.'[236]

The Eastern Industries case was the start of a quarrel between the WVHA and the RSHA which was to last until the end of the Third Reich, the RSHA trying to liquidate as many Jews as possible and the WVHA to retain all those fit for work. Höss commented: 'In the view of the RSHA every new labour camp and every additional thousand workers increased the risk that one day they might be set free or somehow contrive to remain alive.' Nevertheless Pohl was in the stronger position, for Himmler supported him with increasingly urgent demands for prisoners for the armament industry.[237] The more violent this quarrel, the more perplexed the men in control of the gas chambers became. Hardest hit by the battle was Adolf Eichmann, the RSHA's senior liquidator; to add to his troubles, resistance from the European States was growing stronger and an increasing number of SS leaders were suffering twinges of conscience.

Initially it looked as if a series of surprise actions would enable Eichmann and his minions to sweep up the Jews of Europe and pack them into the death trains for Auschwitz. In January 1942 Heydrich had held a conference, known from its location as the Wannsee Conference, at which he had ordered the inclusion of all European Jews in the murder programme.[238] From that moment Adolf Eichmann had only one aim in life – to be death's most reliable and indefatigable collector and transport agent.

The centre of the web was Gestapo Desk IV B 4 with Obersturmbannführer Eichmann at its head, located in the cavernous, gloomy, rooms of No 116 Kurfürstenstrasse, Berlin, formerly a masonic lodge. From this building ran the strands which enmeshed the entire continent to draw European Jewry to its doom. At Eichmann's side was a staff of cold-blooded executioners, ready at any moment to carry his orders abroad. His organization had its repercussions on other German and foreign institutions; as he opened his drag-net campaign Eichmann was assured of the support of German diplomacy, which brought pressure to bear on foreign governments to hand over their Jewish nationals; the Reichsbahn provided the deportation trains; Eichmann had representatives attached to the Sicherheitspolizei commanders in the occupied territories and to German diplomatic missions abroad. All were standing ready to act at any moment on orders from the Kurfürstenstrasse (see Appendix 7).

The death-march of the Jews from central and western Europe had begun even before the Wannsee conference. The first trainloads of German Jews had been dispatched by Eichmann's headquarters in October 1941; by November Jews from Germany proper and from Austria were reaching the Minsk, Riga and Lodz ghettos, all of which were scheduled for destruction.[239] One or two deportee trains were enough to decimate German Jewry. The Final Solution juggernaut then turned westwards, the first victims being the Jews of Holland. There Reichskommissar Arthur Seyss-Inquart was in charge of the German civil administration and he did not wear the uniform of an SS-Obergruppenführer for nothing. The way was clear for the liquidators. From May 1942 the Jews of Holland were forced to wear the Star of David; a month later Eichmann's deportation trains began to arrive and by July they were on their way eastwards. Dutch Jewry was exterminated with unparalleled precision – of 110,000 Jews deported, only 6,000 survived.[240]

Eichmann's men then turned their attention southwards – to Belgium and France. Here, however, hunting became more difficult, for in both countries Wehrmacht generals were in charge and one could never be sure whether they would not, even at this stage, oppose the liquidation programme. As in Poland and Russia the fate of the Jews depended to a large extent on the attitude of the Wehrmacht and once again, as in the East, the response from the military was uneven. Fortunately for the Jews of France and Belgium it was less definite than that in the Balkans; there the partisan war turned the German military commanders into virtual accomplices of the 'Final Solution'; the battle against the Serbian partisans was so savage that the liquidators felt safe in leaving the military to shoot the 20,000 Serbian Jews held as hostages.[241] Martin Luther, an Under-Secretary in the Foreign Office and its senior anti-Semite, commented sneeringly: 'In other territories other military commanders have taken care of considerably larger numbers of Jews without even mentioning it.'[242] The soldiers simply did as they were told. On October 2nd, 1941, for instance, a motorized column of 342 Infantry Division was ambushed by partisans near Topola;[243] thereupon General Franz Böhme of the Mountain Troops, Commanding General in Serbia, had 2,100 Jews shot in reprisal.[244] By the end of the month, the figure had risen to 5,000 – all liquidated by the Wehrmacht.[245] But the military were unwilling to execute the remaining 15,000 Jewish women and children because – as Gruppenführer Dr Harald Turner, Head of the civil administration, obligingly explained – 'It was contrary to the viewpoint of the German soldier . . . to take women as hostages.'[246] The RSHA gas vans did the rest – hardly a Serbian Jew survived.[247]

The German generals in Greece were in equally close touch with the RSHA minions. Lieutenant-General von Krenzki, C-in-C Salonika-Aegean area, was the first to strike against the Jews in the German occupation zone; there were 55,000 of them (in the remainder of Greece, occupied by the Italians, there were 13,000 Jews and in the north-east corner, occupied by the Bulgarians, 5,000). Von Krenzki rounded up 7,000 Jews for work on fortifications;[248] then early in 1943 Eichmann sent to Greece two emissaries, Dieter Wisliceny and Anton Brunner, to organize transports to Auschwitz and again the military helped;[249] the Army was used to clear the Salonika ghetto,[250] Jews were moved north-eastwards in Wehrmacht trains;[251] the German 'Admiral Aegean' made shipping available to carry the last remaining Jews from the Greek islands to the gas chambers.[252]

The German generals in western Europe, on the other hand, differed from their Balkan counterparts. C-in-C Belgium and Northern France was General Alexander von Falkenhausen who 'till his own arrest in July 1944, more than held his own against Security Police interference.'[253]

Belgium was the first country where the tempo of extermination began to slacken. Eichmann's executioners could report only partial successes to Berlin; of the 52,000 Jews living in Belgium, 24,000 were murdered, but hardly a single Jew possessing Belgian nationality was handed over to the death factories in the East.[254]

General Carl-Heinrich von Stülpnagel, the Military Governor, France, was equally unwilling to assist the annihilation programme, repeatedly refusing to make troops available to SS-Standartenführer Dr Helmut Knochen, the Sicherheitspolizei Commander in France.[255] Nevertheless Stülpnagel could hardly have saved the French Jews from the fate of their countrymen in Serbia and Greece had not the French themselves been determined to protect the Jews from Knochen's thugs. Even the puppet government in Vichy refused to assist in the Final Solution; although Pierre Laval, the wily Head of the Government, did not yet know that murder was the purpose of Jewish 're-settlement' in the East, he barred the way to the hunters. Nevertheless he had to pay a considerable price – as a last resort he was ready to sacrifice the stateless Jews, but under no circumstances would he hand over French citizens of Jewish descent.[256]

On July 6th, 1942 Hauptsturmführer Theodor Dannecker, Eichmann's representative in Paris, triumphantly reported to Berlin that the French Government was prepared to relinquish the stateless Jews.[257] But the rejoicing was shortlived. 12,000 Jews from Paris were, indeed, shipped eastwards[258] but in the provinces Eichmann's death wagons remained empty. The Sicherheitspolizei was compelled to rely upon the cooperation of the French gendarmerie and so the French could sabotage Eichmann's programme. In Bordeaux, for instance, a major operation against the stateless Jews was arranged for mid-July but the gendarmes only produced 150 victims.[259] Dannecker's section received a furious call from Eichmann; Obersturmführer Heinz Röthke took it and on July 15th noted down Eichmann as saying: 'Such a thing had never happened to him before. The matter was very "blameworthy". He must consider whether to abandon France altogether as a forwarding area.'[260]

Six months later, however, Eichmann saw an opportunity to get his claws on his prey. In November 1942 the Allies landed in French North Africa and German troops thereupon moved into unoccupied France – the last remnant of French autonomy had disappeared. Eichmann's manhunters promptly moved into Southern France. There, however, the much-despised Italian Army taught them a lesson, proving that even in the era of mass murder, humanity and the honour of an officer still had some meaning; the Italians were now occupying Southern France east of the Rhone and their officers cried halt to the annihilation of the Jews.

The Italian Army's refusal to take action against the Jews in the areas which it occupied (Greece and Croatia for instance), had already been made plain. The Chief of the Italian General Staff had told a Todt Organization leader; 'Anti-Jewish excesses are not compatible with the honour of the Italian Army'[261] – a sentiment one would have wished to hear from the mouth of a German general. In innumerable cases the Italian soldiers had assisted the Jews: in Greece, General Geloso, commanding the Italian Second Army, refused to sanction the wearing of the Star of David in his occupation area; in Athens he posted a guard on the Synagogue and the Jewish Community Centre to deter a Greek anti-Semitic organization from instigating anti-Jewish riots.[262] In Salonika, which was German-occupied, the Italian Consulate saved hundreds of Jews by granting them Italian nationality.[263] In summer 1941, on the pretext of pursuing partisans, an Italian unit penetrated into Inner Croatia to save a group of Jews from murder by the Croat Fascists; following a protest by the Croat Government, the unit's officers were court-martialled but sentenced only to a few days' arrest.[264]

In their new occupation zone in France the Italian Army authorities stopped any anti-Jewish action. Assisted by the French Administration, the Germans had begun to arrest Jews but the Italians reacted immediately. In February 1943, for instance, the Police Chief of Lyons placed 300 Jews in an internment camp for subsequent transport to Auschwitz; an Italian General promptly compelled him to release them.[265] Early in March the French gendarmerie arrested a number of Jews in the Italian zone, but the Italians prevented them being carted off to Germany;[266] Italian troops surrounded the gendarmerie barracks in Annecy until the arrested Jews were released.[267]

Knochen, the local Sicherheitspolizei commander, lamented: 'Throughout France the "Final Solution of the Jewish question" decreed for the whole of Europe is being seriously hampered by the Italian position,' and he appealed to the German C-in-C West to bring the Italians to reason.[268] Suddenly, however, the German generals seemed to be of the same mind as their Italian colleagues. Lieutenant-General Blumentritt, Chief-of-Staff to C-in-C West, informed Knochen: 'If the Italian Government appears to have other views, C-in-C West can take no decision in this matter.'[269]

Eichmann thereupon appealed to the Foreign Ministry for help. Ribbentrop dutifully got busy, complaining to Rome about sabotage by the

Italian generals and asking Mussolini for his assistance.[270] Instead of clearing the matter up, however, the Duce proved a vexation to his allies; he dispatched to Southern France Guido Lospinoso, the Inspector General of the Italian Police, but the latter's primary object seemed to be to avoid all contact with the Germans.[271] Eichmann and his people soon realized why. Lospinoso had brought with him an assistant named Donati, President of the Franco-Italian bank and a confidant of the Vatican. Assisted by the Holy See, Lospinoso and Donati intended to pass across into Switzerland the 30,000 Jews who had meanwhile taken refuge in the Italian zone.[272] The Jew-murderers reacted violently, for Obersturmführer Röthke had the horrifying suspicion that 'Donati is possibly even a full Jew'.[273] Röthke produced a plan to kidnap Donati from the Italian headquarters in Nice and carry him off to Marseilles. Before it could be carried out, however, Donati had taken an aeroplane to Rome.[274]

The capitulation of Italy in the summer of 1943 of course deprived the French Jews of their Italian protectors. Nevertheless the humanity of the Italian generals had assisted 80 per cent of the 300,000 Jews of France to escape the extermination camps.[275] Moreover, Italian resistance to the Final Solution marked a turning point; it coincided with two events which reduced both the tempo and the scope of the murder programme – these were Adolf Hitler's sinking fortunes of war and the revelations, issuing primarily from the Vatican, of the true nature of Eichmann's 're-settlement' in the East.

When Nazi Germany's opportunist allies realized that they were passengers in a sinking ship, the SS murderers spell was broken. In quick succession Germany's satellites withdrew from the Jewish pogrom: in autumn 1942 the Slovak Government stopped all deportations of Jews to the East; the official reason given was that, via the Vatican, information had filtered through concerning the real fate of the Slovak Jews deported to Poland supposedly for 're-settlement'; moreover Eichmann had refused to allow a Slovak Commission of Inquiry to visit supposed Jewish settlements in the East.[276] In December 1942 the Government of Rumania, whose anti-Semites had been even more murderous than the German, refused any further surrender of Jews to Germany.[277] In April 1943 Czar Boris III of Bulgaria ordered all deportation of Jews to stop – not a single Bulgarian Jew was delivered to the mass exterminators.[278]

The remainder of the annihilation programme proceeded only in fits and starts. As a reprisal for Italian sabotage Eichmann planned to arrest all the Jews of Rome during the night of October 16th–17th, 1943, but even this did not succeed – of the 8,000 Roman Jews only 1,259 could be found.[279] Obersturmbannführer Herbert Kappler, the Police attaché in charge of the operation, wired on October 17th: 'Attitude of Italian population definitely one of passive resistance; numerous cases of active assistance to Jews. No sign during operation of anti-Semitic section of population; normal man-in-street only; even some instances of attempts to drag police officers away from Jews.'[280]

Europe's resistance to the Final Solution was undoubtedly growing. Even some of Himmler's immediate entourage were affected and – carefully camouflaged of course – joined the ranks of the 'decent'. The first was Himmler's masseur, Felix Kersten. When, on July 15th, 1942, he heard that Hitler was now demanding surrender of Finland's Jews and that Himmler was to visit Helsinki to put this requirement to the Government, Kersten at once warned the Finnish Legation in Berlin.[281]

On July 29th Himmler, accompanied by Kersten, flew to Finland but before Himmler could open his conversations with the Finnish Government, Kersten went to Witting, the Foreign Minister, and suggested a method of parrying Himmler's attack: he should say that the Jewish problem was so important a question that it could only be decided by Parliament – which, however, did not meet again until November. The Finns adopted Kersten's tactics and Himmler was persuaded to wait until November. On December 14th the Reichsführer once more reverted to the Finns and asked Kersten what was happening to the Finnish Final Solution. Kersten had a new argument ready: the Finnish war situation was so bad that the Government dared not recall Parliament and submit to it so thorny a problem. On September 18th, 1943, Himmler returned to the charge yet again. He growled angrily to Kersten: 'What does this twopenny-halfpenny State think it's doing, refusing to comply with the Führer's desires!' The Finnish Jews were saved – the first move by Kersten, to whom thousands and thousands of European Jews were later to owe their lives.[282]

SS-Brigadeführer Eggert Reeder, Head of Military Administration at the headquarters of C-in-C Belgium and Northern France, also had second thoughts about the programme. As early as March 1942 he had rejected Knochen's proposal to introduce the Star of David in Belgium;[283] in September 1943 he took it upon himself to order the release of Belgian Jews assembled in the Dossin barracks at Malines for transport to Auschwitz.[284]

Even hardened supporters of Hitler like SS-Gruppenführer Wilhelm Stuckart, State Secretary in the Reich Ministry of the Interior, attempted to salve their consciences. Under gentle pressure from Dr Bernhard Lösener, his Counsellor, he attempted to save two fringe categories of German Jewry whose fate had not yet been finally decided – the 107,000 'Mischlinge' ['half-castes'] and the 28,000 Jews 'in mixed marriages'.[285] The Ministry of the Interior held several laborious conferences with Eichmann and the exterminators of the RSHA in an attempt to stop them liquidating the 'Mischlinge'.[286] When the RSHA refused to give way, Stuckart took refuge in a last desperate proposal – sterilization instead of killing. In September 1942 Lösener drafted a personal memorandum from Stuckart to Himmler;[287] it is a typical illustration of the extreme methods and deceptive phraseology which anyone wishing to help Jews in Germany had to use.

Lösener made adroit use of Himmler's devotion to the cult of his Germanic ancestors. In Stuckart's name he submitted that in the case of the 'Mischlinge' it must be remembered that 'deporting the half-Jews would mean not only abandoning that half of the blood which is German but actually making a present of it to the enemies of Germany'; in addition the 'Mischlinge' had 'in most cases made every effort to work for German interests'. Moreover the 'psychological and political repercussions' must be considered since, if the 'Mischlinge' were treated as Jews, 'an increased psychological burden for their parents and relatives would result'. Lösener concluded: 'I cannot therefore regard the evacuation plan as being in the true interests of Germany and would prefer to see the half-Jews sterilized and so die out naturally'. The sting came in the tail: 'neither evacuation nor sterilization could of course be undertaken until after the war.'[288]

The Stuckart-Lösener letter caught the Reichsführer in a weak moment. Himmler forbade liquidation and the majority of the 'Mischlinge' were saved. Even the Nuremberg War Crimes Tribunal accepted Stuckart's letter, particularly as he was able to prove something which he had carefully concealed when writing it – he had previously been assured by SS-Gruppenführer Dr Conti, State Secretary for the Health Service, that sterilization of the 'Mischlinge' was in fact impracticable.[289]

The most striking example of the scepticism from which many SS leaders were now suffering, however, was that of SS Gruppenführer Dr Werner Best, the Gestapo's ex-Legal Adviser and now Reich Plenipotentiary in Copenhagen, who played an active part in sabotaging the extermination of Danish Jewry. Early in September 1943 Best learned that Hitler had ordered the evacuation of the 6,500 Danish Jews.[290] He immediately dispatched a telegram to the Foreign Ministry arguing against the operation: 'The King and Parliament would cease to take part in the government of the country. In addition we cannot discount the possibility of a general strike.'[291]

Nevertheless Hitler and Himmler insisted upon striking their blow against the Danish Jews. On September 18th, Best gave a further warning: 'From the political point of view the evacuation of Jews will undoubtedly lead to a serious increase in the state of tension in Denmark. There may be riots and possibly a general strike.'[292] Ribbentrop was so impressed by Best's gloomy prognostications that he submitted them to Hitler. The answer came back via Ambassador Hewel, the Foreign Ministry's representative in the Führer's headquarters: 'The Fuhrer doubts whether the operation will have the results anticipated.'[293] The operation proceeded. Two Ordnungspolizei battalions were dispatched to Denmark and the *Wartheland* docked in Copenhagen to take the Jewish prisoners on board.[294]

Best then decided to resist. The Reich Plenipotentiary rebelled against his Führer – naturally after his own manner, cautiously feeling his way and with not a little cynical double-dealing. As soon as he heard the date of the operation, he let his shipping expert, Georg Ferdinand Duckwitz, into the picture and told him to warn the Jews. Although he was an old Party member formerly on the staff of Alfred Rosenberg and wearing the Golden Party Badge, Duckwitz lost no time in doing so. On September 27th he met the Danish Resistance leaders in Copenhagen and asked them to alert the leaders of the Danish-Jewish community.[295] By the grapevine the word went round through synagogues and Jewish homes. The Jews went to ground and then, in one of the most remarkable rescue operations which a nation has ever undertaken for a minority, were shipped across the Kattegat to safety in Sweden.[296]

Best did something else to protect the Jews. He instructed the Sicherheitspolizei commander that his men were not to enter Jewish houses but merely to ring the door-bell. He justified his action later by arguing that 'since the vast majority of Jews are no longer living in their own houses, breaking into empty dwellings would have made an unpleasant impression and might have given rise to thefts which would then have been laid at our door.'[297] The anti-Jewish action of October 1st and 2nd, 1943 was therefore inevitably a failure. The Sicherheitspolizei captured only a few of the older Jews whom Best's warning had not reached. Only 477 Jews were evacuated – out of 6,500. Best contrived to arrange that these Jews were sent to the so-called Old People's Concentration Camp, Theresienstadt, where most of them survived to the end of the war.[298]

As an ex-Gestapo pen-pusher however, Best could not forgo his little camouflage joke. As if the Sicherheitspolizei had just carried out a large and successful operation against world Jewry he dutifully reported to

Berlin: '1. Anti-Jewish action in Denmark carried out without incident during the night October 1st/2nd, 1943. 2. As of today Denmark can be regarded as free of Jews.'[299] When the Berlin exterminators screamed to high heaven that only very few Jews had been arrested, Best, with his tongue in his cheek, replied on October 5th, 1943: 'The Sicherheitspolizei Commander and I had foreseen that only very few Jews would be caught. Since the real object of action in Denmark was to free the country of Jews rather than have a good man-hunt, it must be recorded that the operation achieved its object.'[300]

Adolf Eichmann could no longer understand what was going on. First there had been Wilhelm Stuckart and now here was another SS leader wrecking what was supposed to be the Final Solution. He told his Israeli interrogator: 'I remember this very well because I was astounded at the time and said: "Now, that same Dr Best was once Head of Amt I in the RSHA and at that time he gave us a great talk about the tasks and aims of the police"; and then I said to myself: "But, look you, now he's in Denmark and now he's against his master's orders." '[301]

Eichmann's very ordinary, petty but evil little brain was incapable of understanding such curious goings-on. One even more bitter disappointment, however, awaited him before he ended his career as a hangman; when he came to deal with Hungarian Jewry, he found that they had another protector – and his name was Heinrich Himmler.

15

THE IMPOTENCE OF POWER

THE destruction of European Jewry demonstrated even to the sceptics the frightful power over defenceless human beings possessed by the SS in Adolf Hitler's Germany. With its numerous organizations the SS wrapped its tentacles round the Reich like an octopus. With the SD and the Gestapo, the Waffen-SS and the 'Reich Commissar for the strengthening of Germanism', Ahnenerbe [Ancestral Heritage] and 'Lebensborn', concentration camps and industrial enterprises, hardly an aspect of the nation's life was closed to Himmler's bureaucrats and minions. The structure of the SS organizations became increasingly labyrinthine, the whole SS machine increasingly complex and convoluted.

The extent of SS influence was largely concealed by the continuous switching of responsibility from one part of the vast organization to another. The Party's or Allgemeine [General]-SS had long since sunk into insignificance; the Army had swept up sixty per cent of its members[1] and the remainder either paraded for evening instruction or lined the streets – in either case without much enthusiasm; they were practically indistinguishable from the Nazi veterans of the SA or NSKK [National-Sozialistische Kraftfahr Korps – the Party Motor Transport Organization]. But specialized SS organizations appeared in place of the Allgemeine SS, less obtrusive but far more influential.

The success story of the RSHA is perhaps the clearest indication of the extent to which the SS ruled the life of Germany. Under the pressure of the RSHA security machine, the legal rights of the German citizen shrank with each year of war. On the outbreak of the war the RSHA claimed the right to order summary executions to 'correct' sentences by the normal courts, blocking protests from the Ministry of Justice by the statement that under a Führer order the Reichsfuhrer-SS was entitled to use all methods to guarantee the security of the State, including summary executions for offences against defence regulations.[2] So long as Dr Franz Gürtner, a German Nationalist whom Hitler treated with some respect, was still Minister of Justice, the power of the RSHA was kept within bounds. On Gürtner's death in January 1941, however, his place was taken by Franz Schlegelberger, the Permanent Secretary, a weak man with only acting rank, and the RSHA seized the opportunity to deal the judiciary a blow from which it never recovered.

In autumn 1942 Heydrich, in addition to all his other offices, was appointed acting Reich Protector of Bohemia and Moravia. The Czechs were restive and Hitler had told him to act ruthlessly, so Heydrich proposed to usher in his régime with a spectacular trial designed to show the Czech serfs that their new overlord meant business. As candidate for the dock, Heydrich selected General Alois Elias, head of the Protectorate's puppet government in Prague. The SD had long suspected that he was secretly working both with Czech resistance and with the émigré Czechoslovak Government in London.[3]

Ever since mid-1940 the RSHA had been urging the dismissal of Elias and his trial before a summary court, but Freiherr von Neurath, the Reich Protector, who was a moderate, had resisted and refused to take proceedings against him. Even Ernst Lautz, a Nazi lawyer and senior State Attorney of the People's Court, regarded the RSHA's evidence against Elias as inadequate to justify a trial.[4]

But Heydrich had his own plan. He knew that Dr Otto Thierack, an 'old fighter', the first National-Socialist Minister of Justice in Saxony and now President of the People's Court, was an ambitious man and that his aim was to become Reich Minister of Justice; Heydrich calculated that Thierack would be quite prepared to join in a little intrigue if he thought that it would bring him the coveted appointment. On September 27th, 1941 Heydrich and Thierack agreed on the arrest of Elias and his arraignment before the People's Court; Lautz, the sceptical attorney, was to be kept out of the proceedings and the case for the prosecution would be conducted by the Sicherheitspolizei.[5] At one stroke the RSHA had thus almost fulfilled one of their long-standing dreams: the man who was about to become Reich Minister of Justice had in effect agreed that State Attorneys, the men whose thinking was conditioned by the normal legal system, should be completely excluded from the case; he was therefore a supporter of complete freedom of action for the police and they would now be able to appear in court in the role of State Attorney. Thierack in fact was prepared to sell the law down the river. When it was all over he told Rothenberger, the Ministry's State Secretary, that he had agreed with Heydrich that 'should he become Reich Minister of Justice, he would make over to the Reichsführer the duties of the State Attorneys'.[6]

The drama in Prague was staged exactly as agreed in Berlin. Thierack waited until his unsuspecting State Attorney went off for the weekend; meanwhile in Prague, Heydrich arrested Elias, and SS-Obersturmbannführer Dr Hans Geschke, Head of the Gestapo Leitstelle in Prague, took over the case for the prosecution.[7] Before the legal experts in Berlin had realized what was happening in Prague, Heydrich had hustled through his grim travesty of justice. Elias was arrested on September 28th; the next day Geschke indicted him; on September 30th, Division I of the People's Court moved to Prague; on October 1st, at 10 AM sharp proceedings against Elias opened; four hours later sentence was pronounced. The verdict was death for attempted high treason together with action in aid of the enemy.[8]

Otto Thierack had given good service and so could claim his reward; on August 20th, 1942 the grateful Dictator appointed him Reich Minister of Justice.[9] The new Minister of course kept in close touch with the SS. Although the rank-and-file lawyers prevented him handing over all the duties of State Attorneys, he contrived to make over a whole series of the judiciary's preserves to the Reichsführer-SS. In an agreement with Himmler dated September 18th, 1942, Thierack conceded to the RSHA the privilege of 'correcting' sentences of the courts by means of Gestapo 'special treatment'; he also agreed that persons sentenced by the normal courts to more than eight years imprisonment should be handed over to the police;[10] at the beginning of November 1942

Thierack handed over to the Sicherheitspolizei complete judicial responsibility for Poles and Jews in the re-incorporated Eastern Territories;[11] in summer 1943 he agreed that all Jews under German sovereignty should come under the jurisdiction of the RSHA.[12]

Though theoretically under the Reich Ministry of the Interior, the power of the RSHA grew unchecked. Certain of the traditionally minded bureaucrats in the Ministry had made some attempt to bring it under control but from August 1943 even this internal opposition was silenced, for Himmler was then appointed Minister of the Interior in succession to Wilhelm Frick, who was anti-SS and had fallen out of favour.[13] Many of the Ministry's most important responsibilities were thereupon transferred to the RSHA. Abteilung I of the Ministry, for instance, lost to its Prinz-Albrecht-Strasse rivals all real authority in the constitutional, legislative and administrative fields.[14]

One of the chief sufferers from Himmler's new access of power was Hauptamt Orpo. Hitherto its traditionalist officials, lawyers and officers had kept their distance from the RSHA and the Sicherheitspolizei; as a result of an internal streamlining operation, however, euphemistically termed 'clarification of responsibilities', Hauptamt Orpo had to relinquish to the RSHA all control over the criminal police.[15] Worse still, the police reporting and registry system, general questions of police law and police organization, all of which had been Orpo responsibilities, were swallowed up by the RSHA. Politically Hauptamt Orpo was now completely in the shade.[16]

No sooner had he become Minister of the Interior than Himmler disbanded the Administration and Legal Section in Hauptamt Orpo; its self-willed head, Werner Bracht, had obstructed him often enough. The tiresome nest of lawyers was turned into an 'economic and administrative office', at the head of which Himmler placed an 'old fighter', SS-Gruppenführer August Frank.[17] At about the same time Kurt Daluege, the head of the Orpo and one of Himmler's rivals, fell seriously ill and so the Reichsführer was able to abolish the last remnants of Orpo independence.[18] In summer 1944 Orpo welfare questions were transferred to the SS and even administrative police law was removed from it and given to the RSHA.[19]

The expansion of the RSHA, however, was only one indication among many of the growing power of the SS. Himmler's organizing ability had produced another colossus which showed how deeply embedded the SS had become in the whole Nazi system of tyranny – this was the WVHA [Wirtschaftsverwaltungshauptamt – Economic and Administrative Department].

The WVHA originated from the SS administrative office – part of the

SS-Hauptamt which had dealt with all administrative questions concerning the Allgemeine-SS ever since 1934.[20] To head it Himmler had appointed Oswald Pohl, an ex-Naval Paymaster and a slick but dogmatic tyrant; he looked like Mussolini, whose unscrupulous ambition he shared. Brigadeführer Pohl proved to be an inventive organizer and his empire was soon expanding. At an early stage he assumed administrative responsibility for the Totenkopfverbände and the Verfügungstruppe; he finally became financial administrator of the entire SS, taking over the 'Hauptamt Haushalt and Bauten [Budget and Buildings Department] of the Reichsführer-SS and Chief of the German Police within the Reich Ministry of the Interior' – a State institution which gave him the rank of Director in the Ministry.[21]

By 1939 Pohl, who had meanwhile been promoted SS-Gruppenführer, had become so powerful a figure that Himmler freed him from the straitjacket of the SS-Hauptamt, giving him his own Hauptamt, known as 'Verwaltung und Wirtschaft' [Administration and Economics].[22] Three years later, by which time administration of the concentration camps had also been placed under Pohl, Hauptamt Verwaltung and Wirtschaft was amalgamated with Hauptamt Haushalt und Bauten to form the WVHA.[23] So in a remarkably short time, Pohl had worked himself up until, Heydrich expected, he was the most powerful man among the Heads of the SS Hauptämter.

Four potent departments placed Pohl's hand firmly on the levers of power in the SS empire: he was in charge of the entire administration and supply of the Waffen-SS; he controlled the 20 concentration camps and 165 labour camps;[24] he directed all SS and Police building projects; he was in charge of all SS economic enterprises. In fact Pohl could see his Hauptamt developing into one of the most powerful economic forces in Germany – primarily because the SS business concerns could call upon the pool of labour provided by the concentration-camp prisoners.

SS-owned firms had been launched early on by qualified businessmen such as the brothers Georg and Hans Lörner, and SS-Hauptsturmführer Franz Eirenschmalz, a building tycoon.[25] By the outbreak of war there were four great SS concerns: the Deutsche Erd- und Steinwerke GmbH [German Excavation and Quarrying Company Ltd] producing building materials; it owned 14 stone, brick and clinker works with a total turnover in 1943 of 14,822,800 marks;[26] second, the Deutsche Ausrüstungwerke GmbH [German Equipment Co Ltd]; this owned all plant located in the concentration camps and dealt with a variety of trades from bread-making to cutlery, woodworking and iron foundries;[27] third, the Deutsche Versuchsanstalt für Ernährung und

Verpflegung GmbH [German Experimental Establishment for Foodstuffs and Nutrition Ltd]; for Himmler, with his belief in the medicinal qualities of herbs and his insistence upon surrounding the concentration camps with gardens of herbs, this was a favourite concern; later, however, it also dealt with Estates, Forestry and Fisheries where experiments were carried on with new but more innocuous foodstuffs;[28] fourth, the Gesellschaft für Textil- und Lederverwertung GmbH [Society for Exploitation of Textile and Leather Work Ltd]; this concern was centred on Ravensbrück women's concentration camp and its primary activity was the production of uniforms for the Waffen-SS; its turnover in 1943 was over nine million marks.[29]

Pohl grouped all these four concerns together into one holding company, Deutsche Wirtschaftsbetriebe [German Industrial Undertakings – DWB].[30] The formation of the DWB was typical of the technique of capitalist infiltration used by the WVHA to establish a hold over many fringe areas of the German economy. Outwardly the SS did not appear either as owner or manager of these firms; in the case of the DWB, for instance, the members of the board were shown as a certain ministerial director named Oswald Pohl and a businessman named Georg Lörner.[31] Only by thumbing through the SS lists was it possible to elucidate that SS-Obergruppenführer Pohl was head of the WVHA and SS-Gruppenführer Lörner his deputy.[32] Enno Georg, who has written a valuable and exhaustive account of these SS economic undertakings, points out that by various commercial-law subterfuges, the SS were highly successful in concealing their interest in the firms, at the same time reaping all the advantages of a major business undertaking by presenting them as privately organized cartels under public law.[33]

Pohl was realistic enough to know that he could not force his way into all areas of the economy. He therefore drew up a priority programme, setting out those branches of production in which he intended to establish an SS monopoly. First on the list was the mineral-water business, which was centred in the Sudetenland and was mostly in Jewish or British ownership; under cover of the Aryanization decrees, Pohl's representatives took possession of a number of such firms – Grün and Heinrich Mattoni, for instance.[34] He then turned his attention to German firms, laying hands on Niederselters and Apollinaris.[35] By 1944 Pohl was in control of 75 per cent of the German mineral-water market.[36]

The Sudetenland was also the scene of the second and equally successful venture by the WVHA capitalists. Emil Gerstel, the largest furniture manufacturer in Czechoslovakia, also fell into their hands as being an ex-Jewish undertaking; it formed the foundation for an SS-owned furniture industry. In this case, however, the WVHA had to cover their tracks carefully. The Reich Ministry of Economics had laid down that Gerstel should be taken over not by the SS but by a company to be formed by established German furniture manufacturers: Dr Kurt May, a furniture manufacturer from Stuttgart, together with two others in the same line of business, accordingly set up a German firm to take over Gerstel. What the Ministry of Economics did not know, however, was that in his spare time May was an SS-Untersturmführer and head of Amt W IV in the WVHA. He and his two henchmen forthwith made over their interests in the new company to the SS (through the DWB).[37] By taking over a number of other firms including the major Jewish concern of Drucker, the SS built itself up to a predominant position in the furniture market,[38] eventually forming Deutsche Heimgestaltung eV [German Home Furnishing Ltd]; this put cheap home furnishings on the market and drew up a production programme to which many non-SS furniture firms adhered.[39]

The third area to be invaded by the SS captains of industry was that of building materials. Here they could make use of the concerns in the German-occupied Eastern territories and the workshops in the Jewish ghettos of Poland. A company known as Ostdeutsche Baustoffwerke GmbH [East German Building Materials Ltd] was set up in Poznan, running no fewer than 313 ex-Polish or ex-Jewish brickworks in the re-incorporated territories; in 1943 its turnover was 11,000,000 marks.[40] In Eastern Upper Silesia and the Government-General, Klinker-Zement GmbH [Roughcast Cement Ltd] formed by Pohl took over brickworks, lime kilns, cement works and china factories.[41] Until the last frightful phase of the 'Final Solution' Ostindustrie GmbH [Eastern Industries Ltd], formed in 1943, did its best to make use of Jewish labour and businesses in the ghettos.[42] The Deutsche Ausrüstungswerke GmbH, one of DWB's subsidiaries, took over woodworking firms and iron foundries in Poland and even made inroads into textiles, printing and shoemaking.[43] In fact there was hardly a field of business activity in which Pohl's minions did not try their luck. Shale oil, bookbinding, estate management in Russia, jam factories – Pohl's Hauptamt had a finger in them all.

All this was under the control of Amtsgruppe W (Industrial Directorate) in the WVHA. Amstgruppe C was no less successful; it laid the foundation of an SS armaments industry. Amtsgruppe C was in charge of the SS-Police building programme and at its head was one of the most unscrupulous careerists ever to wear SS uniform.

His name was Hans Kammler, he was a qualified engineer and his ambition was abnormal even by SS standards; he would build gas chambers in Auschwitz or launching ramps for flying bombs with equal attention to detail. He eventually became a Gruppenführer but in spite of his exalted position bore no loyalty to the SS; for him the Order was nothing but a ladder for his own advancement.

This did not worry Pohl; he was quite prepared to recruit into the WVHA men who cared nothing for the SS and he kept them as long as they seemed useful, Amtsgruppe W, for instance, was run by a totally apolitical chartered accountant, Dr Hans Hohberg, who never belonged to any Nazi formation and never wore SS uniform;[44] Kammler also came from outside the SS. He was a civil servant who had long held the post of Director of Works in the Reich Ministry of Civil Aviation; in 1941 Himmler persuaded him to transfer to the SS, together with a staff of construction experts from the Luftwaffe.[45] He was given the rank of SS-Standartenführer and took over Amtsgruppe C in the WVHA where he produced an ambitious building programme which, by 1942, was already employing 175,00 men from the concentration and prisoner-of-war camps.[46]

Construction of supply depots, concentration-camp gas chambers, ammunition storage and barracks for the Waffen-SS was not enough to satisfy Kammler. He flew higher. Speer, the Armaments Minister, recalled: 'When Kammler took on his first job, I did not realize that it was he who had been earmarked as my successor.'[47]

Himmler's and Kammler's ambitions coincided: one of the former's dreams was to build up his own armaments industry and so make the SS units independent of equipment allocations from the ever-mistrustful Wehrmacht; Kammler saw himself at the head of a super-Ministry of Armaments. Both these ambitions were to be at least partially satisfied.

From 1943 Kammler was under orders to accelerate construction of arms factories, including underground workshops in the more important cases.[48] With his expert building gangs, his army of concentration-camp slaves and the extensive SS training areas available to him in the east, he soon became an indispensable figure in SS armament planning. He set up the Kammler Special Staff, gradually divorced Amtsgruppe C from the rest of the WVHA and refused to take orders from anyone other than the Reichsführer himself.[49] By 1944 Gruppenführer Kammler was calling himself 'Representative of the Reichsführer-SS'. On many occasions his construction experts paved the way for Himmler into the innermost recesses of armaments policy. Kammler's tasks were legion: construction of an underground Führer headquarters in Thuringia, construction of underground hangars for assembly of aircraft and flying bombs, participation in the manufacture of the Me 262 jet fighter and, finally control of the top secret miracle weapon to which Greater Germany was to look for salvation – the V1 and V2 rockets.[50]

When Himmler became Commander-in-Chief of the Replacement Army after July 20th, 1944, he handed over to Kammler technical direction of the V2 weapons which had been developed by the Army; in September 1944 Himmler took over tactical command of the two Army Missile Units, Group North and Group South.[51] By December 31st, 1944 1,561 V2 rockets had been fired on London and Antwerp.[52] Early in 1945 the Luftwaffe relinquished to Kammler command of 5 AA Division and with it control of the V1 programme; he was now entitled to call himself 'General Commanding a Specialized Army Corps' and to register the greatest prestige victory possible for an SS man – he became responsible to Hitler personally.[53]

Kammler's meteoric career was an illustration of the central position to which the SS and its leaders had risen among the power groups of the Third Reich. Almost every SS organization could tell a success story similar to that of the RSHA or WVHA – and inevitably therefore the idea was mooted that the day might not be far distant when the SS would take over the entire State. Its accumulation of prestige, exalted positions and highly placed dignitaries has led certain historians to ascribe to the SS such omnipotence that the entire Third Reich has been made to appear as a tributary of the SS Order.[54] Any such notion, however, betrays a misunderstanding of the practice of leadership in the totalitarian State.

The majority of historians have read into the Third Reich's system of government a degree of planning, organization and system, in other words a degree of orderliness, which was in fact totally foreign to the rulers of Hitler Germany. The Führer dictatorship was essentially based, not upon authority and organization, but on a complete lack of any hierarchy or structure. Nothing was more abhorrent to Hitler than the appearance of new organizational structures, for they would inevitably exert a constricting influence upon what was known as 'the dynamic will of the leadership'. Deliberately and instinctively, Hitler refused to permit any intervening hierarchical level between himself and the masses – any such intervention could only have detracted from the unique and supreme position of the Führer.

The hallmark of the Nazi régime was 'absence of system' (Masaryk's description of the Stalin régime)[55]; the weight of power was continually shifting among the paladins; communication and coordination between lower-level leaders was barred: the rivalries among the Nazi potentates were artificially kept alive. Hannah Arendt says: 'the will of the Führer can be embodied everywhere and at all times and he himself is not tied to any hierarchy, not even the one he might have established himself'.[56] Refusal to permit devolution of authority to the lower levels was a method of guaranteeing the personal dominance of the Führer – for dynamism was then his prerogative alone. Though outwardly resembling a pyramid of power, the hierarchy of Party functionaries in fact possessed no inherent authority; in the words of Hannah Arendt, the expert on totalitarianism, an action was legitimized 'not because it was done in execution of orders issuing from this or that authority but because it was done in "fulfilment of the will of the leadership".'[57]

In this unsystematic system the SS and its numerous organizations might occupy powerful positions but the absence of established authority continually allowed counterweights to emerge to prevent the SS from attaining any overriding position of predominance. Whether it was the Party, the SA or the Wehrmacht, there were always rivals to apply restraints and prevent the power-hungry SS from flying too high. Even the Wehrmacht, which had been politically emasculated as a result of the Blomberg-Fritsch crisis of 1938, invariably found ways and means to offset any SS claim to predominance. Right to the end of the war the Wehrmacht retained its privileged position. Nevertheless there was clearly a latent conflict between SS and Wehrmacht and this was first reflected in the field of occupation policy for German-occupied Europe; as soon as the German armies moved into Poland, this conflict arose.

From the outset the Wehrmacht had demanded full powers in occupied Polish territory; it had also insisted that the Sicherheitspolizei's Einsatzgruppen working in Poland should (at least during operations) be subordinate to the Wehrmacht. A military administration was in fact set up but disagreements between the Wehrmacht and Himmler's murder commandos became so acute that the senior soldiers were only too glad when responsibility for government in Poland was removed from them by Hitler.[58] Nevertheless on the next occasion the Army's demands, as put forward by its Commander-in-Chief, Colonel-General von Brauchitsch, were even stiffer. Before the Norwegian Campaign he submitted to Hitler a demand that plenary powers should once more be accorded to the Wehrmacht; Einsatzgruppen were not to be allowed in Norway.[59]

Ostensibly Hitler accepted the military demands and Heydrich's bloodhounds were not permitted to take part in the Norwegian campaign. Only ten days after the conclusion of operations, however, the

Dictator broke his word, appointing a Reich Commissar, the fire-eating Gauleiter Josef Terboven. Terboven was admittedly one of the anti-SS Party members, but simultaneously an HSSPF was appointed to Oslo, and he immediately summoned a number of Einsatzkommandos.[60] The process was repeated after the attack on Holland; Einsatzkommandos were only admitted after nomination of a Reich Commissar by Hitler. This time, however, the appointment was a clear victory for the SS: the Reich Commissar in question was Dr Arthur Seyss-Inquart and he wore the uniform of an SS-Gruppenführer.[61]

In Belgium and France, on the other hand, the military contrived to maintain their position of authority. No Einsatzkommandos were allowed while operations were in progress; OKH [Army High Command] eventually agreed to accept a Sicherheitspolizei detachment of ten men but only after representations from Göring and on condition that the men wore Wehrmacht uniform.[62] The detachment commander was SS-Obersturmbannführer Dr Helmut Knochen; he set up headquarters in the Hotel du Louvre, Paris, but General Otto von Stülpnagel, the Military Governor, France, with 2,500 men of the Field Security Police under his command, set out to ensure that Knochen's activities were severely restricted.[63]

Heydrich's nightmare was that 'led by the retired and reserve officers in the counter-espionage offices who were not always politically reliable', the Army might set up its own police organization independent of the RSHA.[64] He therefore produced the standard RSHA demand for all occupied territories – appointment of an HSSPF to command the local police units and be responsible to Himmler alone.[65] The Army refused; it was, however, willing to accept a 'representative of the Sicherheitspolizei and SD'. SS-Brigadeführer Dr Max Thomas was appointed,[66] but he soon became too active for the liking of the military, and they booted him out again.

The SS leaders had good reason to adopt cautious tactics towards the Wehrmacht since additional occupation areas were now under the latter's control. After the Balkan campaign, for instance, military governments were installed in Greece and Jugoslavia and they were not prepared to concede the SS much voice in affairs.[67] With growing suspicion SS headquarters watched the Wehrmacht's attempts to insulate itself from SS influence. Himmler did in fact think that he had a reliable Fifth Column inside the military organization in the shape of the senior SS commanders who acted as Military Administration Advisers in certain of the military districts in western and south-eastern Europe. But the SS luck was out. Hardly one of them proved effective. The worst thorn in Himmler's flesh was SS-Brigadeführer Eggert

Reeder, Head of Military Administration on the staff of C-in-C Belgium and Northern France.

Reeder was an ex-Regierungspräsident and an uncompromising supporter of the well-tried Prussian–German bureaucratic tradition. Himmler and his numerous emissaries were continually finding it necessary to remind Reeder that he was an Honorary SS Commander and that his policy should therefore be palatable to the SS.[68] The Prinz-Albrecht-Strasse was particularly incensed by Reeder's comparatively mild occupation policy and in this he was supported by the anti-Nazi von Falkenhausen, the military commander. Himmler was continually having 'to remonstrate about matters to which I do not normally have to refer in the case of SS officers', as he wrote to Reeder on February 16th, 1943;[69] SS-Gruppenführer Gottlob Berger, Head of the SS Hauptamt and Himmler's most reliable mouthpiece, said that Reeder appeared 'not to realize that his policy was a Belgian one; he should change his policy and make it a "Reich policy".'[70]

Reeder simply shrugged off Himmler's admonitions. He relied largely upon his adviser, an Administrative Officer [Oberkriegsverwaltungsrat] named Franz Thedieck, a right-wing Catholic and anti-Nazi, who scandalized the SS leaders by demonstratively going to church in Wehrmacht uniform (he later became State Secretary in the Federal Ministry in Bonn). Himmler complained again. 'You had promised SS-Gruppenführer Berger that by December 31st, 1942 you would dismiss your staff officer,[71] whom we regard as undesirable if not downright mischievous in the capacity of adviser on political matters in Belgium. This promise has not been kept.' Reeder never kept it.[72]

Himmler was equally disappointed by SS-Brigadeführer Dr Werner Best, head of the Military Section on the staff of the Military Governor, France; though he had been a co-founder of the RSHA, Best was all too frequently found on the side of the more cautious occupation policy adopted by the military. Nevertheless in July 1942 the soldiers got rid of him by an organizational subterfuge. On the arrival of Oberg as HSSPF France, the military decided to clear their decks of SS men. The administrative staff, Paris, was reduced in size and Best, who was an ex-Under Secretary [Ministerialrat], found himself doing a tuppeny-halfpenny job as a desk officer. He departed of his own accord.[73]

In Serbia the military adopted similar tactics against SS-Gruppenführer Dr Harald Turner, a fanatical National-Socialist and anti-Semite, head of the Military Administration on the staff of the Plenipotentiary Commanding General, Belgrade. On March 31st, 1942 SS-Obersturmbannführer Dr Georg Kiesel, Turner's staff officer, reported to Berlin: 'There is no doubt that attempts are now being made by the

Wehrmacht to force Gruppenführer Turner out of the military administration; the fact is that he does not suit them because, being an SS Commander, he is regarded as too dangerous.'[74] From an informer in the office of C-in-C South-East, Kiesel had heard that, as in Paris, the administrative staff was to be downgraded to an administrative section in order to force Turner out of Serbia. The reason adduced was the same as in Paris: appointment of an HSSPF.[75]

The military now opened a 'personal insult' campaign against Turner, described by Kiesel as a 'war of nerves'.[76] C-in-C South-East proposed to throw Turner out of his official residence, forbade him to sign administrative documents and refused to forward one of his reports because 'it contained certain criticisms of the Military Command which are regarded as subversive'.[77] Then Colonel Hermann Foertsch, Chief of Staff to C-in-C South-East, delivered the *coup de grâce*, writing to Turner: 'I can foresee that in the long run the development of the situation in Serbia will neither satisfy nor provide adequate employment for a man of your experience and capabilities.'[78]

Turner complained to the Reichsführer and Himmler succeeded in preventing the Army from carrying out its proposed staff reorganization.[79] The soldiers had more or less given the game up for lost when they found an unexpected ally in the HSSPF Serbia, Gruppenführer August Meyszner; he apparently preferred to side with the military rather than his fellow SS man. The two SS commanders became involved in so bitter a struggle about prerogatives and prestige that in Turner's words 'interested parties in Belgrade could hardly conceal their satisfaction'.[80] Whether the subject was control of the local Serbian Police, disposal of the property of murdered Jews, or priorities in the anti-partisan war, the HSSPF was continually making representations to the military to call 'their' Chief Administrative Officer to order.[81]

Meyszner was clearly one of those SS commanders – mostly ex-police or ex-Army officers – who had never overcome a secret longing to rejoin their old military comrades-in-arms. Neither the splendour of the SS uniform nor the SS élite mystique could quite stifle their private conviction that basically the Wehrmacht was the only force in the country which could legitimately bear arms. Even Karl Wolff, the most senior HSSPF once said that 'as an ex-regular Guards officer he had always been torn between his duty to the SS and his attachment to the Wehrmacht'.[82] Arthur Nebe, who was an ex-Lieutenant in the Engineers, was similarly inclined; when commanding Einsatzgruppe B he tended to pay far more attention to the view of anti-Nazi officers on the staff of Army Group Centre than to his orders from the RSHA.[83] Even Gruppenführer Oberg, the HSSPF France, could never conceal the esteem in which he held his wartime fellow-officer, the anti-Nazi General Carl-Heinrich von Stülpnagel. After the collapse of the July 20th plot in 1944 he saved many of the conspirators from the Gestapo and Stülpnagel himself said: 'If Oberg could have done as he liked, I believe he would have been on our side.'[84]

For many SS leaders the Wehrmacht was still the oracle on military matters and they would frequently accept a General's opinion without question, regarding him as the expert. This attitude of mind became almost an insidious disease sapping the arrogant self-confidence characteristic of so many SS leaders. The most striking example was perhaps Gruppenführer Gerret Korsemann, HSSPF Central Russia, whose behaviour caused Himmler some embarrassment. In summer 1943 the word went round that Korsemann had made an over-hasty getaway during the retreat from the Caucasus and had behaved 'like a frightened rabbit or just a plain coward'.[85] He evidently considered that there was nothing out of order in asking the Wehrmacht to give him a clean bill of health. On June 30th, 1943 he wrote a lengthy letter to Field-Marshal von Kleist under whose command he was: 'Honoured Field-Marshal,' the letter began; the Field-Marshal's 'obedient servant' then 'permitted himself to submit' that the Field-Marshal might 'write a short letter showing that I remained at my post not only as long as was necessary but in fact considerably longer and that I only withdrew with the Field-Marshal's agreement and when in practice I had no further task to perform.'[86] Berger of the SS-Hauptamt exploded: 'The stupidity and ingratiating tone of this letter are an insult to the SS in general and the Reichsführer in particular';[87] Himmler was so incensed that Korsemann was relieved and dispatched to the Waffen-SS as a punishment.[88]

Himmler punished any 'ingratiating attitude' towards the Wehrmacht with all the more severity since he suspected that the generals were exploiting their established position to expand their sphere of influence and block the growth of the SS. Moreover, alongside the Wehrmacht the Reichsführer saw another enemy of the SS emerging, a force which for years had been searching for an ally in its anti-SS campaign – the SA.

The unhappy survivors of the Röhm putsch had been relegated to the status of an old comrades association but the SA's hatred for the SS murderers was still boiling. Even Viktor Lutze, the Chief-of-Staff of the SA, would never forget Hitler's bloody excursion. He was determined to revenge himself on the SS murderers who had assassinated SA men in rows in the cellars of the SS torture houses. But the SA was too weak to challenge the SS unaided. Lutze could think of only one sure ally – the Wehrmacht.

Lutze had wanted the SA and Wehrmacht to strike against the SS immediately after the fall of von Blomberg and von Fritsch. In May 1938 at the foundation-stone laying ceremony of the Volkswagen factory in Wolfsburg, he had drawn aside General Ulex, a well-known anti-Nazi, and told him that the Fritsch case must be used to bring down Himmler who, he said, was already building up a private army in order to seize the succession from Hitler.[89] When the General asked what the attitude of the SA would be in the event of Wehrmacht action against the SS, Lutze exclaimed spontaneously: 'Unconditionally on the side of the Wehrmacht!' What if Hitler supported Himmler, Ulex asked. Lutze replied: 'The Führer must of course be spared as far as possible.' Ulex took Lutze's answer to mean: 'If he will not go along, he must go down too.' Ulex declared himself ready to transmit Lutze's plan to von Fritsch and his successor, von Brauchitsch, but stipulated that Lutze first provide proof that the Gestapo had used force to extract evidence against von Fritsch from Schmidt, the blackmailer.[90]

'A week or two later,' Ulex records, 'the Commander of SA Standarte Feldherrnhalle came to see me. On Lutze's instructions he informed me that his Chief was now in a position to bring proof that Schmidt's statements had been made under pressure from Himmler.' Ulex thereupon went to von Fritsch and von Brauchitsch but neither was willing to take part in Lutze's plans for a putsch, Brauchitsch saying: 'If these gentlemen want to do it, they must do it alone.' The Commander-in-Chief of the Army, torn between his aversion to the régime and his sense of military duty, was once more placing his confidence in Hitler. But his credulity did not last long. He was later to have many occasions to recall his remark to Ulex: 'I assure you that I will not rest until I have cleaned out the Himmler pigsty.'[91]

Lutze made continuous efforts to win over the vacillating C-in-C Army to his plan. His wife was related to the General[92] and so he was continually hanging around him pouring anti-SS poison into his ear. The more menacing the war situation became and the more dangerously the power of the SS grew, the greater the urgency with which Lutze pressed his case. Senior members of the Party were well aware that Lutze was hand-in-glove with the military. Goebbels noted in his diary: 'Unfortunately Lutze allowed his wife and the family's friendship with Brauchitsch to manoeuvre him into excessive opposition to the SS. Everywhere he criticizes and grumbles. Everywhere he feels that his SA has been put in the shade. He has got into the wrong hands.'[93]

As early as March 12th, 1940 Berger noted: 'The attitude of Lutze, the Chief-of-Staff, is gradually becoming a danger to the SS, if not to the Party. His "communal evenings" particularly those attended by the

Wehrmacht, are invariably used for anti-SS propaganda – and in a form unworthy of any decent person.'[94] Berger continued that, when meeting Wehrmacht officers in public, Lutze 'adopted an intolerable attitude towards the Reichsführer' and he ended: 'In my view it is necessary to place Lutze under observation.'[95]

Himmler's minions watched their enemy's every move. Not a detail escaped them. Lutze, for instance, had referred approvingly to a remark by Kerrl, the Reich Minister for Church Affairs, to the effect that Hitler had broken his promise of religious tolerance;[96] Lutze kept too many horses in his stables;[97] Lutze had ridiculed the SS as dagger-carrying numbskulls saying 'We want ideas-merchants, not dagger-merchants'[98] – everything was noted down and reported to the Party Chancellery. SS headquarters did not fail to observe that Lutze had meanwhile found a new ally – Hans Frank, the overlord of Poland and another enemy of the SS; Frank was only too willing to play off the SA against the tiresome SS-Police formations in the Government-General.

Initially Frank had set up a so-called 'special branch', a sort of private police force responsible to him alone and available for use by any Head of a District. After a two-year battle, however, Krüger, HSSPF Cracow and Frank's bitterest rival, had succeeded in removing control of the 'special branch' from the Governor-General.[99] At this moment – the end of 1942 – the SA offered itself to Frank as a new security service. Oberführer Pelz, the SA officer responsible for the Eastern territories, even attempted to take over Krüger's police duties, proposing that the SA be allowed into the Government-General in formed units to act as an auxiliary police force, clearly in the hope that the SA might counterbalance the SS and police formations.[100] On Himmler's instructions Krüger returned a flat negative.[101] But the SA had another card up its sleeve. Pelz offered his unit to the Headquarters of Air Region VIII, located in Cracow. The manoeuvre would have put the necessary weapons (machine guns and anti-aircraft guns) into the hands of the SA but at the last moment Krüger heard of the plan and managed to persuade the Air Region to withdraw its agreement.[102] Yet again the SA returned to the charge; it applied to the Reich Ministry for the East for approval to set up a construction service in all occupied Eastern territories. Berger, the watchdog, described the application as 'illegal' and once more Himmler was able to scotch his adversary's intrigue.[103]

When, however, in February 1943, Himmler heard that Lutze had gone off to Frank's 'kingdom' and had taken up residence in the Governor-General's villa in Bad Kryniza, he was seized with something approaching panic.[104] On February 26th, 1943 he wrote a letter of complaint to Bormann: 'I regard Lutze's visit to a spa in the Government-General as unfortunate; I consider it would be better if he took his cure in some German spa.'[105]

A few months later Lutze was killed in a road accident.[106] The SS had lost a dangerous enemy; nevertheless the SA remained as a centre of anti-SS opposition to whom anyone involved in a struggle with the SS turned for assistance. Alfred Rosenberg, the Minister for the East, together with SA leaders and prominent Party members, was the next to take up the cudgels against excessive SS influence in the German-occupied East. Berger spied another dangerous anti-SS conspiracy forming. 'I note to my astonishment,' he reported to Himmler, 'that a whole collection of Gauleiter are ranging themselves around Rosenberg and that he is regarded by the SA as the ultimate "defender of the rights of man". There are many senior Party leaders who consider the Reichsführer's position to be too powerful and who regard the development of the SS with a jaundiced eye.'[107]

The Russian neo-colonialists closed their ranks firmly against the SS. Of the ten Commissars-General in the eastern administration, two were Gauleiter, two SA-Obergruppenführer, one an NSKK Obergruppenführer, one a senior Party official, two officials of the Labour Service, and two civil servants – there was not a single SS man.[108] Enemies of the SS were everywhere, and opponents were to be found even in the most senior posts. In the Ukraine there was Reich Commissar Erich Koch, whom the SS had tried to sack in the mid-1930s;[109] in the Reich Commissariat 'Ostland' there was Gauleiter Hinrich Lohse, whom Berger described as 'a man without the smallest intelligence' and inspired by 'limitless hatred for the SS';[110] the Reich Commissar-designate Moscow was SA-Obergruppenführer Siegfried Kasche, a Röhm putsch survivor who would seize any opportunity to sabotage the SS.[111]

Motives for the antipathy of all these men to the SS were as varied as their personalities. Koch, for instance, was a crude neo-imperialist and a savage oppressor of the Slav 'sub-humans'; he disliked the SS because he suspected that it did not appreciate his master-race airs. Lohse resisted the SS because its methods bore an unpleasant similarity to those of the OGPU.

When HSSPF Ostland began exporting children from the Baltic States for 'Germanization', Lohse reprimanded him for exceeding his authority and for political ineptitude; on April 13th, 1942 he protested that he found 'this kidnapping of children by the police both provocative and questionable; the Bolshevists also use their police to deport children for

Bolshevist education'.[112] In the Ukraine Koch felt that his HSSPF, Obergruppenführer Prützmann, was spying on him and missed no opportunity of snubbing the man; he was continually trying to reduce Prützmann's authority and even forbade him to accept orders from Himmler. There were frequent shouting matches which would bring Koch's staff running up. Prützmann reported one argument on December 27th, 1942 as follows: 'Koch replied that I was his subordinate and should accept orders only from him. Moreover he would have to get rid of me since he wanted an HSSPF who would do what he said. In addition to criticizing my official actions, Koch made a number of insulting personal accusations; this he clearly did deliberately in order to increase the acrimony of the discussion. Finally I bowed myself out, since Koch declared at the top of his voice that he did not believe a word I said.'[113]

This sniping war between Koch and the SS did however illustrate one thing: the Nazi internal quarrels in the East did not spring solely from sheer lust for power on the part of the SS; SS criticism of the corruption and arrogance of the brown-shirted bosses also played its part and this inevitably brought the SS into increasingly open opposition to the Party.

As a result of the change in the fortunes of war in the East some of the more moderate SS leaders were having second thoughts about the whole master-race concept and felt that the eastern peoples should be treated with more circumspection. In the summer of 1943 even Berger himself emerged as the champion of a more moderate eastern policy; he joined the Ministry for the East as Head of an 'operational staff in charge of political affairs' and became one of Rosenberg's strongest allies against the autocratic Koch.[114] The more the SS eastern policy-makers veered towards tolerance, the more violent became their conflict with Koch and his supporter Bormann, the Head of the Party Chancellery. The SD began to keep records of Koch's atrocities.

The SD reports became so critical and Koch's protests to Himmler so shrill that SS Gruppenführer Thomas, late of France and now Sicherheitspolizei and SD Commander Ukraine, forbade the SD representative on his staff to report further on the Reich Commissar.[115] When the SD reports on Koch continued, Himmler intervened: 'These SD reports must now finally cease; if they do not, the SD will be disbanded and the officer responsible imprisoned.'[116] The reports on Koch ceased.

The fact was that Himmler had suddenly glimpsed a bottomless pit yawning in front of him and he recoiled. The one thing which could really worry him was a head-on collision with the Party.

Ever since the fortunes of war had ceased to smile upon Adolf Hitler the centres of power within the régime had crystallized with increasing clarity. As the months went by SS and Party, starting from opposite poles, had been gnawing their way through the timbers of the Reich towards the central focus of political power – and the moment could not be far distant when they would meet each other face to face. In the words of Professor Trevor-Roper 'Throughout the war the Party machine like the SS had grown; like the SS it had encroached on the functions of the armed forces, especially in matters of administration and supply, fortification and evacuation; like the SS it had become more formidable and more indispensable with every defeat of German arms.'[117] Moreover, since Hess had vanished to England the Party had found in Martin Bormann a leader determined to keep the SS at a distance from the Third Reich's ultimate levers of power. His methods were as unobtrusive as they were dangerous; he sat in the innermost sanctum of the Führer's headquarters, he was the channel of correspondence between Hitler and the Party, he ruled over the serried ranks of Gauleiter and Party functionaries – inconspicuous, ubiquitous and efficient.

For Himmler, the timorous small-timer, there could be no more torturing thought than the possibility that one day he might find himself involved in a duel with the Party. He knew only too well that the Party had no love for him. As long as he could do so without detriment to the prestige of the SS he must avoid open warfare. He had never managed to establish good relations with the Party bureaucracy. The majority of the Party activists were greedy schemers, avid for high-sounding titles and gold-braided uniforms and they despised this moralizing schoolmaster, this desiccated inhuman figure with his clap-trap about an SS Order and Germanism. However many uniformed minions he collected around him, to the Party he remained an outsider. Powerful though he might appear, therefore, the Reichsführer reacted with extreme sensitivity to any criticism from the Party. Though privately he might growl that order would only return to Germany when the last Gauleiter had been hung from a lamp-post,[118] the Party hierarchy had only to clear its throat for Himmler to take fright.

Any number of examples of Himmler's susceptibility on this point can be quoted. He was repeatedly sending to the SD written orders to refrain from investigating Party functionaries or meddling in Party questions.[119] When Bormann's Chancellery complained about anti-Party sallies in the *Schwarze Korps*, he passed the complaints on – to the editors and in writing – with every evidence of vexation. When Gertrud Scholtz-Klink, the Reich women's leader, complained about the *Schwarze Korps* because Michel Mumm, the editorial office wag, had headed a perfectly ordinary announcement of the birth of a child to a local Nazi Group leader with the humorous comment 'Our numbers rise,'[120] an office minute from Himmler gave it to be understood that: 'The Reichsführer-SS desires that no more of Michel Mumm's efforts be published in the *Schwarze Korps* since they all too often lead to complaints.'[121]

Whenever anyone complained, the editors of the *Schwarze Korps* could be sure that a reprimand from Himmler would arrive on their desks. Reichsleiter Karl Fiehler, for instance, objected that 'as used to happen in Jewish rags' the paper was 'seizing avidly upon any opportunity, possible or impossible, to label whole groups of officials as old-fashioned bureaucrats'[122] and Bormann demanded that attacks on individual Party members should cease.[123] On May 2nd, 1941 Himmler accordingly wrote: 'The reason is that this once highly respectable newspaper has sunk to a kitchen gossip level. Once and for all stop these stupid little digs at people; they interest no one except, one supposes, the gentlemen who write them and who apparently derive some inner satisfaction therefrom.'[124]

Himmler had a compelling private reason for remaining on good terms with Bormann. By 1940 he had lost all affection for his nervy shrewish wife Marga, and his ex-secretary Hedwig Potthast, an attractive girl from Cologne whom he had known since 1937, had become his mistress.[125] She was twenty-eight, the daughter of a businessman, and after graduating at the Industrial College in Mannheim, had joined the Reichsführer's personal staff as a secretary in the mid-1930s;[126] she soon came to exert a humanizing and relaxing influence on the stiff prim Himmler.[127] Initially Himmler wished to get a divorce but could not quite bring himself to do so. The liaison had the usual results and early in 1942 Hedwig Potthast was expecting the birth of her first child, Helge (another daughter, Nanette Dorothea, was born in 1944).[128]

This produced a tricky problem for Himmler. Hedwig was lodging with a family, but she obviously could not continue there now that she was pregnant; he had to find her somewhere to live.[129] The problem was all the more urgent since Hedwig's parents, not realizing how far the affair had gone, were continually urging her to give Himmler up.[130] Being a married man, they said, Himmler could never provide a respectable home for Haschen. Hedwig's sister-in-law Hilde, whose husband had been killed on the Eastern Front, became the intermediary between the girl and her parents 'For your parents' sake I would wish to see you married as soon as possible,' she said[131] – and in another letter: 'I fear, Hedwig, that there can never be a reconciliation [with the parents]. They would forgive everything at any time if you would give him up or if he would make himself a free man for your sake. What they cannot swallow is that you should go on living with him.'[132] Hilde rubbed the point home: 'He is after all married and your parents regard your relationship as dishonest towards his wife and disrespectful towards you. Your mother asked me whether his wife knew about it and unfortunately I had to tell her that as far as I knew this was not yet the case. She regarded this as proof of cold feet. Your parents are quite terribly distressed about it all.'[133]

If Himmler was not to lose his Hedwig he had to find her somewhere to live. But how? He was lord of the SS empire, he was master of the SS economic enterprises and he was ruler of the greatest police machine in German history – but he had no private capital. He could think of nothing other than to do what other Party members did – apply for a loan to the Party Chancellery. Bormann was generous and allowed Himmler 80,000 marks[134] and with this sum he built a house for Hedwig Potthast in Berchtesgaden-Schönau near the Königssee.[135] It was named 'Haus Schneewinkellehen' and was the basis of a temporary alliance between Himmler and Bormann, for Himmler's lonely mistress became friendly with Bormann's wife Gerda, who lived nearby.[136]

Like their womenfolk, Bormann and Himmler kept in close touch. One of Gerda Bormann's letters to her husband says 'Oh, Daddy, it doesn't bear imagining what would happen if you and Heinrich didn't see to everything. The Führer would never be able to do it alone. So you two must keep well and take care of yourselves.'[137] Martin Bormann took care. He took care that 'Uncle Heinrich' did not become over-powerful, he encouraged him when he was having an attack of depression, he upbraided him if he ever allowed himself to criticize The Chief (Hitler). On one occasion Himmler lamented that Hitler was being unfair to him; he was apparentely thought good for nothing but to raise new divisions for the Führer. Bormann calmed him down but at the same time warned him not to carry criticism of Adolf Hitler too far; to Gerda he wrote: 'His chilly way of criticizing is unpleasant. When all is said and done the Führer is the Führer. Where should we be without him?'[138]

So long as no vital SS interest was at stake, the Reichsführer had no intention of allowing the rapacity of his underlings to bring him into collision with this mentor who also controlled the only door to his wayward demi-god, Hitler. Himmler forbade any criticism of the Party.

But Himmler had not reckoned upon the overweening ambition of those of his subordinates who had no private reasons to treat the Party gently – and of these the outstanding example was Otto Ohlendorf whose ideas on the Party were quite different. He was the archetype of the schizophrenic SS intellectual; in the same breath he could direct a vast army of spies and dream of the disbandment of the Party to make way for a cultural Order of National-Socialist noblemen. He was one of the most controversial characters in the entire SS world; Himmler regarded him as an intelligent machine but for the historian he is a puzzle – he directed the murder of 70,000 Jews[139] and at the same time was appalled by the crude methods of the brown-shirted bosses. To Himmler's misfortune this was the man at the head of the Inland-SD.

Ohlendorf's friends later tried to present him as a sort of Resistance fighter inside the SS, as the mouthpiece of a 'positive opposition'.[140] They carefully omitted to mention that this opposition was involuntary; Ohlendorf was the victim rather than the master of a chain of events which he himself had initiated. As already related, Ohlendorf had had the idea of instituting a sort of secret Gallup poll to produce unvarnished accounts of all movements of opinion within Germany and these were made known to senior leaders in the 'Reports from the Reich' issued two or three times per week. Here inevitably lay the germ of serious conflict; the SD was forbidden to investigate the Party; if, however, the SD 'Reports from the Reich' were to cover all so-called 'spheres of life', how could they omit the most important political sphere of life – the Party?

With satisfaction mixed with consternation, Ohlendorf realized that hardly a detail of the Party's squabbles escaped his observers. The SD faithfully recorded the megalomania and arrogance of the bosses, the ineffectiveness of Party propaganda and mismanagement by Gau or District headquarters. Vainly he sought to put a brake on the mechanism which he himself had set in motion, assuring senior SD leaders that 'by far his greatest worry' was the fear lest the SD reports give the impression that the Party was 'something negative or hostile' and that 'the Führer, the Reichsführer and the SS were opposed to the Party bureaucracy'.[141]

In every order he protested that the whole purpose of the SD was to reinforce the rule of National-Socialism. 'The legal position,' he said in an SD directive of 1941, must 'invariably be consonant with the political and ideological principles of National-Socialism.' He proclaimed that the law 'had not yet succeeded in bringing the administration of justice entirely into line with the political requirements for the security of our order of society'.[142]

On the basic question of human liberties his thinking hardly differed from that of the barbaric manipulators of the law like Roland Freisler. In a draft for a lecture to be given in October 1942 he described Hans

Frank, the opponent of the police State, as an accomplice of British plutocrats and with his own perverse brilliance proved that the illegal was merely a superior form of legality. The object of the law, he argued, was to protect the community, not the individual; the protection of the law was synonymous with the protection of the Reich; wherever the latter was endangered by ideologically unreliable judges, the police must undertake the 'correction of inadequate sentences' and 'counteract the prevailing leniency in the administration of justice'. He referred to the protection of the law as 'that well-worn phrase'.[143]

In the light of such fanatical National-Socialist orthodoxy Ohlendorf, the puritan, spied all sort of inadequacies, stupidities and depravities disfiguring his idealized picture of National-Socialism. He could not share the calculated optimism of those around him; every fresh report from his informers reinforced his conviction that the Party was suffering from a cancer which would infect the still healthy parts of the régime. Himmler ruminated: 'He has trouble with his liver and gall-bladder. His reports are always gloomy; he has the pessimistic outlook which goes with physical suffering. Liver and gall-bladder troubles always have that effect on the mind.'[144] It never occurred to Himmler that the cause of Ohlendorf's suffering was the gloomy reading made by the SD daily reports. Every page proved that public opinion was turning against the Party and the régime.

A report from SD Aussenstelle Bunde, May 13th, 1941 read: 'Hardly anything has produced so paralysing a shock as the news that the Führer's Deputy [Hess] has flown to England. The craziest rumours are going round and people simply do not believe that some mental aberration can in fact have been the reason. Other people talk of a moral defeat, of another major breach of faith by one of the "old fighters".'[145]

Report from SD Aussenstelle Minden, July 24th, 1941: 'The initial effect upon the majority of the population of Sunday's event – war with Russia – has been one of paralysis. Moreover the fact that the Führer called for God's blessing upon this struggle has contributed to the state of public opinion, which can hardly be described as rosy.'[146]

The more the fortunes of war turned against Germany the more pessimistic the SD reports became and the more often was their criticism directed primarily against the propaganda put out by Goebbels and the Party. Report of January 12th, 1942: 'According to the attached reports from SD Aussenstelle Erfurt the population's reaction to the propaganda appearing in the Press over the last few weeks has been particularly unfavourable. Especially in the *Thüringer Gauzeitung* both the headlines and the comments on individual reports have been so unrealistic and the conclusions drawn so fanciful that the newspaper can hardly continue to be taken seriously.'[147]

'The article by Dr Goebbels in *Reich* of January 11th, 1942 has evoked no applause from the population. His statement that Churchill's place is on the variety stage and not at the head of an empire is liable to lead to underestimation of our enemy. As German propaganda's supreme director Dr Goebbels should really now cease to indulge in such fatuities.'[148] Goebbels in fact became the standard Aunt Sally of the SD reports; on another of his articles SD Erfurt commented: 'Such remarks might perhaps have been acceptable from a street warden during an air-raid practice; coming from the Reich Minister of Propaganda they can only be described as sub-standard.'[149]

Ohlendorf's 'Reports from the Reich' soon became known in the Party and the Party organization men took fright. A wave of Party indignation, touched off by certain prominent Gauleiter, descended on the SD's investigation system. Leading Nazi functionaries were continually complaining to Martin Bormann and accusing the Reichsführer-SS of allowing the SD to exceed its authority. As the months passed the tone of the complaints became sharper until they might have been referring to agents of a foreign power. Hans Frank, the Governor-General of Poland, for instance, voiced 'most serious misgiving concerning the so-called confidential information reports about the Government-General which the so-called SD continuously brandishes about the Reich'. They were 'simply low-level spy stories'.[150] On November 30th, 1942 Gauleiter Albert Florian fulminated: 'My suspicion, hitherto unfortunately lacking evidence, that the SD was in fact rummaging around in Party matters is now fully substantiated. I am therefore compelled to take my own measures. I propose to forbid any political director or member of my staff to undertake any duty on behalf of the SD; alternatively I shall make such action dependent upon approval by the District Governor concerned or by myself.'[151]

On January 22nd, 1943 Gauleiter Carl Weinrich stated: 'I refuse once and for all to allow the SD to poke its nose into my affairs. After all we are not in Russia and do not need to be shadowed by an OGPU.'[152]

The SD now found itself the target for a general attack by the Party functionaries, employing every form of subtlety and designed to uncover and paralyse its informer network. At a meeting of his local Group leaders Kampe, the Kreisleiter [District Leader] of Danzig, called out 'Who among you is a so-called contact man for the SD?' When Pohle, the local Group leader from Praust, admitted as much, Kampe loosed a flood of invective on his head; Richard Hildebrandt, the HSSPF, reported that 'Kampe's description of the contact man compared him to a stateless, characterless Intelligence agent'. Kampe's anti-SD outburst was greeted with thunderous applause by the other local Group leaders, one shouting 'Spy!' and another 'Cheka methods!' One Group leader confided to Hildebrandt: 'I must say that I was really astounded at the hatred of the SS among the political leaders.'[153]

Any SD informer discovered by the indignant Party sleuths was faced with an ultimatum – to make up his mind whether he belonged to the Party or the SS – and some Nazi officials imposed a complete boycott on the SD.

As the Party complaints increased in vehemence Himmler gave way. On March 18th, 1943 he sent a letter to Bormann assuring him that 'as before' the SD had 'the strictest orders not to concern itself with internal Party matters'.[154] Bormann declared himself satisfied with Himmler's assurance – he knew that Himmler disliked the intellectual Ohlendorf more than any other SS leader.

'To be quite frank,' Himmler confided to Kersten, 'I don't care for the man. He has no sense of humour. He is one of those unbearable people who always know better. Having his Gold Party Badge and being one of the first recruits to the SS, he regards himself as the Galahad of National-Socialism.'[155] Rudolf Brandt, Himmler's personal assistant, said that Himmler 'feels that Ohlendorf is continually watching over him like a second Reichsführer; he is a man who always knows better and has the ability to propound detailed arguments on any subject'.[156] Otto Ohlendorf was undoubtedly the last man for whom Himmler would risk a quarrel with the Party. He cut the SD down to size; SD planning was continuously being upset by some pronouncement from Himmler.

The 'Reports from the Reich' frequently came back to Ohlendorf mangled by Himmler; the Reichsführer repeatedly threatened to have Ohlendorf arrested and the Inland-SD disbanded if it continued to deal with Party matters.[157] Although they were probably the most realistic reflections of the true position, he refused to show the reports to Hitler, saying to Kersten: 'They are usually so pessimistic that this is quite out of the question; they would only impair the Führer's capacity for action.'

'Supposing they are true?' Kersten asked.

'That doesn't matter,' Himmler replied. 'Details which are unhelpful must be kept from the Führer, however important they may appear.'[158]

But Ohlendorf showed no inclination to obey his Reichsführer's orders and the SD continued to keep watch on the Party functionaries. The much-abused Goebbels, together with Martin Bormann, thereupon decided that a steam-hammer must be used to crack this nut. Goebbels demanded that the 'Reports from the Reich' either be banned or at least coordinated with the reports of the Reich propaganda offices – which of course were under his orders. The readers of the SD reports, Goebbels said, who included officials in Government offices, were being given information about Party matters and this was the responsibility of the Party Chancellery alone.[159]

Goebbels fired the first shot in the anti-SD campaign – he banned distribution of the reports within his Ministry; Hans Fritzsche, the Director of Broadcasting, remembers him saying that they were 'calculated to give to leading Party and State circles a defeatist impression of the people's morale and the prospects of the war'.[160] Himmler withdrew an inch or two. On May 12th, 1943 Goebbels noted in his diary: 'Himmler is now ready to have the SD report stopped . . . as its effect is too defeatist.'[161] Here, however, Goebbels was being premature – Himmler waited to see what Bormann would do.

For some time Bormann had made no move but then something happened which radically altered his relationship with Himmler – in August 1943 Himmler was appointed Reich Minister of the Interior. Party and SS were now face to face; the confrontation between the two power groups began.

It was soon borne in on Himmler that something had changed. Bormann now joined the anti-SD ranks and demanded strict adherence to Party orders – and these prescribed that both the formulation of opinions on internal Party matters and evaluation of the political reliability of Government officials were the business of the Party alone. Gradually the SD's enemies closed in; in summer 1943 the distribution list of the 'Reports from the Reich' was severely restricted and a year later the reports were banned altogether.[162] Simultaneously Bormann forbade both full-time and part-time Party functionaries to work with the SD and shortly thereafter the Labour Front followed suit – the SA, as we have seen, had already done so.[163]

One would have expected Himmler to protest against the emasculation of his SD and at last mobilize the power which he undoubtedly possessed. But he did nothing of the sort: he made no move at all. Ohlendorf raged: 'He had power but in practice he made no use of it in Germany; he and his power were a pricked balloon.'[164] Himmler, the tactician, could think of only one method of saving the SD: negotiations with the Party Chancellery for a new SD field of activity had already begun, and he allowed them to drag on, hoping for some miracle to appear. At the end of the war he was still negotiating.[165] Evidently he had no faith in their success, for he had long since lopped certain responsibilities in the field of Police Law off the Reich Ministry of the Interior and given them to the SD in order to ensure that it had something to do and therefore some justification for existence.[166]

This withdrawal by Himmler was a good example of a flaw in the SS system which was usually concealed by the façade of totalitarian solidarity. The SS never dared to wage open warfare against the Party because its leaders did not really agree where their true interests lay. The monolithic unity of the SS was in fact no more than a myth carefully cultivated by the SS propagandists.

Himmler was under no illusions that his dream of unshakable SS unity was anything but a figment of the imagination. As early as 1940 he had confided to the officers of the Leibstandarte the 'anxieties which sometimes beset me . . . This Waffen-SS will live only if the SS as a whole lives – if the entire Corps becomes a real Order living according to these laws and realizing that one part without the other is unthinkable.'[167] Speaking to SS-Gruppenführer in Poznan in October 1943 he was even more explicit: 'Doom! – if a split develops between the SS and the police. Doom! – if some well-meaning but misguided notion of their responsibilities leads the Hauptämter to try to make themselves independent each with their own channel of command to their subordinates. I sincerely believe that if that were so and if one day I were to be shot down, it would be the end of the SS,' and he continued with his gloomy picture of the decline of the SS: 'Doom! – if the separate Hauptämter or the individual heads of department have a false picture of their mission . . . Doom! – if we ever allow these ties [between the various SS organizations] to loosen; then you may be sure that in a generation or less all would sink back into its old mediocrity.'[168]

Such desperate appeals for unity showed that Himmler resembled the entrepreneur obsessed with the expansion of his business who sets up ever more numerous and ever larger installations and then finds that he is in danger of losing control of them all. Similarly Himmler, a timorous and mistrustful being anyway, must sometimes have wondered whether he was still master in his own house. The more dynamic and rapacious the SS empire became, the more obvious it was that its component parts were gathering a momentum of their own and visibly divorcing themselves from Himmler; the more self-assertive subordinates acted as if they were independent authorities. Moreover the continuous growth of the SS organization forced Himmler to accept into his Order men who by no means measured up to the standards of pure-blooded National-Socialism.

Even the senior ranks gradually became filled with so heterogeneous a collection of men that the SS turned into a curiously pluralistic organization for a totalitarian dictatorship under the Führer. It resembled a gigantic sponge, sucking up men of the most contradictory characters –

so contradictory that it frequently had difficulty in presenting a solid front to the outside world. Andreas Schmidt, leader of the German minority in Rumania and son-in-law to Gottlob Berger, complained indignantly: 'It is unfortunately a fact that in difficult times even members of the SS do not present a common front; when times are difficult they intrigue all the more, thus considerably increasing already existing difficulties.'[169]

The multifarious interests of the SS subsidiary organizations, and the conviction dinned into them over the years that they belonged to a superior and select group of men, had built up a superiority complex which at times worked against the overall interests of the Order. Thirsting for power and prestige, SS leaders often fought each other to the detriment of the SS as a whole and there were even instances of naked cabalistic intrigue causing senior SS commanders to oppose the interests and orders of Himmler. The appointment of the HSSPF [Höhere SS- und Polizeiführer – Senior SS and Police Commanders] is a good illustration of Himmler's difficulty in asserting his authority in the jungle of the warring SS cliques. The HSSPF were his most important representatives and yet it was all he could do to ensure that they were treated with proper respect; in many instances insults and contempt were the order of the day.

Himmler had created the post of HSSPF in 1937 with two objects; on the 'Land' level (paralleling Himmler at the centre) to amalgamate the SS and police into one State Protection Corps; secondly, as Himmler's representatives, to supervise all SS units.[170] By creating the HSSPF Himmler had hoped to keep ahead of developments. As the SS continued to expand and spawn fresh organization, Himmler was haunted by the nightmare that the individual components of the SS empire might claim their independence and the senior bureaucrats of the subsidiary organizations, the heads of the SS Hauptämter, might undermine his position as the supreme autocrat. Himmler therefore regarded the HSSPF not only as the cement binding together the pluralist SS society but also as the counterweight to the growing power of the Hauptämter.

The Berlin Hauptämter accordingly left no stone unturned to reduce these viceroys of the SS Sultan to the status of delegates with sonorous titles but without power. Moreover the traditionalist official administration refused to allow the upstart HSSPF any disciplinary authority under administrative law, and to conceal his purpose from the recalcitrant administration Himmler was forced to restrict the HSSPF to purely representative functions.[171] Accordingly their SS rivals initially had an easy run.

In occupied Europe, however, where the obstacle of an established administration did not exist, Himmler could give his HSSPF more authority; yet even here pretending that the HSSPF did not exist became a recognized sport for local SS units. The SS and Police Hauptämter took precautions to ensure that the HSSPF did not become over-powerful. Hauptamt Orpo, for instance, repeatedly refused to grant them authority to punish or promote personnel of the Ordnungspolizei;[172] the Chief of the Ordnungspolizei insisted that in Russia the HSSPF were subordinate to him.[173] SS commanders repeatedly showed that they did not take Himmler's representatives very seriously. The local concentration-camp Commandant in Hamburg, for instance, refused to tell his HSSPF how many prisoners he had, saying that he was pledged to secrecy; SS-Oberführer Leo von Jena, Commanding 8 SS Totenkopf Standarte, disputed the right of Krüger, the HSSPF, to demand from his reports on the strength, dispositions and morale of his troops.[174]

The fiercest resistance against the attempts by the HSSPF to exercise command authority came from the Waffen-SS. When Krüger ordered von Jena to take up new positions for a proposed operation against Polish partisans, Jena refused and referred Krüger to the Inspector General of Reinforced Totenkopf Standarte, who alone was authorized to order changes of this nature.[175] Himmler was so vexed by the unruliness of his subordinates that he issued additional orders concerning the authority of the HSSPF; in the case of the Waffen-SS, he said, it appeared that existing orders 'in practice' permitted the HSSPF 'to assist the Waffen-SS' but that 'otherwise they were looked upon as tiresome outsiders'.[176] On March 16th, 1942 Himmler warned the refractory heads of the Hauptämter: 'I would like all my heads of department to think whether they would themselves wish to be an HSSPF under such degrading conditions of impotence. I would also ask them to consider what the SS and police would look like in ten years time if I allowed such a state of affairs to continue.'[177] Himmler then armed his satraps with increased plenary powers. In their areas the HSSPF were given authority over all Allgemeine-SS offices, commanders of the Ordnungspolizei, the Sicherheitspolizei and SD, and overall representatives of VOMI and the RKF Staff Department.[178] A draft order of January 1943 prepared by Himmler's Personal Staff, laid down that the HSSPF were 'responsible for seeing that all offices of the Allgemeine-SS, the Waffen-SS, the Ordnungspolizei and the SD act in a manner worthy of the SS and present a good appearance'.[179] So the HSSPF were now entitled to claim that they alone were responsible for all that went on within the SS in their respective areas.[180]

Nevertheless the Hauptämter contrived to chip away at the authority of the HSSPF; 'provisional service regulations' for HSSPF dated January 8th, 1943, for instance, stated that all members of the SS were under the HSSPF 'for matters of general behaviour in accordance with SS standards'; 'orders and instructions on technical matters', however, could be issued 'to those SS members for whom they were technically responsible' only by the Hauptämter.[181] When the HSSPF complained that they were still being sabotaged by the Hauptämter, Himmler extended their authority yet again. Local SS leaders were ordered to report to their HSSPF before any duty trip to their Hauptamt, and applications for leave also had to be countersigned by the HSSPF.[182] Nevertheless Himmler was only too well aware that the authority of his HSSPF was often as fictitious as the unity of the SS. In 1943 he declaimed: 'This SS Order with all its ramifications, all its basic organizations . . . must continue even under the tenth Reichsführer-SS . . . all must remain as one block, one body, one Order.'[183] The files of the innumerable disciplinary and arbitration Courts, however, show that in practice the Order was little better than an arena in which the most diverse and antagonistic elements struggled for mastery – hardly a single senior SS leader was not accusing one of his colleagues of disloyalty to the policy or ideology of the SS.

In such a maze of individual and factional interests true solidarity was hardly possible. Even Himmler could not impose unity on such perplexing multiplicity. The SS leaders' rugged individualism was proof even against the person of the Reichsführer himself. In fact 'Reichsheini' with his inelegant semi-comic figure, found it difficult to assert his authority when face to face with his subordinates. For this reason Himmler disliked receiving several people at a time; he felt more secure behind his mountains of files and the incessant barrage of orders which he loosed upon his realm.

However, Himmler had his own methods of curbing the impetuosity of his subordinates. Reprimands in severe schoolmasterish style, a spy system covering even the most senior SS leaders and the distribution of orders to the widest possible circle of his subordinates, combined to form a control system calculated to nip in the bud the growth of any new centres of power within the SS. His continuous warnings and scoldings were intended constantly to remind the SS leaders that the Reichsführer was the sole source of their power.

Himmler to SS-Brigadeführer Hintze: 'I have given you this chance to be an HSSPF; if your lack of self-control, drunkenness and megalomania prevent you making use of it, it is your own fault if you get no further.'[184] Shortly thereafter a further reprimand: 'Report to SS-

Obergruppenführer Jeckeln as instructed. Don't make so many speeches and get on with your job.'[185] To SS-Oberführer Professor Arnold Waldschmidt, 'as an old Party member and SS man, I expect you in future to represent the views of the Führer faithfully and without question. Although you have done great damage to the reputation of Germanism and of the SS, I do not propose to proceed further on this occasion. Until further notice, however, you will not receive authorization for journeys abroad.'[186]

Even the most reliable Obergruppenführer received their reprimands. To HSSPF South-West: 'In this serious moment I request you at last to display that energy and drive necessary to avert panic situations.'[187] To Oberstgruppenführer Kurt Daluege, his old crony and rival: 'I implore you to strike with an iron hand and abolish totally that spirit of officialdom still to be found here and there; have it out by the roots.'[188] He even intervened in the private lives of his officers; on May 16th, 1944 he wrote to HSSPF Denmark: 'Dear Pancke, I request you to discipline your wife and to stop her voicing her opinions loud and clear in the most improbable places concerning this or that political occurrence in the Gau or concerning the Gauleiter himself. In general I have the impression that in your marriage you do not exert sufficient control and that you have not educated your young wife in the manner which I have a right to expect from an SS leader.'[189]

Senior SS officers were kept under observation and any irregularity in their private lives was noted. Many of them were persecuted by anonymous letters which Himmler took with extreme seriousness.

One SS leader kept watch upon another. Obergruppenführer Wolff faced Gruppenführer Kaltenbrunner with a report to the effect that he was misusing Government petrol for journeys to his home;[190] Brigadeführer Ohlendorf presented Obergruppenführer Wolff with a report showing that official vehicles were delivering an extraordinary number of geese and ducks to Wolff's house.[191] Himmler distrusted even the older SS commanders, employing outsiders to keep an eye on them. In 1940 he discovered a super-watchdog who was not even a member of the SS and who rapidly became its most hated and most exploited figure.[192]

The whipping-boy was named Dr Richard Korherr, a devout Catholic and one of the most brilliant statisticians in the Reich. Nazi District Headquarters Würzburg described him as 'a timorous personality somewhat shy, irritable and sensitive'[193] – hardly the man to clamp down on the forceful self-seekers of the Hauptämter. Exactly this, however, was what Himmler proposed to the unsuspecting Korherr; as 'Inspector for Statistics attached to the Reichsführer-SS and Chief of the German Police and Reich Commissar for the strengthening of Germanism', he was to check information and reports coming from the Hauptämter. In a solid phalanx the heads of the Hauptämter prepared to run this intruder out of business. Even the dutiful Berger, normally so concerned for his Reichsführer's prestige, attempted to muzzle Himmler's watchdog, saying 'you, Korherr, join me. I will make you a Standartenführer'. But Korherr refused.[194]

Korherr soon uncovered the falsehoods, both great and small, with which the heads of the Hauptämter embellished their success stories to Himmler. He told Himmler: 'Without the smallest detriment to the work of the offices I could now extract from the SS Hauptämter three battle-strength divisions';[195] he pointed out that a report from Lebensborn on infant mortality was a 'stinking lie from beginning to end'.[196] Dr Gregor Ebner, the head of Lebensborn, had reported that the infant mortality rate in his maternity home was four per cent, two per cent lower than the average in Germany at the time. Korherr discovered that the actual mortality rate in the Lebensborn homes was eight per cent. Furiously Ebner demanded that the tiresome Korherr be placed under arrest.[197]

Finally one of the Hauptamt Chiefs resorted to physical violence. On August 12th, 1943 Obergruppenführer Richard Hildebrandt, the new Head of the RuSHA, summoned Korherr and accused him of claiming the right to pass judgement upon the Hauptämter. The subsequent scene was reported to Himmler by Korherr as follows: 'I made as if to go, when Obergruppenführer Hildebrandt said "I will have no more of your insolence." I threw back: "The insolence is on your side," saluted and made for the door. Obergruppenführer Hildebrandt followed and gave me two resounding smacks, one on each cheek. As far as I remember he then said "And now get out", though I could not swear to it. I departed without a word or any attempt to retaliate.'[198]

Seething with anger, Korherr awaited satisfaction, but the weeks went by and the Reichsführer made no move to support his statistician. All Himmler could extract from Hildebrandt was a half-hearted apology addressed, not to Korherr, but to Himmler: 'Honoured Reichsführer, I respectfully request you to express my regret to Oberregierungsrat Doctor Korherr for the physical assault which I made upon him. Heil Hitler! Yours: Hildebrandt.'[199]

Richard Korherr had learned his lesson. Himmler was clearly in no position to protect his own inspector. Korherr took himself off to the neighbourhood of Regensburg where, on Himmler's orders, he set up a scientific statistical institute – out of reach of the Heads of the Hauptämter.[200] The Korherr episode showed how independent the

Hauptämter had become within the SS. In fact they only closed their ranks if some common danger threatened; in normal circumstances they operated separately and each went its own way. After the war SS-Oberführer Reinecke said: 'Instead of working more closely together, as Himmler had intended, these organizations, due to their varied tasks, steadily drifted away from each other.'[201]

Frequently they pursued totally contradictory policies, for instance: the RSHA pressed for the total annihilation of all Jews but the WVHA advocated the preservation of all Jews capable of work;[202] in occupation policy in Russia the RSHA clung to the 'Russian sub-human' theory whereas the SS Hauptamt pressed for the formation of a Russian shadow army under German leadership;[203] on questions of State security (such as monitoring enemy broadcasts) the Gestapo adopted a much tougher line than the SD;[204] the WVHA strove to exempt its various concerns from all control by the State, whereas a group of SS officers led by Ohlendorf visualized stricter supervision of SS economic undertakings by the Reich authorities.[205] In Rumania there were no fewer than four lines of SS policy: the SS Hauptamt wished to recruit the maximum number of 'racial Germans'; VOMI thought similarly but was even more radical; the VDA [Verein Deutscher in Ausland – Union of Germans Abroad] was opposed to VOMI; and finally the Consul General (an SS-Oberführer) pursued a policy all his own.[206] The clearest example, however, of the tendency towards independence shown by the various parts of the SS is the story of the Führungshauptamt [Operational Headquarters], the headquarters of the armed force which carried the SS terror on to the battlefields of Europe, and yet increasingly divorced itself from the ideology of the SS Order: this was the Waffen-SS.

16

THE WAFFEN-SS

IN March 1942 the RSHA forwarded to Himmler a secret SD report showing what the Germans thought of Adolf Hitler's most merciless and most feared force of armed men. 'Basically,' the report said, 'it may be stated that by its achievements the Waffen-SS has won its place in the popular esteem. Particular reference is made to the good comradeship and excellent relations between officers, NCOs and men.'

On the other hand, the SD indicated 'voices are to be heard saying that the Waffen-SS possesses no trained officers and that SS men are therefore "recklessly sacrificed". The Waffen-SS is said to "rush on regardless" because it thinks that it must "get ahead" of the Wehrmacht.' Worse still: 'Critical voices are to be heard saying that the Waffen-SS is a sort of "military watchdog". SS men are trained to be brutal and ruthless, apparently so that they can be used against other German formations if necessary.' General impression: 'The Waffen-SS is the most ruthless force; it takes no prisoners but totally annihilates its enemy.'[1]

The popular picture of the Waffen-SS as presented by the SD was accurate; this force, which more than any other SS formation reflected the heterogeneous character, the horror and the idealism of Himmler's Order, was regarded by many Germans with a mixture of admiration and fear. The Waffen-SS was the Imperial Guard of the National-Socialist régime; in the Second World War its soldiers scored one military success after another, but its commanders were too rugged and too independent to accept their Reichsführer's ideological fantasies without demur.

The Waffen-SS had been conceived as the Party's Brigade of Guards; it had been trained for the merciless fanatical war of ideology; but as the years went by its divorce from the remainder of the Order became increasingly obvious. The daily grind of World War II turned the Reichsführer's legionaries into practically normal soldiers, almost indistinguishable from those of the Wehrmacht. The collective judgement of the Nuremberg Court, however, branded the Waffen-SS as an 'Army of Outlaws' (Felix Steiner's title) and a collection of political fanatics. The Waffen-SS soldiers found themselves stripped of their military character and equated with the RSHA's murder commandos and the concentration-camp torturers.

The ex-Wehrmacht officers could have corrected this distorted picture of the Waffen-SS but the majority preferred to hold their tongues. Many were apparently unable to remember that they had once been glad to have the élite Waffen-SS Divisions fighting alongside them. Some even contributed to this blanket condemnation of the SS troops. Field-Marshal Kesselring described the formation of the Waffen-SS as 'the game of a spoilt child';[2] General Westphal complained that the Waffen-SS had 'diverted the best-quality reinforcements and newly trained men from the Army';[3] Field-Marshal von Manstein grumbled that it 'paid a toll of blood incommensurate with its actual gains'.

Some of the senior soldiers apparently suffered from lapses of memory. During the defensive battles west of Kharkov in August 1943 von Manstein acknowledged that by throwing back the Soviet forces which had broken through in the Bielgorod-Valki area, the SS Division 'Das Reich' had made a German counter-offensive possible. In his memoirs, however, he is silent on the subject.[5]

Such deliberate discretion provoked a counter-offensive from the ex-Waffen-SS commanders; as memoir-writers the SS Generals proved worthy competitors of the Wehrmacht – at least in so far as calculated loss of memory was concerned. The leading Waffen-SS apologists were Obergruppenführer and Colonel-General (retired) Paul Hausser, his late fellow General, Felix Steiner, and the spokesmen of the 'Mutual Aid Society for ex-soldiers of the Waffen-SS', all of whom attempted to prove the unprovable – that the Waffen-SS had never been anything but a purely military force. The worst offenders were the 'Mutual Aid Society'; by quoting fictitious extracts from Hitler's speeches and falsifying dates, they have attempted to prove that the background to the Waffen-SS and its predecessor the SS-Verfügungstruppe (VT) was entirely non-political. The VT, they say, was formed only after the proclamation of universal military service in 1935 and was a 'fourth arm of the Service', a 'modern experimental force'.[6]

In fact the history of the Waffen-SS goes back much further – to the first months following the National-Socialist seizure of power, when the SS started to form armed units. Even at this early stage battle groups armed with personal weapons appeared in the Abschnitte and Oberabschnitte of the Allgemeine-SS; they were designed to ensure that the SA army treated the SS with proper respect and to terrorize the democratic opposition which, though defeated, was still active.

As a general rule in each SS Abschnitt some 100 armed SS men formed themselves into a so-called 'Headquarters Guard', a title which in itself shows that initially the primary purpose of these units was to satisfy some local SS leader's desire for martial pomp and circumstance; in many cases Himmler was not even consulted. Once a Headquarters Guard was fully trained it called itself a Sonderkommando [special detachment] and acted as an auxiliary police force, the object here being to get its pay carried on the local police budget.[7] If a Sonderkommando rose to more than company strength, it was entitled to call itself a Politische Bereitschaft [political alarm squad]; it was then organized on full military lines with sections, platoons, Stürme [companies] and Sturmbanne [battalions].[8]

The entire country was eventually covered by a network of Politische Bereitschaften training armed SS men for the practice of political terror on the home front. In Wolterdingen, Arolsen, Ellwangen, Leisnig, Württemberg and Saxony, for example, Politische Bereitschaften practised for the German civil war,[9] which for a few hours on June 30th, 1934 threatened to become a gruesome reality.

Among these political warriors from the Allgemeine-SS, the best-known unit was one created by Adolf Hitler himself. He had formed a 'Headquarters Guard' for his personal protection and placed at its head a shrewd and effective Upper Bavarian SS-Gruppenführer, Josef ('Sepp') Dietrich. Dietrich, born in 1892, had had a varied career – farm labourer, waiter, NCO in a tank unit, policeman, foreman in a tobacco factory, customs officer and petrol-pump attendant;[10] he was one of those quick-witted Bavarian toughs who rode in Hitler's Mercedes during his oratorical tours of Germany, and whom the Party wags dubbed the 'chauffeureska'.[11] Hitler found a variety of jobs for his versatile bodyguard to do; when he joined the Party in 1928, Dietrich worked as a dispatcher in the Nazi-owned publishing firm, Franz Eher of Munich; he then organized the SS in Southern Bavaria and in 1931 became head of SS Oberabschnitt North in Hamburg; on the Nazi seizure of power he was summoned to the Chancellery as Hitler's chief bodyguard.[12]

On March 17th, 1933, on Hitler's instructions, Dietrich formed the 'SS Headquarters Guard Berlin' consisting of 120 selected men from Hitler's former bodyguard in Munich; initially it was housed in the Alexander Barracks near the Friedrichstrasse underground station.[13] From this unit sprang the most memorable force in National-Socialist military history – the 'Leibstandarte Adolf Hitler'. Initially its development hardly differed from that of the other Politische Bereitschaften; it grew to a strength of two companies and was then organized as an SS Sonderkommando; in spring 1933 it was re-named 'Guard Battalion Berlin' and moved to the barracks of the former Cadet College, Berlin-Lichterfelde; shortly thereafter it was reinforced by three additional companies trained in the military manoeuvre area at Jüterbog.[14]

No 9 Infantry Regiment Potsdam took care of the Leibstandarte's military training,[15] for the requirements of modern war were well beyond the capacity of ex-Sergeant-Major Dietrich. The sceptics subsequently required much convincing that the first Colonel-General of the Waffen-SS possessed any great military qualities. Dietrich's friends were reduced to arguing that he had once served in a tank regiment, undoubtedly possessed exceptional moral courage, and his rugged independence and nonchalant disregard for orders from Himmler made him highly popular with his men; he was therefore a sort of natural soldier, they said. In fact he was barely fit to command a regiment. Wilhelm

Bittrich, the ex-Obergruppenführer, recalls: 'I once spent an hour and a half trying to explain a situation to Sepp Dietrich with the aid of a map. It was quite useless. He understood nothing at all.'[16]

Such failings on the part of his guard commander left Hitler unmoved. The new unit was intended to be, not a military fighting formation but the Third Reich's Household Troops, and ceremonial unit. Very soon it assumed responsibility for the protection of Hitler's person in a manner obvious for all the world to see. Later it provided the personnel on duty inside the new Reich Chancellery. The double sentries in their black uniform with white belts, white gloves and white shirts posted at the entrance to Hitler's study[17] symbolized the opening of a new era – the formation of a second armed force parallel to the Wehrmacht.

At the Nuremberg Party Rally in September 1933 Hitler named the guard battalion after himself; henceforth it was permitted to call itself the Leibstandarte Adolf Hitler.[18] Two months later, on the tenth anniversary of the Munich beer-cellar putsch, the Leibstandarte swore eternal allegiance to its patron.[19] Hardly a soul perceived, however, that both in military and in constitutional terms a miniature revolution had taken place; the men of the Leibstandarte had sworn their oath to the Chancellor, Adolf Hitler, whereas constitutionally the President of the Reich was sole Commander-in-Chief of all armed forces; nowhere was it laid down that the Reich Chancellor might maintain a private army.[20] Though the Leibstandarte was only a few hundred strong at the time, Hitler's action illustrated the duality which was to be the hallmark of the later Waffen-SS; he had created a unit under his exclusive personal command – one day he could use it as a military force, the next as an instrument of political terror, if necessary even against the nation's constitutional armed forces, the Reichswehr.

Anyone who doubted whether this was in fact the case was given his lesson on that bloody Saturday, June 30th, 1934. Two companies of the Leibstandarte moved to Bavaria with orders to seize and arrest the SA leaders assembled in Bad Wiessee.[21] Then in the courtyard of Stadelheim Prison, Munich, a special detachment under Dietrich mowed down six prominent SA commanders,[22] while in Berlin roving commandos of the Leibstandarte hunted anti-Nazis and executed them in the courtyard of the Lichterfelde Barracks. The Politische Bereitschaften also took part in the bloody chase. Politische Bereitschaft SS 3 (Saxony) murdered nine unpopular Party members; other Bereitschaften in West and South Germany arrested suspect SA leaders.[23]

The intervention of the Politische Bereitschaften whetted Himmler's ambition to form a large-scale armed force. Hitler agreed and promised the Reichsführer sufficient equipment from confiscated SA stocks to form a sizeable body – and this in spite of the fact that the Reichswehr Generals were already grumbling that the SS was starting to compete with them as a military unit. Hitler proceeded with sufficient caution, however, to avoid open criticism from Reichswehr headquarters; he allowed Himmler only three armed SS regiments and, with his eye on the Wehrmacht, vetoed a proposal to form them into a division with artillery and pioneer units.[24]

Subsequent instructions both from Hitler and Army headquarters prescribed that the primary task of the future SS-Verfügungstruppe was the *internal* security of the régime; the Verfügungstruppe remained part of the SS and therefore of the Party; only in the event of war was it to be used for military purposes, for which the Reichswehr was responsible for training it; its actual role was to be decided only on mobilization 'in the light of the existing internal political situation and the level of efficiency reached by the SS regiments' – in the words of an instruction of September 24th, 1934 from the Reich Defence Minister (as the Minister of War was entitled at the time). Nevertheless this same instruction recognized the right of the SS to form 'a standing armed force for such special internal political tasks as may be allotted to the SS by the Führer.'[25]

Here was the formal admission that the Verfügungstruppe was intended to be the régime's armed State Police. Himmler now only needed to amalgamate the Leibstandarte and the Politische Bereitschaften into a single force and the foundation would be laid for the future SS army. It was soon borne in upon the Reichsführer, however, that he was not going to be able to form his force from the men of the Allgemeine-SS alone. He needed the craftsmen of war, the military experts; under Sergeant-Major types like Sepp Dietrich his troops would never be an élite.

Here he was faced with a dilemma. He required experienced professional soldiers, but they were unlikely to join a force hardly distinguishable from the police. He was therefore forced to camouflage the real purpose of the Verfügungstruppe and turn it to purposes of a more traditional nature than Hitler's and the Reichswehr's instructions visualized – there can be no other explanation for the fact that even today the senior Waffen-SS commanders seriously believe that from the outset they were serving in a normal military force.

This deceptive picture of a new Imperial Guard attracted certain ex-officers into the ranks of the Verfügungstruppe. Paul Scharfe, the SS judge, even recruited a real Reichswehr general; during SA manoeuvres in Odenwald he met his old war-time comrade Paul Hausser masquerading in the uniform of an SA-Standartenführer; Scharfe inquired whether he would like to join the SS. Hausser would.[26]

A greater contrast to the bull-necked Dietrich could hardly be imagined. Hausser was a tall lean Brandenburger, born in 1880, son of an officer, reared in the Prussian cadet corps and a qualified General Staff Officer; outwardly he was the typical Prussian officer – elegant, educated and with a gift for sarcasm which had made him many enemies in the Reichswehr.[27] His military career had been one of normal promotion and prescribed routine – infantry training, staff college, staff officer with troops on the Western and Eastern Fronts in the First World War, Chief of Staff Wehrkreis II, Commanding Officer 10 Infantry Regiment, Infantry Commander Magdeburg and finally, in January 1932, retirement in the rank of Lieutenant-General.[28] As an ultra-conservative retired officer he could think of nothing better to do than join the German nationalist ex-soldiers association, 'Stahlhelm', where he was immediately appointed local Commander Berlin-Brandenburg – a post which in his own words was 'a "natural" for a retired Reichswehr General.'[29] When the Stahlhelm was forcibly amalgamated with the SA he happily accepted from Röhm the rank of reserve SA-Standartenführer; equally happily he accepted from Himmler the uniform of an SS-Standartenführer.[30]

Himmler sensed that this ex-Reichswehr General possessed the craftsman's technical ability which he must have for the early stages of his programme. On December 14th, 1934 he had issued a directive reorganizing the Politische Bereitschaften into battalions and amalgamating them with the Leibstandarte to form the SS-Verfügungstruppe.[31] Standartenführer Hausser was a key figure in this reorganization; he was to instil into the SS soldiers that which they lacked – discipline, obedience, drill, battle-worthiness – in other words military know-how.

Early in 1935 in one of the Duke of Brunswick's old castles Hausser opened an SS Cadet School to train the young entry who one day would assume command of the regiments and battalions of the SS army. It was not the first of its kind; on October 1st, 1934 Paul Lettow, another ex-Reichswehr officer, had already initiated the first course at the Bad Tölz SS Cadet School.[32] Hausser quickly realized that only by adopting the training methods and outlook of the Reichswehr could he create an effective force: 'I considered that the SS force must be formed on the well-tried training regulations of the Reichswehr.'[33]

Hausser's solid groundwork in Brunswick attracted a sufficient number of ex-police officers, time-expired Reichswehr sergeant-majors and young military enthusiasts to form the officer and NCO cadre of the future SS Army. The cadres were distributed to the scattered battalions and these were gradually formed into regiments. In Munich three Sturmbanne went to form No 1 SS Regiment, the 'Deutschland', organized and equipped as a horse-drawn infantry regiment; in Hamburg another three Sturmbanne formed No 2 SS Regiment, the 'Germania'; in Berlin the Leibstandarte expanded into a motorized infantry regiment and in 1938 the fourth Infantry Regiment formed in Vienna – 3 SS Regiment, 'Der Führer'.[34] By mid-summer 1936 the Verfügungstruppe had so far taken shape that Himmler felt himself entitled to appoint an official head of his miniature SS army: on October 1st, 1936 SS-Brigadeführer Hausser was appointed Inspector of the Verfügungstruppe.[35]

In spite of this sonorous title, Hausser was by no means master in his own house. He created a sort of divisional staff to supervise the equipment and training of his troops, but on paper he was under the SS-Hauptamt and the SS military princelings were not initially prepared to recognize his authority too easily. The Oberabschnitt commanders of the Allgemeine-SS were reluctant to relinquish control of their armed units – they had, after all, formed them as Politische Bereitschaften.[36] A Himmler order of September 17th, 1936 laid down that the powers of the Inspectorate covered training only and would not affect the 'territorial prerogatives of the SS-Oberabschnitt over the VT units located in their areas'.[37] Even though backed by Himmler, Hausser had to exercise caution in asserting his authority over the SS Oberabschnitte.

Hardly had he settled his outside quarrels, however, than an obstreperous opponent appeared within his own ranks: Dietrich, the Commander of the Leibstandarte, evinced no inclination to be ordered about by the Prussian, Hausser. Even Himmler was hesitant to call Dietrich to order. In his Directive on the Verfügungstruppe he had prudently laid down that inspection of the Leibstandarte was his own prerogative and that the Inspector was merely 'authorized to attend Leibstandarte parades'[38] – proof enough that Himmler was resigned to the fact that Dietrich's guardsmen were not going to obey his orders. 'Reichsheini's' authority frequently ended at the barrack gate of Lichterfelde.

Himmler once wrote in agitation: 'My dear Sepp, this is of course another impossibility. Your officers are good enough to recognize me personally; otherwise, however, the Leibstandarte is a complete law unto itself; it does and allows anything it likes without taking the slightest notice of orders from above.'[39] Vexations caused by the Leibstandarte were endless – frequent brawls with Wehrmacht soldiers,[40] insulting remarks to other members of the Verfügungstruppe,[41] recruitment of national servicemen without the Wehrmacht's approval.[42] The Head of the SS-Hauptamt tore his hair: 'If, contrary to all orders, instructions and assurances, the Leibstandarte chooses to act in this arbitrary manner, I foresee great difficulties.'[43] Once more Himmler warned Dietrich: 'For the last time I ask you to stop these things. I can no more admit to the Wehrmacht that I am unable to get the Leibstandarte to conform to the orders and instructions valid for the entire Verfügungstruppe than I can tolerate continuance of these extravagances on the part of the Leibstandarte.'[44]

Although the 'Asphalt Soldiers', as the Verfügungstruppe nicknamed the Leibstandarte, lacked any basic military training, Dietrich's refusal to cooperate forced even Hausser to withdraw for a time. Nevertheless, as they were continuously employed on parades and sentry duty, it soon became abundantly clear that the Leibstandarte was devoid of even the rudiments of battle training.[45] Finally even Dietrich realized that no soldier was taking the Leibstandarte seriously and he was eventually persuaded to allow Hausser more freedom of action. In 1938 he agreed to an exchange of battalion and company commanders between the Verfügungstruppe and the Leibstandarte. Gradually Hausser's training staff managed to put some military order into the unit.[46]

Ex-General Hausser however, was not to be allowed to set the military tone for the Verfügungstruppe all by himself. Ex-soldiers and National-Socialist hotheads were soon pouring into the Verfügungstruppe and, unlike Hausser, they thought it by no means desirable to ape the Reichswehr. The newcomers believed that the Verfügungstruppe's mission in life was to form the core of the new Reich's revolutionary army, destined to take over from the supposedly hidebound Wehrmacht. They brought to the Verfügungstruppe a certain dynamism and the arrogance of the élite Imperial Guard; the blind fervour of the growing Hitler Youth generation combined with the reforming zeal of ex-officer heretics to produce a sense of mission and superiority.

The leading brain among the military reformers was SS-Sturmbannführer Felix Steiner; he was an ex-Reichswehr officer whose experiences on the Western Front in the First World War had turned him into a rebel against the conservative doctrines of the Army. During the breakthrough battles of 1918 he had witnessed the failure of the static mass armies and the advent of a new military formation – the assault detachment or mobile battle group.[47]

To escape from the deadly immobility of trench warfare with one mass army facing another in a mutual battle of attrition, the German front-line officers had hit upon the idea of withdrawing their best men from the trenches and forming them into battle groups. These so-called 'storm battalions' were to stiffen the spine of the mass army, to be the keep of the defence and the spearhead of the attack. The battle groups were trained for fighting at close quarters; they were equipped with flame-throwers, machine guns, pistols, hand grenades and spades, and they quickly learnt what was later to be known as 'military teamwork' – cooperation on the sub-unit level.[48] At the time twenty-year-old Second Lieutenant Steiner from East Prussia, son of an émigré family from Salzburg and now Company Commander of a machine-gun marksman detachment,[49] was lying behind his machine gun; he thought he could see the dawn of a new era in military history; he believed that the future belonged neither to the amorphous mass nor to the traditional single-combat champions but to an élite fighting in groups.

But Steiner was wrong. The post-war Reichswehr generals thought as did the later SS-Brigadeführer Hausser: in their view the storm battalions had been an emergency measure and could never be more than temporary and exceptional expedients within the framework of a normal army.[50] Steiner, promoted Captain in 1927 and serving as a Company Commander in No 1 Infantry Regiment in Königsberg from 1932, found himself increasingly in opposition to the Reichswehr doctrine.[51] The Generals wished to wage the next war as they had the last one – with a citizen army based on universal military service. Steiner, however, was still a believer in the idea of a military élite. Total war, Steiner thought, required mass armies only for defensive operations; the decisive role belonged to mobile operational formations of high-class élite troops, to a select ultra-modern force which 'by blows of lightning rapidity would split the enemy into fragments and then destroy the dislocated remnants.'[52]

For Steiner, with his élite theory, Hausser's Verfügungstruppe was the logical destination; it was the specialized force of the future of which he had always dreamed. He was given command of the proposed VT regiment 'Deutschland' and in a matter of months had become the intellectual counterbalance to Hausser, the Reichswehr traditionalist.[53] Initially Steiner tried out his reforms with one battalion only. He demoted mechanical barrack-square drill from its place of primary importance and centred his training on sport and athletics, aiming to turn his soldiers into cross-country experts of the 'hunter-poacher-athlete type' described by Liddell Hart as the ideal modern infantryman.[54]

He was also insistent upon reducing the distinctions between officers and the rank and file, thereby promoting a spirit of comradeship in face of the hardships and discomforts of battle training or of war itself. Officers, NCOs and men competed in teams against each other – a further method of eliminating differences in rank.[55] The officer selection system also promoted a unit spirit. The SS cadet schools had abandoned the Wehrmacht system whereby officer candidates were accepted at an early age provided they could show the requisite educational qualifications. The future SS officers had to serve for two years in the ranks before going to the Military Academy; no preference was given to education or background – before 1938 forty per cent of SS cadets had not matriculated.[56] Steiner and his fellow SS commanders made it abundantly clear that they were abandoning the Wehrmacht's ways: in SS barracks, doors of rooms and cupboards were left open as a matter of principle,[57] administrative officers had to undergo a period of military training before being released to their technical schools[58] and in the words of the American historian George H. Stein, they 'fostered among officers, NCOs and enlisted men a sense of fellowship and mutual respect generally unknown in the Army.'[59]

In his training for war Steiner introduced numerous innovations. Unlike the Wehrmacht the basic military unit in his view was not the section but the battle group; Steiner wished to organize his entire regiment in battle groups, sufficiently mobile to come rapidly to grips with the enemy but nevertheless capable of retaining their regimental organization.[60] Instead of the Wehrmacht's regulation rifle he introduced handier and more mobile weapons, primarily sub-machine-guns, hand grenades and explosives. A new battledress, the camouflage blouse and camouflage suit, replaced the field service dress of the Army.[61] Gradually Steiner created a force of military athletes, a 'supple adaptable type of soldier, athletic of bearing, capable of more than average endurance on the march and in combat,' as Steiner later described his men.[62] Even the Wehrmacht's eyebrows rose. Troops who could cover three kilometres (1·88 miles) in twenty minutes – such a thing was unheard of.[63]

The success of Steiner's modernization was so obvious that the Verfügungstruppe began to look upon him as their real commander. Himmler too, always easily influenced by anything new, made Steiner 'definitely his favourite baby', as Hausser put it.[64] To begin with, at any rate, Himmler was prepared to overlook the fact that Steiner treated his Reichsführer with scant respect, refused to marry and also refused to leave the Church – a 'must' for any senior SS officer:[65] Himmler was almost invariably ready to tolerate the ideas of his cantankerous soldier.

For years Steiner held his place as the star turn of the Verfügungstruppe because he was one of the very few professional soldiers in the SS. Even the euphoria of the Verfügungstruppe expansion could not conceal the fact that the new force lacked experienced officers with the aptitude for command and the social standing born of generations of military service. In the Reichswehr 49 per cent of the officer corps came of military families but in the Verfügungstruppe the proportion was only 5 per cent; barely 2 per cent of the Wehrmacht officers came of peasant stock, but 90 per cent of the Verfügungstruppe commanders had been brought up on the land.[66] The Verfügungstruppe never made its mark on the bourgeoisie and the town-dwellers; it remained an army of peasants and artisans. In Schleswig-Holstein, Lower Saxony, Franconia and the Saar, one out of every three farmers' sons joined the Verfügungstruppe or, later, the Waffen-SS.[67]

The Verfügungstruppe's recruits and its new commanders sought to compensate for their lack of military tradition by enthusiasm and devotion to the Hitler cult; many of them therefore came to believe that in contrast to the 'reactionary' Wehrmacht, the Verfügungstruppe was the only reliable armed force in the National-Socialist State. Steiner's tactical reforms had implanted in his men the idea that they were a military élite far superior to the Wehrmacht: similarly the new commanders, brought up in the Hitler Youth and indoctrinated in the SS cadet colleges, instilled into their troops a National-Socialist ideological fervour which brought them into barely concealed opposition to 'the old fogeys', as Röhm had once called the Reichswehr generals. Enmity towards the Army became almost an elixir of life to the Verfügungstruppe, for in the early stages the Wehrmacht succeeded in tying the hands of this unwelcome competitor.

The Army generals had never recognized the Verfügungstruppe as a fourth arm of the service; on the contrary, they feared that a second force under the control of Himmler, already in charge of the entire police machine, might rapidly develop into a deadly threat to the existence of the Wehrmacht.[68] There were many little signs – brawls between members of the Verfügungstruppe and Wehrmacht, slanderous gossip in SS messes against General Freiherr von Fritsch, the anti-Nazi C-in-C of the Army, incidents between the Army and the SS when sharing manoeuvre areas; for Army headquarters all these indicated a threat that one day the Army might lose to the SS its monopoly as the sole bearer of arms within the nation.[69] On February 1st, 1938 General von Fritsch noted: 'all sources agree that the attitude of the SS Verfügungstruppe towards the Army is frigid if not hostile. One cannot avoid the impression that this hostile attitude is deliberately cultivated.'[70]

Fritsch and the Army generals had pressed Hitler so hard that the

Dictator temporarily forbade any further expansion of the SS troops and even denied them full recognition as military formations. So the Verfügungstruppe found its way blocked by the Wehrmacht; it was not allowed to form a Division;[71] it was refused artillery;[72] it was forbidden to publish recruiting notices in the Press;[73] the Army had the right to inspect SS units.[74] To cap it all, these provisions were valid only until the outbreak of war; then Hitler would decide whether to place the Verfügungstruppe under the Army as a formed body or disband it and distribute its members individually to Wehrmacht units.[75] No more bitter fate could threaten a military formation, particularly one which prided itself on being both an élite and the core of the future German defence force.

An unexpected crisis within the Wehrmacht now came to the assistance of the Verfügungstruppe. In February 1938 its enemy von Fritsch and the Reich Minister of War, von Blomberg, both fell and Hitler seized command of the Wehrmacht. Six months later the Verfügungstruppe's anxiety over its future was at an end: on August 17th, 1938 Hitler signed a decree which in effect announced the birth of the future Waffen-SS, for it recognized the Verfügungstruppe as a permanent force both in peace and in war. The VT was to be available for 'certain special internal political tasks which are the responsibility of the Reichsführer-SS and Chief of the German Police, and these I reserve the right to allot to him myself as occasion demands; in addition certain formations should be available for mobile employment under the Army in the event of war.'[76] The Verfügungstruppe had arrived. Brigadeführer Leo Petri of the SS Hauptamt noted in triumph: 'the Wehrmacht has been forced to recognize that the pertinacity of the Reichsführer-SS in the pursuit of his aims is stronger than its own resistance to the innovations of the Third Reich.'[77]

Even at the time, professional soldiers such as Hausser and Steiner probably subscribed to the Hitler decree only with considerable reservations; after all, for them it closed the door to their only object in life – to be soldiers following a purely military profession. Hausser, Steiner and the other ex-professional soldiers may have differed on technical military questions but they had one thing in common – they wanted to devote themselves to an exclusively military job; they wanted to be soldiers 'like the rest'; nothing could have been more foreign to them than Petri's triumphal cry about the victory of the 'party troops', nothing could have seemed to them more degrading than their Reichsführer's concept of the Verfügungstruppe as merely one among many links in the chain of his precious State Protection Corps.

Nevertheless the Verfügungstruppe became and remained a force for the protection of the régime; all ideological instruction drummed into Himmler's soldiers the notion that they must be ready, if necessary, to protect Adolf Hitler's State even against their own fellow-countrymen. In the words of an official SS document, they were told that the Verfügungstruppe was 'the visible armed force of the National-Socialist Party'; recruiting pamphlets urged every 'healthy young man of German blood' to join the Verfügungstruppe, but with the proviso that unconditional acceptance of National-Socialist ideology was essential.[78] Educational instruction was designed to ensure that the Verfügungstruppe soldier was a fanatical Nazi, unquestioningly obedient and ready to carry out any order from the Dictator-Chancellor. A flood of anti-Christian propaganda was loosed on the heads of the men to compel them to renounce all the rules of bourgeois Christian morality and to sever all ties with the Church.

The Verfügungstruppe became a stronghold of that atheism peculiar to the SS which, in their perverse terminology, the Nazi propagandists christened 'Gottgläubigkeit' [belief in God]. By the end of 1938 53·6 per cent of Verfügungstruppe men had left the Church, a figure surpassed only by the even more rabid Totenkopfverbände with 69 per cent.[79] Many men were literally compelled to leave the Church. A typical case was that of one Franz Waldmann from Spessart, a Catholic, whose troubles later even came to the ears of OKW. He had volunteered for the Verfügungstruppe because, as his Catholic priest later wrote, his father thought it was 'like joining the Guards'.

The priest's report to his Diocese continued: no sooner had Waldmann joined than 'pressure was brought to bear upon him to leave the Church. He told his mother that some thirty of them refused. They were then subjected to a martyrdom which young men could hardly be expected to endure. On every parade and during every instructional period the cry was "One pace forward anyone who has not yet left the Church!" Every opportunity was taken to humiliate and ridicule them. Franz countered by saying that religion was not the point; what mattered was how he did his duty. One by one his fellows gave way under the pressure until Franz was alone. About this time one of his friends wrote to his father saying that Franz could not stand it any longer. Even he was now weary of the struggle.' Shortly thereafter the priest heard that Franz Waldmann had left the Church. In October 1942 he was killed in Finland. During his last leave he had told his mother: 'Day by day I was compelled to renounce my faith. I would never go back to my unit, even though I like the life. After the war I want to be free again, to be like I was before.'[80]

The SS unit of Radolfzell (about one thousand strong) provided a good illustration of the progress of anti-Church propaganda in the Verfügungstruppe and the later Waffen-SS; of 300 Catholics the church-leavers totalled 4 in 1937, 3 in 1938, 67 in 1940 and 129 in 1942.[81] In a letter of protest to OKW, Kosch, the Vicar-General in the Archbishop of Freiburg's Chancellery, complained: 'In these barracks mass exits from the Church are the regular sequel to an ideological course of instruction. This can hardly be due to individual crises of conscience.'[82] The young Verfügungstruppe officers were continually called upon to prove their uncompromising opposition to the Christian message of reconciliation and tolerance, which the SS regarded as un-German. From the outset they were ordered to abjure the Christian faith as a destructive, effeminate and 'Jewish' doctrine. On leaving the Cadet School the young officers had to write essays on such subjects as 'Responsibility of Christianity for the decline of the Ostrogoths and Vandals' or 'Effect of Christianity on Ancestor Worship among our people.' Himmler called such exercises 'advanced education';[83] they were supposed to ensure that mentally as well as physically the Verfügungstruppe officers belonged to an 'ideological force'.

The men of the Verfügungstruppe were told that they must be ready at any moment to act ruthlessly within their own country in order to prevent another November 1918. Educational material still being distributed to the SS Panzergrenadier Division 'Hohenstaufen' in October 1943 stated that the lessons of history 'showed the necessity for an unflinching force at the disposal of the leadership of the Reich in any situation, even when this implies maintenance of order at home by the use of all methods.'[84] This was no empty statement. On November 9th, 1938, when barbarism engulfed the Jews of Germany, one of Heydrich's urgent teleprinter messages ordered the Verfügungstruppe into the most shameful operation yet undertaken by Germans in uniform.[85] On November 14th, 1939 SD-Oberabschnitt Danube in Vienna reported to the SD-Hauptamt Berlin: 'Mobile detachments of the Verfügungstruppe drove up to the synagogues and placed stocks of hand grenades in position preparatory to setting fire to the buildings.' In the 'Kristallnacht' story, participation by the Verfügungstruppe was the exception; nevertheless this incident showed the type of function SS headquarters thought suitable for the VT.[86]

Himmler had never regarded the Verfügungstruppe as anything other than an instrument of internal political power. It was to protect the régime and form a counterweight to the Wehrmacht, which he never regarded as totally reliable; in the event of a military putsch the Verfügungstruppe, together with the police and Allgemeine SS units, would suppress a *coup d'état*. But the idea of the Verfügungstruppe as a political force was destroyed by Hitler's World War. The Dictator's adventurist policy drove it onto the battlefield – as a military fighting formation.

On August 19th, 1939 OKW transmitted to the Verfügungstruppe Inspectorate an order from Hitler: 'With immediate effect, units of the SS-Verfügungstruppe are placed under the Commander-in-Chief of the Army. The Commander-in-Chief of the Army will lay down their employment in accordance with the directives given by me.'[87] For one campaign at least the men of the Verfügungstruppe were permitted to nurse their illusion that they were no different from normal soldiers. Hausser, the Inspector, arranged to be posted as liaison officer to Major General Werner Kempf's division (a normal Army formation) and never returned to the world of the SS-Hauptämter in Berlin.[88] His frustrating days as Inspector were over; now Paul Hausser could once more be what he had always wanted to be – a General commanding troops.

Steiner's Infantry Regiment, 'Deutschland', an artillery regiment and other units of the Verfügungstruppe were also included in Kempf's semi-armoured division.[89] The Leibstandarte Motorized Infantry Regiment and the 'Germania' Regiment were incorporated in Army formations for the attack on Poland.[90] Steiner's unit distinguished itself during 3rd Army's advance on Mlava and Modlin;[91] the Leibstandarte took part in the battle of Bzura in central Poland;[92] 'Germania' moved forward on Lwow with 14th Army.[93]

The Army critics, however, found the SS troops' performance unsatisfactory. The Verfügungstruppe suffered considerably heavier losses than comparable army formations, and it soon became evident that the SS troops were not trained to fight as part of a Division, nor were the Verfügungstruppe officers capable of commanding their men in complicated operations.[94] The Verfügungstruppe could justifiably retort that in the Polish campaign the Army had starved them of heavy weapons and kept them short of supplies; nevertheless, even the SS military were dissatisfied with the performance of their troops.[95] There was only one solution: the Verfügungstruppe must form a Division with its own heavy weapons and supply services – but this solution was blocked by the OKW Generals, still determined to keep Himmler's force as small as possible.

OKW could in effect dictate the numerical strength of the Verfügungstruppe. Each year it laid down the numbers from each annual class to be allotted to individual arms of the service by the local Wehrbezirkskommando [Defence District Headquarters – WBK], the mustering authority for national servicemen; the last word lay with the

WBK; no man could be called up to a unit until the WBK concerned had released him.[96] This rule also applied to the Verfügungstruppe. OKW could not deny the SS the necessary replacements for their field units but the Wehrmacht could lay down a ceiling sufficiently low to prevent the Verfügungstruppe from expanding – and the OKW Generals made full use of this privilege.[97]

At this point the Verfügungstruppe commanders received a powerful reinforcement in the shape of an energetic Swabian who was both sufficiently astute and unscrupulous to free the Verfügungstruppe from its Wehrmacht shackles – SS-Brigadeführer Gottlob Berger appeared on the scene, and he was the real founder of the Waffen-SS. Since the end of the Thousand Year Reich, however, he has been treated by the ex-SS Generals as a kind of leper: 'Berger? He had nothing whatsoever to do with the Waffen-SS,' Felix Steiner exclaimed shortly before his death;[98] ex-Obergruppenführer Bittrich shuddered at the mere name: 'A mountebank, a swindler.'[99]

Such vitriolic reactions give one to suspect that Berger did not fit into the 'we-were-all-simple-soldiers' theme of the Waffen-SS apologists. The 'Duke of Swabia', as the SS called Berger,[100] was one of the earliest recruits to National-Socialism and the SA[101] and he regarded the SS units primarily as the military arm of the Party and of National-Socialism. Born in 1896, son of a saw-mill owner, Berger had volunteered in the First World War and had been severely wounded as a second lieutenant commanding a battle group; he was an expert athletics instructor and well-versed in military affairs[102] – yet the professional officers of the Verfügungstruppe always kept him at arm's length. They disliked him for his typically Swabian loquacity and for his position as Himmler's *éminence grise*. For years he had been regarded as the most faithful of a faithful band, a man who thought it his duty to warn his Reichsführer of any disloyalty among his closest collaborators, and in particular among the Verfügungstruppe military men. He once wrote in a minute to Himmler, for instance, that in many regiments 'and in particular on the staff of the Verfügungstruppe' people had 'attempted to bypass the Reichsführer-SS – I have witnessed this myself and as a result clashed with Hausser at the time.'[103] With a mixture of machiavellianism, shrewdness and frankness Berger became Himmler's principal adviser; he weaned his master away from many a crazy idea (particularly on eastern policy) but he clung to him, for 'my Reichsführer confides in me and tells me things personally which he would never do unless he was completely at ease' – as he wrote to Himmler on March 9th, 1943.[104]

He clung faithfully to Himmler because his career depended upon that of his master. He had already failed in the SA; in spring 1933 he had been involved in a quarrel with the younger SA element, had been brought before an arbitration court and had subsequently resigned; after the Röhm upheaval he had spied an opportunity to recapture some leading position in the SA.[105]

Berger had given SA Headquarters the written assurance that 'I shall always regard the SA as Number One and shall never be on the side of those who wish to destroy the SA.'[106] Only a week or two later, however, he had become someone else's disciple; he accepted a post under SA-Obergruppenführer Krüger (who later transferred to the SS) who was regarded as a traitor by the SA because of his equivocal role in the Röhm putsch; one year later Berger had finally joined the SS.[107] On December 7th, 1934 SA-Gruppenführer Hanns Ludin, once a friend of Berger, explained to the special Court convened by Supreme SA Headquarters that Berger suffered from 'a not inconsiderable self-conceit', was 'loud-mouthed' and gave evidence of a 'deplorable lack of self-criticism and soldierly modesty'.[108] Between the SA leaders and the renegade Berger there developed an implacable hatred which was to have dire consequences for the Waffen-SS. At a later stage three SA-Gruppenführer (Ludin, von Jagow and Beckerle), all members of the SA Arbitration Court which had sat on Berger's case,[109] were in charge of German legations in the Balkans; they sabotaged Berger's Waffen-SS recruiting programme – and without the assistance of the Foreign Ministry Berger was powerless to obtain any 'racial Germans' for his units.

Recruitment for the SS troops was one of Berger's most important tasks. In 1938 he had become head of the recruiting office in the SS Hauptamt[110] and he shared Himmler's ambition to build up the Verfügungstruppe into a full-scale army; he had accordingly given much thought to the expansion of the armed SS units. When, therefore, the Wehrmacht's opposition threatened to torpedo the Verfügungstruppe's expansion programme, Berger knew what to do. In the formations responsible to the 'Reichsführer-SS and Chief of the German police' three categories of men were exempt from service in the Wehrmacht; first, the concentration-camp guards, the 'Totenkopfverbände', secondly their wartime reinforcements (the so-called 'police reinforcements' or 'Reinforced Totenkopf Standarten'), and thirdly a section of the Ordnungspolizei.[111] Two Hitler orders now gave Berger the opportunity to build up the Waffen-SS from sources over which the Wehrmacht had no control; a decree of August 17th, 1938 provided that parts of the Totenkopfverbände would reinforce the Verfügungstruppe in the event of war; a further decree of May 18th,

1939 permitted Himmler to call up 50,000 men of the Allgemeine SS as 'Reinforced Totenkopf Standarten'.[112]

The plan which Berger proposed to Himmler provided for immediate duplication of the armed SS and formation of two full battle-strength divisions; in addition, if Hitler would sanction transfer of the Totenkopfverbände and Ordnungspolizei units into the Verfügungstruppe, Himmler would then have three to four divisions available in a very short time.[113] Hitler approved Berger's plan since theoretically the proposal did not infringe the recruiting rules laid down by the touchy Wehrmacht. Berger and the Verfügungstruppe Inspectorate were therefore free to start formation of an entirely new army; it was also given a new name – Waffen-SS.[114]

Berger's subterfuge, however, linked the Verfügungstruppe with the most disreputable organization in the entire SS, a process which many Verfügungstruppe commanders regarded as an insult to any soldier. Under SS-Gruppenführer Theodor Eicke the Totenkopfverbände had been deliberately schooled in the antithesis of militarism. They and the Verfügungstruppe originated from the same source, the Politische Bereitschaften,[115] but since then no love had been lost between the two members of the family. The Verfügungstruppe was trying to be a military force, whereas the Totenkopfverbände affected an anti-military outlook; the result had been many a tavern brawl.[116]

Eicke was an irascible Alsatian, the murderer of Röhm and the inventor of bureaucratized concentration-camp terror. One of his objects in life was to turn his Totenkopfverbände into a sort of counter-force to the Verfügungstruppe. As an ex-paymaster in the Imperial Army he was imbued with an undying hatred of the professional officers whom he now saw in command of the Verfügungstruppe as well as the Army.[117] He had been dismissed from the Army, had been a failure in the police and was written off by the Party as a querulous individual – so he instilled into his men all the pent-up resentments for which he himself could find no outlet. They were willing pupils; the uneducated yokels and embittered unemployed, who provided the majority of his army of thugs, accepted without demur 'Papa' Eicke's hate tirades against Jews, Marxists and professional soldiers.

The brown uniform which Eicke's men wore, in place of the regulation SS black, showed that they posssessed some sort of special status. Himmler had given his head concentration-camp guard almost complete autonomy; as 'Inspector of Concentration Camps and Commander of SS Guard Formations' Eicke was responsible to the Reichsführer-SS alone.[118] He formed a guard unit in each concentration camp, outside the control of the Allgemeine-SS and initially entitled a Sturmbann. On

March 29th, 1936, by which time they totalled 3,500 men, they were officially designated 'Totenkopfverbände'.[119] In April 1937 Eicke formed his five Sturmbanne into three Totenkopfstandarten – 'Oberbayern' located in Dachau, 'Brandenburg' located in Oranienburg, and 'Thuringia' located in Weimar for Buchenwald; in 1938 a fourth Standarte was added – 'Ostmark' located in Linz.[120]

Eicke kept jealous watch to ensure that no professional officer infiltrated into his organization to dispute his command of the Totenkopfverbände; he was continually warning his men against the 'ludicrous attempt to ape a military organization'.[121] In 1937 one of his orders stated: 'We belong neither to the Army nor to the police nor to the Verfügungstruppe ... men of the Totenkopfverbände consider themselves members of the Allgemeine-SS and cannot therefore be commanded either by officers or NCOs . . . henceforth commanders who act like officers, junior officers who act like NCOs, and men who act like private soldiers will be posted to the Allgemeine-SS.'[122]

Such was the mentality in which Eicke had schooled the corps of thugs which was now to be combined with the Verfügungstruppe. But with their eyes set on their own expansion the SS military brushed the problem aside, just as Himmler ignored the lack of ideological reliability among the men streaming into the Waffen-SS from the Ordnungspolizei. 'They are no National-Socialists,' he said, 'they are neither SS men nor selected personnel . . . they were simply called up like men of some construction battalion.'[123]

Though the Waffen-SS was fast becoming a remarkably heterogeneous force, Berger and his organizers formed division after division. The SS army gradually took shape; in late September 1939 SS-Brigadeführer and Police Major-General Karl Pfeffer-Wildenbruch formed an SS/Police Division from members of the Ordnungspolizei together with certain specialized Army units.[124] On October 10th SS-Gruppenführer Hausser commenced formation of a motorized Verfügungstruppe division (later named 'Das Reich') from the three SS regiments 'Deutschland', 'Germania' and 'Der Führer'.[125] On November 1st SS-Gruppenführer Eicke formed the 'Totenkopf' division from certain of his Totenkopfstandarten and parts of the 'police reinforcements'.[126] The Leibstandarte initially remained as a motorized infantry regiment, only becoming a division in 1942.[127]

So at one stroke Berger had succeeded in creating a sizeable SS armed force. When it left for the Polish campaign the Verfügungstruppe had been 18,000 strong; now Himmler had no fewer than 100,000 armed men.[128] Simultaneously Berger created the 'Waffen-SS reinforcement office', for the vital question now was whether he would be able to obtain adequate replacements for the SS field formations and the Totenkopfstandarten. Berger set up recruiting offices in the seventeen SS-Oberabschnitte and opened negotiations with the Wehrmacht;[129] his object was to persuade OKW to agree to the formation of larger SS reserve units in the hope that one day he might be able to expand the Waffen-SS yet again.

But the Wehrmacht at first refused to recognize the Totenkopfstandarten as military units – they had after all originally been intended for police work. OKW was prepared to release only a limited number of conscripts as replacements for the Totenkopfstandarten or the police units; it allowed Berger to recruit 20-year-olds for the Waffen-SS field units,[130] but reserved the right to decide whether a man so recruited should in fact be released for service in the SS. The Wehrmacht had thus placed a further spoke in Berger's wheel; however many applicants might report for service in the Waffen-SS, the Wehrbezirkskommando released on average only one-third of them.[131]

The more persistently Berger pressed the Wehrmacht, the more firmly did OKW reject his plans for expansion. On March 8th, 1940 OKW laid down the units which it would henceforth recognize as part of the Waffen-SS – the Leibstandarte, the three SS divisions, the Totenkopfstandarten, the replacement units and the cadet schools.[132] Even Hitler supported his generals in this case. In his eyes the Waffen-SS was still a militarized police force of élite National-Socialists and it must be ready at any time to defend the régime.

Hitler was counting upon a short war and a rapid victory; in addition he had no wish to scare his professional soldiers with the bogey of a second Wehrmacht. Accordingly (at least until June 1942) he opposed all the major expansion plans of the Waffen-SS. He forbade formation of an SS army corps, he laid down that the strength of the Waffen-SS was not to exceed 5–10 per cent of the peacetime strength of the Army.[133] He was continually emphasizing what the Waffen-SS was *not* to be – a purely military force. In a secret decree issued on August 6th, 1940 he gave his own view on the 'necessity for the Waffen-SS'; the expansion of the Greater German Reich, he said, necessitated 'the creation of an armed state police capable, whatever the situation, of representing and enforcing the authority of the Reich in the interior of the country.'[134]

The rebuff administered by the Führer's headquarters was clear enough but Berger was not to be deterred. His own position had meanwhile grown in importance; on June 1st, 1940, he had been promoted Head of the SS-Hauptamt and had thus become the man mainly responsible for the Waffen-SS.[135] After the western campaign command of the

Waffen-SS had been divided between two Hauptämter. On August 15th, 1940 the Verfügungstruppe Inspectorate had turned into the Führungshauptamt, the 'headquarters for the military command of the Waffen-SS', in the words of the basic order;[136] the SS-Hauptamt, however, remained responsible for ideological education, recruiting and, most important of all, replacements for the Waffen-SS.[137]

Berger therefore looked around for new methods of expanding his army. Since the Wehrmacht refused him any further replacement units, he must now draw his recruits from some source outside the control of the OKW generals. He found just such a source. Beyond the borders of the Reich, primarily in the Balkans, lived hundreds of thousands of 'racial Germans', who were citizens of other states but nevertheless intoxicated by Hitler's campaigns of conquest and captivated by the propaganda on 'greater Germany'. These were the men to be drawn into the Waffen-SS; no Wehrmacht general could forbid their recruitment as a gigantic reserve for Himmler's legions.

Berger started with his own family – his son-in-law was Andreas Schmidt, leader of the German minority in Rumania. He was an ultra-Nazi, typical of the immature young fanatics intoxicated by the Hitler cult and he immediately promised his father-in-law that he would recruit the Germans of Rumania into the Waffen-SS. In the spring of 1940 Schmidt, assisted by Berger's minions, contrived to smuggle 1,000 Germans out of Rumania under the noses of the Rumanian authorities, who were keeping sharp watch to ensure that no Rumanian liable for military service deserted to some foreign army.[138] Berger was so elated by his successes in Rumania that in August 1940 he proposed to Himmler that all the Germans in south-eastern Europe fit for military service (there were 1,500,000 of them) be directed into the Waffen-SS – with or without the agreement of their Governments.[139]

Berger's methods of press-ganging the 'racial Germans' into the Waffen-SS were highly imaginative. The SS 'volunteers' were camouflaged as casual labourers, they were hidden in German hospital trains, they were swept up by the supply columns of the SS divisions as they carved their way across south-eastern Europe.[140] Berger's Hauptamt later concluded agreements with various foreign Governments permitting Germans to volunteer for the Waffen-SS and officially leave their country of origin on certain agreed conditions. The Balkan states did not always observe the agreements and in such cases Berger's minions would re-start their recruit-smuggling operations.[141]

In Berger's empire, however, volunteering was an elastic notion. Where the siren song of propaganda failed, strong-arm squads came to the assistance of the Nazi majority leaders. Berger commented 'If a minority is even passably well led, all will volunteer; those who do not volunteer will have their houses broken up.'[142] In the later years of the war sheer press-gang methods were used. Germany forced upon the Balkan States agreements providing that all men of German blood should legally complete their military service in the German Army – for preference in the Waffen-SS.[143] By the end of 1943 25 per cent of Waffen-SS manpower was 'racial German' and by the end of the war 310,000 of them, drawn from all parts of Europe, were serving in SS units.[144]

Meanwhile Berger had had the idea of tapping a new and even more remarkable reservoir of recruits – the countries known to the SS as 'Germanic'. The early German blitz victories had electrified many of the young men of northern and western Europe; in a matter of weeks a whole world, the world of bourgeois democracy, had collapsed before their eyes. To many of the simpler minds the conquerors who marched through the streets of Oslo, Brussels or The Hague, were the youthful standard-bearers of a new era.

In many a young Belgian, Dutchman or Norwegian there awoke the urge to conform, the desire not to miss the opportunity of climbing on the band-wagon of the new era. They were not of course invariably the blue-eyed idealists of Waffen-SS legend. As well as the urge for adventure a powerful motive was the prospect of a career and of becoming 'warrior peasants' ruling millions of 'Slav sub-humans'. Political ideas were decisive only for a minority; of the 125,000 West Europeans who fought in the Waffen-SS barely a third belonged to the pro-Nazi nationalist parties where subservience to the new German masters was to be seen in its crudest form.[145]

Whatever their motives, men streamed into the recruiting offices which, from mid-1940, Berger set up in all the occupied countries of western and northern Europe – little did he think what political and ideological results the introduction of so diverse a collection of races would have on the SS and on its relationship to Adolf Hitler. He was concerned solely with numbers, and on this score he was more than satisfied. By the end of 1940 the SS-Hauptamt had set up a training camp at Sennheim in Alsace where SS volunteers from all the countries of Europe were drilled – both in arms and in ideology.[146] By spring 1941 the first major non-German formation had been constituted, the SS Division 'Viking' composed of Flemish, Dutch, Danish and Norwegian volunteers with German commanders and cadres.'[147]

The 'Germanic' Waffen-SS soon turned into a sort of European Army; new nationalities were continually being brought in – and diluting the purity of its National-Socialism in the process. Berger even recruited in the East; fezzes and Cossack caps lent a curious appearance to Himmler's army of ideological puritans. The Reichsführer's anti-Slav prejudices had to be circumvented – initially the sight of 'Eastern subhumans' in the uniform of the Waffen-SS seemed to Himmler a shameful breach of faith with Germanism. The persuasive Berger, however, eventually argued Himmler into acceptance of all eastern Europeans as German plunder; first came the Baltic peoples, then the Ukrainians and finally even Russians and other races, culminating in the Balkan Moslems. Eventually no fewer than 200,000 members of these races were serving in the Waffen-SS.[148]

Year by year Berger's recruiting list lengthened; year by year the Waffen-SS army swelled to more explosive proportions – mid-1940 – 100,000 men, 1941 – 220,000, 1942 – 330,000, 1943 – 540,000, 1944 – 910,000.[149] Berger's influx of recruits eventually enabled the officers of the Führungshauptamt to bury the detested label of armed State Police; the Waffen-SS entered upon a victorious career of which there are few parallels in the history of the war. Even in the 1940 campaign in the West the SS proved that it could hold its own with the crack divisions of the Army. The SS military athletes stormed through Holland, Belgium and France – fanatical, irresistible, disdainful of losses and impelled by a blind fury in the assault which distinguished Himmler's army from all other formations of the German Wehrmacht. The first Iron Cross of the campaign was won by SS-Obersturmführer Kraas of the Leibstandarte;[150] it was the shadow of things to come – again and again SS units spearheaded the attack and swept the German invasion forward. Sepp Dietrich's Leibstandarte in particular displayed a nonchalance, towards both the enemy and its own superior officers, that was totally foreign to the Wehrmacht.

During the pursuit of the British forces towards Dunkirk the Leibstandarte was ordered to cross the heavily defended Aa Canal and seize the town of Watten. On the afternoon of May 24th, 1940, however, the Führer's headquarters countermanded the crossing. Dietrich simply disregarded Hitler's order and a few hours later his troops were over the canal.[151] At a later stage of the campaign the Leibstandarte headed the pursuit of the beaten enemy; as advance guard to Colonel-General von Kleist's Panzer Group it stormed southwards to prevent the French from forming a line of resistance along the Loire. In a wide southward sweep the regiment reached St Etienne, leaving the main body of the German Army far behind.[152]

The other SS formations were equally successful; the 'Der Führer' Regiment forced the Grebbe line in Holland; the Verfügungstruppe Division chased the enemy right up to the Spanish frontier; the Totenkopf Division seized a crossing over the Seine and bridgeheads over the Loire.[153]

The Army generals observed the SS thirst for battle with mingled admiration and dismay; to the traditionally minded these new soldiers seemed to herald a new form of warfare which made a mockery of all reasonable and calculable tactics. Many regarded the SS troops as did Werner Picht, the sociologist, who commented that they were 'not a new form of front-line soldier but an oath-bound community, available to the Führer for any mission.'[154] General Erich Hoepner, an armoured-formation commander, gave perhaps the crispest expression to the regular officers' criticism of the SS; when Eicke, commanding the Totenkopf Division which was under Hoepner at the time, reported that a certain order to attack had been carried out and that in doing so human life had counted for nothing, the ex-cavalryman retorted: 'That's a butcher's outlook.'[155]

Army officers were appalled by the fact that the Waffen-SS commanders had clearly never learnt to exercise any form of caution in the use of the men entrusted to them. Many, though of course not all, SS commanders simply put into practice in the field the lesson they had learned in the cadet schools – that the soldier's supreme duty was to deal out and to accept death.[156] The SS formations accordingly suffered losses on a scale unknown to the Army. Just before the Battle of France began officer casualties in the SS divisions were found to have been so heavy that replacement officers had to be drafted in straight from the cadet schools.[157]

Despite these obvious failings on the part of the SS the Wehrmacht leaders sensed danger. A rival to the Wehrmacht had appeared on the battlefield and its *élan* inevitably impressed the Dictator in his field headquarters. On July 19th, 1940 in a speech to the Reichstag Hitler publicly acknowledged that 'the brave divisions and Standarten of the Waffen-SS' had been used.[158] Praise from the Dictator, their own successes and, even more, the aloofness of their military rivals reinforced the corps spirit of the SS and it was an arrogant spirit, looking down upon the military world around it with the guardsman's traditional contempt for the common soldiery. With each battle the Waffen-SS visibly reinforced its claim to the mantle of the nation's military élite. Though the SS soldiers had been schooled to be especially faithful and uncompromising fighters for National-Socialism, in their own eyes they were no different from the American 'Leathernecks' or the later French 'Paras' – surrounded by an aura of toughness and masculinity, inspired by a sense of belonging to an aristocratic minority, a closed community with its own rules and loyalties.

SS-Gruppenführer Hans Jüttner, the Chief-of-Staff and later Head of the Führungshauptamt, was insistent that the Waffen-SS formations must meet the standards and requirements of the Wehrmacht and that all traces of their former police character must be eliminated. The main stumbling-block here was Eicke, whose pseudo-revolutionary anti-militarism no longer squared with the imperial-guard concept. With increasing severity the Führungshauptamt demanded that the Totenkopf Division Commander adhere strictly to the orders of Waffen-SS headquarters (formed in summer 1940).[159] Eicke complained to Obergruppenführer Wolff that there was a 'hate against him' in Berlin – 'ever since I left Germany certain circles have been doing their best to undermine the Reichsführer's confidence in me, which I have enjoyed for years.'[160]

Jüttner in fact considered that, for the sake of the reputation of the Waffen-SS, the dilettante ex-paymaster should be relieved of command of his division. Too much explosive evidence was piling up; the Totenkopf Division had been guilty of the first major war crime in the West on May 26th, 1940 – a Company Commander of No 2 Regiment had shot one hundred British prisoners of war during the fighting in north-west France;[161] in many units of the division the barbaric methods characteristic of the concentration-camp guards persisted; Eicke secretly obtained additional weapons for his division from the Dachau and Oranienburg concentration camps;[162] he made unauthorized purchases of trucks in unoccupied France because the Wehrmacht refused to motorize his division, which was still horse-drawn.[163] Finally in August 1940, when certain men of his division were to be released, Eicke demanded a declaration from them binding them never to voice complaints regarding conditions within the division. This was too much for Jüttner, and Eicke was called to order. Waffen-SS Headquarters ordered him to withdraw the declarations immediately.[164] On Jüttner's orders SS legal officers interrogated the men who had carried out Eicke's secret weapons forays and all the division's unauthorized vehicles were confiscated. Simultaneously Jüttner threatened that, in the event of further insubordination, Eicke's weapons traffickers would be summoned before the competent SS-Police court.[165]

In a fury, Eicke retorted that hitherto he had in principle been responsible to the Reichsführer alone and that Jüttner should therefore regard any agreement to conform as a concession. He continued: 'The tone adopted towards a senior SS officer and Divisional Commander in the letters from your office is not that to which even hardened soldiers are accustomed.'[166] But Jüttner persisted. The Führungshauptamt interrogated ex-members of the division and compiled a comprehensive critique of Eicke's methods of command. Once more Eicke protested, writing to Jüttner of attacks 'by expert pen-pushers on your staff and silly gossip by their spiteful friends'. He concluded: 'When inquiries are made regarding conditions in an SS operational division which has left 23 officers and 370 NCOs and men dead on the battlefield, and when the purpose of the inquiry is simply to obtain incriminating evidence against decent SS officers and men, this is pure Marxism and the result is to undermine confidence.'[167]

At times even Himmler took part in the anti-Eicke campaign. One of Eicke's Divisional Orders showed that 'for general edification' even regimental commanders were being punished for trivial offences, and the names of senior officers who contracted venereal disease were being announced in public. Himmler blew up: 'Dear Eicke, when I read something like this, I doubt your reason. These are moments when I question your capacity to command a division.'[168] Nevertheless Himmler would not allow Jüttner to relieve Eicke of his command. Eicke swallowed the reproof and retained his division.

Meanwhile the Führungshauptamt pushed on with the expansion of the SS army and by spring 1941 it consisted of four divisions and one brigade. At this point World War II turned eastwards; the SS formations were summoned to the Balkans and once more SS troops spearheaded the German invading armies. The Leibstandarte broke through from southern Serbia into Albania, stormed through Thessaly and forced the passage into the Peloponnese. In central Serbia 'Das Reich' took Belgrade by *coup de main* and overran the Bacska.[169]

The SS formations had hardly come to rest, however, before the Führer's headquarters teleprinters were tapping out new orders. Adolf Hitler had decided to attack the Soviet Union.

Himmler's army now numbered 160,000 men;[170] it moved into its assembly areas on the eastern frontier of the German zone ready for the Third Reich's final catastrophic adventure. The Leibstandarte and the 'Viking' Division were allotted to Army Group South, 'Das Reich' to Army Group Centre, and the Totenkopf and Police Divisions to Army Group North.[171] On June 22nd, 1941 at 3.15 AM the Waffen-SS set foot upon the battleground of its greatest achievements; the real saga of the SS army was about to open. Before it did so, however, a shadow had fallen upon the Waffen-SS of which it was never to rid itself: Himmler had issued an instruction indirectly linking all forces of the Waffen-SS with the murkiest corner of the entire SS empire – the concentration camps.

On April 22nd, 1941 Himmler laid down the units which he intended to regard as part of the Waffen-SS. Hitherto he had accepted OKW's decision that the Waffen-SS consisted solely of the fighting formation, their replacement units, the Totenkopf Standarten and the three cadet schools in Brunswick, Bad Tölz and Klagenfurt. But now, on the eve of the Eastern campaign and in control of four divisions, Himmler felt himself strong enough arbitrarily to extend the meaning of the term 'Waffen-SS'. In a Führungshauptamt directive he set out 179 units and agencies all now to be considered an integral part of the Waffen-SS – and they included the concentration camps, their administrative staffs and the Totenkopf guard units,[172] in other words all those organizations which had been formed in 1939 when Eicke's Totenkopfverbände were relieved from concentration-camp duty; their personnel consisted of men unfit for service from the Allgemeine-SS and Kyffhäuserbund and the SA.[173]

From now on the concentration-camp guards ranked as members of the Waffen-SS. They carried the same pay-books, they wore the same uniform as the true Waffen-SS[174] which, with its fighting formations at the front, had never been implicated in the terror régime of the concentration camps. Moreover the hangmen and the soldiers had something else in common – the Führungshauptamt was responsible for the equipment and military training of the guard units, and all transfers between concentration camps now had to pass via Waffen-SS Headquarters. Worse still – pending transfer to the WVHA – the Concentration Camp Inspectorate, the headquarters of all concentration camps, was temporarily included in the Führungshauptamt (from autumn 1940 to spring 1942).[175]

But did the Waffen-SS soldiers protest against this insult? Did they rise in wrath when their military organization was equated with the executioners of the torture factories and extermination camps? They accepted Himmler's order without a word: they fell into line, held their tongues, and remained dumb – as they had done at the end of 1939 when the Verfügungstruppe was amalgamated with Eicke's 6,500 thugs from the concentration camps and the Waffen-SS thus received an injection of the poison of an inhuman and barbaric attitude to prisoners learnt and practised over the years.[176] They remained dumb – as they did later when the 50,000 men of the 'Reinforced Totenkopf Standarten,' also trained in the concentration camps and the standard-bearers of political terror throughout German-occupied Europe, joined the Waffen-SS as cadres for new divisions.[177] They remained dumb as they did later in the war when many a sinister figure from the eerie empire of terror and mass extermination was transferred to the Waffen-SS – Hauptsturmführer Bothmann with his liquidation commando which had murdered 300,000 Jews in the Kulmhof gas vans[178] – the 2,500 men from the extermination staff of Auschwitz[179] – the 1,500 guards from Sachsenhausen.[180]

The Waffen-SS commanders probably comforted themselves with the thought that the discipline and sense of honour of their troops would enable them to keep their distance from the SS political underworld. But they could not keep the slate quite clean: the Waffen-SS had to provide units (some 1,500 men) to assist in forming the Einsatzgruppen murder squads;[181] certain of their reserve units took part in the more grisly SS operations such as the suppression of the Warsaw ghetto revolt;[182] they had to accept official Waffen-SS status for a penal brigade composed of poachers, professional criminals and men under sentence of court-martial, commanded by a friend of Berger's Doctor Oskar Dirlewanger.[183]

Nevertheless the SS military thought that they could keep their escutcheon clean and in this they were supported even by Himmler; early in April 1941 he made a gesture showing that he still wished to keep the Waffen-SS fighting formations separate from the machine of terror.[184] He created a sort of Waffen-SS within the Waffen-SS, a private army which he intended to use for his own political strategy.[185] Immediately they entered the operations zone, the Waffen-SS fighting formations came under command of the Army; this special force, however, was subject to Himmler alone; he could, of course, make it available to the Army but equally he could remove it at any time he thought fit.[186] The main body of Himmler's army consisted of the Totenkopf Standarten, which OKW had initially refused to recognize as Waffen-SS units. Himmler organized the majority of the Standarten into infantry and cavalry brigades under the direct orders of the Reichsführer-SS.[187] He chose SS-Brigadeführer Knoblauch as Chief-of-Staff and in May 1941 formed the 'Headquarters Staff Reichsführer-SS' [Kommandostab];[188] the troops were for use in rear of the Front against partisans and Jews.

But the martial dreams of Himmler's middle age melted away as quickly as had those of his youth. The eastern campaign demanded more and more formations. Regiment by regiment Himmler's private army was swallowed up and by mid-1942 all its units had been incorporated in the field army.[189] As a result of the formation of the 'Headquarters Staff', however, the gap between Himmler and the professional commanders of the Waffen-SS widened. Moreover the farther the SS divisions penetrated into the endless expanses of Russia, the more visibly did Himmler's military men become divorced from the orders and fantasies of their Reichsführer.

The SS soldiers were living in another world, a cruel remorseless world, aeons removed from the ideological verbiage of the SS. Driven by belief in their Führer and in the ultimate victory of Germany, the SS formations stormed through the steppes, marshes and forests of Russia, both heroes and victims of a ghastly chapter of human error and hallucination. They won for themselves a select place in the annals of war. Whether in the south, the centre or the north, wherever the enemy recovered sufficiently from his surprise to stand and fight, wherever he launched a counter-attack and tore gaps in the German attacking front, orders went out for the SS formations.

Once more the SS divisions spearheaded the German armies. The Leibstandarte seized a bridgehead over the Dnieper; it broke through the Soviet defences of the Crimea at Perekop and stormed Taganrog and Rostov.[190] The 'Viking' division pursued the enemy to the shores of the Sea of Azov: 'Das Reich' broke through the Moscow defences south of Borodino and came within a few miles of the Soviet capital.[191] Then, when the Soviets launched their first major counter-attacks late in 1941, the Waffen-SS provided an unparalleled example of tenacity. Hammered by 'Stalin organs', tanks and massed infantry, the SS more than justified their reputation as the eastern army's fire brigade.

In January 1942 after the Soviet breakthrough west of Moscow, strong Soviet forces moved forward in rear of Army Group Centre. General Model, C-in-C 9th Army, thereupon moved the SS regiment 'Der Führer' under Obersturmbannführer Otto Kumm into the bend of the Volga near Rzhev. The regiment was to form a thin screen linking the Front with the Army formations farther west and it was to hold until Model had concentrated sufficient troops in the south to deal the enemy an annihilating blow. In a temperature of minus 52 Centigrade the SS men held on, driving the enemy back day after day, hour after hour. By February 18th Model had won his victory. When his regiment was relieved, Kumm met his Army commander. Model said: 'I know what your regiment must have been through, Kumm. But I still can't do without it. How strong is it now?' Kumm pointed to the window: 'My regiment is on parade outside!' There stood 35 men, all that remained of 2,000.[192]

Even Theodor Eicke now proved that he could turn soldier. Since being promoted SS-Obergruppenführer the ex-concentration-camp guard had become a changed man. He shut himself up in his billet for days at a time, cut the tactical signs out of the situation maps and played a war game with them on the floor of his room – all in deadly secret lest his senior General Staff officer notice his suddenly acquired taste for military matters.[193] When Soviet forces cut off the Totenkopf division and five other Army divisions at Demyansk south of Lake Ilmen on February 8th, 1942, they found that in Eicke they were facing a tough, clever opponent.[194] Field-Marshal Busch described the fact that the Germans encircled at Demyansk held out for months primarily to 'the energetic leadership of Obergruppenführer Eicke'.[195] Then the SS soldiers showed their offensive spirit once more; together with Army formations they broke through into the pocket and relieved the defenders of Demyansk.

Demyansk, Rzhev, the Mius River, Lake Ladoga, Volkov – all these names were linked with the military exploits of a force which had gained an almost legendary reputation on both sides, evoking superstitious fear on the one hand and jealous admiration on the other. Both friend and foe were agreed that the Waffen-SS possessed military qualities equalled by few other forces and surpassed by none.

When taken prisoner in autumn 1941 the Russian Major-General Artemenko, Commander of XXVII Army Corps, said that the SS division 'Viking' had shown greater fortitude than any other formation on either side; the Russians had breathed a sigh of relief, he said, when the division was relieved by Army units.[196] General Wohler, C-in-C of the German 8th Army, thought similarly, becoming almost lyrical in his praise of the SS formations under his command; they had 'stood like a rock in the Army', he said and had withstood the enemy 'with unshakeable fortitude'.[197] In a letter to Himmler, General von Mackensen, commanding III Panzer Corps, extolled the Leibstandarte for its 'discipline, refreshing, cheerful energy and unshakeable steadfastness in crisis.' 'A real élite unit,' he concluded.[198]

Not all Army officers, however, were prepared to agree with such panegyrics. Rivalry and jealousy were the feelings uppermost in the breasts of many professional soldiers as they saw the Waffen-SS pushing itself into the forefront and clearly obtaining favoured treatment from the leaders of the State. The Army's aversion to the Waffen-SS was an open secret. Waffen-SS commanders already suspected the Army of deliberately allotting the most dangerous hot-spots to the Waffen-SS in order to 'burn up' their tiresome rival.

Eicke fulminated that the SS would 'emerge from these battles so weak that it would never get on its feet again';[199] even Himmler later detected an intention 'on the part of many people of ill-will' to 'butcher this unwelcome force and get rid of it for some future development.'[200] SS-Oberführer Simon, a regimental commander in the Totenkopf division, had positive proof that the staff of II Corps had deliberately withheld orders from the Führer's headquarters for the relief of the Danish volunteers and the cadres of No 2 Totenkopf infantry regiment in order to avoid having to relieve these units with Army troops.[201] Eicke grumbled that it was high time that 'our men were released from the grip of a malicious, jealous gang.'[202]

In the case of many officers, however, jealousy was not the only reason for their frosty reserve. The military detected in this new force a fanaticism foreign to the military tradition and directed not only against the enemy in the field but also against helpless prisoners and the civilian population. In many cases Waffen-SS units broke the rules of military ethics which those soldiers with any feeling for tradition were trying to preserve despite all the bestialities of this war. Stories of barbaric treatment of prisoners-of-war and civilians by SS units were as numerous as the tales of SS bravery. Apologists for the Waffen-SS later protested that the troops were merely reacting to the inhuman Soviet methods of warfare. German troops had in fact found in captured files orders by Soviet Army and Corps headquarters proving that German prisoners had been murdered by the Russians. For instance – report from Headquarters Russian 26 Division, July 13th, 1941: 'The enemy left about 400 dead behind on the battlefield; about 80 men surrendered and were shot.'[203] Report from 33 Army, December 8th, 1941: '100 prisoners of war captured by the GM Infantry Division were shot by orders of the Commissar of the Division in view of the complicated situation.'[204] Liquidation of German prisoners of war became so widespread that order No 0068 of December 2nd, 1941, from the Chief-of-Staff Soviet Coastal Army Sebastopol contained this: 'As a rule the troop formations exterminate prisoners without interrogation and without transferring them to the divisional staff. Prisoners may only be exterminated in the case of resistance or escape. Besides, the shooting of prisoners at the place of capture or at the front line, which is being practised most extensively, acts as a deterrent to soldiers of the enemy wanting to desert to us.'[205] On March 29th, 1942 the Leibstandarte War Graves Officer reported that in the courtyard of the former GPU headquarters in Taganrog six members of No 3 Company of the Leibstandarte had been found murdered; all had been thrown down a well shaft; the medical report stated: 'Four fingers of the right hand missing (presumably hacked off), skull smashed (presumably when thrown down the well) . . . Spine broken . . . chest smashed in.'[206]

The SS apologists ignore the fact that both sides were guilty of crimes against prisoners of war; moreover the aggressor, who in this instance had decided upon the liquidation of whole categories of prisoners *before* operations commenced (the Commissar Order), could send his prisoners to the rear more easily than the disorganized defender. In any case the brutal reprisals for Soviet crimes taken by Waffen-SS soldiers were out of all proportion, and repugnant to many of their fellow-countrymen. In fairness, however, it must be said that senior Waffen-SS commanders, including even Sepp Dietrich, tried to prevent reprisals against prisoners – 'We owe it to the title on our sleeve,' Dietrich said.[207] But the order did not penetrate to each individual soldier.

As a result of the introduction of unsoldierly types drawn from the cesspool of political fanaticism – the former members of the Totenkopf-verbände or the exchange personnel from the concentration camps for instance – combined with the fury of battle and a certain relaxation of discipline, the Waffen-SS became apt to use all types of inhuman methods of warfare. Its military record was continually being tarnished by crime; a fortnight after the opening of the Russian campaign the 'Viking' division shot 600 Jews in Galicia as a reprisal for Soviet crimes;[208] in summer 1943 the 'Prinz Eugen' division liquidated the inhabitants of Kosutica because Einsatzkommando 2 reported that the troops had 'apparently' been fired on from the church;[209] in spring 1944 the SS/Police division destroyed Klissura in northern Greece after one of their units had been ambushed;[210] in June 1944 a company of 'Das Reich', searching for an SS commander who had been captured by the *maquis*, destroyed the village of Oradoursur-Glane in south-west France, killing the entire population[211]; two months later during the battles in Normandy the SS Panzer division 'Hitlerjugend' shot 64 Canadian and British prisoners of war.[212]

Explicable though such brutalities may be, the fact remains that similar crimes were seldom committed by the Wehrmacht. Reports on Wehrmacht and Waffen-SS misdemeanours collated by the Allgemeine Wehrmachtamt [General Armed Forces office – AW] of OKW underline the difference. On August 2nd, 1943 AW stated: 'In the period covered by this report 151 cases of this nature came to notice. In 19 cases the culprits belonged to the Army, in 53 cases to the Waffen-SS, while in 79 cases the culprits' unit could not be established. The number of cases of rape is high. After interrogation of the victims and of witnesses, the Field Security Police and in certain instances the SS Patrol Service [Streifendienst], reported 18 proven cases of rape. In 12 cases the culprits were members of the Waffen-SS; in the other 6 the culprits' arm of the service could not be clearly established.'[213]

In parts of the Ukraine the Waffen-SS behaved with such savagery that the people deserted their villages and took refuge with the Soviet Army. The AW noted: 'The inhabitants of this town and the surrounding district are in a state of permanent indignation over thefts of livestock, assaults on inhabitants and rape of women and girls.'[214] On May 30th, 1943 two Russian officials begged the Town Mayor of Rogosyanka to order the Waffen-SS 'not to beat up the population, to refrain from requisitioning and to cease plaguing the villagers'. They concluded:

'Prior to the arrival of the SS the population was most favourably disposed towards the troops and towards Adolf Hitler.'[215]

From other areas also reports of brutality and high-handed actions by the Waffen-SS began to arrive. In November 1942 the Rumanian General Staff protested that 'racial German' members of the Waffen-SS were beating up Rumanian officials, violating Rumanian laws and intriguing against the authority of the Rumanian State. A telegram from Böhme, the Police Attaché, Bucharest, stated: 'Based on these proven instances, the Rumanian Great General Staff asserts that these misdemeanours and incidents are the work primarily of members of the Waffen-SS . . . the Great General Staff considers it necessary that both sides should respect the good order and discipline prevalent in this country.'[216] In the Balkans even the RSHA Einsatzkommando protested against the inhuman methods of warfare of the SS divisions. On July 15th, 1943 SS-Sturmbannführer Reinholz of Einsatzkommando 2 reported that the Waffen-SS methods had 'begun to have an injurious effect upon German interests in this area.'[217] In conversation with a Croat Minister SS-Brigadeführer Ritter von Oberkamp, commander of the 'Prinz Eugen' division, attempted to pass off some outrage committed by his unit as an 'error'; SS-Oberführer Fromm, who was also present, threw back at him: 'Since you arrived there has unfortunately been one "error" after another.'[218] Many of these 'errors' were due to the fact that as the Waffen-SS swelled and division after division was formed, discipline inevitably relaxed – and the SS swelled because its successes, together with his own sinking fortunes, caused Adolf Hitler to lift all restrictions on it. As the years went by the Waffen-SS became the tyrant's last hope; Hitler clung in desperation to the belief that only the invincible SS troops could save him from catastrophe.

As early as the spring of 1942 Hitler had agreed to the formation of a new SS division, the 'Prinz Eugen';[219] shortly thereafter the 'Florian Geyer' division was formed from the SS cavalry brigade[220] and by that autumn Hitler was allowing the Waffen-SS to do as it liked. The result was the 'Hohenstaufen' Panzergrenadier division, initially consisting of 70 per cent conscripts;[221] then the 'Frundsberg',[222] a new 'Germanic' division named 'Nordland',[223] the 'Hitlerjugend',[224] and a Bosnian division[225] – the Waffen-SS grew and grew. Moreover the SS now managed to break the OKW stranglehold on equipment. The Army had so far been careful to ensure that the Wehrmacht had priority over the Waffen-SS in the distribution of modern weapons, but Hitler now reversed the position, allocating to the Waffen-SS all the latest equipment from assault guns to armoured troop carriers.[226]

Finally the Waffen-SS succeeded in eliminating the deficiency to which it ascribed its heavy losses in men and material – lack of armour. Even in late 1941 Arthur Phleps, the ex-Rumanian General and at the time a regimental commander in the 'Viking' division, had implored Felix Steiner to 'get us tanks; without them this magnificent force will be ruined'.[227] Slowly, and in the face of continual resistance from the Wehrmacht, the three original Waffen-SS divisions (the Leibstandarte, 'Das Reich' and 'Totenkopf') were re-equipped as Panzer divisions;[228] and the first SS Panzer Corps allowed to the Waffen-SS was constituted under the command of Paul Hausser.[229] Additional Panzer Corps followed.[230] In March 1943 Obergruppenführer Hausser at the head of his armoured formations charged through the Ukraine and fulfilled Hitler's wildest hopes. The Corps repulsed a major Soviet attack in the Kharkov area and in summer 1943 spearheaded the southern front in the last major German offensive in Russia.[231]

A year later the Waffen-SS divisions had become the crack formations on the Eastern Front. In the view of Stein, the American historian, they 'had on two separate occasions prevented another Stalingrad'[232] by breaking up menacing Soviet envelopment moves: at Cherkassy in January 1944 Soviet forces had surrounded two German Corps; they were relieved by army formations together with the SS division 'Viking'; at Kamenetz-Podolsk an entire German Panzer Army was surrounded and eventually relieved by Hausser's Corps, which had in the meantime been moved to France and recalled.[233] Stein says: 'Wherever they were committed they attacked; sometimes with great success and sometimes with little or none. But whatever the outcome of the individual action, the end result was to delay the enemy advance.'[234] The military triumphs of the Waffen-SS, however, could not conceal the fact that the force had long since been 'burnt to a cinder', in the words of Steiner, the commander of the 'Viking' division.[235] The armour had come too late. By 1943 one-third of the original Waffen-SS divisions had fallen in Russia.[236] They had suffered losses which would have broken the back of any other force. Between June 22nd and November 19th, 1941 they lost 1,239 officers and 35,377 men, of whom 13,037 were killed.[237] During the break-out from the Cherkassy pocket, 'Viking' lost all its tanks, all its equipment and half its men.[238] In February 1943 Eicke, commanding the Totenkopf division, fell near Kharkov and similar casualties in other divisions began to affect efficiency. On November 15th, 1941 'Totenkopf' reported: 'The losses so far suffered in battle have deprived this formation of nearly 60 per cent of the vital officer and NCO cadre. Losses in NCOs are catastrophic . . . a company which has lost its old experienced NCOs and section commanders cannot attack. It is unreliable in defence because its backbone is not there. There are already companies in this division incapable of reconnoitring in front of their sectors.'[239]

As their manpower losses mounted, the SS divisions' cries for assistance became more strident; moreover the quality of the replacements provided by the SS-Hauptamt recruiting centres was so low that both the fighting efficiency and quality of the force were affected. The early Waffen-SS soldiers had gone to war with enthusiasm, inspired by the Hitler cult and in the conviction that they were serving a new, more egalitarian Germany. They were young idealists under the spell of a sort of ecstasy, and nothing seemed more natural to them than to devote themselves and sacrifice themselves to what they called 'Führer and Reich'. The seal was set on their tragic error – the error of an entire generation – by the graves and wooden crosses in the lonely expanses of Russia. Behind these early crusaders followed a new wave of actual or ostensible volunteers, but they lacked the naïve credulity of their predecessors, now dead. Many of them had been press-ganged or lured into service and they soldiered with reluctance. They had joined the Waffen-SS without enthusiasm, they were badly trained and they had turned into sceptics; they brought to the Waffen-SS a mentality far removed from that of the Verfügungstruppe pioneers.

With righteous National-Socialist indignation the Führungshauptamt recorded in spring 1943: 'Morale is bad. Unmistakable signs of home and church influences. General attitude: if I am conscripted I can do nothing about it, but volunteer I will not. Fear of active service.'[240] Berger could no longer provide the replacements required by the military for his sources had long since been exhausted. The reservoir of volunteers had dried up as quickly in the case of the Waffen-SS as in that of the Wehrmacht and from 1942 onwards the Waffen-SS had to rely on conscripts.[241] Every report from the recruiting centres confirmed that, horrified by the reports of its savage methods of warfare and its towering casualty figures, the Germans were now anti-Waffen-SS.

In February 1943 Waffen-SS headquarters collated thirteen reports from the recruiting centres and they told a story of total failure.[242] Recruiting Centre South-East (Breslau): 'Readiness to enlist not good. No enthusiasm for military service. Young men do not wish to volunteer. Instances of a definite anti-Waffen-SS attitude.'[243] Recruiting Centre South (Munich): 'Readiness to enlist leaves much to be desired, sometimes giving impression of passive resistance. Men do not wish to volunteer but to wait until they are conscripted.'[244] Recruiting Centre Main (Nuremberg): 'Readiness to enlist small, at times catastrophic. The young men are not only anti-Waffen-SS but basically opposed to any form of military service.'[245] The anti-Christian propaganda so long drummed into the Waffen-SS now began to boomerang. Parents and churches paralysed recruiting; even fear of the Gestapo did not prevent men from opting out of Himmler's army.

SS Recruiting Centre North-East: 'Influence of parents and church negative.'[246] Baltic II: 'Home influence unfavourable.'[247] South: 'Many youngsters forbidden by their parents to join the Waffen-SS.'[248] Hamburg: 'Parents generally anti-Waffen-SS.'[249] Vienna: 'Church influence very strong. One man said: "The priest told us that the SS was atheist and if we joined it we should go to hell." '[250] Berger reported to Himmler that at a Leibstandarte passing-out parade almost all officer cadets had refused to become Waffen-SS officers. One, a youngster from Hanover, had said: 'We didn't want war. We had enough to eat and still have. Let those who haven't enough to eat carry on with this war.' Berger added: 'Reichsführer, these are not isolated instances.'[251]

Gloomily, Himmler accepted Berger's jeremiads. On May 14th, 1943 he lamented: 'In my view the overall conclusion is that the youth of our people has clearly and deliberately been poisoned by Christian education and we have obviously not countered it by sufficiently positive ideological education, particularly now in wartime.'[252] Nevertheless Berger refused to accept that all recruiting was at an end and he found two allies prepared to hound their members into volunteering: the pre-military training camps of the Hitler Youth and the Labour Service Camps; here he was free to recruit at his will.[253]

To be sure that he was ahead of the Wehrmacht's mustering commissions in the hunt for new recruits, Berger ordered all members of certain annual intakes to present themselves for preliminary mustering for the Waffen-SS. SS recruiting officers appeared, determined to force every young man in the Labour Service into the Waffen-SS. On February 24th, 1943 a number of young men failed to appear for a Waffen-SS lecture in a Labour Service agricultural school at Halle. An SS officer commented: 'If these people joined the SS they would forthwith be shot; this is nothing else but sabotage and desertion.'[254] Others at the school were confronted with printed forms pledging them to join the Waffen-SS. When one man objected that he must first talk to his father, the SS officer replied: 'We don't have anything more to do with those old fogeys. You've all got to sign or I shall let no one leave.' To another man he said: 'You pigs seem to think that others are being shot to bits out there for the pleasure of allowing you to skrimshank here.' Practically everybody signed.[255]

Writing to his father a Labour Service man complained: 'Dear Papa, today I have witnessed the dirtiest trick I have ever seen.' Three SS men and a policeman had appeared in the camp demanding that all the inmates register on the Waffen-SS recruiting list. The letter continued: 'About 60 men were forced to sign, failing which they were given a reprimand or three days under arrest. All sorts of threats were used. Everybody was frightfully indignant. One or two just departed, some even through the window. The policeman stood at the door and would let no one out. The whole camp is furious. I've had enough; I've changed completely.' The father sent the letter on to Himmler.[256]

The headquarters of the Moselle Gau reported to the Party Chancellery: 'We understand that all Labour Service men over 5 feet 5 inches were paraded and a certain number selected; whether they wished to or not, they were then forced to "volunteer" for the Waffen-SS on the pretext that the SS delegation had come direct from the Führer's headquarters.'[257] On March 30th, 1943 the acting commander of V Army Corps reported 'numerous complaints that the Waffen-SS is using unauthorized recruiting methods.'[258] Report from Sassbach-Achern: 'When no one came forward even after the demand had been repeated five times, it was stated that no one might leave the hall who had not volunteered for one of the Waffen-SS formations.'[259] Canvassing among apprentices in a Mulhouse factory, SS officers threatened that 'in the case of refusal their parents would be expelled from Alsace.'[260]

The units, however, were horrified when they saw the replacements with which they were expected to face the increasingly severe fighting in prospect. In August 1941 and again in March 1942 Jüttner protested to Berger against the 'totally unacceptable replacements' provided by the SS-Hauptamt.[261] In September 1942 he was even more outspoken, referring to crude recruiting methods which produced men either obtained on false pretences or simply press-ganged. Units were continually being plagued by complaints from families demanding the return of relatives press-ganged into the Waffen-SS.[262]

In addition commanders complained about the miserable training standard of their recruits. 'A considerable proportion of the men reach the front knowing nothing,' Eicke reported: 'their listless uninterested faces are eloquent. One can see that they have had no strenuous training to fit them for battle.'[263] The fighting commanders may have been dissatisfied with the replacements mustered from Germany but Berger's protégés, the 'racial German' volunteers, were worse. Headquarters of the 'Florian Geyer' SS cavalry division observed in 1943 that the racial Germans showed 'a striking indifference and mulishness' which was affecting the morale of the troops.[264]

Initially the racial German volunteers from Rumania and Croatia had been glad to join the Waffen-SS (unlike their counterparts from Hungary) but they were soon disillusioned.[265] The headquarters of the 'Florian Geyer' division thought it 'perfectly possible that many of the racial German volunteers do not regard this war as their own nor consider service in the Waffen-SS as their duty to the German people.'[266] Eicke's opinion of them was even lower: 'A large number of the racial Germans can only be described as intellectually sub-standard. Many can neither write nor read German. They do not understand the words of command and are inclined to insubordination and malingering. Orders issued are generally not carried out, the excuse being that they did not understand what their officer wanted. This is an invitation to cowardice.'[267] Fighting efficiency was eventually so badly affected by the attitude of the racial Germans that a low percentage of racial Germans was considered the mark of a good SS division.[268]

In the eyes of the SS commanders this vexatious recruiting situation was partially offset by the enthusiasm for the Waffen-SS shown by the European volunteers. The 200,000 non-Germans in the Waffen-SS gave it a multi-racial aura and reintroduced some of that idealism which the commanders found so sadly lacking. But the daily wartime grind quickly damped enthusiasm. Even the cry of 'anti-Bolshevist crusade', to which all could subscribe, could not conceal the fact that the Waffen-SS was not, as it liked to think, the political and military expression of a spontaneous European movement.

Drawn from a variety of countries and with a variety of ideologies, the SS volunteers suddenly found themselves under training by a force of strict Prussian drill-sergeants reared in the blinkers of totalitarianism. In the Waffen-SS these foreigners were thrown together with men who had no understanding of the habits and views of other races. Complaints soon began to pile up that officers and NCOs of the Waffen-SS were treating their foreign volunteers in the most overbearing master-race manner. Resistance to the over-Germanic training methods of the Waffen-SS came primarily from the Flemish, the Norwegians and the Dutch.[269] Even Himmler castigated the 'iniquitous and psychologically mistaken treatment' of his non-German Germans and threatened that 'officers and NCOs who offend against the future of Germanism must be ruthlessly demoted and expelled.'[270] In Norway ex-Waffen-SS men banded together to keep out Berger's recruiting officers;[271] from early 1943 applications by Dutchmen, Danes and Belgians for release from the Waffen-SS increased sharply.[272]

'It is simply incomprehensible how little influence Waffen-SS methods have had upon the men's ideological attitude,' Amt VI of the SS-Hauptamt lamented in October 1942.[273] In many cases outright enemies of the SS were wearing Waffen-SS uniform. The field postal censorship office, for instance, intercepted a letter from a Dutch SS cadet named 't Veer telling a friend in Amsterdam that he was 'twice as optimistic since our friends [the Allies] have established a foothold on Italian soil.' Himmler ordered: 'This man must immediately be brought before an SS court.'[274] Leon Degrelle, the Rexist leader and Belgian Waffen-SS hero, an SS-Sturmbannführer decorated with the Oak Leaves, had in fact only joined the Waffen-SS in order to thwart Himmler's plan to separate Flemish-speaking Belgium from the rest of the country and incorporate it in the Reich.[275] Voorhoeve, the director of National-Socialist propaganda in Holland, was anti-German and opposed to SS Germanic policy; he told a friend that only by joining this 'squad of damned idiots' could SS plans be countered.[276] Rauter, the HSSPF, warned: 'Acceptance of this man into the Waffen-SS is highly dangerous. Should he return to Holland as a "hero" it would be very difficult for us to oppose so distinguished a front-line soldier.'[277]

Even the more simple-minded among the European volunteers began to realize that they had been lured by promises which were not being kept. Many of them had joined the Waffen-SS because they believed in the promises made by Berger's recruiting squads that by serving the Germans in war they would assure their country's independence in Adolf Hitler's new Europe. The Waffen-SS commanders supported these aspirations, but the door was soon closed by Hitler. As the months went by, therefore, the officers' position *vis-à-vis* the European volunteers became more and more untenable. Commanders took refuge in a variety of expedients: the Bad Tölz cadet school was turned into a European military academy[278] where non-Germans were even permitted to criticize the National-Socialist Party programme; in Holland it was proposed to erect a 'memorial to the Germanic warrior';[279] plans for a pan-European future appeared – and all the time these officers knew that they were drawing for their men a picture of a future which would never materialize.

The world in which the Waffen-SS commanders had once believed collapsed. The ideological lifeline linking the army of Steiner, Hausser, Bittrich and Dietrich to the SS parted – not suddenly but gradually, becoming more tenuous and tattered month by month. With their faith in Hitler wavering, despairing of final victory, handicapped by second-rate reinforcements and wrestling with a crisis of conscience over the European volunteers, the SS army fell a prey to ideological doubts, unsure whether it still belonged to the SS. The SS formations were now following only their own banners and they were led by commanders whose loyalty to the leadership of the State was faltering.

They still trotted out the stereotyped phrases about Führer and

Reich, loyalty and final victory, but in their heart of hearts they withdrew into themselves and became a force owing allegiance to none – no longer SS and not yet Wehrmacht. In this they shared the traditional fate of an imperial guard which, in the words of Rolf Bigler, the Swiss sociologist, is invariably characterized by 'a special relationship to official authority and consequently to the government.'[280] So among the hardships and disappointments of war, for the men of the Waffen-SS the unit became their real home; the divisional symbol, the bitter battles, the memory of fallen comrades formed a mystical bond holding the unit together, a closed circle into which no stranger might penetrate. It was the same with the commanders. Seldom have German formations been led by more self-assured or haughtier generals. The SS generals gave many examples of robust self-reliance.

In February 1943, for instance, Paul Hausser and his II SS Panzer Corps were ordered to stop the enemy then massing against Kharkov and to hold the city at all costs. By February 12th, however, the Russians had succeeded in working round behind the German formations and Hausser's corps was faced with encirclement at any moment. Hausser thereupon asked permission from Lanz, his Army commander, to evacuate Kharkov and withdraw. Lanz's headquarters refused, pointing out that Hitler had forbidden any retrograde movement. On February 15th OKH sent a radio message to Kharkov referring once more to the Führer's order and forbidding Hausser to evacuate Kharkov. Then Hausser took his own decision. About 12.50 PM on February 15th he gave the order to withdraw – contrary to his Führer's explicit instructions. As a result his Panzer corps was saved from annihilation and Field-Marshal van Manstein was able to use it later for a counter-offensive. Hitler grumbled about the insubordinate SS General but left him undisturbed.[281]

SS generals frequently disregarded the orders of the Army. During the German advance in southern Russia OKW accused Dietrich, the commander of the Leibstandarte, of 'charging into Rostov' contrary to orders 'purely to gain a prestige victory' – as Berger noted in the file;[282] the insubordination of another SS commander drew an order from Field-Marshal von Kleist in classic terms. 'The commander of the "Viking" division,' he radioed, 'is 1: to be informed that the Army will not have positions occupied contrary to orders; 2: to report how it comes about that, without reporting the fact, he has occupied a position other than that expressly ordered by Corps headquarters.'[283]

Few had more reason to complain of the SS generals' independent ways than Himmler himself. Suspiciously he watched the Waffen-SS withdrawing into its own world. On November 23rd, 1942 Maximilian von Herff, Head of the SS Personnel Office, commented on the senior officers of the Führungshauptamt: 'There is a circle centred around Jüttner which must be watched, since it could become dangerous one day. This is the Petri–von Jena–Hansen group. Neither their thoughts nor their desires are those of the SS. They simply wish to be an imperial guard; anything else is a side issue in their eyes.'[284]

The Reichsführer-SS had never had any very close relationship with his troops but he was sufficiently sensitive to perceive the increasing estrangement between his fighting force and the rest of his Order. It can hardly have surprised him. As early as March 5th, 1952 he had prophesied: 'I see here a major danger – that the Waffen-SS will start to lead its own existence, pleading "exigency of war" just as the Wehrmacht used earlier to plead "national defence requirement." '[285] On many previous occasions the Reichsführer-SS had been worried by the fact that the Waffen-SS led its own existence. There were many small signs – the manifest aversion of Waffen-SS officers to social contact with men of the Allgemeine-SS, the tendency to use Wehrmacht instead of SS ranks, contrary to Himmler's order, and the alacrity with which Waffen-SS units placed themselves under Wehrmacht orders, again contrary to the Reichsführer's explicit instructions.

When 600 Waffen-SS men placed themselves under the Wehrmacht Commandant Berlin during an air raid, Himmler was furious: 'If a single other Waffen-SS man places himself under the command of the Wehrmacht and the Waffen-SS thereby stabs me, the Reichsführer-SS, in the back, I shall have the SS Garrison Commander Berlin not only relieved at once but arrested.'[286] But the Waffen-SS officers were not to be persuaded to renounce what Himmler called the 'Wehrmacht outlook. Sturmbannführer Loh, Waffen-SS Garrison Commander Nuremberg, refused on principle all contact with offices of the Allgemeine-SS and SD. On October 10th, 1941 the SD-Abschnitt Nuremberg reported: 'As SS-Oberabschnitt Commander, SS-Brigadeführer Dr Martin has done all in his power to weld the SS as a whole into one block ... his attempts to include the Waffen-SS have failed in face of the obdurate and incomprehensible attitude of the above-named SS-Sturmbannführer Loh.'[287] In vain Himmler drew the attention of his soldiers to the fact that the SS Order was the real home of the Waffen-SS. In August 1941 he commanded that only SS badges of rank be used in the SS divisions.[288] Steiner was reprimanded for invariably signing his Corps Orders 'General Steiner'.[289] On this point, nevertheless, Himmler had eventually to give way somewhat to his military men. He agreed that senior Waffen-SS officers from Brigadeführer upwards might use Wehrmacht ranks in addition to their SS titles.[290] But he was more outspoken in criticizing ideological backsliding on the part of his generals. Sharply worded orders descended on Waffen-SS headquarters urging every SS officer to train his soldiers 'to be more fanatical and convinced standard-bearers of the National-Socialist ideology and of the concept of our Führer Adolf Hitler'; and then a threat: 'I shall judge capacity to command a unit not only by ability to train it well militarily but also by ability to educate every individual officer, NCO and man to be a convinced, steadfast ideological fighter in every situation.'[291]

Hardly a single SS General took any notice. Berger found it astonishing 'that there are people in the SS who simply take no notice of an explicit order from the Reichsführer.'[292] In many divisions the ideological instruction ordered by Himmler simply did not take place and the more assiduous SS commanders who tried to carry it out became a laughing stock. In 1944 the ideological instructor of 13 SS Division complained that his 'honour as an SS leader and officer had been impugned' because his political work 'was largely disregarded by the divisional staff'.[293] On October 2nd, 1943, a secret SS-Hauptamt informer put it more crudely: 'It's enough to make you vomit. I'm always hearing: "SS spirit! Shit! It's non-existent".'[294]

As the frequency of such reports increased, so did Himmler's suspicion that he was surrounded by ungrateful generals who already had a foot in the other camp – that of the Wehrmacht. One after another he saw his generals as apostates from the SS Order.

Berger noted that Obergruppenführer Phleps, commanding the SS Mountain Corps, had become 'most peculiar'; he excluded from his staff conferences non-military National-Socialists such as Andreas Schmidt, the minority group leader.[295] Obergruppenführer Höfle's servile attitude to the Wehrmacht so infuriated Himmler that, although he was an old comrade from the days of the November 1923 putsch, Himmler ceased to address him with the familiar 'du' and threatened him with the direst punishments. 'Herr Höfle. This letter is the final warning before I dismiss you. As a subordinate you are as indisciplined as you are weak in carrying out your orders. I have the impression that you are complete wax in the hands of your staff. You will notify concisely and convincingly in writing – without any excuses or explanations – whether you are now prepared to obey your instructions and to pay more attention to the orders you receive from me than to the whisperings of your staff or the directives of the loyal Army authorities.'[296]

His Reichsführer's outbursts of rage left Höfle unmoved. Similarly Obergruppenführer Bittrich, now Commander of II SS Panzer Corps, when dismissed by Himmler for critical utterances after the Normandy battle, refused to leave his post and was supported by the Commander-in-Chief West, Field-Marshal Model.[297] Particularly exasperating to Himmler was the fact that his one-time favourite, SS-Obergruppenführer and Waffen-SS General Felix Steiner, now joined the ranks of the Reichsführer's critics.

'You are my most insubordinate general,' Himmler once exclaimed, after hearing that Steiner had referred to him as a 'sleazy romantic'.[298] Henceforth Himmler watched the crusty East Prussian with mistrust. He had already observed that Steiner had surrounded himself with SS officers who did more than merely ridicule the spindly-legged figure of 'Reichsheini' in uniform. As early as 1940 Himmler had been taken aback when Steiner, then commanding the 'Deutschland' Verfügungstruppe regiment, had voiced loud criticism in the officers' mess of Hitler's strategy in the Western Campaign – so loud that Himmler had dispatched Höfle to tell him to hold his tongue.[299] Himmler was also incensed by the critical comments of SS-Sturmbannführer Reichel, Steiner's senior staff officer, who, according to the Reichsführer, exercised 'an extraordinarily unfortunate influence on morale among the officers of the [Viking] division.'[300] He gave Steiner his reasons in August 1942: 'In particular I regard it as impossible in the long run that Reichel should shoot his mouth off, criticizing the actions not only of the authorities in general but even of the Führer and also of myself.'[301] Standartenführer Gille, Steiner's Artillery Commander, was also in the Reichsführer's bad books. Gille was an entirely non-political officer who would have nothing to do with ideology. To Obersturmbannführer Fick, the divisional ideological observer, he growled: 'Wearing of the brown shirt is not permitted in this aristocratic artillery regiment. I'll put a clean-out squad into your room.'[302]

Himmler did his best to bring his one-time favourite general to heel. He threatened. He coaxed. He implored. He appealed to Steiner's sense of gratitude. He dispatched emissaries to talk the General round. 'I think it is generally recognized,' he confided to Berger, 'that I have always shown the greatest possible leniency towards the vainglory now characteristic of the soldiers and in particular of the average General.'[303] Appealing to Steiner's gratitude Himmler pointed out that 'he must realize that he had become an Obergruppenführer and Waffen-SS General at the age of 47, whereas in the Army I doubt whether you would have become a general at all.' Would he therefore be so good as to 'cease calling himself General, taking his SS rank of Obergruppenführer for granted, and use "Gruppenführer" or "Obergruppenführer", the ranks to which he has been promoted as a revolutionary commander.'[304] And more threateningly: 'The Reichsführer desires that he [Steiner] put a stop once and for all to the scandalous expressions used about me, the Reichsführer, by many in the "Viking" Division when talking in the mess, etc. I will no longer tolerate these things.'[305]

But Himmler's admonitions fell on deaf ears. Berger gave up the struggle, recognizing 'that SS-Gruppenführer Steiner is simply not to be controlled. He does what he wants and will not be talked to.'[306] The last straw was the news that Steiner was now greeting his men simply with 'Heil' instead of the obligatory 'Heil Hitler' and was even criticizing the SS 'Russian sub-humans' policy: Berger was instructed 'to establish whether Steiner is lacking in loyalty towards the Reichsführer.'[307] Berger was able to reassure Himmler.[308]

But loyalty was an elastic term in the Waffen-SS. Himmler and Berger were unaware that a few days earlier (June 1943) in a Berlin café Felix Steiner had met an old friend, the one-time Nazi and now anti-Nazi Fritz Dietlof Graf von der Schulenburg, lately Vice President of the Berlin Police. Steiner and Schulenburg had been friends ever since they had served together in No 1 Infantry Regiment in Königsberg. Schulenburg divulged dangerous thoughts to his friend: 'We shall have to kill Hitler before he ruins Germany totally.'[309] SS-Obergruppenführer Steiner departed deep in thought. The Waffen-SS was headed for the great parting of the ways. The moment of truth – July 20th, 1944 – was only a year away.

17

THE SS AND GERMAN RESISTANCE

IN autumn 1942 information reaching the RSHA caused SS-Gruppenführer Müller, the Head of the Gestapo, to prick up his ears. The Gestapo Leitstelle Munich reported a currency case which, though it seemed at first sight an ordinary misdemeanour, was to have considerable effects upon the whole structure of power in the Third Reich.

On orders from the Customs Investigation Office in Prague, a man named David had been arrested on the old Czechoslovak frontier for carrying 400 dollars without authorization. David stated that he was acting on behalf of an Officer of Military Intelligence [Abwehr] under Admiral Wilhelm Canaris and that he had been commissioned to wind up certain financial dealings with Jews in the Protectorate.[1] From David the trail led to two sources of money, both in the pay of the Abwehr Office Munich – Captain Ickrat and his friend Wilhelm Schmidhuber, a German exporter. Both were placed on the suspect list for breaking currency regulations.[2]

Under pressure Schmidhuber dictated to the Gestapo interrogating officials a statement which showed that this apparent currency offence had political implications. He referred to similar transactions undertaken by Dr Hans von Dohnanyi, a State Attorney working in the Abwehr Central Office under Major-General Hans Oster.[3] Thinking that they had stumbled upon a further Abwehr affair, the Gestapo investigated further. They discovered that von Dohnanyi had provided Jews with papers and money from the Abwehr and allowed them to travel to Switzerland as agents.[4]

Meanwhile Schmidhuber had been arrested by the Gestapo and 'persuaded' to talk further. He indicated that there was some connexion between his activities and the efforts made by Lieutenant Josef Müller of the Munich Abwehr to persuade the Vatican to mediate between Germany and the Allies.[5] Gestapo Müller immediately realized the implications of the Munich report; for the first time the Gestapo had succeeded in penetrating the mighty Abwehr which had so far prevented Müller's organization from becoming Germany's sole secret service and protected the Wehrmacht from the prying eyes of the Gestapo. Moreover in the Gestapo's mind, Major-General Oster, Lieutenant Müller and Dr von Dohnanyi were suspect; they had long been convinced that the OKW Ausland/Abwehr office contained a group of determined enemies of the régime who under Wehrmacht cover – and therefore out of the Gestapo's reach – were planning the downfall of the National-Socialist régime.

Ever since the RSHA had clamped its controls on Germany, it had been at daggers drawn with the Abwehr. Although officially the two organizations collaborated, Abwehr officers were always criticizing the unscrupulous Gestapo methods of suppressing so-called enemies and they thwarted all attempts by SS headquarters to amalgamate the political and military secret services (SD and Abwehr) under the RSHA. The RSHA had already compiled what Heydrich called the 'ammunition pack' which the Gestapo brains trust would open when the time seemed ripe to give the enemy the *coup de grâce*.[6] The 'pack' contained secret dossiers recording numerous indications of anti-régime activity by

Oster, Dohnanyi and Müller. Oster was a monarchist and a sort of Chief-of-Staff of the Abwehr; he had organized an internal political information service which provided the leaders of German resistance with reports of anti-régime sentiment; it was so effective that von Hentig, a foreign service officer, had referred in somewhat highly-coloured terms to 'supervision of the entire Party by the Wehrmacht's Abwehr'.[7] Dr von Dohnanyi, a lawyer, had been on the RSHA's black list ever since 1938, when he had helped to uncover the Gestapo intrigue against Colonel-General von Fritsch; he was also known to be in close contact with the anti-Hitler circle led by Ludwig Beck, the late Army Chief-of-Staff, and Carl Goerdeler, the ex-Burgomaster.[8] Lieutenant Josef Müller was a Catholic, later a co-founder of the Christian Socialist Union; he had long been under Gestapo and SD observation on suspicion of having divulged to the Belgian Legation in the Vatican the date of the German offensive in the West (May 10th, 1940).[9]

All this led Gestapo Müller to think that the Munich currency case offered an opportunity to disgrace the Abwehr. But nothing must reveal his true political motives; the Gestapo must give the impression that it was simply inquiring into a breach of currency regulations. Since the Gestapo could not pursue its investigations inside the Abwehr, Müller handed the case over to the Wehrmacht but at the same time ensured that the Gestapo had a hand in the game by appointing an observer, Kriminalkommissar Sonderegger.[10] The Reich Military Court, oblivious of the Gestapo's manoeuvre, nominated as investigating officer the senior Judge Advocate, Dr Manfred Roeder, who had already shown his ability as an investigator of anti-Nazi resistance in the case of the Soviet 'Rote Kapelle' espionage ring.[11]

On April 5th, 1943 Roeder and Sonderegger presented themselves to Canaris. Roeder produced an arrest warrant for Dohnanyi and explained to the Admiral that he was authorized by the Reich Military Court to search Dohnanyi's office.[12] A few minutes later the three men were in Dohnanyi's room. Roeder's unexpected visit exposed a fatal weakness to which the anti-Hitler conspirators were prone. Only a few days earlier Arthur Nebe, the Head of the Kripo, who had been in contact with the internal German resistance for years, had warned the Abwehr that Gestapo Müller was planning a coup, but Dohnanyi was still taken by surprise. Roeder went to Dohnanyi's desk and extracted a disorderly pile of documents. Among them was a file on Dohnanyi's Jewish agents in Switzerland and notes on peace talks in Rome and Stockholm undertaken by Abwehr officers together with Pastor Dietrich Bonhoeffer, who was already under Gestapo observation.[13] Sonderegger noticed that Oster was staring at Dohnanyi's desk as if transfixed. A file lay upon it.

Dohnanyi hissed to Oster 'Those papers; those papers.' Slowly Oster drew nearer to the desk and reached out to snatch the papers.[14] 'Stop,' Sonderegger shouted, pointing to Oster. Roeder turned round and grasped the position at once. He requested Admiral Canaris to order Oster to relinquish the papers and after some initial hesitation Oster complied.[15]

Roeder read the paper. On it Dohnanyi and Oster had worked out a code by which a meeting between Bonhoeffer and certain pro-Allied politicians, planned to take place in a foreign country, could be presented as perfectly harmless. This scene in Dohnanyi's room heralded the end of the Abwehr's independence. Oster, the opposition's most important informant next to Nebe, was dismissed and cashiered; Dohnanyi, Josef Müller and Bonhoeffer were arrested.[16]

In January 1944 the Gestapo brought off another coup against the imprudent Abwehr conspirators. Gestapo Müller broke up a resistance ring centred around Hanna Solf, the widow of the former Ambassador to Japan, and in the process arrested certain members of the Abwehr office; they included Kiep, the ex-minister, Graf von Moltke, a military administrative officer and Captain Gehre.[17] Hardly had the Abwehr recovered from this new blow than it fell victim to its own weakness once more. The Abwehr representatives in Switzerland, Sweden and Turkey deserted to the Allies.[18]

When the desertions were reported to Hitler, he heaped curses on the head of the Abwehr. He was heard to say that Admiral Canaris' organization had failed all along the line. SS-Gruppenführer Fegelein, Himmler's representative in the Führer's headquarters and Hitler's future brother-in-law, partly as a joke remarked that 'the whole business' ought to be handed over to the Reichsführer-SS. Hitler seized on the idea and summoned Himmler.[19] In a matter of minutes the fate of the Abwehr was decided: at the end of February 1944, Himmler was commissioned by his Führer to amalgamate the Abwehr and the SD. The Wehrmacht had lost a decisive battle to the SS.[20] The mighty German Wehrmacht had lost its Intelligence organization and become the only army in the world without its own Secret Service. Military counter-espionage was henceforth a prerogative of the SS – which of course was jubilant.

Curiously enough, however, the victor did not take his anticipated revenge. Gestapo Müller, who was eager to clean out the 'gang of traitors' in Canaris' office, was not placed in charge of the Abwehr; instead the job went to Müller's bitterest rival, SS-Brigadeführer Walter Schellenberg, Head of Amt VI (Ausland-SD) in the RSHA. The relationship between Schellenberg and Admiral Canaris had long been curiously ambivalent; the Admiral appreciated the young man's exceptional intelligence; his feelings were almost paternal. In return Schellenberg respected Canaris as a man – an unusual attitude for the cold SD intellectual.[21]

Even during his most violent quarrels with Heydrich, Schellenberg's master, the Admiral would listen to the young man's advice. 'Was I too outspoken again?' he would often ask when he met Schellenberg on his morning ride in the Berlin Tiergarten.[22] Canaris knew that, as far as he was concerned, there were certain rules of loyalty which Schellenberg would never break. The Foreign Ministry Head of Intelligence, an ultra-Nazi of the Ribbentrop school, once asked Schellenberg whether Canaris was really a crafty old fox or a genuine supporter of the Nazi régime. Schellenberg cut him short, saying that there was no doubt of the Admiral's loyalty.[23] (Schellenberg never wavered in this conviction – not even on July 23rd, 1944 when Müller deliberately selected him to arrest the Admiral as an accomplice of the July 20th conspirators.[24] Schellenberg knew better. Perhaps he even knew of the telephone conversation between Canaris and Graf Stauffenberg who made the attack on Hitler; when, on the afternoon of July 20th, Stauffenberg informed the Admiral of the supposedly successful attack on Hitler, Canaris exclaimed: 'Dead? Good God! Who did it? The Russians?')[25]

Nevertheless Schellenberg regarded the end of the Abwehr as a personal triumph, a victory for his Ausland-SD. At last his dream looked like coming true – a unified super Secret Service; he could visualize himself as the master mind of an espionage empire which would put the much-envied British 'Intelligence Service' in the shade.[26] Here was further proof of the fact that Walter Schellenberg was one of the most ambitious and unpredictable figures in SS headquarters; even the other RSHA heads of division regarded him as a dangerous outsider who was best avoided. Through the SD's spy system this Saarbrücken lawyer had worked his way first into the SS and then into favour with Heydrich, to whom he was bound by a sort of love-hate relationship.[27]

The RSHA had initially regarded Schellenberg as Heydrich's office factotum; later, however, they realized that behind the almost feminine sensitivity of this well-groomed and well-read barrister lay a strength of will capable of asserting itself even in face of the fearsome Heydrich. Moreover he had contrived to reinsure with Himmler; the Reichsführer liked this wily 'Benjamin', as he used to call Schellenberg.[28] During a flight to Vienna Schellenberg had once seized his Reichsführer by the tunic when Himmler thoughtlessly leant back against the door handle.[29] Himmler had felt confident in Schellenberg's sense and circumspection ever since.

In spite of these close ties with the most powerful personalities in the SS, Schellenberg was shrewd enough not to 'lay at the feet of the totalitarian State the tribute of his loyalty unto death'.[30] He had no intention of shedding his last drop of blood for the National-Socialist State. The versatility and adaptibility which had won this penniless son of a middle-class family a place among the SD élite enabled him to turn his back on the Hitler régime as soon as he saw the writing on the wall heralding the Nazi *Götterdämmerung*. He had been aware of the Reich's real situation ever since he had forced his way into the higher echelons of the SS Intelligence Service. In 1940 he had taken over the Abwehr Polizei [Counter-Espionage Police] when Werner Best was dismissed, but had then fallen out so badly with his master, the sour, brutal, Gestapo Müller,[31] that he must have been only too glad to take over the Ausland-SD in 1942 as successor to Heinz Jost.[32]

As Head of the Foreign Intelligence Service, Schellenberg displayed such talent that when Himmler was given the task of amalgamating the SD and the Abwehr his mind turned to his 'Benjamin' and so in spring 1944 Schellenberg set to work to form a unified Secret Service under the RSHA.[33] But he did not parade his sense of triumph before the vanquished Abwehr. He dismantled the Abwehr machine with the utmost caution; almost to a man Canaris' old staff was carefully given its niche in the RSHA.[34] On the surface nothing had changed except, apparently, the senior posts.[35]

Even Canaris was initially left in peace by the Gestapo. He was first confined in Burg Lauenstein under a sort of parole, but after a discussion with Schellenberg he was allowed to return to Berlin as head of the OKW Special Staff for Economic Warfare.[36] The SS even brought themselves to sing the praises of their fallen enemy. Early in May 1944 in a castle near Salzburg Himmler and Keitel, the Chief of OKW, celebrated the birth of the new era for the Secret Service in the presence of a crowd of SS leaders; on this occasion the Reichsführer referred to 'the valuable work of the Military Abwehr'.[37] The majority of the Abwehr officers had no inkling why Schellenberg was treating the Canaris men with such leniency. Only gradually did the fantastic truth emerge – Schellenberg, the Head of the SD, was pursuing a policy surprisingly similar to that of the Abwehr conspirators.

On this eve of July 20th, 1944 hardly a soul knew that the Abwehr and the Ausland-SD were working on parallel lines. Both had ceased to believe in an ultimate German victory; both wanted a separate peace with the Allies; both were ready to do away with Adolf Hitler in the interests of German survival.

The Abwehr's critical analyses of the war situation checked with the

SD's enemy Intelligence and morale reports. Moreover both organizations were equally frustrated. Canaris had continually complained that his situation reports were no longer read in the Führer's headquarters; from mid-1944 the SD was not even allowed to submit its 'Reports from the Reich' which were intended for the top-level leaders.[38] In their search for an escape from Hitler's war, SD and Abwehr often found themselves using the same deep dark paths, the same intermediaries, the same Allied agents.

At least in some degree the two were heading in the same direction; on the one hand the conscience of the German officer corps was in revolt, on the other the cold-blooded rationalists of the SD were taking avoiding action. So close was their alliance that the SS apologists later maintained that the two wanted the same thing; after the war, Werner Best considered that the same tragic fate had overtaken both the Abwehr and the SD. 'It was a tragedy for both of us,' he said, 'that for the sake of our people we created a régime which made a good start and registered considerable initial successes but then, for unforeseen reasons – Hitler's obsession with his gift of prophecy – led us to catastrophe.'[39]

This reading of the situation, of course, ignores the vast moral difference between the conspirators of July 20th, who acted primarily on ethical grounds, and the SS technologists of power; nevertheless Best's words reflect the bitterness and disillusionment into which the drab reality of the Third Reich had plunged the lieutenants of the Führer dictatorship. Best's remark about 'Hitler's obsession with his gift of prophecy' provides a clue to the attitude of the SS, or at least certain of its leaders, up to July 20th, 1944. In their heart of hearts many SS leaders had lost faith in the man to whom they had sworn blind, fanatical loyalty – Adolf Hitler.

Devotion to this 'greatest brain of all time', as Himmler called his idol,[40] was the only thing which lent the SS Order any sense or purpose in the eyes of its leaders. To guard the life of Adolf Hitler, to carry out his orders ruthlessly, to be the executors of his last will and testament – for them this was the sacred mission of the SS. Many of its leaders had been disgusted by the kaleidoscope of the Weimar democracy with its apparent disorder, so they dreamed of an orderly 'Völkisch' State directed by the genius of a Führer towering over his century and administered by a technologist class of unsentimental 'realists' (their favourite expression) translating into action the directives of the leadership. For them the totalitarian State was the only salvation; they hoped that it would bring about the much-trumpeted orderliness and national discipline. But close proximity to the régime's manipulators of power brought many SS leaders down to earth. They soon perceived that the democratic party struggles had been replaced, not by single coordinated direction from the Führer dictatorship, but by wranglings about precedence among a plethora of Nazi potentates whom Hitler rode on a long rein in order to maintain his own position as the supreme autocrat.

For the SD intellectuals the most disillusioning aspect was that the Dictator proved by no means the supremely realistic statesman they had envisaged in their clinically efficient world. Instead of rationalism, instead of the SD's golden rule of realism, they found their Head of State possessed by a brutal urge to conquer, an uncontrollable lust for power, drawing his inspiration from the crudest nineteenth-century biological nationalism and ruled by a racialist colonizing mania which broke all bounds of nationalistic doctrine, even as interpreted by the SS leaders.

The first tiny crack, noticeable only to the initiated, in the relationship between Hitler and the SS leaders, occurred when the Dictator, intoxicated by his success, incorporated into his empire the first non-German people – the Czechs of the 'remainder of Czechoslovakia'. The rape of Prague staggered not only the outside world but certain SS leaders as well. SS-Standartenführer Reinhard Höhn, for instance, met Oberführer Best on a morning ride in the Berlin Tiergarten in March 1939: 'Höhn, my friend,' Best confided to him, 'this is the end. So far people have believed us when we said that National-Socialism was the incarnation of the racial concept and that this racial concept had certain limits. With the move into Prague, however, National-Socialism has turned to imperialism.'[41]

Of course neither the thoughts nor the deeds of the SS leaders showed any trace of these fleeting doubts in public; the SS followed Hitler into his world of fantasy; it followed him in his campaigns of conquest and genocide. Nevertheless, it was symptomatic that even Himmler, insulated though he was by his ecstatic Hitler worship, at times showed signs of an unmistakable unease – and that as early as summer 1939. In his heart of hearts Himmler was a timorous being and Hitler's suicidal career into the abyss of war gave him food for thought. During the 1938 Sudeten crisis he had been a front-ranking jingoist, egging the Dictator on in his policy of aggression; but when Hitler engineered the Danzig quarrel Himmler was assailed by a feeling that his master was gambling too high.

On the Danzig question Himmler allied himself with Göring, who was opposed to Hitler's policy of naked force; consequently he came into collision with Ribbentrop, whom he regarded as the most sinister of all Hitler's advisers. Early in April he journeyed to Danzig to counsel moderation to Albert Forster, the bellicose Gauleiter and overlord of the Free Port.[42] Baron Guy de la Tournelle, the French Consul General, reported to Paris that Himmler was determined to oust Forster[43] but in spite of the support of Greiser, the President of the Danzig Senate and Forster's rival, he did not succeed. At this time even the Polish Ambassador to Berlin ranked Himmler as one of the opponents of war.[44] On July 26th, 1939 Burckhardt, the Swiss League of Nations Commissioner in Danzig, wrote to the Secretary-General that there was talk abroad 'that Hitler was now isolated by Himmler and Goebbels. This was inaccurate but it was true that since the autumn and particularly since the November Jewish pogrom, Himmler had changed front; he now stood much closer to Göring and was opposed to Goebbels and his propaganda methods.'[45]

Later Himmler dutifully fell in behind Hitler's war policy but he retained his aversion to Ribbentrop, on whose shoulders he placed responsibility for Germany's fateful course towards war – to absolve his idol Hitler from any blame. Certain of Hitler's entourage were labouring under the delusion that peace with the Allies could be quickly achieved if only Ribbentrop could be got rid of. Göring once said: 'This is not our war; it's Ribbentrop's!'[46] And many in SS Headquarters thought this way. In October 1939 Ulrich von Hassell, the ex-Ambassador and one of the leaders of German resistance, heard of it. When he met Graf Welczek, the ex-German Ambassador to Paris, he told him that they were trying to end the war as soon as possible. Hassell noted: 'His [Welczek's] sphere of activity includes members of the SS High Command – Stuckart and Höhn. He maintained that these two men thought fundamentally as we [the opposition] do and were already considering whether Ribbentrop should not be thrown to the wolves. The formation of a new Cabinet was under consideration there.'[47]

Such little indications, sporadic though they were, showed that the men of SS headquarters by no means shared that blind confidence in victory of the thousands upon thousands of young SS men whom they dispatched to face the horrors and massacres of the Second World War. Even at the height of the German victories Hassell noted: 'Since the SS view the outcome of the war very realistically, that is sceptically,' SS headquarters was unable to subscribe to the regulation Nazi jingoism.[48]

Not that they had any doubts about the essential validity of Hitler's power policy. As always, the SS stood ready to carry out even the most barbaric order from its Führer. Whether the task was to annihilate the Jewish people, to launch a fresh offensive on the battlefield, to liberate

Mussolini from captivity or prevent the defection of a German satellite, the SS never hesitated.

Many an SS leader found that common sense prevented him from placing himself unreservedly at the disposal of the Führer dictatorship. The SD élite was simply too intelligent to swallow the poisonous doctrine of naked force preached from the Führer's headquarters by the apostle of 'Lebensraum'. In occupation policy, certain significant shades of difference appeared between the SS concept of rule and Hitler's simple master-and-slave concept. The coldly calculating technicians of power, whose task was to rule conquered Europe with their police machine and at the same time to pacify it, found their task complicated by Hitler's uncompromising 'Lebensraum' imperialism; inevitably its naked policy of conquest would one day rouse the subject people to resist their German masters.

Hitler's instructions for the treatment of occupied Russia were in general valid for the rest of Europe; the basic point he said, was 'to carve up the gigantic cake so that we may first dominate it, secondly administer it and thirdly exploit it'.[49] His world contained, apart from Germany, no autonomous peoples or states but simply a collection of satrapies under a centralized super-dictatorship. Speaking to the Reichsleiter and Gauleiter in 1944 Hitler had said that the 'rubbish of small states' must be liquidated as soon as possible; 'the Germans alone' could really organize Europe. He was not prepared to allow the occupied states even a minimum of national autonomy,[50] saying: 'The road to self-government leads to independence; one cannot keep by democratic institutions what one has acquired by force'.[51]

The SS version of this programme was a more intelligent, though morally no less questionable, policy, best described by the current phrase 'stick and carrot'. The SS occupation policy experts hoped to produce a grudging consensus between rulers and ruled by continuous alternation between severity and leniency. Werner Best's ideas, for instance, were very different from those of his master with his scorn for the 'rubbish of small states'; in 1942 Best wrote in the periodical *Reich, Volksordnung, Lebensraum:* 'as regards the relationship of a great power to other peoples in an area, it must be remembered that in the long term no people has been able to exercise leadership without or against the consent of the led . . . men can be neither coerced nor duped . . . The highest degree of self-expression to which a people can aspire is to be the strongest among a group of peoples living in the same area, to work towards the same destiny in close cooperation with its allies, to have as its object the creation of a single great demographic area in which it will still be the leader in accordance with the natural laws of existence; by this means lasting natural development can be assured instead of decline, the inevitable consequence of a short-term master-race hallucination.'[52]

Heydrich was the first to put this specifically SS occupation policy to the test. In September 1941, although already Head of the SD and Director of the RSHA, he was nominated acting (and in practice actual) Reich Protector of Bohemia and Moravia.

Heydrich introduced himself to the Czechs with a wave of terror which earned him the name of the 'Butcher of Prague'. He engineered the first fake trial in Nazi history, having the Czech Premier, Alois Elias, condemned to death within a few hours. Meanwhile Gestapo commandos broke up the Czech resistance groups and arrested opposition elements;[53] shortly before his arrival the pro-Western and Communist resistance groups had combined, but in a bare two weeks Heydrich had practically destroyed the Czech resistance movement.[54] Daily he reported the 'victories' of his terror campaign to the Führer's Headquarters.

No sooner had he achieved his immediate purpose, however, than Heydrich brought the summary courts of justice to an end. The Reich Protector presented a new face to his terrorized subjects. Heydrich the butcher was replaced by Heydrich the benefactor. He declared political persecution at an end and began to woo the Czech workers and peasants, playing them off against the bourgeois intelligentsia whom he regarded as the main focus of potential resistance.[55] Having been commissioned to raise Czech industrial and agricultural production, he abolished many of the regulations stamping the Czechs as second-class citizens.

Heydrich raised the fat ration for 2,000,000 Czech industrial workers, released 200,000 pairs of shoes for workers in the armaments industry, and requisitioned luxury hotels in Bohemia's world-famous spas as holiday homes for Czech workers.[56] Simultaneously he reorganized the Czech social-security system, which was far inferior to the German. Charles Wighton, Heydrich's British biographer, says that 'for the first time even in democratic Czechoslovakia he made them [the workers and peasants] socially acceptable.'[57] With his wife Lina, the Protector received a stream of Czech delegations, giving many the erroneous impression that the Czechs had accepted German domination.[58]

In London the Czech Government-in-exile under Eduard Beneš was taken aback by the reports of Heydrich's achievements. Peace in the Protectorate threatened to paralyse the Czech émigré democrats, for the more the population of Bohemia and Moravia seemed prepared passively to accept their German masters, the more untenable did the position of the Government-in-exile become in negotiations with the Allies.[59] Only if there was an active resistance movement in the Protectorate could the Government-in-exile assert any claim to Allied consideration of Czech interests in a post-war settlement. However, so long as the Germans under Heydrich continued their flexible occupation policy, there would be no resistance. The Czech exiles drew the sober conclusion – Heydrich must be liquidated; only the murder of the mighty Reich Protector was likely to call forth that German brutality without which Czech resistance had neither purpose nor incentive.

In December 1941 the émigré Cabinet in London decided that Heydrich must die. Two Czech NCOs, Jan Kubis and Josef Gabcik, were selected for the task of murdering the Protector and shortly after Christmas they were dropped into the Protectorate from a British aircraft.[60] Kubis and Gabcik had been well prepared for their mission. They had been sent to a school for spies near Manchester, had been trained in sabotage at Cambusdarroch in Northern Scotland and been given final training at the Villa Pellasis near Dorking; they planned to murder Heydrich somewhere along his short daily drive to Prague from Panenske-Breschen, his summer residence.[61]

As the assassination spot Kubis and Gabcik chose the Prague suburb of Holešovice, where the Dresden–Prague road traces a hairpin bend down to the Troja bridge. While negotiating the bend Heydrich's car, which was always unescorted, would naturally have to reduce speed. This was the moment which Kubis and Gabcik, now reinforced by two more saboteurs, intended to use.[62] The four men distributed themselves around the curve, each armed with a Sten gun and a supply of hand grenades concealed under their mackintoshes. Valcik, another of the gang, was posted three hundred yards before the turn to give warn- of Heydrich's arrival by whistle signal.[63]

On the morning of May 27th, 1942 all was ready; 9.30 AM, Heydrich's usual time of arrival, passed and the Protector's green Mercedes convertible did not appear. An hour went by and they were becoming nervous. Then Gabcik and Kubis heard the signal. Gabcik unbuttoned his coat, grasped his Sten gun and sprang into the roadway. As the Mercedes turned the corner, he raised his gun and aimed. He could see everything quite clearly through the windscreen – Heydrich's pale face and the head of Klein, the driver. He pressed the trigger – nothing happened, he cocked the gun again – again nothing. A desperate shout came from Kubis standing behind him. Kubis pulled out a hand-grenade and lobbed it at the car as it slithered to a halt. The bomb hit the back of the car and wrecked it.[64] Apparently unharmed, Heydrich leapt out of the convertible roaring something to his driver. At the first sight of Gabcik he had stood up in the car and dragged his service revolver out of the holster. Now he jumped out into the road and set off, shouting and shooting, after his attackers who were now on the run; he was 'the central figure in a scene which might have been taken from any Western.'[65] Heydrich was gaining on Kubis when the Czech saw his chance; two trams were approaching from opposite directions and Kubis managed to slip behind one of them before Heydrich reached him. He jumped on a bicycle which had been left in readiness and escaped. Heydrich then turned on the second attacker. Gabcik had been slow to recover from his dismay at the failure of his sub-machine-gun; now he suddenly realized his danger. Drawing his revolver from his pocket he jumped back, firing as he went; turning and shooting, diving from cover to cover, he fled.[66] Then he saw Heydrich throw his revolver to the ground; his ammunition was exhausted. Suddenly he clapped his right hand to his hip and staggered. Gabcik made good his escape. Now at last it became clear that the attackers had not missed Heydrich; Kubis' grenade had driven leatherwork and steel springs from the car's upholstery into Heydrich's ribs and stomach; particles of horsehair had even penetrated the spleen. The doctors were unable to save Reinhard Heydrich: on June 4th, 1942 he died of his wounds.[67] All that remained of the lord of the greatest system of terror in German history was his death mask, a picture of a machiavellianism peculiar to the SS. One of the first to see the mask was Dr Bernhard Wehner, a criminal police official ordered to Prague to investigate the affair; he noted later: 'Deceptive features of uncanny spirituality and entirely perverted beauty, like a Renaissance cardinal.'[68]

The Government-in-exile in London, however, got what it wanted. A wave of terror descended on Bohemia and Moravia, one of the most agonizing in the history of the Third Reich. 10,000 Czechs were arrested; at least 1,300 were shot, including all male inhabitants of the village of Lidice near Prague which was supposed to have harboured Heydrich's attackers. The village was razed to the ground. Heydrich's assailants were in fact among the victims of these wild, fanatical reprisals, but this was purely a matter of chance.[69] After the war the British Labour MP, R. T. Paget, pronounced 'Partisans often deliberately provoke reprisals in order that hatred of the occupier may be intensified and more people may be induced to resist. This was our general idea when we flew in a party to murder Heydrich in Czechoslovakia. The main Czech resistance movement was the direct result of the consequent SS reprisals.'[70]

Among those who fell heir to Heydrich's occupation policy, one at least was determined to avoid such barbaric reprisals in future. Ironically, among the men destined both to continue and refine the policy initiated by Heydrich was one whom he had hated more than any other SS leader – Dr Werner Best, Heydrich's co-founder of the Gestapo machine, now an SS-Gruppenführer and, since August 1942, a Director in the Foreign Ministry.[71]

As a result of a German–Danish crisis in late 1942 Best had been dispatched to Copenhagen. Though occupied, the Danes had retained their constitutional machinery and Hitler felt that he had been publicly insulted by the Royal House and the Danish Government; he proposed to take the opportunity to insist upon acceptance into the Government of the small group of Danish Nazis. In the autumn the Dictator broke off relations with the Danish Royal House and recalled his two most important representatives, the Reich Plenipotentiary and the German Military Commander. He proposed to appoint a more rabid National-Socialist as Reich Plenipotentiary who was to demand the resignation of the Danish Government and acceptance of the National-Socialists into a new Cabinet.[72]

For this task von Ribbentrop selected SS-Gruppenführer Best; he had, after all, a reputation as an energetic operator. Best, however, soon realized that Hitler's demands were bound to wreck German occupation policy in Denmark. The Danish Parliament would never agree to the nomination of Nazi Ministers. Best accordingly did what no other Foreign Ministry diplomat had dared to do – he ignored the Führer's order and came to an agreement with the Danish politicians; they formed a new Cabinet, dropping one or two ministers who were suspect to the Germans and Best, as a *quid pro quo*, did not insist on the inclusion of the Danish Nazis;[73] in fact he made clear to them that they were hindering rather than helping German occupation policy. When Parliamentary elections were held in March 1943 and the Nazis won only three seats, Best persuaded their leader, Frits Clausen, to leave Copenhagen and more or less to retire into private life.[74]

Best quietly and unobtrusively pursued the policy which seemed to him most effective. He was determined to ensure good order and stability in his area and to do so was prepared to act against all disturbers of the peace, the Allies, the Danish resistance – and Hitler.

His flexible policy, based on cold logic though it was, soon encountered resistance from Hitler. The Führer's headquarters had accepted the sacrifice of the Danish Nazis, but the supposedly weak-kneed treatment of the Danish resistance infuriated the Dictator. In fact a course of events similar to that in Prague now repeated itself in Denmark. Danish resistance fighters trained in England started guerilla warfare against the German occupation authority in Best's model protectorate. Again the primary object was to provoke German reprisals against the still hesitant population. Best the diplomat, however, avoided all unnecessary severity. He allowed the military and the Sicherheitspolizei to carry out only transient, limited reprisals. In his reports to the Foreign Ministry he even tended to minimize the real extent of the resistance to avoid some wild reaction on the part of Hitler. That he feared more than he did the partisans.[75]

Meanwhile, however, the situation reports from the military commander Denmark to the OKW operations staff painted so black a picture of Danish resistance that Hitler began to suspect his plenipotentiary of deceiving him. Furiously he demanded the most servere reprisals against the Danish partisans, for Denmark was important to him as a bridge to Norway.[76] Best was ordered to present the Danish Government with an ultimatum demanding the institution of summary courts to deal with the resistance and the introduction of the death penalty for attacks on the German occupation forces. Best declared at once that the Danish Government would never accept this ultimatum[77] and a few days later he was proved right; the Danish Cabinet rejected it and on August 29th, 1943 resigned in a body. The German military commander thereupon proclaimed a state of emergency.[78]

Looking at the situation soberly and realistically Best, the technician of power, was convinced that Hitler's policy of force could be of help only to the partisans. When, therefore, the Dictator proceeded to introduce into Denmark the standard savage anti-partisan methods, it was clear that a collision was unavoidable. On December 30th, 1943 Best was summoned to the Führer's headquarters. Hitler explained that the terror in Denmark could only be broken by intensified counter-terror; he therefore ordered that sabotage by the Danish resistance should be answered by German reprisals; for every German attacked, five partisans, or persons who had assisted them with money or otherwise, were to be liquidated. Best objected that counter-terror was not the way to deal with the Danes. With so law-abiding a people, he said, the best method of making the saboteurs unpopular was to take action only against terrorists who had been arrested and condemned under the laws of war. Hitler, who anyway regarded lawyers as the most despicable people on earth, was infuriated by Best's legal arguments. The order for counter-terror was confirmed.[79]

A wave of severe German reprisals descended upon Denmark and, however great his scepticism regarding the policy, Best could not avoid becoming involved with other leading German functionaries in some responsibility for the crimes committed. He was in fact forced to take part in a programme of reprisals which he found abhorrent. Nevertheless he continued to try to reduce the tempo of the terror campaign. In collusion with the Commander of the Sicherheitspolizei he reduced Hitler's reprisal ratio from 5:1 to 1:1 and gradually introduced German Courts-martial.[80]

His Plenipotentiary's evasive manoeuvres did not escape Hitler's notice. Only July 3rd, 1944 Ribbentrop cabled to Best: 'In view of the reports on the situation in Denmark, the Führer has voiced very sharp criticism of the policy you have so far adopted towards the Danes. The Führer considers that the institution of legal courts is responsible for present developments in Denmark.' Threateningly Ribbentrop demanded an immediate detailed report, in particular on the question why 'contrary to the Führer's instructions you have continued to deal with sabotage activity by legal proceedings instead of simply by counter-terror.'[81] Once more Best was summoned to his Führer and on July 5th found himself facing Hitler: 'These gentlemen always think they are cleverer than me,' the Dictator growled. Hitler renewed his order for counter-terror and insisted that the Reich Plenipotentiary had no business to follow a policy of his own. When Best started to object, Hitler screamed: 'I will not listen.' SS-Gruppenführer Best saluted and left the room.[82] A few hours later he had glaring proof of the illogicality of the Nazi totalitarian State. When he explained the position to Ribbentrop, the latter suddenly turned pensive and then gave him the grotesque advice: 'Do what you think is right and sensible. But the Führer's orders must be carried out.'[83]

The Best episode was the first clear demonstration that, where occupation policy was concerned, Hitler's ideas and those of the SS were not invariably identical. The next area in which differences began to appear was the treatment of the so-called 'Germanic' peoples; though both Hitler and the SS used the phraseology of Nazi dogma, the two were in fact working on different principles. In spite of all the Germanic claptrap, Hitler was still the German nationalist of the imperial era, who regarded any supra-national institution as a betrayal of Germany; the SS leaders, on the other hand, were genuinely striving for a Great German Reich which, in a vague sort of way, they hoped and believed would produce a new epoch of international brotherhood transcending national boundaries – though under German leadership, of course.

In one of his moments of enthusiasm, Himmler said that he could quite well imagine that the next Reichsführer-SS might not be a German; Hitler, on the other hand, would ridicule Himmler's passion for Germanic experimentation;[84] in his view, unless he had been ideologically brainwashed, every non-German SS volunteer must 'feel himself a traitor to his people'.[85] These two remarks alone give one to think that in contrast to Hitler's nationalistic programme, the SS leant 'towards a policy conceived in quite different terms; one of greater autonomy' (Paul Kluke's phrase). Kluke also found Himmler 'far more prepared to remove the Nordic elements from the non-German races, in other words to carry out those biological fishing expeditions among other peoples which Hitler himself found so dubious'.[86]

As Himmler became more deeply involved in his Germanic programme and came to occupy a key position in occupation policy in relation to those countries which the SS called 'Nordic-Germanic', the divergence between the SS and Hitler inevitably became more pronounced. The requirement for 'Germanic' volunteers for the Waffen-SS and the tangle of warring Nazi cliques in the German-occupied territories had caused Hitler to appoint Himmler as a sort of overlord for the Germanic countries. A Führer decree stated: 'The Reichsführer-SS carries sole responsibility for negotiation on common Germanic Völkisch requirements with the Germanic Völkisch groups in the occupied territories.'[87] A 'Germanische Leitstelle' [Germanic Office – GL] was set up in the SS-Hauptamt under Dr Franz Riedweg, a Swiss military medical officer and son-in-law to the Field-Marshal von Blomberg who had been dismissed in 1938.[88] The GL maintained out-stations in Oslo, Copenhagen, The Hague and Brussels, and set up a network of pan-German SS cells.

The GL out-stations canvassed for Waffen-SS recruits, they checked 'Germanic' applicants for the Allgemeine-SS, they set up educational establishments, they bought up publishing firms, they published newspapers, they kept in touch with local Nazi leaders who were opposed to their official Party headquarters.[89] Already the SS Germanic fanatics could see the great Germanic empire forming. Gottlob Berger, Head of the SS-Hauptamt, said: 'The Germanic volunteers in the Waffen-SS, together with the members of the Germanic SS, will one day form the foundation upon which the Germanic empire will be built.'[90] The minutes of a Commanders' Conference in the SS-Hauptamt, on October 8th, 1942, laid down the SS programme: 'Responsibility for the entire Germanic area will be conferred on the Reichsführer. It must therefore be our task to prepare the way for our leader in order that later he may be able to unite the Germanic countries in the Germanic empire. These countries should enter our Germanic empire without renouncing their nationality or their culture.'[91]

The Dictator's innate nationalistic instincts, however, ran counter to the imperialistic illusions of the SS Germanists; Hitler showed no inclination to grant the Germanic countries even that measure of autonomy which the SS leaders were prepared to concede. The majority of the German-occupied countries were still legally in a state of war with the Reich and with Hitler unwilling to make any definite pronouncement about the measure of national sovereignty to be allowed these countries in the proposed 'Germanic Empire of the German Nation', the SS 'Greater Germany' propaganda naturally proved totally ineffective.

The problem was not one of ideology alone; Hitler's refusal to make any pronouncement affected the actual practical work of the SS – and that on a subject which was difficult anyway. Since the dictator refused to speak the saving word, the Waffen-SS recruiters found themselves paralysed by Adolf Hitler. The GL reports continued to emphasize that unless Hitler soon gave the Germanic countries some assurance regarding their national independence, SS recruiting would come to a complete standstill. In 1943 Berger reported on the situation in Norway: 'The supply of volunteers has dried up completely. In spite of all our efforts, we are no longer in a position to obtain volunteers because the basis for recruitment is lacking.' As the months went by, he continued, Norwegian SS men were asking with increasing urgency 'the old question: what will become of us after the war?'[92]

Desperately Berger urged his Reichsführer to ask Hitler to conclude a peace treaty with occupied Norway. Writing to Himmler on September 25th, 1943 he said: 'Since it is essential that we tap the manpower resources of the Germanic countries, I believe that in view of the forthcoming recruiting campaign, I am justified in re-opening this question, in spite of the fact that the Führer has previously given a negative reply.'[93] Once more Hitler refused. Only later was he persuaded to allow Terboven, the Reich Commissar in Norway, to issue a declaration holding out to the Norwegian people some prospects of internal sovereignty – but its terms were vague and the future to which it referred even more nebulous. The SS leaders were not taken in by Hitler's meaningless verbiage. A combined report from Amt III of the RSHA and the GL Norway set out what the Norwegians thought of Hitler's declaration: 'It is so elastic that whoever is in power can make it mean what he likes. In practice, therefore, it has changed nothing.'[94]

Hitler's policy of silence tempted SS leaders to take the law into their own hands and make political promises to their Germanic subjects. As early as summer 1942 Obergruppenführer Jeckeln, the HSSPF Ostland, was telling Latvian officers that 'in a great Germanic empire the Latvian people too would have their place in the sun'. He was even more explicit: 'Latvia has already been granted self-government; no restrictions are placed upon its cultural life; even its economy is already beginning to revive. After the war Latvia will continue to enjoy similar independence and in close association with the Reich will once more blossom in every way.'[95] The Ministry for the East indignantly refused to accept such political extravagances on the part of SS leaders. On August 14th, 1942 Meyer, the acting Minister, protested: 'It cannot be the business of an HSSPF to give public expression to views about the possibility of development in the status of Latvia under constitutional law.'[96]

Jeckeln was not the only SS leader to realize that if the ground was not to be cut from under his feet, he must use his own initiative to offset Hitler's blanket orders. Other local SS governors walked the tightrope between officially authorized policy and the wrath of the Dictator. SS-Gruppenführer Wächter, Governor of Galicia, for instance, considered that the Poles should be treated with moderation, whereas the orders from on high called for deportations to make room for German settlers;[97] his colleague, Curt von Gottberg, Commissar-General in White Ruthenia, demanded a measure of self-government for the Russians, whereas Hitler's theme was that any internal autonomy would undermine German rule.[98]

The last great drama which, more than any other single event, finally loosened the ties between Hitler and the SS and produced an unconscious change in the mentality of many SS leaders, was the war against Russia. It carried the SS to the Baltic States, Galicia and White Ruthenia and the story of events in these areas leads direct to the July 20th plot.

Initially Hitler and SS headquarters had been completely at one in their ideas on Russia. Both wished to carve up the 'gigantic Russian cake' to decimate the peoples of the East and settle Germans in the areas thus released. The SS ideological instructors preached that the Slav millions were uncultured sub-humans with the habits of vermin. A brochure entitled *The Sub-Human*, issued by Berger's ideological craftsmen, explained to SS men why the Slavs were not in fact human beings. 'To the outward eye the sub-human is biologically an entirely similar creation of nature; he has hands, feet and a sort of brain with eyes and a mouth. In fact, however, he is a totally different and a frightful creature, a caricature of a man with features similar to those of a human being but intellectually and morally lower than any animal. This creature is actuated by a ghastly chaos of savage, unrestrained passions – limitless destructiveness, primitive lust and shameless vulgarity.'[99]

The murders by the Einsatzgruppen, the mass shootings of Soviet prisoners-of-war by the Gestapo, atrocities by individual soldiers and units of the Waffen-SS against the Russian civilian population – all this proved that the theory down in black and white was meant in deadly earnest. The SS became the scourge of German-occupied Russia. Thousands of SS eyes watched to ensure that no German soldier fraternized with the Slav sub-human. The RSHA's spies and detachments were busy frustrating every effort by the German soldiers and administrators to persuade the inhabitants of the East to work for the Reich by guarantees of some measure of self-government. In Himmler's eyes such efforts were a betrayal of the German mission in the East. He saw anyone prepared to accept Russians as auxiliaries or, still worse, allies in the anti-Soviet crusade, as a saboteur of his programme for German rule in the East. Systematically he opposed any tendency to grant the Eastern peoples a measure of self-government. SS-Einsatzkommandos broke up the Ukrainian National Government which had been formed by agreement with the Wehrmacht, and arrested its leaders;[100] in White Ruthenia the Sicherheitspolizei liquidated a nationalist group which Gauleiter Kube, Gottberg's predecessor, hoped to use to build up an indigenous administration;[101] SS headquarters rejected all offers by captured Soviet generals to fight with the Germans against Stalin.[102]

Even the strictest ideological vigilance, however, could not prevent the Germans from being confronted with the realities of the situation. Two sobering years of bloody war in Russia provided cruel proof of the falsity of the tale about 'sub-humans'. As early as August 1942 in its 'Reports from the Reich' the SD noted that the feeling was growing among the German people 'that we have been victims of delusion. The main and startling impression is of the vast mass of Soviet weapons, their technical quality and the gigantic Soviet effort of industrialization – all in sharp contrast to the previous picture of the Soviet Union. People are asking themselves how Bolshevism has managed to produce all this.'[103]

The Waffen-SS commanders were among the first to protest against the false doctrine that the Russians were 'sub-humans'; every day spent in the slime and mud of the Russian front proved to their men what fighting against Russians really meant. Anger at the claptrap of the ideologists gave rise to bitter memoranda to the Reichsführer. Felix Steiner, for instance, commanding the 'Viking' Division, told Himmler that the war could only be won if people such as the Ukrainians were granted autonomy and allowed to fight at the side of the German Army against the Soviet enemy. Himmler rejected the idea: 'Do not forget that in 1918 these splendid Ukrainians murdered Field-Marshal von Eichhorn.'[104] When Gunter d'Alquen's SS war reporters began to criticize the stale 'sub-human' theme and advocate 'Europe' as the new slogan, Himmler exploded, referring to 'stupid twaddle about a

European community in which even the Ukrainians and Russians would be included . . . I refuse once and for all to allow the SS to subscribe in any way to this policy . . . which has been specifically rejected by the Führer.'[105] Himmler's attitude, however, was not dictated by ideology alone; he feared the Dictator's wrath. Hitler refused to meet the national desires of the eastern peoples in any way and he had already clashed with Himmler over a statement concerning autonomy for the Baltic States.

The origin of the disagreement was a plan to raise recruits for the Waffen-SS in Estonia, Latvia and Lithuania. Himmler's international lawyers persuaded him that general mobilization was incompatible with the status of an occupied country and so he set to work to obtain a measure of autonomy for the Baltic States.[106] The three Baltic countries were to be given their own sovereignty under the 'protection' of the Greater German Reich, which would continue to control military and foreign affairs. But in the Führer's headquarters Himmler failed to gain his point. On February 8th, 1943 Hitler turned down the proposal, to the relief of Bormann, the Head of the Party Chancellery, who feared that such an expansion of the SS might affect the position of the Party.[107]

As time went on, however, a sort of conspiracy of common sense involved the SS ever more closely in the problem of German occupation policy in the East; in face of the realities of the eastern campaign the SS anti-Russian dogma began to look more and more part-worn. The next stage of the struggle for autonomy for the Baltic States provided a good illustration; under the leadership of Rudolf Bangerskis, ex-Minister of War in Latvia, so many Baltic volunteers were streaming into the Waffen-SS that Himmler felt that he owed it to his Baltic brigades to take up the struggle for autonomy once more.[108] In November 1943 he faced his Führer again but again Hitler refused. Rosenberg, the Minister for the East, noted: 'In the course of the discussion the Führer repeatedly interjected that it was self-evident that he could not evacuate these countries, that there could of course be no talk about this. He was also inherently opposed to making such far-reaching concessions in difficult times.'[109]

So Himmler had lost once more. Nevertheless, 'this breach in the "anti-eastern" stand of the SS was to provide an important precedent.'[110] Himmler's appetite for new SS recruits drawn from the populations of the East had been whetted and now there was no holding him; step by step he retreated from the 'sub-human' ideology and Germans drawn from a series of races were press-ganged into the SS.

After the Balts came the turn of the Ukranians. In spring 1943

SS-Brigadeführer Dr Otto Wächter the Governor of Galicia, had begun to recruit Ukrainians into an SS volunteer division entitled 'Galicia'.[111] Himmler agreed, for in his eyes Galicia had no connexion with Ukrainian nationalism since it consisted of the West Ukrainian areas which had formerly been part of the Austro-Hungarian Monarchy and reputedly had always been pro-German.

When no fewer than 100,000 Ukrainians volunteered, Wächter petitioned Himmler to change the name 'Galicia' to 'Ukraine'.[112] Himmler was horrified – this sounded like encouragement of Ukrainian nationalism; it sounded like betrayal of the German colonizing mission in the East. And what would the Führer say? On July 14th, 1943 he decreed: 'To all Heads of Hauptamt. In referring to the Galician Division, I forbid use of the term "Ukrainian Division" or mention of Ukrainian nationality.'[113] Wächter protested: to refuse the division the name 'Ukraine', he wrote to Himmler on July 30th, would be tantamount to a German attempt to de-nationalize the Ukrainians; this was not in the German interest; it would predispose the Ukrainians to listen to Bolshevist blandishments.[114] Himmler re-affirmed his order, though he did agree not to punish anyone who used the title 'Ukraine'. When Wächter continued to object, Himmler refused to discuss the matter further.[115] In 1945, however, he gave ground once more, agreeing that the Galician Division be entitled 'First Division of the Ukrainian National Army';[116] the Ukrainian General Schandruk was the first 'sub-human' to wear the uniform of an SS-Gruppenführer.[117]

An increasing number of eastern races were now found to be 'SS-worthy'. After the Ukrainians came a brigade under the Russian adventurer Kaminski,[118] then a White Russian SS Division,[119] then the Cossack formations commanded by Lieutenant-General von Pannwitz;[120] finally even Soviet Moslems appeared in ranks of the Waffen-SS.[121] The dramatic demise of the 'sub-human' doctrine finally attracted a group of officers who were experts on eastern affairs, Nazis but nevertheless friends of Russia; for two years they had been trying in vain to offer Germany's political and military leaders a secret weapon which they hoped would produce a decisive turn of events in the eastern campaign.

At an early stage certain Army officers both in the General Staff and the Abwehr had proposed that Germany constitute a Russian Liberation Army from the mass of Soviet prisoners of war; its members were first to be given an assurance that the Russia of the future would be granted full sovereignty and then they could be employed to fight the common Soviet enemy, not as 'volunteer auxiliaries' but as full-scale allies of Germany. Chance had provided the planners with a Commander for such a Russian Army – Lieutenant-General Andrei Andreievich … the defender of Moscow in the 1941 winter battle, C-in-C of 2 Soviet Shock Army at Volkov, taken prisoner in 1942; he had declared himself ready to join forces with the Germans against Stalin. Supported by a number of young German officers acting on their own initiative, he began to recruit in the prisoner-of-war camps and his first speeches brought an unexpectedly large number of applicants.[122]

Hitler's reaction to the idea of a Vlassov army, however, was one of rage and contempt. He refused to have any truck with Russian nationalism; even discussion of the subject ran counter to his colonial policy, whose only object was exploitation. On June 8th, 1943 he said: 'I will never build up a Russian Army. That is fantasy of the first order. Let no one imagine that we have any need to form a Russian State, that everything would then be in order, that we should get a million men. We should get nothing, not one man. We should merely have committed a monumental folly.'[123]

Vlassov's military friends capitulated, leaving only a small group of incorrigible Russian enthusiasts still believing in the possibility of a Vlassov movement. The group included one or two Hitler Youth leaders, certain National-Socialist intellectuals, a few officers and a woman named Melitta Wiedemann who was determined to introduce her hero Vlassov to some important personality in the Third Reich.[124] Melitta Wiedemann had been born in Saint Petersburg; she had been a secretary in the editorial office of Goebbels' paper *Der Angriff* and was now a leader-writer for the anti-Comintern journal *Die Aktion*. She hit upon the desperate notion that the Vlassov Movement could only be helped by its bitterest enemy, the SS. With an unerring feel for National-Socialist realities, she selected the SS leader whom she thought had the courage to promote the Vlassov movement in spite of all resistance – Wächter, the Governor of Galicia. She arranged for Vlassov and Wächter to meet in her parents' house; Wächter was attracted by the Russian and promised to help her.[125]

But Himmler could not bring himself to abandon his own dogma or deviate from the orders of his Führer. 'We must never swallow the idea of this Russian General,' he said. 'We would be creating a new Russian nation organized with our own help.'[126] Carefully though Vlassov's friends pleaded their case, Himmler remained deaf to their entreaties. Melitta Wiedemann, however, persisted. With the mighty head of the SS clinging helplessly to his obsolete doctrines, she harried him with letters and memoranda. Letter to Himmler dated May 26th, 1943: 'The theory that the eastern peoples and, above all, the Russians are sub-humans has been disproved in practice. They fight well. They sacrifice everything for their country. Their weapons are at least as good as ours . . . if we wish to have millions of men labouring for the Reich in the East and vast armies of eastern forces at the front, it is absolutely essential that this sub-human theory disappear from our propaganda.'[127] October 5th, 1943: 'Our use of the word sub-human has enabled Stalin to declare a national war. Hatred of us is frightful . . . As against this it is absolutely certain that the entire Russian peasantry, the greater part of the intelligentsia and all middle-and senior-level commanders of the Red Army are enemies of Bolshevism and in particular of Stalin. By our policy we have faced these men with a tragic dilemma: either to fight for Stalin or to see their people and therefore themselves condemned to form part of a colonial empire, where the inhabitants are murdered, robbed, labelled as sub-humans and reduced to the status of serfs for generations to come, whereas in fact they are one of the most gifted peoples of the white race.' The only solution was a change of German policy in the East, constitution of nation-states and of a Russian Liberation Army. She concluded: 'The only real danger lies in obdurate persistence in the present policy and failure to realize the causes of our present sinking fortunes of war.'[128]

When Melitta Wiedemann asked for an interview with Himmler he evaded the issue, taking refuge, as so often when embarrassed, behind the Führer's orders. Rudolf Brandt, his personal assistant, had to write to the lady: 'In particular I would not wish to go into this matter further since I can tell you that, in the matter of Vlassov, the Führer has already given clear instructions.'[129]

As far as the SS was concerned the Vlassov movement would have been condemned to total failure had it not been sponsored by Standartenführer Gunter d'Alquen, the head SS war reporter. He used a mixture of shock therapy and native cunning to wean Himmler slowly away from his Führer's anti-Russian dream-world. On a flight to the front in September 1943, Himmler showed d'Alquen the 'sub-human' brochure. D'Alquen thought for a moment and then acted the disgruntled SS trooper. The document was 'a flop', he growled and then, in the argot of the private soldier: 'Our men out there don't know where they're going to leave their arses and believe you me if our men saw this brochure, they would ask loud and clear: these people who are attacking us and have better tanks than ours, are good at tactics and red hot at strategy, are they just simple sub-humans? What sort of super-men are we, then? Look what these sub-humans are doing for their country and the sacrifices they're making! Look at the beating they take.'

Himmler retorted: 'What's this rubbish you're talking?', and d'Alquen told him: 'Reichsführer, that's the sort of thing I hear from our men wherever I go nowadays. After two years of war against our present enemy, we can't go on any longer with such theories.'[130] Himmler broke off the conversation in a fury. Nevertheless the outburst had shaken him, for a few days later he summoned d'Alquen and authorized him to take members of the Vlassov movement to the front and initiate psychological warfare against the Soviet Army – but only within Hitler's prescribed limits – a promise to Soviet deserters of entry into a Russian Liberation Army which did not exist and, if Hitler had his way, never would.[131]

D'Alquen kept any doubts about this order to himself and went to work. His first venture was 'Operation Winter Fairy-Tale', launched in the corps area of another critic of the 'sub-human' doctrine, Obergruppenführer Steiner; it was the first of many propaganda operations which ultimately succeeded in luring numbers of Soviet deserters to the German side.[132] 'Winter Fairy-Tale' also opened a breach in Himmler's ideological defensive front and gradually he withdrew his objections in face of d'Alquen's arguments. D'Alquen was permitted to include in his propaganda army increasingly prominent figures from Vlassov's camp and eventually he succeeded in persuading Himmler to recognize Vlassov himself.'[133] Only in October 1943 Himmler had shouted: 'This butcher's apprentice is a dangerous Bolshevist,'[134] but a year later he thought differently. Vlassov was permitted to form two Russian divisions and Himmler wrote to the ex-'sub-human': 'I wish you all success in the interests of our common cause.'[135]

Himmler was still on tenterhooks lest he get another bad mark from his Führer for this flirtation with Vlassov; but as the Nazi fortunes sank, all those who still laboured under the delusion that there might still be a change in German eastern policy began to see in this alliance between the ex-Soviet General and the SS an indication that the SS might be their last sheet-anchor. Memorandum after memorandum in the files of Himmler's staff prove that the National-Socialist critics of Hitler's policy of conquest saw the SS as the only possible instrument of reform. At the same time these memoranda present a deplorable picture of both the situation and efficiency of the Nazi régime.

Melitta Wiedemann renewed her pressure: 'The tempo at which developments regarding Vlassov are proceeding bears no relation to the methods of an authoritarian state; it is a tempo of indecision and missed opportunities.'[136] SS-Gruppenführer von Gottberg, Governor of White Ruthenia, struck a more resigned note: 'I would point out that ever since the winter of 1941–2 I have continued to advocate both verbally and in writing the necessity of a change in our basic attitude. In view of the mentality of the Eastern peoples, who think only of the present, no nation has ever had a more favourable opportunity to bring the war in the East to a rapid conclusion than that now existing.'[137]

The severest critic of German occupation policy was Alfred E. Frauenfeld, the ex-Gauleiter, now Commissar-General in the Crimea. (He used such strong language that even so harsh a critic of the Nazi régime as Robert Kempner, the Nuremberg prosecutor, exclaimed in astonishment: 'But that's a staggering thing you've written there!'[138]) Frauenfeld described German occupation policy as 'a masterpiece of ineptitude; within a year it has achieved the considerable and astonishing feat of turning a completely pro-German people, who welcomed us as liberators, into partisans roaming the forests and marshes; its influence upon the course of events in the East has been wholly negative . . . policy of ruthless brutality . . . methods used centuries ago against black slaves . . . makes a mockery of any sensible policy . . . Proof of total lack of instinct in handling foreign people . . . the acme of stupidity . . . proof that those who parade their brutality and give themselves master-race airs are at heart uneducated louts.'[139]

Bormann, the head of the Party Chancellery, forwarded Frauenfeld's memorandum to Himmler – it was, after all, primarily a criticism of the SS anti-Slav doctrine. On March 26th, 1944 Himmler noted on it: 'Frauenfeld is not far wrong.'[140] Gradually, even the most fervent National-Socialist in the SS came round to the bitter realization that the totalitarian State was not even in a position to apply the most elementary rules of psychological warfare. Incapable of reform, entangled in the struggle of the régime's warring power groups and exposed to the growing superiority of the Allies both in the East and in the West, Hitler's Germany was tottering to its doom.

For the SS leaders, however, the question whether any future for the SS was conceivable in the post-Hitler period became increasingly insistent as the Reich's position deteriorated. The SD's 'Reports from the Reich' left no doubt that the Germans were longing for peace and quiet and the end of Hitler's senseless war.

'Report from the Reich', February 10th, 1944: 'In spite of all his stupidity and obtuseness, the enemy is getting his claws upon us and no one can imagine how we can shake him off again, however often he has been or may be "cracked over the head".'[141]

'Report from the Reich', April 6th, 1944: 'In this uneasy period of waiting for invasion and retribution and also for a change of fortunes in the East, many are wondering what would happen if we could no longer hold out. People are asking themselves whether the many severe sacrifices and hardships which the war demands and will continue to demand are worth it . . . people are gradually beginning to long for peace.'[142]

'Report from the Reich', April 20th, 1944: 'The continual pressure, alarm at developments in the East and the continually deferred hope of "a saving miracle" are gradually producing signs of weariness among the people. In general people are "fed to the back teeth" with the war. Desire for a rapid end to the war is everywhere very great.'[143]

Those of the SS leaders who read these secret SD reports must inevitably have wondered what would become of the SS on the day when everything in which they had believed collapsed. The SS leaders had long since begun to think about the unthinkable. To many the thought of Germany without Hitler no longer seemed revolutionary. The war had demolished many of their illusions; the daily grind of the régime and above all the eastern campaign had destroyed the old identity of view between Adolf Hitler and his SS. Even the SS leaders could no longer evade the question with which every person in authority found himself confronted in 1944 – whether to allow the country to be completely wrecked for the sake of a criminal régime.

But the SS would not have been the SS had its answer to this question been unanimous. The reactions of authoritative SS leaders ranged from a demand for the removal of Hitler to berserk defence of the régime. They fell into five groups: first a small circle centred around Arthur Nebe of the RKPA – for years he and his associates had been in touch with the internal German resistance, including the actual conspirators of July 20th, 1944; scondly, the senior Waffen-SS generals – they were opposed to the murder of Hitler, but wished to work with the Wehrmacht in removing Hitler from military command and concluding an armistice with the Western Allies; thirdly a circle grouped around Walter Schellenberg, the head of the SD – they wished (for a time with Himmler's approval) to conclude peace with the Allies, handing over Hitler if necessary; fourthly, a larger circle of SS leaders, ranging from Werner Best to Otto Ohlendorf – they were opposed to any violent change of régime in wartime but nevertheless believed in the possibility of reform after the war. Finally the 'to-the-bitter-end' fanatics led by Ernst Kaltenbrunner, Heydrich's successor, and Heinrich Müller, head of the Gestapo – they stood for savage suppression of even the smallest criticism of the régime.

The Nebe circle had been anti-Hitler ever since 1938, the high-tension period of the Sudeten crisis. For the first time certain anti-Nazi generals had then given serious consideration to a project for halting the march to catastrophe by a military putsch and the removal of Hitler.[144]

At that time Hans-Bernd Gisevius, an anti-Nazi civil servant, had introduced his friend Nebe into a circle of the resistance which included Colonel-General Beck, since retired, and Hans Oster, later of the Abwehr.[145] Nebe was then head of the Kripo (he later became an SS-Gruppenführer and head of a division in the RSHA); he viewed the resistance with suspicion and scepticism for, as an experienced criminal police officer, what he saw in his secret meetings with Oster and Beck gave him the impression that the conspirators were dilettantes.

Nebe, who was used to covering his tracks, was appalled by the levity with which the conspirators, apparently almost in public, were planning the removal of Hitler. He never drove to a conspirators' meeting in an official car; he would leave his car in a sidestreet, observe the vicinity of the meeting points with care and then suddenly appear in the midst of the conspirators.[146] Goerdeler, the over-garrulous head of the resistance, never even knew the name of the SS leader to whom the opposition owed its information from the RSHA. If Goerdeler threatened to appear at a conference when Nebe was present, the cautious police officer disappeared in good time.[147]

Whatever Nebe's reasons for joining the resistance – fear for his own future or anxiety for the country – he remained loyal to the conspiracy. In late 1941, when commanding an Einsatzgruppe, he could see no escape from the Nazi régime and his own guilt other than in the murder of Hitler.[148] From this time on he was continuously urging the plotters to carry out their attack on Hitler; each time the coup was planned and as often called off, he had a squad of police officers ready to open the Berlin ministries to the conspirators' army units on D-day.[149] Such measures could not of course be taken without the complicity of other SS members of the police. Nebe recruited his friend Hans Lobbes, an SS-Sturmbannführer and executive director in the RKPA;[150] the Gestapo furnished another anti-Nazi, SS-Brigadeführer Paul Kanstein. In 1937 Kanstein had taken over the Gestapo Leitstelle Berlin and had immediately become a key figure in all plans for an anti-Nazi putsch. He (an SS man, be it noted) had mended the broken fences btween two prominent conspirators, Graf von Helldorf, the Berlin Police President and his Deputy, Fritz-Dietlof Graf von der Schulenburg,[151] thereby ensuring that the Berlin police would at least not be found in the anti-conspiracy camp. The putschists gave him his reward – had the July 20th, 1944 coup succeeded, Kanstein, the ex-Gestapo official, would have become head of the new Sicherheitspolizei in post-Hitler Germany.[152]

Loosely connected to this circle in Berlin were a number of other SS officers working on their own. Sturmbannführer Hartmut Plaas, for instance, an official in Göring's telephone-tapping organization known as the 'Air Research Office', warned the conspirators that they were under increasingly strict Gestapo observation;[153] Sturmbannführer Hans-Viktor Graf von Salviati, head of the remount office in the SS-Hauptamt and, from 1941, ADC to Field-Marshal von Rundstedt, was another sympathizer;[154] so was Max Frauendorfer, an SS officer and old Party member who was president of the 'Labour Division' in the Government-General of Poland – a sort of Ministry of Labour.[155] The common denominator between all these men distinguishing them from the other SS critics of Hitler, was moral indignation with a régime characterized by contempt for human rights and by self-destructive megalomania; on ethical grounds they revolted against the irresponsibility of the men in charge of Germany. Von Hassell noted in his diary that Frauendorfer impressed him 'because of his boundless despair about all he had lived through in Poland; it was so terrible that he could not endure it.'[156]

Since undercover assistance appeared to be forthcoming from within Heinrich Himmler's empire, some of the resisters felt that, risky though it was, they must try to recruit more SS men; when the putsch took place, after all, the attitude of the SS might well decide the success or failure of the *coup d'etat*. Canaris had already voiced the opinion that as so many attempts on Hitler's life had failed, there was now no alternative but to try to involve Himmler in action against the dictator and have a 'frank discussion' with him.[157] Field-Marshal von Bock had also declared that he would only collaborate if Himmler took part in the putsch.[158]

Goerdeler thereupon asked the advice of his friend, Jakob Wallenberg, the Swedish banker. Wallenberg asked: 'Does Himmler know what you're doing?' Goerdeler replied: 'I don't know.' (On hearing subsequently that a favourable opportunity for the attack upon Hitler had been missed because Himmler, who was also to be liquidated, was not present on that day, Wallenberg advised Goerdeler: 'But leave Himmler out of your assassination plans. If you act against Hitler alone, Himmler won't stop you.'[159])

In autumn 1943 von der Schulenburg took soundings in the SS-Hauptamt, asking Obersturmbannführer Riedweg of the Germanische Leitstelle for the names of SS officers with whom he could discuss the political situation frankly. Riedweg referred him to Hildebrandt, one of the HSSPF, and to two Waffen-SS generals, Hausser and Steiner.[160] Schulenburg had already contacted Steiner who had been his company commander in No 1 Infantry Regiment. Meeting in a Berlin café, he had told the SS General that Hitler must be eliminated by force if the total collapse of the Reich was to be prevented, but Steiner did not agree; he pointed out to Schulenburg that the Eastern Front was already cracking at every joint, that the Western Allies' invasion might come at any moment and that a change of régime was therefore only possible if the entire Wehrmacht was behind the putsch – an unlikely contingency.[161] Certain of the conspirators, however, were not prepared to take this as the last word from the SS-Generals. Marie-Louise ('Puppi') Sarre, for instance, who worked with von Hassell, was convinced that 'the National-Socialist spirit of the Waffen-SS was becoming increasingly doubtful. They feel themselves at one with the fighting troops of the Wehrmacht.'[162] She was right. Only a few weeks later Steiner and his Chief-of-Staff, SS-Oberführer Joachim Ziegler, held a three-day meeting with Melitta Wiedemann when they discussed how Hitler could be got rid of. They had even evolved a vague plan: during its move to the Eastern Front, Steiner's III 'Germanic' Panzer Corps was to kidnap Hitler in his headquarters, 'Wolfsschanze', and 'declare him mentally deranged, publicizing his crimes' (Melitta Wiedemann's description). A year later the Waffen-SS commanders were prepared to tell the resistance what they really thought; then they gave Field-Marshal Rommel their word that they would support him in a revolt against Hitler. But they had not reached that stage in 1943 and Schulenburg met with no success.

Equally fruitless were the efforts of Dr Jens Peter Jessen, the Professor of Political Science, to win over his former pupil and friend, Otto Ohlendorf, now an SS-Gruppenführer and head of Amt III in the RSHA. Jessen and Ohlendorf had once worked together for National-Socialism but Hitler's war and drift into constitutional and political crime had driven the two apart. Basically both were still National-Socialists according to their lights, but they differed on the central issue: whether a régime which issued orders for murders in millions, and was now sacrificing the fatherland for one man's fanatical determination to survive, should continue to exist.

Ohlendorf, who after all had commanded an Einsatzgruppe, would have answered this question in the affirmative, although he found many aspects of the Third Reich as distasteful as did Jessen. He was the author of the 'Reports from the Reich' and was regarded in National-Socialist circles as 'the mouthpiece of an opposition which would otherwise remain dumb,' as Fritzsche, the propaganda spokesman, described him with some justification.[163] He persisted in supporting the proscribed theosophist movement and was therefore an object of continual suspicion to Gestapo Müller;[164] he was friendly with Wilhelm Ahlmann, the anti-Nazi banker who later committed suicide when proved to have been in contact with Stauffenberg, Hitler's would-be assassin;[165] he had his own private plan for a future National-Socialist Germany in which the NSDAP was to be no more than a cipher. He collected letters from disillusioned youngsters at the front and contacted their authors; he envisioned the post-war régime taking its cue from the Hitler Youth Leaders and front-line soldiers with an NSDAP purged, freed from power politics and administrative responsibilities, and acting solely as a 'temple of wisdom' – a political brains trust.[166]

Though these were the directions in which his mind was turning, Ohlendorf still could not conceive that Germany could be anything other than the realm of the NSDAP and the Reich of Adolf Hitler. He regarded any doubts on the subject as mortal sins against the fatherland and the 'community'. Even in his death-cell in Nuremberg in 1948, he was still fulminating against 'the many people who had renounced their heritage and veiled the oath they had sworn to the Führer in a tissue of treachery and mendacity.'[167] Even his one-time collaborator, Jessen, incurred his wrath for such supposed treachery. When the Gestapo later arrested the professor, Ohlendorf did not move a finger. But the sleepless night he spent when Jessen was hanged – that Ohlendorf would not forget. (Nor did he forget his conscience-stricken promise henceforth to share his salary with the Jessen family.[168])

Men such as Höhn and Best, Stuckart and Streckenbach reacted in the same way as Ohlendorf. None of them was capable of breaking loose from the still-compelling magic of Hitler and of acting to stave off catastrophe and ruin. Dimly they may have realized what the popular Führer State of their dreams had become, but they could not bring themselves to turn their backs on a lifetime of illusion, error and guilt.

But there was one SS leader who was both sufficiently unscrupulous and sufficiently clear-sighted to cast overboard all that he and his fellows had once worshipped – Brigadeführer Walter Schellenberg. He watched every move by the anti-Nazi conspirators and knitted them into his own plans – plans designed to ensure that when catastrophe came, he, Schellenberg, would be on the right side.

Ever since June 1941, when he was appointed to a senior post in the SD Foreign Intelligence Service (initially as Deputy Head), Schellenberg had regarded the prospects of outright German victory with scepticism. The SD reports provided far too realistic a picture of the enemy's growing war effort to permit any wishful thinking. As early as autumn 1941 he had begun cautiously and tentatively to probe the possibilities of a separate peace with the Western Allies and for this purpose he used a circle of anti-Nazi resisters, who, using international channels, had been carrying on confidential discussions with the Allies or with pro-Allied foreigners ever since the outbreak of war. There were many curiously fortuitous connexions between these anti-Nazis and SS headquarters. Dr Carl Langbehn, for instance, a Berlin attorney and a member of the Beck-Goerdeler opposition group, was in contact with Himmler via his daughter who was a school friend of Himmler's daughter, Gudrun;[169] Jessen, one of the advocates of a *coup d'état*, was still friendly with Höhn, to whom he had once recommended his pupil Ohlendorf;[170] even von Hassell could claim some connexion with Himmler – Schuhknecht his ex-chauffeur was now in Himmler's service.[171]

Schellenberg thought it wise to listen in to these secret discussions between the anti-Nazis and their foreign friends. In late summer 1941 Stallforth, an American banker, arrived in Berlin and informed von Hassell that Roosevelt would only make a gesture to the Germans if they first removed Hitler. Calmly the SD listened;[172] Group B of the Ausland-SD in the RSHA dutifully noted down all the secret agreements between Hassell and his American opposite number. On October 11th, 1941 they heard Stallforth telling Miss Boensel, his secretary, over the telephone to 'inform Herr von Hassell [referred to as Howe] that his proposals had been very favourably received. Would von Hassell please let him know whether he could come to Lisbon with some authoritative personality and there discuss matters with leading Americans.'[173] The code names and abbreviations used in the letters between Hassell and Stallforth, which the SD intercepted, caused Schellenberg's office no trouble. Group D noted: ' "The man in the South" must be Mussolini. "Ph" refers to Phillips, the American Ambassador in Rome.'[174]

The SD were so well informed about these secret negotiations that they began talking to the Americans themselves. Von Hassell was taken aback when an SD man named Danfeld brought him warm greetings from Stallforth. Hassell noted: 'This particular SS man, still very young, showed himself remarkably well-informed in foreign political matters, sober in judgement and astonishingly free in his comments. He remained an hour and a half and broached certain subjects which I thought it more discreet not to discuss. My general impression was that people in Himmler's entourage are very worried and are searching around for some loophole.'[175]

Schellenberg did not yet think the time ripe to reveal his far-reaching plans to Himmler. The German armies in Russia were still winning victory after victory and the Russian campaign would decide whether Hitler would succeed in bringing about an early end to the war. On a trip through Spain and Portugal in April 1942 Schellenberg told the two police attachés, Winzer in Madrid and Schroeder in Lisbon, that the die would be cast in the forthcoming summer; if the German armies broke through in Southern Russia and in Egypt, then the war was decided; if they did not, the Reich had lost the gamble.[176]

When the midsummer reports on both operations painted an increasingly gloomy picture, Schellenberg had his answer. In his memoirs he says that as early as August 1942 he sought out Himmler in his command post at Vinnitsa in the Ukraine and put to him the question: 'Reichsführer, in which drawer of your desk do you keep your alternative solution for ending the war?'

Himmler retorted: 'Have you gone mad? Are you losing your nerve?'

Schellenberg said: 'Reichsführer, I knew you'd go on like this. In fact I thought it might be even worse.'

Himmler then calmed down, Schellenberg says, and asked him to work out a plan. Schellenberg proposed that, profiting from the tension between Russia and the Western Powers, secret peace discussions be opened with the Western Allies; a prior condition, however, was that Ribbentrop, the Foreign Minister, must disappear, for he, as Stallforth had confirmed, was regarded in the West as 'primarily responsible for the war'. Himmler apparently agreed to Schellenberg's plan – 'he even grasped my hand and promised that by Christmas (1942) Ribbentrop would have been relieved of his post.'[177]

Whether or not this conversation actually took place, the fact remains that from late summer 1942 Schellenberg and Himmler, assisted by Felix Kersten, Himmler's masseur, and Obergruppenführer Karl Wolff, head of his Personal Staff, seriously attempted to bring about a separate peace with the West, at the price, if necessary, of the deposition of Hitler. Himmler had for some time been toying with the alluring thought that, should the war situation worsen, his mission might be to replace Hitler and bring peace to Germany and the world. The idea had flashed through his mind and he had, as quickly, put it behind him – the Reichsführer-SS could never be unfaithful to the 'greatest brain of all time'. But the insidious thought returned again and again. In May 1942, Burckhardt, the Swiss, told Ilse von Hassell, the wife of the ex-Ambassador and daughter of von Tirpitz, that 'an agent of Himmler's had come to him to find out whether England would perhaps make peace with Himmler instead of Hitler';[178] on April 9th, 1942 Count Ciano, the Italian Foreign Minister, noted in his diary: 'Himmler, who was an extremist in the past but now feels the real pulse of the people, wants a compromise peace.'[179]

That Himmler, the agent of the most gruesome crimes of the century, should seriously have believed that the world would be prepared to regard him as a peace negotiator, today seems a fantastic idea. At the time, however, things looked different; people wished to see Himmler at the conference table precisely because they believed he had the power. Many statesmen secretly thought like José Maria Doussinague, the Director General of the Spanish Foreign Ministry; he included Himmler 'among those who seek a peaceful accommodation with the Allies in order to forestall a Soviet Russian invasion. They are entirely agreed that the disappearance of Hitler and his immediate entourage is an essential condition. Himmler could bring this about. Consequently the key to peace negotiations lies in his hands.'[180]

Although Himmler shrank from the horrifying prospect of falling out of step with his Führer, nevertheless in summer 1942 he provided himself with a weapon capable of eliminating the dictator if necessary; this was a 26-page medical report showing that Hitler was suffering from the after-effects of syphilis and was threatened with creeping paralysis.[181] When walking one evening with the head of the Criminal Biological Institute of the RKPA, Nebe had asked: 'Tell me, doctor, can one justifiably say that the Führer is mentally ill?'[182] Himmler now put a similar question to Kersten and the answer came back pat: Adolf Hitler's place was in a hospital for nervous diseases, not in the Führer's headquarters.[183] But Himmler could not bring himself to take a definite decision, replying: 'I can't make a move against the Führer – I who am Reichsführer of the SS whose motto is "my honour is loyalty".'[184]

Schellenberg, however, had no such scruples. Using numerous channels he initiated an operation aiming at two things: discussions with the Americans and the jettisoning of Ribbentrop. A variegated cross-section of society was included in his plans. For his battle against Ribbentrop he used Martin Luther, a corrupt Under-Secretary in the Foreign Ministry; he dispatched Langbehn to neutral countries to contact the Allies;[185] via SS-Oberführer Fritz Kranefuss, the ambitious secretary of the 'Friends of the Reichsführer-SS', he used the international connexions of the businessmen belonging to the 'Friends';[186] last but not least he listened to a member of the most illustrious European aristocracy – Prince Max-Egon Hohenlohe-Langenburg, who figured on his list of agents as No 144/7957.[187]

The Prince, born in 1897, had retired from the Army as a 2nd Lieutenant, married the Spanish Marquesa de Belvis de las Navas and had been living in Spain for years.[188] His reason for keeping in contact with the SD was to preserve his family possessions – the Hohenlohes owned vast estates in the Sudetenland and the Prince was determined to preserve them in face of all upheavals and changing personalities. As a result, during the Sudeten crisis of 1938 he had opted for Hitler and made his not inconsiderable diplomatic abilities available to the SD. Now in wartime he was quick to seize any chance of a compromise peace which would preserve the Hohenlohe fortunes in the Sudetenland.[189]

His proprietary instincts, however, were not the Prince's only motives for taking a hand in Schellenberg's game. He was a member of the European aristocracy and his background was one of traditional diplomacy – in the nineteenth century, after all, the Hohenlohes had provided a German Chancellor, a French Marshal, a Roman Catholic Cardinal, a number of Austro-Hungarian Field-Marshals, Generals of Prussia and Baden, hereditary Marshals of Württemberg and ADCs General to the Russian Czar, so Prince Max-Egon Hohenlohe was a believer in the old European concert of powers and he was quite prepared to use senior National-Socialist functionaries to tell the potentates of the Third Reich a few home truths.

In a memorandum of September 1939, submitted to Göring, he said: 'In initiating World War II Germany has started from false premises and has miscalculated in every way. She did not calculate that England and France would fight for Poland, overlooking the fact that Poland is not the point – it is something quite different – the maintenance and assurance of peace in Europe.' Quite unabashed he continued: 'Even at this late stage the possibility of an overall solution must be borne in mind. It must include: re-establishment of confidence, a guarantee for the respect of treaties, disarmament under mutual control and possibly withdrawal from Czechoslovakia and its reconstitution as a demilitarized State.' He ended with a warning: 'Roosevelt might still be prepared to mediate, but it will soon be too late.'[190]

Working with SS-Oberführer Höhn, the Prince prepared a memorandum urging influential Nazi leaders and others to initiate some peace move; Ambassador Hewel, a long-standing Nazi and now the Foreign Ministry representative in Hitler's headquarters, was also working with Hohenlohe and Höhn; he even had certain of the memoranda re-typed on the Führer's special machine and submitted to the Dictator. But Hitler threw them out indignantly as 'defeatist scribblings' and warned Höhn off.[191] Nevertheless the Prince continued to work for a separate peace with the Western Allies. He journeyed to Switzerland where Allied diplomats evinced interest in his proposals; he also gained the sympathy of the Vatican, which frequently used him as a channel of communication for warning messages to the Third Reich.[192]

Urged by the Vatican, Prince Hohenlohe now prepared a memorandum which he handed to Hewel when the latter visited Spain at the end of 1941. He said: 'It is now quite clear that Adolf Hitler is under the thumb of the Prussian generals and Prussian methods are being used in the treatment of the subject peoples. Each month that goes by will show the people that Europe is ruled by Prussian generals; they will have personal experience of the brutal methods of force used by Prussian generals and they will become ripe for rebellion. Every time men are shot, the word will go round and ultimately all Europe will form a single great moral defensive front. Germany . . . can only retreat step by step. Then the great moment will come when the peoples will rise for their war of liberation.'[193] The Reich, he continued, would lose this war unless it moderated its policy and sought an accommodation with the peoples and powers of Europe.

Göring read the Prince's memorandum but had not the courage to go against his Führer's policy. So Hohenlohe looked around for some better ally – and found him in Schellenberg. Hohenlohe made Schellenberg's acquaintance in 1942 and immediately realized that he was determined to do away with Hitler if need be. Although the Prince will not today admit to having played any important role in Schellenberg's plan, he remembers his line of argument very well: 'Schellenberg went so far as to tell me that he knew that the West would never make peace with Hitler and therefore some internal changes in Germany were necessary. Later in the conversation he told me that he hoped Hitler would be patriotic enough to subordinate his own interests to those of the German people. If he did not, he must be removed by force.'[194]

Hohenlohe had little difficulty in putting Schellenberg in touch with American negotiators. One of his business friends, an SS man referred to in the SD files as 'Alfonso', had connexions with Americans in Lisbon and after a few preliminary questions, the latter showed interest in Schellenberg's proposals.[195] In December 1942 'Alfonso' met the American negotiators in Lisbon and told them that his principals were ready for a separate peace with the West provided Germany was allowed to pursue the war in the East and drive Russia out of Europe. The Americans considered the SD proposal worth discussing, provided Alfonso's masters could guarantee an internal political change in Germany such as would allow the Western Governments to pacify public opinion. During the discussions the Americans' demands became increasingly centred upon the person of Hitler. The essential condition, they said, was that he must be handed over alive to the Allies; only thus could the growth of a posthumous Hitler myth be avoided and lasting peace ensured.[196]

Even Schellenberg was taken aback by this demand but having put his hand to the plough, he had no alternative. The Reich's situation was deteriorating month by month; in November 1942 British and American troops had landed in North Africa, producing a dangerous threat to the Afrika Korps; in the East the Stalingrad disaster was looming. Schellenberg's reply must have sounded so forthcoming to the Americans in Lisbon that they were prepared to continue negotiations. They referred him to the man Hohenlohe called 'the most influential White House man in Europe' – Allen W. Dulles, the US special representative in Berne, later head of the US Secret Service.[197] Hohenlohe told Schellenberg: 'He is a tall, burly, sporting type of about 45, healthy-looking with good teeth and a fresh simple open-hearted manner';[198] another SD report stated: 'It may be assumed with certainty, and has been confirmed by investigation, that if faced with serious negotiators, Mr Bull (the SD code name for Dulles) would never do anything underhand.'[199]

Before Schellenberg could dispatch his emissaries to Berne, however, a time bomb which he himself had primed, exploded and jeopardized all his carefully laid intrigue. Luther, his accomplice in the Foreign Ministry, together with a group of young diplomats, loosed their attack on Ribbentrop.

SA-Brigadeführer Martin Luther was one of the most ill-bred and most hated figures in the Foreign Ministry; he owed his career to his friendship with Ribbentrop, which had brought him promotion to the rank of Under-Secretary of State and the post of head of the section dealing with relations between the Foreign Ministry, the Party and the SS; at the same time he had a hand in the annihilation of the Jews.[200] Though initially on bad terms with the RSHA, Luther had swung over into the anti-Ribbentrop camp primarily under pressure from a group of young Foreign Ministry bureaucrats who had persuaded him that Ribbentrop must go in order to prepare the way for peace negotiations. One of the anti-Ribbentrop conspirators, Counsellor Walther Kieser, who had known Schellenberg at university, told Schellenberg what was afoot and the latter immediately encouraged him to go all out in his criticism of Ribbentrop. The next day Luther called Schellenberg for confirmation of this conversation. Speaking to Luther in January 1943 Schellenberg was even more explicit; Walther Gödde, one of Luther's staff, noted that Schellenberg had already made an initial, but still tenuous, contact with the American Secret Service and it was 'now essential to bring down Ribbentrop if progress was to be made with the Americans'. Walter Büttner, the leader of the anti-Ribbentrop conspiracy in the Foreign Ministry, then contacted Schellenberg and made preparations for the *coup*.[201] At this point, however, Schröder, the Head of the Foreign Ministry Personnel Office, heard of Luther's plans and informed von Weizsäcker, the Secretary of State.[202]

Büttner recalls that 'On February 8th, 1943 Schellenberg again asked his opposite number to call and assured him that Himmler was prepared to urge upon Hitler the dismissal of Ribbentrop. He would, however, like a statement in writing of the Luther group's arguments. These had, in fact, been explained verbally early in February and were now dictated in Schellenberg's presence.' The primary point made was that Ribbentrop was mentally ill and incapable of fulfilling the functions of his office. But Himmler once more relapsed into indecision and before he could make up his mind to act, Ribbentrop, who was well informed, struck back, summoning Luther and accusing him of treachery. Shortly thereafter Luther and his fellow-conspirators in the Foreign Ministry were arrested; Luther was sent to a concentration camp, Büttner and the others to the front. Just before his arrest on February 10th, 1943 Luther, still the typical Berliner, called Büttner on the telephone and said: 'It is all over for us; order two wreaths from Grieneisen' (the Berlin undertaker).[203]

In vain Schellenberg appealed to Himmler to save Luther from the concentration camp and to make use of the incident to bring down Ribbentrop. Himmler wavered. Wolff, the Head of his Personal Staff, hit upon a face-saving formula good enough to justify Himmler's inactivity in the eyes of any SS man: 'But Reichsführer, you cannot let SS-Obergruppenführer Joachim von Ribbentrop, one of the highest-ranking members of our Order, be kicked out by this scoundrel Luther.'[204] Schellenberg now had to try and keep conversations going with the Americans, even though Ribbentrop was still in the saddle. On January 15th, 1943 Hohenlohe (known as Paul) and an SD officer (code name Bauer) had started negotiations with Dulles.[205] Like the other Americans, Dulles stressed that the elimination of Hitler was essential. He was obviously hinting to Schellenberg's man that with Hitler still there Germany was lost. Reporting Dulles' statements, Hohenlohe recorded that 'acceptance of Hitler as undisputed ruler of Greater Germany was hardly conceivable in view of the inflamed state of public opinion in the Anglo-Saxon countries. They would have no confidence in the permanency or reliability of agreements made with him.'[206] If, however, Dulles' argument continued, Hitler were to be deposed, a peace settlement recognizing neither victor nor vanquished might be arranged. Dulles was quite prepared to hold out to his opposite numbers the hope that a powerful German State should remain as a factor in the orderly reconstruction of Europe; there was no question of its division nor of its separation from Austria. On the other hand the power of Prussia within the German State must be reduced to an acceptable level. 'Mr Bull did not seem to attach much importance to the Czech question; on the other hand he favoured enlargement of Poland eastwards and the maintenance both of Rumania and a strong Hungary as a *cordon sanitaire* against Bolshevism and Panslavism . . . He regarded a Greater Germany, federated on American lines and allied to a Danube confederation, as the best guarantee for the orderly reconstruction of central and eastern Europe.'[207]

The fact remained that Dulles was prepared to continue talking to Schellenberg's representatives. He told Prince Hohenlohe that he had instructed the American Embassy in Madrid to make itself available to him at all times, the contact being Butterworth, the Counsellor. 'Alfonso', the SS Lisbon contact, was also authorized to call Dulles at any time, using an agreed code word.[208]

It soon became clear, however, that the British Government did not approve of the American discussions with the SD. Numerous reports confirm that the Americans were still willing to negotiate and the SD was later convinced that Schellenberg's game had failed primarily owing to British resistance. On June 10th, 1943 SS-Obersturmführer Ernst Kienast reported from American sources in Hungary:

1. The US desires an agreement with the Reich on the following basis:
   (a) Germany to retain the Germanic North and East
   (b) The US to occupy Italy, approximately as far north as Florence
   (c) Thereafter the US would take no further interest in a war in Europe.
2. This plan was . . . ventilated in Spain.
3. This plan collapsed before it was ever put to the Reich owing to British disapproval.[209]

Schellenberg's people now set about using the neutrals to overcome British resistance. Hohenlohe let senior officials of the Spanish Foreign Ministry into the secret and was assured of their support for a plan to replace Hitler by Himmler. Doussinague, the Permanent Secretary, noted: 'We were told that the US Government was well aware that it lay in Himmler's power to bring about a radical political change in Germany, provided that this was not synonymous with total military defeat. The Americans were confident that he was both willing and able to eliminate the leading personalities in the German Government.'[210] But England said 'no' to the Spanish mediators too. When Doussinague attempted to sell the plan to Yencken, First Secretary in the British Embassy in Madrid, the latter brushed him off with: 'I am most astonished that Catholic Spain should be prepared to sit down to peace discussions with the SS, the champion of German atheism.'[211]

As a result of his setbacks in Spain, Schellenberg, with Himmler trailing hesitantly behind him, peddled his peace proposals in a wider forum. His emissaries appeared in a number of neutral countries, holding out prospects of Hitler's downfall and his replacement by his faithful SS Chief. In May and June 1943 Himmler agreed that contact should be made with Jakob Wallenberg, the Swedish banker, to examine the possibilities of a separate peace under SS auspices.[212] That summer Schellenberg dispatched Langbehn, a member of the resistance, to Stockholm for talks with Soviet diplomats (he had already been negotiating in Stockholm with British and American representatives).[213] In late summer, Langbehn conferred in Berne with Gero von Gaevernitz, a German-American member of Dulles' staff.[214] In October Kersten went to Stockholm and discussed a seven-point American peace plan with Hewitt, the American special envoy, but could not persuade Himmler to see Hewitt personally; by December 9th, when Himmler did finally make up his mind to meet the American, Hewitt had already left.[215] On December 25th, 1943 the British Ambassador in Moscow told Harriman, his American colleague, that via Sweden the British Government had been 'informed of Himmler's desire to gain contact'; Himmler had apparently declared his readiness to send a representative to Great Britain to find out how England interpreted the phrase 'unconditional surrender'. The British replied that the words required no interpretation.[216]

The continual stumbling block was the question of how the SS could get rid of Hitler in order to clear the way for peace. The division of opinion was clear: Schellenberg was prepared to take the consequences, whatever they might be; Himmler, on the other hand, recoiled from the thought that he or the SS should take the life of his beloved Führer. Once more Wolff produced the face-saver. He proposed to wait and find out what those who were clearly working for the downfall of the régime proposed to do with Hitler. Possibly – it cannot be proved – this was cover for a sophisticated plan to allow Hitler to be eliminated by the anti-Nazis, who could then themselves be neutralized.

Contact was quickly established with the internal German resistance. Langbehn, who was both a friend of Himmler and a member of the anti-régime conspiracy, had access to the Berlin 'Wednesday Club', the meeting-place of the most active opponents of the régime, Jessen, von Hassell and Colonel-General Beck, the most senior military officer in the resistance.[217] Another member of this circle was the Prussian Finance Minister, Dr Johannes Popitz, an energetic, intelligent but at times highly controversial advocate of a *coup d'état.* On Wolff's instruction he was asked by Langbehn whether it would not be worthwhile to explain the opposition's ideas quite openly to Himmler. Popitz found Langbehn's SS contacts somewhat sinister. He ruminated: 'He can do anything with these people and yet he's their bitterest enemy; sometimes I believe they know it.'[218] Nevertheless he accepted Langbehn's proposal.

As chance would have it, at exactly this time (summer 1943) the thoughts of the dissidents were running parallel to those of Himmler's entourage but in the opposite direction. In spite of the resistance pressure upon them to take the decisive step, the Wehrmacht generals were still evading the issue; the conspirators therefore turned to the idea of using the other great power factor, the SS, to strike against Hitler and the Party. Von Hassell noted that 'people are discussing more frequently the possibility of using the SS to overthrow the régime if all other means fail. They argue that this might not only put this organization into our hands but would also prevent domestic disorders. They say that afterwards the SS will of course be dissolved too. The first question is whether Himmler and company would dare to play such a game and cooperate in the friendly manner desired; secondly what effect this procedure would have abroad, for every foreigner justly regards the SS as the very incarnation of the Devil.'[219] Even among the resistance leaders the 'Himmler solution' was not without its opponents, but Beck, many of the soldiers (Olbricht, Witzleben and Tresckow), and temporarily even Goerdeler, subscribed to it.[220] Popitz was therefore deputed to enlist Himmler in the plan for a *coup d'état.*

On August 26th, 1943 Popitz, accompanied by Langbehn, presented himself at the Reich Ministry of the Interior; Langbehn remained in the anteroom with Wolff, while Popitz in a long interview with Himmler explained that the war could no longer be won, that Hitler must be relieved of his position and a strong personality (meaning Himmler) must assume the duty of making peace with the West. Adroitly he appealed to Himmler's sense of mission. According to the subsequent case for the prosecution against Popitz he said that the people 'were wondering: what does Himmler want, does he want to start a campaign of terror or does he really want to establish order? If he wants to do the latter quietly and reasonably, the State would be on firm foundations.'[221] While Hitler was still there, Popitz continued, the Reich could not be saved. The 'essential condition was that the Führer should go; he should be more or less pensioned off as honorary president' – this at least was the way Himmler put it in a later speech (after July 20th, 1944) when he was trying to gloss over his part in the affair.[222]

Meanwhile in the anteroom Langbehn was working on Wolff using similar arguments. It was time, he said, that Germany once more became a State based on the rule of law and directed by intelligent, honest and far-sighted men – giving it to be understood, of course, that among such men were the SS leaders.[223] After the failure of the July 20th putsch, Himmler thought it wise to give an assemblage of Gauleiter and Reichsleiter his own version of these remarkable discussions with the resistance – remarkable at least for a Hitler supporter; he had immediately gone to the Führer, he told them, and reported everything; Hitler had, however, instructed him not to strike yet but to continue to watch the Popitz circle.[224]

In fact, Himmler's reaction bore little relation to his subsequent version of the affair. On August 26th he agreed to meet Popitz again;[225] the latter for his part went off to Field-Marshal von Witzleben and asked him (again according to the case for the prosecution against Popitz) 'whether he [Popitz] might give his [Witzleben's] name as the future military Commander-in-Chief, should the plan for collaboration with the Reichsführer-SS prove feasible.'[226]

On August 27th Wolff summoned Langbehn once more and discussed with him details of further meetings with leading members of the resistance.[227] The discussions progressed so favourably that a few days later Langbehn departed for Switzerland with instructions from Wolff.[228]

In Switzerland Langbehn met Gero von Gaevernitz of Dulles' office and told him that a senior SS leader on Himmler's staff (he was of course referring to Wolff) was party to a plan which aimed to reduce Hitler's still unlimited power; it was hoped thereby to create conditions which would facilitate discussions with the Western Powers.[229] At this moment, however, all the plans – both of the conspirators and of Himmler – were upset. In early September 1943 the Gestapo, the most fanatical protector of the régime in the whole of Himmler's empire, deciphered a radio message which, according to Dulles, originated 'from some Allied agency neither American nor British' – and it revealed the secret of Langbehn's discussions in Switzerland. The Gestapo forwarded the message to the Führer's headquarters without first showing it to Himmler;[230] whether this was chance or intrigue against the vacillating Reichsführer, Himmler was compelled to break off all relations with the resistance for fear Hitler should react. He had Langbehn arrested and sent to a concentration camp; he never received Popitz again.[231]

Schellenberg, however, continued to pursue his plans for the complete elimination of Hitler. He had contacted certain American military circles in Spain and had discussed with them a fantastic project referred to by the Madrid newspaper *Pueblo* as 'Operation KN' (Kidnapping) – a plan in fact to kidnap Hitler and hand him over to the Allies. According to the Spanish paper the SS leaders and the American military had 'reached full agreement to carry out the kidnapping plan. Technical and organizational details had been worked out and a complete organization prepared with bases in Madrid, Lisbon and on the Mediterranean coast near Valencia.'[232] But the plan never progressed beyond the discussion stage. The talks with the Allies were conducted by Paul Winzer, the police attaché in Madrid, who even attempted to recruit the Catholic Church to help. The Church was not unforthcoming; Father Conrado Simonsen, a liaison officer for the highest Vatican circles, placed himself at Winzer's disposal together with helpers, couriers and money from Spain, Portugal and South America.[233] The plan was only pigeon-holed in May 1944 when Winzer's head courier, a Frenchman named Letellier, stole the secret papers connected with Operation KN from Winzer's safe and sold them to an Allied Secret Service; meanwhile the SD had undoubtedly realized that in view of the close guard kept on Hitler, the kidnapping plan was not technically feasible.[234]

Nevertheless Schellenberg's negotiations in Spain did achieve one thing; they reinforced the feeling in Allied circles that only Himmler and the SS could bring the Hitler system down. Even the British authorities now began to show interest in the so-called 'Himmler Solution'. On April 3rd, 1944 SS-Brigadeführer Kranefuss noted that 'in English circles the Reichsführer-SS and the SS are apparently the subjects of numerous rumours and schemings.'[235] An SD informer (name unknown) located in Lisbon reported that the British now considered that a change of régime in Germany could be brought about only by the SS, not by the Wehrmacht. The report read: 'During the last year, the attention of these [British] circles has been increasingly focused upon the SS and the Waffen-SS in particular. Reports that there is a possible or potential or even acute difference of opinion between the Führer and the SS or Waffen-SS can clearly be traced back to English sources.' The informer continued that according to his British sources, the Waffen-SS generals were becoming noticeably more critical of Hitler; 'this stems from their estimate of the war situation.' Early in January 1944, he continued, a rumour had been current in Lisbon that 'Waffen-SS generals, including a general who was decorated with the Oak Leaves to the Knights Cross in late autumn,' had been in negotiation with the British.'[236]

The author can hardly have realized that his report was to prove prophetic. Three months later the commanders of the SS formations in the West formed themselves into the first formal group of SS officers prepared to disobey Adolf Hitler. And their motive was exactly that which the Lisbon SD man had ascribed to the SS generals – their estimate of the war situation.

Ever since June 6th, 1944 the Normandy battle had been in the process of destroying the Waffen-SS commanders' last illusion concerning Hitler and the real situation of the Reich. SS regiment after SS regiment wasted away, sacrificed by a Führer immured in his eerie dream-world in Wolfsschanze and impervious to demands for withdrawal or reports of the enemy's material superiority and the exhaustion of the German troops. The SS Imperial Guard was in danger of total destruction, for the greater part of the Waffen-SS was fighting in the West – six divisions in all including the Leibstandarte, forming I SS Panzer Corps under Sepp Dietrich, and II SS Panzer Corps under Paul Hausser.[237] The prospect of losing their troops altogether made even the SS generals ripe for participation in the anti-Hitler conspiracy. Even so they might have hesitated, had they not met in Field-Marshal Erwin Rommel, now Commander-in-Chief of Army Group B, a soldier who like them had scaled the heights and plumbed the depths of Hitler discipleship. Early in 1944 Rommel had still been impervious to the arguments of the opposition but by May he knew that it was now a struggle for existence.

Time was pressing. Rommel estimated that the German defensive front in Normandy might hold for three weeks, but that then a breakthrough by the American forces and the loss of France must be reckoned with.[238] Realization of this bitter conclusion led him to give support to a plan worked out by anti-Nazi officers on the staff of Army Group B even before the invasion had begun. Led by Lieutenant-General Hans Speidel, Rommel's Chief-of-Staff, a 'mobilization timetable' had been drafted envisaging evacuation of the occupied territories in the West without a fight, withdrawal of the German Army behind the Siegfried line and the transfer to the Allies of administrative authority in the occupied territories. The central point of the plan was 'the arrest of Adolf Hitler and his arraignment before a German court.'[239]

By early July Rommel had made up his mind to carry out the programme. On the 9th he ordered Lieutenant-Colonel Caesar von Hofacker, the head planner of the military opposition in the West and a cousin of Stauffenberg, to draft a missive to the Allies in his, Rommel's, name, informing them that the German Army in the West would cease hostilities on its own initiative and withdraw to the Reich.[240] But what would be the attitude of the Waffen-SS, those six divisions which formed the backbone of Army Group B? Rommel wished to be quite sure. Tirelessly he toured the front, questioning commanding generals and senior commanders. One after the other they declared themselves ready to break with Hitler. Moreover the Waffen-SS generals were no exception. Even Party veterans such as Sepp Dietrich could no longer hide their heads in the sand; according to Speidel, Dietrich manifested his discontent with the high command and demanded 'independent action if the front is broken.'[241] SS-Obergruppenführer Hausser, who had meanwhile assumed command of 7th Army, joined in the criticism of Hitler and his senseless 'hang-on-at-all-costs' strategy.[242]

The most outspoken was Obergruppenführer Wilhelm Bittrich who had assumed command of II SS Panzer Corps in succession to Hausser. As he returned to his command post during the night of July 15th–16th, 1944, Field-Marshal Rommel was announced. Bittrich, who was renowned in the Waffen-SS for his sharp tongue, did not mince his words: 'My knowledge is not restricted to Normandy, Field-Marshal. I know how bad things are on the Eastern Front too. There is no more objective leadership there. All that's happening is the crudest gimmickry.' He growled on: 'Up there they don't realize the danger because they're not in touch and therefore can't estimate the situation correctly. Every day I see young men being killed unnecessarily because they're badly led from above, so in future I'm not going to carry out senseless orders and shall act as the situation demands.' Rommel interrupted him and told Bittrich of his own plans. 'I too know that it can't go on like this. But soundings have been taken with the enemy and they lead me to hope that we can make a planned withdrawal from occupied France back to the Siegfried line.' Without hesitation Bittrich subscribed to the anti-Hitler pact: 'Field-Marshal,' he said, 'if this is so, I am with you and so is II SS Panzer Corps. My commanders think exactly as I do.'[243]

Unfortunately the anti-Hitler alliance between the Waffen-SS commanders and the Army in the West collapsed as soon as it had been formed. On July 17th, while on the road behind the German front in Normandy, Rommel was severely wounded by a British ground-attack aircraft; the military opposition in the West had lost its leading figure.[244] Three days later the unity of purpose achieved between the SS generals and the anti-Nazi Army generals in the West was destroyed by the action of Colonel Claus Graf Schenk von Stauffenberg, Chief-of-Staff to Commander-in-Chief Replacement Army, when he set off the bomb under Hitler's conference table. Rommel and the SS generals had agreed on one condition for their rebellion in the West – that Hitler should not be murdered; the whole basis of that agreement was now gone.

The assassination attempt in the Führer's headquarters took the SS political leaders by surprise no less than it did the rebellious generals.

Himmler and Schellenberg seemed semi-paralysed by the military putsch; hours passed before they recovered themselves sufficiently to take counter-measures – which they then did ruthlessly although the *coup d'état* had long since miscarried. Seeing that for months the SS leaders had been negotiating with the resistance and knew most of the secrets of the anti-Nazi opposition, their evident bewilderment sets the historian a pretty puzzle. How was it possible that the accessories of the July 20th movement could be so completely taken by surprise by Stauffenberg's action? Many have subscribed to the facile theory that the SS leaders' surprise was merely a piece of play-acting – in fact, they say, Himmler and his closest collaborators were merely awaiting the success of Stauffenberg's action to join the rebels.[245] The theory is based upon supposition only; there is no concrete proof.

Study of SS headquarters' files shows that neither Himmler's Personal Staff nor the RSHA had ever suspected the circle of conspirators centred around Stauffenberg. The July 20th movement fell into three groups; a circle of conservative officials and retired officers (the Beck-Goerdeler group); a circle of right-wing Christian intellectuals and socialist politicians (the Kreisau circle); and a circle of young regular officers grouped around Stauffenberg and formed early in autumn 1943. The Gestapo knew of only the first two groups. Detailed information on the Beck-Goerdeler group is to be found in the Gestapo files; men such as Beck, Goerdeler, Langbehn and Oster were well known to Gestapo Müller. As early as 1943 Himmler had warned Canaris, the head of the Abwehr, that he now knew who was behind the anti-régime opposition in the Army and that we would 'run people like Beck and Goerdeler out of business quick enough.'[246] The Kreisau circle too held no secrets for the Gestapo since its leader, Helmuth James Graf von Moltke, and other members had been arrested in 1944.

Only Stauffenberg's group of officers remained unknown to the RSHA, for they worked under Wehrmacht cover and were therefore protected from the Gestapo investigators. So little did Himmler suspect Stauffenberg that during a visit to the Führer's headquarters in mid-June 1944 he helped the severely handicapped Stauffenberg off with his coat and carried his heavy briefcase – the same case in which Stauffenberg later put the bomb with which he intended to murder Hitler.[247] Himmler had known Stauffenberg since early June 1944 and regarded him as a capable staff officer who merited promotion. In mid-July when Colonel-General Guderian told Himmler that the General Staff must be manned by officers with fighting experience and that Stauffenberg should be Chief-of-Staff, Himmler at once volunteered to recommend him to Hitler.[248]

There can be no doubt that Himmler knew nothing of Stauffenberg's plans. He did not even suspect when, at about 1 PM his driver, Sturmbannführer Lukas, stormed into the sleeping-quarters of the Reichsführer's field headquarters, shouting: 'Attempt on the Führer! Attempt on the Führer!'[249] Stauffenberg's bomb had exploded in Hitler's briefing hut at 12.42 PM, but Stauffenberg himself had left shortly before. Just after the explosion he was stopped by a suspicious guard at the outer checkpoint of the Führer's headquarters but a telephone call had sufficed to send him on his way to carry out his putsch.[250]

Himmler was still in total ignorance. Even when, a few moments later, he rushed over to the Führer's headquarters to congratulate Hitler on his escape, he was still on a false trail; he suspected a Todt Organization construction group working in the headquarters of having built the bomb into the floor of the briefing hut.[251] Only considerably later did he take notice of a statement by a sergeant-major working in the camp telephone exchange who had observed that Colonel von Stauffenberg had left in a hurry. Even when the suspected criminal landed in Berlin, Himmler failed to have him arrested.[252]

Eventually someone from the Führer's headquarters called Kaltenbrunner and hinted that it might be worth finding out from Colonel von Stauffenberg in the Bendlerstrasse (OKW headquarters) why he had left Wolfsschanze so hurriedly. Kaltenbrunner dispatched to the conspirators' headquarters, which was bristling with armed men, a lone body, Oberführer Dr Piffrader; the only result of this manoeuvre was to deprive Kaltenbrunner of Piffrader's services for some time – Stauffenberg simply waved his unsuspecting visitor away and had him locked up.[253]

This incident shows something of the bewilderment reigning in the SS camp. For years the SS had been girding its loins to deal with a *coup d'état*; for years the Sicherheitspolizei and SD had been battling against the so-called enemies of the State. But now a few hours were enough to destroy, at least temporarily, the myth of the alert, vigilant, all-powerful SS. The RSHA wildly overestimated the strength of the putschists in the Bendlerstrasse and during the afternoon of July 20th Berlin SS Headquarters was as if paralysed. Nebe's Criminal Police squads swarmed out to assist Stauffenberg's Army units to cordon off the Government quarter,[254] but the Leibstandarte companies remained prudently in their barracks at Lichterfeld.[255] No unit of the Waffen-SS or Ordnungspolizei hurried to the Prinz-Albrecht-Strasse to assist their RSHA masters, who were reduced to standing at the windows biting their nails and watching the Wehrmacht battalions, alerted by the conspirators' code word 'Valkyrie', as they marched by. In the provinces and the German-occupied territories the SS Police formations were even more ineffective.

At 6.20 PM Colonel Heinrich Kodré, Chief-of-Staff to Wehrkreis XVII (Vienna) received a teleprinter message from the Bendlerstrasse telling him to arrest all senior Party and Police officials in Austria because 'an unscrupulous clique of chairborne Party leaders has attempted to use this situation [the attack on Hitler] to stab the fighting front in the back and seize power for their own selfish purposes.'[256] Shortly thereafter the teleprinter produced another order from the putschists: 'The following are immediately to be relieved of their offices and placed in strict solitary confinment: all Gauleiter, Reichsstatthalter, Ministers, Oberpräsidenten, Police Presidents, HSSPF, Heads of Gestapo and SS officers.' The message continued: 'Should there be doubt regarding the willingness of commanders of Waffen-SS formations to obey or should they appear undesirable, they are to be taken into protective custody and replaced by Army officers. Waffen-SS formations whose unconditional acceptance of orders is in doubt are to be ruthlessly disarmed.'[257]

Kodré read these orders with some embarrassment; his was the entire responsibility, for his commanding general was on a journey and the latter's deputy away. By the use of a little cunning combined with Viennese charm, however, he succeeded in persuading the mighty SS and Police functionaries to bow to the inevitable. He summoned them to an urgent conference in the General's room at 8 PM[258] and arrested them all – but with every military courtesy. And they came, every one – Querner the HSSPF, Schumann the General of Police, the Deputy Inspector of the Sicherheitspolizei and SD, the Waffen-SS Garrison Commander.[259]

These worthies soon recovered from their surprise. Obergruppenführer Querner and Gotzmann, the Police President, forthwith placed themselves at the disposal of the new régime;[260] Querner was almost indignant when Kodré assured him that he was only acting as instructed by a teleprinter message from the Bendlerstrasse which the Obergruppenführer might see if he liked; Querner waved the idea away, saying: 'If you tell me so, of course I believe you.'[261] In short the mighty policemen made no difficulties. They remained as prisoners in their respective rooms passing the time in small talk. Even when, at about 9.30 PM, a final telephone conversation with Berlin proved that the putsch had failed, the SS leaders made no fuss of any sort.[262]

The military asked their prisoners' pardon, referred to the unfortunate orders from Berlin and bowed the SS dignitaries out. Kodré later recalled that 'none of those present, even subsequently, complained in any way nor have they ever expressed a feeling that they were in the right and had been wrongly arrested.'[263]

In Paris the SS and Police were similarly stampeded by the putschists. At about the time that Colonel Kodré was taking his leave of his prisoners in Vienna, detachments of Security Regiment No 1 under Lieutenant-Colonel von Kraewel were preparing to strike against the Sicherheitspolizei posts in Paris.[264] Major-General Brehmer, Deputy Garrison Commander, Paris, a long-standing Nazi and wearer of the 'Blood Order', personally carried out the arrests of the senior SS leaders in France – Carl-Albrecht Oberg, the HSSPF, and Standartenführer Helmut Knochen, Head of the Sicherheitspolizei. A few minutes sufficed for the change of régime. By 11 PM Oberg and Knochen were in a locked room of the Continental Hotel drinking brandy and listening to the radio;[265] 1,200 men of the Sicherheitspolizei had been incarcerated in the Wehrmacht prison at Fresnes and in the casemates of the old Fort de l'Est.[266]

In the Raphael Hotel the officers of the Paris garrison were just celebrating their victory over the SS when a broadcast speech by Hitler and orders from Field-Marshal von Kluge, Commander-in-Chief West, put an end to all hopes of a *coup d'état*. Kluge had at one time been in close contact with the opposition but had then fallen under the spell of Hitler once more. When he heard of the arrest of the Sicherheitspolizei personnel in Paris, he dismissed General von Stülpnagel, the anti-Nazi Military Governor in France, and ordered the immediate release of Oberg's people.[267]

At 1.30 AM on July 21st Lieutenant General Freiherr von Boineburg-Lengsfeld, the Garrison Commander, Paris, set off to release the two SS leaders. Meanwhile in their hotel room Oberg and Knochen had also heard Hitler's speech. When the General told them that they were free again, Oberg jumped up shouting: 'What damned game is this you're playing at, Boineburg?' Boineburg replied that von Stülpnagel would explain everything in the Raphael Hotel.[268] Oberg stumped indignantly through the bar of the Raphael and, as General von Stülpnagel rose, was about to fly at him when Ambassador Otto Abetz, who was also present, intervened saying: 'What happens in Berlin is one thing. Here what matters is that the Normandy battle is raging and so here we Germans must show a united front.'[269]

Oberg looked sulky but gradually calmed down. That night there occurred what Ritter von Schramm, the military historian, describes as one of the miracles of July 20th, 1944 – SS and Wehrmacht secretly joined forces against the SS persecutors. 'To save what could still be saved, they built up a common front against Himmler's RSHA', Schramm says.[270] Knochen invented a face-saving story for Himmler and the outside world – the arrest of the Sicherheitspolizei men, so the story ran, had simply been an exercise, agreed beforehand between SS-Gruppenführer Oberg and General von Stülpnagel.[271]

For a few hours longer Oberg and the Army were able to protect the Paris putschists from the RSHA. Even when orders began to arrive from Himmler, Oberg attempted to help; he selected with care the military members of the commission of inquiry to examine the conduct of officers; he listened to General Blumentritt, Chief-of-Staff to C-in-C West and an accomplice of the conspirators, and so limited the scope of the inquisition from the outset.[272] Oberg did what he could for Stülpnagel, whom Field-Marshal von Kluge had reported to the Führer's headquarters as one of the leading putschists; Stülpnagel was ordered to report to Berlin and tried to commit suicide on the journey; Oberg caught him up and promised to protect his family from reprisals.[273] Nevertheless Oberg was powerless to prevent the Gestapo from laying hands on the leaders of the putsch in France, Hofacker, Colonels Finckh and von Linstow, Dr Ernst Röchling, and Kreuter, a secret-service official. Thanks to Oberg, however, the majority of the conspirators and their accomplices were spared the journey to the Prinz-Albrecht-Strasse and thence to death. Von Schramm says: 'The leaders of the surprise action against the Paris security service on July 20th all escaped with their lives. Not one hair fell from the head of any of the responsible officers.'[274]

The Waffen-SS commanders also took part in the rescue operation. Three senior officers of the post-war German Army (the Bundeswehr) owe their lives to the action of SS generals; Sepp Dietrich intervened with the RSHA to obtain the release of Speidel;[275] Obergruppenführer Lombard saved Graf Kielmansegg, then a colonel on the General Staff, from Gestapo arrest;[276] Major-General Heusinger also owed his freedom to SS intervention.[277]

When Obergruppenführer Bittrich, who had been in collusion with Rommel, heard on the radio that Colonel-General Erich Hoepner, his former commander in the eastern campaign, had been condemned to death by hanging, he leapt from his chair in a great state of indignation, raging; 'That is the end of the German Army! Never in the history of the German Army has an officer been hanged for treason – they have always been shot.' Bittrich's Chief-of-Staff, an Army officer seconded to the Waffen-SS, hissed to him: 'General, I must ask you not to speak like this in public.' But Bittrich waved him away with: 'Oh, leave me alone!' The outburst was reported to Himmler who at once ordered Bittrich to relinquish his command. General Eberbach, however, Commander-in-Chief of V Panzer Army and Bittrich's immediate superior, refused to release him, saying that the situation at the front was too critical; Himmler could do nothing since, when at the front, the Waffen-SS was under command of the Army and his authority over his own troops was therefore limited. Nevertheless, he continued to try to rid himself of his refractory SS General. During the Arnhem battle a few weeks later, he saw a new opportunity. He dispatched his old friend Karl Gebhardt, the SS/Police Medical Officer-in-Chief and a Lieutenant-General in the Waffen-SS, to Bittrich with orders for him to report forthwith to the Reichsführer-SS. Once more, however, the Army refused to accept Himmler's authority. Field-Marshal Model, the new Commander-in-Chief West, declared himself opposed to Bittrich's recall and even retained him after the withdrawal from France. Himmler never succeeded in disciplining his insubordinate general.[278]

The Bittrich setback, however, was one of the few suffered by Himmler in his extermination campaign against the conspirators of July 20th, 1944 and their accomplices. Pitilessly he struck against suspected traitors and their families; the bloodiest purge in German military history began.

As early as 1.0 PM on July 20th Kersten realized to his despair that Himmler had once more become the fanatical disciple of his Führer – the same Führer whom he had so lately planned to depose with the help of the dissidents. Now all his doubts and hesitations were gone; he said to Kersten: 'Now my hour has come. I will round up all the reactionary gang and have already given orders for the traitors' arrest.'[279] When Kersten wondered whether Hitler's escape was really beneficial to Germany, Himmler retorted: 'What's that you're saying, Kersten? Is that your real opinion? You oughtn't even to think that, still less say so. By preserving the Führer Providence has given us a sign. The Führer lives, invulnerable – Providence has spared him to us so that we may bring the war to a triumphant conclusion under his leadership.'[280]

In a sort of religious frenzy he rushed over to the Führer's headquarters and set the Gestapo death machine going in top gear. He sensed that fortune was smiling on him. He never left the side of his idol for a moment; yet, spellbound though he was, he kept his wits about him sufficiently to submit for Hitler's approval decrees making him, Heinrich Himmler, the second most powerful man in the Reich.

On the afternoon of July 20th Hitler was in a high state of excitement; reports indicated the spread of the revolutionary movement. This was the moment seized upon by Himmler to submit to him a document nominating the Reichsführer-SS as Commander-in-Chief of the Replacement Army. Hitler signed – he was in a state to sign anything which would ensure the annihilation of the conspirators. He screamed: 'Shoot anyone who resists, no matter who he is. The fate of the nation is at stake. Be merciless.' Himmler clicked his heels, saying: 'My Führer, you can rely on me.'[281] His master's faithful watchdog rushed out; and at 4.30 PM Himmler landed in Berlin.[282] The Führer's inquisitor was clever enough to give the conspirators enough rope to hang themselves but no sooner had Keitel, the Head of OKW, countermanded their orders by telephone, than Himmler let loose the terror of a counter-putsch. He moved the remaining units of the Leibstandarte and the SS-Standarte Saarow into the Government quarter; he set up a special 'July 20th Commission' and gathered up the reins of the Replacement Army, of which he was now in charge.[283] The Gestapo bloodhounds combed every corner; the slightest suspicion was enough for any German to find himself in the Prinz-Albrecht-Strasse interrogation cells. Savage and arbitrary police action was the order of the day; the iron curtain descended even upon innocent families. Hardly one of the resistance leaders escaped the régime's vengeance. By the evening of July 20th Stauffenberg and his group had already been shot in the Bendlerstrasse by officers loyal to Hitler but the remaining members of the resistance trod the martyr's road – Gestapo prison, concentration camp, fake trial under the lash of Roland Freisler's tongue, and finally the gallows.

The death-mills of the RSHA also swept up the SS leaders who had been in contact with the Beck-Goerdeler group. On July 24th Nebe, the Head of the Kripo, fled in the (erroneous) belief that the Gestapo had discovered his secret;[284] for months he was hunted by his own Criminal Police until eventually he was betrayed by a jealous woman friend and arrested in November 1944.[285] Colonels Hansen and von Freytag-Loringhoven, ex-Abwehr and now in Schellenberg's 'Amt Mil', were also victims;[286] SS-Sturmbannführer Plaas had been arrested even before the putsch and was executed on July 19th.[287] Von Salviati, the SS cavalry leader, was betrayed by his diary. He was a special target for Himmler's thirst for revenge. The Reichsführer instituted special investigation proceedings against Salviati conducted by the senior judge advocate; in the words of von Herff, Head of the SS Personnel Department, he was 'an incorrigible enemy of National-Socialism and of the Führer';[288] Himmler added: 'If the People's Court had not condemned him, I would have had Salviati shot as a disloyal SS man.'[289]

Among the anti-Nazi SS conspirators, however, Brigadeführer Kanstein escaped. He, it will be remembered, was the conspirators' Sicherheitspolizei Chief-designate; he was interrogated for hours in the RSHA, but was eventually released on an order from Stuckart, the Permanent Secretary of the Ministry of the Interior and an SS Obergruppenführer. Kaltenbrunner was furious and never forgave Stuckart for his interference.[290]

Yet the more savagely Himmler's thugs acted against the resistance leaders, the more reticent did he himself become. His renewed confidence in Adolf Hitler was short-lived. The old doubts which had affected his loyalty to his Führer raised their heads once more. A crazy notion took possession of him; might it not be possible, even now, to bring about peace via the men condemned to death for the assassination attempt – in fact to use the international contacts of the Beck–Goerdeler group? Himmler continually postponed the executions and initiated an eerie sequence of discussions with the victims. Goerdeler, Popitz and Graf von der Schulenburg were permitted to write learned theses setting out their reasons for opposing Hitler.[291]

Callously the victims' lives were prolonged while the SS considered whether to assume the mantle of the opposition. In October 1944 Himmler allowed Schellenberg to contact the Swedish banker, Jakob Wallenberg.[292] Himmler was now ready to use Goerdeler's contact with Wallenberg, hitherto considered a mortal crime, if he could thereby resume discussions with the Allies. But Wallenberg was not to be wooed by Schellenberg. Himmler persisted nevertheless. He summoned Goerdeler and urged him to render one last service to his country.[293]

Wilhelm Brandenburg, Goerdeler's guard, tells the story: 'One day Goerdeler received an offer from the highest quarters [Himmler]; one might almost call it a mission. He was invited to use his close personal and political contacts and friendship with the Swedish financier Wallenberg in Stockholm and the Zionist leader, Dr Weizmann, and via them to the King of Sweden. In other words he was to do what he and his circle would most probably have done had the *coup d'état* succeeded – pave the way for contact with Churchill and so bring about a rapid end to the war on acceptable terms.'[294] Goerdeler was ready, if Himmler would allow him to go to Sweden, but Himmler would not risk that. He and Goerdeler met once more but could not reach agreement.[295]

So Himmler broke off his discussions with Goerdeler. On February 2nd, 1945 the German resistance martyr went to the gallows.[296] Heinrich Himmler, however, could now no longer escape from the régime which he wished both to defend and to remove. He and his SS order remained prisoners of their wishful thinking and of their fanaticism – to the bitter end.

18

THE END

IN autumn 1944 Gebhard Himmler, the civil servant, met his brother Heinrich. Heinrich had a bad cold, but was nevertheless preparing to go to a conference of senior Nazi leaders. 'You should take care of yourself,' his brother said, 'Why not postpone the Conference?' In a somewhat offended tone the Reichsführer replied: 'Have you ever heard of Easter being postponed because the Pope had a cold?'[1]

The answer shows how Heinrich Himmler was living in a dream-world, obsessed by a sort of missionary fervour. He had been the principal beneficiary of the failure of the July 20th putsch and now occupied an unparalleled position of power. To many it seemed that he was merely waiting for the death of Adolf Hitler to place himself at the head of the State. A mere list of his offices is enough to show the power he now wielded: he was lord of the SS – next to the Party the most important organization in the Third Reich; he controlled the Police and the Secret Service; he was in charge of the Ministry of the Interior; as the 'Reich Commissar for the Strengthening of Germanism' he was responsible for the régime's racial policy; he supervised relations between the Reich and Nazi movements in the so-called Germanic countries; 38 Waffen-SS divisions owed allegiance to him, even if only on paper; as head of the armaments industry and Commander-in-Chief of the Replacement Army he commanded all armed forces in the home country; one of his Obergruppenführer, Gottlob Berger, administered the Wehrmacht's prisoner-of-war camps.[2]

Himmler's power was in fact such that even at the time many succombed to the belief that, behind the ageing and decaying Hitler, he alone was responsible for holding the disintegrating régime together. Late in 1944 the world Press from Stockholm to San Francisco carried the headline 'Himmler – Dictator of Germany'.[3] Anyone who did not have personal experience of the gruesome and grotesque realities of National-Socialism's final phase may be forgiven for thinking that, in its last months, Hitler Germany was ruled from the SS barracks. Even a decade later Karl O. Paetel considered that: 'Ten months before the end, the SS finally held Germany in its grip. In 1944–5 no agency of the economy, the State or the Party could stand in the way of the SS. The

Order had taken possession, sometimes openly, sometimes more discreetly, of all power. All that was not part of it was, in its view, no more than an instrument. At the end of 1944 there were only two men who mattered in Germany: Adolf Hitler and Heinrich Himmler.'[4]

One man at least believed in this specious story of SS omnipotence – its own Grand Master. To him it seemed that the hour had come when he could purge National-Socialist Germany of all 'treachery' and all doubts, of those satanic powers which, in his distorted view, had so far prevented Germany's final victory. In a sort of ecstasy he proclaimed in August 1944: 'What we are waging now is a sacred war of the people.'[5]

With threats, mobile courts martial and strident 'rifle-in-hand' propaganda, Himmler mobilized the last levies – copying the Soviet system. He even publicly acknowledged his debt to his Bolshevist mentors, recommending to the generals an SD study entitled *Soviet measures for the successful defence of Leningrad* as an indication of the lines on which the German defensive battle should be fought.[6] To the officers of a 'Grenadier Division' he thundered: 'I give you the authority to seize every man who turns back, if necessary to tie him up and throw him on a supply wagon . . . put the best, the most energetic and the most brutal officers of the division in charge. They will soon round up such a rabble. They will put anyone who answers back up against a wall.'[7]

In his mobilization measures for his fanatical 'last man, last round' strategy, Himmler was influenced by his long-standing hatred of the professional officer. Immediately after July 20th Hitler ordered him to form 15 new divisions and Himmler saw here a unique chance to create a new Wehrmacht, the 'National-Socialist People's Army'.[8] The men of these new formations were scraped together from factories and school classrooms and Himmler deliberately organized them on non-Army lines; fervent young Nazis with only the sketchiest of training were appointed to officer the units; the authority of the 'National-Socialist Leadership Officers', the Nazi version of the political commissars, was increased; even unit nomenclature demonstrated that Himmler's 'revolutionary army' was something different. Formations were entitled 'People's Grenadier Divisions' and 'People's Artillery Corps'.[9]

'True marriage between Party and Wehrmacht has today become a living reality' the *Völkischer Beobachter* proclaimed.[10] Himmler was determined to shield his people's army from any infiltration by regular officers. No 'People's Officer' might be transferred to another unit; the new formations were invariably to remain under the jurisdiction of the Commander-in-Chief of the Replacement Army (Himmler). 'The army which must win this war is the National-Socialist People's Army,' he said.[11]

Simultaneously he infiltrated spies and informers into the remainder of the Replacement Army to report to him even the slightest deviation from the 'last man, last round' policy. Speaking to Gauleiter in Poznan on August 3rd, 1944 he announced that he would be ruthless in bringing to justice any doubters in ultimate victory. And he knew where to begin: 'There is a greater or smaller proportion, five, ten, fifteen per cent perhaps, who are real swine, people who belong to the officers' clique. These we should seek out and, if they are against us, bring them to justice sooner or later.'[12] Throughout the Wehrmacht the SD spies kept their ears to the ground for any defeatist murmurs. The HSSPF were ordered to maintain regularly checked lists, showing whether the senior Wehrmacht officers in any particular locality were reliable and were applying the spur to their men to hold on until 'final victory'.[13]

Report from Obergruppenführer Gutenberger, HSSPF West: 'Colonel Feind, Düren – lax in his attitude to duty and should be dismissed . . . Lieut-Colonel Bührmann, Krefeld 60J – unwilling to take responsibility, no power of decision. Dismissal urgently necessary . . . Colonel Kaehler, Neuss – politically colourless, no power of decision, dismissal necessary.'[14] From Obergruppenführer Hofmann, HSSPF South-West 'Lieut-Colonel Graf, Schlettstadt – politically unreliable, dismissal urgently requested . . . Lieut-Colonel von Hornstein, Rastatt – should be dismissed, said to have a Jewish grandmother.'[15] The all-seeing eye of the RSHA even watched unit officers. SD informers, mostly NCOs and men from the Allgemeine-SS, sent in detailed reports describing 'lack of planning in the higher military echelons . . . valuable troops and resources lying idle . . . disastrous irresponsibility in high places.'[16]

On November 14th, 1944 the SD-Hauptaussenstelle Mannheim reported to the SD commander Strasbourg: 'Reference the situation in 205 Tank Battalion now at Dossenwald camp near Schwetzingen and in particular the unsuitable personality of the commander, Hirschberger – aged 29: further information best obtained from junior officers of the battalion.'[17] The informer in this battalion missed nothing. Regarding the 'National Socialist Leadership Officer' he reported: 'Even today this officer is given insufficient scope. Many simply do not possess the necessary backbone. Officers, NCOs and even the men are wondering about this situation. They think that we should quite simply take our tune from the example of the Bolshevist army.'[18] Regarding the officers: 'Wasting their time in the mess is still their main occupation today. After being stationed in France, all they think of is drink and women. Many have no political education whatsoever.'[19] Concerning the attitude to the National-Socialist officer: 'With this officer clique, social standing is still the most important criterion for promotion of an NCO to officer rank. So far precautions have been taken to exclude avowed National-Socialists.'[20]

Informers were employed to report whether court-martial sentences on so-called 'saboteurs of the war effort' measured up to Himmler's severe standards and the reports were collated in Group A2 Amt III of the RSHA; when the RSHA began demanding to see the records of court-martial proceedings in doubtful cases, however, the Army jibbed, causing Kaltenbrunner to write to Himmler on October 17th, 1944 'I therefore propose that henceforth all records and sentences of courts-martial be forwarded to the RSHA on demand; further that SD Abschnitte or Lietabschnitte be entitled to see the proceedings of divisional courts held in their area.'[21] Such interference with the prerogatives of the Wehrmacht, however, was too much even for Himmler; even the military yes-men such as Keitel of OKW were still missing on the Wehrmacht's rights, tattered though they had now become. In the margin of Kaltenbrunner's letter, Himmler scribbled: 'No, unwise.'[22]

Himmler felt that time was on his side. Like a drowning man Hitler clung desperately to the belief that the pugnacity of the SS would save him from catastrophe and that only Himmler could achieve what the Wehrmacht generals had failed to do. The extent of Hitler's empire was growing ominously smaller; the 1944 summer offensive had brought the Red Army to the Vistula and East Prussia; in September British and American forces appeared on the original Western frontier of Germany. The Dictator was sustained only by his faith in the magic and terror of his SS.

And initially Himmler in fact accomplished what his Führer expected of him. During September and October, with his peculiar brand of organizational talent, he collected 500,000 fresh soldiers and dispatched them to the front, hurriedly and miserably trained though they were.[23] Even before this he had produced from the Replacement Army six brigades hitherto reserved for internal security duties.[24] He drew up fantastic plans for the defence of every German house; he even worked out a scheme, known as 'Werewolf,' for an organization of fanatical Nazi partisans; he dreamed of an alpine fortress in Southern Germany as the last impregnable refuge of the National-Socialist élite. On September 10th he plastered the country with posters: 'Every deserter ... will find his just punishment. Furthermore his ignominious behaviour will entail the most severe consequences for his family.'[25] Soon his summary courts were on the move to write the fulfilment of the Reichsführer's gruesome prophecy in letters of blood. The more desperate the battle both in East and West became, the more bestially did the death mills of Himmler's Sonderkommandos grind, the more frequently were victims of the summary courts to be seen hanging from trees with a placard: 'I am a deserter' or 'I am hanging here because I left my unit without permission.'[26]

Wherever Hitler saw a new catastrophe looming at the front, the Reichsführer-SS moved his cohorts in to the counter-attack. Three times the Dictator summoned his Imperial Guard and three times they brought the enemy to a halt.

By August 1st, 1944 the Soviet armies had reached the Vistula on a broad front and their reconnaissance detachments were already in the Warsaw suburb of Praga west of the river. Thus encouraged, General Bor-Komorowski, the Polish insurgent leader, called his 35,000 partisans on to the Warsaw streets to fight the Germans. The revolt in Warsaw was a major threat since it cut communications to 9th Army, still fighting farther east.[27] The city had not been declared part of the Army operations zone and so Colonel-General Guderian, the Army Chief-of-Staff, applied to Hitler to have Warsaw placed under the Wehrmacht so that the Army might put down the revolt. Hitler refused; the task was allotted to Himmler as Commander-in-Chief of the Replacement Army.[28]

Himmler ordered to the Warsaw front the head of his anti-partisan formations, SS Obergruppenführer von dem Bach-Zelewski, who put down the Polish revolt with his usual brutality. Bach-Zelewski mobilized the most notorious formations in the SS – twelve police companies under SS-Gruppenführer Heinz Reinefahrt, the regiment commanded by SS-Oberführer Dr Oskar Dirlewanger (composed of poachers and convicted criminals) and a force of Russian ex-prisoners of war under the White Russian, SS-Brigadeführer Bronislav Kaminski.[29] The story of the horrors perpetrated by Dirlewanger's and Kaminski's men even reached the Führer's headquarters. In his memoirs Guderian says; 'What I learnt . . . was so appalling that I felt myself bound to inform Hitler about it that same evening and to demand the removal of the two brigades from the Eastern Front.' Even Gruppenführer Fegelein, Himmler's chief representative, confirmed the story, saying: 'It is true, *mein Führer*, those men are real scoundrels.'[30]

Grudgingly Hitler gave way to Guderian but not before giving Bach-Zelewski the opportunity of shooting the freebooter Kaminski as 'a possibly dangerous witness' (Guderian's words).[31] The exploit confirmed the Dictator in his opinion that 'this Bach-Zelewski is one of the cleverest of men.'[32]

The ashes of the Warsaw rising were still smouldering when a new crisis in rear of the Eastern Front brought another order to the SS from Hitler. Encouraged by the Russians, the Slovak politicians and some units of the Slovak Army revolted, threatening to bar the way to German formations withdrawing from Galicia.[33] Before the revolt had spread throughout the country, however, and before the hesitant Bratislava Government had made up its mind, the SS struck once more. The SD arrested the leading revolutionaries and the SS training school in Bohemia and Moravia formed itself into an armoured regiment and marched.[34]

The training-school regiment captured Neusohl, the centre of the revolt; meanwhile 18 SS-Panzer-Grenadier division, known as 'Horst Wessel', together with the newly-formed SS division 'Galicia', moved in from the East; Army units and the Dirlewanger regiment arrived later. From Berlin Himmler summoned the most faithful of all his followers, Gottlob Berger, the head of the SS-Hauptamt, and he took over as the new Wehrmacht Commander-in-Chief Slovakia.[35] Assisted by Einsatzgruppe H under SS-Obersturmbannführer Dr Josef Witiska, Berger took only four weeks to re-establish behind the front the perfect peace characteristic of German rule.[36] The Slovak Government 'dwindled from a puppet régime to a shadow.'[37] Together with the Wehrmacht the SS was now in effect the ruler of the satellite states.

When Berger reported back from his mission in Slovakia, he found in the Führer's headquarters a giant SS officer awaiting a new mission from Hitler. The Dictator had summoned to Wolfsschanze the man who had become a legend in the SS – Sturmbannführer Otto Skorzeny, destined to lead the SD's last international coup.

Skorzeny had been born in Vienna in 1908. He trained as an engineer and became manager of a scaffolding business; in 1939 he joined the Luftwaffe and later transferred to the Leibstandarte;[38] he then moved to the Ausland-SD where he was put in charge of sabotage operations[39] and became a sort of father-figure for all those Germans who hoped that some Secret-Service gimmick would produce a change in the fortunes of war. His almost mythical reputation dated from Sunday September 12th, 1943 when, at the head of German parachute troops, he had rescued Mussolini from his Carabinieri guards in a mountain hotel in the Gran Sasso, one of the most inhospitable parts of Italy, where the ex-Dictator had been incarcerated by the Badoglio Government. Skorzeny had greeted the Duce with the words: 'The Führer has sent me.'[40] Now a year later Hitler proposed to dispatch his guerrilla leader to another ally, but with a very different mission – to arrest him and remove him from the scene.

Hitler's orders to Skorzeny ran: 'We have received secret reports that the Head of the Hungarian State, Admiral Horthy, is attempting to get in touch with our enemies with a view to a separate peace . . . You, Skorzeny, must be prepared to seize the Citadel of Budapest [the Burgberg – Horthy's residence] if he betrays his alliance with us.'[41]

Skorzeny changed into mufti and set off for Hungary with a passport in the name of Dr Wolff.[42] On the way he thought up a code name for the operation; he had forgotten to tell the commanders of his paratroop units to take bazookas with them and so he christened the operation 'Panzerfaust' [Bazooka].[43] On reporting to Obergruppenführer Dr Winkelmann, the HSSPF Hungary, however, Skorzeny learnt that the situation had taken a dramatic turn; on August 30th, 1944 Horthy had dismissed Hungary's pro-German Government and replaced it by a Cabinet, under Field-Marshal Geza Lakatos, clearly intended to prepare for Hungary's withdrawal from the war. Barely a month later Field-Marshal Farago was on the way to Moscow to arrange an armistice with the Russians.[44]

Farago signed his agreement with the Russians on October 11th,[45] but Winkelmann was fore-armed. Ever since the installation of the Lakatos Government, which he regarded as a 'sign of treachery',[46] he had taken precautions to ensure that, should Hungary try to change sides, a Nazi-run Government would suddenly take the place of the Horthy régime.[47] Since late August Ferenc Szalasi, the Hungarian Nazi leader, had been prepared to take over;[48] the SD was holding ready three million leaflets proclaiming the new Nazi Government;[49] SS-Untersturmführer Erich Kernmayr with a special squad was waiting to seize Budapest radio station.[50]

Winkelmann was unwilling to wait further and decided to forestall the Hungarians. He reported: 'On Friday, October 6th, 1944, knowing that treachery was round the corner but also that no major action could take place for military reasons, I took the decision to clarify the situation.'[51] The decision was – 'arrest Horthy's entourage as soon as possible.'[52] Winkelmann, SS-Oberführer Hans Geschke (the Sicherheitspolizei Commander for Hungary) and Skorzeny drew up a plan of campaign and on the morning of October 10th they struck.

As Field-Marshal Bakay, commmander of I Hungarian Army Corps stationed in Budapest and Horthy's principal military adviser, returned to his apartment he was kidnapped by Geschke's thugs.[53] Horthy thereupon nominated Field-Marshal Aggteleki to succeed Bakay but he too disappeared without trace.[54] The German plan also included the kidnapping of Nikolaus (Nikki) Horthy, the Regent's son whom the SD had been shadowing for some time on suspicion of attempts to negotiate an armistice with representatives of Tito, the leader of the Yugoslav partisans. The SD in Budapest had drawn up a typically SD plan. They proposed to capture Horthy *in flagrante delicto*, while actually negotiating with Tito's representatives, carry him off and then blackmail his father into agreement to continue to fight at Germany's side and install a pro-German Government.[55] The kidnapping operation was given the code name 'Operation Mouse' – young Horthy's nickname 'Nikki' had been misheard as 'Mickey' and so the wags of the Budapest SD christened the operation 'Mickey Mouse'.[56]

Two SD men were disguised as officers of Tito's army and quickly gained contact with Nikolaus Horthy. They agreed on a secret meeting on October 13th but the premature appearance in Budapest of an SD Commander known to Nikki made him suspicious and he called the meeting off.[57] He did, however, agree to a further meeting to take place on October 15th in the office of the Director of the Hungarian 'Danube Ports Association'. Nikolaus took his precautions; he was accompanied by five Honved [Hungarian National Guard] officers to watch the door of the building; a Honved company was posted a couple of streets away.[58]

But the Germans had made their preparations too. The previous day an SD commando had taken up residence in a *pension* one floor above the Ports Association's offices and in a side street Skorzeny had posted a company of his men in closed trucks.[59] The kidnapping of Horthy was planned for 10.10 AM. Just after 10.00 Skorzeny, again in mufti, drove up to the building which young Horthy had just entered. Horthy's car was parked in front of the entrance and behind it was a jeep in which sat three Hungarian officers invisible to passers-by.[60]

Two SD men then approached the building. As they did so the three Honved Officers realized the danger and fired. One of the SD men collapsed, dead.[61] At this moment the muzzles of Hungarian rifles and sub-machine-guns appeared through the windows of the building, and Skorzeny's car came under heavy fire. Skorzeny drew his revolver and summoned his men. They occupied the opposite side of the square and, as the Hungarians moved forward, drove them back into the neighbouring houses. The alarm had hardly reached the Honved troops nearby, however, when the SD men already located in the building ran out with Horthy and the Director of the Ports Association both handcuffed. The two prisoners were hustled into a truck and a few minutes later were in the air heading for Mauthausen concentration camp.[62]

'Operation Bazooka' now got underway. At midday Dr Veesenmayer, the German Minister and also an SS officer, announced himself to Admiral Horthy with the demand that he forthwith declare himself for or against the Reich.[63] SS-Brigadeführer Veesenmayer did not feel comfortable in his role of blackmailer; he had already been critical of Winkelmann's crude methods and Kaltenbrunner, the head of the RSHA, had once denounced him for 'defeatism'.[64] He did not, as Winkelmann later complained, 'fire the biggest gun, which he should have done according to the plan; he did not tell the old man that at the slightest sign of treachery his son would be put against the wall.'[65] The conscience-stricken Minister held his tongue, thereby jeopardizing the entire operation – at 2 PM Radio Budapest announced that Hungary had signed an armistice with the Soviet Union.[66]

Meanwhile, however, Winkelmann had taken control of Budapest. To the threatening rumble of forty German tanks[67] Untersturmführer Kernmayr occupied the Budapest radio station and proclaimed the new Nazi régime;[68] German troops occupied all key points in the city and Skorzeny now prepared to deal the Horthy régime its death-blow. He alerted 22 SS Cavalry Division which cordoned off all approaches to the Burgberg, Horthy's fortress;[69] he then deployed his parachute troops and early on October 16th they moved into the attack. Sharp at 6 AM Skorzeny and his men scaled the escarpment and were soon in control of the situation. Skorzeny reported: 'We reached the Burgberg without firing a shot. The whole operation had not taken more than half an hour.'[70] In fact he could have spared himself the trouble, for shortly before 4 AM Veesenmayer had reported to Winkelmann that Horthy was prepared to hand over power to the Nazi leader, Szalasi.[71] Hungary was to continue to bleed for Hitler.

Once more the SS had shown that it could still snatch Pyrrhic victories to feed Hitler's 'last man, last round' mania. And the more spectacular these SS successes, the higher Himmler rose in that extraordinary and melancholy court at the Führer's headquarters – a nest of intrigue increasingly reminiscent of some oriental fable.

October 1944 was the month in which Himmler's power reached its zenith. The Dictator showed his gratitude for his imperial guard's victories in Poland, Slovakia and Hungary: on November 8th, 1944 Himmler was granted the privilege of taking Hitler's place for the delivery of the traditional speech commemorating the Munich beer-cellar putsch.[72] Himmler was entranced by his own power; the sense of being the principal and apparently indispensable assistant of his Führer intoxicated him. Trevor-Roper says sarcastically that the decline of the Reich had 'brought Himmler to God' – that God was Hitler, whose removal in the interests of peace Himmler had been considering only a few months before but for whom he was now ready to demand the most horrifying offerings of blood.

'In the course of the last year,' he confided to Schwerin von Krosigk, the Finance Minister, 'I have learned to believe in miracles again. The Führer's escape on July 20th was a miracle.'[73] With a ghastly, grotesque show of optimism he suppressed any doubts he might have had in the Dictator. To Kersten, who was notoriously sceptical, he proclaimed: 'All Hitler's calculations will prove themselves correct. He is, after all, still the greatest genius of all time. He knows exactly the day when we shall be victorious. On January 26th next year we shall once more stand on the shores of the Atlantic.'[74] When Guderian, the Army Chief-of-Staff, objected that he did not know where to find the troops to contain the next Russian offensive, Himmler simply laughed at so much unnecessary anxiety and lack of faith saying: 'You know, my dear Colonel-General, I don't really believe the Russians will attack at all. It's all an enormous bluff.'[75]

For a moment it seemed as if the Reich really was ruled by only two men – Hitler and Himmler, but the picture of Himmler's power was deceptive. Trevor-Roper says: 'Nevertheless in spite of these apparent accessions of power, Himmler was in fact in decline.'[76] Those who believe in the Hitler-Himmler theory have forgotten another man who was watching with buring jealousy every step taken by his rival Himmler. Martin Bormann, Head of the Party Chancellery, managing director of the Nazi Party, the Dictator's *éminence grise* and doorkeeper of his private office, blocked the rise of 'Uncle Heinrich', as he liked to call Himmler.

The quarrel over the powers of the Inland SD had already shown that Bormann's influence in the Führer's headquarters was growing apace. The more the Reich shrank under its enemies' hammer blows, the more strident became the orders issued in rear of the front by Bormann's 'birds of paradise' brigade. Bormann watched jealously to ensure that Himmler and his HSSPF did not infringe the Party's prerogatives. He intervened whenever some Gauleiter complained that SS interference was a challenge to his authority. Speer, the Armaments Minister, recalls that 'Bormann immediately reported such cases to Hitler and exploited them to fortify his own position.'[77] Hitler shared Bormann's view that as the war moved on to German territory political leadership was increasingly the prerogative of the Party and so Bormann began to dispatch his emissaries to the more important military headquarters. In the Führer's headquarters the Wehrmacht was now discredited – and its place was taken, not by the SS but by the Gauleiter.

Among the most rabid of these was Erich Koch, who had been driven out of the Ukraine into his native East Prussia; he was the first to show what the Party leaders understood by home defence, Bormann style. As Reich Defence Commissar in his Gau, he made himself literally the overlord of East Prussia,[78] diregarding both the Wehrmacht and the SS, whom he treated with equal contempt. Without informing the responsible Army Group under Colonel-General Reinhardt, he constructed defensive positions; using invalids, old-age pensioners and teenagers, he formed a private army which he called the 'Volkssturm' [Home Guard]; he requisitioned the armaments factories in East Prussia and refused any expert military advice for the Volkssturm.[79] Koch even extracted from the Führer's headquarters an agreement that he should carry out the functions to which Himmler and the SS laid claim – he reported on officers and men and took charge of the search for deserters.[80]

Dilettante and megalomaniac though he was, Koch's success inspired Hitler and Bormann to give the Party nation-wide charge of this final levy. Guderian had proposed that a static Home Guard be formed in the East under the Army, but Hitler's version of this was a Volkssturm on the Koch model under the Party – and at its head, of course, Martin Bormann.[81] On September 26th Bormann instructed the Gauleiter to start immediate preparations for the formation of a Volkssturm.[82] Three weeks later, on the anniversary of the Battle of Leipzig (October 18th, 1813), it was officially constituted by Hitler decree[83] – and a by-product of this last desperate measure by the Nazi régime was a reduction in the power of Himmler; as Commander-in-Chief of the Replacement Army he was responsible only for the organization, training and equipment of the Volkssturm; recruiting and political leadership were Bormann's preserve.[84]

Bormann now brought another of Himmler's rivals into the game – Goebbels. Before July 20th Goebbels had ruminated: 'The Army for Himmler, and for me the civilian direction of the war. That is a combination which could re-kindle the power of our war leadership.'[85] After the attack on Hitler, however, Goebbels realized that Bormann was the stronger of the two and therefore threw in his lot with him. Bormann succeeded in getting Goebbels nominated Reich Plenipotentiary for Total War.[86] In December he was commissioned to investigate the Wehrmacht's manpower position and recommend unit moves to the Führer's headquarters – another clear interference with Himmler's prerogatives as Commander-in-Chief of the Replacement Army.[87]

Nevertheless, so long as Himmler was still frequenting the Führer's headquarters and therefore available to counter Bormann's backstairs influence, the power of the Reichsführer was inevitably a source of disquiet to the party Chancellery. There was only one solution – Himmler must be removed from the Dictator's immediate entourage. Bormann had an idea. He knew that Himmler, once an Army cadet, had always secretly longed to be at the head of a fighting formation; ever since World War I had denied the Landshut student his war experience, a warlord's career had been his dream. Martin Bormann gave it him – and it formed the prelude to Himmler's downfall.

By late November British and American forces had driven into Alsace and the German 19th Army was confined to a bridgehead on the left bank of the Rhine. The problem therefore was to create a fall-back position on the right bank through which the remnants of 19th Army might withdraw if necessary and which would hold any further enemy offensive. The Führer's headquarters decided to form a new Army Group in the area between Karlsruhe and the Swiss frontier[88] – and Bormann proposed Himmler as its Commander-in-Chief. The horrified soldiers were forced to swallow the appointment since Hitler and Bormann pointed out that only Himmler, in his capacity as C-in-C of the Replacement Army, could provide the necessary forces for the new Army Group: since the problem was primarily to form a stop line, as Head of the Police Himmler was ideally suited for the post.[89]

Himmler was appointed early in December. The 'Commander-in-Chief Upper Rhine' was radiant and entirely oblivious of the fact that Bormann was holding a knife to his throat. Now at last Himmler could fulfil the dream of his youth; now Himmler, the warlord, would bring about the great turning point in the Second World War. Initially he contrived by his industry and organizing ability to deceive many even among the soldiers. He quickly formed a defensive front, mobilized units from his Replacement Army to reinforce Army Group Upper Rhine and soon assembled a heterogeneous force of stragglers, home guard men, customs officials, anti-aircraft auxiliaries and battalions of non-Germans from the East.[90] He did indeed seem to have a superstitious aversion to leaving his headquarters in the Black Forest, but nevertheless he was clearly preparing himself for the great battle. Meanwhile he contented himself with more trivial victories over the enemy within his own ranks: he dismissed Army and corps commanders on pretexts of inefficiency and refused to recognize that Commander-in-Chief West, who was responsible for the entire Western Front, had any authority over his Army-Group[91] (see Appendix 8).

So busy was he fighting the great decisive battle in the West – though only on paper – from his headquarters, that the collapse of his authority both in the SS and in Germany passed him by. The Reichsführer's disappearance into the Black Forest was the signal for many SS leaders to try their luck with his rival Bormann, who was obviously more powerful. Highly influential SS men were among the deserters – SS-Gruppenführer Hermann Fegelein, for instance (Himmler's personal representative in the Führer's headquarters, who was married to Gretel Braun, Eva's sister), and Obergruppenführer Kaltenbrunner, the Head of the RSHA.

Kaltenbrunner's defection was not without irony, for he was a second-rater selected by Himmler to head the Prinz-Albrecht-Strasse solely in order to ensure that there should not be another Heydrich.[92] He was an attorney from Linz, tall, scar-faced and a chain smoker; when he was appointed in January 1943 after Heydrich's death, hardly anyone knew him; he had been in charge of SS-Oberabschnitt Danube and gossip had it that he owed his career to the fact that by 1938 the semi-Fascist Austrian police had eliminated all his predecessors.[93] In addition Himmler ensured that Kaltenbrunner did not possess the power of his predecessor, Heydrich. He removed from the RSHA responsibility for personnel and economic questions and transferred them to two of its rivals – the SS Personnel Hauptamt and the WVHA.[94]

When Kaltenbrunner took over the RSHA he found that his Heads of Division had more authority than their new master. To his old classmate, Skorzeny, he complained that he was 'often bypassed' by his independent Heads of Division and 'learnt many things only when they were over'; Skorzeny remarked: 'It struck me that this man . . . was not feeling quite at his ease.'[95] Kaltenbrunner made blatant attempts to turn on his Austrian charm, but this could not conceal the fact that he was striving feverishly to recover his predecessor's power. By 1944 he was considered the second most powerful man in the SS: even Himmler sometimes shuddered, as had Canaris the Head of the Abwehr, at the sight of Kaltenbrunner's coarse, unmanicured hands.[96]

His alliance with Bormann, however, gave Kaltenbrunner a privilege which even Heydrich had not enjoyed. He became a constant visitor to the Führer's headquarters and Hitler gave him orders direct – not through Himmler. This was something entirely new – Kaltenbrunner acted as if he was responsible to his Führer alone in matters of RSHA policy.[97]

The Himmler loyalists realized the implications of Kaltenbrunner's defection. They warned the Reichsführer againsts the machinations of the Bormann clique and attempted to rouse Himmler from his warlord daydreams. On December 21st, 1944 Gottlob Berger wrote to him: 'I request you to cut short your time as Commander-in-Chief Upper Rhine and return to the Führer's headquarters. I am actuated in this request not only by the knowledge that rumours are being assiduously cultivated in certain quarters – that the Reichsführer-SS is in disfavour and that, via Keitel, the Wehrmacht is calling the tune – but also because I sense that when the Reichsführer-SS is not in the headquarters, our political work . . . suffers badly.'[98] The loyalists in the 'Kurt Eggers' Standarte, the Waffen-SS propaganda squad, were also restless. Standartenführer Gunter d'Alquen's staff was ordered to prepare a memorandum for Himmler demanding that the SS put an end to the 'Bormann monopoly'.[99]

But Himmler, frozen in his martial pose, disregarded these warnings. He was sure of his role as crown prince; be believed firmly in his right to the succession. Only later did he realize that Bormann and the OKW had out-manoeuvred him; they had given him a military command only to ensure that he would fail.[100] But in late 1944 he would not believe it; a military future seemed to lie before him. When, in early January 1945, an opportunity offered to display his military qualities, he pushed himself forward as if possessed.

In a limited counter-offensive two mobile divisions of the neighbouring Army Group had succeeded in penetrating the French Maginot Line near Hagenau and breaking into northern Alsace. Spurred on by this success, Himmler worked out an ambitious plan: he requested the Führer's headquarters to allot him the two divisions and with them he proposed to recapture Strasbourg. He stressed that his 19th Army still retained a bridgehead in central Alsace; if this was reinforced with the two divisions now near Hagenau, he said, there would be little difficulty in re-taking Strasbourg. Contrary to the advice of Commander-in-Chief West, the Führer's headquarters approved the plan and General Himmler's orders went out.[101]

In an intricate move the two divisions at Hagenau were moved south along the Rhine, but before they could occupy their new positions the Allies had recovered from their setback in northern Alsace.[102] Even so, the Americans were so surprised by Himmler's attack (he penetrated to within a few miles of Strasbourg) that General Eisenhower, the Allied Commander-in-Chief, toyed with the idea of evacuating the city and withdrawing his right flank behind the Vosges. Frey, the Mayor of Strasbourg, however, protested and the Allies held the city.[103] The German attack bogged down. On January 20th the Allies moved in to counter-attack, rolled up Himmler's bridgehead west of the Rhine and a month later had driven the last German soldier across the river.[104]

Himmler's failure as a military commander was obvious, but Bormann had another command in store for his rival: it was to involve Himmler even more irrevocably in the military catastrophe of the sinking régime and expose him to outbursts of rage from the mistrustful Dictator. He was given another shadow army, this time on the Eastern Front – Army Group Vistula.

On January 12th, 1945, the Soviets launched the attack at which

Himmler had so lately scoffed, and it proved to be the greatest offensive in military history. Three million Russians over-ran 750,000 poorly armed German soldiers and in a few days the entire German front lay in ribbons. The Army Groups of Marshals Chernyakovsky and Rokossovsky drove forward to Königsberg and Marshal Koniev reached Sagan.[105] Panic seized the German defenders; apart from a coastal strip, East Prussia went down in a welter of refugee columns, the screams of women being raped, and the murderous sentences of German summary courts; Army Group North had almost ceased to exist.[106]

In the north-east the Soviet armies had opened a yawning gap between the German Army Groups North and Centre. The area between the Oder and the Vistula, barely defended by a few scattered formations, reserve units and home guard detachments and with no coordinating headquarters,[107] lay wide open to the Russians. On January 23rd, therefore, Guderian, the Chief-of-Staff, proposed that a new Army Group staff be formed in Pomerania to coordinate the forces located between the Vistula and the Oder and form a new defensive front. He suggested that this 'Army Group Vistula' be entrusted to Field-Marshal Freiherr von Weichs, whose staff had been thrown up by the shrinkage of the Balkan theatre of war.[108]

Hitler agreed but thought Guderian's candidate for the command gave a 'tired impression'. He knew someone better – Himmler. No one could defend the area better than the Head of the SS. Guderian protested. 'This preposterous suggestion appalled me,' he says, 'and I used such argumentative powers as I possessed in an attempt to stop such an idiocy being perpetrated on the unfortunate Eastern Front. It was all in vain.'[109] Hitler insisted that Himmler had run his affairs very well on the Upper Rhine; being in charge of the Replacement Army, moreover, he could call direct on its resources. When Guderian attempted to provide Himmler, who knew nothing of strategy, with minimal experienced General Staff assistance, Hitler scotched this idea too. As Chief-of-Staff Himmler chose SS-Brigadeführer Heinz Lammerding, a courageous but inexperienced tank general of the Waffen-SS; he surrounded himself with SS officers and only later accepted Army officers on his staff.[110]

Nevertheless, as he left on January 24th to set up his headquarters in Deutsch-Krone, Himmler had lost that megalomaniac confidence which had governed his warlord daydreams on the Upper Rhine.[111] He went eastwards in fear – fear of the Dictator's ungovernable rages and of his vindictiveness. Himmler knew only too well that he could not afford another defeat if he was not to risk all that he had so carefully built up over the years. He had no time to lose; immediately and continuously, he must be able to report victories. So he departed on his new mission in a mixture of fear and fanatical determination.

He assembled the last forces from the Replacement Army; he had the lines of communication combed for fit soldiers by squads of SS and police; he formed new Waffen-SS formations although the existing divisions were already down to brigade strength; he summoned proven SS generals such as Obergruppenführer Steiner to his Army Group.[112] To offset his lack of troops he relied on the meaningless pathos of 'last man, last round' appeals and martial announcements giving the civil population an impression of strength in which not even he himself believed. 'The task now before us,' he told the commanding generals and divisional commanders of his Army Group, 'is one our ancestors have faced a hundred times in battle against Avars, Mongols and, in the south-east, Turks and Tartars. Even in those days, the only reliable allies were our own strength and our stout hearts.'[113] Through the *Pommersche Zeitung*, the local Party newspaper, he announced: 'Miracles are being worked as a result of full use of all available resources in men and weapons and the employment of all our strength in the rearward area. The population of South Pomerania has recognized the task of the hour; the front is holding and becoming stronger daily.'[114]

Even the sound and fury of his own propaganda, however, could not conceal from Himmler the fact that he was headed for a catastrophe. He was a superstitious being who, more than any other Nazi potentate, believed in the stars and the prophesies of astrologers, and now he saw himself under an unlucky star. He dispatched X SS Army Corps to the Oder-Warthe bend to hold the Soviet drive towards the Oder but the operation was doomed to failure. On January 29th Zhukov's men appeared in front of the Oder position and quickly overran it.[115] Desperately Himmler attempted a counter-attack to offset his reverse on the Oder. He launched his best SS units in a flanking attack against Zhukov's army in the Schneidemühl area – a hopeless operation from the outset.[116] The Germans were driven back once more. Haunted by defeat and no longer sure of his Führer's favour, warlord Himmler took refuge in his sickbed. His visits to the SS hospital at Hohenlychen, run by his old friend Karl Gebhardt, became more frequent; the C-in-C of the Army Group now only appeared in his headquarters for a few hours a day and by 10 PM the war was over as far as he was concerned – he slept long and no officer dared wake him.[117]

Now that Himmler had more or less eliminated himself, Guderian decided to attempt one last stroke with Army Group Vistula. His plan was to launch a surprise attack against the Soviet armies in the Arnswalde area, defeat them north of the Warthe, clear Pomerania of Russians and so secure the lines of communication to West Prussia. To carry out this plan, Guderian proposed to attach to Himmler's staff a new chief of operations, General Walter Wenck, presumably hoping in practice to remove the command from Himmler. On February 13th he submitted his plan to Hitler in the Reich Chancellery[118] but the Dictator was quick to see through his game. Himmler was present and, pale and embarrassed, was forced to listen to the Dictator and the Chief-of-Staff discussing his military qualities. The argument became heated and harsh words were used.

Guderian: 'General Wenck must be attached to the Reichsführer's staff since otherwise there can be no prospect of the attack succeeding.'

Hitler: 'The Reichsführer is man enough to carry out the attack on his own.'

Guderian: 'The Reichsführer has neither the requisite experience nor a sufficiently competent staff to control the attack single-handed. The presence of General Wenck is therefore essential.'

Hitler: 'I don't permit you to tell me that the Reichsführer is incapable of performing his duties.'

Guderian: 'I must insist on the attachment of General Wenck to the Army Group staff so that he may ensure that the operations are competently carried out.'

For two hours Hitler and Guderian shouted at each other, neither willing to give way. Furiously Hitler paced up and down and then suddenly he stopped in front of Himmler and said: 'Well, Himmler, General Wenck will arrive at your headquarters tonight and take charge of the attack.' He looked at Guderian with a dry laugh; 'Now please continue with the conference. The General Staff has won a battle this day.'[119]

The end of Himmler's power was in sight, though Guderian's plan failed, for four days later Wenck was involved in a car crash and the attack miscarried.[120] Nevertheless Guderian continued his efforts to get rid of Himmler from the Army of the East; twice he asked Hitler to relieve the Commander-in-Chief Vistula and twice the Dictator refused.[121] In desperation Guderian decided to propose to Himmler himself that he should resign. When he reached the headquarters, however (which had meanwhile moved to Prenzlau), and asked to see the Commander-in-Chief of the Army Group he was told that Himmler had been in his friend Gebhardt's clinic for weeks suffering from 'severe influenza'. Brigadeführer Lammerding asked: 'Can't you rid us of our Commander?'[122]

Guderian could. On March 18th he presented himself to Himmler who, when he recognized his visitor, shrank beneath the bedclothes, coughing. But Guderian comforted him, assuring him that he fully understood that with all his other responsible posts the Reichsführer could hardly attend to the little job of commanding an Army Group, particularly when his health was so bad. The fallen warlord took note: but recoiled again immediately. What would the Führer say, he mumbled, looking expectantly at Guderian. Guderian offered to help: if the Reichsführer had no objection, he Guderian, on his own initiative would ask the Führer to release the Reichsführer from command of the Army Group.[123] On March 20th, 1945 the thing was done. Almost without a murmur Hitler agreed to the proposal that Colonel-General Gotthard Heinrici, Commander-in-Chief I Panzer Army, should assume command of Army Group Vistula in place of the Reichsführer SS.[124] Himmler's vision of himself as warlord was extinguished.

Hardly a soul realized, however, that March 20th, 1945 was a moment of leave-taking: Heinrich Himmler's departure from his life-long idol, the renunciation of the demigod to whom he had been prepared to offer the most grisly blood sacrifices, the awakening from a life of self-deception unparalleled in history. From that day onwards Himmler was determined to save what he thought still might be saved – his own skin, his SS Order and the illusions of his murky career. Himmler would not have been Himmler had he not withdrawn into a new world of illusion and it told him that he was the man whose mission it was to bring peace to the world and guide post-war Germany, liberated from Hitler, into a new era.

The first to learn of this change of heart was Colonel-General Heinrici when he arrived at the Prenzlau headquarters on March 22nd to take over. In some embarrassment Himmler explained what he was leaving behind him, but when Heinrici asked for a 'general political orientation' all Himmler's old confidence returned. He was a changed man. The head of the SS seized Heinrici by the arm and led him conspiratorially to a sofa in the corner of his office. Then he whispered: 'The moment has now come to initiate negotiations with our Western enemies. I have already taken the first steps; my negotiators have already established contact.'[125]

For the first time Himmler had revealed to an outsider the secret which he had hitherto guarded so carefully: through contacts in Sweden and Switzerland he had been trying for months to gain contact with the Allies and arrange a separate peace with the Western powers. Hitherto the Germans had seen only one of the two faces presented by the SS. Now, to the initiated at least, the other face revealed itself and what the initiated saw was bitter and grotesque. The SS had brutally punished any who expressed doubt in ultimate victory; with their pathetic appeals and suicidal operations they had spurred the Germans on to resist to the end. Now these same SS were seeking to save their own skins by secret trafficking with the enemy because they themselves no longer believed in victory. This grotesque change of heart, moreover, had its macabre side, for in their haste to capitulate the SS leaders looked for salvation to the very people whom they had set out to exterminate to the last man. Their Jewish hostages, they calculated, could be both their intermediaries and their guarantors, their lever for the initiation of discussions with the West.

The fact that many SS leaders, including Himmler, harboured such illusions was due in no small measure to a fat, busy and somewhat boastful Balt who never tired of urging the SS and its Reichsführer to break with Adolf Hitler – Felix Kersten, Himmler's masseur. Born in Dorpat in 1898 of a Brandenburg family, Kersten was both a *bon viveur* and a philanthropist; for years he had exerted on Himmler an influence comparable only to that of the astrologer Seni on Wallenstein; just as the Italian could exorcise the seventeenth-century warlord's nightmares of the powers of evil, so 'the man with the miraculous hands', as Joseph Kessel called him, could relieve Himmler of his almost intolerably painful stomach cramps.

With the sensitive pressure of his hands Kersten could relieve men of pain. As a young man in Finland he had studied manual therapy, whose theory, according to its supporters, is that many maladies result from nervous tension and can be cured by relaxation of the nerves. Having qualified as a masseur in Finland, Kersten had moved to Berlin where he had become a fashionable practitioner. When Dr Ko, the Chinese master masseur, once allowed Kersten to practise upon him, he exclaimed: 'My young friend, you understand nothing as yet, but I have waited thirty years for you. You have the gift.'[126]

Kersten's miraculous hands worked wonders and brought him the most profitable posts ever captured by any Berlin medical practitioner during the 1920s. His reputation spread rapidly across Europe, assisted by the fact that his undoubted ability, and insistence upon an adequate financial return for his labours, was allied to a courtly, aristocratic manner. The role of personal physician to illustrious potentates came naturally to him – Alexander Westberg, personal physician to the Czar of Russia, was one of his patrons.[127] In 1928 he was appointed personal physician to the Dutch royal family[128] and eleven years later he assumed responsibility for the most dangerous patient imaginable for any medical man in the Third Reich – the Reichsführer-SS, Heinrich Himmler.

Kersten had been introduced to Himmler by one of his patients, August Rosterg, a potash manufacturer and member of the 'Friends of the Reichsführer-SS.' According to Achim Besgen, Kersten's biographer, in March 1939 Kersten 'established that Himmler was suffering from a most painful disturbance of the nervous system; he was in great pain but Kersten was able to relieve him in a few minutes.' Himmler found this instantaneous cure almost incomprehensible saying: 'I have consulted many German professors and none of them could help me. Please help me, Professor.' Kersten explained to his new patient that he was neither a professor nor a doctor; nevertheless he allowed himself to be engaged as the ogre's personal physician.[129]

Kersten now hardly left Himmler's side. He had soon realized that his pain-killing hands gave him a power over Himmler which ended only where the magic of Adolf Hitler began. Himmler was open to any proposal from Kersten; no sooner had the masseur's fingers sunk into the Reichsführer's tortured body than even Himmler showed that he was still a human being. With every soothing movement of his hand Kersten could extract some unusual concession from his patient – in one case the release of some individual from a concentration camp, in another permission for some fugitive to leave Germany, in yet another the rescue of thousands of Jews from the 'final solution' machine. Kersten was always on hand to help, and frequently achieved the impossible. The list of those who owed their lives to him grew continually. For instance he saved Theodor Steltzer, later Minister-President of Schleswig-Holstein, from execution;[130] he stopped the annihilation of Finland's Jews; he prevented the theft of the Dutch art treasures;[131] he channelled the Scandinavian concentration-camp prisoners to neutral Sweden.

Eventually Himmler had such confidence in his cosmopolitan personal physician that by 1943 Kersten could act entirely on his own. He was allowed to leave his country house, Hartzwalde, north of Berlin, and move to Stockholm; using the code number 145 he was authorized to call Himmler at any moment.[132] The post-war world found Felix Kersten's story so fantastic and improbable that in 1947 the Dutch Government set up an historical commission under Professor Nicolaas Wilhelmus Posthumus, Director of the War History Institute, to inquire into the activities of the ex-Dutch Royal Physician. For three years the Commission interrogated both friends and enemies of Kersten; they examined the archives of many countries and Kersten's 800-page diary. In 1950 Posthumus pronounced judgement: Felix Kersten had rendered such outstanding service to mankind and to peace that he, Professor Posthumus, would make bold to say that history knew no comparable example of courageous philanthropy.[133] A major contributory factor to the Professor's conclusion was the adroitness with which Kersten contrived to instil into Himmler from early 1944 the erroneous belief that only by halting his murder programme could he gain sympathy and the ear of the Western Allies. With Himmler vacillating between subservience to Hitler and his own determination to survive, Kersten gradually weaned him away from the extreme 'Final Solution' policy, eventually persuading him that on the day when the Jewish annihilation programme halted, the door to negotiations with the Western powers would open automatically. Himmler was only too ready to believe Kersten's story.

Professor Posthumus was told by an SS-Obergruppenführer whose name he does not divulge: 'At dinner in Hegewaldheim [East Prussia] in early summer 1944 Kersten brought up the Jewish question. He did so without any preamble. The conversation was extremely lively and sharp words were used. Kersten was dogmatic. I was there myself. Kersten worried away like a terrier until Himmler finally agreed to make a fundamental change in the whole Jewish business – in favour of the Jews. "You will be pleased, Kersten," Himmler said at the end.'[134]

One of the first to see that something had changed was Adolf Eichmann, the 'Final Solution' expert. With his henchmen Krumey, Dannecker, Wisliceny, Nowak, Hunsche and Abromeit he had moved to Hungary in March 1944 to stage the final act in the genocide drama, the annihilation of Hungarian Jewry.[135] Since the Soviet armies were approaching, Eichmann urged his German and Hungarian executioners to hurry. Hungary's 900,000 Jews were driven into ghettos and the country was divided into six deportation zones: the indefatigable Eichmann had already ordered up his death trains from the Reichsbahn. The funeral procession to Auschwitz was ready to start.[136] Eichmann was preparing to move the Jews in the first two zones when he came into collision with another SS authority.

SS-Hauptsturmführer Otto Clages, head of the SD in Hungary, sensing that the end of the Thousand Year Reich was approaching, was searching in some trepidation for a method of insuring his own future after the catastrophe. His staff in Budapest included certain ex-members of Admiral Canaris' Abwehr. From them Clages learnt that they possessed contacts to a Zionist organization prepared to pay vast sums of money if Germany would put a stop to its extermination programme.[137]

In January 1943 three Zionists, Otto Komoly, an engineer, Rezso Kastner, a journalist, and Joel Brand, a dealer in knitwear, had formed a group which they called 'Waadat Ezra Vö-Hazzalah Bo-Budapest' (Waadah for short) meaning 'Jewish Rescue Committee, Budapest'. Their object was to assist the Jews of Germany, Poland and Slovakia to escape to Hungary, and from there to send them on their way to Palestine.[138] It occurred to them that they might be able to save the Jews by bribing the SS executioners and Kastner and Brand soon realized that behind the monolithic façade of the SS were men only too ready to be bought. The head executioner in Slovakia was SS-Hauptsturmführer Wisliceny who had already brought corruption in the SS to a fine art. In 1942 he had proposed that as part of the 'Europe Plan' the surviving European Jews (Poland excepted) should be spared from the 'Final Solution' if 'World Jewry' would pay a ransom of two to three million dollars.[139] When Waadah now heard that this same Wisliceny was a member of Eichmann's Special Einsatzkommando for Budapest, Kastner and Brand were full of hope that a little bribery might ease the lot of the Hungarian Jews. Early in April 1944 Kastner sought out Wisliceny and put to him a deal which he accepted at once.[140] Against payment of four million marks Wisliceny promised to allow 600 Jews to emigrate to Palestine. Kastner's committee paid the ransom, whereupon Wisliceny revoked, contemptuously rejecting all Kastner's pleas.[141]

Nevertheless Waadah pursued its ransom plan and looked for some more reliable opposite number in the army of murderers. In doing so Brand contacted, among others, members of the German Abwehr and it was by this means that early in April 1944 Clages of the SD heard of Waadah's proposal. He passed on the offer to Himmler, recommending the Reichsführer to negotiate with the Jewish Rescue Committee deliveries of war material for the Waffen-SS. This clearly roused Himmler's acquisitive instincts, for a few days later Eichmann received an order from the highest quarters to contact Joel Brand.[142]

Was avarice Himmler's only motive? Initially undoubtedly it was. It seems, however, that other considerations soon began to weigh and he began to wonder whether he might not be able to contact the Allies via Brand the Zionist and Waadah; Kastner and Brand after all had proclaimed that behind them stood the money and power of what the superstitious SS called 'World Jewry'. Brand's cousin, Andreas Biss, a Hungarian businessman and an active supporter of Waadah, who later became the most knowledgeable historian of the 'Final Solution' in Hungary, saw 'ever more clearly the picture of a Heinrich Himmler who initially hoped that his contact with us would bring him weapons and equipment to reinforce and expand his SS, but who then – not much later – was aiming at re-insurance via Washington. Moreover, as I noted later, this re-insurance was confined to himself alone and entirely excluded his Führer, Adolf Hitler.'[143]

As he read Himmler's order telling him to hold out to Waadah the prospect of an end to the murder programme, Eichmann must have been assailed by a small feeling of unease. On April 25th he summoned Brand

and proposed to him that the Hungarian Jews be struck out of the programme if World Jewry paid a price – and not in money but in kind. Eichmann's bill amounted to 10,000 trucks, 2 million cases of soap, 200 tons of tea and 200 tons of coffee.[144] Brand, Eichmann stipulated, was to go to Istanbul and there negotiate the deliveries with the representatives of the Jewish World Organization. At the same time, however, deportation of the Hungarian Jews would begin and would only be halted when Brand could produce World Jewry's agreement.[145] With many misgivings Waadah agreed but demanded that as a token of goodwill Eichmann should dispatch 'a sample train'. Brand's arrival in Istanbul, they said, must coincide with the arrival in some neutral country of 600 to 1,200 Hungarian Jews. Eichmann agreed and on May 17th, 1944 Brand left for Istanbul.[146]

Hardly had Brand packed his bags than Eichmann began to hunt the Jews of Hungary into his trains to Auschwitz. Brand was due back in Budapest in a fortnight at the latest and by that time, so Eichmann swore to himself, the majority of Hungarian Jewry must have been liquidated.[147] With the morbid persistence of a man who sees himself cheated of his ambition in life, Eichmann dispatched train after train to Auschwitz. His little mind had grasped the fact that the days of the 'Final Solution' were numbered; Kaltenbrunner and Gestapo Müller, his immediate superiors, were still firmly behind the murder programme, but a new tone was detectable in Himmler's instructions. So his deportation orders became more urgent and the Hungarian ghettos were emptied with increasing rapidity. By June 7th Zones 1 and 2 had been cleared and 289,357 Jews murdered in the gas chambers of Upper Silesia; by June 17th Zone 3 was clear and 50,805 Jews had been murdered in Auschwitz; by June 30th Zone 4 was free, with another 41,499 Jews murdered.[148]

Meanwhile Brand had apparently disappeared without trace (he had been cold-shouldered by the Jewish representatives in Istanbul and arrested by the British on his way through Syria).[149] And now there was no holding Eichmann. He used every method to sabotage the agreed transport of Jews abroad. He refused to assemble in Budapest the Jews selected for the 'sample train'. He was continually trying to reduce the number of Jews selected. He refused to allow Jews to leave Portugal as previously agreed.[150] No subterfuge was too devious for him if it would deny a few Jews their liberty. In vain Kastner appealed to the agreements already concluded; in vain he called for assistance from Clages. At last in desperation he turned to another of Himmler's Budapest representatives whom Eichmann regarded as his bitterest rival.

SS-Obersturmbannführer Kurt Becher was in charge of an armaments commission of the SS-Führungshauptamt whose job it was to obtain equipment for the Waffen-SS.[151] By a quirk of fate he was to put a spoke in the wheel of Eichmann's murder programme. While looking for 20,000 horses for the Waffen-SS, Becher made the acquaintance of a banker, Dr Franz Chorin, one of the shareholders of the largest industrial concern in Hungary, the Jewish-controlled Manfred Weiss works. Chorin was a connoisseur of horses and Becher a dedicated horseman; on receiving a couple of useful tips on sources of good horseflesh, Becher was only too willing to repay the good turn.[152]

The horse business brought the two so close together that Chorin eventually confided to Becher the troubles of the late Manfred Weiss family. Most of the Jewish members of the family wished to leave Hungary before they were caught by Eichmann's death machine and Chorin proposed that Becher might help – and do the SS a good turn in the process. Becher and the Weiss firm reached an agreement in which humanity and blackmail both played their parts: the SS took over the stock (55 per cent of the share capital) held by the 'Aryan' members of the Weiss family and allowed 48 (including 35 Jewish) members of the family to leave for Portugal, paying them compensation of 3,000,000 marks and retaining nine members of the family as hostages.[153] On May 17th, 1944 the agreement was signed and the Jewish industrial dynasty travelled to freedom.[154]

The agreement sparked off a deadly enmity between Becher and Eichmann, who now saw his 'Final Solution' programme being jeopardized by a fellow representative of Himmler. The Hungarian puppet government was already protesting against Becher's interference with the Hungarian economy and Eichmann was enraged by Becher's coup, for behind it he sensed a principle which to him was anathema – rescue of the Jews by ransom. In Becher's action Eichmann saw confirmation of his suspicion that, as the Nazi régime went down, even the Reichsführer was becoming 'soft' on the Jewish problem. Moreover Becher personified all that Eichmann hated – he was the 'SS Officer in kid gloves'. Even his smart uniform and his important position could not conceal the fact that Eichmann, the petit bourgeois, was still only on the fringe of society and he could not stand the sight of Becher, the businessman's son, the product of established Hamburg society, the SS cavalryman, the welcome guest in feudal mansions. To cap it all, by his agreement with Weiss this man had now become the last hope of the Jews.[155]

To Waadah Becher was exactly the man for whom they had been waiting to switch off Eichmann's death machine. He had a direct line to Himmler (he signed his letters 'the Reichsführer's most obedient Becher') and his negotiations over the Weiss family were precisely on the lines of Waadah's original programme. Kastner contrived to get in touch with him and sell him the idea of the sample train. In late July Becher flew off to see Himmler and returned with authority to negotiate with Waadah in Eichmann's stead.[156] Becher took up the 'sample train' plan with energy. He demanded a deposit of a certain sum in Hungary, the remainder to be paid when the train reached its destination. The price per head was $1,000. Kastner accepted.[157] On June 30th the train left Budapest carrying 1,684 Jews.[158]

Nevertheless Eichmann was not to be defeated. On his own authority he diverted the train to Belsen concentration camp,[159] and meanwhile Himmler changed course once more. Reports appearing in the British and American Press on Joel Brand's mission and the 'trucks-for-Jews' deal showed clearly that neither the Jewish organizations nor the Allied Governments were in a mood to do business.[160] Triumphantly Eichmann threatened Waadah that 'the inmates of the sample train now located in Belsen would be moved to Auschwitz in a week's time and there fed into the "mill" as they arrived' unless by that time Brand had returned to Budapest carrying the agreement of the Jewish World Organization.[161] Kastner and Biss rushed to their friend Becher to ask for help; but Becher cold-shouldered them; the 'Reichsführer's most obedient Becher' had sensed the wind of change from Himmler's headquarters and refused to assist.[162] This time, however, Clages of the SD came to the rescue. He asked Biss to draft a memorandum setting out Waadah's new financial proposals and forwarded it to Himmler.[163] On July 26th, 1944 he told Biss that 'my memorandum has been favourably received in Berlin and Himmler has given instructions for deportations from Hungary to cease until further notice' – at least this is what Biss says in his memoirs.[164] So an initial success had been achieved; the death march to Auschwitz was halted for a time.

At this point Becher plucked up his courage once more and flew off to see Himmler again. The latter agreed that 500 Jews from the sample train might go abroad immediately; regarding the finance for the transfer of the remainder, Becher was to discuss matters with representatives of the Jewish-American Aid Organization, the 'American Joint Distribution Committee' in Switzerland.[165] At last Himmler could see the door to negotiations with the Western powers opening a crack. Being convinced that America was in the grip of world Jewry, Himmler genuinely believed that if an offer of negotiations was made by Waadah, the 'American Joint Distribution Committee' could provide a direct line to the White House in Washington and that this would lead to a separate peace between Germany and the Western Allies. Waadah did its best to foster this crazy notion. Biss recalls: 'We were continually referring to

President Roosevelt as our benefactor.'[166] The gullible Himmler swallowed Waadah's every word on their fictitious relationship with Washington.

The SS leaders now proceeded to bring pressure to bear on their Jewish partners to open the door to negotiations with the West. After all, Clages said to Biss, the rescue of a few hundred thousand Jews was not the point; the Swiss negotiations might lead to 'a development of international and historic significance'.[167] But Becher soon saw through Waadah's propaganda game. At his first meeting on August 21st, 1944 with the Swiss Federal banker Saly Mayer in the frontier town of St Margarethe, Becher realized that the Jewish organizations were not to be persuaded to agree to the trucks-for-Jews deal. Mayer was only willing to talk if Himmler first announced the official end of the murder programme and had released all the inmates of the sample train.[168]

A single report from Becher to Himmler would have sufficed to bring the negotiations with the Distribution Committee to an end but Becher did not tell his Reichsführer the true situation. He glossed over Mayer's unforthcoming statements and so dragged the vacillating, hesitating and timorous Himmler ever deeper into the jungle of anti-Hitler intrigue.[169] Whether Becher was genuinely concerned for the fate of the Jews, or whether he himself believed in the possibility of a separate peace once Hitler had gone, the fact remains that he played Waadah's game. When Hauptsturmführer Max Grüson, Becher's aide, saw Mayer on September 1st, he begged the Swiss to make at least one or two concessions, even at the risk of being disowned by the Joint Distribution Committee.[170]

But Mayer and the Distribution Committee would give no concrete assurances and Becher would have had to admit the failure of his efforts, had not Roosevelt announced at the end of September that he was dispatching Roswell D. McClellan, the Quaker leader, to Switzerland as his personal representative – with the specific purpose of participating in the negotiations between the SS and the Distribution Committee.[171] This was precisely the news for which Himmler had been waiting for months. He reacted at once; on September 30th he informed Waadah that he had finally authorized suspension of the 'actions' in Auschwitz (which was anyway now threatened by advancing Soviet Forces); in mid-October he decided that the remaining inmates of the sample train might leave for Switzerland whether the ransom had been paid or not.

For a moment it looked as if the United States would respond to Himmler's gesture. McClellan expressed a desire to meet Becher, and the US legation in Berne busied itself obtaining Swiss entry visas for Himmler's representatives.[172] On November 5th, 1944 McClellan and Becher met in the Savoy Hotel, Baur-en-Ville, Zurich.[173] Biss reports: 'That this meeting took place at all, when the Allies had agreed that all negotiations with Germany should be tripartite and based on unconditional surrender, must have seemed to Himmler an important – if not the most important – result of his contact with us. Technically, moreover, the meeting was a breach of the Teheran Agreement whereby the Western Allies had agreed with Stalin to maintain a complete boycott of the Third Reich.'[174]

But the hopes which Himmler and Becher had placed in these discussions did not materialize. Himmler recalled Eichmann from Hungary and, in December, the remaining members of the Budapest sample train arrived in Switzerland; further negotiations foundered, however, on the refusal of the Jewish organizations to repay Himmler's gesture either in money or in kind.[175] There was, however, another SS leader who, as we have seen, had long been trying to move his Reichsführer to take action against Adolf Hitler and he found encouragement in these Swiss negotiations.

For more than two years SS-Brigadeführer Walter Schellenberg, Head of the Ausland-SD, had been urging Himmler to do something to put an end to the war and guarantee the SS some future in the post-Hitler world. Like Himmler, he believed that the way to negotiations with the Allies lay via the Jewish hostages and he therefore sought the acquaintanceship of prominent Jews abroad. In Montreux he contacted the Sternbuch brothers, two orthodox Jews representing the American Rabbinate in Switzerland.[176] Like Becher, Schellenberg offered them the chance of rescuing Jews from the grip of Himmler. From the Sternbuchs Schellenberg's contacts led to Dr Jean-Marie Musy, President of the Swiss Altbund, who was disposed, for humanitarian reasons, to take a hand in Schellenberg's double-faced game.[177]

Early in October 1944 Musy declared himself ready to go to Germany and discuss the fate of the Jews with Himmler.[178] The two met near Vienna. After some initial hesitation, Himmler declared himself ready gradually to release all Jews in German custody and allow them to travel to Switzerland.[179] In his memoirs Schellenberg states that Himmler thereupon dictated in his presence an instruction to Kaltenbrunner, the Head of the RSHA, that the lives of all Jews in concentration camps were to be spared.[180] At the Nuremberg trial, however, Becher, now a corn merchant in Bremen, claimed that he was responsible; he could even remember Himmler's exact words: 'By this order, which becomes effective immediately, I forbid any extermination of Jews and order that on the contrary care should be given to weak and sick persons.'[181]

Whoever was responsible, the fact remains that Himmler had issued an order liable to bring him into sharp conflict with Hitler. It amounted to nothing less than total disregard of Adolf Hitler's directive that the final solution of the Jewish question was to be pursued without regard to the war situation. Heinrich Himmler had taken the first step on the road away from his demigod. Schellenberg kept up the pressure. Now was the moment when he must finally cut the ties between the Dictator and his Chief of Police. The next move was made by Kersten, who was doing his utmost to bring about Schellenberg's dream of weaning Himmler away from his Führer. Kersten had just received an appeal for assistance from the Swedish Government, which was in a state of acute political embarrassment.

The Swedes were being subjected to increasing Allied pressure to enter the war against Hitler and, in the hope of postponing a decision, the Swedish Government had decided to undertake a spectacular rescue operation. Sweden declared herself ready to provide food for all inmates of concentration camps and accept any prisoners released.[182] The Swedish Foreign Ministry applied to Himmler but he rejected all Swedish offers of help. The Foreign Minister, von Günther, thereupon turned to Kersten who was living in Stockholm, and asked him to assist. Kersten worked on his patient so persistently that Himmler eventually gave way.[183] On December 8th, 1944, in Himmler's command post at Triberg in the Black Forest, Kersten and Himmler concluded an agreement. Its provisions were that all Scandinavian concentration-camp prisoners should be moved to an assembly camp at Neuengamme near Hamburg; the prisoners were to be fed by the Swedish Red Cross; 1,000 Dutch, 800 French, 500 Polish, 400 Belgian, 50 Danish and 50 Norwegian women were to be released; all transport to be carried out in Swedish buses.[184]

Günther tendered his thanks to Kersten and passed the word to Himmler that Sweden would make the buses and transport personnel available. This was on January 1st, 1945.[185] But the Swedes were in no hurry, obviously hoping that the rapidly developing war situation would save them the necessity of carrying out this burdensome rescue operation. Not until February 5th did Günther make his next move, informing Kersten that the transport operation would be under the direction of Count Folke Bernadotte, a nephew of the King of Sweden and Vice-President of the Swedish Red Cross.[186] Further weeks passed in inactivity with Schellenberg and Kersten impatiently awaiting the arrival of the man who, they intended, should finally prise Himmler loose from his Führer.

At last, on February 16th, 1945, Count Bernadotte left Bromma Airport, Stockholm, and flew to besieged and burning Hitler Germany.[187]

The first SS officer to greet him on his arrival at Tempelhof Airport was Walter Schellenberg and he accompanied the Count to Kaltenbrunner, whom protocol dictated should be the first port of call.[188] Bernadotte recognized at once that Schellenberg had only one object – to leave the sinking ship. In his memoirs he says: 'I am quite willing to admit that from the first I felt a certain confidence in Schellenberg.'[189] Nevertheless, Schellenberg did not find it easy to win Bernadotte over to his and Kersten's plan. Moreover Himmler was still hesitant and regarded the arrival of the Swede with a mixture of curiosity and fear – fear because he knew that Kaltenbrunner was watching Schellenberg's every move with suspicion. At Kaltenbrunner's instigation Fegelein had inquired of the Dictator how Bernadotte's visit should be handled and had received the answer: 'One cannot accomplish anything with this sort of nonsense in a total war.'[190] Schellenberg had to argue with his master at great length before Himmler could be persuaded to receive Bernadotte but finally, on February 19th, the introduction was made in the SS Hospital at Hohenlychen.[191]

Himmler emphasized at the outset: 'I have sworn loyalty to Adolf Hitler and as a soldier and as a German I cannot go back on my oath. Because of this, I cannot do anything in opposition to the Führer's plans and wishes.'[192] After two and a half hours, however, he thought somewhat differently. He allowed Bernadotte to move a proportion of the Scandinavian concentration-camp prisoners to Norway and confirmed what he had already agreed with Kersten, namely that the Swedish Red Cross might provide food for the Nordic prisoners.[193]

No sooner had Bernadotte flown back to Sweden than Schellenberg turned on his Reichsführer the full force of his indefatigable argumentative powers. Ceaselessly he hammered at Himmler, always with the same argument – finish with Hitler, finish with the war. Trevor-Roper describes the process thus: 'In the niche of Himmler's private worship, from which the idol of Hitler was thus gradually crumbling away, Schellenberg substituted slowly and tentatively, and against stubborn and despairing resistance from the worshipper, a new and even more appropriate image: the image of Himmler himself crowned as the second Führer, the second incarnation of the spirit of Aryan Germany.'[194] Tirelessly Schellenberg urged that use must now be made of Bernadotte and that he should be dispatched to General Eisenhower's headquarters with an offer of capitulation. Himmler recoiled in horror. Nevertheless he was so shaken by Schellenberg's arguments that he gave his tormentor permission to use his own initiative in persuading Bernadotte to undertake the mission to the Allies.

On April 2nd Bernadotte visited Himmler once more.[195] At a certain point Himmler was called to the telephone in the next room and Schellenberg seized his moment to ask 'if I could not see Eisenhower to discuss with him the possibilities of arranging a capitulation on the Western Front.'[196] Bernadotte refused, saying that the initiative must come from Himmler. But Schellenberg now went to work on Bernadotte; on the way back to Berlin he 'talked the whole way in a confidential but rather forced manner'.[197] Bernadotte was prepared to go to Eisenhower only if Himmler would declare himself Hitler's successor, dissolve the NSDAP and release all Scandinavian prisoners. He says: 'Personally I never imagined that Himmler would accept these conditions but Schellenberg did not hesitate. He told me that he would try to induce his Chief to accept them.'[198] Schellenberg went to work again; in his view Himmler's stock in the Führer's headquarters had now fallen so low that his master had no other choice but to strike against Hitler to save his own skin.

'So you are demanding that I depose the Führer?' asked Himmler. 'Yes,' replied Schellenberg.[199] He knew, however, that Himmler would never make up his mind unless it could be proved to him that Adolf Hitler's life was nearly at an end anyway, so he sent his friend Max de Crinis, Professor of Medicine and Director of the Neurological Clinic of the Berlin Charité, to tell the Reichsführer that Hitler was a very sick man, almost totally paralysed and suffering from Parkinson's disease. Himmler's conclusion was: 'Schellenberg, I believe nothing more can be done with Hitler.'[200]

But Himmler was still unable to make up his mind. He dreamed of himself as the saviour of Germany but could not break loose from his Nazi superstitions. He planned the death of the Dictator but could not free himself from Hitler's influence. He knew that the war was lost but exhorted the Germans to hold on. As late as April 1st he was telling the Hamburg Nazi City Council that disagreements among the Allies and the imminent entry into service of the German jet fighters would produce a decisive breathing-space.[201] On April 13th, when he heard that Obergruppenführer Karl Wolff, his HSSPF in Italy, had been negotiating with Allen Dulles in Switzerland, his immediate reaction was 'disloyalty to the Führer.'[202]

Wolff had been on close personal terms with Himmler, having served him for years, first as senior aide and then as Head of his Personal Staff; he knew all the murkiest secrets of SS headquarters. Yet that same night Himmler called him peremptorily to account, ordering him to report in person forthwith. Wolff agreed, but then sent his master a letter informing him drily that he could not come.[203] On April 14th Himmler once more called Wolff at his headquarters on Lake

Garda. Twice he ordered Wolff to report at once and twice Wolff ignored the order.[204] Then Wolff asked Dulles' advice and the American recommended him to place himself out of Himmler's reach and take refuge in Switzerland with his family.[205] Wolff, however, decided otherwise; trusting to his personal charm, he took the risk of meeting Himmler. He wished to find out how much Himmler knew of his negotiations with the Allies.[206]

Wolff's journey to Berlin might well have been a journey to death, for he had dared to do what no other of Adolf Hitler's generals had done – he had agreed with the enemy on the capitulation of one million German soldiers.

Though Wolff was a Nazi 'Believer in God,' an audience of Pope Pius XII in April 1944 had marked a turning point in his life. SS-Standartenführer Dr Eugen Dollmann, a historian, interpreter and Wolff's liaison officer to Mussolini's republic, had used his contacts in Roman society to arrange an audience and the Pope was impressed by Wolff. 'How much misery might have been avoided if God had led you to me earlier,' he said.[207] Wolff could never forget the Pope's parting words: 'You are steering a difficult course, General Wolff. Allow me to send you on your dangerous road with my blessing on you and your family.' Even at that time Wolff had hinted that he had long since known that Germany was defeated and that, using his own special channels, he might be able to bring fighting in Italy to an end.[208]

Negotiations had in fact reached an advanced stage as early as February. Here again Dollmann, with his knowledge of Italy and his manifold connexions, had been the intermediary. One of his contacts, Baron Luigi Parilli, a Milan businessman with numerous influential Swiss friends, had passed the word to Swiss Secret-Service officers and thence to Dulles in Berne, that the commanders of the German Army in Italy would be interested in a cessation of hostilities.[209] Dulles demanded some gesture of good-will and Wolff immediately released two of his most prominent prisoners, leaders of the Italian partisan movement.[210] Dollmann then went to Switzerland and negotiated with the Americans. He was followed by Wolff.[211] The decision was taken on March 8th, 1945 – SS-Obergruppenführer Wolff agreed to a German capitulation in Italy.[212] Inhibited by a perverted sense of loyalty to their oaths as officers, however, the German Army commanders postponed the actual signing from week to week. First Field-Marshal Kesselring and then Colonel-General von Vietinghoff, his successor as Commander-in-Chief in Italy, took fright[213] and meanwhile news of Wolff's visits to Switzerland reached Himmler.[214]

So on his flight to Berlin Wolff was wondering whether Hitler knew of his pact with Dulles and whether therefore he would be arrested when he arrived: he landed near Berlin on April 16th, the day on which Zhukov launched his last great attack on Berlin – and so opened the final chapter in the history of the Third Reich.[215]

A few hours later Wolff was in Himmler's presence. But Himmler could not bring himself openly to accuse his 'little Wolff' of treachery and left it to his old friend Gebhardt to interrogate his HSSPF. The two withdrew to the Adlon Hotel in Berlin.[216] Wolff had thought up a convincing story. Yes, he had negotiated with Dulles but only on an exchange of prisoners of war; moreover he had only been following the Führer's instructions, given him in February, to seize every opportunity of playing the Allies off against each other. That was what he, Obergruppenführer Wolff, had been doing.[217]

Himmler accepted Wolff's story, relieved that his old friend had not been disloyal to the Führer. Suddenly, however, Kaltenbrunner, the Head of the RSHA, entered the room with an ominous request that he might speak with Himmler alone. Kaltenbrunner was the bearer of dangerous news for Wolff; an informer had just reported that Wolff had been negotiating with Cardinal Schuster of Milan for the capitulation of the German Army in Italy and that the entire German Southern Front might collapse at any moment. With Kaltenbrunner urging him on, Himmler turned furiously on Wolff but the latter assured them: 'I have never personally negotiated with Cardinal Schuster concerning capitulation.' Nevertheless Wolff's back was against the wall. He realized that only a bold move could save him.[218]

Wolff therefore acted the injured innocent, saying that he must now ask the Reichsführer and Comrade Kaltenbrunner to accompany him to the Führer and in his presence repeat their scandalous statements. There and only there would he justify himself. Himmler went white; he did not dare go to Hitler. He decided that it would suffice if Kaltenbrunner accompanied Wolff to the Führer's bunker.[219]

The two SS men entered the bunker at 3 AM on April 18th, 1945. In the corridor they met Hitler shuffling along and he greeted Wolff: 'Ah! You're here Wolff. Good. Please wait until the briefing is over.'[220]

At 4 AM the two were summoned to Hitler. Casually the Dictator asked what Wolff had been doing with Dulles. Wolff explained that on February 6th he, the Führer, had told him in the presence of the Foreign Minister that, should the introduction of the new secret weapons be delayed, the next step should be to negotiate with the Allies. 'Now I am happy to be able to report to you, my Führer,' he said, 'that I have succeeded in opening doors through Mr Dulles to the

President, Prime Minister Churchill and Field-Marshal Alexander. I request instructions for the future.' Hitler accepted Wolff's story and ordered him to report again in the afternoon when he explained his plans for the future – incomprehensible ravings which clearly confirmed to Wolff that Adolf Hitler was near losing his reason.[221]

For a moment the tyrant gazed searchingly at his visitor and then held out his trembling hand. His final words were: 'Go back to Italy. Keep up your relationship with the Americans but see that you get better terms. Stall a bit. Give my best wishes to my friend the Duce. To you my thanks and my appreciation.'[222] Wolff was saved. Hurriedly he flew back to his Italian headquarters, there to sign the capitulation on April 29th. Dollmann now found that he had 'time to fulfil my vow; while Wolff was away I had sworn that, should we be saved, I would light a candle to my Madonna del Rosario who was ever present in my thoughts.'[223]

Himmler's 'little Wolff' was not the only SS leader to desert Adolf Hitler. Three SS-Obergruppenführer, Felix Steiner, Curt von Gottberg and Richard Hildebrandt, were considering a plan to murder him and so put an end to the war.[224] Even Kaltenbrunner, the régime's watchdog, had sent SS-Sturmbannführer Dr Wilhelm Höttl to Switzerland at the end of February to offer Dulles the surrender of Austria.[225] The most striking proof that the ties between Hitler and the SS were now cut, however, was provided by the Waffen-SS.

At the end of March the last great attack (in Hungary) by 6 SS Panzer Army under Sepp Dietrich had collapsed in face of the enemy's overwhelming superiority and the Dictator's contempt and rage had descended on the heads of his beloved Waffen-SS. Field-Marshal Keitel telegraphed to Dietrich: 'The Führer believes that the troops have not fought as the situation demanded and orders that the SS divisions "Adolf Hitler", "Das Reich", "Totenkopf" and "Hohenstaufen" be stripped of their armbands' (carrying the name of the division).[226]

The Waffen-SS soldiers were so incensed that they implicitly believed the current story – Dietrich was said to have summoned his divisional commanders, slammed Keitel's telegram on the table and shouted: 'That's all the thanks you get for all you've done in the last five years.' He proposed to return his decorations to Hitler and tell the Führer that rather than carry out his order he would shoot himself. The only known fact is that Dietrich ignored his Führer's order. He did not go as far as did a certain SS-Sturmbannführer commanding the assault group which had penetrated farthest into the enemy positions during the Hungary offensive. When he heard of Hitler's order he turned furiously to his officers saying: 'Let's take a chamber pot, put all our medals in it and tie around it the ribbon of the "Götz von Berlichingen"* division.'[227]

This was a somewhat crude method of giving notice that the SS had renounced the tyrant still crouched in his bunker in Berlin, bent on self-destruction. For thousands upon thousands of SS men their whole world was collapsing. Small groups of fanatics fought on, hounding themselves senselessly into death, the scourge and terror of the civil population to the very end; but the mass of the SS Order was not prepared to commit their officially ordered suicide. At the battle of Waterloo when Napoleon's Old Guard had fired its last cartridge and, surrounded by British cavalry, was summoned to lay down its arms, the French General Cambronne is supposed to have said: 'The Guard dies, it does not surrender.' Though the remark was never in fact made, it was and is the motto of every Imperial Guard; it is the essence and justification of a military élite. But Hitler's Guard did not fire its last cartridge; the SS surrendered before it was totally surrounded by the enemy. Little by little the SS commanders gave up the fight.

In blind self-torturing indecision, however, Himmler was still feeling his way through the moonscape of the Nazi régime, driven fearfully hither and thither between the urgings of his adviser Schellenberg and the ghostly figure in the Führer's bunker. Schellenberg would not let go: Himmler must make up his mind at last. Schellenberg had found a new ally in Graf Schwerin von Krosigk, the Finance Minister, who on April 19th implored Himmler to liberate Germany from the madman in the Reich Chancellery and make peace.[228] Meanwhile Schellenberg and Franz Seldte, the ex-Stahlhelm leader, drew up a Government programme for Himmler providing for the deposition of Hitler, the dissolution of the Party, the abolition of the People's Courts and negotiations for capitulation.[229] When even this appeal did not rouse Himmler to act, Schellenberg summoned yet another ally. Kersten arrived from Stockholm, bringing with him the most memorable visitor imaginable for the Reichsführer-SS – Norbert Masur, the official representative of the Jewish World Congress. On April 19th Schellenberg met Masur at Tempelhof Airfield and a few hours later they reached Kersten's estate, Hartzwalde.[230]

But Himmler could not be contacted. He was already on his way to the Führer's bunker, for it was April 20th, 1945, Hitler's birthday. Himmler was determined to pay his last reverence to his Führer. The Head of the SS could not be absent from the eerie birthday court which the Dictator held in the courtyard of the Reich Chancellery.[231] On the

* Götz von Berlichingen was a choleric knight in Goethe's play, who said to the Bishop of Bamberg, 'Kiss my arse.'

return journey, however, Himmler once more adopted the pose of the determined saviour of Germany. 'Have you contacts to General Eisenhower?' he asked Kersten when he arrived at Hartzwalde. Kersten had not. Himmler thereupon asked whether he was willing to go to Eisenhower and negotiate the capitulation. Kersten, obviously prompted by Schellenberg, suggested Count Bernadotte as the most suitable personality to make contact with Eisenhower.[232] A few hours later (on April 21st) Bernadotte arrived, hurriedly summoned by Schellenberg, but Himmler's courage had evaporated once more. 'The military situation is grave, very grave,' Himmler whispered, but he made no mention of the Eisenhower plan. Bernadotte departed in puzzlement.[233]

No one in the Führer's headquarters realized at this time how close the faithful Himmler was to deserting his Führer. On the contrary, immured in his Chancellery the Dictator pinned his last desperate, crazy hopes upon the SS, now personified for him by one man – Steiner. 'Steiner, Steiner,' Hitler kept mumbling, searching across the map with his magnifying glass. His quivering finger came to rest at a point north-east of Berlin where Felix Steiner, SS-Obergruppenführer and General of the Waffen-SS, had made a stand with a handful of worn-out units.[234] 'Army Group Steiner' – this was the force which Hitler believed would liberate Berlin from the Soviet armies, now almost entirely surrounding the city.

On April 21st Hitler ordered Steiner to move south to Eberswalde, break through the Soviet flank and re-establish the crumbling German defences south-east of Berlin. 'You will see. The Russians will suffer their greatest defeat, the bloodiest defeat of their history, before the gates of Berlin.'[235] Hitler warned him: 'It is expressly forbidden to fall back to the West. Officers who do not comply unconditionally with this order are to be arrested and shot immediately. You, Steiner, are answerable with your head for execution of this order.'[236]

Throughout April 22nd Hitler waited for Steiner to launch his great offensive. Hour after hour went by but Steiner failed to issue the order to attack. To send 10,000 men into battle against 100,000 seemed to him to be total lunacy.[237] Again and again Hitler inquired how far Steiner's attack had progressed. The soldiers of the staff knew only too well that Steiner would never attack but they kept their knowledge to themselves. Not until the afternoon did Hitler learn the truth.[238] Then he cracked. Screaming and raging, he accused his staff of treachery and cowardice. Everyone had let him down, first the Wehrmacht, now even the SS. The National-Socialist concept was lost; it had no further purpose. He would not leave Berlin but would die in his capital. Transfixed, the staff gazed at their Führer as, shaken by sobs and howling, he suddenly slumped back in his chair.[239]

But no one was prepared to suggest to the madman that he abdicate and surrender. Everyone attempted to uphold the broken Führer, everyone had a word of encouragement – and leading them was Heinrich Himmler who, when informed over the telephone of the Dictator's outburst of rage, begged Hitler to leave Berlin and continue the battle in southern Germany. Then, one after another, they turned on the unhappy Steiner, urging him to make the last sacrifice for his Führer. Keitel, Jodl, Krebs – all were only too ready to descend on Steiner's headquarters and drive him into the attack; they requested, they implored, they threatened.[240] Colonel-General Heinrici, whose only concern was that the front should hold, urged: 'But Steiner, this is for your Führer; he is relying on you to save him!' Keitel threatened Steiner This attack is nonsense – murder. Do what you want to me.'[241] Still with his Marshal's baton but Steiner remained firm: 'No, I won't do it. Hitler waited for reports from Steiner but on April 27th he gave up hope. He ordered the dismissal of Obergruppenführer Steiner and his replacement by an Army officer, Lieutenant-General Holste.[242] Yet once more Steiner sabotaged a Führer order: he persuaded Holste to leave him in command.[243]

Twenty-four hours later an officer of the Ministry of Propaganda arrived in the Führer's bunker with a report substantiating all Hitler's nightmares. Lorenz had intercepted a dispatch from Paul Scott Rankine, Reuter's correspondent in San Francisco, to the effect that the Reichsführer-SS Heinrich Himmler had offered the Western Allies the capitulation of Germany. Walter Schellenberg had finally triumphed over his timorous idolatrous master.[244]

The men in the Führer's bunker were paralysed by the news. At this point Werner Naumann, State Secretary in the Propaganda Ministry, was called to the telephone and returned with an even more circumstantial, though still unconfirmed, report. Radio Stockholm had just announced that Himmler was already negotiating with the Anglo-American High Command.[245] The Dictator looked up. A whimper escaped him – the full extent of SS villainy had been revealed. Now he knew why Steiner had not attacked, why the SS offensive in Hungary had broken down, why Himmler had failed on the Vistula. It was all a gigantic conspiracy engineered by that evil intriguer whom he had once called the 'faithful Heinrich'. But as long as blood ran in his veins he still had the strength to smash the traitors. 'A traitor must never succeed me as Führer,' he screamed; he summoned Field-Marshal Ritter von Greim and ordered him to fly out of beleaguered Berlin and arrest Himmler at all costs.[246]

Hitler would no longer tolerate any SS officer in his presence; every SS man was suspect as a member of the vast gang of traitors. On hearing that his brother-in-law Hermann Fegelein, an SS-Gruppenführer and Himmler's chief representative, had left the bunker on his own and been seen in civilian clothes, he had him shot in the courtyard of the Reich Chancellery.[247] In his last will and testament he declaimed: 'Before my death I expel from the Party and all his offices of State the former Reichsführer-SS and Minister of the Interior Heinrich Himmler . . . By secretly negotiating with the enemy without my knowledge and against my will, as also by attempting illegally to seize power in the State, Göring and Himmler have done the country and the people immeasurable harm, quite apart from their infidelity to me personally.'[248]

Two days later Adolf Hitler was dead, but his faithless servant still believed in a future in which he, Heinrich Himmler, would direct the fate of Germany. The Allies had long since rejected Himmler's unilateral offer of capitulation, yet the Reichsführer continued to hope.

He imagined himself founding a new Nazi party to be known as the 'Party of National Union'.[249] He planned a post-war Government in which one of the Ministers was to be Otto Ohlendorf, the head of the Inland SD, with whom he had so long been at loggerheads.[250] He drew up a new Government programme. But as the Great German Reich disintegrated under the Allies' armoured thrusts, so Himmler's hopes and hallucinations shrank to a more modest scale. He started determined to be the Führer of post-war Germany. Then he coveted the position of No 2 to Karl Dönitz, Hitler's successor, and fled to his headquarters in Flensburg.[251] Then he was prepared to be content with the post of Chief of Police.[252] Finally the job of Minister-President in Schleswig-Holstein seemed adequate.[253]

When Admiral Dönitz's rump régime collapsed, Himmler realized that he was a lost man. Graf Schwerin von Krosigk knew what he must be feeling – he was keeping control of himself only with difficulty mumbling: 'Discipline, gentlemen, discipline.'[254] Von Krosigk told him: 'It must not happen that the Reichsführer decks himself out with a false name and a false beard. There is no other way for you but to go to Montgomery and say "Here I am." It is then that you must assume the responsibility for your men.'[255]

Himmler, however, was proposing to do exactly what von Krosigk had warned him against. On May 20th, 1945 he put on an eye-patch and Field Security Police uniform, carrying in his pocket a pass in the name of Heinrich Hitzinger, a man not unlike Himmler who had been condemned to death by a People's Court.[256] Then the Reichsführer-SS set forth on his exit from history. With a few faithful followers including Ohlendorf, Brandt, his personal assistant, Karl Gebhardt and Grothmann, his aide, Himmler marched through Holstein, crossed the Elbe and attempted to slip through the British check points. But the British had their eyes open. On May 23rd Himmler's little group was captured and at 2 PM British Military Police handed them over to interrogation camp No 031 near Lüneburg.[257]

When the new arrivals were paraded in front of Captain Tom Selvester, the Camp Commandant, three of them caught his eye. Two were tall but the third was 'a small miserable-looking and shabbily dressed man.' He ordered the three to step forward, the two larger men he dispatched to solitary confinement then – in Selvester's own words – 'the small man who was wearing a black patch over his left eye removed the patch and put on a pair of spectacles. His identity was at once obvious and he said "Heinrich Himmler" in a very quiet voice.'[258]

Selvester immediately alerted Military Intelligence. Two officers of the Intelligence Corps soon appeared. They were followed that evening by Colonel Michael Murphy, head of Secret Intelligence on Field-Marshal Montgomery's staff. Murphy immediately suspected that Himmler had poison concealed somewhere and that he would take it the moment he was left unguarded. The British had in fact already found a phial of poison in Himmler's clothing, but Murphy was still not satisfied. He summoned a doctor, who examined Himmler once more. Himmler opened his mouth and the doctor caught a glimpse of something black between his teeth. As the doctor began to twist his head towards the light Himmler turned and snapped his teeth together with a crunch. The hidden phial of cyanide burst and in a few seconds Himmler breathed his last.[259]

May 23rd, 1945: Heinrich Himmler was dead: the history of the SS was at an end. In the smoke of National-Socialism's funeral pyre the SS Order dissolved, that fearsome instrument, symbol of an epoch, for in the SS had been reflected all the crime to which men can be led by lust for power, glorification of the State, the cult of personality and undiscriminating servility.

Only a few SS leaders followed their Grand Master's example and committed suicide. Globocnik took poison;[260] Grawitz, the SS Medical Officer-in-Chief, blew himself and his family up with a couple of hand-grenades;[261] Conti, the denouncer of Stennes, committed suicide in his cell in Nuremberg;[262] Friedrich-Welhelm Krüger, the HSSPF, committed suicide[263] and Prützmann, another HSSPF, did the same, not far from Himmler's camp.[264] The Allied Military Tribunals and the

European People's Courts laid hands on the most important of Himmler's minions and exacted due vengeance.

Many SS leaders were executed: Höss, the Commandant of Auschwitz,[265] Jeckeln and Rauter, the HSSPF;[266] Kaltenbrunner, Pohl and Daluege, the heads of the Hauptämter;[267] Ohlendorf and Naumann, Commanders of Einsatzgruppen;[268] Greiser, Forster and Seyss-Inquart, Honorary SS commanders.[269] The majority of the SS leaders, however, were treated with remarkable leniency. There survived: 16 out of 30 HSSPF, 8 out of 12 Heads of Hauptämter, 3 out of 6 Heads of Division in the RSHA, 3 out of 8 Commanders of Einsatzgruppen in Russia. The majority of the survivors were sentenced to periods of imprisonment but later pardoned and released. Some of the murkiest figures of the SS underworld escaped completely, the most notable being Eichmann who, however, was tracked down by Israeli agents in 1960 and condemned to death in Jerusalem two years later. Many of his most important minions, however, managed to disappear – Alois Brunner, Günther, Dannecker and Röthke; Gestapo Müller and Glücks, the Inspector of Concentration Camps, also vanished.

The mass of SS men, however, went into captivity to meet a fate which could be alleviated neither by the sentence of a court nor by some pronouncement of innocence. In the wooden huts and on the parade grounds of the Allied prisoner-of-war camps a great debate began – and it is not finished yet – the debate of the disillusioned and the defeated, the defiant and the retrospective, the ashamed and the broken. They were tortured by a sense of guilt and sin. Many were unable to still the nagging question: how had it come to pass that with enthusiasm and self-surrender young men had turned into unthinking instruments of force, into slaves to a perverted notion of loyalty and honour which had made every member of the SS a morally defenceless executive functionary of the Führer's will?

They could, of course, excuse themselves personally and shrug off the burden of collective guilt by saying that of one million SS men at most 50,000 had actually taken part in the more gruesome crimes.[270] But such an answer did not satisfy many; they dug deeper. Something had happened to make them susceptible to the call of barbarism, to the lust for power of unscrupulous small-timers concealed behind a façade of patriotism and socialism. The history of the SS unrolled itself before their eyes like a film. It told of a lost generation, brought up in the black pessimism of the anti-bourgeois cultural reaction and therefore attracted to an Order which promised them action and adventure as members of a primitive community serving a supposed genius and an ideal.

They had entered the SS Order because it satisfied two innate yearnings peculiar to the Germans: the yearning to belong to a military community promising fame, security and the glitter of martial exercises, and the yearning to form part of a secret élite, an all-powerful secret society. To many Germans, after all, the words 'politics' and 'government' meant simply the rule of occult forces, secret circles and *éminences grises*. The SS Order was the answer to such daydreams; anyone who joined the SS became overnight one of the lords of the nation, a member of a secret society of selected noblemen, the main prop of the National-Socialist State.

They had been devoted disciples because they believed in what was preached to them – 'popular togetherness' [Volksgemeinschaft], service to their country and a new social order. And they did not perceive the gradual debasement of the élite order into a bodyguard of thugs serving no other purpose than to do the dirty work for an unscrupulous unbridled dictator and his clique. The mental anguish of the SS dated from the 'Röhm putsch' of June 30th, 1934, the day of the SA murders; that was the start of the journey into the abyss, of the slow destruction of everything – of freedom, decency, humanity, and finally of the word which was always on the lips of the SS knights, the Reich.

In one of these prison-camp discussions, the former SS-Untersturmführer Erich Kernmeyr shouted: 'When our troops marched into Czechoslovakia after Munich did we say "No" in our heart of hearts? Did we then say "no" even to ourselves? No, a thousand times no! We were intoxicated by a vision of world power. It gripped the people like a great frenzy. The frenzy of power.'[271] This march of the devotees of power knew no limits and disregarded all norms; its effects were all the more disastrous in that these youthful standard-bearers of this supposedly new Germany were not simply under the spell of the Dictator's magic; they were also swayed by that old German belief that Government can do not wrong and if it does, then, by differentiating between his private life and his official duty, a citizen can emerge unsullied from any task laid upon him by the State.

So the bloody history of the SS is but another page in that of the old German nation-state; the acts and deeds of the SS are but an illustration of the hypertrophy of nationalism and State omnipotence. Have the Germans, and have the ex-SS-men, learnt their lesson? The historian would not make so bold as to give an answer. But the questions remain and will continue to nag at us. For one thing is certain – the history of the SS will continue to stalk the Germans, a record of terrifying lust for power. So long as Germany has a future, that history will stand as a warning and a challenge.

APPENDIX I

NOTES

ABBREVIATIONS

BDC Microfilm

Files of the Berlin Documentary Centre, on microfilm in the National Archives, Washington (Groups 580, 611).

Central Archives

Files of the Central Archives of the NSDAP, on microfilm in the Hoover Institution on War, Revolution and Peace, Stanford University.

IMT

Record of International Military Tribunal, Nuremberg.

RFSS Microfilm

Files of the Personal Staff of the 'Reichsführer-SS and Chief of the German Police', on microfilm in the National Archives, Washington (Group T-175).

RSHA

Anschriftenverzeichnis des Reichssicherheitshauptamtes.

CHAPTER ONE

1. IMT Vol. XXI, pp 500–501.
2. Himmler: *Die Schutzstaffel als anti-bolschewistische Kampforganisation*, p 29.
3. *SS Liederbuch* [Song Book] p 18.
4. IMT Vol. XXI p 502. Also RSHA, October 1st, 1941, RFSS Microfilm No 463. Jacques Delarue: *The History of the Gestapo*, p 197.
5. Dienstaltersliste der Schutzstaffel der NSDAP, Nov 9th, 1944, p 61. Hilberg: *The Destruction of the European Jews*, p 134.
6. Martin Broszat: *Anatomy of the SS State*, pp 503–4.
7. Paul Hausser: *Waffen-SS im Einsatz*, p 16.
8. Letter of Sept 23rd, 1947 from Dr Heinrich Malz, ex-adviser in the RSHA.
9. Hauptsturmführer Kähne, for instance, was not allowed to defend himself against the cigarette manufacturer Theodor Schmiedeberg because the SS leaders were afraid that SS secrets might emerge in court. See letter of Aug 6th, 1941 from

Chef der Sicherheitspolizei und des SD (hereafter referred to as CSSD) to FRSS Private Office, RFSS Microfilm No 25.

10. Enno Georg: *Die Wirtschaftlichen Unternehmungen der SS*, p 139.
11. Hannah Arendt: *The Origins of Totalitarianism*, p 372, Note 80.
12. Werner Bross: *Gespräche mit Hermann Göring während des Nürnberger Prozesses*, pp 265, 288.
13. Reinhard Henkys: *Die nationalsozialistischen Gewaltverbrechen*, pp 173, 176.
14. IMT Vol XXII, p 516.
15. IMT Vol XXII, p 517.
16. Felix Steiner: *Die Armee der Geächteten*, Plesse Verlag, Göttingen 1963.
17. Erich Kern: *Der grosse Rausch, Russlandfeldzug 1941–45*, Verlag Lothar Leberecht, Waiblingen 1948.
18. IMT Vol XX, p 368.
19. IMT Vol XX, pp 343—4.
20. Ibid.
21. Eugen Kogon: *Der SS Staat*, p 32. The book has been translated into English under the title *The Theory and Practice of Hell*, but not all the quotations given, which are from the 1965 edition, occur in the English version.
22. Kogon: *The Theory and Practice of Hell*, p 18.
23. Kogon: Ibid, p 29.
24. Kogon: *Der SS Staat*, pp 23 and 26.
25. Letter of October 24th, 1948 from Ohlendorf to Dr Heinrich Malz.
26. Gerald Reitlinger: *The Final Solution*, p 5.
27. Comer Clarke: *Eichmann, the Man and his Crimes*, p 25.
28. Joseph Kessel: *The Man with the Miraculous Hands*, p. 4.
29. *Deutsche Zeitung*, Aug. 15th, 1956.
30. Kogon: *Theory and Practice of Hell*, p 260.
31. Ibid, p 25.
32. Ibid.
33. Elie Cohen: *Human Behaviour in the Concentration Camp*, p 233.
34. Ibid, p 236.
35. Karl O. Paetel: 'Die SS', *Vierteljahrshefte für Zeitgeschichte*, Jan. 1954, p 25.
36. Ermenhild Neusüss-Hunkel: *Die SS*, p 118.
37. Hilberg: op cit, p 134.
38. Neusüss-Hunkel: op cit, pp 105 and 111.
39. Letter of Feb. 26th, 1949 from Dr Aschenhauer, a lawyer, to Bishop Neuhäusler.
40. Hans Rothfels: *Die deutsche Opposition gegen Hitler*, pp 112, 227.
41. Raul Hilberg: *The Destruction of the European Jews*, Quadrangle Books, Chicago; W. H. Allen, London 1961.
42. Alexander Dallin: *German Rule in Russia 1941–45*, Macmillan, New York 1957.
43. Jacques Delarue: *The History of the Gestapo* (translated by Mervyn Savill), Macdonald, London 1964.
44. Edward Crankshaw: *The Gestapo*, Putnam, London 1956.
45. Jacques Bénoist-Méchin: *Histoire de l'Armée Allemande*, Albin Michel, Paris 1964–6.
46. Hannah Arendt: *Eichmann in*

Jerusalem, Viking Press, New York 1963.
47. Enno Georg: *Die wirtschaftlichen Unternehmungen der SS*, Deutsche Verlagsanstalt, Stuttgart 1963.
48. Helmut Krausnick, Hans Buchheim, Martin Broszat, Hans-Adolf Jacobsen: *Anatomy of the SS State*, Collins, London 1968.
49. Buchheim and others: op cit, p xv.
50. George H. Stein: *The Waffen-SS*, Cornell University Press, Ithaca, New York; Oxford University Press, London 1966.
51. Stein: op cit, p vii. It should be mentioned here that Horst Pelckmann, defence counsel for the SS at Nuremberg, did try to present a less stylized picture of the SS.
52. Paetel: op cit, p 20.
53. Kogon: *Der SS Staat*, p 32.
54. Buchheim: *SS und Polizei im NS-Staat*, pp 16–17.
55. Trevor-Roper: *The Last Days of Hitler*, p 2.
56. Hannah Arendt: *The Origins of Totalitarianism*, p 398, Note 29.
57. Arendt: *Elemente und Ursprünge totaler Herrschaft*, p 646 (not in English translation).
58. Buchheim: *Totalitäre Herrschaft*, p 115.
59. Statement by Otto Ohlendorf, October 8th, 1947, in the official record of Case X, Nuremberg Trials 2nd series p 486 (Reference: American Military Tribunal, M-IL-I-I-Caming (Int Lea) Court IIa Case X).
60. Ibid.
61. Trevor-Roper: op cit, p 2.
62. Werner Best: *Die deutsche Abwehrpolizei bis 1945*, p 19.
63. Paul Seabury: *The Wilhelmstrasse*, p 127.
64. Dallin: op cit, pp 168–72.
65. Letter of April 17th, 1943 from Hildebrandt to Himmler, RFSS Microfilm 117.
66. Heinz Boberach: *Meldungen aus dem Reich*, Vol XXVII.
67. Martin Broszat: *Nationalsozialistische Polenpolitik, 1939–45*, pp 83, 84.
68. Viktor Lutze's diary, *Frankfurter Rundschau*, May 16th, 1957.
69. Walter Schellenberg: *Memoirs*, p 179.
70. Bullock: *Hitler, A Study in Tyranny*, p 269.
71. Report by the Commander of the Sicherheitspolizei and SD in White Ruthenia, RFSS Microfilm 59.
72. Robert Kempner: *Eichmann und Komplizen*, pp 373–80.
73. Achim Besgen: *Der stille Befehl*.
74. Ibid, pp 28, 29.
75. IMT Vol XX, p 418.
76. Correspondence between Himmler and Reeder, RFSS Microfilm 56.
77. Quarterly report of the Nuremberg SD Sector, October 10th, 1941, RFSS Microfilm 406.
78. Letter of April 2nd, 1943, from Berger to Rudolf Brandt, RFSS Microfilm 117.
79. Ibid.
80. Correspondence between Ohlendorf and Wolff, Brandt and d'Alquen 1942–3, RFSS Microfilm 275.

81. Rudolf Höss: *Kommandant in Auschwitz*, p 130.
82. Jürgen Thorwald: *Wen sie verderben wollen*, p 360. Reitlinger: *The House built on Sand*, p 355. Dallin: op cit, p 605.
83. Dr Korherr's private papers.
84. Enno Georg: op cit, pp 51 et seq.
85. Ibid, pp 37–8.

CHAPTER TWO

1. Ernst Deuerlein: *Der Hitler-Putsch*, p 30.
2. Deuerlein: 'Hitler's Eintritt in die Politik und die Reichswehr', *Vierteljahrshefte für Zeitgeschichte*, No 2, April 1959, p 185.
3. Ibid, p 184.
4. Ibid, p 208. Heinrich Bennecke: *Hitler und die SA*, p 15.
5. Bennecke: op cit, p 19.
6. Ibid, p 19. Hans Volz: *Daten der Geschichte der NSDAP*, p 5.
7. Ernst Röhm: *Die Geschichte eines Hochverräters*, p 86.
8. Werner Maser: *Die Frühgeschichte der NSDAP*, pp 189–90. Deuerlein: op cit, p 26.
9. Röhm: op cit, p 114.
10. Bennecke: op cit, pp 13–14.
11. Konrad Heiden: *Geschichte des Nationalsozialismus*, p 83.
12. Bennecke: op cit, p 13.
13. Ibid, p 16.
14. Heiden: op cit, p 86.
15. Ibid, p 98.
16. Röhm: op cit, p 115.
17. Ibid, p 125.
18. Bennecke: op cit, p 27.
19. Ibid.
20. Ibid, p 28.
21. Ibid, p 27.
22. Ernst von Salomon: *Der Fragebogen*, p 398.
23. Heiden: op cit, p 87. Bennecke: op cit, p 28.
24. Röhm: op cit, p 173.
25. Heiden: op cit, p 87.
26. Ibid, p 99.
27. Bennecke: op cit, p 31. Heiden: op cit, p 81.
28. Bennecke: op cit, pp 54–5.
29. Ibid, pp 54, 56, 68.
30. Ibid, p 54.
31. Ibid, p 66.
32. Volz: op cit, p 11. Röhm: op cit, p 149.
33. Bennecke: op cit, pp. 86, 88.
34. Ibid, p 236.
35. Volz: op cit, p 120.
36. Ibid.
37. Ibid.
38. Ibid.
39. Ibid. Josef Wulf: *Die SS*, p 2.
40. Maser: op cit, p 357.
41. Ibid, p 303.
42. Letter of October 14th, 1966 from Herr Otto Eichinger.
43. Maser: op cit, p 308.
44. Reitlinger: *The SS*, p 13.
45. Deuerlein: *Der Hitler-Putsch*, p 99.
46. Maser: op cit, p 443.
47. Bennecke: op cit, p 92.
48. Maser: op cit, p 448.
49. Ibid, p 445.
50. Ibid.
51. Ibid, p 448. Volz: op cit, p 122.
52. Maser: op cit, p 445. Bennecke: op cit, p 52.
53. Maser: op cit, p 445.
54. Ibid, p 446.
55. Bennecke: op cit, p 94.

56. Maser: op cit, pp 448 and 456.
57. Bennecke: op cit, p 94.
58. Maser: op cit, p 458.
59. Ibid, p 459.
60. Ibid.
61. Ibid, p 461.
62. Ibid, p 460.
63. Volz: op cit, pp 10–11.
64. Röhm: op cit, p 206.
65. Ibid, p 275.
66. Bennecke: op cit, p 110.
67. Ibid.
68. Ibid, p 111.
69. Röhm: op cit, pp 324, 327.
70. Ibid, p 329.
71. Bennecke: op cit, p 62.
72. Röhm: op cit, p 338.
73. Ibid, p 293.
74. Ibid, p 336.
75. Volz: op cit, p 12.
76. Bennecke: op cit, p 117.
77. Ibid.
78. Röhm: op cit, p 341.
79. Bennecke: op cit, p 120.
80. Reitlinger: *The SS*, p 13.
81. Volz: op cit, p 122.
82. Bennecke: op cit, p 127.
83. Buchheim: *SS und Polizei im NS-Staat*, p 27.
84. 'Uns ist der Kampf', Official SS Brochure, RFSS Microfilm 161.
85. Walter Görlitz and Herbert A. Quint: *Adolf Hitler*, p 251.
86. Bennecke: op cit, p 125.
87. Circular No 1 of September 21st, 1925 from SS headquarters, BDC Microfilm No 87. See also Edgar Erwin Knoebel: *Racial Illusion and Military Necessity*, p 3.
88. Knoebel: op cit, p 3. Gunter d'Alquen: *Die SS*, p 7.
89. Guidelines for the formation of the National-Socialist 'Schutzstaffel' issued by SS headquarters (no date), BDC Microfilm 87.
90. Ibid.
91. *Völkischer Beobachter*, November 27th, 1925.
92. Letter from Schreck to Party Headquarters, Sept 27th, 1925, BDC Microfilm 87.
93. Undated memorandum by Julius Schreck, Central Archives Microfilm 17.
94. Address by Rosenwink, Central Archives Microfilm 17.
95. Ibid.
96. Ibid.
97. Ibid.
98. Neusüss-Hunkel: op cit, p 7.
99. NSK-Wahlsonderdienst, April 5th, 1938, Sheet 5, BDC Microfilm 87. Buchheim: *SS und Polizei*, p 28.
100. Volz: op cit, p 122.
101. Bennecke: op cit, p 128.
102. Ibid, pp 128–9.
103. Volz: op cit, p 122. Bennecke: op cit, pp 130–1–2.
104. Bennecke: op cit, pp 132, 239.
105. Letter of May 20th, 1926, from Ernst Wagner to Hitler, BDC Microfilm 87.
106. Ibid.
107. Guidelines for the SS, BDC Microfilm 87.
108. Circular No 1, dated April 14th, 1926, BDC Microfilm 87.
109. Wagner to Hitler, May 20th, 1926, BDC Microfilm 87.
110. NSK-Wahlsonderdienst, April 5th, 1938, Sheet 5, BDC Microfilm 87.
111. Bennecke: op cit, pp 239–40.
112. SA Order No 1, Jan 16th, 1931, BDC Microfilm 87.
113. Gunther d'Alquen: op cit, p 8.
114. Bennecke: op cit, p 239.

115. SS HQ memorandum, BDC Microfilm 87.
116. Heiden: op cit, p 28.
117. Ibid.
118. Order No 1 from SS headquarters, September 13th, 1927, BDC Microfilm 87.
119. Ibid.
120. Situation report of May 7th, 1929 from Police headquarters Munich, BDC Microfilm 87.
121. Ibid.
122. Heiden: op cit, p 28.
123. *SS Song-book*, p 4.
124. Heiden: op cit, p 27.
125. Roger Manvell and Heinrich Fraenkel: *Heinrich Himmler*, p 17.

CHAPTER THREE

1. Albert Krebs: *Tendenzen und Gestalten der NSDAP*, p 209.
2. Ibid, p 210.
3. Ibid, p 209.
4. Hossbach: *Zwischen Wehrmacht und Hitler*, 1934–8, p 33.
5. Guderian: *Panzer Leader*, p 446.
6. Carl J. Burckhardt: *Meine Danziger Mission 1937–9*, p 123.
7 Alfred Rosenberg: *Letzte Aufzeichnungen*, p 102.
8. Walter Dornberger: *V2 – der Schuss ins Weltall*, pp 196, 202.
9. Count Folke Bernadotte: *The Fall of the Curtain*, p 20.
10. Trevor-Roper: *The Last Days of Hitler*, p 20.
11. As an example see Willi Frischauer: *Himmler*, p 20.
12. Manvell and Fraenkel: *Heinrich Himmler*, pp 1–2.
13. Letter from Margarete Himmler to Heinrich Himmler, April 11th, 1928, Central Archives, Microfilm 98.
14. Ernst Himmler qualified as an engineer and became a senior technician in the Berlin Radio; he died in 1945. Gebhard Himmler was a civil servant in the Reich Ministry of Education and is now working in the Europe/Afghanistan Cultural Institute, Munich.
15. Verbal information Jan 29th, 1966, from a close relative of Himmler who wishes to remain anonymous.
16. Himmler to his mother, June 2nd, 1921, Central Archives, Microfilm 98.
17. Heinrich Himmler to Ernst Himmler, November 14th, 1920, Central Archives, Microfilm 98.
18. Himmler to Paula Stölzle, April 18th, 1923, Central Archives, Microfilm 98.
19. Letter from Max Blüml to Himmler, March 14th, 1924, Central Archives, Microfilm 98.
20. Ibid.
21. Letter from Himmler to Rössner, March 12th, 1924, Central Archives, Microfilm 98.
22. Letter from Himmler to Paula Stölzle, April 13th, 1923, Central Archives Microfilm 98.
23. Manvell and Fraenkel: op cit, p 1.
24. Ibid.
25. Ibid, p 255 Note 2.

26. Werner T. Angress and Bradley F. Smith: 'Diaries of Heinrich Himmler's Early Years,' *Journal of Modern History*, September 1959. This article by two American historians gives some most informative sidelights on the character of the man who was later to be Reichsführer-SS.
27. Ibid, p 214.
28. Verbal information, Jan 29th, 1966, from a close relative who wishes to remain anonymous.
29. Questionnaire regarding Heinrich Himmler completed by his father, June 26th, 1917, Central Archives, Microfilm 98.
30. Manvell and Fraenkel: op cit, p 4.
31. Angress and Smith: op cit, p 207.
32. Manvell and Fraenkel: op cit, p 4.
33. Letter of June 11th, 1917 to Gebhard Himmler from the Keeper of the Purse to the Dowager Princess Arnulf of Bavaria, Central Archives, Microfilm 98.
34. Letter of June 17th, 1919 from Heinrich Himmler to the depot of 11 Bavarian Infantry Regiment, Central Archives, Microfilm 98.
35. Manvell and Fraenkel: op cit, p 255, Note 4.
36. Josef Wulf: *Heinrich Himmler*, p 8.
37. See letter of June 17th, 1919 (Note 34 above).
38. Ibid.
39. Ernst Deuerlein: *Der Hitler-Putsch*, pp 19–20.
40. Ibid, p 20.
41. Cuno Horkenbach: *Das deutsche Reich von 1918 bis heute*, Vol I, p 65.
42. Deuerlein: op cit, p 22.
43. Angress and Smith: op cit, p 208.
44. Ibid.
45. Letter of June 17th, 1919 from Himmler (Note 34 above).
46. Manvell and Fraenkel: op cit, p 5.
47. Wulf: op cit, p 8.
48. Wulf: *Die SS*, p 9.
49. Angress and Smith: op cit, p 208.
50. Ibid.
51. Ibid.
52. Ibid, p 209.
53. Receipt dated May 16th, 1920 from No 14 'Alarm' Company, Central Archives, Microfilm 98.
54. Angress and Smith: op cit, p 208.
55. Ibid, p 210.
56. Ibid.
57. Ibid, p 217.
58. Ibid.
59. Ibid, p 211.
60. Verbal information, Jan 29th, 1966, from a relative who wishes to remain anonymous.
61. Angress and Smith: op cit, p 217.
62. Ibid.
63. Ibid.
64. Ibid.
65. Besgen: *Der stille Befehl*, p 77.
66. Letter of Dec 14th, 1966 from Herr Theodor Rosenfeld.
67. Letter of Aug 15th, 1950 from Herr Hans Knipp.
68. Letter from Robert Kistler to Himmler, Jan 4th, 1919, Central Archives, Microfilm 98.
69. Angress and Smith: op cit, p 209.

70. Ibid.
71. Ibid.
72. General assembly of the NSDAP on Jan 21st, 1921. See Volz: op cit, p 4.
73. Angress and Smith: op cit, p 213.
74. Ibid.
75. Himmler's membership cards in Central Archives, Microfilm 98.
76. Angress and Smith: op cit, p 219.
77. Ibid, p 220.
78. Ibid.
79. Ibid, p 221.
80. Ibid, p 216.
81. Ibid.
82. Ibid.
83. Ibid.
84. Letter from Himmler to his parents, July 28th, 1922, Central Archives, Microfilm 98.
85. Röhm: *Die Geschichte eines Hochverräters*, p 86.
86. Ibid, p 115.
87. Angress and Smith: op cit, p 211.
88. Ibid.
89. Certificate for Heinrich Himmler, dated Aug 30th, 1923, from the Stickstoff-Land-GmbH, Landwirtschaftlicher Betrieb, Schleissheim, Central Archives, Microfilm 98.
90. Angress and Smith: op cit, p 211.
91. See note 89 above.
92. Röhm: op cit, p 221.
93. Angress and Smith: op cit, p 211.
94. Röhm: op cit, p 233.
95. Ibid, p 234.
96. Ibid.
97. Ibid.
98. Ibid, pp 237–9.
99. Ibid, p 240.
100. Ibid, p 243.
101. Ibid, p 242.
102. See Chapter 5.
103. Röhm: op cit, p 242.
104. Ibid, p 244.
105. Ibid.
106. Letter of Nov 18th, 1923 to Himmler from 'L.M.', Central Archives, Microfilm 98.
107. Ibid.
108. The other group called itself 'Grossdeutsche Volksgemeinschaft' [Greater Germany Peoples Community]; Alfred Rosenberg and Julius Streicher were among its more prominent members.
109. Volz: op cit, p 16.
110. Ibid. Also Krebs: op cit, p 183.
111. Angress and Smith: op cit, p 222.
112. Ibid, pp 221–2.
113. Letter of Aug 22nd, 1942 from Himmler to Robert Kistler, Central Archives, Microfilm 98.
114. Volz: op cit, p 17.
115. Letter of Aug 22nd, 1924, see Note 113 above.
116. Angress and Smith: pp 223–4.
117. Ibid, p 215.
118. Ibid.
119. Ibid, p 210.
120. Letter of Dec 30th, 1927 from Margarete Himmler to Heinrich Himmler, Central Archives, Microfilm 98.
121. Ibid, letter of Jan 3rd, 1928.
122. Volz: op cit, p 12.
123. Ibid, p 122.
124. Manvell and Fraenkel: op cit, p 14.
125. Frischauer: *Himmler*, p 23.
126. Manvell and Fraenkel: op cit, p 16.
127. Verbal information, Jan 29th

1966 from relative who wishes to remain anonymous.
128. Frischauer: op cit, p 24.
129. Besgen: op cit, p 72.
130. Bernadotte: op cit, p 28.
131. Letter of Nov 2nd, 1927 from Frau M. Sieguth to Himmler, Central Archives, Microfilm 98.
132. Ibid, letter from Margarete Himmler, Feb 26th, 1928.
133. *Reichsführer-SS und Chef der Deutschen Polizei*, SS official abridged biography of Himmler, undated, Central Archives, Microfilm 229.
134. Heinrich Himmler: *Völkische Bauernpolitik*, undated, Central Archives, Microfilm 98.
135. Joachim C. Fest: *Das Gesicht des Dritten Reiches*, p 163.
136. Ibid.
137. Heinrich Himmler: *Das Zusammenleben*, undated, Central Archives, Microfilm 98.
138. Ibid.
139. Kersten: op cit, p 299.
140. Himmler: *Völkische Bauernpolitik*, Central Archives, Microfilm 98.
141. Ibid.
142. Walter Z. Laqueur: *Young Germany*, p 158.
143. Ibid.
144. Ibid.
145. Ibid, p 31 (Note).
146. Ibid, p 158. Degener: *Wer ist wer* [*Who's Who*] 1935 edition.
147. *Blut und Boden*, documentary film issued by the Head of the Rasse- und Siedlungshauptamt [Race and Resettlement Department], undated, Part II, p 5, RFSS Microfilm 161.
148. Ibid, p 25.
149. Ibid, Part I, p 17.
150. Laqueur: op cit, p 75.
151. Volz: op cit, p 29.
152. Verbal information, Jan 29th, 1966 from relative who wishes to remain anonymous.
153. Ibid.
154. Ibid.
155. Ibid.
156. Ibid.
157. Certified copy of Heinrich and Margarete Himmler's marriage certificate provided by the Registrar's office, Berlin-Schöneberg, Jan 7th, 1960.
158. Information from anonymous relative Jan 29th, 1966. See Note 152 above.
159. Letter of Feb 26th, 1928 from Margarete Himmler to Heinrich Himmler, Central Archives, Microfilm 98.
160. Manvell and Fraenkel: op cit, p 17.
161. Ibid.
162. Letter of May 6th, 1929 from Margarete to Heinrich Himmler, Central Archives, Microfilm 98.
163. Ibid, undated letter.
164. Manvell and Fraenkel: op cit, p 17.
165. Letter of Feb 26th, 1928 from Margarete to Heinrich Himmler, Central Archives, Microfilm 98.
166. Ibid, letter of Feb 2nd, 1928.
167. Ibid, letter of Feb 16th, 1928.
168. Ibid, undated letter.
169. Ibid, letter of March 20th (year not given).
170. SS Seniority List, July 1st, 1935, p 2.

CHAPTER FOUR

1. Haase: *Der Nationalsozialistische Orden*, undated, Central Archives, Microfilm 98.
2. Knoebel: *Racial Illusion and Military Necessity*, University of Colorado thesis 1965, p 8.
3. 'Die Schutzstaffel', address of Jan 18th, 1943, RFSS Microfilm 155.
4. Knoebel: op cit, p 9.
5. IMT Vol XXIX, p 208.
6. Ibid.
7. Ibid.
8. Ibid.
9. Röhm: op cit, p 88.
10. IMT Vol XXIX, p 209.
11. Ernst Jünger: *Krieg und Krieger*, p 106.
12. Arendt: op cit, p 327.
13. Ernst Jünger: *Der Kampf als inneres Erlebnis*, p 2.
14. Jünger: *Krieg und Krieger*, p 119.
15. *Das Schwarze Korps*, Nov 26th, 1942.
16. Jünger: *Krieg und Krieger*, pp 120–21.
17. Emphasized particularly by Paetel: op cit, p 29.
18. Reitlinger: *The SS*, p 76. Also Interpress, Biographical Service No 86 of 1951.
19. IMT Vol XX, pp 283–5.
20. *Wer ist wer*, 1935 edition.
21. Josef Wulf: *Das Dritte Reich und seine Vollstrecker*, p 227.
22. *Frankfurter Allgemeine Zeitung*, July 14th, 1964.
23. Delarue: op cit, p 235.
24. Krebs: *Tendenzen und Gestalten der NSDAP*, p 209.
25. Letter from Himmler to Röhm, Jan 29th, 1930, RFSS Microfilm 199.
26. Ibid.
27. Knoebel: op cit, p 17.
28. Bennecke: *Hitler und die SA*, p 239.
29. Ibid.
30. Ibid, pp 239–40.
31. Letter from Stennes to Röhm, Feb 28th, 1931, Central Archives, Microfilm 17.
32. Anonymous SA leaflet, Feb 25th, 1931, Central Archives, Microfilm 17.
33. Volz: op cit, p 124. Bennecke: op cit, p 153.
34. Notice to all SS men of No 3 Sturm, No III Sturmbann, No 5 Standarte, undated (probably late 1930) RFSS Microfilm 15.
35. 'National-Socialist Self-defence Formations' report from Munich Police Headquarters to the Bavarian Ministry of the Interior, Dec 22nd, 1931, Central Archives, Microfilm 17.
36. Notice to all SS men (see Note 34 above), p 5.
37. Supplement issued by OSAF Deputy South to Party and SA Supreme Headquarters Order of Nov 7th, 1930, Central Archives, Microfilm 17.
38. Order from Party and SA Supreme HQ. See Note 37.
39. Heiden: *Geschichte des Nazionalsozialismus*, p 189.
40. Görlitz and Quint: *Adolf Hitler*, p 256.
41. Paetel: op cit, p 5.
42. Heiden: op cit, p 282.
43. Ibid, p 203.
44. Ibid, p 204.
45. Görlitz and Quint: op cit, 260. *Führerlexikon*, p 77.
46. Rosenberg: op cit, p 35.

47. Heiden: op cit, pp 202–3.
48. Görlitz and Quint: op cit, p 258.
49. Ibid, p 258–9.
50. Görlitz and Quint: op cit, p 258.
51. Hans-Joachim Neufeldt, Jürgen Huck and Georg Tessin: *Zur Geschichte der Ordnungspolizei 1936–1945*, p 107.
52. Martin Broszat: 'Die Anfänge der Berliner NSDAP 1926–7', *Vierteljahrshefte für Zeitgeschichte*, Folio Jan 1st, 1960, p 89.
53. Ibid.
54. Broszat: op cit, p 90.
55. Ibid.
56. Ibid. Volz: op cit, p 33.
57. Görlitz and Quint: op cit, p 423.
58. Karl-Dietrich Bracher, Wolfgang Sauer and Gerhard Schulz: *Die nationalsozialistische Machtergreifung*, p 843.
59. Ibid, p 840.
60. Ibid.
61. Volz: op cit, pp 123, 263.
62. Ibid, pp 123, 192.
63. Görlitz and Quint: op cit, p 263.
64. Bennecke: op cit, p 154. Bracher, Sauer and Schulz: op cit, p 848.
65. Heiden: op cit, p 279.
66. Ibid, pp 279–83.
67. Manvell and Fraenkel: *Heinrich Himmler*, p 19.
68. Ibid.
69. Undated and unsigned report on the early history of the Berlin SS, clearly originating from Berlin SS circles, BDC Microfilm 87.
70. Packebusch's SS register in Tobias' papers. Letters from Daluege dated Aug 20th, 1938 and Jan 9th, 1939, also in Tobias' archives.
71. Bennecke: op cit, p 148.
72. Letter of Feb 28th, 1931 from Stennes to Röhm, Central Archives, Microfilm 17.
73. See Bennecke: op cit, pp 169 et seq on the close connexion between the rising unemployment and the increase in Nazi votes.
74. Bracher, Sauer and Schulz: op cit, p 47.
75. Ibid, pp 847–8.
76. See numerous anonymous leaflets by revolutionary Berlin SA men in Central Archives, Microfilm 17.
77. Leaflet drafted by unknown Party members and SA men, May 31st, 1931, Central Archives, Microfilm 17.
78. Bennecke: op cit, p 146.
79. OSAF Deputy South, Memorandum on proposed reorganization of SA Command, Sept 19th 1930, BDC Microfilm 85.
80. Report by Munich Police Headquarters, Oct 24th, 1930, BDC Microfilm 85. *Münchner Post*, Sept 4th, 1930.
81. Ibid.
82. Leaflet by Dresden SA men, March 20th, 1931, Central Archives, Microfilm 17.
83. *Münchner Post*, Sept 4th, 1930.
84. Report from Munich Police Headquarters, Oct 24th, 1930, BDC Microfilm
85. Ibid.
86. Ibid.
87. Ibid. Krebs: op cit, p 167.
88. Heiden: op cit, p 284; *Wahrheiten der Woche* (Stennes' supporters paper) Oct 10th, 1931,

Central Archives Microfilm.
89. *Völkischer Beobachter*, Sept 4th, 1930.
90. Letter from Conti to Pfeffer, Sept 8th, 1930, Central Archives Microfilm 17.
91. Ibid.
92. Heiden: op cit, p 198.
93. Ibid.
94. Bracher, Sauer and Schulz: op cit, p 349.
95. Ibid.
96. Bennecke: op cit, p 164.
97. Letter from Daluege dated Jan 9th, 1939, Tobias' papers.
98. Letter from Daluege to Röhm, April 1st, 1931, Central Archives Microfilm 17.
99. Görlitz and Quint: op cit, p 312.
100. *Hamburger Fremdenblatt*, April 2nd, 1931.
101. *Hamburger Echo*, April 3rd, 4th, 5th, 1931.
102. Ibid, April 3rd, 4th.
103. Ibid, April 3rd.
104. Special announcement issued by Stennes, undated, Central Archives Microfilm 17. *Hamburger Echo*, April 2nd, 3rd, 4th, 10th, 1931. *Hamburger Nachrichten*, April 4th, 1931.
105. Bracher, Sauer and Schulz: op cit, p 852. Horkenbach: *Das deutsche Reich von 1918 bis heute*, Vol III, p 125.
106. Horkenbach: op cit, Vol III, p 128.
107. Wulf: *Das Dritte Reich und seine Vollstrecker*, pp 225 and 228.
108. Buchheim: *Anatomy of the SS State*, p 142.
109. Leaders' Conference June 13th–14th, 1931, SS headquarters Report, BDC Microfilm 87.
110. Provisional SS duty regulations, June 1931, BDC Microfilm 87.
111. Ibid.
112. Ibid.
113. SS Sector order No 4, March 21st, 1931, BDC Microfilm 87.
114. Letter from Wagener to OSAF Deputies, Oct 3rd, 1930, BDC Microfilm 85.
115. Letter from Schreck to Party Headquarters, Sept 24th, 1925, BDC Microfilm 87.
116. Provisional SS duty regulations, June 1931, BDC Microfilm 87.
117. Ibid.
118. Shlomo Aronson: *Heydrich und die Anfänge des SD und der Gestapo (1931–5)*, p 87.
119. SS Order A 53, Oct 10th, 1931, BDC Microfilm 87.
120. See Chapter 8.
121. Order 114/32a from SA Supreme Commander, Jan 25th, 1932, Central Archives Microfilm 17.
122. Ibid.
123. Ibid.
124. Röhm: op cit, p 261.
125. Letter from Röhm to Heimsoth, Dec 3rd, 1928, Central Archives Microfilm 85.
126. *Münchner Post*, June 30th, 1931.
127. Ibid.
128. Bennecke: op cit, pp 165–6.
129. Judgement of the Criminal Division of the Munich Civil Court in November 1934, case against Peter Granninger and others, Central Archives Microfilm 17.
130. Ibid, p 4.
131. Ibid, p 9.

132. Ibid, p 5.
133. Görlitz and Quint: op cit, p 313.
134. Ibid. *Münchner Post*, June 24th and 27th, 1931.
135. Open letter from Dr Helmut Klotz, ex-NSDAP Reichstag deputy, March 1932, Central Archives Microfilm 85.
136. Ibid. Also letter of July 4th, 1934, from SA-Oberführer Hans Kallenbach to Reichsleiter Fiehler, Central Archives, Microfilm 17.
137. Friedrich Stampfer: 'Erfahrungun und Erkenntnisse' quoted from *Die andere Zeitung* No 50 Dec 1959.
138. Copy of an article in *Flammenzeichen* of Nov 5th, 1932. Central Archives, Microfilm 17.
139. Ibid.
140. *Glück und Ende des Nationalsozialisten Bell*, pp 21–2.
141. Press report on the Danzeisen case, July 1932, RFSS Microfilm 476.
142. Supplement to Danzeisen case, statement by Karl Horn, May 18th, 1932, RFSS Microfilm 467.
143. Press report, July 1932, RFSS Microfilm 467.
144. Murder letter, March 14th, 1932, RFSS Microfilm 467.
145. Ibid.
146. Ibid.
147. In the Granninger case the Munich court certified that there was no proof of homosexual acts on the part of du Moulin-Eckart and released him. Judgement on Granninger and others, RFSS Microfilm 17.
148. Statement by Karl Horn, pp 7, 8, RFSS Microfilm 467.
149. Ibid, p 9.
150. Ibid, p 10.
151. Ibid, p 11.
152. Ibid, p 12.
153. Ibid, p 14.
154. Wilhelm Högener: *Die verratene Republik*, p 325.
155. *Die andere Zeitung*, No 12 of 1950.
156. Ibid.
157. See Horn files, RFSS Microfilm 467.
158. *Münchner Post*, Nov 18th, 1932.
159. Letter of Oct 5th, 1932 from Martin Bormann to Rudolf Hess, Central Archives, Microfilm 17.
160. Ibid.
161. Knoebel: op cit, p 17.
162. Führer Conference June 13th–14th, 1931, Report by SS headquarters, BDC Microfilm 87.

CHAPTER FIVE

1. Görlitz and Quint: *Adolf Hitler*, pp 382, 389.
2. Ibid.
3. Buchheim: *SS und Polizei im NS-Staat*, p 35.
4. Horkenbach: *Das deutsche Reich von 1918 bis heute*, Vol IV, p 929.
5. Rudolf Diels: *Lucifer ante Portas*, p 179.
6. *Der Spiegel*, 'Das Spiel ist aus – Arthur Nebe' (hereafter referred to as 'Nebe series') Feb 9th, 1950.

7. Ibid.
8. Ibid.
9. Ibid. Also issue of Feb 23rd, 1950.
10. Ibid.
11. Franz Neumann: *Behemoth*, p 47.
12. Ibid.
13. Ibid.
14. Robert L. Koehl: *RKFVD, German Resettlement and Population Policy 1939–45*, p 14.
15. Ibid, pp 13–19.
16. Görlitz and Quint: op cit, p 387.
17. Ibid.
18. Ibid.
19. Bracher, Sauer and Schulz: *Die nationalsozialistische Machtergreifung*, p 925.
20. Ibid.
21. Görlitz and Quint: op cit, p 276.
22. Diels: op cit, p 229.
23. For Goebbels' increasing power see Bullock: op cit, p 312.
24. Görlitz and Quint: op cit, p 399.
25. Kersten: *Totenkopf und Treue*, p 245.
26. Görlitz and Quint: op cit, p 399.
27. Ibid.
28. Bracher, Sauer and Schulz: op cit, p 588.
29. Ibid, p 589.
30. Trevor-Roper: op cit, p 1.
31. Fritz Tobias: *Der Reichstagsbrand*, p 135 (not in English translation).
32. Ibid, pp 135–6.
33. Ibid, p 136.
34. Ibid, p 135.
35. Ibid.
36. Diels: op cit, p 71.
37. Bullock: *Hitler, a Study in Tyranny*, p 256.
38. Stein: *The Waffen-SS*, p 4.
39. Ibid: p 5.
40. Ibid.
41. Buchheim: *SS und Polizei im NS-Staat*, p 30.
42. K–G. Klietman: *Die Waffen-SS*, p 54.
43. Ibid.
44. Ibid, p 53.
45. Konrad Himmler's registration card, Record (Vol I) of Infanterie-Leib-Regiment, Munich War Ministry Archives, Central Archives, Microfilm 98.
46. Buchheim: *Anatomy of the SS State*, p 148.
47. Ibid (Broszat), p 414.
48. Ibid, p 405.
49. IMT Vol XXIX, p 226.
50. Ibid.
51. Best: *Heinrich Himmler*, p 2.
52. Ibid.
53. Aronson: *Heydrich und die Anfänge des SD und der Gestapo 1931–5*, pp 177 et seq.
54. Tobias: *The Reichstag Fire*, p 260.
55. Bracher, Sauer and Schulz: op cit, p 865.
56. Buchheim: *Anatomy of the SS State*, p 145.
57. Diels: op cit, p 217.
58. Ibid, pp 166, 228.
59. Delarue: op cit, p 34.
60. Buchheim: *Anatomy of the SS State*, pp 145–6.
61. Ibid.
62. Ibid (Broszat), pp 402–3.
63. Ibid (Buchheim), p 146.
64. Ibid. Diels: op cit, p 228.
65. Buchheim: *Anatomy of the SS State*, pp 145–6.
66. Delarue: op cit, p 38. Crankshaw: *Gestapo*, p 15.

67. Horkenbach: op cit, Vol IV, p 66.
68. Bracher, Sauer and Schulz: op cit, p 868.
69. Ibid, p 872.
70. Ibid, p 868.
71. Diels: op cit, p 224.
72. Bracher, Sauer and Schulz: op cit, p 873.
73. Diels: op cit, pp 255–6.
74. Bracher, Sauer and Schulz: op cit, p 865.
75. Ibid.
76. Diels: op cit, p 253.
77. Ibid.
78. Ibid.
79. Ibid, p 257.
80. Ibid, p 311.
81. Ibid, p 327.
82. Ibid, p 249.
83. Ibid.
84. Manvell and Fraenkel: *Göring*, p 50.
85. *Wahrheiten der Woche*, Oct 10th, 1931, Central Archives, Microfilm 17.
86. Ibid.
87. Diels: op cit, p 250.
88. Ibid.
89. Wheeler-Bennett: *The Nemesis of Power*, p 227 footnote.
90. Diels: op cit, p 257.
91. Ibid, p 262.
92. 'Nebe series', Nov 17th, 1949, p 24.
93. Ibid.
94. Ibid, p 23.
95. Ibid, pp 23–4.
96. *Völkischer Beobachter*, June 10th, 1933.
97. Martin H. Sommerfeldt: *Ich war dabei*, p 57.
98. H. B. Gisevius: *To the Bitter End*, p 145.
99. 'Nebe Series', Nov 17th, 1949, p 25.
100. Ibid.
101. Charles Wighton: *Heydrich*, p 61.
102. Diels: op cit, p 328.
103. Ibid.
104. Ibid, p 330.
105. Ibid.
106. Ibid.
107. Wighton: op cit, p 61.
108. Ibid, p 62.
109. Diels: op cit, p 328.
110. Günter Plum: 'Staatspolizei und innere Verwaltung', *Vierteljahrshefte für Zeitgeschichte*, Issue 2 of 1965, p 205.
111. Bracher, Sauer and Schulz: op cit, p 600.
112. Ibid, p 601.
113. Neufeldt, op cit, p 5.
114. Bracher, Sauer and Schulz: op cit, p 601.
115. Buchheim: *Anatomy of the SS State*, p 146.
116. Plum: op cit, pp 193–5.
117. Buchheim: *SS und Polizei im NS-Staat*, pp 36–40.
118. Bracher, Sauer and Schulz: op cit, p 598.
119. Ibid, p 601.
120. Ibid.
121. Ibid, p 602.
122. Ibid, p 603.
123. Buchheim: *Anatomy of the SS State*, p 151.
124. Diels: op cit, p 412.
125. Ibid.

CHAPTER SIX

1. Hermann Rauschning: *Gespräche mit Hitler*, p 144 (not in English translation).
2. Hossbach: *Zwischen Wehrmacht*

und Hitler 1934–1938, p 57.
3. Rauschning: *Hitler speaks*, p 155.
4. Bracher, Sauer and Schulz: *Die nationalsozialistische Machtergreifung*, p 853.
5. 'National-Sozialistische Selbstschutzverbände', Report from Munich Police Headquarters to the Bavarian Ministry of the Interior, Central Archives, Microfilm 17.
6. Ibid.
7. Bennecke: *Die Reichswehr und der 'Röhm-Putsch'*, p 27. Bracher, Sauer and Schulz: op cit, p 888.
8. Görlitz and Quint: *Adolf Hitler*, pp 318–19.
9. Bracher, Sauer and Schulz: op cit, p 940.
10. Ibid, p 939.
11. Ibid, p 886.
12. Ibid, p 880.
13. Ibid, p 886.
14. Ibid, p 891.
15. Ibid, p 939.
16. Ibid, pp 890, 893.
17. Ibid, p 893.
18. Ibid, p 894.
19. Ibid, p 941.
20. Announcement of Dec 1st, 1933 signed by Hitler, Central Archives, Microfilm 17.
21. Helmut Krausnick: 'Der 30 Juni 1934', in *Das Parlament 30 June*, 1954, p 320.
22. Bracher, Sauer and Schulz: op cit, p 904.
23. Krausnick: op cit, p 318.
24. Bracher, Sauer and Schulz: op cit, p 924.
25. Krausnick: op cit, p 319.
26. Bracher, Sauer and Schulz: op cit, p 943. Krausnick: op cit, p 319.
27. Bracher, Sauer and Schulz: op cit, p 943.
28. Edgar Röhricht: *Pflicht und Gewissen*, p 63.
29. Krausnick: op cit, p 319.
30. *Der Spiegel*, May 15th, 1957, p 22. 'Der Furcht so fern, dem Tod so nahe'.
31. Krausnick: op cit, p 319.
32. Ibid.
33. Hermann Foertsch: *Schuld und Verhängnis*, p 48.
34. *Der Spiegel*, May 15th, 1957, p 23.
35. Reitlinger: *The SS*, p 55.
36. See Lutze's allusions in Aug 1935 – end of this chapter.
37. Case for the prosecution against Josef Dietrich and Michael Lippert, Munich Provincial Court I, July 4th, 1956, p 35.
38. Bracher, Sauer and Schulz: op cit, p 928.
39. Wighton: *Heydrich*, p 46.
40. Bracher, Sauer and Schulz: op cit, p 929.
41. See Chapter 10.
42. Anonymous: *Glück und Ende des Nationalsozialisten Bell*, p 22.
43. Krausnick: op cit, p 321.
44. Case against Dietrich, p 46.
45. Ibid, p 45. Bennecke: *Die Reichswehr und der 'Röhm-Putsch'*, pp 46–7.
46. Case against Dietrich, p 45.
47. Ibid, p 47.
48. Ibid, p 41.
49. Bracher, Sauer and Schulz: op cit, p 951.
51. Record of interrogation of Max Jüttner April 8th, 1949, Proceedings of Provincial Court I, Munich, p 4.
52. Ernst von Salomon: *Der Fragebogen*, p 438.

53. Ibid.
54. Case against Dietrich, p 41.
55. Statement by Patzig in *Der Tagesspiegel*, May 10th, 1957.
56. Bracher, Sauer and Schulz: op cit, p 951.
57. Ibid.
58. Felix Steiner: *Die Armee der Geächteten*, p 48.
59. Case against Dietrich, p 49.
60. Ibid.
61. Ibid.
62. Bracher, Sauer and Schulz: op cit, p 954.
63. Case against Dietrich, p 50.
64. Ibid. Also Bracher, Sauer and Schulz: op cit, p 954.
65. Ibid. Also *Der Spiegel*, May 15th, 1957, p 22.
66. Krausnick: op cit, p 321.
67. Bennecke in *Die Reichswehr und der 'Röhm-Putsch'*, p 57, emphasizes the importance of the role played by Gauleiter Wagner.
68. Bracher, Sauer and Schulz: op cit, p 954.
69. Sommerfeldt: *Ich war dabei*, p 76.
70. Bracher, Sauer and Schulz: op cit, p 952. Krausnick: op cit, p 320.
71. Bennecke: *Röhm-Putsch*, pp 43–4.
72. Letter of June 12th, 1934, from Höfle to Röhm, Central Archives, Microfilm 17.
73. Bennecke: *Röhm-Putsch*, p 54.
74. Bracher, Sauer and Schulz: op cit, p 952.
75. Krausnick: op cit, p 320.
76. Ibid.
77. Wheeler-Bennett: *The Nemesis of Power*, p 311.
78. Papen: *Der Wahrheit eine Gasse*, p 346 (not in English translation). *Süddeutsche Zeitung*, June 30th, 1964.
79. Keesing's Contemporary Archives, No 34/1486.
80. Papen: *Memoirs*, p 310.
81. Ibid.
82. Sommerfeldt: *Ich war dabei*, p 58.
83. See Papen: op cit, pp 247–8.
84. *Völkischer Beobachter*, June 1st, 1934.
85. Sommerfeldt: op cit, p 69.
86. Wheeler-Bennett: op cit, p 319.
87. Ibid, pp 319–20.
88. Ibid, p 320.
89. Ibid.
90. Lutze's diary, published in *Frankfurter Rundschau*, May 14th, 1957.
91. Ibid.
92. Case against Dietrich, p 54.
93. Ibid.
94. Ibid, pp 54, 61.
95. Ibid, p 61.
96. Krausnick: op cit, p 321; case against Dietrich, p 52.
97. Bracher, Sauer and Schulz: op cit, p 956.
98. Ibid.
99. Krausnick: op cit, p 321. Case against Dietrich, p 52.
100. Bracher, Sauer and Schulz: op cit, p 959.
101. Westphal: *The German Army in the West*, p 9.
102. *Die Welt*, May 30th–31st, 1957.
103. Peter Bor: *Gespräche mit Halder*, p 125.
104. Statement by Heinrici, *Abendpost*, May 7th, 1957.
105. Foertsch: op cit, p 52.
106. Bennecke: *Röhm-Putsch*, p 52. Case against Dietrich, p 53.

107. Case against Dietrich, p 55.
108. Bracher, Sauer and Schulz: op cit, p 958.
109. Bennecke: *Röhm-Putsch*, p 49.
110. Bracher, Sauer and Schulz: op cit, p 958. Foertsch: op cit, p 49. Krausnick: op cit, p 321.
111. Bracher, Sauer and Schulz: op cit, p 958.
112. Ibid, p 959.
113. Letter of May 27th, 1949 from Karl Schreyer to Munich Police Headquarters, p 5; Proceedings of Provincial Court I, Munich.
114. Bracher, Sauer and Schulz: op cit, p 959.
115. *Blick in die Zeit*, July 7th, 1934.
116. Even the latest German historians seem to accept this (see Bracher, Sauer and Schulz: op cit, p 959).
117. *Völkischer Beobachter*, June 26th, 1934.
118. *Der Spiegel*, May 15th, 1957, p 23.
119. Wheeler-Bennett: op cit, p 321.
120. *Völkischer Beobachter*, June 27th, 1934.
121. Lutze's diary published in *Frankfurter Rundschau*, May 14th, 1957.
122. Case against Dietrich, p 59.
123. *Der Spiegel*, May 15th, 1957, p 24.
124. Lutze's Diary – *Frankfurter Rundschau*, May 14th, 1957.
125. Ibid.
126. Ibid.
127. Case against Dietrich, p 59.
128. Ibid, p 52.
129. Ibid.
130. Ibid, pp 54, 56. Lutze's diary.
131. Bracher, Sauer and Schulz: op cit, p 945.
132. Ibid, p 960.
133. Case against Dietrich, pp 61 et seq.
134. Ibid, p 60, Lutze's diary.
135. Ibid, p 57.
136. Statement by Dietrich, *Abendpost*, May 7th, 1957.
137. Case against Dietrich, p 60.
138. Ibid.
139. Ibid.
140. Judgement of the Assize Court, State Court I, Munich on Josef Dietrich and Michael Lippert, May 14th, 1957, p 20.
141. Ibid.
142. Case against Dietrich, p 60.
143. Bennecke: *Röhm-Putsch*, p 53.
144. Ibid, p 54.
145. Ibid.
146. Ibid.
147. *Völkischer Beobachter*, July 1st, 1934. Case against Dietrich p 58. Statement by Martina Schmid, *Abendpost*, May 7th, 1957.
148. Bracher, Sauer and Schulz: op cit, p 960.
149. *Abendpost*, May 7th, 1957.
150. Case against Dietrich, p 80.
151. *Abendpost*, May 7th, 1957.
152. Interrogation of Brückner, Traunstein Court, May 30th, 1949, p 2.
153. *Hannoversche Anzeiger*, June 30th, 1934.
154. Lutze's diary.
155. Case against Dietrich, p 77; *Süddeutsche Zeitung*, May 8th, 1957.
156. Statement by Martina Schmid, *Abendpost*, May 7th, 1957.
157. Ibid.
158. *Der Spiegel*, May 15th, 1957, p 25. Krausnick: op cit, p 323. Lutze's diary in *Frankfurter*

Rundschau, May 14th, 1957.
159. Bennecke: *Röhm-Putsch*, p 57.
160. *Der Spiegel*, May 15th, 1957, p 25.
161. Lutze's diary in *Frankfurter Rundschau*, May 14th, 1957.
162. Ibid.
163. Ibid.
164. *Völkischer Beobachter*, July 3rd, 1934.
165. Lutze's diary in *Frankfurter Rundschau*, May 14th, 1957.
166. Ibid.
167. Interrogation of Brückner, p 3.
168. Ibid.
169. Ibid.
170. Ibid.
171. Written submission by Dr Robert Koch, Jan 25th, 1949, proceedings of State Court I, Munich, p 1.
172. Ibid.
173. Written submission by Max Jüttner, p 3.
174. Ibid.
175. List of entrants to Munich prison, Proceedings of State Court I, Munich.
176. Submission by Max Jüttner, p 3.
177. Ibid.
178. *Der Spiegel*, May 15th, 1957, p 27.
179. Bullock: op cit, p 305.
180. Ibid.
181. *Der Spiegel*, May 15th, 1957, p 27.
182. Ibid. Also Bullock: op cit, p 306.
183. Judgement on Dietrich, p 60.
184. Letter from Schreyer to Munich Police Headquarters, p 3.
185. Ibid, p 4.
186. Judgement on Dietrich, p 11.
187. Ibid.
188. Ibid, p 12.
189. Ibid.
190. Bracher, Sauer and Schulz: op cit, p 961. *Der Spiegel*, May 15th, 1957, p 27.
191. Lutze's diary in *Frankfurter Rundschau*, May 15th, 1957.
192. Judgement on Dietrich, pp 12–13.
193. Ibid, p 13.
194. List of entrants to Munich prison. Proceedings of State Court I, Munich.
195. Judgement on Dietrich, p 61.
196. Ibid, p 64.
197. Statement by Dietrich, *Die Welt*, May 7th, 1957.
198. Case against Dietrich, p 65.
199. Ibid.
200. Ibid, pp 3, 72.
201. Ibid, p 67.
202. Ibid.
203. Ibid, p 68.
204. Ibid.
205. Judgement on Dietrich, p 15.
206. Case against Dietrich, p 69.
207. Judgement on Dietrich, p 16.
208. Case against Dietrich, pp 70, 72. Statement by Dietrich, *Frankfurter Allgemeine Zeitung*, May 7th, 1957.
209. Case against Dietrich, pp 72–3–4.
210. Papen: op cit, p 315.
211. Gisevius: *To the Bitter End*, pp 276 et seq.
212. Papen: op cit, p 316.
213. Robert Kempner: *SS im Kreuzverhör*, p 257.
214. Ibid, p 256.
215. Ibid, p 257.
216. Ibid.
217. Ibid, pp 257–8.
218. Ibid, p 255.
219. Ibid, pp 258–9.
220. Ibid, p 259.

221. Wheeler-Bennett: op cit, p 232.
222. Salomon: op cit, p 440.
223. Wheeler-Bennett: op cit, p 324.
224. *Süddeutsche Zeitung*, June 19th, 1961. Prosecution of Bach-Zelewski, pp 3 et seq.
225. *Der Spiegel*, May 15th, 1957, p 29.
226. Statement by Dr Schaeffer, *Frankfurter Rundschau*, May 23rd, 1957.
227. Report by Dr Walter Schaeffer, an ex-State Attorney [Generalstaatsanwalt], Nov 29th, 1945, in Schaeffer's private collection. Affidavit (also in Schaeffer's collection) by Dr Werner von Haacke, another State Attorney [Oberstaatsanwalt] Feb 15th, 1957.
228. Verbal information from Dr Werner von Haacke, Sept 9th, 1965.
229. G. M. Gilbert: *The Psychology of Dictatorship*, p 69.
230. Ibid, p 95.
231. Bracher, Sauer and Schulz: op cit, p 921. Krebs: *Tendenzen und Gestalten*, pp 192–3.
232. *Der Spiegel*, May 15th, 1957, p 27.
233. Bullock: op cit, p 303. Schreyer's statement, p 7.
234. *Der Spiegel*, May 15th, 1957, pp 27–8.
235. François-Poncet: *The Fateful Years*, p 139.
236. Krausnick, op cit, p 320.
237. Ibid, p 323; *Völkischer Beobachter*, July 3rd, 1934.
238. Bracher, Sauer and Schulz: op cit, p 960. Papen: *Die Wahrheit eine Gasse*, p 355 (not in English translation).
239. Papen: op cit, p 316.
240. Bennecke: *Röhm-Putsche*, p 61.
241. *Die Welt*, May 4th, 1957.
242. Sommerfeldt: op cit, pp 72, 73, 76.
243. Gisevius: *Bis zum bitteren Ende*, p 155 (not in English translation). Case against Dietrich, p 61.
244. Von Ribbentrop: *Memoirs*, p 34 (Note).
245. Record of ministerial discussion, July 3rd, 1934, p 7 – in Tobias papers.
246. Deposition by Max Jüttner, p 5.
247. Lutze's diary in *Frankfurter Rundschau*, May 15th, 1957.
248. Bennecke: *Röhm-Putsch*, p 89.
249. Paul Schulz: *Meine Erschiessung am 30 Juni, 1934*, pp 13 et seq.
250. Ibid, p 9.
251. Ibid, p 12.
252. Ibid, p 14.
253. Ibid, p 22.
254. Ibid. Also report by Otto Grub on events of June 30th to July 4th, 1934, p 2 – in Tobias papers.
255. Ibid, p 25. Grub report, p 4.
256. Ibid, p 35.
257. Case against Dietrich, p 4.
258. Ibid.
259. Deposition by Koch, p 3.
260. Ibid, p 4.
261. Statement by Lippert, *Stuttgarter Zeitung*, May 7th, 1957.
262. *Völkischer Beobachter*, July 1st, 1934.
263. *Süddeutsche Zeitung*, March 30th–31st, May 11th and May 14th, 1947. *Frankfurter Rundschau*, May 8th, 1957.
264. Letter from Schreyer, p 6.

265. Ibid.
266. Ibid.
267. See Bennecke: *Röhm-Putsch*, pp 87–8.
268. *Schulthess' calendar of European history 1934*, p 184.
269. Record of meeting of Ministers, July 3rd, 1934, p 8.
270. *Frankfurter Allgemeine Zeitung*, May 10th, 1957.
271. *Der Spiegel*, May 15th, 1957, p 29.
272. Bennecke: *Röhm-Putsch*, p 65.
273. *Der Spiegel*, May 15th, 1957, p 29.
274. Kramary: *Stauffenbery, The Life and Death of an Officer*, p 49.
275. Foertsch, op cit, pp 57–8.
276. Buchheim: *SS und Polizei im NS-Staat*, pp 62–3.
277. *Völkischer Beobachter*, July 26th, 1934.
278. Klietmann: op cit, p 15.
279. Koehl: op cit, p 21.
280. Order from SA Supreme Commander July 2nd, 1934, BDC Microfilm 85.
281. Ibid, July 14th, 1934.
282. Ibid, Aug 9th, 1934.
283. Report by SA-Sturmführer Hermann Baecke, No 3116/34, Central Archives, Microfilm 17.
284. 'Die Vorgänge anlässlich der Röhm-revolte', Supplementary report by commander of Standarte 168, July 27th, 1934, Central Archives, Microfilm 17.
285. Report to Sturm 3/R 168, July 2nd, 1934, Central Archives, Microfilm 17.
286. Report by SS-Standartenführer Schulz, Aug 21st, 1935, RFSS Microfilm 33.
287. Ibid, pp 6–7.

CHAPTER SEVEN

1. Kersten: *Totenkopf und Treue*, pp 245–6.
2. Schellenberg: *Memoirs*, p 21.
3. IMT Document, 45–55.
4. Konrad Heiden: *Geburt des Dritten Reiches*, p 29.
5. Quoted from the *Stuttgarter Zeitung*, June 30th, 1964.
6. Quoted from the *Frankfurter Allgemeine Zeitung*, June 30th, 1964.
7. *NSDAP Organization Handbook*, Tables 43 and 32.
8. Ibid, pp 435, 52. (See also Table of Ranks, p 652, this volume).
9. Himmler: *Die Schutzstaffel*, p 24.
10. Robert Koehl: 'The Character of the Nazi SS', *Journal of Modern History*, Sept 1960, p 282.
11. SS Seniority List, 1945.
12. Ibid, 1944.
13. German State Archives: Der Adel im deutschen Offizierkorps, Statistische Übersicht, p 12.
14. Georg: *Die wirtschaftlichen Unternehmungen der SS*, p 55.
15. Paul Hausser: *Wie andere Soldaten auch.*
16. Verbal information from Felix Steiner, Jan 29th, 1966.
17. Klietmann: op cit, p 421. Stein: *Die Waffen-SS*, p 13.
18. Josef Wulf, for instance, in *Die SS*, pp 93 et seq.
19. SS Seniority List, 1944.

20. Ibid.
21. Letter of Sept 2nd, 1943, from Edda Ciano to Himmler, RFSS Microfilm 33.
22. See Plum: *Staatspolizei und innere Verwaltung, 1934–1936* pp 198–206.
23. Correspondence between Himmler and Reeder, RFSS Microfilm 56.
24. Walter Hagen (alias Wilhelm Höttl): *Die geheime Front*, pp 141–58. SS Seniority List, 1944.
25. Boberach: *Meldungen aws dem Reich*, pp xxvii et seq.
26. Undated statement before the International Military Tribunal by the rider von Woykosky-Buedau – in Tobias' papers.
27. Undated submission by Woykosky-Buedau entitled 'Entwicklung der SS-Reiterei' – in Tobias' papers.
28. Ibid.
29. *Das Schwarze Korps*, March 6th, 1935.
30. *Süddeutsche Zeitung*, June 19th, 1961.
31. Case against Bach-Zelewski, p 10; *Die Welt*, Dec 24th, 1958.
32. Hassell: op cit, p 359.
33. Written information from Frida Fätkenheuer, Nov 13th, 1966.
34. SS Seniority List, 1944.
35. *Das Schwarze Korps*, Series 16 1935.
36. Wheeler-Bennett: *The Nemesis of Power*, pp 77 et seq.
37. Letter of July 2nd, 1941 from Berger to Himmler, describing a discussion with Schwarz – in Wulf's papers.
38. SS Order A 53 from Reichsführer-SS dated Oct 10th 1931, BDC Microfilm 97.
39. Salomon: *Der Fragebogen*, p 477.
40. Emil Helfferich: *Ein Leben*, Vol IV, pp 26–7.
41. Ibid, p 15.
42. Ibid, p 26.
43. Ibid, p 25.
44. Ibid, p 27. Bernt Engelmann: *Deutschland-Report*, pp 91–3.
45. Engelmann: op cit, p 69. Michael H. Kater: *Der 'Freundeskreis Himmler'*, p 2.
46. Helfferich: op cit, p 28.
47. Kater: op cit, p 7.
48. Helfferich: op cit, p 28. Kater, op cit, p 8.
49. Engelmann: op cit, p 92.
50. Buchheim: *Anatomy of the SS State*, p 255.
51. Ibid.
52. Order from Wittje to SS Abschnitte IX and XVIII, March 1st, 1933, Central Archives, Microfilm 17.
53. Wilhelm Ehrmann, Declaration of entry Jan 1st, 1934. Letter of Nov 15th, 1933, from Himmler, forbidding canvassing in writing – both from BDC Microfilm 10. Neusüss-Hunkel: *Die SS*, p 17.
54. Letter of Aug 7th, 1933, from Himmler on the subject of Sponsoring Members' badges. Letter of April 7th, 1934 from Wittje to all Oberabschnitt Press Officers. Undated FM Membership Book. Copy of FM Periodical – all in BDC Microfilm 10. See also Knoebel: *Racial Illusion and Military Necessity*, p 4.
55. Letter from Pohl to Schwarz, undated – approx. end 1936, RFSS Microfilm 131.

56. Letter of July 2nd, 1941 from Berger to Himmler, describing a discussion with Schwarz – in Wulf's papers.
57. Political report of Jan 4th, 1937, by Gauleitung Munich/Upper Bavaria on Kriminaloberinspektor Heinrich Müller – Wulf's papers.
58. Ibid.
59. Letter of Jan 11th, 1943 from RSHA to Reichsführer SS Private Office, RFSS Microfilm 56.
60. Ibid, Jan 19th, 1943. Wulf: *Die SS*, p 79.
61. IMT Vol XXIX, p 210.
62. Ibid.
63. Ibid.
64. Ibid, p 212.
65. Report of Aug 21st, 1935 by SS-Standartenführer Schulz, RFSS Microfilm 33.
66. *Das Schwarze Korps*, May 22nd, 1935.
67. Report by SS-Standartenführer Schulz: see Note 65 above.
68. Knoebel: op cit, p 38.
69. Ibid, p 23.
70. IMT Vol XXIX, p 210.
71. Knoebel: op cit, p 19.
72. Ibid, p 23.
73. Letters from Himmler to Berger, Oct 2nd, 1943, and Berger to Himmler, Oct 22nd, 1943, RFSS Microfilm 128.
74. Reitlinger: *The SS*, pp 14–15.
75. Schellenberg: op cit, p 32.
76. Paetel: 'Die SS', in *Vierteljahrshefte für Zeitgechichte* 1, 1954, p 16.
77. *Brockhaus' Conversations-Lexikon*, Leipzig 1885.
78. OMGUS (Office of US Military Government) Public Safety Branch, Survey of Nazi Criminal Organization.
79. Buchheim: *Anatomy of the SS State*, p 256.
80. See Chapter 16.
81. OMGUS Survey (see Note 78 above).
82. Points noted during official inspection trips, address by Gruppenführer Zech at a Gruppenführer Conference in Berlin, Jan 23rd–25th, 1939, RFSS Microfilm 17.
83. Ibid.
84. Ibid.
85. Knoebel: op cit, p 15.
86. Ibid.
87. Ibid, pp 15–17.
88. Besgen: *Der stille Befehl*, p 75.
89. IMT Vol XXIX, p 211.
90. Ibid.
91. Knoebel: op cit, p 15.
92. 'Der Weg des SS-Mannes', directives drafted by Himmler, undated (approx. 1935), pp 13–27, RFSS Microfilm 155.
93. Helfferich: op cit, p 36.
94. 'Der Weg des SS-Mannes' (see Note 92 above), pp 13–27.
95. Ibid, pp 16, 19, 23.
96. Ibid, p 5.
97. Order dealing with engagements and marriages in 'Uns ist der Kampf', undated (approx. 1942), RFSS Microfilm 161.
98. 'Thoughts on SS jurisdiction' address by Scharfe at Gruppenführer Conference, Berlin, Jan 23rd–25th, 1939, RFSS Microfilm 17.
99. Ibid, pp 7–8.
100. 'Das Ehrengesetz der SS', in 'Uns ist der Kampf' (see Note 97 above).
101. Letter from Himmler to the SS-Gericht [SS Legal Service], July

26th, 1938, RFSS Microfilm 161.
102. Record of proceedings in the Buchhold case by Hauptsturmführer Günther Bleyl, June 22nd, 1943; note by Bleyl, June 22nd, 1943, RFSS Microfilm 131.
103. This point is emphasized in Neusüss-Hunkel: op cit, p 21.
104. Cover note to rules for the grant of the SS Death's Head ring, Aug 1st, 1939, RFSS Microfilm 15. SS Seniority List, 1944.
105. Neusüss-Hunkel: op cit, p 22.
106. SS Seniority List, 1944.
107. Besgen: op cit, p 75.
108. Knoebel: op cit, p 30.
109. Letter to Pohl of July 17th, 1937 – in Wulf's papers.
110. Ibid.
111. Ibid.
112. Verbal information from Ruprecht, the castle warden.
113. Ibid.
114. Trevor Roper: op cit, p 23.
115. Verbal information from Ruprecht.
116. Ibid.
117. W. Segin: *Geschichte der Wewelsburg*, p 14.
118. Ibid, p 10.
119. Frischauer: *Himmler*, pp 67–8.
120. Heiner Lichtenstein, 'Wo Himmler residieren wollte', West German Radio Jan 30th, 1965, script pp 15–16.
121. Ibid, pp 3, 6.
122. Enno Georg: op cit, p 22. (Taubert should not be confused with Sigfred Taubert, head of the German Booksellers Association's Exhibition and Book Fair Organization).
123. Ibid.
124. Inhabitants of Wewelsburg village can still remember this rumour.
125. Georg: op cit, p 22.
126. IMT Vol XXIX, p 225.
127. Georg: op cit, p 21.
128. IMT Vol XXIX, p 225. Georg: op cit, p 21.
129. IMT Vol XXIX, p 225.
130. Georg: op cit, p 23.
131. Wulf: *Die SS*, p 18.
132. *Das Schwarze Korps*, July 1937.
133. Georg: op cit, p 23.
134. Helfferich: op cit, p 31.
135. Besgen: op cit, p 76.
136. Ibid, p 74.
137. Neusüss-Hunkel: op cit, p 119.
138. Ibid, p 71.
139. Address by Zechs, pp 7–8, RFSS Microfilm 17.
140. Address by Standartenführer Dr Cäsar 'Education Experiences', Gruppenführer Conference, Berlin, Jan 25th, 1939, RFSS Microfilm 17.
141. Ibid.
142. 'Der Weg des SS Mannes', pp 6–7.
143. Knoebel: op cit, p 21.
144. Speech by Himmler, Nov 8th, 1936.
145. Knoebel: op cit, p 31.
146. Ibid, pp 30–31.
147. Himmler: *Die Schutzstaffel als antibolschewistische Kampforganisation*, p 22.
148. Speech by Himmler, Nov 8th, 1936, RFSS Microfilm 89.
149. Knoebel: op cit, p 22.
150. Ibid.
151. Ibid.
152. Ibid.
153. Ibid, p 35.
154. Ibid, p 36.

155. Ibid.
156. Verbal information from ex-Obergruppenführer Wilhelm Bittrich, Jan 29th, 1966.
157. Numbers of married SS men and total numbers of children, return as at Jan 1st, 1939, franked by Himmler's Personal Staff, RFSS Microfilm 25.
158. 'Two Years Work in Lebensborn', address by Standartenführer Dr Ebener, Berlin Gruppenführer Conference, Jan 25th, 1939, RFSS Microfilm 17.
159. Ibid.
160. Knoebel: op cit, p 41.
161. See Bundesarchiv statistical review 'Der Adel im Deutschen Offizierkorps', p 12.
162. 'Administrative and Economic Situation, end 1936' – Report by Brigadeführer Pohl, p 2, RFSS Microfilm 131.
163. Ibid.
164. Annual Report of SS Personnel Chancellery, Dec 31st, 1938, p 2 RFSS Microfilm 17.
165. Ibid, p 3.
166. Report on the SS Leaders School, Munich-Dachau, Appendix to SS Personnel Chancellery Annual Report (see Note 164 above), p 4.
167. Lutz Graf Schwerin von Krosigk: *Es geschah in Deutchsland*, p 250.
168. Ernst Jünger: *Der Kampf als inneres Erlebnis*, p 78.
169. Werner Best: 'Der Krieg und das Recht' in Jünger, *Krieg und Krieger*, 1930.
170. Ibid, p 152.
171. Buchheim: *Anatomy of the SS State*, p 329.
172. Ibid, p 328.
173. Ibid.

CHAPTER EIGHT

1. Wulf: *Die SS*, pp 45–6.
2. Buchheim: *Anatomy of the SS State*, p 166.
3. The document is in Wulf's papers.
4. Gercke's memorandum, p 1.
5. Burckhardt: *Meiner Danziger Mission 1937–1939*, p 57.
6. Reitlinger: *The Final Solution*, p 13.
7. Michael Freund, quoted from Ulrich Popplow's 'Reinhard Heydrich oder die Aufnordung durch den Sport' in *Olympisches Feuer*, Aug 1963, p 14.
8. Reitlinger: *The SS*, p 35.
9. H. G. Adler: *Theresienstadt 1941–45*, p 645.
10. Kersten: *Totenkopf und Treue*, pp 97–8.
11. Burckhardt: op cit, p 55.
12. Ibid, p 57.
13. Michael Freund: *Deutschland unterm Hakenkreuz*, p 336.
14. Kersten: op cit, p 98.
15. Verbal information from Bruno Streckenbach, Jan 21st, 1966.
16. Popplow: op cit, p 15.
17. Ibid.
18. Ibid, p 18.
19. 'Nebe Series', Feb 9th, 1950.
20. Ibid.
21. Verbal information from Streckenbach, Jan 21st, 1966.
22. Kersten: op cit, pp 90–91. 'Nebe Series', Jan 9th, 1950.
23. Kersten: op cit, p 90.
24. Ibid.
25. Fest: *Das Gesicht des dritten Reiches*, p 141. Wighton:

Heydrich, p 81.
26. Popplow: op cit, p 16.
27. Fest: op cit, p 139.
28. Statement by Rudolf Diels, *Frankfurter Allgemeine Zeitung*, May 9th, 1957.
29. Wighton: op cit, pp 93–4.
30. Burckhardt: op cit, p 56.
31. 'Nebe Series', Feb 9th, 1950, p 23.
32. Aronson: *Heydrich und die Anfänge des SD und der Gestapo*, p 1.
33. Wighton: op cit, p 27.
34. Ibid, p 29.
35. Abshagen: *Canaris, Patriot und Weltburger*, p 77.
36. Ibid, pp 146–7.
37. Ibid, p 58.
38. Aronson: op cit, pp 23, 42.
39. Abshagen: op cit, p 80.
40. Aronson: op cit, p 38.
41. Wighton: op cit, p 33.
42. Aronson: op cit, p 31.
43. Ibid, p 43. 'Nebe Series', Feb 9th, 1950.
44. Aronson: op cit, p 46. Manvell and Fraenkel: *Himmler*, p 26.
45. Aronson: op cit, p 47. 'Nebe Series', Feb 9th, 1950, p 23.
46. Ibid. Wighton, op cit, p 34.
47. Aronson: op cit, p 48.
48. *Der Spiegel*, No 9 of 1950, p 42.
49. Ibid, p 61.
50. Ibid, p 42.
51. Wighton: op cit, p 34.
52. Aronson: op cit, p 51.
53. Verbal information from Streckenbach, Jan 21st, 1966.
54. Wighton: op cit, p 35.
55. Hagen: *Die geheime Front*, p 41.
56. Aronson: op cit, p 51.
57. 'Nebe Series', Feb 9th, 1950, p 23.
58. Ibid.
59. Wulf: *Die SS*, p 44.
60. Ibid.
61. Aronson: op cit, pp 86–7.
62. Ibid, p 87.
63. Ibid, p 86.
64. Ibid, p 87.
65. Ibid, p 89. 'Nebe Series', Feb 9th, 1950, p 23.
66. Ibid, p 98.
67. Ibid, p 92.
68. Buchheim: *Anatomy of the SS State*, p 142.
69. Aronson: op cit, p 89.
70. Ibid.
71. Ibid, p 98.
72. SS Seniority List.
73. Kersten: op cit, p 99.
74. Schellenberg: *Memoirs*, p 30.
75. Kersten: op cit, p 99.
76. Ibid, p 98.
77. Hagen: op cit, p 86.
78. Alfred Schweder: *Politische Polizei*, p 145.
79. Werner Best: *Die Deutsche Polizei*, p 29.
80. Ibid, p 44.
81. Wulf: *Die SS*, p 55.
82. Ibid.
83. Buchheim: *Anatomy of the SS State*, p 147.
84. Ibid, p 148.
85. Ibid.
86. Ibid, pp 147–8.
87. Ibid, p 148.
88. Broszat: *Anatomy of the SS State*, p 404–5.
89. Ibid, p 401–2.
90. IMT Vol XXIX, p 217.
91. Broszat: op cit, p 416.
92. Ibid, p 424.
93. Buchheim: *Anatomy of the SS State*, p 151.
94. Ibid, p 170.
95. Aronson: op cit, p 175.
96. Ibid.

97. Buchheim: *Anatomy of the SS State*, p 167.
98. Aronson: op cit, p 176.
99. Ibid, p 177.
100. Ibid, pp 154 et seq. SS Seniority List, 1935.
101. Ibid, pp 154–5. Verbal information from Streckenbach, Jan 21st, 1966.
102. Ibid, p 155.
103. Political appreciation on Senior Criminal Inspector Heinrich Müller, Headquarters of Munich-Upper Bavaria Gau, Jan 4th, 1934 – in Wulf's papers.
104. Ibid.
105. Ibid.
106. Political appreciation on Müller by the local Nazi Group office in Pasing, Dec 28th, 1936 – in Wulf's papers.
107. Aronson: op cit, p 117.
108. Ibid, pp ix and x.
109. SS Seniority List, 1934.
110. Kaltenbrunner Report. *Spiegelbild einer Verschwörung*, p 245.
111. Ibid, p 244. 'Nebe Series', Nov 17th, 1949, p 23.
112. Ibid, p 244.
113. Ibid, p 240. 'Nebe Series', Nov 17th, 1949, p 23.
114. 'Nebe Series', Nov 17th, 1949, p 24.
115. Ibid, p 25.
116. Aronson: op cit, pp 236–236*c*.
117. Jünger: *Krieg und Krieger*, p 152.
118. Ibid, p 157.
119. Ibid, pp 153, 158.
120. Horkenbach: *Das deutsche Reich von 1918 bis Heute*, Vol II, p 364.
121. Ibid, p 346.
122. Aronson: op cit, pp 249–50.
123. Ibid, pp ixx *c*, 253. Verbal information from Werner Best, Feb 5th, 1966.
124. Verbal information from Best.
125. IMT Vol XXI, p 501.
126. Buchheim: *SS und Polizei im NS-Staat*, pp 32–4.
127. Aronson: op cit, p 137.
128. Buchheim: *Anatomy of the SS State*, p 146. Helmut Schlierbach: *Die Politische Polizei in Preussen*, p 48. Aronson: op cit, p 294.
129. Buchheim: op cit, pp 146–7.
130. Schlierbach: op cit, p 53.
131. Ibid, pp 41–2.
132. Reinhard Heydrich: *Wandlungen unseres Kampfes*, pp 4, 5, 14.
133. Schweder: op cit, p 14.
134. 'Politische Polizei', Memorandum by Kriminalkommissar Wendzio, p 7, RFSS Microfilm 432.
135. Letter of July 7th, 1938 from Heydrich to all Gestapoleitstellen and Stellen, RFSS Microfilm 491.
136. Ibid.
137. Diels: op cit, pp 160, 167. Aronson (op cit) gives a figure of approx 35 men for 1933.
138. Buchheim: *SS und Polizei im NS-Staat*, p 79. Schlierbach: op cit, p 61.
139. Buchheim: *Anatomy of the SS State*, p 244.
140. Best: *Die deutsche Abwehrpolizei*, p 44.
141. 'Wesen der Geheimen Staatspolizei' – author and date unknown, RFSS Microfilm 432.
142. Ibid.
143. Letter of July 26th, 1937 from Best to Regierungspräsidenten and Police Presidents, RFSS

Microfilm 403.
144. 'Wesen der Geheimen Staatspolizei' (see Note 141 above).
145. Broszat: *Anatomy of the SS State*, p 425.
146. Ibid, p 427.
147. Verbal information from Werner von Haacke.
148. IMT Vol XX, p 471.
149. Ibid, pp 455–6.
150. Broszat: op cit, p 430.
151. Ibid.
152. IMT Vol XX, p 456.
153. Ibid, p 458.
154. Ibid.
155. Ibid.
156. Aronson: op cit, pp 257 and 272.
157. Diels: op cit, p 310. Verbal information from Werner von Haacke.
158. Diels: op cit, p 396.
159. Ibid, p 400. Hubert Schorn; *Der Richter im Dritten Reich*, pp 672–3.
160. Verbal information from Dr Walter Schaeffer, Jan 24th, 1966.
161. Diels: op cit, p 399.
162. Schorn: op cit, pp 107 and 642. Broszat: op cit, pp 422–3.
163. Martin Broszat: 'Zur Perversion der Strafjustiz im Dritten Reich' *Vierteljahrschefte für Zeitgeschichte*, Oct 1958, p 390.
164. Schorn: op cit, p 11.
165. Broszat: 'Perversion der Strafjustiz', p 392. Schorn: op cit, p 193.
166. Hans Frank: *Im Angesicht des Galgens*, p 160.
167. Ibid, p 161.
168. Broszat: *Anatomy of the SS State*, p 424.
169. Schorn: op cit, p 80.
170. Ibid, p 91.
171. Plum: *Staatspolizei und innere Verwaltung 1934–1936*, pp 200–201.
172. Ibid, p 202.
173. Letter of Aug 5th, 1935 from Best to all Gestapo offices, RFSS Microfilm 139.
174. Werner Best: *Die Deutsche Polizei*, p 26.
175. Helmut Krausnick: 'Wehrmacht und Nationalsozialismus' *Das Parlament*, Nov 9th, 1955, p 672.
176. Plum: op cit, pp 198 and 206.
177. Ibid, p 200.
178. Ibid, p 198.
179. Aronson: op cit, p 372. Plum: op cit, p 221.
180. Plum: op cit, p 221.
181. Ibid, p 198.
182. Ibid, pp 213–14.
183. Buchheim: *Anatomy of the SS State*, p 154.
184. Ibid. Schlierbach: op cit, p 55.
185. Plum: op cit, p 203.
186. Neufeldt: *Zur Geschichte der Ordnungspolizei 1936–1945*, p 9.
187. Ibid, p 17.
188. Ibid, p 14.
189. Ibid, p 15.
190. Ibid, p 16.
191. Ibid, p 17. Schlierbach: op cit p 82.
192. Buchheim: *SS und Polizei im NS-Staat*, p 55.

CHAPTER NINE

1. Broszat: *Anatomy of the SS State*, p 448.
2. Ibid.
3. Ibid. Broszat: *Perversion der*

Strafjustiz, p 395.
4. 'Nebe Series', Nov 24th, 1949, p 28.
5. Best: *Die Deutsche Polizei*, p 37.
6. Ibid.
7. Ibid, p 38.
8. Even Best admits as much – *Die Deutsche Polizei*, p 37.
9. Ibid, p 38.
10. Broszat: *Perversion der Strafjustiz*, p 391.
11. Ibid.
12. Ibid.
13. Neufeldt: *Zur Geschichte der Ordnungspolizei 1936–1945*, p 25.
14. Ibid, p 21.
15. Best: *Die Deutsche Abwehrpolizei*, pp 29–30. Buchheim: *Anatomy of the SS State*, pp 163–4.
16. Best: op cit, p 29.
17. Address instructions for encoded correspondence, Issue of May 10th, 1941, RFSS Microfilm 463. Friedrich Zipfel: *Kirchenkampf in Deutschland 1933–34*, p 148.
18. Buchheim: *SS und Polizei im NS-Staat*, pp 52–3.
19. Best: *Die Deutsche Polizei*, p 21.
20. Schweder: *Politische Polizei*, p 156.
21. Schlierbach: *Die politische Polizei in Preussen*, pp 88–93.
22. 'Wesen der Geheimen Staatspolizei', undated, RFSS Microfilm 432.
23. Broszat: *Anatomy of the SS State*, p 418.
24. Ibid, pp 446–7.
25. Broszat: *Perversion der Strafjustiz*, p 395.
26. Ibid, p. 395.
27. Broszat: *Anatomy of the SS State*, pp 443–50. Best: *Die Deutsche Polizei*, pp 39–40.
28. Kogon: *The Theory and Practice of Hell*, p 30.
29. Henkys: *Die nationalsozialistische Gewaltverbrechen*, p 47.
30. Ibid, pp 47, 48, 50.
31. IMT Vol XX, pp 132–3.
32. Schlierbach: op cit, p 61.
33. Kogon (op cit. p 40) wrongly assumes that the post of Concentration Camp Inspector was created by Heydrich and that Eicke's office was at No 7 Prinz-Albrecht-Strasse. In fact Eicke's office was in Block, F, No 129 Friedrichstrasse, Berlin NW7 (see also Broszat: *Anatomy of the SS State*, p 443).
34. IMT Vol XX, p 133.
35. Broszat: *Anatomy of the SS State*, p 405.
36. Aronson: *Heydrich und die Anfänge des SD und der Gestapo*, pp 171–2.
37. Ibid, p 171.
38. Broszat: *Anatomy of the SS State*, p 431.
39. Benedikt Kautsky: *Teufel und Verdammte*, pp 91–2.
40. Broszat: *Anatomy of the SS State*, p 437.
41. Ibid, pp 432–3.
42. Rudolf Höss: *Kommandant in Auschwitz*, p 58.
43. Buchheim: *Anatomy of the SS State*, pp 228, 256.
44. Ibid, p 256.
45. Broszat: *Anatomy of the SS State*, pp 444–5.
46. Ibid, p 436.
47. Ibid.
48. Ibid, p 433.
49. Kautsky: op cit, p 87.

50. Buchheim: op cit, p 260.
51. Ibid.
52. Ibid, p 261.
53. Ibid.
54. Neufeldt: op cit, p 8.
55. Ibid, p 5.
56. Ibid, p 36.
57. Buchheim: *SS und Polizei im NS-Staat*, p 91.
58. Neufeldt: op cit, p 76.
59. Ibid, p 42.
60. Buchheim: *Anatomy of the SS State*, pp 186–7. Letter from Pflomm to Bracht, Feb 18th, 1943; letter from Pflomm to Wolff, April 3rd, 1943, RFSS Microfilm 31.
61. Buchheim: *Anatomy of the SS State*, p 194.
62. Ibid, p 185.
63. Letter of Feb 18th, 1943 from Pflomm to Bracht. Buchheim: *Anatomy of the SS State*, p 186.
64. 'Nebe Series', Dec 1st, 1949, p 22.
65. Ibid.
66. 'Wesen der Geheimen Staatspolizei', p 5.
67. IMT Vol XX, p 128.
68. See Chapter 4, this volume.
69. 'Illegal information organization', Report of Mar 31st, 1937 (probably from Munich Police Headquarters), pp 9–10, RFSS Microfilm 467.
70. Ibid, pp 5–6.
71. Ibid, p 6.
72. Ibid, p 3.
73. Ibid, p 6.
74. Ibid, p 7.
75. Wulf: *Die SS*, p 118.
76. Adolf Eichmann: Record of interrogation, Vol 1 Folio 44.
77. 'How I came to be employed in Russia'; deposition (undated) by Otto Ohlendorf at his trial (in the private papers of Frau Käthe Ohlendorf).
78. Aronson: op cit, p 250.
79. Ibid, pp 279–80.
80. Ibid, pp 281–2.
81. Kogon: op cit, p 21.
82. Aronson: op cit, pp 280–1.
83. Ibid, p 382.
84. On the psychology of the SD élite see Zipfel: *Kirchenkampf in Deutschland 1933–1945*, pp 165 et seq.
85. Schorn: *Der Richter im Dritten Reich*, p 29.
86. Laqueur: *Young Germany*, p 199.
87. Statement by Ohlendorf, Oct 8th, 1947, American Military Tribunal No II A, Case IX. (Reference M-IL-I-I Caming (In Lea) Court II*a*, Case IX.)
88. Ibid, p 488.
89. Ohlendorf to his wife, Frau Käthe Ohlendorf, Feb 6th, 1934, Ohlendorf documents, Book 1a, Ohlendorf trial.
90. Statement by Ohlendorf (see Note 87 above), p 490.
91. Aronson: op cit, p 343.
92. Ibid, p 269.
93. Ibid, p 232.
94. Ibid, p 271.
95. Verbal information from Prof. Reinhard Höhn, Nov 15th, 1966.
96. Aronson: op cit, p 355.
97. Delarue: *History of the Gestapo*, p 208.
98. Aronson: op cit, p 360. Schellenberg: *Memoirs*, pp 19–20.
99. Verbal information from Dr Werner Best, Feb 5th, 1966.
100. Werner Best: *Reinhard Heydrich*, p 3.
101. Schorn: op cit, p 11.
102. IMT Vol XX, p 194.

103. Ibid, pp 141–2.
104. Aronson: op cit, p 360.
105. Ibid, p 275.
106. Ibid, pp 96–7. Wulf: *Die SS*, p 43.
107. Ibid, p 344.
108. Ibid, p 94.
109. Ibid.
110. Ibid, p 93.
111. Ibid, p 355.
112. Boberach: *Meldungen aus dem Reich*, p xiii.
113. Aronson: op cit, p 346.
114. Ibid, p 75.
115. Zipfel: op cit, p 379.
116. Ibid, pp 383–4.
117. Ibid, p 384.
118. Ibid, p 383.
119. IMT Vol XX, p 194.
120. Boberach: op cit, p xxiv.
121. Schlierbach: op cit, p 25.
122. Wendzio: 'Politische Polizei', RFSS Microfilm 432.
123. Eichmann: Record of interrogations Vol 1, p 76.
124. Evaluation system used by Amt VI of the RSHA, worked out by Schellenberg Aug 10th, 1942, RFSS Microfilm 463.
125. Wulf: *Die SS*, p 123.
126. Aronson: op cit, p 332.
127. Ibid, p 333.
128. IMT Vol XXIX, p 223.
129. Letter from Grillenberger to Amt I, SD-Hauptamt, Jan 26th, 1938, RFSS Microfilm 411.
130. Wulf: *Die SS*, pp 124–5.
131. Office minute by Desk II 112, Dec 29th, 1937, RFSS Microfilm 411.
132. Office minute by Hagen, undated (approx 1937–8), RFSS Microfilm 411.
133. Office minute by Hagen, Jan 8th, 1938, RFSS Microfilm 411.
134. Verbal information from Gunther d'Alquen, June 30th–July 1st, 1966.
135. Ibid.
136. Ibid.
137. Ibid.
138. Wulf: *Die SS*, pp 108–9.
139. *Das Schwarze Korps*, Jan 21st, 1937.
140. Ibid, Aug 27th, 1935.
141. Ibid, May 28th, 1936.
142. Ibid, June 5th, 1935 and Apr 22nd, 1937.
143. Ibid, Aug 27th, 1936
144. Ibid, Feb 18th, 1937.
145. Letter from editor's office *Schwarze Korps*, June 21st, 1938, RFSS Microfilm 509.
146. Letter from Paul Koch to editor *Schwarze Korps*, June 7th, 1938. Letter *Schwarze Korps* to Six June 21st, 1938. Letter Desk II 112 to SD Führer East, July 8th, 1938. Letter Desk II 112 to *Schwarze Korps*.
147. Minute from aus den Ruthen to SD Hauptamt, Apr 14th, 1938. Letter from Desk II 112 to aus den Ruthen, Apr 21st, 1938, RFSS Microfilm 509.
148. Note by Hagen, June 17th, 1938, RFSS Microfilm 509.
149. *Das Schwarze Korps*, July 16th, 1936.
150. Ibid, Aug 7th, 1935.
151. Ibid, Jan 5th, 1939.
152. Ibid, Feb 13th, 1941.
153. Ibid, July 11th, 1940.
154. Letter from d'Alquen to Ohlendorf, Sept 25th, 1942, RFSS Microfilm 275.
155. Comment by RSHA Amt III on d'Alquen's letter of Sept 25th, 1942, RFSS Microfilm 275.
156. Ibid, p 7.
157. Letter from d'Alquen to Ohlen-

dorf, July 22nd, 1942, RFSS Microfilm 275.

158. Letter from Ohlendorf to d'Alquen, Aug 14th, 1942, RFSS Microfilm 275.
159. Ibid.

CHAPTER TEN

1. 'Grundsätzliche Gedanken zur Neugliederung' drafted by Schellenberg, undated (approx summer 1939), RFSS Microfilm 432.
2. Boberach: *Meldungen aus dem Reich*, pp xiii, xiv.
3. Ibid, p xiv.
4. 'Die Eigenständigkeit des Sicherheitsdienstes', undated, RFSS Microfilm 239.
5. Wighton: *Heydrich*, p 115.
6. Ibid. *Hamburger Morgenpost*, Feb 3rd, 1965.
7. Wighton: op cit, p 116.
8. Ibid.
9. Ibid, p 117.
10. Ibid. *Hamburger Morgenpost*, Feb 3rd, 1965.
11. Werner Best: *Wilhelm Canaris*, p 6.
12. Letters from Hagen and Eichmann, Nov 4th, 1937, RFSS Microfilm 411.
13. Ibid.
14. Ibid.
15. Abshagen: *Canaris, Patriot und Weltburger*, p 94.
16. Ibid, pp 19, 51, 68, 139.
17. Karl Bartz: *Die Tragödie der deutschen Abwehr*, p 80.
18. Abshagen: op cit, p 147.
19. Werner Best: *Die deutsche Abwehrpolizei bis 1945*, pp 19, 19a, 19b.
20. Best: *Wilhelm Canaris*, p 6. Gerd Buchheit: *Der deutsche Geheimdienst*, pp 158 et seq.
21. Hagen: *Die geheime Front*, p 57.
22. See Delarue: *History of the Gestapo*, p 187.
23. Schellenberg: *Memoirs*, p 46.
24. Ibid, p 47.
25. Ibid, p 49.
26. Hagen: op cit, p 54; 'Braver, dummer Klim', *Der Spiegel*, Nov 8th, 1961, p 68.
27. B. H. Liddel Hart: *The Red Army*, p 69.
28. 'Die Politische Lage in der Roten Armee', issued by Head of SD Hauptamt 1938, RFSS Microfilm 467.
29. *Die Welt*, Jan 4th, 1962.
30. Karl Spalcke: 'Der Fall Tuchatschewski' in *Die Gegenwart*, Jan 25th, 1958.
31. *Der Spiegel*, Nov 8th, 1961, p 70.
32. Ibid, p 71.
33. Ibid.
34. Ibid.
35. Ibid.
36. Ibid.
37. Hagen (Höttl): op cit, p 62.
38. Schellenberg: op cit, p 49.
39. *Der Spiegel*, Nov 8th, 1961, p 68.
40. Hagen: op cit, p 62.
41. Spalcke: op cit, p 47.
42. Abshagen: op cit, p 169.
43. Buchheim: *SS und Polizei im NS-Staat*, pp 62–3.
44. Buchheim: *Anatomy of the SS State*, p 171.
45. Ibid.

46. Boberach: op cit, p xiii. Ohlendorf's statement, Oct 8th, 1967, pp 496 et seq.
47. Ohlendorf's statement, p 490.
48. Verbal statement by Gunter d'Alquen, Nov 1966.
49. Ohlendorf's statement, pp 484 et seq.
50. Boberach: op cit, p xiii.
51. Ohlendorf's statement, p 490.
52. Ibid, p 491.
53. Ibid.
54. 'Die Wirtschaft im nationalsozialistischen Staat', undated memorandum by Ohlendorf, in Frau Käthe Ohlendorf's private papers.
55. Ohlendorf's statement, p 491.
56. Boberach: op cit, p xiii.
57. Ohlendorf's plea in mitigation, July 1950, p 40 (Frau Ohlendorf's private papers).
58. Helmut Heiber: *Walter Frank*, pp 430 et seq.
59. Ibid, pp 441, 444.
60. Verbal information from Professor Höhn, Nov 1966.
61. Affidavit by Karl Wolff, Sept 13th, 1947, Ohlendorf documents Book IV.
62. Ibid. Kersten: op cit, p 209.
63. Sworn statement by Luitpold Schallermeier, Aug 21st, 1947, Ohlendorf documents, Book IV.
64. Ohlendorf's statement, Oct 8th, 1947, p 492.
65. Boberach, op cit, p xiv.
66. Ohlendorf's statement, Oct 8th, 1947, p 493.
67. Ibid.
68. Verbal information from Frau Käthe Ohlendorf Jan 26th, 1966.
69. Memorandum drafted by Schellenberg 'Reorganization of the SD with a view to its fusion with the Sicherheitspolizei', Feb 24th, 1939, RFSS Microfilm 239.
70. Judgement of court set up by Supreme Commander of the Wehrmacht in the case of Freiherr von Fritsch, March 18th, 1938, p 3 (in the private papers of Fabian von Schlabrendorf).
71. Ibid, pp 9–10.
72. Ibid, p 3.
73. Ibid. Adolf Graf von Kielmansegg; *Der Fritschprozess 1938*, pp 53 and 56.
74. Ibid, p 3.
75. Ibid.
76. Verbal information from Dr Werner Best, Feb 5th, 1966.
77. Judgement of court (see Note 70 above), pp 4–9.
78. Ibid.
79. Ibid.
80. Ibid, p 11.
81. *Der Spiegel*, No 36 of 1965, p 46.
82. Hossbach: *Zwischen Wehrmacht und Hitler 1934–1938*, p 126.
83. Ibid, p 103.
84. Krausnick: *Wehrmacht und Nationalsozialismus*, p 666.
85. Foertsch: *Schuld und Verhängnis*, p 90. Krausnick: op cit, p 677.
86. Foertsch: op cit, p 76.
87. Ibid. Hossbach: op cit, p 188.
88. Hossbach: op cit, p 190.
89. Ibid, p 218.
90. Foertsch: op cit, pp 91, 138.
91. Kielmansegg: op cit, pp 34–5.
92. Graf von der Goltz: 'Die Entlassung des Generalobersten Freiherr von Fritsch'.
93. Foertsch: op cit, p 128.
94. Walter Görlitz: *Generalfeldmarschall Keitel, Verbrecher*

oder Offizier?, pp 86, 88.
95. Ibid, p 102.
96. Letter from Curt Hellmuth Müller, Dec 9th, 1949.
97. Ibid.
98. Ibid.
99. Ibid.
100. Görlitz: *Keitel*, p 103.
101. Ibid.
102. Hossbach: op cit, p 123.
103. Ibid, p 124.
104. Ibid, p 123.
105. Ibid.
106. Krausnick: *Wehrmacht und Nationalsozialismus*, p 679.
107. Hossbach: op cit, p 123.
108. Foertsch: op cit, p 141.
109. Ibid, p 102.
110. Ibid, pp 90–91.
111. Hossbach, op cit, pp 126–7.
112. Quoted from Werner Picht: *Vom Wesen des Krieges und vom Kriegswesen der Deutschen*, p 225.
113. Wilhelm Treue: script of radio talk 'The Fritsch Affair', p 35.
114. Hossbach: op cit, p 129.
115. Ibid.
116. Ibid.
117. Foertsch: op cit, p 138.
118. Ibid, p 128.
119. Görlitz: *Keittel*, p 106.
120. Foertsch: op cit, p 88.
121. Ibid, p 138.
122. Görlitz: *Keitel*, p 107.
123. Kielmansegg: op cit, p 38.
124. Foertsch: op cit, p 88.
125. Ibid, pp 88–9.
126. Görlitz: *Keitel*, p 109.
127. Foertsch: op cit, p 106.
128. Ibid, p 105.
129. Ibid, p 118.
130. Ibid.
131. Heinrich Rosenberger: 'Die Entlassung des Generalobersten Freiherrn von Fritsch' in *Deutsche Rundschau*, Nov 1946, pp 91–2.
132. Ibid.
133. Kielmansegg: op cit, pp 48–9.
134. Judgement of Court (see Note 70), p 28.
135. Ibid, p 29.
136. Ibid, p 1.
137. Kielmansegg: op cit, p 50.
138. Foertsch: op cit, p 100.
139. Ibid.
140. Verbal information from Dr Werner Best, Feb 5th, 1966.
141. Ibid.
142. Gisevius: *To the Bitter End*, p 243.
143. Schellenberg: op cit, p 32.
144. Foertsch: op cit, p 120.
145. Judgement of Court, p 23.
146. Gisevius: *Bis zum bitteren Ende*, p 274 (not in English translation).
147. Foertsch: op cit, p 105.
148. Abshagen: op cit, p 178.
149. Schellenberg: op cit, p 33.
150. Krausnick: *Wehrmacht und Nationalsozialismus*, p 678.
151. Gisevius: *Bis zum bitteren Ende*, p 280 (not in English translation).
152. Krausnick: op cit, p 681.
153. Judgement of Court, pp 31–4.
154. Kielmansegg: op cit, p 80.
155. Judgement of Court, p 18.
156. Foertsch: op cit, p 121. Kielmansegg: op cit, p 82.
157. Foertsch: op cit, p 122.
158. Ibid.
159. Kielmansegg: op cit, pp 87–8.
160. Foertsch: op cit, p 125.
161. Kielmansegg: op cit, p 90.
162. Foertsch: op cit, p 124.
163. Judgement of Court, p 1.
164. Wolfgang Foerster: *Generaloberst Ludwig Beck*, p 92.

165. Ibid, p 169.
166. Foertsch: op cit, p 129.
167. Wheeler-Bennett: *Nemesis of Power*, p 381.
168. Foertsch: op cit, p 129.
169. Ibid.
170. 'Nebe Series', Dec 29th, 1949, p 404.
171. Schellenberg: op cit, p 34.
172. Verbal information from Bruno Streckenbach, Jan 21st, 1966.
173. Verbal information from Paul Hausser, Jan 31st, 1966.
174. Draft of an address by Brigadeführer Petri headed 'General experiences of the call-up of reinforcements for the SS-Totenkopfverbände in September 1933 and of the mass employment of the Allgemeine SS' – initialled by Himmler Jan 22nd, 1939, RFSS Microfilm 17.
175. Wighton: op cit, p 150.
176. Abshagen: op cit, pp 185–6.
177. Görlitz: *Keitel*, p. 407.
178. Comment by Schellenberg on Heydrich's proposals for reorganization of the SD and Sicherheitspolizei, Apr 4th, 1939, RFSS Microfilm 239.
179. Buchheim: *Anatomy of the SS State*, p 209.
180. Ibid, pp 209–10.
181. Ibid, p 185.
182. Ibid, pp 213–14.
183. Best: *Die Deutsche Polizei*, pp 85, 87.
184. Zipfel: op cit, pp 159, 164.
185. 'Reorganization of the Sicherheitsdienst Reichsführer-SS with a view to organizational and personnel assimilation to the Sicherheitspolizei'; memorandum drafted by Schellenberg, Feb 24th, 1939, RFSS Microfilm 239.
186. Letter from Pohl to Schwarz, undated (approx. end 1936), RFSS Microfilm 131.
187. Ibid.
188. Zipfel: op cit, p 146.
189. Letter from Schellenberg to Heydrich, Feb 27th, 1939, RFSS Microfilm 239.
190. Note by Schellenberg, dated Apr 4th, 1939, recommending formation of a working party to discuss SD problems, RFSS Microfilm 239.
191. Buchheim: *SS und Polizei im NS-Staat*, p 61.
192. See Note 185 above.
193. 'Comment on SS-Brigadeführer Best's latest draft on career structure', note by Schellenberg dated Aug 28th, 1939, RFSS Microfilm 239.
194. As evidence of Schellenberg's campaign against Best, see his note on SD careers, Feb 28th, 1939, RFSS Microfilm 239.
195. *Deutsches Recht*, Folio 8–9, Apr 15th, 1939.
196. Ibid, p 198 (Best's article 'Kritik und Apologie des Juristen').
197. Letter from Schellenberg to Heydrich, Apr 25th, 1939, RFSS Microfilm 239.
198. Ibid.
199. Verbal information from Dr Werner Best, Feb 5th, 1966.
200. Schellenberg: *Memoiren*, p 34 (not in English translation).
201. Ohlendorf's statement, Oct. 8th, 1947, p 496.
202. The Reich Ministry of the Interior, for instance, initially, took no official cognizance of the formation of the RSHA (see Neufeldt: op cit, p 21).
203. Buchheim: *Anatomy of the SS State*, pp 137–40.

204. Ibid.
205. Ibid.
206. Ibid.
207. Ibid.
208. Ibid.
209. Ohlendorf's statement, Oct 8th, 1947, pp 495–6.
210. Ibid, p 496.
211. Ibid.
212. Verbal information from Dr Werner Best, Feb 5th, 1966.
213. Ibid.
214. Letter from Best to Heydrich, Apr 15th, 1942 (in Wulf's papers).
215. Verbal information from Dr Werner Best, Feb 5th, 1966.
216. Buchheim: *Anatomy of the SS State*, p 194.

CHAPTER ELEVEN

1. Hans-Adolf Jacobsen: *1939–45, Der Zweite Weltkrieg in Chronik und Documenten*, p 115.
2. Ibid, p 116.
3. Shirer: *The Rise and Fall of the Third Reich*, p 532.
4. Ibid.
5. Ibid.
6. Halder's diary, Vol I, p 19.
7. Helmut Arntz: 'Die Menschenverluste im Zweiten Weltkrieg', in *Bilanz des Zweiten Weltkrieges*, p 446.
8. Jürgen Runzheimer: 'Der Überfall auf den Sender Gleiwitz' in *Vierteljahrshefte für Zeitgeschichte*, No. 4 of 1962, p 419
9. Jürgen Thorwald: 'Der Mann, der den Krieg auslöste' in *Der Stern*, June 7th, 1953.
10. Ibid.
11. Ibid.
12. *Der Spiegel*, Nov 13th, 1963.
13. Ibid, p 73.
14. Raimund Schnabel: *Macht ohne Moral*, p 384.
15. Thorwald: op cit, p 14.
16. *Der Spiegel*, Nov 13th, 1963, p 71.
17. Ibid.
18. Runzheimer: op cit, p 420.
19. Ibid.
20. Ibid, pp 411, 413.
21. Thorwald: op cit, pp 14 et seq.
22. Ibid.
23. Schnabel, op cit, p 386.
24. Ibid.
25. Ibid.
26. Ibid.
27. Shirer: op cit, p 547.
28. Rudi Strauch: *Sir Neville Henderson*, p 278.
29. Ludwig Denne: *Das Danzig-Problem in der deutschen Aussenpolitik 1934–39*, p 278.
30. Runzheimer: op cit, p 425.
31. Shirer: op cit, p 557.
32. Helmuth Greiner: *Die oberste Wehrmachtführung*, pp 46–7.
33. 'Nebe Series', Dec 29th, 1949, p 27. Letter of Feb 6th, 1967 from Herr Jürgen Runzheimer.
34. Letter of Feb 6th, 1967 from Herr Jürgen Runzheimer. (I should like to take this opportunity of thanking Herr Runzheimer for his assistance and recommending to the reader his study 'Die Grenzzwischenfälle am Aug 30th, 1939,' in *Vierteljahrshefte für Zeitgeschichte*.
35. Shirer: op cit, p 569.

36. *Der Spiegel*, Nov 13th, 1963, p74.
37. Ibid. Runzheimer: op cit, p 425.
38. *Der Spiegel*, Nov 13th, 1963, pp 74–5.
39. Runzheimer: op cit, p 415.
40. *Der Spiegel*, Nov 13th, 1963, p 74.
41. Ibid, pp 74–5. Runzheimer: op cit, p 415.
42. Ibid, p 75.
43. Schnabel: op cit, p 390.
44. *Völkischer Beobachter*, Sept 1st, 1939.
45. Quoted from Thorwald: op cit, p 14.
46. Runzheimer: op cit, p 409.
47. Ibid.
48. Ibid.
49. 'Nebe Series' Dec 29th, 1949, p 27.
50. Ibid.
51. Knoebel: *Racial Illusion and Military Necessity*, p 226.
52. Buchheim: *SS und Polizei im NS-Staat*, p 168.
53. 'Die Erhebung der österreichischen Nationalsozialisten im Juli 1934', Report by the Reichsführer-SS Historical Commission, p 68.
54. Adolf Eichmann: Record of proceedings, Vol 1, Col 36.
55. 'Die Erhebung' (see Note 53), p 68.
56. Ibid.
57. Ibid.
58. Ibid, p 69.
59. Ibid, p 67.
60. Ibid, p 71.
61. Ibid, p 70.
62. Ibid.
63. Ibid.
64. Ibid.
65. Ibid.
66. Ibid.
67. Ibid, p 77. Gordon Shepherd: *Dollfuss*, p 235.
68. Shepherd: op cit, pp 213, 233.
69. Letter from Wächter to the Supreme Party Court of the NSDAP, May 31st, 1938, RFSS Microfilm 32.
70. Shepherd: op cit, p 237.
71. Ibid.
72. Ibid.
73. Letter from Wächter to Supreme Party Court, p 8, RFSS Microfilm 32.
74. Ibid, pp 7–8.
75. Submission by Wächter at the Hamburg trial Jan 1937, pp 4–5, RFSS Microfilm 32.
76. Ibid, p 4.
77. Ibid, p 7.
78. Ibid, p 5.
79. Ibid.
80. Ibid.
81. Hellmuth Auerbach: 'Eine nationsozialistische Stimme zum Wiener Putsch vom 25 Juli 1934', in *Vierteljahrshefte für Zeitgeschichte*, Apr 1964, p 204.
82. Wächter's submission (see Note 75), p 8.
83. Shepherd: op cit, p 243.
84. 'Die Erhebung' (see Note 53), p 81.
85. Stepherd: op cit, p 243.
86. 'Die Erhebung', p 84.
87. Ibid, pp 81–2.
88. Ibid, p 81.
89. Wächter's letter to Supreme Party Court, p 10.
90. 'Die Erhebung', p 82.
91. Ibid, p 84.
92. Ibid, p 85.
93. Ibid.
94. Shepherd: op cit, p 249–50.
95. 'Die Erhebung', p 85.
96. Ibid, p 88.
97. Ibid.

98. Ibid, p 89.
99. Ibid, pp 89, 94, 96.
100. Ibid, pp 94, 96.
101. Ibid, p 92.
102. Shepherd: op cit, p 309.
103. Ibid, p 310. 'Die Erhebung', p 102.
104. Ibid, p 311.
105. 'Die Erhebung', p 128.
106. Ibid, p 132. Wächter's submission (see Note 75) p 10.
107. Ibid, p 132.
108. Wächter's submission, p 10.
109. 'Die Erhebung', p 140.
110. Papen: *Memoirs*, pp 337–8.
111. Bullock: op cit, p 328.
112. Wächter's submission, pp 10–11.
113. Volz: *Daten der Geschichte der NSDAP*, p 34. Louis de Jong: *Die deutsche Fünfte Kolonne im Zweiten Weltkrieg*, p. 260.
114. Ibid, p 263.
115. Ibid.
116. MacAlister Brown: 'The Third Reich's mobilization of the German Fifth Column in Eastern Europe' in *Journal of Central European Affairs*, July 1959, p 129.
117. de Jong: op cit, p 264. Koehl: op cit, pp 36–7.
118. Buchheim: *Anatomy of the SS State*, p 284. Robert Koehl: 'Towards an SS Typology: Social Engineers' in *American Journal of Economics and Sociology*, No 18, Jan 1959, p 117.
119. Koehl: *RKFVD*, p 39.
120. Ibid, p 27.
121. de Jong: op cit, p 264.
122. Ibid.
123. Ibid.
124. Ibid.
125. Neusüss-Hunkel: *Die SS*, pp 81–2.
126. *Organisationsbuch der NSDAP*, p 151.
127. Heinrich Orb: *Nationalsozialismus*, p 389.
128. Wulf: *Die SS*, p 96.
129. Ribbentrop: *Memoirs*, p 22. Von Papen: *Memoirs*, p 235.
130. Ribbentrop: op cit, p 22 (Note).
131. Ribbentrop: *Zwischen London and Moskau*, p 37 (not in English translation).
132. Neusüss-Hunkel: op cit, p 82.
133. Seabury: *The Wilhelmstrasse*, p 108.
134. Ibid.
135. Ibid, p 106.
136. Ernst-Günther Krätschmer: *Die Ritterkreuzträger der Waffen-SS*, p 208.
137. Erich Kordt: *Nicht aus den Akten*, p 188.
138. Ibid. Weizsäcker was made SS-Brigadeführer in 1942 (see SS Seniority List, 1944).
139. Kordt: op cit, p 188. Woermann was promoted SS-Oberführer in 1942 (see SS Seniority List 1944).
140. Kordt: op cit, p 188.
141. Ibid.
142. Kempner: *SS im Kreuzverhör*, pp 244–5.
143. Verbal information from Dr Werner Best, Feb 5th, 1966.
144. Hagen (alias Höttl): *Die geheime Front*, p 142.
145. Ibid.
146. Ibid, pp 123, 131.
147. Kurt Glaser: *Die Tschechoslowakei*, p 52.
148. Hagen: op cit, p 126.
149. Ibid, p 138.
150. Ibid, pp 144, 146.
151. Ibid, p 156.
152. SS Seniority List 1944.

153. Brown: op cit, p 133.
154. Hagen: op cit, p 174.
155. Ibid.
156. Ibid, p 175.
157. Ibid.
158. Ibid, p 541.
159. Ibid.
160. Letter from Keppler to Himmler, July 11th, 1939, RFSS Microfilm 32.
161. Bullock: *Hitler, a Study in Tyranny*, p 483.
162. Hagen: op cit, p 76.
163. Ibid, p 177.
164. Letter from Keppler to Himmler, July 11th, 1939, RFSS Microfilm 32.
165. de Jong: op cit, p 148.
166. Ribbentrop: op cit, p 82.
167. Seabury: *The Wilhelmstrasse*, p 194.
168. de Jong: op cit, p 168.
169. 'Wenn ihr einmarschiert, schiessen wir', *Der Spiegel* No 18, 1963, pp 77 et seq.
170. Hagen: op cit, pp 280 et seq.
171. Letter from Heydrich to the Foreign Ministry, June 20th, 1941, RFSS Microfilm 199.
172. Seabury: op cit, p 129; Ribbentrop op cit, p 82.
173. Führer order, Sept 3rd, 1939, RFSS Microfilm 199.
174. Schellenberg: *Memoirs*, p 82.
175. S. Payne Best: *The Venlo Incident*, pp 7–8. Schellenberg: op cit, pp 82–3.
176. Schellenberg: op cit, p 83.
177. Ibid, p 85.
178. Ibid.
179. Ibid.
180. Ibid, p 86.
181. Ibid, p 88.
182. Ibid, p 91.
183. Ibid, p 94.
184. Dr Werner Best: *Joachim von Ribbentrop*, p 2.
185. Manuscript for discussion 'Das bestellte Attentat', July 26th, 1965, Channel I German TV, p 5.
186. Schellenberg: op cit, p 94.
187. Ibid, p 95.
188. Ibid, p 96.
189. Ibid, p 97.
190. Ibid, pp 101, 103.
191. Ibid, p 104.
192. Ibid.
193. Ibid.
194. 'Nebe Series', Jan 5th, 1950, p 24. Dr Albrecht Böhme: 'Das Bürgerbräuattentat' (MS), p 5. See also, by the same author 'Das Attentat auf Hitler im Bürgerbräukeller, kein Werk des englischen Geheimdienstes', in *Die Kriminalistik*, No 10, 1966.
195. Böhme: MS pp 6–7 (see Note 194 above).
196. Record of interrogation of Elser, *Der Stern*, May 10th, 1966.
197. 'Nebe Series', Jan 5th, 1950, p 24. Böhme MS, p 11.
198. Schellenberg: op cit, p 110.
199. *Der Stern*, May 17th, 1964, p 84.
200. Böhme: MS pp 9–10 (see Note 194 above).
201. Statement by Haber in *Bild am Sonntag*, Dec 6th, 1959.
202. Schellenberg: op cit, p 91 (German original – not in English translation).
203. 'Das bestellte Attentat', p 26 (see Note 185 above).
204. Schellenberg: op cit, p 179.
205. Hagen: op cit, p 283.
206. Ibid, p 206.
207. Martin Broszat: 'Das Dritte Reich und die rumänische Judenpolitik' in *Gutachten des*

Instituts für Zeitgeschichte, p 121.
208. Hagen: op cit, pp 288–9.
209. Broszat: op cit, p 124.
210. Hagen: op cit, p 290.
211. Ibid. Broszat: op cit, p 126.
212. Letter from Andreas Schmidt to Berger, Sept 24th, 1943, RFSS Microfilm 128.
213. Hagen: op cit, p 282.
214. Letter from Heydrich to Foreign Ministry, June 20th, 1941, RFSS Microfilm 199.
215. Seabury: op cit, p 128.
216. Ibid.
217. Letter from Ribbentrop to Himmler Sept 6th, 1942, RFSS Microfilm 117.
218. Seabury: op cit, pp 127, 194.
219. Verbal information from Dr Werner Best, Feb 5th, 1966.

CHAPTER TWELVE

1. Helmut Krausnick and others: 'Denkschrift Himmlers über die Behandlung der Fremdvölkischen im Osten' in *Vierteljahrshefte für Zeitgeschichte*, Apr 1957, p 194.
2. Ibid, p 196.
3. Ibid, p 198.
4. Ibid, p 197.
5. Ibid.
6. Helmut Heiber: 'Der Generalplan Ost' in *Vierteljahrshefte für Zeitgeschichte*, Issue 3 of 1958, p 284.
7. Kersten: *Totenkopf und Treue*. p 132.
8. Neusüss-Hunkel: *Die SS*. p 72.
9. Ibid, p 71.
10. Ibid, p 72.
11. Koehl: *RKFVD*, p 27.
12. Ibid, p 43. *Gutachten des Institut für Zeitgeschichte*, p 246.
13. Ibid, p 42.
14. Ibid, p 43.
15. *Mein Kampf* (James Murphy's translation, Hurst & Blackett, 1939), p 533.
16. Martin Broszat: *Nationalsozialistische Polenpolitik 1939–45*, p 21.
17. Case for the prosecution against Karl Wolff for participation in mass murder, Public Prosecutor's Office, Provincial Court Munich II, Ref. 10a JS 39/60, p 86.
18. Buchheim: *Anatomy of the SS State*, pp 176–7.
19. Ibid.
20. Ibid.
21. Ibid.
22. Wulf: *Die SS*, pp 242–3.
23. Ibid, p 239.
24. Ibid.
25. Ibid, p 240.
26. Ibid.
27. Ibid.
28. Helmut Krausnick: 'Hitler und die Morde in Polen' in *Vierteljahrshefte für Zeitgeschichte*, April 1963, p 198.
29. Ibid.
30. Ibid.
31. Ibid, p 205.
32. Ibid, p 207.
33. Case against Wolff (see Note 17 above), p 87.
34. Ibid, pp 87–8. Wulf: *Die SS*, p 246.

35. Krausnick: op cit, p 203.
36. Broszat: *Nationalsozialistische Polenpolitik*, p 28.
37. Ibid, p 45.
38. Ibid, p 39.
39. Ibid, p 45.
40. Ibid.
41. Ibid, p 44.
42. Note by Schellenberg following a Heads of Section conference on Sept 27th, 1940, RFSS Microfilm 239.
43. de Jong: *Die deutsche Fünfte Kolonne im Zweiten Weltkrieg*, p 54.
44. Ibid, pp 55–6.
45. Ibid, p 57.
46. Ibid.
47. Broszat: op cit, p 47.
48. Ibid, p 60.
49. Ibid, p 28.
50. Ibid, pp 29, 45, 46.
51. Ibid, p 61.
52. Ibid.
53. Ibid.
54. Henkys: *Die nationalsozialistischen Gewaltverbrechen*, p 82.
55. Krausnick: 'Hitler und die Morde in Polen', p 203.
56. Ibid, p 198.
57. Reitlinger: *The Final Solution*, p 37.
58. Hilberg: *The Destruction of the European Jews*, pp 127–8.
59. Case against Wolff, p 90.
60. Broszat: *Nationalsozialistiche Polenpolitik*, p 27.
61. Krausnick: op cit, p 203.
62. Broszat: op cit, p 28.
63. Case against Wolff, p 94.
64. Ibid.
65. Broszat: op cit, p 29.
66. Hilberg: op cit, pp 129–31.
67. Krausnick: op cit, p 202. Broszat: op cit, p 22.
68. Broszat: op cit, p 29.
69. Ibid.
70. Ibid, p 58.
71. Ibid.
72. Buchheim: *Anatomy of the SS State*, pp 213–14.
73. Broszat: op cit, p 58.
74. Ibid, pp 28, 58.
75. Ibid, p 58.
76. Ibid.
77. Ibid.
78. Krausnick: op cit, p 203.
79. Broszat: op cit, p 78.
80. Ibid, pp 74–5–6.
81. Krausnick: op cit, p 204.
82. Broszat: op cit, p 41.
83. Ibid.
84. Ibid.
85. Schnabel: *Macht ohne Moral*, p 395.
86. Ibid, p 396.
87. Wulf: *Das Dritte Reich und seine Diener*, p 518.
88. Hilberg: op cit, p 127. Broszat: op cit, p 40.
89. Broszat: op cit, p 204.
90. Krausnick: op cit, p 205.
91. Broszat: op cit, p 76.
92. Krausnick: op cit, p 204.
93. Koehl: *RKFVD*, pp 100, 101, 72.
94. Hans Buchheim: 'Rechtsstellung und Organisation des Reichskommissars für die Festigung deutschen Volkstums' in *Gutachten des Instituts für Zeitgeschichte*, p 275.
95. Ibid.
96. Koehl: 'SS Typology', p 115; *RKFVD*, p 48.
97. Buchheim: *Rechtsstellung RKF*, p 276.
98. Ibid.
99. Ibid, p 245.
100. Ibid.
101. Ibid.

102. Koehl: *RKFVD*, p 49.
103. Ibid.
104. Ibid, p 50.
105. Buchheim: *Anatomy of the SS State*, pp 274–6. Decree of the Führer and Reich Chancellor for the Strengthening of Germanism, Oct 7th, 1939, RFSS Microfilm 239.
106. Ibid.
107. Buchheim: *Rechtsstellung RKF*, p 245.
108. Ibid, p 247.
109. Ibid, pp 245–7.
110. Ibid, p 261.
111. Ibid, p 267.
112. Ibid, p 265.
113. Koehl: *RKFVD*, p 62.
114. Buchheim: *Rechtsstellung RKF*, pp 248–9.
115. Koehl: *RKFVD*, pp 62–3.
116. Ibid, p 63.
117. Ibid.
118. Wulf: *Die SS*, p 186.
119. Koehl: *RKFVD*, pp 56, 73.
120. Buchheim: *Rechtsstellung RKF*, p 270.
121. Ibid.
122. Koehl: *RKFVD*, p 59.
123. Ibid.
124. Wulf: *Die SS*, p 182.
125. Broszat: *Nationalsozialistische Polenpolitik*, pp 63–4.
126. Koehl: *RKFVD*, p 121.
127. Ibid, p 130.
128. Ibid, p 86.
129. Ibid, pp 216–7.
130. Buchheim: *Rechtsstellung RKF*, p 271. Koehl: op cit, pp 120–1.
131. Wulf: *Die SS*, p 195.
132. Ibid, p 197.
133. Ibid, p 200.
134. Ibid.
135. Ibid, pp 101–2. Koehl: *RKFVD*, p 144.
136. Ibid, pp 205–6.
137. Koehl: *RKFVD*, pp 212–3.
138. Broszat: *Nationalsozialistische Polenpolitik*, p 93.
139. Ibid.
140. Letter from Willich to Kaltenbrunner, Apr 16th, 1943, RFSS Microfilm 117.
141. Broszat: op cit, p 93.
142. Koehl: *RKFVD*, p 146.
143. Heiber: *Generalplan Ost*, p 285.
144. Ibid, pp 298–9.
145. Ibid, p 291.
146. Ibid, pp 291–2.
147. Ibid, p 297.
148. Ibid, p 246.
149. Kersten: op cit, p 133.
150. Ibid.
151. Wulf: *Das Dritte Reich und seine Vollstrecker*, p 262.
152. Ibid, p 271.
153. Koehl: *RKFVD*, p 133.
154. Ibid, pp 226–7.
155. Ibid, p 227.
156. Ibid, p 134.
157. Ibid, p 152.
158. Gilbert: *The Psychology of Dictatorship*, p 143.
159. IMT Vol XXIX, p 443.
160. Ibid, p 444.
161. Ibid.
162. Ibid, p 455.
163. Ibid.
164. Koehl: *RKFVD*, p 130.
165. Broszat: *Nationalsozialistische Polenpolitik*, p 183.
166. Verbal information from Gottlob Berger, Feb 1st, 1966.
167. Broszat, op cit, p 81.
168. IMT Vol XXIX, p 507.
169. Ibid, p 379.
170. Broszat: op cit, p 82.
171. Letter from Reinecke to Himmler, Dec 1st, 1941, RFSS, Microfilm 125.

172. Ibid.
173. Ibid.
174. Ibid.
175. Ibid.
176. Ibid.
177. Ibid.
178. Broszat: op cit, p 82.
179. Office minute by Himmler dated Mar 5th, 1942, RFSS Microfilm 125.
180. Ibid.
181. Letter from Frank to Lammers, Mar 10th, 1942, RFSS Microfilm 125.
182. Lammers to Himmler Mar 7th, 1942. Führer decree on prerogatives of the Reichsführer-SS and Chief of the German Police in the Government General, RFSS Microfilm 125. Broszat: *Nationalsozialistische Polenpolitik*, p 83. Hilberg: op cit, p 132.
183. IMT Vol XXIX, p 514.
184. Gilbert: op cit, p 147.
185. IMT Vol XXIX, p 520.
186. Ibid, pp 527, 519.
187. Ibid, p 533.
188. Ibid, p 537.
189. Ibid, p 534.
190. Ibid, p 555.
191. Ibid, p 559.
192. Wulf: *Das Dritte Reich und seine Vollstrecker*, pp 171–2.
193. Broszat: *Nationalsozialistische Polenpolitik*, p 84.

CHAPTER THIRTEEN

1. Kersten: *Totenkopf und Treue*, p 119.
2. Ibid.
3. Ibid, p 120.
4. Ibid, p 161.
5. Ibid, pp 161–2.
6. Hans Lamm: *Uber die innere und äussere Entwicklung des deutschen Judentums im Dritten Reich*, p 94.
7. Ibid, p 95.
8. See Wighton: *Heydrich*, p 162
9. Henry A. Zeiger: *The Case against Adolf Eichmann*, p 100.
10. Case against Wolff, p 108. Krausnick: *Denkschrift Himmlers*, pp 194 et seq.
11. 'Des nationalsozialistichen Menschen Ehre und Ehrenschutz', in *Deutsche Justiz* of 1938, p 1660.
12. Krausnick: *Anatomy of the SS State*, pp 11–12.
13. Buchheim: *Das Dritte Reich*, p 41.
14. Wilhelm Schallmayer: *Verebung und Auslese im Lebenslauf der Völker*.
15. Krausnick: op cit, p 14.
16. Himmler: *Die Schutzstaffel als antibolschewistische Kampforganization*, p 3.
17. 'Judentum, Freimaurerei, Bolschewismus' Part 1, issued by Head of RuSHA, undated (approx 1936), pp 19 et seq and 39, RFSS Microfilm 161.
18. *Das Schwarze Korps*, June 5th, 1935.
19. Ibid.
20. Gestapo memorandum, Oct 2nd, 1935, RFSS Microfilm 402.
21. Eichmann: Record of interrogation, Vol 1, Col 328.
22. Office minute by Hagen, July 21st, 1938, RFSS Microfilm 509.

23. Office minute by Hagen, undated, RFSS Microfilm 509.
24. Office minute by Hagen, undated (approx. summer 1938), RFSS Microfilm 415.
25. Ibid.
26. Verbal information from Leopold von Mildenstein, Nov 20th, 1966.
27. Reinhard Höhn: *Artur Mahraun*, p 61.
28. Lamm: op cit, p 72.
29. Ibid, p 53.
30. Ibid, p 42.
31. Ibid, pp 37–40.
32. Ibid, p 45.
33. *Völkischer Beobachter*, May 9th, 1935.
34. *Jüdischer Rundschau*, July 2nd, 1935.
35. Lamm: op cit, p 48.
36. Ibid, p 215.
37. Ibid, p 144.
38. *Jüdischer Rundschau*, April 28th, 1933.
39. Lamm: op cit, p 161.
40. Ibid, p 156.
41. Ibid, p 149. Eichmann: Record of interrogation Vol 1, Col 67.
42. *Das Schwarze Korps*, May 15th, 1935.
43. Lamm: op cit, p 233.
44. Eichmann: Record of interrogation, Vol 1, Cols 61 et seq.
45. 'Die Organisation der Judenheit, ihre Verbindungen und politische Bedeutung' – notes for an address by Hagen, Sept 23rd, 1938, p 2, RFSS Microfilm 411.
46. Ibid.
47. Ibid, pp 9–10.
48. Eichmann: Record of interrogation, Vol 1, Cols 6, 11, 61, 62.
49. Ibid, Col 63.
50. Ibid, Col 26. Ahrendt: *Eichmann in Jerusalem*, pp 57–8. Reitlinger: *The Final Solution*, pp 23–27.
51. Verbal information from von Mildenstein, Nov 20th, 1966.
52. Eichmann: Record of interrogation, Vol 1, Col 68.
53. Bracha Habas: *The Gate-breakers*, p 49.
54. Arendt: *Eichmann in Jerusalem*, pp 36–7. Kempner: *Eichmann und Komplizen*, p 39.
55. 'Die Zionistiche Weltorganisation', Report prepared by Eichmann and Hagen, Oct 20th, 1936, RFSS Microfilm 411.
56. Ibid, Part II, p 1.
57. Hagen's notes (see Note 45 above), Part B, p 36.
58. Statement on oath by Dr H. Ehlich, Ohlendorf trial, Document volume, p 2 (in Frau Käthe Ohlendorf's private papers).
59. 'Die Zionistische Weltorganisation' (see Note 55 above), Part II, p 3.
60. Eichmann: Record of Hearings, Vol 1, Col 69. Report on trip to Egypt and Palestine by Eichmann and Hagen Nov 4th, 1937, Part I, pp 1–2, Part IV, p 2.
61. 'Die Zionistische Weltorganisation' Part I, p 7.
62. Hagen's report, June 17th, 1937, RFSS Microfilm 411.
63. Ibid.
64. Eichmann: Record of Hearings, Vol 1, Col 90. Hagen report June 17th, 1937.
65. Hagen report, p 4.
66. Ibid.
67. Ibid.

68. Ibid.
69. Eichmann: Record of interrogation, Vol 1, Col 90. Report on trip to Egypt and Palestine.
70. Ibid (Eichmann).
71. Ibid.
72. Report on Egypt and Palestine, p 1.
73. Ibid, p 33.
74. Ibid, p 32.
75. Eichmann: Record of interrogation, Vol 1, Col 94.
76. Ibid, Cols 94, 96, 108.
77. Ibid, Col 101.
78. Ibid, Cols 103, 107, 108. Kempner: *Eichmann und Komplizen*, p 218.
79. Arendt: *Eichmann in Jerusalem*, pp 39–40.
80. Ibid, p 40. Kempner: op cit, p 45.
81. Letter from Hagen, June 24th, 1938, RFSS Microfilm 411.
82. Arendt: *Eichmann in Jerusalem*, p 39. 'Das Judentum in Deutschland', Memorandum by Desk II 112, June 15th, 1939, RFSS Microfilm 411.
83. Note by Eichmann, June 7th, 1938, RFSS Microfilm 415.
84. Ibid. Letter from Hiemer to Eichmann, May 30th, 1938, RFSS Microfilm 415.
85. Letter from Hagen to Eichmann, June 28th, 1938, RFSS Microfilm 415.
86. Ibid.
87. Letter from Six to Desk II 112, June 23rd, 1938, RFSS Microfilm 415.
88. Lionel Kochan: *Pogrom*, pp 36 et seq.
89. German Foreign Policy Documents, Series D 1937–45, Vol V, pp 98, 115, 141.
90. Kochan: op cit, p 38.
91. Hermann Graml: 'Der 9 November 1938' in *Das Parlament*, Nov 11th, 1953, p 7.
92. Ibid.
93. Hilberg: *The Destruction of the European Jews*, p 23.
94. Kochan: op cit, p 51.
95. IMT Vol XX, p 292.
96. IMT Vol XIV, p 422.
97. Kochan: op cit, pp 52–3.
98. 'Urkunden zur Judenpolitik des Dritten Reiches' in *Das Parlament*, Nov 10th, 1954, p 582.
99. Ibid.
100. Kochan: op cit, p 106.
101. Ibid, p 55. Graml: op cit, p 9.
102. Ibid.
103. IMT Vol XX, p 133.
104. IMT Vol XLII, pp 511–13, Vol XXI, p 354. Kochan: op cit, p 55.
105. Graml: op cit, p 9.
106. IMT Vol XLII, p 512.
107. Ibid.
108. Ibid, p 511.
109. IMT Vol XXXI, p 516.
110. IMT Vol XXI, p 392.
111. Statement on oath by Fritz Schulz, Sept 30th, 1947, Ohlendorf trial, document book (in Frau Käthe Ohlendorf's private papers).
112. Statement by Hafiz Khan, *Frankfurter Allgemeine Zeitung*, Sept 15th, 1964.
113. IMT Vol XX, p 294.
114. Hassell: *Vom anderen Deutschland*, p 34.
115. Ibid, p 27.
116. Graml: op cit, p 15.
117. IMT Vol IX, p 277. Kochan: op cit, p 107.
118. 'Urkunden zur Judenpolitik des Dritten Reiches', p 585.
119. IMT Vol IX, p 277.

120. IMT Vol XXI, p 392.
121. Burckhardt: op cit, p 227.
122. Ibid, p 228.
123. Ibid.
124. Ibid, p 230.
125. Schellenberg: *Memoiren*, p 59 (not in English translation).
126. Burckhardt: *Meine Danziger Mission 1937–1939*, p 230.
127. Ibid, p 124.
128. 'Urkunden zur Judenpolitik', p 585.
129. IMT Vol XXVI, p 266.
130. Krausnick: *Anatomy of the SS State*, p 46.
131. Ibid, p 43.
132. Lamm: op cit, pp 81, 217.
133. Ibid, p 223.
134. Ibid. Poliakov and Wulf: *Das Dritte Reich und die Juden*, p 120.
135. Ibid. *Keesing's Contemporary Archives 1937*, p 3240B.
136. Habas: op cit, p 71; *Schulthess' Europäische Geschichtskalender 1938*, p 541, and 1939, p 354. Jon and David Kimche: *The Secret Roads*, p 40.
137. Habas: op cit, p 23. Kimche: op cit, p 40.
138. Kimche: op cit, p 15. Habas: op cit, p 48.
139. 'Das Judentum in Deutschland', Memorandum by Desk II 112, June 15th, 1939, RFSS Microfilm 411.
140. *German Foreign Policy Documents*, Series D, Vol V, pp 780, 784.
141. Kimche: op cit, p 31.
142. Ibid, p 32.
143. Ibid.
144. Ibid, p 39.
145. Ibid, pp 33, 34, 35. Habas, op cit, pp 61, 63.
146. Ibid, pp 35, 39.
147. Ibid, p 41.
148. Ibid.
149. Ibid, pp 41–2. *Schulthess 1939*, p 362.
150. Ibid, p 43.
151. Krausnick: *Anatomy of the SS State*, p 48.
152. Eichmann: Record of Interrogation, Vol 1, Cols 126–7.
153. Krausnick: op cit, p 48.
154. Eichmann: Record of Interrogation, Vol 1, Cols 127, 128, 132.
155. Ibid, Col 128.
156. Ibid, Col 121.
157. Ibid, Col 124.
158. Office note on conference of heads of Ämter and Einsatzgruppen, Sept 27th, 1939, RFSS Microfilm 239.
159. Ibid.
160. Case against Wolff, pp 90–91.
161. Eichmann: Record of Interrogation, Vol 1, Col 125. Reitlinger: *The Final Solution*, pp 43 et seq.
162. Krausnick: *Anatomy of the SS State*, p 54. Reitlinger: op cit, p 42. Hilberg: op cit, p 138.
163. Eichmann: Record of Interrogation, Vol 1, Col 121.
164. Hilberg: op cit, pp 138–9.
165. Reitlinger: op cit, p 45.
166. Krausnick: op cit, pp 56–7. Reitlinger: op cit, pp 76 et seq.
167. Eichmann: Record of Interrogation, Vol 1, Col 137.
168. Reitlinger: op cit, p 77.
169. Ibid, p 76. *German Foreign Policy Documents*, Series D, Vol IV, pp 420–1.
170. Bernhard Lösener: 'Als Rassereferent im Reichsministerium des Innern' in *Vierteljahrshefte für Zeitgeschichte*, 1961, Issue 3, pp 296 et seq.

171. Paul Schmidt: *Hitler's Interpreter*, p 178.
172. Eichmann: Record of Interrogation, Vol 1 Col 140.

CHAPTER FOURTEEN

1. *German Foreign Policy Documents*, Series D, Vol IV, p 170.
2. Domarus: *Hitler Reden und Proklamationen 1932–45*, Vol II, p 1058.
3. Krausnick: *Anatomy of the SS State*, p 63.
4. Ibid, p 60.
5. Warlimont: *Inside Hitler's Headquarters*, pp 150–1. Jacobsen: *Anatomy of the SS State*, pp 512–14. Uhlig: 'Der verbrecherische Befehl' in *Das Parlament*, July 17th, 1957, p 431.
6. Warlimont: op cit, pp 157–9.
7. Schellenberg: *Memoirs*, p 210.
8. Uhlig: op cit, p 432. Warlimont: op cit, p 161.
9. Jacobsen: *Anatomy of the SS State*, p 532. Warlimont: op cit. p 162.
10. Warlimont: op cit, pp 158–60. Uhlig: op cit, p 432. Schellenberg: op cit, pp 213–14. Hilberg: op cit, p 183.
11. Warlimont: op cit, pp 158–9. Uhlig: op cit, p 432.
12. Warlimont: op cit, pp 158–9.
13. Jacobsen: *Anatomie des SS Staates*, Vol 2, p 206 (not in English translation).
14. 'Nebe Series', Feb 2nd, 1950, p 24.
15. Ibid.
16. Hans-Bernd Gisevius: *Wo ist Nebe?*, p 240.
17. Ibid, p 244.
18. Krausnick: *Anatomy of the SS State*, p 64.
19. 'Nebe Series', Feb 2nd, 1950, p 25.
20. Verbal information from Frau Käthe Ohlendorf, Jan 26th, 1966.
21. Hilberg: *The Destruction of the European Jews*, p 189. Statement by Ohlendorf, IMT Vol XLII, p 446.
22. Reitlinger: *The Final Solution*, p 186.
23. Ibid, p 192. Kempner: *SS im Kreuzverhör*, p 281.
24. Ibid, pp 192 et seq.
25. Wulf: *Die SS*, pp 273 et seq.
26. Kempner: *SS im Kreuzverhör*, pp 284 et seq.
27. Bomhard: IMT Vol XLII, pp 636, 644.
28. 'Nebe Series', Feb 2nd, 1950, p 24.
29. Case against Wolff, p 128. Reitlinger: op cit, p 189.
30. Hilberg: op cit, p 189.
31. Ibid.
32. Ohlendorf's statement, IMT Vol IV, p 313. Aubrey Dixon and Otto Heilbrunn: *Communist Guerilla Warfare*, p 99. Kempner: *SS im Kreuzverhör*, p 19.
33. 'Nebe Series', Feb 2nd, 1950, p 24.
34. Ibid.
35. Krausnick: *Anatomy of the SS State*, p 63.
36. Ohlendorf's plea in mitigation, p 28.
37. Ibid, pp 29–30.
38. Wulf: *Die SS*, p 252. Hilberg: op cit, p 188.

39. Wulf: *Die SS*, 261.
40. Hilberg: op cit, pp 189–90.
41. Ibid, p 207.
42. Ibid, p 190.
43. Ibid, p 191.
44. Kempner: *SS im Kreuzverhör*, p 28.
45. Case against Wolff, p 143.
46. Kempner: op cit, p 25.
47. Ibid, p 22.
48. Ibid.
49. Ibid, p 23.
50. Ibid.
51. Ibid, p 28.
52. Ibid, p 29.
53. Ibid.
54. IMT Vol VII, p 535. Henkys: *Die nationalsozialistischen Gewalverbrechen*, p 117.
55. Henkys: op cit, p 117.
56. Ibid, p 118.
57. Ibid, p 120.
58. Krausnick: *Anatomy of the SS State*, p 64. Henkys: op cit, pp 114–16.
59. Ibid, p 66. Case against Wolff, p 122.
60. Ibid, p 62. Hilberg: op cit, pp 193, 243.
61. Hilberg: op cit, p 196.
62. Ibid, pp 196, 225.
63. Reitlinger: op cit, p 192.
64. Ibid, p 187.
65. 'Nebe Series', Feb 2nd, 1950, p 26. Gisevius: *Wo ist Nebe?*, p 244.
66. 'Nebe Series', Feb 2nd, 1950, p 26.
67. Case against Wolff, p 161.
68. Quoted from *Süddeutsche Zeitung*, July 25th, 1964.
69. Quoted from *Frankfurter Rundschau*, July 10th, 1958. *Abendpost*, July 14th, 1961.
70. Letter from Herf to Maximilian von Herff, July 29th, 1943, RFSS Microfilm 38.
71. Hilberg: op cit, p 440.
72. Wulf: *Die SS*, p 269.
73. Poliakov and Wulf: *Das Dritte Reich und seine Diener*, p 383.
74. IMT Vol XXIX, p 145.
75. Case against Wolff, p 317.
76. Ibid, pp 317–18.
77. Kersten: op cit, p 151.
78. Buchheim: *Anatomy of the SS State*, p 338.
79. Case against Wolff, p 365.
80. Hilberg: op cit, pp 218–19.
81. Crankshaw: *Gestapo*, pp 128–9.
82. Hilberg: op cit, pp 209–10. Reitlinger: op cit, pp 207–8. Crankshaw, op cit, p 129.
83. Hilberg: op cit, p 215.
84. Ibid.
85. Ibid.
86. Ibid, p 217.
87. Ibid, p 216.
88. Ibid, p 217.
89. Ibid. Reitlinger: op cit, p 232.
90. 'Niederschrift über Beobachtungen während meines Besuches in Italien vom 11 bis 14 Oktober 1942', memorandum by Himmler dated Oct 22nd, 1942, RFSS Microfilm 69.
91. Hilberg: op cit, p 196.
92. Ibid, p 197.
93. Ibid.
94. Ibid, p 198.
95. IMT Vol XXXV, p 85.
96. Hilberg: op cit, p 198.
97. Ibid.
98. Dixon and Heilbrunn: op cit, pp 143–4.
99. Hilberg: op cit, p 199.
100. Ibid, p 224.
101. Bor: *Gespräche mit Halder*, p 197.
102. Reitlinger: *The House built on*

Sand, p 233; *The Final Solution*, p 189.
103. Reitlinger: *The House built on Sand*, p 232.
104. Hilberg: op cit, pp 242–3.
105. Ibid, p 243.
106. Ibid, p 244.
107. Ibid, p 251.
108. See detailed accounts of individual operations in Hilberg (op cit) and Reitlinger (*The House built on Sand*).
109. Hilberg: op cit, p 250.
110. Case against Wolff, p 137. IMT Vol XXXVII, p 670.
111. IMT Vol XXVII, p 4.
112. Ibid, p 6.
113. Ibid, p 3.
114. Ibid.
115. Helmut Heiber: 'Aus den Akten des Gauleiters Kube' in *Vierteljahrshefte für Zeitgeschichte*, Issue I, 1956, p 68.
116. Ibid.
117. Ibid, p 67.
118. Letter from Strauch to Bach-Zelewski, July 25th, 1943, RFSS Microfilm 59.
119. Office minute by Strauch, July 20th, 1943, RFSS Microfilm 59.
120. Ibid.
121. Heiber: 'Aus den Akten des Gauleiters Kube', p 84.
122. Ibid.
123. Hilberg: op cit, p 254.
124. Letter from Strauch to Bach-Zelewski, July 25th, 1943.
125. Heiber: op cit, p 76.
126. IMT Vol XXXVIII, p 373.
127. Ibid, p 371.
128. Heiber: op cit, p 77. Reitlinger: op cit, pp 288–9.
129. Hilberg: op cit, p 254.
130. Ibid, pp 256, 767.
131. Henkys: op cit, p 124.
132. Hilberg: op cit, p 309. Henkys: op cit, p 95. Poliakov and Wulf: op cit, p 197. Case against Wolff, p 221.
133. Henkys: op cit, p 97. Reitlinger: op cit, p 137.
134. Reitlinger: op cit, p 137.
135. Ibid, p 139.
136. Eichmann: Record of Interrogation, Vol 1, Cols 175–7.
137. Henkys: op cit, p 86.
138. Case against Wolff: p 198. IMT Vol XXIX, pp 502 et seq.
139. Henkys: op cit, p 65. Reitlinger: op cit, pp 129 et seq.
140. Buchheim: *Anatomy of the SS State*, pp 223–4.
141. Hilberg: op cit, p 562.
142. Ibid.
143. Gerstein Report (quoted in Poliakov and Wulf: op cit, 106).
144. Poliakov and Wulf: op cit, p 104.
145. Ibid.
146. Ibid, p 108. Henkys: op cit, p 109.
147. Henkys: op cit, p 110.
148. Case against Wolff, p 210.
149. IMT Vol XXVII, pp 341 et seq. Höss: op cit, p 159.
150. Hilberg: op cit, p 567.
151. Poliakov and Wulf: op cit, p 106.
152. Ibid, pp 106–7.
153. Höss: *Kommandant in Auschwitz*, pp 176–7.
154. Letter from Himmler to Krüger, July 19th, 1942, RFSS Microfilm 122.
155. Case against Wolff, p 226.
156. Poliakov and Wulf: op cit, p 104.
157. Wolff trial, Hassler's statement, Aug 20th, 1964, quoted from

Süddeutsche Zeitung, Aug 21st, 1964.

158. Krausnick: *Anatomy of the SS State*, p 105.
159. Ibid.
160. Ibid, p 108.
161. Ibid, p 108–9. Case against Wolff, pp 230, 233.
162. Case against Wolff, p 234.
163. Ibid, p 235.
164. Krausnick: op cit, p 110.
165. Ibid, p 111.
166. From *Süddeutsche Zeitung*, Sept 3rd, 1964.
167. Case against Wolff, p 206. Henkys: op cit, pp 95, 103, 106, 108, 111. Krausnick: op cit, pp 103–4.
168. Henkys: op cit, p 107.
169. Ibid, p 110.
170. Statement in evidence during the Auschwitz trial, Oct 15th, 1964, quoted from *Frankfurter Allgemeine Zeitung*, Oct 16th, 1964.
171. Henkys: op cit, p 92.
172. *Frankfurter Algemeine Zeitung*, May 25th, 1964.
173. *Frankfurter Rundschau*, Nov 6th, 1964.
174. *Frankfurter Allgemeine Zeitung*, Dec 1st, 1964. Henkys: op cit, p 208.
175. From *Die Zeit*, Aug 27th, 1965.
176. Statement in evidence by Dr Lingens-Reiner during the Auschwitz trial, quoted from *Frankfurter Allgemeine Zeitung*, Mar 3rd, 1964.
177. Hannah Arendt: 'Organisierte Schuld' in *Die Wandlung*, No 4, 1945/6, p 341.
178. From *Die Zeit*, June 25th, 1965.
179. Buchheim: *Anatomy of the SS State*, p 351.
180. Ibid, p 353.
181. Ibid, p 365.
182. Ibid, p 352.
183. Verbal information from Dr Konrad Morgen, Feb 3rd, 1966.
184. 'Nebe Series', Feb 23rd, 1950, p 24.
185. 'Lady mit Lampenschirm', *Der Spiegel*, Feb 16th, 1950, p 12.
186. Testimony by Günter Reinecke, IMT Vol XX, pp 419 et seq, 436–7, 496 et seq. Statement by Dr Konrad Morgen, IMT Vol XLII, pp 551 et seq, 563 et seq. Statement by Dr Werner Paulmann, IMT Vol XLII, pp 543 et seq.
187. Reinecke: IMT Vol XX, p 505.
188. *Der Spiegel*, Feb 16th, 1950, p 12.
189. Ibid.
190. Ibid. Verbal information from Dr Konrad Morgen, Feb 3rd 1966. IMT Vol XX, pp 510 et seq.
191. Ibid.
192. *Der Spiegel*, Feb 16th, 1950, pp 13–14. IMT Vol XX, pp 506 et seq.
193. 'Nebe Series', Feb 23rd, 1950, p 24.
194. Hilberg: op cit, p 579.
195. Statement by Dr Konrad Morgen, *Süddeutsche Zeitung*, Mar 11th, 1964, p 3.
196. Ibid.
197. IMT Vol XLII, p 552.
198. IMT Vol XX, pp 439—40.
199. Ibid.
200. Ibid, p 508.
201. IMT Vol XLII, p 556. IMT Vol XX, pp 489, 438.
202. Hilberg: op cit, p 579.

203. IMT Vol XLII, p 556.
204. IMT Vol XLII, p 548. Hilberg: op cit, p 579.
205. IMT Vol XLII, p 556. IMT Vol XX, p 489.
206. IMT Vol XX, p 378. Verbal information from 'Central Office for investigation of National-Socialist crimes', Ludwigsburg, Dec 15th, 1966.
207. Hilberg: op cit, p 579.
208. Ibid.
209. Statement by Dr Morgen, *Frankfurter Allgemeine Zeitung*, Mar 16th, 1965.
210. IMT Vol XX, p 507. Verbal information from Dr Konrad Morgen, Feb 3rd, 1966.
211. IMT Vol XX, p 442.
212. IMT Vol XXIX, p 146.
213. Höss: op cit, p 17.
214. Hannah Arendt: 'Organisierte Schuld', pp 340, 342.
215. Höss: op cit, p 129.
216. Ibid, p 111.
217. Ibid, p 133.
218. Ibid.
219. Statement by Schultz, *Süddeutsche Zeitung*, Aug 28th, 1964.
220. Hilberg: op cit, p 332.
221. Höss: op cit, p 124.
222. Gilbert: op cit, p 255.
223. Georg: *Die wirtschaftlichen Unternehmungen der SS*, pp 38–9.
224. Ibid, p 32.
225. IMT Vol XXXVIII, pp 363–4.
226. Georg: op cit, p 114.
227. Ibid, p 111.
228. Ibid, p 110.
229. Ibid, p 114.
230. Jan Triska: 'Work redeems' in *Journal of Central European Affairs*, April 1959, p 15.
231. Georg: op cit, pp 58, 61.
232. Henkys: op cit, p 88.
233. Georg: op cit, p 93.
234. Hilberg: op cit, p 340.
235. Georg: op cit, p 97.
236. Ibid.
237. Höss: op cit, pp 138–9.
238. Hilberg: op cit, p 264.
239. Henkys: op cit, p 136.
240. Ibid. Reitlinger: op cit, p 329.
241. Kempner: *Eichmann und Komplizen*, p 293. Hilberg: op cit, p 441.
242. Reitlinger: op cit, p 360.
243. Hilberg: op cit, p 437.
244. Ibid.
245. Ibid, p 441.
246. Ibid.
247. Henkys op cit, p 144.
248. Hilberg: op cit, pp 442–3. Henkys: op cit, p 147.
249. Ibid, p 443. Reitlinger: op cit, p 371.
250. Ibid, pp 446 et seq.
251. Ibid, p 446.
252. Ibid, p 451.
253. Reitlinger: op cit, p 342.
254. Hilberg: op cit, p 384. Henkys: op cit, p 138. Reitlinger: op cit, pp 342 et seq. Hannah Arendt: *Eichmann in Jerusalem*, p 150.
255. Reitlinger: op cit, p 309.
256. Henkys: op cit, p 139.
257. Kempner: *Eichmann und Komplizen*, p 208.
258. Henkys: op cit, p 140.
259. Kempner: op cit, p 208.
260. Ibid, p 209.
261. Renzo de Felice: *Storia degli ebrei italiani sotto il fascismo*, p 460.
262. Ibid, p 459.
263. Ibid.
264. Ibid, p 460.
265. Hilberg: op cit, p 414.
266. Ibid, p 415.

267. Ibid.
268. Kempner: *Eichmann und Komplizen*, p 321.
269. Ibid.
270. Ibid, p 323.
271. Felice: op cit, p 462. Hilberg: op cit, pp 415–6.
272. Kempner: op cit, p 329. Felice: op cit, p 462. Reitlinger: op cit, p 324.
273. Hilberg: op cit, p 416.
274. Ibid.
275. Reitlinger: op cit, p 328.
276. Ibid, p 390. Henkys: op cit, p 144. Hilberg: op cit, p 470.
277. Ibid, p 404. Henkys: op cit, p 149.
278. Hilberg: op cit, p 483. Henkys: op cit, p 148.
279. Hilberg: op cit, p 429. Case against Wolff, p 285.
280. Case against Wolff, pp 285–6. Henkys: op cit, p 143.
281. Besgen: op cit, p 28. Kersten: op cit, p 144.
282. Besgen: op cit, pp 28–9.
283. Reitlinger: op cit, pp 342–5. Hilberg: op cit, p 384.
284. Reitlinger: op cit, pp 342–5.
285. Lösener: 'Als Rassereferent im Reichsministerium des Innern' in *Vierteljahrshefte für Zeitgeschichte*, No 4 1963. Hilberg: op cit, pp 268, 277.
286. Hilberg: op cit, pp 269, 270, 273.
287. Lösener: op cit, p 298.
288. Ibid, pp 299–300.
289. Ibid, pp 300, 302. Hilberg: op cit, p 270.
290. Henkys: op cit, p 142. Hilberg: op cit, p 357. Werner Best: *Die deutsche Politik in Dänemark*, p 47. Kempner: *Eichmann und Komplizen*, pp 372–3.
291. Best: op cit, p 48.
292. Ibid.
293. Ibid, p 50.
294. Ibid, p 49. Kempner: op cit, p 374.
295. Ibid, p 51. Kempner: op cit, p 377.
296. Henkys: op cit, p 142.
297. Kempner: op cit, p 379. Reitlinger: op cit, pp 347–8 (footnote).
298. Kempner: op cit, p 375. Reitlinger: op cit, pp 349–50. Henkys: op cit, p 142.
299. Kempner: op cit, p 376.
300. Ibid, pp 378–80.
301. Eichmann: Record of Interrogation, Vol 1, Col 251.

CHAPTER FIFTEEN

1. Knoebel: *Racial Illusion and Military Necessity*, p 226.
2. Broszat: *Zur Perversion der Strafjustiz im Dritten Reich*, p 408.
3. Helmut Heiber: 'Zur Justiz im Dritten Reich – Der Fall Elias', *Vierteljahrshefte für Zeitgeschichte*, No 4 of 1955, pp 275–7, 279.
4. Ibid, p 279.
5. Ibid, pp 231–2.
6. Ibid, p 282.
7. Ibid.
8. Ibid, pp 287, 290.
9. Broszat: *Perversion der Strafjustiz*, p 403.
10. Ibid, p 404.
11. Ibid.

12. Broszat: *Anatomy of the SS State*, p 413.
13. Neufeldt and others: *Zur Geschichte der Ordnungspolizei*, p 31.
14. Ibid, pp 31–2.
15. Ibid, p 31.
16. Ibid.
17. Ibid, pp 43, 109.
18. Ibid, p 32.
19. Ibid.
20. Georg: *Die Wirtschaftlichen Unternehmungen der SS*, p 25.
21. Buchheim: *Anatomy of the SS State*, p 298. Georg: op cit, p 29.
22. Buchheim: op cit, p 298.
23. Ibid, p 299.
24. Georg: op cit, p 41.
25. Ibid, p 37.
26. Ibid, pp 42, 44, 56.
27. Ibid, pp 58, 62.
28. Ibid, pp 62, 64.
29. Ibid, pp 66, 69.
30. Ibid, p 70.
31. Ibid, p 71.
32. Ibid, pp 30–31 (WVHA organization table).
33. Ibid, p 131.
34. Ibid, pp 72–4.
35. Ibid, p 74.
36. Ibid, pp 75–6.
37. Ibid, pp 79–81.
38. Ibid, pp 80, 82.
39. Ibid, pp 80–81.
40. Ibid, p 87.
41. Ibid, p 88.
42. Ibid, pp 92–3.
43. Ibid, p 97.
44. Ibid, p 130.
45. Ibid, p 37.
46. Ibid.
47. David Irving: *The Mare's Nest*, p 123.
48. Georg: op cit, p 38.
49. Ibid.
50. Ibid.
51. Irving: op cit, p 283.
52. Ibid, p 294 (footnote).
53. Ibid, pp 260, 295.
54. Paetel, for instance, in *Die SS*, p 20.
55. Arendt: *The Origins of Totalitarianism*, p 395.
56. Ibid, p 405.
57. Arendt: *Elementer und Ursprünge totalitärer Herrschaft*, p 642 (not in English version).
58. Krausnick: *Hitler und die Morde in Polen*, p 197.
59. Ibid, p 198.
60. Ibid, p 200.
61. Ibid.
62. Ibid, p 201. Delarue: op cit, p 219.
63. Delarue: op cit, pp 219–20.
64. Krausnick: op cit, p 201.
65. Ibid.
66. Ibid.
67. Hilberg: op cit, pp 434–5.
68. See correspondence between Himmler and Reeder referred to below, RFSS Microfilm 56.
69. Letter from Himmler to Reeder, Feb 16th, 1943, RFSS Microfilm 56.
70. Letter from Berger to Rudolf Brandt, Feb 25th, 1943, RFSS Microfilm 56.
71. Letter from Reeder to Himmler, Feb 20th, 1943, RFSS Microfilm 56.
72. Letter from Himmler to Reeder, Feb 16th, 1943.
73. Werner Best: *Erinnerungen aus dem besetzten Frankreich 1940–1942*, p 27. Verbal information from Dr Best, Feb 5th 1966.
74. Letter from Kiesel, Mar 31st, 1942, RFSS Microfilm 72.

75. Ibid.
76. Ibid.
77. Letter from Foertsch to Turner, Dec 29th, 1941, RFSS Microfilm 72.
78. Letter from Foertsch to Turner, Feb 2nd, 1942, RFSS Microfilm 72.
79. Letter from Turner to Meyszner, Aug 29th, 1942, RFSS Microfilm 140.
80. Ibid.
81. Ibid.
82. *Bild-Zeitung*, July 1st, 1964.
83. Fabian von Schlabrendorff: *The Secret War against Hitler*, p 137.
84. Eberhard Jäckel: *Frankreich in Hitler's Europa*, p 342.
85. Letter from Korsemann to von Kleist, June 30th, 1943 (in Wulf's papers).
86. Ibid.
87. Letter from Berger to von Herff, July 6th, 1943 (in Wulf's papers).
88. Letter from Himmler to Korsemann, July 5th, 1943 (in Wulf's papers).
89. Krausnick: *Wehrmacht und Nationalsozialismus*, p 681.
90. Ibid.
91. Ibid.
92. *The Goebbels Diaries*, p 284.
93. Ibid, pp 284, 102.
94. Letter from Berger to Rudolf Brandt, Mar 12th, 1940, RFSS Microfilm 33.
95. Ibid.
96. Letter from Berger to Himmler, Nov 24th, 1941, RFSS Microfilm 117.
97. Letter from Himmler to Bormann, Feb 1940, RFSS Microfilm 33.
98. Letter from Weitzel to Himmler, April 17th, 1938, RFSS Microfilm 33.
99. Broszat: 'Der Sonderdienst im General Gouvernement' in *Gutachten des Instituts für Zeitgeschichte*, pp 408–10.
100. Letter from Krüger to Himmler, Oct 10th, 1942, RFSS Microfilm 128.
101. Ibid.
102. Ibid.
103. Letter from Berger to Himmler, Nov 21st, 1942, RFSS Microfilm 128.
104. Letter from Himmler to Bormann, Feb 26th, 1943, RFSS Microfilm 33.
105. Ibid.
106. *Archiv für Publizistische Arbeit*, Aug 26th, 1943.
107. Letter from Berger to Himmler, Oct 10th, 1942, RFSS Microfilm 22.
108. Hilberg: op cit, p 230.
109. Albert Krebs: *Fritz-Dietlof Graf von der Schulenburg*, pp 130–31.
110. Letter from Berger to Himmler, Nov 20th, 1943, RFSS Microfilm 22.
111. Letter from Berger to Himmler, Oct 30th, 1943, RFSS Microfilm 22.
112. Letter from Lohse to HSSPF Ostland, Apr 13th, 1942, RFSS Microfilm 155.
113. Letter from Himmler to Koch, Oct 9th, 1942, RFSS Microfilm 56.
114. Dallin: *German Rule in Russia*, p 174.
115. Statement by Hans Ehlich at the Ohlendorf trial, Sept 20th, 1947, (in Frau Käthe Ohlendorf's private papers).
116. Ibid.

117. Trevor-Roper: *The Last Days of Hitler*, p 42.
118. 'Nebe Series', Jan 19th, 1950, p 22.
119. Boberach: op cit, p xvii.
120. Ortsgruppenleiter Löcken to Frau Scholtz-Klink, June 27th, 1938, RFSS Microfilm 69.
121. Office minute, July 4th, 1938, RFSS Microfilm 69.
122. Letter from Karl Fiehler to Frick, Apr 19th, 1941, RFSS Microfilm 69.
123. Letter from Bormann to Himmler, Apr 28th, 1941, RFSS Microfilm 69.
124. Letter from Himmler to editor *Schwarze Korps*, May 2nd, 1941, RFSS Microfilm 69.
125. Information, Jan 29th, 1966, from a close relative of Himmler who wishes to remain anonymous.
126. Certificate dated July 27th, 1937, and identity card dated May 23rd, 1933, from Industrial College, Mannheim. Telegram from Himmler to Hedwig Potthast, Dec 5th, 1937 – all in Central Archives, Microfilm 99.
127. Information from close relative of Himmler (see Note 125 above).
128. Certificate of guardianship for Helge and Nanette Dorothea Potthast, Sept 12th, 1944, from Berlin-Charlottenburg District Court, Central Archives, Microfilm 99.
129. Certificate from District Court acknowledging Hedwig Potthast's renunciation of the Church, June 2nd, 1939, Central Archives, Microfilm 99.
130. See correspondence quoted below between Hedwig Potthast and Hilde Potthast, Central Archives, Microfilm 99.
131. Letter from Hilde Potthast to Hedwig Potthast, Mar 26th, 1942, Central Archives, Microfilm 99.
132. Hilde Potthast to Hedwig Potthast, May 8th, 1942, Central Archives, Microfilm 99.
133. Ibid.
134. Schellenberg: *Memoirs*, p 358.
135. See certificate of guardianship (Note 128 above).
136. See letter from Gerda Bormann to her husband, Sept 21st, 1944 in Trevor-Roper: *The Bormann Letters*, p 119.
137. Trevor-Roper: op cit, p 126.
138. Ibid, p 2.
139. Hilberg: op cit, p 256.
140. Statement by Dr Justus Beyer at the Ohlendorf trial, Oct 22nd, 1947 (in Frau Käthe Ohlendorf's private papers).
141. Boberach: op cit, p xviii.
142. Ibid, p xxii.
143. Peter Schneider: Rechtssicherheit und richterliche Unabhängigkeit aus der Sicht des SD' in *Vierteljahrshefte für Zeitgeschichte*, No 4, 1956, p 416.
144. Kersten: op cit, p 215.
145. Memorandum from SD Aussenstelle Bünde to SD Abschnitt Bielefeld, May 13th, 1941, RFSS Microfilm 269.
146. Memorandum from SD Aussenstelle Minden to SD Abschnitt Bielefeld, June 24th, 1941, RFSS Microfilm 269.
147. Memorandum from SD Aussenstelle Erfurt to SD Hauptaussenstelle Weimar, Jan 12th, 1942, RFSS Microfilm 269.

148. Ibid.
149. Memorandum SD Aussenstelle Erfurt to SD Hauptaussenstelle Weimar, Jan 5th, 1942, RFSS Microfilm 269.
150. IMT Vol XXIX, p 514.
151. Letter from Florian to Bormann, Nov 30th, 1942, RFSS Microfilm 59.
152. Letter from Weinrich to Party Chancellery, Jan 22nd, 1943, RFSS Microfilm 59.
153. Letter from Hildebrandt to Himmler Apr 17th, 1943, RFSS Microfilm 117.
154. Boberach: *Meldungen aus dem Reich*, p xviii.
155. Kersten: *Totenkopf und Treue*, p 215.
156. Ibid, p 209.
157. Ohlendorf's statement, Oct 8th, 1947, p 508 (in Frau Käthe Ohlendorf's private papers).
158. Kersten: op cit, p 216.
159. Boberach: op cit, p xxvi.
160. Statement by Hans Fritzsche at the Ohlendorf trial Aug 18th, 1947, p 510 (in Frau Käthe Ohlendorf's private papers).
161. *Goebbels Diaries*, p 293.
162. Boberach: op cit, p xxvi.
163. Ibid, p xxviii.
164. Ohlendorf's statement, Oct 8th, 1947, p 510 (in Frau Käthe Ohlendorf's private papers).
165. Boberach: op cit, p xvii.
166. Ibid.
167. IMT Vol XXIX, p 107.
168. Buchheim: *Anatomy of the SS State*, pp 227–8.
169. Letter from Andreas Schmidt to Gottlob Berger, Sept 24th, 1943, RFSS Microfilm 128.
170. Buchheim: *Anatomy of the SS State*, pp 213–14.
171. Buchheim: 'Die Höhere SS-und Polizeiführer' in *Vierteljahrshefte für Zeitgeschichte*, No 4, 1963 pp 362–4.
172. Ibid, p 387.
173. Ibid.
174. Buchheim: *Anatomy of the SS State*, p 231.
175. Ibid.
176. Ibid, p 232.
177. Ibid, p 235.
178. Ibid, p 219.
179. Draft on prerogatives of the HSSPF, Jan 8th, 1943, RFSS Microfilm 119.
180. Ibid.
181. Ibid.
182. Buchheim: *Anatomy of the SS State*, pp 237–8.
183. Ibid, p 228.
184. Letter from Himmler to Hintze, May 11th, 1944, RFSS Microfilm 56.
185. Teleprinter message from Himmler to Hintze, undated, RFSS Microfilm 56.
186. Letter from Himmler to Waldschmidt, Apr 20th, 1944, RFS Microfilm 33.
187. Letter from Himmler to Hofmann, Nov 29th, 1944, RFSS Microfilm 56.
188. Letter from Himmler to Daluege, Feb 4th, 1943, RFSS Microfilm 60.
189. Letter from Himmler to Pancke, May 16th, 1944, RFSS Microfilm 56.
190. Letter from Wolff to Kaltenbrunner, Nov 23rd, 1942; anonymous letter to editor *Schwarze Korps* (both in Wulf's papers).
191. Letter from Ohlendorf to Wolff, Aug 6th, 1942, RFSS Microfilm 122.
192. Verbal information from Dr

Richard Korherr, Mar 8th, 1966.

193. Questionnaire on Korherr, District HQ Würzburg, Personnel Office, dated Sept 30th, 1940 (in Korherr's private papers).
194. Verbal information from Dr Richard Korherr, Mar 8th 1966.
195. Ibid.
196. Ibid.
197. Ibid.
198. Letter from Korherr to Himmler, Aug 13th, 1943 (in Dr Korherr's papers).
199. Letter from Hildebrandt to Himmler, undated (in Dr Korherr's papers).
200. Verbal information from Dr Korherr, Mar 8th, 1966.
201. IMT Vol XX, p 426.
202. Höss: op cit, p 138.
203. Reitlinger: *The House built on Sand*, pp 355, 358.
204. Letter from Müller to Sicherheitspolizei and SD Commanders, Aug 28th, 1941, RFSS Microfilm 491. Letter from SD Leitabschnitt Munich, Mar 8th, 1943, RFSS Microfilm 269.
205. See statement by Dr Hans Hohberg, July 11th, 1947. Files of US Military Court II, Case IV.
206. See correspondence between Berger and his son-in-law Andreas Schmidt, RFSS Microfilm 128.

CHAPTER SIXTEEN

1. Memorandum from Streckenbach to Himmler, approx Mar 9th, 1942, RFSS Microfilm 140.
2. Kesselring: *Gedanken zum Zweiten Weltkrieg*, p 164.
3. Westphal: *The German Army in the West*, p 54.
4. von Manstein: *Lost Victories*, p 188.
5. Stein: *The Waffen-SS*, p 215. OKW Reports 1943, Vol II, p 1010.
6. *Wiking-Ruf* No 6 of 1955, pp 13 et seq; No 7 of 1955, pp 10 et seq.
7. Hausser: *Soldaten wie andere auch* (uncorrected MS), p 2. Buchheim: *SS und Polizei im NS-Staat*, pp 29–30.
8. Hausser: op cit, p 2.
9. Hausser: *Waffen-SS im Einsatz*, p 10. Klietmann: *Die Waffen-SS*, pp 53–4.
10. Judgement on Dietrich, p 4.
11. Stein: op cit, p 4.
12. Judgement on Dietrich, p 4.
13. Klietmann: op cit, p 71. Hausser: *Soldaten*, p 2.
14. Klietmann: op cit, pp 71, 51.
15. Hausser: *Soldaten*, p 2.
16. Verbal information from Wilhelm Bittrich, Jan 29th, 1966.
17. Stein: op cit, p 5.
18. Ibid.
19. Ibid.
20. Görlitz: *Die Waffen-SS*, p 9.
21. See Chapter 6, this volume.
22. See Chapter 6, this volume.
23. Klietmann: op cit, p 53.
24. Ibid, p 15.
25. Hausser: *Soldaten*, p 107.
26. Verbal information from Paul Hausser, Jan 31st, 1966.
27. Hausser: *Soldaten*, p 1. Verbal

information from Paul Hausser, Jan 31st, 1966.
28. Letter from Paul Hausser, Feb 10th, 1966.
29. Verbal information from Paul Hausser, Jan 31st, 1966.
30. Ibid.
31. Klietmann: op cit, p 18.
32. Ibid, p 421. Hausser: *Soldaten*, p 33.
33. Verbal information from Paul Hausser, Jan 31st, 1966.
34. Klietmann: op cit, p 21. Buchheim: *SS und Polizei im NS-Staat*, pp 167–8.
35. Hausser: *Soldaten*, p 10.
36. Stein: op cit, p 10.
37. Letter from Himmler to all SS-Oberabschnitte, Sept 17th, 1936, RFSS Microfilm 155.
38. Ibid.
39. Letter from Himmler to Dietrich, undated, RFSS Microfilm 33.
40. Verbal information from Felix Steiner, Jan 28th, 1966.
41. Ibid.
42. Letter from Heissmeyer to Himmler, July 18th, 1938, RFSS Microfilm 33.
43. Ibid.
44. Letter from Himmler to Dietrich, July 2nd, 1938, RFSS Microfilm 33.
45. Steiner: *Armee der Geächteten*, p 70.
46. Verbal information from Wilhelm Bittrich, Jan 29th, 1966.
47. Verbal information from Felix Steiner, Jan 28th, 1966.
48. Ibid.
49. Steiner: op cit, p 351.
50. Verbal information from Paul Hausser, Jan 31st, 1966.
51. Steiner: op cit, p 351.
52. Ibid, p 39.
53. Verbal information from Felix Steiner and Paul Hausser, Jan/Feb 1966.
54. Steiner: *Von Clausewitz bis Bulganin*, p 69.
55. Verbal information from Felix Steiner, Jan 28th, 1966.
56. Stein: op cit, p 13.
57. Hausser: *Soldaten*, p 22.
58. Verbal information from Felix Steiner, Jan 28th, 1966.
59. Stein: op cit, p 13.
60. Article entitled 'Die reformerischen Leistungen der ehemaligen Waffen-SS', probably written by Steiner, *Wiking-Ruf* No 4, of 1955, p 12.
61. Ibid.
62. Steiner: *Von Clausewitz bis Bulganin*, p 234.
63. Steiner: *Die Armee der Geächteten*, p 92.
64. Verbal information from Paul Hausser, Jan 31st, 1966.
65. Verbal information from Felix Steiner, Jan 28th, 1966.
66. Karl Demeter: *The German Officer Corps*, pp 54–6 and 268. Steiner: *Die Armee der Geächteten*, pp 96–7.
67. *Wiking-Ruf* article (see Note 60 above), p 12.
68. See Krausnick: *Wehrmacht und Nationalsozialismus*, pp 669 et seq.
69. Ibid.
70. Foertsch: op cit, p 148.
71. Krausnick: *Wehrmacht und Nationalsozialismus*, p 669.
72. Ibid.
73. Buchheim: *Anatomy of the SS State*, p 259.
74. Ibid.
75. Hossbach: op cit, p 32.
76. Klietmann: op cit, pp 26–7.
77. Address by Gruppenführer

Petri, Jan 1939, entitled 'Experiences of the initiation of expansion of the SS-Totenkopfverbände in September 1938 and of large-scale employment of the Allgemeine SS'.
78. SS pamphlet 'Uns ist der Kampf', undated (approx. 1942), RFSS Microfilm 161.
79. Knoebel: op cit, p 35.
80. Letter from OKW to Himmler, Dec 7th, 1942. Letter from Archbishop of Freiburg's Chancellery to OKW, Nov 25th, 1942.
81. Letter from Archbishop of Freiburg to OKW, Nov 25th, 1942.
82. Ibid.
83. Draft (dated Jan 16th, 1939) of an address for Gruppenführer conference, Jan 23rd–25th, 1939, RFSS Microfilm 17. Half-yearly report on advanced education of VT officers graduating from SS Cadet Colleges, Apr 5th, 1938, RFSS Microfilm 69.
84. Ideological instruction for the month of Oct 1943, syllabus of SS Panzergrenadier Division 'Hohenstaufen', Sept 18th, 1943, RFSS Microfilm 161.
85. IMT Vol XXX, p 516.
86. Eichmann: Record of Interrogation, Vol II, Col 1683.
87. Hausser: *Soldaten*, p 21.
88. Ibid, p 50.
89. Ibid, p 20.
90. Ibid.
91. Ibid, p 49.
92. Ibid, p 50.
93. Ibid.
94. Stein: op cit, p 28.
95. Ibid.
96. Ibid, p 35.
97. Ibid, p 40.
98. Verbally from Felix Steiner, Jan 28th, 1966.
99. Verbally from Wilhelm Bittrich, Jan 29th, 1966.
100. Verbally from Felix Steiner, Jan 28th, 1966.
101. Gottlob Berger's autobiography, undated, in Wulf's papers.
102. Ibid.
103. Letter from Berger to Himmler, July 28th, 1943, RFSS Microfilm 56.
104. Letter from Berger to Himmler, Mar 9, 1943, RFSS Microfilm 117.
105. Berger's autobiography.
106. Letter from Berger to Hanns Ludin, Nov 13th, 1934 (in Wulf's papers).
107. Berger's autobiography.
108. Letter from Ludin to SA Supreme Headquarters Special Court, Dec 7th, 1934 (in Wulf's papers).
109. Ibid.
110. Personal file, 'SS Brigadeführer Berger, Gottlob' undated (approx. 1940) in Wulf's papers.
111. Buchheim: *Anatomy of the SS State*, pp 260–62.
112. Stein: op cit, p 33.
113. Ibid, pp 38 et seq.
114. Klietmann: op cit, p 37.
115. Buchheim: *SS und Polizei im NS-Staat*, 165–7.
116. Ibid.
117. Aronson: op cit, p 171.
118. Buchheim: *Anatomy of the SS State*, p 228.
119. Ibid, p 258.
120. Ibid.
121. Ibid, pp 331, 333.
122. Ibid, p 331.
123. Speech by Himmler, June 19th, 1942, RFSS Microfilm 89.

124. Klietmann: op cit, pp 131, 123.
125. Ibid, pp 104, 87.
126. Ibid, pp 107, 108, 121.
127. Ibid, p 72.
128. Neusüss-Hunkel: op cit, pp 72, 499.
129. Hausser: *Soldaten*, p 76. Stein: op cit, p 36.
130. Stein: op cit, p 40.
131. Ibid, p 46.
132. OKW Secret Order, Mar 8th, 1940, 'Wehrdienstverhältnis und Wehrüberwachung der Angehörigen der Waffen-SS während des Krieges', RFSS Microfilm 119.
133. Hausser: *Waffen-SS im Einsatz*, p 16.
134. Seraphim: 'SS Verfügungstruppe und Wehrmacht', in *Wehrwissenschaftliche Rundschau*, No 12, 1955.
135. Klietmann: op cit, p 44.
136. Ibid, p 45.
137. Ibid, p 46.
138. Stein: op cit, p 169.
139. Ibid.
140. Robert Herzog: *Die Volksdeutschen in der Waffen-SS*, p 4.
141. Ibid.
142. Ibid, p 5.
143. Ibid, p 6.
144. Stein: op cit, p 153. Klietmann: op cit, p 506.
145. Stein: op cit, p 138.
146. Ibid, p 146.
147. Klietmann: op cit, p 133.
148. Hausser: *Soldaten*, p 62.
149. Ibid.
150. Stein: op cit, p 63.
151. Guderian: op cit, p 117.
152. Klietmann: op cit, p 76.
153. Hausser: *Waffen-SS im Einsatz*, pp 33, 39, 40.
154. Picht: *Vom Wesen des Krieges und vom Kriegswesen der Deutschen*, p 248.
155. Görlitz: *Die Waffen-SS*, p 19.
156. *Das Schwarze Korps*, Nov 26th, 1942.
157. Stein: op cit, p 81.
158. Ibid, p 90.
159. Letter from Jüttner to Eicke, Oct 24th, 1940, RFSS Microfilm 107.
160. Letter from Eicke to Wolff, Oct 9th, 1940, RFSS Microfilm 107.
161. Cyril Jolly: *The Vengeance of Private Pooley*.
162. See correspondence between Eicke and Jüttner, Autumn 1940.
163. Verbal information from Gunter d'Alquen, Nov 1966.
164. Letter from Jüttner to Eicke, Oct 24th, 1940.
165. Ibid.
166. Letter from Eicke to Wolff, Oct 22nd, 1940, RFSS Microfilm 107.
167. Ibid.
168. Letter from Himmler to Eicke, Jan 30, 1941, RFSS Microfilm 108.
169. Klietmann: op cit, pp 76, 70, 90.
170. Ibid, p 501.
171. Ibid, pp 184, 90, 110, 130.
172. Hausser: *Soldaten*, Documents 19 and 20.
173. Buchheim: *SS und Polizei im NS-Staat*, pp 182–3.
174. Stein: op cit, p 111.
175. Buchheim: *Anatomy of the SS State*, p 273.
176. Stein: op cit, p 258.
177. Ibid, p 259.
178. Görlitz: *Die Waffen-SS*, p 18.

179. Stein: op cit, p 261.
180. Ibid.
181. Ibid, p 264.
182. Görlitz: op cit, p 18.
183. Stein: op cit, pp 266–8.
184. Ibid, p 103.
185. Hausser: *Soldaten*, p 55, Buchheim: *Anatomy of the SS State*, pp 270–1.
186. Stein: op cit, p 103.
187. Ibid, p 109.
188. Klietmann: op cit, p 393.
189. Ibid, p 395.
190. Ibid, p 78. Hausser: *Waffen-SS im Einsatz*, p 46.
191. Ibid, p 90.
192. Steiner: *Armee der Geächteten*, pp 162, 164.
193. Verbal information from Gunter d'Alquen, Nov 1966.
194. Steiner: op cit, pp 164 et seq.
195. Letter from Busch to Himmler, May 4th, 1942, RFSS Microfilm 108. Steiner: op cit, p 165.
196. Teleprinter message from Heydrich to Himmler, Nov 6th, 1941, RFSS Microfilm 108. Steiner: *Die Freiwilligen*, pp 377 et seq.
197. Stein: op cit, p 216.
198. Letter from Mackensen to Himmler, Dec 26th, 1941, RFSS Microfilm 108.
199. Letter from Eicke to Jüttner, Aug 5th, 1942, RFSS Microfilm 107.
200. 'T.E.': 'Die Rede Himmlers vor den Gauleitern am 3 Aug. 1944', in *Vierteljahrshefte für Zeitgeschichte*, No 4, 1953, p 372.
201. Letter from Simon to Eicke, Aug 2nd, 1942, RFSS Microfilm 108.
202. Letter from Eicke to Jüttner, Aug 5th, 1942, RFSS Microfilm 107.
203. Dixon and Heilbrunn: *Communist Guerilla Warfare*, p 107.
204. Ibid.
205. Ibid.
206. Letter from War Graves Officer of the Leibstandarte to Divisional Headquarters, Mar 29th, 1942, RFSS Microfilm 108.
207. Letter to the author from Wilhelm Keilhaus, Mar 4th, 1967.
208. Stein, op cit, p 272.
209. Letter from von Reinholz to Einsatzgruppe E, July 15th, 1943, RFSS Microfilm 140.
210. Görlitz: *Die Waffen-SS*, p 27. Stein: op cit, p 277.
211. See the latest account of historical investigation on this subject in Jäckel: *Frankreich in Hitlers Europa*, pp 326–8.
212. Stein: op cit, p 277.
213. Letter to Wolff from Allgemeines Wehrmachtsamt of OKW, Aug 2nd, 1943, RFSS Microfilm 122.
214. Ibid.
215. Ibid.
216. Letter from Dr Plötz to Brandt, Nov 17th, 1942, RFSS Microfilm 140.
217. Letter from Reinholz to Einsatzgruppe E, July 15th, 1943.
218. Note for the file by Kumm on conversation with Reichsführer-SS and Obergruppenführer Phleps on July 28th, 1943, undated, RFSS Microfilm 140.
219. Klietmann: op cit, p 151.
220. Ibid, p 157.
221. Ibid, p 165.
222. Ibid, p 169.
223. Ibid, p 178.
224. Ibid, p 181.
225. Ibid, p 187.
226. Stein: op cit, p 206.

227. Steiner: *Armee der Geächteten*, p 173.
228. Stein: op cit, p 209.
229. Klietmann: op cit, pp 59–61.
230. Ibid, pp 49, 61 et seq.
231. Ibid, p 60.
232. Stein, op cit, p 218.
233. Ibid, p 217.
234. Ibid, p 213.
235. Steiner: *Armee der Geächteten*, p 173.
236. Estimate by Steiner during interview with the author.
237. Stein: op cit, p 134.
238. Ibid, p 217.
239. Letter from Eicke to Führungshauptamt, Nov 15th, 1941, RFSS Microfilm 108.
240. Copy of summarized report forwarded to Himmler by SS-Führungshauptamt, May 11th, 1943, RFSS Microfilm 131.
241. Stein: op cit, p 204.
242. Summarized report (see Note 240 above).
243. Ibid.
244. Ibid.
245. Ibid.
246. Ibid.
247. Ibid.
248. Ibid.
249. Ibid.
250. Ibid.
251. Letter from Berger to Himmler, Apr 18th, 1943, RFSS Microfilm 131.
252. Letter from Himmler to Bormann, May 14th, 1943, RFSS Microfilm 131.
253. Stein: op cit, p 204.
254. Letter from Kallmeyer, a Labour Service Leader, to Simon, Head of the Labour Service, Feb 26th, 1943, RFSS Microfilm 70.
255. Ibid.
256. Letter to his father from some young man unknown, undated, registered in by Himmler's Personal Staff as No 1319, RFSS Microfilm 70.
257. Letter from Bormann to Himmler, Feb 24th, 1943, RFSS Microfilm 70.
258. Letter from Acting Commander V Corps to OKW, Mar 30th, 1943, RFSS Microfilm 70.
259. Ibid.
260. Ibid.
261. Stein: op cit, p 172.
262. Ibid, pp 172–3.
263. Letter from Eicke to Führungshauptamt, Nov 15, 1941, RFSS Microfilm 108.
264. Special instructions for ideological education issued by Section 1a/VI SS Cavalry Division HQ, Apr 5th, 1943, RFSS Microfilm 70.
265. Ibid.
266. Ibid.
267. Letter from Eicke to Führungshauptamt, Nov 15th, 1941.
268. Stein: op cit, p 192.
269. See letter from Himmler to Berger and Jüttner, Apr 13th, 1942, RFSS Microfilm 66.
270. Ibid.
271. Ibid.
272. Letter from Berger to Himmler, Oct 12th, 1942, RFSS Microfilm 66.
273. Ibid.
274. Letter from Himmler to Bender, Feb 22nd, 1944, RFSS Microfilm 22.
275. Knoebel: op cit, p 177.
276. Letter from a Dutch SS man named Thoen to the Head of the Dutch SS, undated, forwarded to Himmler, June 16th, 1942, RFSS Microfilm 122.

277. Letter from Rauter to Himmler, June 6th, 1942, RFSS Microfilm 122.
278. Verbal information from Felix Steiner.
279. On morale among the European SS volunteers see extracts from the diary of an unknown SS man in *Christ und Welt*, Aug 10th, 1950.
280. Rolf Bigler: 'Sie wollen ganz anders sein', *Frankfurter Allgemeine Zeitung*, Feb 12th, 1964.
281. Letter to the author from Paul Hausser, Feb 5th, 1967.
282. Letter from Berger to Himmler, Jan 22nd, 1942, RFSS Microfilm 108.
283. Letter from Colonel-General Zeitzler to Himmler, Mar 21st, 1944, RFSS Microfilm 66.
284. Letter from von Herff to Wolff, Nov 23rd, 1942, RFSS Microfilm 70.
285. Buchheim: *Anatomy of the SS State*, p 231.
286. Teleprinter message from Himmler to Jüttner, Feb 10th, 1944, RFSS Microfilm 69.
287. Quarterly report SD Abschnitt Nuremberg, period to Oct 10th, 1941, undated, RFSS Microfilm 406.
288. Verbal information from Felix Steiner, Jan 28th, 1966.
289. Letter from Brandt to Berger, June 21st, 1943, RFSS Microfilm 56.
290. Aide-mémoire on SS ranks issued by Press Office, Reichsführer's Personal Staff, Dec 31st, 1942.
291. SS Order, Feb 24th, 1943, RFSS Microfilm 225.
292. Letter from Berger to Brandt, July 10th, 1944, RFSS Microfilm 64.
293. Memorandum 'Attitude of Section VI of Div. HQ' from Section VI HQ 13 SS Division Apr 10th, 1944, RFSS Microfilm 70.
294. Unsigned letter to 'Dear Willi', Oct 2nd, 1943, RFSS Microfilm 64.
295. Letter from Berger to Himmler, Aug 30th, 1944, RFSS Microfilm 64.
296. Letter from Himmler to Höfle, Dec 30th, 1944, RFSS Microfilm 59.
297. Verbal information from Wilhelm Bittrich, Jan 29th, 1966.
298. Verbal information from Felix Steiner, Jan 28th, 1966.
299. Letter from Himmler to Steiner, Aug 1942, RFSS Microfilm 70.
300. Ibid.
301. Ibid.
302. Letter from Fick to Wolff, Jan 27th, 1942, RFSS Microfilm 38.
303. Letter from Himmler to Berger, July 15th, 1943, RFSS Microfilm 56.
304. Ibid.
305. Ibid.
306. Letter from Berger to Brandt, July 9th, 1943, RFSS Microfilm 56.
307. Letter from Berger to Himmler, July 28th, 1943, RFSS Microfilm 56.
308. Verbal information from Gottlob Berger, Feb 1st, 1966.
309. Steiner: *Armee der Geächteten*, p 271. Krebs: *Fritz-Dietlof Schulenburg*, p 145.

CHAPTER SEVENTEEN

1. Bartz: *Die Tragödie der deutschen Abwehr*, pp 129, 133.
2. Ibid, pp 129, 145.
3. Buchheit: *Der deutsche Geheimdienst*, p 419.
4. Bartz: op cit, p 154.
5. Buchheit: op cit, p 419.
6. Schellenberg: *Memoiren*, p 322 (not in English translation).
7. Buchheit: op cit, p 139. Abshagen: *Canaris*, p 140. Hassell: *Von andern Deutschland*, pp 32–3. (not in English translation).
8. Abshagen: op cit, p 180.
9. Buchheit: op cit, pp 303–4.
10. Bartz: op cit, pp 151, 154.
11. Buchheit: op cit, p 419.
12. Ibid.
13. Buchheit: op cit, p 420
14. Gisevius: *To the Bitter End*, p 472. Buchheit: op cit, p 420.
15. Buchheit: op cit, p 420.
16. Ibid.
17. Gerhard Ritter: *Carl Goerdeler und die deutsche Widerstandsbewegung*, p 372. Gisevius: op cit, pp 472–3.
18. Buchheit: op cit, p 428.
19. Abshagen: op cit, p 368. Buchheit: op cit, p 429.
20. Ibid.
21. Buchheit: op cit, pp 421–2.
22. Schellenberg: *Memoiren*, p 333 (not in English translation).
23. Note by Schellenberg, Jan 30th, 1941, RFSS Microfilm 463.
24. Abshagen: op cit, p 375.
25. Buchheit: op cit, p 438.
26. Verbal information from Bruno Streckenbach, Jan 21st, 1966.
27. Schellenberg: *Memoirs*, p 30.
28. Verbal information from Bruno Streckenbach, Jan 21st, 1966.
29. Schellenberg: *Memoiren*, p 52 (not in English translation).
30. Ibid, p 18.
31. Ibid, p 137.
32. Schellenberg: *Memoirs*, p 222.
33. Buchheit: op cit, pp 429–31.
34. Ibid, pp 430–2. Abshagen: op cit, p 369.
35. Ibid, p 431.
36. Ibid, pp 429, 433. Schellenberg: *Memoiren*, p 333 (not in English translation).
37. Ibid, p 432.
38. See Chapter 15, this volume.
39. Buchheit: op cit, p 415.
40. Besgen: *Der stille Befehl*, p 72.
41. Verbal information from Professor Reinhard Höhn, Jan 15th, 1967.
42. Denne: *Das Danzig-Problem in der deutschen Aussenpolitik*, p 182.
43. Ibid.
44. Burckhardt: op cit, p 334.
45. Ibid.
46. Seabury: op cit, p 135.
47. Hassell: *The von Hassell Diaries*, p 78.
48. Ibid, p 242.
49. IMT Vol XXXVIII, p 88.
50. Goebbels: *Diaries*, p 322.
51. Dallin: *German Rule in Russia*, p 57.
52. Buchheim: *Anatomy of the SS State*, p 369.
53. Heiber: *Zur Justiz im Dritten Reich – Der Fall Elias*, pp 275 et seq.
54. Wighton: *Heydrich*, pp 238–41.
55. Ibid, pp 253 et seq.
56. Ibid, pp 257–8.
57. Ibid, p 259.

58. Ibid.
59. Ibid.
60. Ibid, p 260.
61. Ibid, p 268.
62. Ibid, p 270.
63. Ibid, p 271.
64. Ibid, p 272.
65. Ibid.
66. Ibid.
67. Ibid, p 275.
68. 'Nebe Series', Feb 9th, 1950, p 28.
69. Wighton: op cit, pp 275, 278.
70. Ibid, p 270.
71. Best: *Die deutsche Politik in Dänemark*, pp 10 et seq.
72. Hassell: op cit, pp 245–6. Joergen Haestrup: *Til Landets bedste*, p 25. Best: op cit, pp 8, 11.
73. Hassell: op cit, p 278. Haestrup, op cit, p 25. Best: op cit, p 18.
74. Best: op cit, p 23. Haestrup: op cit, p 25.
75. Best: op cit, pp 30, 74. Haestrup, op cit, p 26.
76. Best: op cit, pp 37–8. Haestrup: op cit, pp 22–3.
77. Best: op cit, pp 40, 42. Haestrup: op cit, pp 23, 533.
78. Best: op cit, p 42. Haestrup: op cit, pp 22, 35, 44, 45.
79. Best: op cit, p 67. Haestrup: op cit, p 288, 320, 321.
80. Best: op cit, p 67. Haestrup: op cit, p 320.
81. Best: op cit, p 83.
82. Ibid, p 84.
83. Ibid.
84. Verbal information from Felix Steiner, Jan 28th, 1966.
85. Paul Kluke: 'Nationalsozialistische Europa-Ideologie' in *Vierteljahrshefte für Zeitgeschichte*, No 3, 1955, p 265.
86. Ibid, p 267.
87. Hans-Dietrich Loock: 'Zur grossgermanischen Politik des Dritten Reiches' in *Vierteljahrshefte für Zeitgeschichte*, No 1, 1960, pp 59–60.
88. Buchheim: *Anatomy of the SS State*, p 234.
89. Loock: op cit, p 61.
90. Record of conference in the SS-Hauptamt held on Oct 10th, 1942, date illegible, RFSS Microfilm 70.
91. Ibid.
92. Letter from Berger to Himmler, June 25th, 1943, RFSS Microfilm 125.
93. Letter from Berger to Himmler, Sept 25th, 1943, RFSS Microfilm 125.
94. Report on effect of declarations made in Norway by Reichskommissar Terboven on behalf of the Führer, undated, registered under No 60–17 in the files of the Reichsführer-SS Personal Staff, RFSS Microfilm 125.
95. Letter from Jeckeln to Lohse, July 30th, 1942, RFSS Microfilm 122.
96. Letter from Meyer to Lohse, Aug 14th, 1942, RFSS Microfilm 122.
97. Basil Dmytryshyn: 'The Nazis and the SS Volunteer Division "Galicia"' in *The American Slavic and East European Review*, July 1956.
98. Dallin: *German Rule in Russia*, p 221.
99. Wulf: *Die SS*, p 162.
100. Dallin: op cit, pp 119–122.
101. Ibid, pp 217–220. Letter from Strauch to von dem Bach-Zelewski, July 25th, 1943, RFSS Microfilm 59.

102. Letter from Himmler to d'Alquen, July 1943, RFSS Microfilm 267.
103. Boberach: op cit, p 287.
104. Steiner: *Armee der Geächteten*, p 179.
105. Letter from Himmler to d'Alquen, July 1943, RFSS Microfilm 267.
106. Dallin: op cit, pp 193–4.
107. Ibid, p 194.
108. Ibid, p 195.
109. Ibid.
110. Ibid, p 194 (footnote).
111. Ibid, p 598. Dmytryshyn: op cit, p 3.
112. Ibid, pp 598–9; Klietmann: op cit, p 194; Dmytryshyn: op cit, p 6.
113. Letter from Himmler to all Heads of Hauptämter, July 14th, 1963, RFSS Microfilm 267.
114. Dmytryshyn: op cit, p 7.
115. Ibid, p 8.
116. Klietmann: op cit, p 193.
117. Reitlinger: *The House built on Sand*, p 365.
118. Dallin: op cit, p 599.
119. Ibid. Klietmann: op cit, p 319.
120. Ibid.
121. Ibid, p 600.
122. Ibid, pp 553–6.
123. Thorwald: *Wen sie verderben wollen*, p 236.
124. Ibid, pp 260 et seq.
125. Ibid, pp 266–7.
126. Letter from Himmler to Bach-Zelewski, Jan 1943, RFSS Microfilm 128.
127. Letter from Melitta Wiedemann to Himmler, May 26th, 1943, RFSS Microfilm 38.
128. Extract taken by Himmler's Personal Staff from letter of Oct 5th, 1943, from Melitta Wiedemann (in Wulf's papers).
129. Letter from Brandt to Melitta Wiedemann, June 30th, 1943, RFSS Microfilm 38.
130. Thorwald: op cit, pp 351–2.
131. Ibid.
132. Ibid, p 355.
133. Ibid, pp 355–80.
134. Dallin: op cit, p 606.
135. Thorwald: op cit, p 433.
136. Letter from Melitta Wiedemann to Brandt, Oct 10th, 1944, RFSS Microfilm 38.
137. Letter from Gottberg to Rosenberg, Aug 31st, 1944, RFSS Microfilm 59.
138. Kempner: *SS im Kreuzverhör*, p 286.
139. Letter from Frauenfeld, Feb 10th, 1944, RFSS Microfilm 125.
140. Letter from Bormann to Himmler, Feb 18th, 1944 and manuscript note thereon by Himmler, Mar 26th, 1944, RFSS Microfilm 56.
141. Boberach: op cit, p 487.
142. Ibid, p 491.
143. Ibid, p 503.
144. Gisevius: *Wo ist Nebe?*, pp 109 et seq.
145. Ibid, pp 110–13.
146. 'Nebe Series', Mar 16th, 1950, p 31.
147. Ibid.
148. Ibid.
149. Ibid.
150. Ibid.
151. Krebs: *Fritz-Dietlof Schulenburg*, p 156.
152. Ibid, p 320.
153. Ibid, p 262.
154. Hassell: *Vom anderen Deutschland*, p 185 (not in English translation).
155. Hassell: op cit, p 152.
156. Ibid, p 250.

157. Ritter: op cit, p 355.
158. Allen Dulles: *Germany's Underground*, p 149.
159. Ritter: op cit, p 429.
160. Krebs: *Fritz-Dietlof Schulenburg*, p 262.
161. Ibid, p 145. Steiner: *Armee der Geächteten*, p 271.
162. Dulles: op cit, p 149.
163. Statement by Hans Fritzsche at the Ohlendorf trial, Aug 18th, 1947 (in Frau Käthe Ohlendorf's papers).
164. Verbal information from Frau Käthe Ohlendorf, Jan 26th, 1966.
165. Statement by Karl Hedrich at the Ohlendorf trial, undated, Document No 4 (in Frau Käthe Ohlendorf's papers).
166. Statement by Dr Hans Rössner at the Ohlendorf trial, Document No 27 (in Frau Käthe Ohlendorf's papers).
167. Letter written by Ohlendorf from Nuremberg, June 8th, 1948 (in Frau Käthe Ohlendorf's papers).
168. Verbal information from Frau Käthe Ohlendorf and Frau Käthe Jessen, Jan 1966.
169. Dulles: op cit, pp 147–8.
170. Ritter: op cit, p 547.
171. Hassell: op cit, p 43.
172. Ibid, p 193.
173. Letter from Heydrich to Ribbentrop, Nov 6th, 1941, RFSS Microfilm 125.
174. Ibid.
175. Hassell: op cit, p 194.
176. Heinrich Brackelmann: *Die SS und die geplante Entführung Hitlers*, p 1.
177. Schellenberg: op cit, pp 351–7.
178. Hassell: op cit, p 177.
179. Ciano: *Diary*, p 455.
180. José M. Doussinague: *España Tenia Razon*, p 295.
181. Kersten: op cit, pp 165–6.
182. 'Nebe Series' Mar 16th, 1950, p 28.
183. Kersten: op cit, p 166.
184. Ibid, p 169.
185. Schellenberg: op cit, pp 365 et seq, 428.
186. See letter from Kranefuss to Brandt, Sept 23rd, 1942, RFSS Microfilm 60. Kranefuss was later the channel for reports from Himmler's contact men in Lisbon and Stockholm (see RFSS Microfilm 22).
187. Letter from SS-Hauptsturmführer Ahrens to Amt VID (Western Group Ausland-SD) of the RSHA, Apr 30th, 1943, in Bezimenski's papers.
188. *Genealogisches Handbuch des Adels*, p 235.
189. Heinrich Brackelmann: *Prinz Hohenlohe*, p 2.
190. Report by Hohenlohe to Hewel, Sept 1939 (in Hohenlohe's papers).
191. Verbal information from Professor Höhn, Feb 1967.
192. Hohenlohe's report, Dec 1941 (in Hohenlohe's papers).
193. Ibid.
194. Letter from Prince Hohenlohe, Feb 1967.
195. Brackelmann: *Die SS und die geplante Entführung Hitlers*, p 2. Letter from Hohenlohe on his meeting with Dulles, mid-Feb 1943 (in Bezimenski's papers).
196. Brackelmann: op cit, pp 2–3.
197. Ibid, p 2.
198. Letter from Hohenlohe to an unnamed SS authority, mid-Feb 1943 (in Bezimenski's papers).
199. Undated SD report on nego-

tiations with Dulles, approx spring 1943 (in Bezimenski's papers).
200. Schellenberg: op cit, p 277. Seabury: op cit, p 132.
201. Letter to the author from Walter Büttner, Feb 1967. Note by Gödde of Luther's staff, undated (in Büttner's papers).
202. Seabury: op cit, p 196.
203. Note by Gödde. Letter to the author from Walter Büttner, Feb 1967. Hassell: op cit, p 263.
204. Schellenberg: op cit, p 368.
205. SD report on negotiations with Dulles, undated and unsigned.
206. Memorandum by Prince Hohenlohe, mid-Feb 1943.
207. Ibid.
208. Ibid.
209. Letter from Kienast to SS-Hauptamt, June 10th, 1943, RFSS Microfilm 45.
210. Doussinague: op cit, p 296.
211. Ibid, p 299.
212. Dieter Ehlers: *Technik und Moral einer Verschwörung*, p 220.
213. Schellenberg: op cit, p 428.
214. Verbal information from Gero von Gaevernitz, Feb 3rd, 1947.
215. Schellenberg: op cit, p 432. Besgen: op cit, pp 33–4.
216. Ehlers: op cit, p 220.
217. Dulles: op cit, p 27.
218. Ibid.
219. Hassell: op cit, p 275.
220. Ehlers: op cit, p 220.
221. Dulles: op cit, p 159.
222. 'T.E.': *Die Rede Himmlers vor den Gauleitern am 3 Aug. 1944*, p 376.
223. Dulles: op cit, p 160.
224. 'T.E.': op cit, p 376.
225. Dulles: op cit, p 160.
226. Ibid.
227. Ibid.
228. Ibid, p 162.
229. Verbal information from Gero von Gaevernitz, Feb 3rd, 1967.
230. Dulles: op cit, p 162.
231. Ibid, p 161.
232. Mario Rodriguez Aragon: 'Operacion KN' in *Pueblo*, Aug 21st, 1958.
233. Brackelmann: *Die SS und die Entführung Hitlers*, p 5.
234. Diary of German Embassy Madrid 1941–5, Vol II, Chapter 7.
235. Letter from von Kranefuss to Brandt, Apr 3rd, 1944, RFSS Microfilm 22.
236. Ibid.
237. Schramm: *Conspiracy among Generals*, pp 31–2.
238. Speidel: *We defended Normandy*, pp 123, 126.
239. Ibid. pp 90–91.
240. Schramm: op cit, p 34.
241. Speidel: op cit, p 125.
242. Schramm: op cit, pp 14, 31.
243. Steiner: *Armee der Geächteten*, pp 188–9.
244. Schramm: *Der 20 Juli in Paris*, p 84 (not in English translation).
245. See Ehlers: op cit, pp 158–9.
246. Schlabrendorff: *The Secret War against Hitler*, p 273.
247. Zeller: *Geist der Freiheit*, p 271.
248. Ibid, p 339.
249. Kersten: op cit, p 201.
250. Zeller: op cit, p 381.
251. Ibid, p 247.
252. Ibid, p 246.
253. Ibid, p 387.
254. Kaltenbrunner Report, pp 27–8.

255. Ehlers: op cit, p 220.
256. Ludwig Jedlicka: *Der 20 Juli in Österriech*, pp 54, 117.
257. Ibid, p 55.
258. Ibid, p 119.
259. Ibid, p 58.
260. Ibid, p 60.
261. Ibid, p 59.
262. Ibid, p 121.
263. Ibid.
264. Schramm: op cit, pp 57, 66.
265. Ibid, p 68–9.
266. Ibid, p 68.
267. Ibid, pp 71, 95–6.
268. Ibid, p 100.
269. Ibid, p 105.
270. Ibid, p 109.
271. Ibid, pp 109–10.
272. Ibid, pp 144–5.
273. Ibid, pp 120 et seq, 170.
274. Ibid, pp 169 et seq.
275. Steiner: *Armee der Geächteten*, p 191.
276. Ibid.
277. Ibid.
278. Ibid, p 190. Verbally from Wilhelm Bittrich, Jan 29th, 1966.
279. Kersten: op cit, p 201.
280. Ibid, p 202.
281. Zeller: op cit, p 251.
282. Ibid, p 249.
283. Ibid, p 251. SS Report on July 20th, in *Nordwestdeutsche Hefte*, Feb 1947, p 3.
284. 'Nebe Series', Mar 30th, 1950, p 20.
285. 'Nebe Series', Apr 6th, 1950, pp 22 et seq.
286. Abshagen: op cit, p 345. Buchheit: op cit, p 426.
287. Krebs: *Fritz-Dietlof Schulenburg*, p 262.
288. Letter from von Herff to Himmler, Oct 9th, 1944, RFSS Microfilm 155.
289. Letter from Himmler to Kaltenbrunner, Oct 14th, 1944, RFSS Microfilm 155.
290. Krebs: op cit, pp 304, 326.
291. Ritter: op cit, p 547.
292. Ibid, p 422.
293. Ibid.
294. Ibid, p 427.
295. Ibid, p 428.
296. Ibid, p 435.

CHAPTER EIGHTEEN

1. Frischauer: op cit, p 225.
2. Patel: 'Die SS' in *Vierteljahrshefte für Zeitgeschichte*, No 1, 1954, p 13.
3. Frischauer: op cit, p 225.
4. Patel in *The Third Reich*, Weidenfeld & Nicolson, 1955, p 661.
5. 'T.E.': *Die Rede Himmlers vor den Gauleitern am 3 Aug. 1944*, p 392.
6. Letter from Himmler to Commanding Generals and Divisional Commanders of Army Group Vistula, Feb 19th, 1945, RFSS Microfilm 59.
7. Reitlinger: *The SS*, p 385.
8. 'T.E.': op cit, p 388.
9. Ibid, p 392. Guderian: *Panzer Leader*, p 364.
10. *Völkischer Beobachter*, Aug 3rd, 1944.
11. 'T.E.': op cit, p 392.
12. Ibid, p 389.
13. Reports by SS-Obergruppenführer Gutenberger, HSSPF West, on senior officers in Wehrkreis VI, RFSS Microfilm 59.

14. Ibid.
15. Report by SS-Obergruppenführer Hofmann, HSSPF Southwest, on senior officers in Wehrkreis V, RFSS Microfilm 59.
16. Report from SD-Hauptaussenstelle Mannheim to SD Commander Strasbourg, Nov 14th, 1944, RFSS Microfilm 269.
17. Ibid.
18. Ibid.
19. Ibid.
20. Ibid.
21. Letter from Kaltenbrunner to Himmler, Oct 17th, 1944, RFSS Microfilm 131.
22. Ibid.
23. Reitlinger: *The SS*, p 387.
24. 'T.E.': op cit, p 389.
25. Manvell and Fraenkel: *Himmler*, pp 201–2.
26. I saw them myself (author).
27. Guderian: op cit, p 355.
28. Ibid.
29. Hanns von Krannhals: *Der Warschauer Aufstand*, 1944, pp 125–6.
30. Guderian: op cit, p 356.
31. Ibid.
32. *Frankfurter Allgemeine Zeitung*, Dec 22nd, 1958.
33. Hagen: op cit, p 189. Reitlinger: *The SS*, pp 377–8.
34. Ibid.
35. Hilberg: *The Destruction of the European Jews*, p 472. Klietmann: *Die Waffen-SS*, p 195.
36. Hilberg: op cit, p 472.
37. Ibid.
38. Skorzeny: *Skorzeny's Special Missions*, pp 7, 8, 12.
39. Ibid, pp 26–7.
40. Ibid, pp 78 et seq, 80.
41. Ibid, p 130.
42. Ibid, p 133.
43. Ibid, p 132.
44. Hagen: op cit, p 369.
45. Nikolaus von Horthy: *Ein Leben für Ungarn*, p 282.
46. Letter from Winkelmann to Himmler, Oct 25th, 1944, RFSS Microfilm 59.
47. Ibid.
48. Ibid.
49. Ibid. Kern: *Der grosse Rausch*, p 156.
50. Kern: op cit, p 156.
51. Letter from Winkelmann to Himmler Oct 25th, 1944.
52. Ibid.
53. Hagen: op cit, p 374. Horthy: op cit, p 282.
54. Horthy: op cit, p 282.
55. Skorzeny: op cit, pp 134–5.
56. Ibid, p 135. Hagen: op cit, p 375.
57. Hagen: op cit, p 375.
58. Ibid, p 376. Skorzeny: op cit, pp 135–6. Letter from Winkelmann to Himmler, Oct 25th, 1944
59. Skorzeny: op cit, pp 135–6.
60. Ibid, p 136.
61. Ibid.
62. Ibid, p 137. Letter from Winkelmann to Himmler, Oct 25th, 1944.
63. Letter from Winkelmann to Himmler, Oct 25th, 1944.
64. Seabury: *The Wilhelmstrasse*, p 195.
65. Letter from Winkelmann to Himmler, Oct 25th, 1944.
66. Hagen: op cit, p 376.
67. von Senger und Etterlin: *24 Panzerdivision*, p 266.
68. Letter from Winkelmann to Himmler, Oct 25th, 1944.
69. Skorzeny: op cit, p 138.
70. Ibid, p 143.
71. Letter from Winkelmann to Himmler, Oct 25th, 1944.

72. *Völkischer Beobachter*, Nov 9th, 1944.
73. Trevor-Roper: *The Last Days of Hitler*, pp 37–8.
74. Kessel: *The Man with the Miraculous Hands*, p 202.
75. Guderian: op cit, p 383.
76. Trevor-Roper: op cit, p 40.
77. Ibid, p 42.
78. Jürgen Thorwald: *Es begann an der Weichsel*, p 17.
79. Thorwald: *Das Ende an der Elbe*, p 17.
80. Ibid.
81. *Keesing's Contemporary Archives.*
82. Reitlinger: *The SS*, p 386.
83 *Keesing's Contemporary Archives.*
84. Reitlinger: *The SS*, p 386.
85. Ibid, p 381.
86. Ibid.
87. Ibid, p 382.
88. Kurt von Tippelskirch: *Geschichte des Zweiten Weltkriegs*, p 521. Westphal: *The German Army in the West*, p 187.
89. Westphal: op cit, pp 187–8.
90. Hausser: *Waffen-SS im Einsatz*, p 185.
91. Westphal: op cit, p 188.
92. Delarue: *History of the Gestapo*, p 286; Reitlinger: *The SS*, pp 236 et seq.
93. Delarue: op cit, pp 283–4, 287.
94. Ohlendorf's statement, Oct 8th, 1947, p 502.
95. Skorzeny: op cit, p 31.
96. Abshagen: op cit, p 356.
97. Delarue: op cit, p 363.
98. Letter from Berger to Himmler, Dec 21st, 1944, RFSS Microfilm 122.
99. Verbal information from Gunter d'Alquen.
100. Best: *Himmler*, p 13.
101. Westphal: op cit, p 189.
102. Ibid.
103. Reitlinger: *The SS*, p 398.
104. Ibid, p 399.
105. Toland: *The Last 100 Days*, pp 4–5.
106. Tippelskirch: op cit, pp 536–7.
107. Ibid, p 539.
108. Guderian: op cit, p 403.
109. Ibid.
110. Ibid, pp 403–4.
111. Reitlinger: *The SS*, p 401.
112. Verbal information from Felix Steiner.
113. Letter from Himmler to Commanding Generals and Divisional Commanders of Army Group Vistula, Feb 19th, 1945.
114. Thorwald: *Es begann an der Weichsel*, p 221.
115. Ibid, p 218.
116. Ibid, p 219.
117. Ibid, p 220.
118. Guderian: op cit, p 413.
119. Ibid, pp 414–5.
120. Ibid, p 415.
121. Thorwald: *Das Ende an der Elbe*, p 10.
122. Guderian: op cit, p 421. Thorwald: op cit, p 11.
123. Guderian: op cit, pp 421–2; Reitlinger: *The SS*, p 412.
124. Thorwald: *Das Ende an der Elbe*, p 7. Toland: op cit, pp 259 et seq.
125. Thorwald: *Das Ende an der Elbe*, pp 18, 21.
126. Kersten: *Totenkopf und Treue*, p 15 (not in English translation). Besgen: op cit, pp 17–18.
127. Besgen: *Der stille Befehl*, p 15.
128. Ibid, p 20.

129. Ibid, pp 21–2. Engelmann: *Deutschland Report*, p 93.
130. Ibid, pp 38–9.
131. Ibid, p 36.
132. Ibid, pp 20, 37.
133. Ibid, pp 14, 65.
134. Ibid, p 53.
135. Arendt: *Eichmann in Jerusalem*, pp 176 et seq.
136. Andreas Biss: *Der Stopp der Endlösung*, p 24.
137. Ibid, pp 48, 24.
138. Ibid, p 25. Hilberg: op cit, p 542.
139. Ibid, pp 34–5.
140. Arendt: *Eichmann in Jerusalem*, p 179.
141. Hilberg: op cit, p 543.
142. Biss: op cit, p 37.
143. Ibid.
144. Ibid, pp 37, 50. Hilberg: op cit, p 544.
145. Ibid, p 51.
146. Ibid, p 53.
147. Ibid, p 59.
148. Hilberg: op cit, p 547.
149. Biss: op cit, p 302.
150. Ibid, p 60.
151. Ibid, p 69.
152. Hilberg: op cit, p 532. *Süddeutsche Zeitung*, Aug 27th, 1966.
153. Hilberg: op cit, p 532.
154. Ibid.
155. Kurt Emmenegger: 'Reichsführers gehorsamster Becher in *Sie und Er*, Jan/Feb 1963, Serial 7.
156. Biss: op cit, pp 106 et seq.
157. Ibid, p 107.
158. Ibid, pp 110, 349.
159. Ibid, p 110.
160. Ibid, p 141.
161. Ibid, p 129.
162. Ibid.
163. Ibid, p 135.
164. Ibid, p 145.
165. Ibid, p 148.
166. Ibid, p 157.
167. Ibid, pp 156–7.
168. Ibid, pp 150–3.
169. Ibid, p 153.
170. Ibid, pp 166–7.
171. Ibid, pp 167, 178, 180.
172. Ibid, pp 178, 180, 201.
173. Ibid, pp 202, 205.
174. Ibid, pp 205–6.
175. Ibid, pp 351 et seq.
176. Schellenberg: *Memoirs*, p 428. Biss: op cit, p 250.
177. Schellenberg: op cit, p 428.
178. Ibid, pp 428–9.
179. Ibid, p 429.
180. Ibid, p 430.
181. IMT Vol XI, p 334.
182. Besgen: op cit, p 43.
183. Ibid.
184. Ibid. Schellenberg: op cit, pp 441–4.
185. Ibid.
186. Ibid.
187. Bernadotte: *The Fall of the Curtain*, p 8.
188. Ibid, p 10.
189. Ibid, pp 12–13.
190. Schellenberg: op cit, p 434.
191. Ibid, p 435.
192. Bernadotte: op cit, p 22.
193. Ibid, pp 23, 26, 29.
194. Trevor-Roper: *The Last Days of Hitler*, pp 96–7.
195. Bernadotte: op cit, p 44.
196. Ibid, p 45.
197. Ibid, p 47.
198. Ibid, p 48.
199. Trevor-Roper: op cit, p 99.
200. Ibid, pp 99–100.
201. Kurt Detlev Möller: *Das letzte Kapital*, pp 55–6.
202. Toland: op cit, p 478.
203. Ibid.
204. Allen Dulles: *The Secret Surrender*, pp 155–6.

205. Toland: op cit, p 478.
206. Verbal information from Gero von Gaevernitz.
207. Eugen Dollmann: *Wie Italien vor dem Bolschewismus gerettet wurde*, pp 4 et seq.
208. Ibid, p 6.
209. Toland: op cit, p 239.
210. Dollmann: *Die Kapitulation von Caserta*, p 19.
211. Ibid, p 24.
212. Ibid.
213. Dulles: op cit, p 165.
214. Toland: op cit, p 478.
215. Ibid.
216. Ibid.
217. Ibid.
218. Ibid, p 479.
219. Ibid.
220. Ibid.
221. Ibid, p 480.
222. Ibid, p 481. Dollmann: *Die Kapitulation von Caserta*, p 40.
223. Dollmann: op cit, p 40.
224. Trevor-Roper: op cit, p 188, footnote.
225. Hagen: op cit, pp 460–1.
226. Toland: op cit, p 338.
227. Ibid.
228. Trevor-Roper: op cit, pp 102, 115 et seq.
229. Ibid, p 117.
230. Besgen: op cit, p 51.
231. Trevor-Roper: op cit, p 123.
232. Besgen: op cit, p 51.
233. Bernadotte: op cit, p 53.
234. Thorwald: *Das Ende an der Elbe*, p 76. Cornelius Ryan: *The Last Battle*, pp 334–5.
235. Thorwald: op cit, p 76. Ryan: op cit, p 335.
236. Klietmann: op cit, pp 56–7. Ryan: op cit, p 335.
237. Toland: op cit, p 420. Thorwald: op cit, p 87.
238. Thorwald: op cit, p 89.
239. Ibid.
240. Ryan: op cit, pp 373–4; Toland: op cit, pp 436–7.
241. Ryan: op cit, p 374. Letter from Gotthard Heinrici, Mar 1st, 1967. Toland: op cit, p 437.
242. Thorwald: op cit, p 143.
243. Felix Steiner: *Die Freiwilligen*, pp 328–9.
244. Trevor-Roper: op cit, p 186. Ryan: op cit, p 392.
245. Ryan: op cit, p 392.
246. Trevor-Roper: op cit, p 189.
247. Toland: op cit, p 520.
248. Hans-Adolf Jacobsen: *1939–1945*, p 532.
249. Trevor-Roper: op cit, p 184.
250. Reitlinger: *The SS*, p 435.
251. Ibid, p 441.
252. Ibid, p 445.
253. Ibid, p 446.
254. Ibid, p 443.
255. Ibid, p 446.
256. Manvell and Fraenkel: *Himmler*, pp 244, 246.
257. Ibid, p 245.
258. Ibid.
259. Ibid, p 248.
260. Hilberg: op cit, p 706. Reitlinger: *Final Solution*, p 357.
261. Ryan: op cit, p 319.
262. Hilberg: op cit, p 694.
263. Reitlinger: *Die Endlösung*, p 586 (German edition only).
264. Reitlinger: *Die Endlösung*, p 589 (German edition only).
265. Hilberg: op cit, p 707.
266. Ibid, pp 708, 712.
267. Reitlinger: *Final Solution*, pp 510, 513, 507.
268. Hilberg: op cit, p 711.
269. Ibid, pp 707, 706, 713.
270. See data passim in Hilberg, op cit, and Reitlinger, *Final Solution*.
271. Kern: op cit, p 187.

APPENDIX 2

TABLE OF SS RANKS

SS	Approximate Equivalent	
	British Army	*U.S. Army*
Reichsführer-SS	Field-Marshal	General of the Army
SS-Oberstgruppenführer	General	General
SS-Obergruppenführer	Lieutenant-General	Lieutenant-General
SS-Gruppenführer	Major-General	Major-General
SS-Brigadeführer	Brigadier	Brigadier-General
SS-Oberführer	Senior Colonel	Senior Colonel
SS-Standartenführer	Colonel	Colonel
SS-Obersturmbannführer	Lieutenant-Colonel	Lieutenant-Colonel
SS-Sturmbannführer	Major	Major
SS-Hauptsturmführer	Captain	Captain
SS-Obersturmführer	Lieutenant	1st Lieutenant
SS-Untersturmführer	2nd Lieutenant	2nd Lieutenant
SS-Sturmscharführer	Regimental Sergeant-Major	Sergeant-Major
SS-Hauptscharführer	Sergeant-Major	Master-Sergeant
SS-Oberscharführer	Quartermaster-Sergeant	Technical Sergeant
SS-Scharführer	Staff Sergeant	Staff Sergeant
SS-Unterscharführer	Sergeant	Sergeant
SS-Rottenführer	Corporal	Corporal
SS-Sturmmann	Lance-Corporal	Corporal
SS-Oberschütze	Senior Private	Private 1st Class
SS-Schütze	Private	Private

APPENDIX 3

PARTITION OF POLAND 1939–42

APPENDIX 4

THE FATE OF GERMAN JEWRY

Jewish population 1933	**503,000**
Emigrants 1933–45	**207,000**
to USA	90,000
to Palestine	50,000
Murdered	**170,000**
(including emigrants to countries occupied by Germany during the war)	
Excess of deaths over births 1933–45	**72,000**
(excluding those murdered)	
Jewish population in 1945	**23,000**

All figures refer to the Jewish population within the 1933 Reich frontiers

APPENDIX 5

EINSATZGRUPPEN IN OCCUPIED RUSSIA (NOVEMBER 1941)

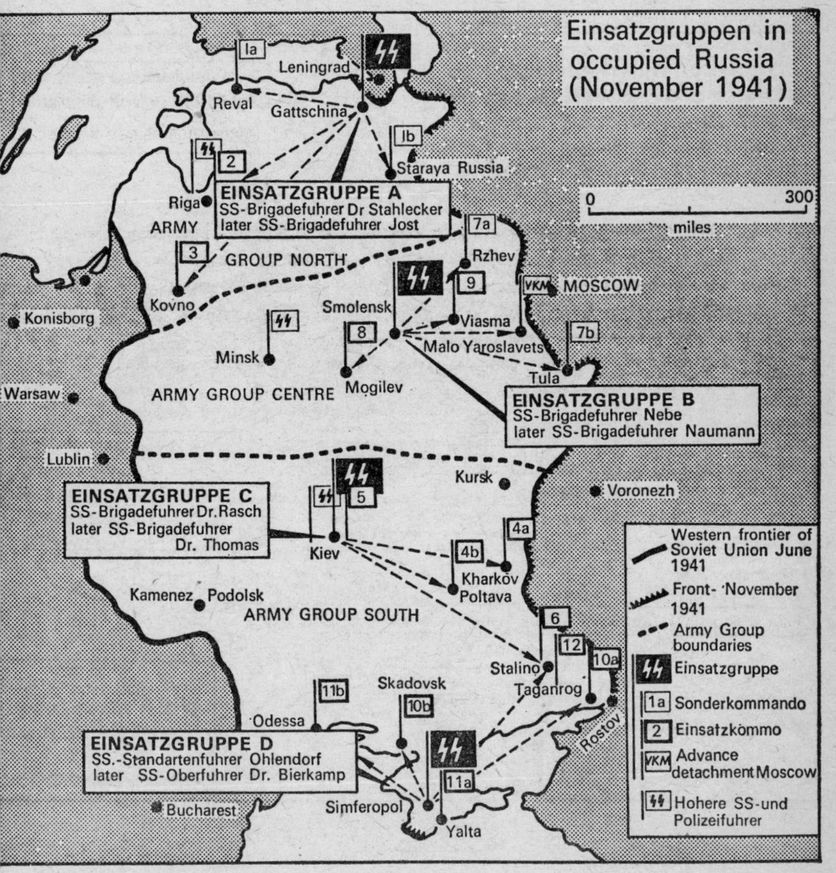

APPENDIX 6

THE DESTRUCTION OF EUROPEAN JEWRY

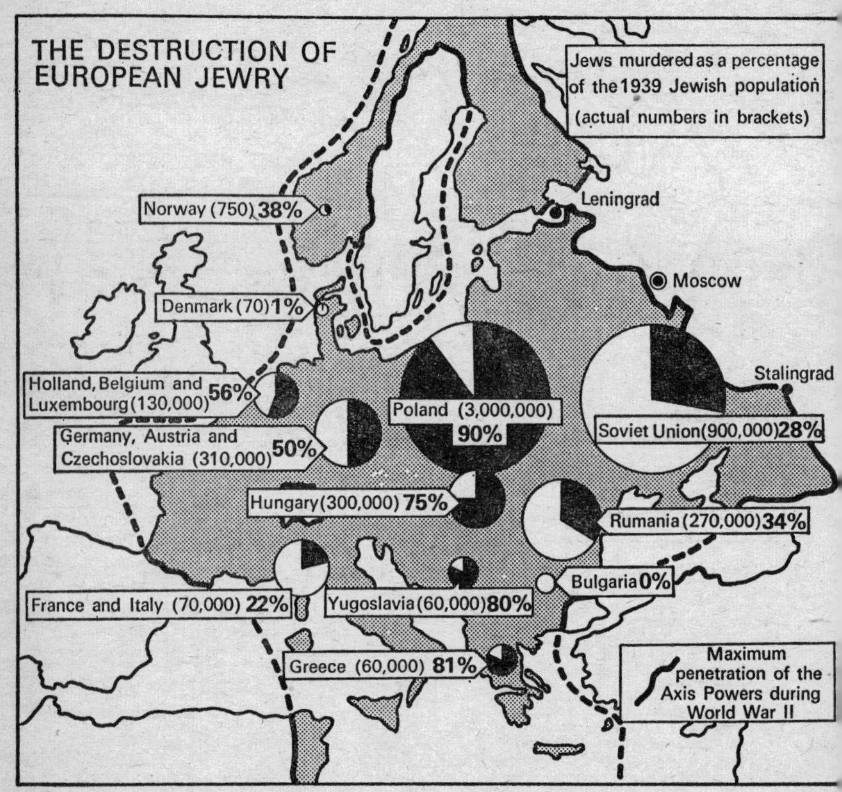

APPENDIX 7

THE VICTIMS OF THE 'FINAL SOLUTION'

Jews murdered in areas under SS control		
Germany (including Austria and the 'Reich Protectorate of Bohemia and Moravia')		250,000
Slovakia		60,000
Denmark and Norway	under	1,000
Holland, Belgium and Luxembourg		130,000
France and Italy		70,000
Soviet Union (including Latvia, Estonia and Lithuania)		900,000
Poland		3,000,000
Yugoslavia		60,000
Greece		60,000
Rumania		270,000
Hungary		300,000
Total		**5,100,000**

These figures are based on those of the American historian, Raul Hilberg, who has extracted them, almost without exception, from SS and Reich Foreign Ministry documents.

APPENDIX 8

THE MILITARY SITUATION AT THE END OF JANUARY 1945

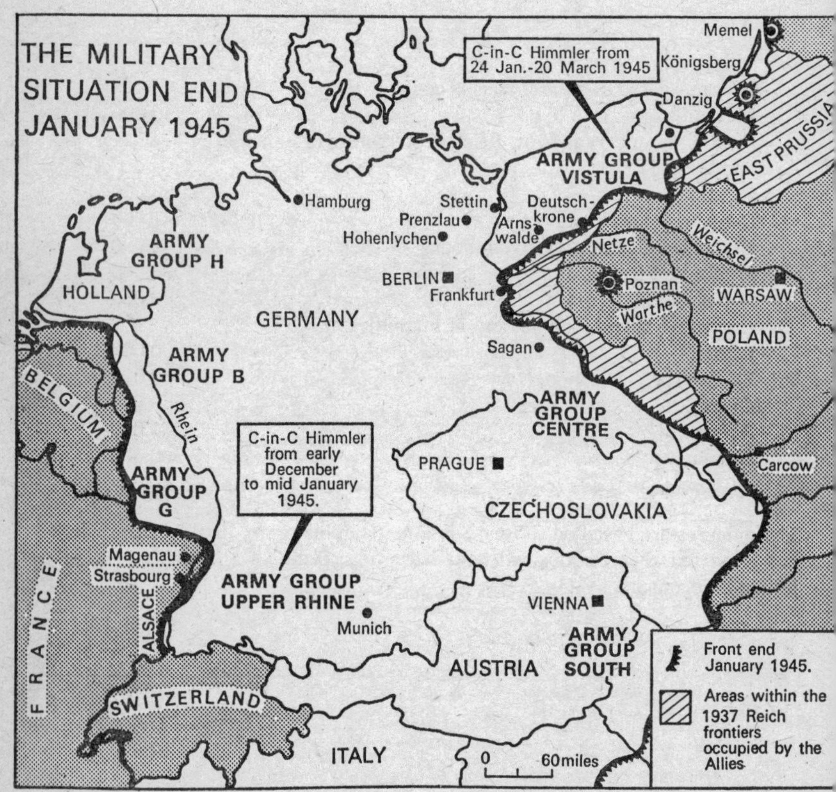

APPENDIX 9

BIBLIOGRAPHY

I. *Unpublished Sources*

Bach-Zelewski, Erich von dem – Public Prosecutor's case for the prosecution, Provincial Court Nuremberg-Fürth – reference Az. la Js 228/60 dated March 11th, 1960.

Best, Werner: Wilhelm Canaris – monograph dated April 10th, 1949.

Best, Werner: Joachim von Ribbentrop – monograph dated March 6th, 1949.

Best, Werner: Reinhard Heydrich – monograph dated September 18th, 1949.

Best, Werner: Reinhard Heydrich – monograph dated October 1st, 1949.

Best, Werner: Die deutsche Politik in Dänemark während der letzten 2½ Kriegsjahre – monograph completed on June 8th, 1960.

Best, Werner: Die deutsche Abwehrpolizei bis 1945.

Best, Werner: Erinnerungen aus dem besetzten Frankreich 1940–1942 – monograph of summer 1951.

Brackelmann, Heinrich: Prinz Hohenlohe.

Brackelmann, Heinrich: Die SS und die geplante Entführung Hitlers.

Der Adel im deutschen Offizierkorps – statistical survey compiled by the Bundesarchiv, Zentralnachweisstelle, Kornelimünster, April 1966.

Diary of the German Embassy Madrid 1941–5.

Dollmann, Eugen: Die Kapitulation von Caserta April 29th, 1945 – supplement by General Hans Röttiger, Frankfurt 1953.

Dollmann, Eugen: Die Kapitulation der deutschen Italien-Armee im Frühjahr 1945, Parts I and II, undated.

Dollmann, Eugen: Wie Italien vor dem Bolschewismus gerettet wurde, undated.

Files of the Personal Staff of the 'Reichsführer-SS and Chief of the German Police', on microfilm in the National Archives, Washington (Group T–175) – referred to as 'RFSS Microfilm'.

Files of the Central Archives of the NSDAP, on microfilm in the Hoover Institution on War, Revolution and Peace, Stanford University – referred to as 'Central Archives'.

Files of the Berlin Document Centre, on microfilm in the National Archives, Washington (Groups 580, 611) – referred to as 'BDC Microfilm'.

Files of the cases against Josef Dietrich and Michael Lippert before Provincial

Court I Munich 1956–7.

Files of Amt VI of the RSHA – in the papers of the Soviet historian Lev A. Bezymenski, Moscow.

Hohenlohe, Prince Max-Egon – private papers.

Interim judgement in case of Gunter d'Alquen July 25th, 1955. De-Nazification Board, Berlin.

Kater, Michael P.: Der 'Freundeskreis Himmler' 1933–45 – submission, Heidelberg 1964.

Memorandum (anonymous) from SS Prisoner of War Camp submitted to Nuremberg Tribunal, dated December 16th, 1945.

von Mildenstein, Leopold: Memorandum April 24th, 1961.

Schaeffer, Dr Walter – private papers.

Wulf, Josef: Die SS.

II. *Published Sources*

Absolon, Rudolf: *Wehrgesetz und Wehrdienst 1935–1945. Das Personalwesen in der Wehrmacht*, Harald Boldt Verlag, Boppard am Rhein, 1960.

Boberach, Heinz: *Meldungen aus dem Reich* (Excerpts from the SD's secret situation reports 1939–44), Hermann Luchterhand Verlag, Neuwied & Berlin 1965.

Degener, Herrmann A. I.: *Degener's Wer ist's?* Verlag Herrmann Degener, Berlin 1935.

Das Deutsche Führerlexikon 1934/35, Verlagsanstalt Otto Stollberg, Berlin 1934.

Die Verfolgung nationalsozialistischer Straftaten im Gebiet der Bundesrepublik Deutschland seit 1945 – issued by the Federal German Ministry of Justice, July 1964.

Dienstaltersliste der Schutzstaffel der NSDAP (SS Seniority List) as at October 1st, 1934, Buchdruckerei Birkner sponsored by Hermes, Munich 1934.

Dienstaltersliste der SS – as at July 1st, 1935, Reichsdruckerei, Berlin 1935.

Dienstaltersliste der SS – as at November 9th, 1944, Reichsdruckerei, Berlin 1944.

Dienstaltersliste der Waffen-SS, SS-Obergrupperführer to SS-Hauptsturmführer – as at July 1st, 1944.

Eichmann, Adolf: Record of interrogation by the Israeli police, six Vols.

Genealogisches Handbuch des Adels, C. A. Starke Verlag, Limburg a. d. Lahn.

Historische Kommission des Reichsführers-SS: *Die Erhebung der österreichischen Nationalsozialisten im Juli 1934*, Europa Verlag, Vienna, Frankfurt, Zurich, 1965.

Horkenbach, Cuno: *Das Deutsche Reich von 1918 bis heute*, Vols 1–3 Verlag für Presse, Wirtschaft und Politik, Berlin 1930–33; Vol 4, Presse und Wirtschaftsverlag, Berlin 1935.

Heiber, Helmut: *Hitlers Lagebesprechungen. Die Protokollfragmente seiner militärischen Konferenzen 1942–45*, Deutsche Verlags-Anstalt Stuttgart 1962.

Institut für Zeitgeschichte – submissions, Selbstverlag des Instituts für Zeitgeschichte, Munich 1958.

International Military Tribunal (referred to as IMT) *Record of the Nuremberg Trials November 14th, 1945 – October 1st, 1946*, 42 Vols, HMSO 1947 – 1949.

Jacobsen, Hans-Adolf: *1939–1945. Der Zweite Weltkrieg in Chronik und Dokumenten*, Wehr und Wissen Verlagsgesellschaft, Darmstadt 1961.

Klietmann, K.-G.: *Die Waffen-SS. Eine Dokumentation*, Verlag 'Der Freiwillige', Osnabrück 1965.

Kaltenbrunner, Ernst: *Spiegelbild einer Verschwörung* – the Kaltenbrunner reports to Bormann and Hitler on the coup of July 20th, 1944. Secret documents from the former RSHA, edited by Archiv Peter für historische und zeitgeschichtliche Dokumentation, Seewald Verlag, Stuttgart 1961.

Keesing's Contemporary Archives 1931–45.

Keilig, Wolf: *Das deutsche Heer 1939–1945. Gliederung, Einsatz, Stellenbesetzung*. 3 Vols, Verlag Hans-Henning Podzun, Bad Nauheim (year not given).

Krätschmer, Ernst-Günther: *Die Ritterkreuzträger der Waffen-SS*, Plesse-Verlag, Göttingen 1957.

Murawski, Erich: *Der deutsche Wehrmachtbericht 1939–1945. Ein Beitrag zur Untersuchung der geistigen Kriegführung*. 2nd edition. Harald Boldt Verlag, Boppard am Rhein 1962.

Oberkommando der Wehrmacht. *Die Berichte des Oberkommandos der Wehrmacht 1 September 1939 – 31 December 1940*, Wiking Verlag, Berlin 1941.

OKW (as above) Reports January 1st – December 31st, 1941, Wiking Verlag Berlin 1942.

Organisationsbuch der NSDAP issued by the Reichsorganisationsleiter of the NSDAP, 5th impression, Zentralverlag der NSDAP, Franz Eher II, Munich 1938.

Picker, H.: *Hitlers Tischgespräche im Führerhauptquartier 1941–1942*, Seewald Verlag, Stuttgart 1963; *Hitler's Table Talks*, Introduction by Professor H. R. Trevor-Roper, translated by Norman Cameron and R. H. Stevens, Weidenfeld & Nicolson, London 1953.

Reichsführer-SS: *Dich ruft die SS*, Verlag Hermann Hillger, Berlin-Grünewald & Leipzig 1943.

Schnabel, Reimund: *Macht ohne Moral. Eine Dokumentation über die SS*, Röderbergverlag, Frankfurt 1957.

Schulthess' Europäischer Geschichtskalendar, issued by Ulrich Thürauf Vol 75 1934, C. H. Beck'sche Verlagsbuchhandlung, Munich 1935.

SS im Einsatz. Eine Dokumentation über die Verbrechen der SS, Kongress-Verlag, East Berlin 1957.

Allgemeines Liederbuch der SS (SS Song Book), Ostenddruckerei, Frankfurt (year not given).

Unsere Ehre heisst Treue. War diary of Reichsführer-SS Operational staff. Activity reports of 1 and 2 SS Infantry Brigades, 1 SS Cavalry Brigade and SS Sonderkommandos, Europa Verlag, Vienna, Frankfurt, Zurich 1965.

Volz, Hans: *Daten der Geschichte der NSDAP*, Verlag A. G. Ploetz, Berlin & Leipzig 1935.

Wet leitet? Die Männer der Wirtschaft und der einschlägigen Verwaltung einschliesslich Adressbuch der Direktoren und Aufsichtsräte 1941/42, Spezialarchiv der deutschen Wirtschaft, Verlag Hoppenstedt & Co, Berlin 1942.

'Urkunden zur Judenpolitik des Dritten Reiches, Dokumente zur Reichskristallnacht', – in *Das Parlament* No 54, 1954.

Wolff, Karl: Case for the prosecution against – Provincial Court Munich II – reference 10a Js 39/60.

III. *Theses*

Aronson, Shlomo: 'Heydrich und die Anfänge des SD und der Gestapo 1931–1935'. Inaugural Dissertation of Faculty of Philosophy in the Free University of Berlin, Berlin 1966.

Knoebel, Edgar Erwin: 'Racial Illusion and Military Necessity: A Study of SS Political Objectives in occupied Belgium'. Thesis submitted to the Faculty of the Graduate School of the University of Colorado 1965.

Lamm, Hans: 'Uber die innere und äussere Entwicklung des deutschen Judentums im Dritten Reich'. Inaugural Dissertation of Faculty of Philosophy in the Friedrich-Alexander University, Erlangen 1951.

Schweder, Alfred: 'Politische Polizei – Wesen und Begriff der politischen Polizei im Metternichschen System, in der Weimarer Republik und im nationalsozialistischen Staat'. Inaugural dissertation for the Doctorate of Law in the Faculty of Law and Economics, University of Rostock, Carl Heymanns Verlag, Berlin 1937.

IV. *Books*

Abshagen, Karl Heinz: *Canaris, Patriot und Weltbürger*, Union Deutsche Verlagsanstalt, Stuttgart 1950.

Adler, H. G.: *Theresienstadt 1941–1945*, J. C. B. Mohr (Paul Siebeck), Tübingen 1955.

d'Alquen, Gunter: *Auf Hieb und Stich*, Zentralverlag der NSDAP, Franz Eher II GmbH, Berlin & Munich 1937.

d'Alquen, Gunter: *Die SS Geschichte, Aufgabe und Organisation der Schutzstaffel der NSDAP*, Junker & Dünnhaupt Verlag, Berlin 1939.

Andreas-Friedrich, Ruth: *Berlin Underground 1939–1945*, Latimer House, London 1948.

Anonymous: *Glück und Ende des Nationalsozialisten Bell*, Verlagsgenossenschaft Ausländischer Arbeiter in der USSR, Moscow & Leningrad 1933.

Arendt, Hannah: *Eichmann in Jerusalem. A report on the Banality of Evil*, Viking Press, New York, 1963.

Arendt, Hannah: *The Origins of Totalitarianism*, Allen & Unwin, London 1958; *Elemente und Ursprünge totaler Herrschaft*, Europäische Verlagsanstalt, Frankfurt 1955.

Armstrong, John: *Ukrainian Nationalism 1939–1945*, Columbia University Press, New York 1955.

Aretin, Erwein Freiherr von: *Fritz Michael Gerlich. Ein Märtyrer unserer Tage*, Verlag Schnell & Steiner, Munich 1949.

Aretin, Erwein Freiherr von: *Krone und Ketten*, Süddeutscher Verlag, Munich 1955.

Bartz, Karl: *Die Tragödie der deutschen Abwehr*, Pilgram Verlag, Salzburg 1955.

Bennecke, Heinrich: *Hitler und die SA*, Günter Olzog Verlag, Munich & Vienna 1962.

Bennecke, Heinrich: *Die Reichswehr und der 'Röhm-Putsch'*, Günter Olzog Verlag, Munich & Vienna 1964.

Benoist-Méchin, Jacques: *Histoire de l'armée allemande*, Albin Michel Paris 1964–6.

Bernadotte, Count Folke: *The Fall of the Curtain*, Cassell & Co, London, Toronto, Melbourne & Sydney 1945.

Besgen, Achim: *Der stille Befehl. Medizinalrat Kersten und das Dritte Reich*, Nymphenburger Verlagshandlung, Munich 1960.

Bezymenski, Lev: *Martin Bormann*, Aurora Verlag, Zurich 1965.

Best, S. Payne: *The Venlo Incident*, Hutchinson & Co, London, New York, Melbourne, Sydney & Cape Town 1950.

Best, Werner: *Die Deutsche Polizei*, L. C. Wittich Verlag, Darmstadt 1941.

Biss, Andreas: *Der Stopp der Endlösung. Kampf gegen Himmler und Eichmann in Budapest*, Seewald Verlag, Stuttgart 1966.

Bor, Peter: *Gespräche mit Halder*, Limes Verlag, Wiesbaden 1950.

Bouhler, Philipp: *Kampf um Deutschland*, Zentralverlag der NSDAP, Berlin 1939.

Bracher, Karl Dietrich: *Die Auflösung der Weimarer Republik*, 1st edition, Ring-Verlag, Stuttgart & Düsseldorf 1955, 3rd edition Ring-Verlag, Villingen/Schwarzwald 1960.

Bracher, Karl Dietrich; Sauer, Wolfgang; Schulz, Gerhard: *Die nationalsozialistische Machtergreifung*, Westdeutscher Verlag, Köln & Oppladen 1960.

Bross, Werner: *Gespräche mit Hermann Göring während des Nürnberger Prozesses*, Wolff Verlag, Flensburg & Hamburg 1950.

Broszat, Martin: *Nationalsozialistische Polenpolitik 1939–45*, Deutsche Verlagsanstalt, Stuttgart 1961.

Buchheim, Hans; Broszat, Martin; Krausnick, Helmut; Jacobsen, Hans-Adolf *Anatomie des SS-Staates*, Walter Verlag, Olten & Freiburg im Breisgau 1965; *The Anatomy of the SS State*, translated R. H. Barry, Marian Jackson & Dorothy Long, Collins, London 1968.

Buchheim, Hans: *Glaubenkrise im Dritten Reich*, Deutsche Verlagsanstalt Stuttgart 1953.

Buchheim, Hans: *SS und Polizei im NS-Staat*, Selbstverlag der Studiengesellschaft für Zeitprobleme, Duisdorf nr Bonn 1964.

Buchheim, Hans: *Totalitäre Herrschaft*, Kösel Verlag, Munich 1962.

Buchheit, Gert: *Der deutsche Geheimdienst*, List Verlag, Munich 1966.

Bullock, Alan: *Hitler. A Study in Tyranny*, Odhams Press, London 1964.

Burckhardt, Carl J.: *Meine Danziger Mission 1937–1939*, Verlag Georg D. W. Callwey, Munich 1960.

Carell, Paul: *Unternehmen Barbarossa*, Verlag Ullstein, Frankfurt, Berlin and Vienna 1963; *Hitler's War on Russia*, translated by Ewald Osers, Harrap, London, 1940.

Carell, Paul: *Verbrannte Erde*, Verlag Ullstein, Frankfurt, Berlin and Vienna 1966.

Ciano, Count Galeazzo: *Ciano's Diary*, Wm Heinemann, London and Toronto 1947.

Clarke, Comer: *Eichmann. The Man and his Crimes*, Ballantine Books, New York 1960.

Cohen, E: *Human Behaviour in the Concentration Camps*, translated from the Dutch by M. H. Braaksma, W. W. Norton & Co, New York 1953.

Cole, Hubert: *Laval*, Wm Heinemann, London, Melbourne and Toronto 1963.

Colvin, Ian: *Chief of Intelligence*, Victor Gollancz, London 1951.

Crankshaw, Edward: *The Gestapo*, Putnam, London 1956.

Craig, Gordon A.: *The Politics of the Prussian Army 1640–1945*, OUP, New York 1964.

Dallin, Alexander: German Rule in Russia *1941–1945*, Macmillan & Co, New York 1957.

De Felice, Renzo: *Storia degli ebrei italiani sotto il fascismo*, Giulio Einaudi, Turin 1961.

Degrelle, Leon: *Die verlorene Legion*, Veritas Verlag, Stuttgart 1952.

Delarue, Jacques: *Histoire de la Gestapo*, Fayard, Paris 1962; *The History of the Gestapo*, translated Mervyn Savill, Macdonald, London 1964.

Demeter, Karl: *Das deutsche Offizierkorps in Gesellschaft und Staat 1650–1945*, Bernard & Graefe Verlag für Wehrwesen, Frankfurt 1962; *The German Officer Corps*, translated by Angus Malcolm, Weidenfeld & Nicolson, London 1965.

Denne, Ludwig: *Das Danzig-Problem in der deutschen Aussenpolitik 1934–1939*, Ludwig Röhrscheid Verlag, Bonn 1959.

Diels, Rudolf: *Lucifer ante portas*, Deutsche Verlagsanstalt, Stuttgart 1950.

Dixon, C. Aubrey; Heilbrunn, Otto: *Communist Guerrilla Warfare*, Allen & Unwin, London 1954.

Domarus, Max: *Hitler. Reden und Proklamationen 1932–1945*, 4 Vols, Süddeutscher Verlag, Munich 1965.

Dönitz, Karl: *Zehn Jahre und Zwanzig Tage*, Athenäum Verlag, Bonn 1958; *Memoirs, Ten Years and Twenty Days*, translated R. H. Stevens, Weidenfeld & Nicolson, London 1959.

Dornberger, Walter: *V2 – Der Schuss ins Weltall*, Bechtle Verlag, Esslingen 1952.

Doussinague, José M.: *España tenia Razon 1939–1945*, Espasa-Calpe SA, Madrid 1950.

Dulles, Allen: *The Secret Surrender*, Weidenfeld & Nicolson, London 1946.

Dulles, Allen: *Germany's Underground*, Macmillan, New York 1947.

Ehlers, Dieter: *Technik und Moral einer Verschwörung, 20 Juli 1944*, Athenäum Verlag, Frankfurt & Bonn 1964.

Engelmann, Bernt: *Deutschland Report*, Ex-libris Buchhandlung GmbH-Verlag, Berlin 1965.

Fest, Joachim C.: *Das Gesicht des Dritten Reiches*, R. Piper & Co Verlag, Munich 1963.

Foerster, Wolfgang: *Generaloberst Ludwig Beck*, Isar Verlag, Munich 1953.

Foertsch, Hermann: *Schuld und Verhängnis. Die Fritsch-Krise im Frühjahr 1938*, Deutsche Verlagsanstalt, Stuttgart 1951.

François-Poncet, André: *The Fateful Years*, translated Jacques Le Clercq Victor Gollancz, London 1948.

Georg, Enno: *Die wirtschaftlichen Unternehmungen der SS*, Deutsche Verlagsanstalt, Stuttgart 1963.

Gilbert, G. M.: *Nuremberg Diary*, New American Library, New York 1947.

Gilbert, G. M.: *The Psychology of Dictatorship*, Ronald Press Co, New York 1950.

Gisevius, Hans-Bernd: *Bis zum bitteren Ende*, Fretz & Wasmuth Verlag, Zurich 1946; *To the Bitter End*, translated Richard & Clara Winstone, Jonathan Cape, London 1948.

Gisevius, Hans-Bernd: *Wo ist Nebe?*, Droemersche Verlagsanstalt AG, Zurich 1966.

Glaser, Kurt: *Die Tschechoslowakei*, Athenäum Verlag, Bonn and Frankfurt 1964.

Goebbels, Joseph: *Tagebücher aus den Jahren 1942–43*, Atlantis Verlag, Zurich 1948: *The Goebbels Diaries*, edited and translated Louis P. Lochner, Hamish Hamilton, London 1948.

Gordon, Harold J.: *The Reichswehr and the German Republic*, OUP, London 1947.

Görlitz, Walter, and Quint, Herbert A.: *Adolf Hitler. Eine Biographie*, Steingruben Verlag GmbH, Stuttgart 1952.

Görlitz, Walter: *Generalfeldmarschall Keitel. Verbrecher oder Offizier?* Musterschmidt Verlag, Göttingen, Berlin, Frankfurt 1961.

Görlitz, Walter, and *Die Waffen-SS*, Arani Verlag GmbH Berlin-Grünewald 1960.

Greiner, Helmuth: *Die Oberste Wehrmachtführung 1939–1943*, Limes Verlag, Wiesbaden 1951.

Groppe, Theodor: *Ein Kampf um Recht und Sitte*, Paulinus Verlag, Trier 1947.

Guderian, Heinz: *Erinnerungen eines Soldaten*, Kurt Vowinckel, Heidelberg 1951; *Panzer Leader*, foreword Sir Basil Liddel Hart, translated Constantine Fitzgibbon, Michael Joseph, London 1952.

Habas, Bracha: *The Gate Breakers*, Thomas Yoseloff, New York, London 1963.

Hagen, Walter: *Die geheime Front*, Nibelungen Verlag, Linz and Vienna 1950.

Haestrup, Jorgen: *Til Landets Bedste*, Gyldendal, Copenhagen 1966.

Hassell, Ulrich von: *Vom anderen Deutschland*, Fischer Bücherei, Frankfurt and Hamburg 1964; *The von Hassell Diaries*, Hamish Hamilton, London 1948.

Hausser, Paul: *Soldaten wie andere auch*, Munin Verlag, Osnabrück 1966.

Hausser, Paul: *Waffen-SS im Einsatz*, Plesse Verlag K. W. Schütz, Göttingen 1953.

Heiber, Helmut: *Adolf Hitler. Eine Biographie*, Colloquium Verlag, Berlin 1960.

Heiber, Helmut: *Walter Frank und sein Reichsinstitut für Geschichte des neuen Deutschlands*, Deutsche Verlagsanstalt, Stuttgart 1967.

Heiden, Konrad: *Geburt des Dritten Reiches*, Europa Verlag AG, Zurich 1934.

Heiden, Konrad: *Geschichte des Nationalsozialismus*, Rowohlt, Berlin 1932.

Helfferich, Emil: *Ein Leben*, Vol 4. Printed as facsimile manuscript by C. L. Mettcker & Sons, Jever 1964.

Henkys, Richard: *Die nationalsozialistischen Gewaltverbrechen*, Kreuz Verlag, Stuttgart & Berlin 1964.

Herzog, Robert: *Die Volksdeutschen in der Waffen-SS*, Institut für Besatzungsfragen, Tübingen, May 1955.

Heusinger, Adolf: *Befehl im Widerstreit*, Rainer Wunderlich Hermann Leinz, Tübingen and Stuttgart 1950.

Hewins, Ralph: *Quisling, Prophet without Honour*, W. H. Allen, London 1965.

Heydrich, Reinhard: *Wandlungen unseres Kampfes*, Verlag Franz Eher II, Munich and Berlin 1935.

Hilberg, Raul: *The Destruction of the European Jews*, Quadrangle Books, Chicago, W. H. Allen, London 1961.

Himmler, Heinrich: *Die Schutzstaffel als antibolschewistische Kampf-organisation*, Zentralverlag der NSDAP, Franz Eher II, Munich 1936.

Hirsch, Kurt: *SS, Gestern, heute und . . .*, Progress Verlag Johann Fladung, Darmstadt 1960.

Hitler, Adolf: *Mein Kampf*, Zentralverlag der NSDAP, Franz Eher II, Munich 1942; translated James Murphy, Hurst & Blackett, London 1939; translated Ralph Manheim, Houghton Mifflin, Boston 1943.

Hoegner, Wilhelm: *Die verratene Republik*, Isar Verlag, Munich 1958.

Höhn, Reinhard: *Arthur Mahraun, der Wegweiser zur Nation*, Schleswig-Holsteinische Verlagsanstalt, Rendsburg 1929.

Hofer, Walther: *Der Nationalsozialismus. Dokumente 1933–1945, Fischer Bücherei No 172.*

Hofmann, Hans Hubert: *Der Hitlerputsch*, Nymphenburger Verlagshandlung, Munich 1961.

Horthy, Nikolaus von: *Ein Leben für Ungarn*, Athenäum Verlag, Bonn, 1953.

Hossbach, Friedrich: *Zwischen Wehrmacht und Hitler 1934–1938*, Wolfenbütteler Verlagsanstalt, Wolfenbüttel and Hannover 1949.

Höss, Rudolf: *Kommandant in Auschwitz*, edited Martin Broszat, Deutscher Taschenbuch Verlag, Munich 1965.

Irving, David: *The Mare's Nest*, Wm Kimbler, London 1964.

Jäckel, Eberhard: *Frankreich in Hitler's Europa*, Deutsche Verlagsanstalt, Stuttgart 1958.

Jaksch, Wenzel: *Europas Weg nach Potsdam*, Deutsche Verlagsanstalt, Stuttgart 1958.

Jedlika, Ludwig: *Der 20 Juli 1944 in Österreich*, Verlag Herold, Vienna and Munich 1965.

Jolly, Cyril: *The Vengeance of Private Pooley*, Wm Heinemann, London 1956.

de Jong, Louis: *Die deutsche Fünfte Kolonne im Zweiten Weltkreig*, Deutsche Verlagsanstalt, Stuttgart 1959.

Jünger, Ernst: *Der Kampf als inneres Erlebnis*, E. S. Mittler & Son, Berlin 1922.

Jünger, Ernst: *Krieg und Krieger*, Junker & Dünnhaupt Verlag, Berlin 1930.

'*Kameraden bis zum Ende*' – History of 4 'DF' SS-Panzergrenadier-Regiment 1939–45, Plesse Verlag, Göttingen 1962.

Kautsky, Benedikt: *Teufel und Verdammte*, Büchergilde Gutenberg, Zurich 1946.

Kempner, Robert M. W.: *Eichmann und Komplizen*, Europa-Verlag AG, Zurich, Stuttgart and Vienna 1961.

Kempner, Robert M. W.: *SS im Kreuzverhör*, Rütten & Loening Verlag, Munich 1964.

Kern, Erich: *Der Grosse Rausch*, Verlag Lothar Leberecht, Waiblingen/Württemberg 1948.

Kerstern, Felix: *Totenkopf und Treue*, Robert Mölich Verlag, Hamburg 1952; *The Kersten Memoirs 1940–1945*, introduction Professor Trevor-Roper, translated Constantine Fitzgibbon & James Oliver, Hutchinsons, London 1956.

Kessel, Joseph: *The Man with Miraculous Hands*, introduction Professor Trevor-Roper, translated from the French Helen Weaver & Leo Raditsa, Farrar, Strauss & Cudahy, New York 1961.

Kesselring, Albert: *Gedanken zum Zweiten Weltkrieg*, Athenäum Verlag, Bonn 1955.

Kesselring, Albert: *Soldat bis zum letzten Tag*, Athenäum Verlag, Bonn 1953; *Memoirs*, translated Lynton Hudson, Wm Kimber, London 1953.

Kielmansegg, Adolf Graf von: *Der Fritschprozess 1938*, Hoffmann & Campe Verlag, Hamburg 1949.

Kimche, Jon: *General Guisans Zweifrontenkrieg*, Verlag Ullstein, Berlin, Frankfurt, Vienna 1962.

Kimche, Jon and David: *The Secret Roads*, Secker & Warburg, London 1955.

Kleist, Peter: *Zwischen Hitler und Stalin 1939–1945*, Athenäum Verlag, Bonn 1950.

Kochan, Lionel: *Pogrom. 10 November 1938*, André Deutsch, London 1957.

Koehl, Robert L.: *RKFVD: German Resettlement and Population Policy 1939–1945*, Harvard University Press, Cambridge, USA 1957.

Kogon, Eugen: *Der SS-Staat*, 1st 100,000 Verlag des Druckhauses Tempelhof, Berlin 1947; 211,000–224,000 Europäische Verlagsanstalt, Frankfurt 1965; *The Theory and Practice of Hell*, translated Heinz Norden, Secker & Warburg, London 1950.

Kordt, Erich: *Nicht aus den Akcen*, Union Deutsche Verlagsgesellschaft, Stuttgart 1950.

Kramarz, Joachim: *Claus Graf Stauffenberg*, Bernard & Graefe Verlag für Wehrwesen, Frankfurt 1965; *Stauffenberg, The Life and Death of an Officer*, introduction Professor Trevor-Roper, translated R. H. Barry, André Deutsch, London 1967.

Krannhals, Hanns von: *Der Warschauer Aufstand 1944*, Bernard & Graefe Verlag für Wehrwesen, Frankfurt 1962.

Krebs, Albert: *Fritz-Dietlof Graf von der Schulenburg*, Leibnitz Verlag, Hamburg 1964.

Krebs, Albert: *Tendenzen und Gestalten der NSDAP*, Deutsche Verlagsanstalt, Stuttgart 1959.

Langbein, Hermann: *Im Namen des deutschen Volkes*, Europa Verlag AG, Vienna, Köln, Stuttgart, Zurich 1963.

Langemann, Hans: *Das Attentat*, Kriminalistik, Verlag für kriminalistische Literatur, Hamburg 1956.

Laqueur, Walter Z.: *Young Germany*, introduction R. H. S. Crossman, Routledge & Paul Kegan, London 1962.

Leverkuehn, Paul: *Der geheime Nachrichtendienst der Wehrmacht im Kriege*, Athenäum Verlag, Frankfurt, Bonn 1964.

Liddell Hart, Sir Basil: (editor): *The Red Army*, Weidenfeld & Nicolson, London 1956.

Macdonald, Bruce J. S.: *The Trial of Kurt Meyer*, Clarke Irwin Co, Toronto 1954.

Manvell, Roger, and Fraenkel, Heinrich: *Heinrich Himmler*, Wm Heinemann, London, Melbourne, Toronto, Cape Town, Auckland 1965.

Manstein, Erich von: *Verlorene Siege*, Athenäum Verlag, Bonn 1958; Lost Victories, translated A. G. Powell, Methuen, London 1958.

Maser, Werner: *Die Frühgeschichte der NSDAP*, Athenäum Verlag, Frankfurt and Bonn 1965.

Meyer, Kurt: *Grenadiere*, 4th edition, Schild Verlag, Munich-Lochhausen 1965.

Mitscherlich, Alexander; Mielke, Fred: *Das Diktat der Menschenverachtung*, Verlag Lambert Schneider, Heidelberg 1947.

Mitscherlich, Alexander; Mielke, Fred: *Medizin ohne Menschlichkeit*, Fischer Bücherei, Frankfurt and Hamburg 1960.

Möller, Kurt Detlev: *Das letzte Kapitel. Geschichte der Kapitulation Hamburgs*, Hoffmann & Campe Verlag, Hamburg 1947.

Müller-Hillebrand, Burkhart: *Das Heer 1933–1945*, 2 Vols, Verlag E. S. Mittler & Son, Frankfurt 1954–6.

Neufeldt, Hans-Joachim; Huck, Jürgen; Tessin, Georg: *Zur Geschichte der Ordnungspolizei 1936–1945*, printed as manuscript, Koblenz 1957.

Neumann, Franz: *Behemoth. The Structure and Practice of National-Socialism*, Victor Gollancz, London 1943.

Neusüss-Hunkel, Ermenhild: *Die SS*, Norddeutsche Verlagsanstalt, Hannover and Frankfurt 1956.

Orb, Heinrich: *Nationalsozialismus, 13 Jahre Machtrausch*, Verlag Otto Walter, Olten 1945.

Paetel, Karl O.: 'The SS' in *The Third Reich* (composite authorship), Weidenfeld & Nicolson, London 1955.

Papen, Franz von: *Der Wahrheit eine Gasse*, Paul List Verlag, Munich 1952; *Memoirs* translated Brian Connell, André Deutsch, London 1952.

Pechel, Rudolf; *Deutscher Widerstand*, Eugen Rentsch Verlag, Erlenbach Zurich 1947.

Picht, Werner: *Vom Wesen des Krieges und vom Kriegswesen der Deutschen*, Friedrich Vorwerk Verlag, Stuttgart 1952.

Piotrowski, Stanislav: *Hans Franks Tagebuch*, Polnischer Verlag der Wissenschaften, Warsaw 1963.

Poliakov, Leon; Wulf Josef: *Das Dritte Reich und seine Diener*, Arani Verlags-GmbH, Berlin-Grünewald 1956.

Poliakov, Leon; Wulf, Josef: *Das Dritte Reich und seine Denker*, Arani Verlags-GmbH, Berlin-Grünewald 1959.

Poliakov, Leon; Wulf, Josef: *Das Dritte Reich und die Juden*, Arani Verlags-GmbH, Berlin-Grünewald 1955.

Quinton, René: *Die Stimme des Krieges*, Der graue Verlag, Berlin and Zurich 1936.

Raeder, Erich: *Mein Leben*, 2 vols, Verlag Fritz Schlichtenmayer, Tübingen 1957; *Struggle for the Sea*, translated E. Fitzgerald, Wm Kimber, London 1959.

Rahn, Rudolf: *Ruheloses Leben*, Diederichs Verlag, Düsseldorf 1949.

Rauschning, Hermann: *Gespräche mit Hitler*, Europa Verlag AG, Zurich, Vienna, New York 1940; *Hitler speaks*, Thornton Butterworth, London 1939.

Reitlinger, Gerald: *The House built on Sand*, Weidenfeld & Nicolson, London 1960.

Reitlinger, Gerald: *The Final Solution*, Valentine Mitchell, London 1953.

Reitlinger, Gerald: *The SS. Alibi of a Nation*, Wm Heinemann, London, Melbourne, Toronto 1956.

Reynolds, Quentin: *Minister of Death. The Eichmann Story*, Viking Press, New York 1960.

Ribbentrop, Joachim von: *Zwischen London und Moskau*, Druffel-Verlag, Leoni am Starnberger See 1961; *The Ribbentrop Memoirs*, introduction Alan Bullock, translated Oliver Watson, Weidenfeld & Nicolson, London 1954.

Ritter, Gerhard: *Carl Goerdeler und die deutsche Widerstandsbewegung*, Deutsche Verlagsanstalt, Stuttgart 1956.

Röhm, Ernst: *Die Geschichte eines Hochverräters*, 3rd edition, Verlag Franz Eher II, Munich 1933.

Röhricht, Edgar: *Pflicht und Gewissen*, W. Kohlhammer Verlag, Stuttgart 1965.

Rosenberg, Alfred: *Letzte Aufzeichnungen*, Plesse Verlag, Göttingen 1955.

Rothfels, Hans: *Die deutsche Opposition gegen Hitler*, Scherpe-Verlag, Krefeld 1949.

Ryan, Cornelius: *The Last Battle*, Simon & Schuster, New York, Collins, London 1966.

Salomon, Ernst von: *Der Fragebogen*, Rohwolt Verlag, Hamburg 1951.

Schallmayer, Wilhelm: *Verrbung und Auslese im Lebenslauf der Völker*, Gustav Fischer Verlag, Jena 1903.

Schellenberg, Walter: *Memoiren*, Verlag für Politik und Wirtschaft, Köln 1956; *The Schellenberg Memoirs*, introduction Alan Bullock, translated Louis Hagen, André Deutsche, London 1961.

Schlabrendorff, Fabian von: *Offiziere gegen Hitler*, edited by Gero von Gaevernitz, Europa Verlag, Zurich 1946; *The Secret War against Hitler*, translated Hilda Simon, Hodder & Stoughton, London 1961.

Schlierbach, Helmut: *Die politische Polizei in Preussen*, Verlag Heinrich & J. Lechte, Emsdetten 1938.

Schmidt, Paul: *Statist auf diplomatische Bühne 1923–45*, Athenäum Verlag, Bonn 1949; *Hitler's Interpreter*, edited R. H. C. Steed, Wm Heinemann, London, Melbourne, Toronto 1951.

Schorn, Hubert: *Der Richter im Dritten Reich*, Vittorio Klostermann, Frankfurt 1959.

Schramm, Wilhelm von: *Der 20 Juli in Paris*, Kindler & Schiermeyer Verlag, Bad Wörishofen 1953; *Conspiracy among Generals*, translated and edited R. T. Clark, Allen & Unwin, London 1956.

Schulz, Paul: *Meine Erschiessung am 30 Juni 1934*, Private publication 1948.

Schwerin von Krosigk, Lutz Graf: *Es geschah in Deutschland*, Rainer Wunderlich Verlag Hermann Leins, Tübingen and Stuttgart 1951.

Seabury, Paul: *The Wilhelmstrasse*, University of California Press, Berkeley and Los Angeles, Cambridge University Press, London 1954.

Segin, W.: *Geschichte der Wewelsburg*, Druck u. Verlag P. N. Esser, Büren. Westphalia 1925.

Shepherd, Gordon: *Dollfuss*, Macmillan & Co, London and New York 1961.

Shirer, William L.: *The Rise and Fall of the Third Reich*, Secker & Warburg, London 1961.

Skorzeny, Otto: *Geheimkommando Skorzeny*, Hansa Verlag Josef Toth, Hamburg 1950; *Skorzeny's Special Missions*, Robert Hale, London 1957.

Sommerfeldt, Martin H.: *Ich war dabei*, Drei Quellen Verlag, Darmstadt 1949.

Speidel, Hans: *Invasion 1944*, Rainer Wunderlich Verlag Hermann Leins, Tübingen and Stuttgart 1951; *We defended Normandy* translated Ian Colvin, Herbert Jenkins, London 1951.

Staff, Ilse: *Justiz im Dritten Reich*, Fischer Bücherei, Feb 1964.

Stein, George H.: *The Waffen-SS*, Cornell University Press, Ithaca, NY 1966.

Steiner, Felix: *Die Armee der Geächteten*, Plesse Verlag, Göttingen 1963.

Steiner, Felix: *von Clausewitz bis Bulganin*, Deutsche Heimat-Verlag, Bielefeld 1956.

Steiner, Felix: *Die Freiwilligen*, Plesse Verlag, Göttingen 1958.

Strasser, Otto: *Hitler und ich*, Johannes Asmus Verlag, Constance 1948.

Strauch, Rudi: *Sir Neville Henderson*, Ludwig Röhrscheid Verlag, Bonn 1959.

Taylor, Telford: *Final Report to Secretary of the Army*, US Department of Army 1949.

Thorwald, Jürgen: *Das Ende an der Elbe*, Droemersche Verlagsanstalt Th. Knaur II, Munich and Zurich 1965.

Thorwald, Jürgen: *Es begann an der Weichsel*, Steingruben-Verlag, Stuttgart 1953.

Thorwald, Jürgen: *Wen sie verderben wollen*, Steingrüben-Verlag, Stuttgart 1952.

Tippelskirch, Kurt von: *Geschichte des Zweiten Weltkriegs*, 2nd edition, Athenäum Verlag, Bonn 1956.

Tobias, Fritz: *Der Reichstagsbrand*, G. Groete'sche Verlags-buchhandlung, Rastatt 1962.

Toland, John: *The Last 100 Days*, Random House, New York, Arthur Barker, London 1965.

Trevor-Roper, Prof. H. R.: *The Bormann Letters*, Weidenfeld & Nicolson, London 1954.

Trevor-Roper, Prof. H. R.: *The Last Days of Hitler*, Macmillan & Co, London and New York, 3rd edition 1956.

Vogelsang, Thilo: *Reichswehr, Staat and NSDAP*, Deutsche Verlagsanstalt, Stuttgart 1962.

Vollmer, Bernhard: *Volksopposition im Polizeistaat*, Deutsche Verlagsanstalt, Stuttgart 1957.

Warlimont, Walter: *Im Hauptquartier der deutschen Wehrmacht 1939–1945*, Bernard & Graefe Verlag, Frankfurt 1962; *Inside Hitler's Headquarters*, translated R. H. Barry, Weidenfeld & Nicolson, London 1964.

Weizsäcker, Ernest von: *Erinnerungen*, Paul List Verlag, Munich, Leipzig and Freiburg 1950.

Westphal, Siegfried: *Heer in Fesseln*, 2nd edition, Athenäum Verlag, Bonn

1952; *The German Army in the West*, Cassell & Co, London 1951.
Wheeler-Bennett, Sir John W.: *The Nemesis of Power*, Macmillan, London St Martin's Press, New York 1953.
Wiesenthal S.: *Grossmufti – Grossagent der Achse*, Ried-Verlag, Salzburg and Vienna 1947.
Wighton, Charles: *Heydrich*, Odhams Press, London 1962.
Wilmot, Chester: *The Struggle for Europe*, Collins, London, Harper Bros, New York 1952.
Wulf, Josef: *Das Dritte Reich und seine Vollstrecker*, Arani Verlags-GmbH, Berlin-Grünewald 1961.
Wulf, Josef: *Heinrich Himmler*, Arani Verlags-GmbH, Berlin-Grünewald 1960.
Henry, A.: *The Case against Adolf Eichmann*: New American Library, New York 1960.
Zeller, Eberhard: *Geist der Freiheit*, Verlag Hermann Rinn, Gotthold Müller Verlag, Munich 1963.
Zipfel, Friedrich: *Gestapo und Sicherheitsdienst*, Arani Verlags-GmbH, Berlin-Grünewald 1960.
Zipfel, Friedrich: *Kirchenkampf in Deutschland 1933–1945*, Walter de Gruyter & Co, Berlin 1965.

V. Periodicals

Adler, H. G.: 'Selbstverwaltung und Widerstand in den Konzentrationslager der SS' – *Vierteljahrshefte für Zeitgeschichte*, No 3 1960.
Angress, Werner T.; Smith, Bradley F.: 'Diaries of Heinrich Himmler's Early Years' – *Journal of Modern History*, No 3 1959.
Auerbach, Helmuth: 'Die Einheit Dirlewanger' – *Vierteljahrsheft für Zeitgeschichte*, No 3 1962.
Auerbach, Helmuth: 'Eine nationalsozialistische Stimme zum Wiener Putsch vom 25 Juli 1934' – *Vierteljahrshefte für Zeitgeschichte* No 2 1964.
Berger, Gottlob: 'Zum Ausbau der Waffen-SS' – *Nation Europa*, No 4 1953.
Best, Werner: 'Kritik und Apologie des Juristen' – *Deutsches Recht*, April 8th–15th, 1939.
Bihl, K.: 'Kommandobehörden, Verbände und selbständige Truppenteile der Waffen-SS' – *Feldgrau* Nos 1, 2 and 3 1961, Nos 3 and 4 1963, Nos 1 and 2 1965.
Bihl, K.: 'Die Waffen-SS, Allgemeines zur Entstehung und Stellung' – *Feldgrau* Nos 5 and 6 1964.
Bihl, Wolfdieter: 'Zur Rechtsstellung der Waffen-SS' – *Wehrwissenschaftliche Rundschau*, No 7 1966.
Broszat, Martin: 'Die Anfänge der Berliner NSDAP 1926/27' – *Vierteljahrshefte für Zeitgeschichte*, No 1 1960.
Broszat, Martin: 'Zur Perversion der Strafjustiz im Dritten Reich' – *Vierteljahrshefte für Zeitgeschichte*, No 4 1958.

Brown, MacAlister: 'The Third Reich's Mobilization of the German Fifth Column in Eastern Europe' – *Journal of Central European affairs*, No 2 1959.

Buchheim, Hans: 'Die Höheren SS- und Polizeiführer' – *Vierteljahrshefte für Zeitgeschichte*, No 4 1963.

'Das Ende einer Illusion' – *Christ und Welt* August 10th–17th, 1950.

Davis, Forrest: 'The Secret History of a Surrender' – *Saturday Evening Post*, September 22nd–29th, 1945.

Deuerlein, Ernst: 'Hitlers Eintritt in die Politik und die Reichswehr' – *Vierteljahrshefte für Zeitgeschichte*, No 2 1959.

Dmytryshyn, Basil: 'The Nazis and the SS Volunteer Division "Galicia" ' – *The American Slavic and East European Review*, No 1 1956.

'T.E.': 'Die Rede Himmlers vor den Gauleitern am 3 August 1944' – *Vierteljahrshefte für Zeitgeschichte*, No 4 1953.

Franz, Georg: 'Munich; Birthplace and Center of the National-Socialist German Workers Party' – *Journal of Modern History*, No 4 1957.

Goltz, Graf von der: 'Die Entlassung des Generalobersten Freiherr von Fritsch' – *Deutsche Rundschau*, No 3 1947.

Graml, Hermann: 'Der 9 November 1938' – *Das Parlament* November 11th, 1953.

Günther, Joachim: 'Die Stufe zum Satanismus' – *Deutsche Rundschau* 1948.

Heiber, Helmut: 'Zur Justiz im Dritten Reich. Der Fall Elias' – *Vierteljahrshefte für Zeitgeschichte*, No 4 1955.

Heiber, Helmut: 'Aus den Akten des Gauleiters Kube' – *Vierteljahrshefte für Zeitgeschichte*, No 1 1956.

Heiber, Helmut: 'Der Generalplan Ost' – *Vierteljahrshefte für Zeitgeschichte*, No 3 1958.

Koehl, Robert: 'Toward an SS Typology: Social Engineers' – *American Journal of Economics and Sociology*, No 18, Jan 1959.

Krausnick, Helmut: 'Denkschrift über die Behandlung der Fremdvölkischen im Osten' – *Vierteljahrshefte für Zeitgeschichte*, No 4 1957.

Krausnick, Helmut: 'Hitler und die Morde in Polen' – *Vierteljahrshefte für Zeitgeschichte*, No 4 1963.

Krausnick, Helmut: 'Wehrmacht und Nationalsozialismus' – *Das Parlament* November 9th, 1955.

Lösener, Bernhard: 'Als Rassereferent im Reichsministerium des Innern' – *Vierteljahrshefte für Zeitgeschichte*, No 3 1961.

Maier, Hedwig: 'Die SS und der 20 Juli' – *Vierteljahrshefte für Zeitgeschichte*, No 3 1966.

Mau, Hermann: 'Die "Zweite Revolution" – der 30 Juni 1934' – *Vierteljahrshefte für Zeitgeschichte*, No 2 1958.

Noack, W.D.: 'Sind Führer der Waffen-SS berechtigt Dienstgrade der Wehrmacht zu verwenden?' – *Militärarchiv*, No 7 1965.

Paetel, Karl O.: 'Die SS (Geschichte und Soziologie)' – *Vierteljahrshefte für Zeitgeschichte*, No 1 1954.

Plum, Günter: 'Staatspolizei und Innere Verwaltung 1934–1936' – *Vierteljahrshefte für Zeitgeschichte*, No 2 1965.

Popplow, Ulrich: 'Reinhard Heydrich oder die Aufnordnung durch die Sport' – *Olympisches Feuer*, No 8 1963.

'Prememoria eines bayerischen Richters zu den Juni-Morden 1934' – *Vierteljahrshefte für Zeitgeschichte*, No 1 1957.

Pruck, Erich F.: 'Die Rehabilitierung von Kommandeuren der Roten Armee' – *Osteuropa*, No 3 1964.

Reitlinger, Gerald: 'The Doubts of Wilhelm Kube' – *Wiener Library Bulletin*, No 5/6 1950.

Rosenberger, Heinrich: 'Die Entlassung des Generalobersten Freiherr von Fritsch' – *Deutsche Rundschau*, No 8 1946.

Runzheimer, Jürgen: 'Der Uberfall auf den Sender Gleiwitz im Jahre 1939' – *Vierteljahrshefte für Zeitgeschichte*, No 4 1962.

Schneider, Peter: 'Rechtssicherheit und richterliche Unabhängigkeit aus der Sicht des SD' – *Vierteljahrshefte für Zeitgeschichte*, No 6 1956.

Seraphim, Hans-Günther: 'SS-Verfügungstruppe und Wehrmacht' – *Wehrwissenschaftliche Rundschau*, No 12 1955.

Spalcke, Karl: 'Der Fall Tuchatschewski' – *Die Gegenwart*, January 25th, 1958.

Der Spiegel: 'Das Spiel ist aus – Arthur Nebe' September 29th, 1949–April 20th, 1950.

Der Spiegel: 'Lady mit Lampenschirm' – February 16th, 1950.

Der Spiegel: 'Der Furcht so fern, dem Tod so nahe' – May 15th, 1957.

Der Spiegel: 'Braver, dummer Klim' – November 8th, 1961.

Der Spiegel: 'Wenn ihr einmarschiert, schiessen wir' – May 1st, 1963.

Der Spiegel: ' "Grossmutter gestorben". Interview mit dem ehemaligen SS-Sturmbannführer Alfred Naujocks' – November 13th, 1963.

'SS-Bericht über den 20 Juli' – *Nordwestdeutsche Hefte*, February 1947.

Thorwald, Jürgen: 'Der Mann der den Krieg auslöste' – *Der Stern*, No 23 1953.

Triska, Jan F.: 'Work redeems': Concentration-camp Labor and Nazi German Economy' – *Journal of Central European Affairs*, No 1 1959.

Uhlig, Heinrich: 'November 9th, 1938' – *Das Parlament*, November 6th, 1963.

Urrisk, Otto R.: 'Uber den Begriff der "Garde" und die Schaffung militärischer "Eliten" ' – *Osterreichische Militärische Zeitschrift*, Nos 2–3 1964.

Wolff, Richard: 'Der Reichstagsbrand 1933' – *Das Parlament*, January 18th, 1956.

VI. *Radio and Television Scripts*

Lichtenstein, Heiner: 'Wo Himmler residieren wollte', West German Radio, Programme 2, January 30th, 1965.

Zipfel, Friedrich: 'Ein Volk in Waffen. Die SA der NSDAP', Radio Bremen, June 6th, 1966.
Kipphardt, Heinar: 'Die Geschichte von Joel Brand', German TV, Channel 2.
Panorama: 'Das bestellte Attentat'; German TV Channel 1, July 26th, 1965.

VII. *Standard Newspapers and Periodicals*

Frankfurter Rundschau 1957.
Hamburger Echo 1934.
Münchner Post 1931, 1932.
Das Schwarze Korps 1935–45.
Völkischer Beobachter 1933–45.
Die Welt 1955–67.
Süddeutsche Zeitung 1955–67.

INDEX

History and Biography

William L. Shirer
THE RISE AND FALL OF THE THIRD REICH 85p

D. C. Watt
A HISTORY OF THE WORLD IN THE 20th CENTURY
PART I 1899-1918 50p

Frank Spencer
A HISTORY OF THE WORLD IN THE 20th CENTURY
PART II 1918-1945 60p

Neville Brown
A HISTORY OF THE WORLD IN THE 20th CENTURY
PART III 1945-1968 50p

Violet Bonham Carter
WINSTON CHURCHILL AS I KNEW HIM (illus) 37½p

Alistair Horne
THE FALL OF PARIS (illus) 62½p

Robert K. Massie
NICHOLAS AND ALEXANDRA 50p

Robert Payne
THE LIFE AND DEATH OF LENIN (illus) 75p
THE RISE AND FALL OF STALIN (illus) 75p

Harrison E. Salisbury
THE 900 DAYS: THE SIEGE OF LENINGRAD 95p

Elizabeth Longford
VICTORIA R. I (illus) 90p

Harold Nicolson
KING GEORGE V (illus) 75p

David Cecil
MELBOURNE (illus) 75p

Leonard Mosley
ON BORROWED TIME (illus) 65p

R. J. Mitchell & M. D. R. Leys
A HISTORY OF THE ENGLISH PEOPLE (illus) 52½p

War Books

Ralph Barker
STRIKE HARD, STRIKE SURE (illus) 25p
Paul Brickhill
THE DAM BUSTERS (illus) 30p
Tim Carew
THE KOREAN WAR – The Story of the Fighting Commonwealth Regiments (illus) 30p
Brian Connell
RETURN OF THE TIGER (illus) 30p
E. H. Cookridge
SET EUROPE ABLAZE (illus) 50p
William Craig
THE FALL OF JAPAN (illus) 40p
Guy Gibson V. C.
ENEMY COAST AHEAD 30p
Alexander McKee
VIMY RIDGE (illus) 30p
C. E. Lucas Phillips
COCKLESHELL HEROES (illus) 25p
Jerrard Tickell
ODETTE (illus) 30p
Edited by H. R. Trevor-Roper
HITLER'S WAR DIRECTIVES 1939-1945 25p
T. J. Waldron & James Gleeson
THE FROGMEN (illus) 25p
Peter Young
WORLD WAR 1939-1945 (illus) 75p